www.brookscole.com

www.brookscole.com is the World Wide Web site for Brooks/Cole and is your direct source to dozens of online resources.

At *www.brookscole.com* you can find out about supplements, demonstration software, and student resources. You can also send e-mail to many of our authors and preview new publications and exciting new technologies.

www.brookscole.com
Changing the way the world learns®

Applied Social Research

A Tool for the Human Services

SIXTH EDITION

Duane R. Monette
Thomas J. Sullivan
Cornell R. DeJong

Northern Michigan University

THOMSON

BROOKS/COLE

Australia • Canada • Mexico • Singapore • Spain
United Kingdom • United States

THOMSON
™

BROOKS/COLE

Executive Editor: Lisa Gebo
Assistant Editor: Alma Dea Michelena
Editorial Assistant: Sheila Walsh
Technology Project Manager: Barry Connoly
Marketing Manager: Caroline Concilla
Marketing Assistant: Mary Ho
Advertising Project Manager: Tami Strang
Project Manager, Editorial Production: Matt Ballantyne
Art Director: Rob Hugel

Print/Media Buyer: Kris Waller
Permissions Editor: Stephanie Lee
Production Service: Carlisle Publishers Services
Compositor: Carlisle Communications, Ltd.
Copy Editor: City Desktop Productions
Cover Designer: Bill Stanton
Cover Image: Impression III (Concert) by Kandinsky © Planet Art
Cover Printer: Coral Graphic Services
Printer: Quebecor World, Kingsport

Printed in Canada
1 2 3 4 5 6 7 08 07 06 05 04

For more information about our products, contact us at:
Thomson Learning Academic Resource Center
1-800-423-0563

For permission to use material from this text or product,
submit a request online at
http://www.thomsonrights.com
Any additional questions about permissions can be submitted by email to
thomsonrights@thomson.com

Library of Congress Control Number: 2004102452

ISBN 0-534-62858-3

Brooks/Cole—Thomson Learning
10 Davis Drive
Belmont, CA 94002-3098
USA

Asia
Thomson Learning
5 Shenton Way #01-01
UIC Building
Singapore 068808

Australia/New Zealand
Thomson Learning
102 Dodds Street
Southbank, Victoria 3006
Australia

Canada
Nelson
1120 Birchmount Road
Toronto, Ontario M1K 5G4
Canada

Europe/Middle East/Africa
Thomson Learning
High Holborn House
50/51 Bedford Row
London WC1R 4LR
United Kingdom

Latin America
Thomson Learning
Seneca, 53
Colonia Polanco
11560 Mexico D.F.
Mexico

Spain/Portugal
Paraninfo
Calle Magallanes, 25
28015 Madrid, Spain

To my mother,
Thanks for everything.

To Nancy,
Who accepted my fleeting presence.

To Susan,
From where the sun now stands, we shall commute no more forever.

Brief Contents

Table of Contents

Research in Practice

Computers in Research

Preface

The social sciences and the human services confront an important challenge as a new millennium begins. Human service programs in today's environment must demonstrate a need for their services, document the quality of services they deliver, explicate a theoretical knowledge base for services, and show evidence of the effectiveness of those services. These expectations mean that human service professionals must be well able to apply social science research methods to practice problems, because it is those research methods that will provide convincing evidence of those needs, quality, and effectiveness.

Students new to the human service field are often unaware of research's contribution to human service delivery. A common question that we hear from our own students is this: "I want a career where I can help people. Why do I need to study research methods?" We know that building a convincing case for the connection between research and practice in the human service curriculum cannot be done in just a paragraph of an introduction, nor can it be accomplished in the first lecture of the semester. Sustaining student interest requires that the connection between research and practice be a constant theme throughout the textbook and the course. Our goal, from the first edition through this sixth one, has been to present the methods of social science research within the context of human service practice. Research is unquestionably a demanding subject, but consistently seeing the connections between research and human service practice can defuse a sense of drudgery and instill enthusiasm in its place.

One of the most rewarding experiences we've enjoyed in writing this textbook and in teaching research has been to witness student apprehensions dissipate with the discovery of new knowledge and the mastery of new ideas. It is our desire to emphasize the connections between research and practice and encourage more students to share that positive growth. Having engaged in both practice and research ourselves, we are convinced that each enterprise has much to offer the other, and we hope that readers will share our enthusiasm for uncovering the parallels and linkages between research and practice.

We have retained the interdisciplinary cooperative effort of the earlier editions: Our professional experience includes the direct provision of human services, the conduct of human service evaluation research, and consultation to help practitioners design and evaluate service. As teaching faculty, we instruct students in basic research methods, practice evaluation, program evaluation, and direct human service practice methods.

As is the case with allies in any human enterprise, disputes, tensions, and disagreements occur between research-as-science and human-service-as-practice. But we have been heartened by the accumulation of excellent examples of research and human service practice working together that have come to our attention and been incorporated in the revision of this text. In this sixth edition, we have incorporated attention to evidence-based practice as an emerging focus in the human services. Evidence-based practice has been gaining in popularity throughout the health and human service professions, and its emphasis on using empirical research to make decisions about practice reinforces the need for researchers and practitioners to collaborate in the design, delivery, and evaluation of human services.

As with earlier editions, our goal is to prepare a book that is useful to those in human service departments who integrate research into the student's practice education as well as to social scientists who emphasize the applied dimension of social science methods.

The special theme of this book, then, is that many parallels and linkages exist between social research and human service practice. We outline these ideas in the first chapter and then carry this theme through the remainder of the book. This textbook is primarily an introduction to social research as it relates to the human services. As such, we have presented all of the topics of scientific research important for such an introduction. But we have also offered a challenge—we hope that students will learn that social research has many parallels with human service practice and that understanding these parallels will make them better practitioners as well as social scientists. The challenge is also to recognize the ways in which the two can be linked—by incorporating research activities into practice and by shaping practice settings into research opportunities.

Features

A number of special features in this book are designed to help develop an appreciation for social research and its importance to the human services.

Research in Practice: Each chapter includes boxed features titled Research in Practice, in which we discuss some special examples where research and practice have been linked. In this way, we emphasize the theme of the book and encourage students to consider the many ways in which this linkage can be achieved.

Computers in Research: Recognizing that computers are an integral part of both research and human service practice, many chapters include boxed features that present some application of computers in research. These inserts require no previous experience with or knowledge of computers, and they are intended to inform students of the general capabilities of software rather than to train them to use particular types of software.

Content on Women and Minorities: We have given additional recognition to the need for human service workers to be knowledgeable of the special needs and problems of women and minorities. To this end, we have addressed in most chapters some special considerations in research methods as they apply to these groups.

Coverage of Both Qualitative and Quantitative Approaches: Throughout the book, we emphasize the diversity of research methods that are applicable to the human services. Qualitative methods are increasingly recognized for their capacity to address the richness and complexity of human behavior that one encounters in the human services. At the same time, quantitative methods offer the human service professional the tools to summarize data, to utilize precise measurement tools, and to generalize from study samples to larger populations. Our purpose is not to champion one approach over the other but to encourage the use of the full range of research methods in the search for knowledge to inform the human services.

Exploring InfoTrac® College Edition and the Internet: We encourage students to go beyond the boundaries of what can be provided in a textbook by exploring additional resources available on the World Wide Web. The Internet has become an increasingly important adjunct to all kinds of research and practice delivery tasks. In every chapter, a feature called Exploring InfoTrac® College Edition and the Internet suggests some specific Web sites that we personally have found to be valuable. We also identify key terms for accessing full-text articles through InfoTrac® College Edition—a fully searchable, online library of hundreds of periodicals that is made available by the publisher of this book.

For Further Reading: Each chapter includes a brief, annotated list of books that students will find useful for pursuing chapter topics in greater depth.

Exercises for Class Discussion: Each chapter ends with a set of exercises in which we present some problem or setting in human service practice and ask questions that call for students to consider the parallels and linkages between research and practice. These exercises can be used as a context for class discussion, or they can serve as out-of-class assignments. Either way, students should find them challenging and stimulating.

Appendix on Library Usage and Information Retrieval: We have included an appendix in which we discuss how to use the library and online information retrieval technologies, focusing specifically on the special needs of students in the human services. Although many college students will be familiar with some of this by the time they take a research methods course, some may find they have a weakness in this area that can be strengthened by studying the appendix. Even those familiar with the library and information retrieval will find some new and useful information relevant to the human services.

Instructor's Manual and Internet Resources: A manual of test items, suggested lecture and class discussion topics, plus other teaching/learning resources are available through the Wadsworth Web site: http://www.wadsworth.com. Information on accessing these materials is also available from your local Wadsworth representative or by contacting the Social Work Editor, Wadsworth/Thompson Learning, 60 Garden Court, Monterey, CA 93940 or by contacting Customer Service at 1-800-923-0563, or support@kdc.com.

New to the Sixth Edition

In approaching this revision of *Applied Social Research,* we have done our best to balance two goals: to add new material and additional features on the one hand and to retain the content and style that has served instructors and students well in past editions. New and exciting studies that illustrate the principles of social science research are continuously appearing in the literature. We've used some of these to update Research in Practice illustrations and to add some new Computers in Research sections. Advances in computer technology and the use of the Internet have transformed not only how research is conducted but how we access and use research as well, and these changes are reflected throughout this new edition. The perspective of the student, the ultimate consumer of the book, has been foremost in our minds as we reviewed each chapter. Where the same point could be made with less elaboration, we've been more concise. Some illustrations have been modified to eliminate confusion, and some content has been reordered to enhance comprehension.

A few changes impact the entire text. Previous editions included a feature called Exploring the Internet, in which we provided tips on accessing information from the Internet and some recommended Web sites. Thanks to a new Internet tool called Info-Trac® College Edition, which is provided by the publisher, this feature is now called Exploring Info-Trac® College Edition and the Internet. InfoTrac® College Edition, which is described more fully in Chapter 1, provides student access to an immense database of research-related literature. We have included a list of search terms in each chapter that we have personally tested with InfoTrac® College Edition and that will enrich the user's understanding of key chapter content. We also specify two or more specific articles that we have located through Info-Trac® College Edition. Of course, we still retain a general guide to the Internet with updated World Wide Web site recommendations.

A modest change that appears throughout the text concerns a change in terminology. We now use the term "single-system" in place of "single-subject" when referring to evaluation studies that use repeated measures of baseline and intervention. Reviewers recommended this change to better communicate that while the focus of such a study is most often one individual, it could as well be one family, group, or community.

Here are the more extensive modifications that mark the sixth edition on a chapter-by-chapter basis:

Chapter 1. We begin the chapter with an updated description of the term *human services,* with emphasis on the collaboration between professionals in the delivery of services. In keeping with this theme of collaboration, Research in Practice 1.2 is new and specifically addresses collaboration between practitioners and researchers. Spurred on by advances in computerization, a development that has shown rapid development throughout the human services is evidence-based practice. A structured, systematic approach to using the results of research to guide practice, evidence-based practice is one excellent example of using research as a tool for the human services. We introduce the model of evidence-based practice in the beginning of the chapter and while discussing the steps in practice intervention. Research in Practice 1.1 has also been revised in light of this model. It is also addressed in a number of subsequent chapters.

Chapter 2. A general principle to which we adhere is that content on minorities and human diversity should be included throughout the text. Research in Practice 2.1 has been substantially updated to reflect current literature on gays and lesbians and to show how research can serve as a resource to practitioners whose delivery of services is impacted by controversies related to sexual orientation. The Computers in Research section in Chapter 2 of the fifth edition has been deleted to make room for new computer material elsewhere in the book.

Chapter 3. Our discussion of research ethics includes new specific content on hallmark events in the development of research ethics, particularly the Belmont Report with its emphasis on the values of respect for persons, beneficence, and justice. The section on court challenges to confidentiality in research has been updated and expanded and now also addresses legislative challenges. Using computers in research and studying "Internet communities" have also generated new ethical challenges, and we have addressed these important topics in a new Computers in Research section.

Chapter 4. This chapter continues our coverage of evidence-based practice through the inclusion of a new Computers In Research section that describes a Cochrane review and a literature search process that can be used both to guide in the formulation of a research problem and to inform practice decisions.

Chapter 5. We have revised our discussion of reliability somewhat in order to introduce the concept of internal reliability and the various approaches to estimating it. The chapter also includes a new Computers in Research section showing how computerized data collection systems can enhance researcher–practitioner collaboration. This replaces the Computers in Research section in the fifth edition, which was somewhat repetitive of material in other parts of the book.

Chapter 6. The discussion on simple random sampling has been modified by relocating to Appendix B the discussion of using random numbers tables to draw a sample. The chapter discussion of simple random sampling now focuses more strictly on the concept and theory of sampling.

Chapter 7. A point of confusion for students has been the distinction between the survey as a general research method and the survey as a data collection tool used with various research approaches, such as experiments and qualitative studies. We address this issue in the introduction to this chapter. More survey research is being conducted using the World Wide Web, so we have updated our coverage of online surveys to reflect changes in this rapidly developing field. In our discussion of interviews, we have elaborated the coverage of controlling interviewers by introducing the concept of interviewer falsification, which is both an issue of ethics and research quality.

Chapter 9. The introductory content on the characteristics of qualitative methods has been reorganized. The basic concepts and key terms are essentially the same, but we have made an effort to eliminate redundancy and to cover the contextual approach, grounded theory, and field research in a more orderly manner. Several new illustrations of participant-observation research have been added. A discussion of handheld computers as an aid to observational research is the focus of a new Computers in Research section.

Chapter 10. In the discussion of external validity, we have updated the discussion on the impact of relying on volunteers as participants in experimental studies by incorporating some recent research on the topic.

Chapter 11. We now use "single-system" in lieu of "single-subject" throughout the text as the term for this special form of quasi-experimental design. We provide a rationale for this change. The discussion of types of designs now distinguishes between reversal designs and withdrawal designs in connection with ABA- and ABAB-type studies. The Computers in Research section has new figures and has been rewritten to make it clearer.

Chapter 17. We have rewritten the section on federal government funding sources to make it consistent with current government practice and terminology. The world of grant writing has been greatly impacted by the availability of Web-based information, and we have included new material on learning about funding opportunities by using the World Wide Web.

Appendix A. "A Guide to the Library" is now "A Guide to Library Use and Information Retrieval." More than just a name change, the appendix reflects the transformation taking place in the world of information access. Whether seeking articles in journals, books, government documents, or Web pages, users today rely heavily on computers and Internet technology. We have extensively revised the appendix to reflect these changes and to make locating information a more efficient and enjoyable process for the student.

Appendix B. The spreadsheet random number–generating illustration has been modified to show how to create a table of four-digit columns just like the illustrative random number table. The presentation of using random numbers to select a sample has been moved here from Chapter 6.

Of course, we have updated recommended readings with new publications, and we have incorporated recent citations from the literature to illustrate key points. New content and reorganization of material are identified in the Instructor's Manual.

Acknowledgments

This book began as an idea born out of our own experience teaching research methods to future professionals in social work, criminal justice, education, health care, and other human service areas as well as students in various social science disciplines. We became convinced that existing books contained some significant shortcomings and that a better textbook could be prepared for students in these fields. Over the years, with each revision, we hope that we have come closer to the ideal of helping students to discover the linkages and parallels between practice and research. The students who have passed through our courses played a major role in shaping our thoughts and the content of this text. Their criticism, their frustration, their questioning, and their desire to learn have all motivated us to revise and improve with each edition. We owe them much.

We are indebted to the many social scientists, social workers, and other researchers who reviewed earlier editions of this book and provided important suggestions on how to improve it. We were also guided in preparing this sixth edition by some additional reviewers. For their insightful comments and helpful suggestions, we wish to thank the following reviewers: Howard Alstein, University of Maryland; Carmen Aponte, State University of New York, Brockport; Ronnie Mahler, Buffalo State College; Phyllis Solomon, University of Pennsylvania; and Spencer Zeiger, University of Alaska, Anchorage.

As authors, we have been gratified to see our interest in and enthusiasm for applying research to practice rewarded with demand for a sixth edition. Such long-standing success could not have been achieved without the support and understanding of some very special people who have tolerated our preoccupation, coped with our irregular schedules, and inspired us when the task seemed dreary. We dedicate this book to you.

Chapter 1

Research in the Human Services

This book is about the use of research in human services. The term **human services** refers to activities with the primary goal of enhancing the relationship between people and societal institutions so that people may maximize their potential and alleviate distress. At the broadest level, the human services include formal systems such as government welfare programs, mental health services, child development and family support programs, addiction prevention and intervention programs, and correctional services of the justice system. At the federal level, many of these programs are funded and administered through the Department of Health and Human Services (DHHS). Likewise, *department of human services* or a similar label designates the agency that administers financial assistance and intervention programs at the state level. In addition to public organizations, many charitable and nongovernmental organizations deliver supportive and ameliorative services, from foster care for children to meals programs for the elderly. All of these programs may be included under the umbrella term of human services. More recently, the term *human services* has come to mean not merely a collage of programs but an organized system. Defined this way, the human services comprise a coordinated or integrated set of programs that are designed to work together across agency and professional boundaries, enabling people to cope with problems and thrive in our complex society. There is an emphasis on working in teams and in collaborative relationships across disciplines. Research is becoming increasingly essential to the delivery of human services and to the professionals who are mandated with the responsibility of making serviced delivery effective, efficient, and responsive to human needs. Consider the following actual case:

> Two months after giving birth to a baby boy, a young mother kills her infant son and disposes of the body by dumping it in the trash. Through a routine visit by a public-health nurse, the tragedy is discovered. In the course of the investigation, it is learned that the mother had made threatening remarks about the child while she was still in the hospital. The local community is outraged. Why was the mother allowed to leave the hospital with the child? Why was there no police intervention? Where was the local community mental health agency? The various human service agencies of the community are called on to do something to make sure that similar events will not happen again.

Do something. But what? The human service professionals charged with taking action can first of all turn to research studies on the nature of child abuse and the effectiveness of child abuse programs in other communities. Second, they can use research to ascertain just how much abuse actually occurs in their community. The community response may be different if this event is isolated. In addition, research can help identify factors that can predict which families are most at risk for some sort of family violence and assess the consequences of abuse in child development. Finally, once a plan is put into operation, research methods can be used to monitor the intervention process to assure that the plan is being carried out faithfully and to evaluate its effectiveness.

Thus, numerous linkages exist between research and human-service practice. By linkages, we mean that research can contribute to the goals of practice just as properly conducted practice can contribute to the goals of research. Because research provides the means for understanding the problems with which professionals work and the means for evaluating change, practitioners in human services are certain to encounter the need to understand, apply, and in some cases conduct research in carrying out the goals of their professions. Some would go farther and argue that the link between research and practice is even more intimate, namely, that there can be—and should be—a fruitful merger of the two. In fact, the notion that scientific research and human-service practice are totally distinct enterprises is gradually disappearing (Gibbs 2003; O'Hare 1991). Two reasons explain this.

First, strong parallels are now recognized between the conduct of research and the conduct of practice. By parallels, we mean that the two endeavors may have similar structures, follow similar processes, and use similar techniques. Practitioners can benefit by incorporating into practice some of the techniques used in research. Both research and practice, for example, are based on observation, but the observations of practitioners are often characterized as unstructured and intuitive. Some of the more precise and structured techniques (discussed in Chapters 7 and 9) that researchers use can be adapted for practice purposes.

Second, properly conducted practice intervention can provide scientifically valid knowledge about human behavior and the effectiveness of intervention. For example, practitioners can scientifically assess the effectiveness of their interventions if those interventions are organized in a manner researchers call *single-system design,* which parallels the scientific experiment. (We discuss single-system designs in Chapter 11.) Some illustrations of how the tasks of research have been incorporated into the very defi-

nition of the human services are provided in Research in Practice 1.1.

The purpose of this book is to introduce students in the human services to social research logic, methods, and design. We do this by emphasizing the parallels and linkages between research and practice. Because research and practice are intertwined, human service professionals need training in the techniques of social research as much as they need to know about group processes or theories of personality. In some situations, human service providers will *consume* social research as they apply the findings of research to practice intervention. Therefore, they need to understand the logic of research and be able to assess research procedures critically to decide whether and in what fashion research findings can be introduced into practice.

RESEARCH IN PRACTICE 1.1

PRACTICE EFFECTIVENESS:

"Scientific Practice" as a Challenge to the Human Services

Three decades ago, the Health Research Group, one of Ralph Nader's public citizen organizations, aimed a challenge in the direction of the human services (Adams and Orgel 1975). The group suggested that people seeking help from human service professionals should demand a written contract at the outset of the relationship specifying the conditions of the therapy, the goals of the intervention, and even the site at which the therapy would take place. They also suggested that the contract specify the character of the practitioner–client relationship, especially regarding the empirical evidence showing what kind of relationship would enhance the achievement of the client's goals. Underlying these recommendations was a demand for a high degree of *accountability* on the part of the helping professions. In the intervening decades, these demands for accountability have become louder and broader in scope, as is illustrated by a number of developments (Cournoyer and Powers 2002):

• The emergence of managed care systems that drive much human service practice and reward use of interventions shown to be effective by research.

• The empowerment of consumer groups such as Nader's Health Research Group and a proposed inter-professional Clients' Bill of Rights that includes the right to "be informed about the options available for treatment interventions and the effectiveness of the recommended treatment." (Joint Initiative of Mental Health Professional Organizations 2000)

• The establishment of accreditation standards by organizations such as the Council on Social Work Education that require schools to prepare students who can use and develop "evidence-based knowledge to provide high quality services." (Council on Social Work Education 2003)

These demands for accountability have motivated human service professionals in such fields as psychology, social work, criminal justice, and nursing to begin defining the human services as *scientific* disciplines (Goldfried and Wolfe 1996; Rosen 1996; Turnbull and Dietz-Uhler 1995). They now use such terms as "scientific practice," "scientist practitioner," and "evidence-based practice." In the field

continued on next page

of community mental health, Abraham Jeger and Robert Slotnick (1982) developed what they called a behavioral–ecological approach to the delivery of mental health services. In presenting this approach, they argued that research should be viewed as an integral part of treatment. Over the ensuing decades, this idea has continued to receive support. For example, integrating research with practice served as the organizing theme of an entire special issue of the journal *Education and Treatment of Children*. In one of the articles, Alisa Bahl and colleagues (1999) discuss treating behavioral problems in children using what they call a data-driven approach. They advocate collecting data not only before and after treatment but also throughout the course of treatment. To illustrate this point, they discuss how they employed Parent–Child Interaction Therapy to treat a six-year-old boy with oppositional defiant disorder. They employed parent and teacher reports, observation during clinic sessions, and parental monitoring during each daily home practice session. The case illustrates the importance of using research procedures not only for the advancement of knowledge but also as an enhancement of service delivery.

On a similar note, the National Association of Social Workers Code of Ethics (1999) emphasizes the responsibility of professionals to employ empirical knowledge in practice and to contribute to the advancement of professional knowledge through re-search. The section on evaluation and research in the NASW Code of Ethics includes the following points:

- Social workers should monitor and evaluate policies, implementation of programs, and practice interventions.
- Social workers should promote and facilitate evaluation and research to contribute to the development of knowledge.
- Social workers should critically examine and keep current with emerging knowledge relevant to social work and fully use evaluation and research evidence in their professional practice.
- Social workers should educate themselves, their students, and their colleagues about responsible research practices.

Similarly, the Council on Social Work Education (2003) calls for social work education to impart an understanding of and appreciation for the necessity of a scientific approach to knowledge building and practice, including evidence-based interventions. Research knowledge is important for developing high-quality services, improving service delivery, and evaluating one's own practice.

In each chapter, we will set aside separate space entitled "Research in Practice," where we will discuss particular instances in which research and practice have been linked. In this fashion, students in the human services can gain a deeper understanding of the many ways in which this linkage might be achieved.

Human service workers are called upon to *collaborate* with researchers who are conducting studies involving agency services, data, or clients. Human service professionals are also expected to *conduct* social research as a part of their overall intervention strategy, so they need to know how to design and carry out scientifically valid research projects.

Research in the Human Services
Goals of Research

The word *research* is applied to many activities: the student who browses in the library for a few hours; the social worker who, while visiting clients about other issues, makes a mental note of some of their social characteristics; the parole officer who routinely inquires about a parolee's family life as a part of an intake interview. All of these people might claim to be doing research. Yet the term as it is commonly used in the social and behavioral sciences has a considerably more precise meaning, according to which none of these activities would be considered scientific research. This is not to say that these activities are unimportant. They may have a variety of uses. However, social research has specific goals that can be achieved only through utilizing proper procedures.

Social research is the systematic examination (or reexamination) of empirical data, collected by someone firsthand, concerning the social or psychological forces operating in a situation. Three major elements characterize this definition. First, social research is *systematic*—that is, all aspects of the research process are carefully planned in advance, and nothing is done in a casual or haphazard fashion. The systematic nature of research is at the core of the scientific method, which is discussed in more detail in Chapter 2. Second, social research involves the collection of *empirical data*—that is, information or facts about the world based on sensory experiences. As such, it should not be confused with philosophizing or speculating, which lack the empirical base of research. Third, social research studies *social and psychological factors* that affect human behavior. Biological, physiological, nutritional, or other such factors would be a part of social research only to the extent that they affect or are affected by social and psychological factors.

Research in the human services generally focuses on one or more of the following goals: description, prediction, explanation, or evaluation. **Descriptive research** has as its goal *description,* or the attempt to discover facts or describe reality. Descriptive research, for example, might deal with such questions as these: What are people's attitudes toward welfare? How widespread is child abuse? How many people avail themselves of the services of home health care workers? Some descriptive research efforts are quite extensive. For example, the National Center for Health Statistics (NCHS) and the Centers for Disease Control and Prevention (CDCP) collect voluminous amounts of data each year for purposes of describing the health status of Americans.

Predictive research focuses on *prediction,* or making projections about what may occur in the future or in other settings. Insurance companies, for example, make use of sophisticated actuarial schemes for predicting the risks involved in insuring people or property. Based on past descriptive research on deaths and injuries, they can project how long people with certain characteristics are likely to live or the degree of likelihood that they will suffer injuries. Such projections can also be made by the NCHS. For example, the NCHS can project that infants and children with particular social characteristics will have an increased likelihood of being undernourished or suffering from infectious or parasitic diseases. Armed with this information, it is possible to devise preventive health-care programs targeted at the high-risk groups.

Explanatory research involves *explanation,* or determining why or how something occurred. Explanatory research, for example, would go beyond describing rates of juvenile delinquency or even predicting who will engage in delinquent acts. Explanatory research would focus on *why* certain people become delinquents. The goal of explanation may appear to be quite similar to that of prediction, but there is a difference: One can make predictions without an accompanying explanation. Insurance companies, for example, make actuarial predictions based on past statistical associations, often without knowing why those associations occurred.

Evaluation research focuses on *evaluation,* or the use of scientific research methods to plan intervention programs, to monitor the implementation of new programs and the operation of existing ones, and to determine how effectively programs or clinical practices achieve their goals. Evaluation research can also determine whether a program has unintended consequences, both desirable and undesirable. In the past few decades, a vast array of social programs has emerged—relating to poverty, child development, crime, alcoholism, delinquency, and the like—that attempts to ameliorate undesirable social conditions. As competition for funds for such programs has increased (especially in the past decade), program directors are often required to justify and defend their programs in terms of cost-effectiveness. Thus, evaluation research is now often an integral part of human service programs.

Applications of Research

Some social research is called **basic** (or **pure**) **research** in that its purpose is to advance knowledge about human behavior with little concern for any immediate, practical benefits that might result. Many sociologists and psychologists conduct basic research. Research in the human services, however, is more likely to be **applied research**—research designed with a practical outcome in mind and with the assumption that some group or society as a whole will gain specific benefits from it. Thus, explaining juvenile delinquency is important to social workers, probation officers, and the police because it can lead to programs intended to alleviate delinquency in a community.

The focus of this book is on applied social research and especially on the linkage of social research with the human services. Although we distinguish between basic and applied research, the line between the two is vague, and, in fact, even pure research can have applications in the human service field. To organize our thinking about the applications of research to the human services, we find it useful to think in terms of five focal areas in which this linkage occurs: understanding human functioning in social environments, needs assessment, assessment of client functioning, program evaluation, and practice effectiveness evaluation. We do not claim that this is the only way to divide the human service field or that our list of areas is exhaustive. These five categories, however, are a helpful aid as we analyze the links between research and practice. We review each area briefly here. Then each Research in Practice insert in this and subsequent chapters emphasizes one of the focal areas.

Behavior and Social Environments.   Human service providers do many things: link people to resources they can use, enhance people's coping abilities, improve the operation of social systems, and participate in the development of social policy, to name only a few. All these activities rest on an understanding of the behavior of the people to whom services are provided and a comprehension of the social environment in which they function. Social research can provide much of this knowledge. For example, an agency providing services to teenagers can turn to research on adolescents in American society for a better understanding of the problems facing their clients. One such area that has received considerable social research is the link between self-esteem and teenage pregnancy (Crockenberg and Soby 1989). Although this research has typically been conducted without any particular practice-intervention goals in mind, the results suggest that raising adolescent self-esteem may be one way to reduce teenage pregnancy rates. The research shows that self-esteem does not seem to change the levels of sexual activity among teenagers, but it does document that teenagers with higher self-esteem—both males and females—are more likely to use contraceptives than are teenagers with low self-esteem. Knowledge of factors that influence adolescent behavior can provide practitioners with insights into how to shape effective intervention strategies to reduce teenage pregnancies. In other words, a wide range of behavioral research, much of it basic research, seems only indirectly linked to practice, but it can inform intervention. Human service providers need to be able to understand and assess this research in terms of whether it is sufficiently valid to incorporate into practice.

Although much research on human behavior and social environments is conducted by behavioral scientists, human-service professionals themselves—therapists, social workers, nurses, and other practitioners—are increasingly doing research of this type.

Needs Assessment.   Social research can also be used to make an accurate assessment of the need for various forms of service and suggest alternative strategies for meeting those needs (McKillip 1987; Rossi, Freeman, and Lipsey 1999). The purpose of this research is to determine whether a problem exists, to indicate the severity of the problem, and to estimate the number and characteristics of people adversely affected by the problem. Needs assessment research is often highly descriptive rather than explanatory or predictive. One illustration of needs assessment research is a project that involved the cooperation of a mental health agency and a local university to collect data from a community about mental health needs and services (Witkin 1984). Labeled a Community Oriented Needs Assessment (CONA), it was based on questionnaires mailed to key informants, interviews of a random sample of community residents, and profiles based on demographic statistics. From the CONA, the mental health agency received community input into client needs, service delivery planning, and evaluation. The data were used to help plan and implement programs and to support requests for additional funds from government and other funding agencies.

Assessment of Client Functioning.

In the provision of human services, assessing the level of functioning of clients is often necessary. What kind of communication problems exist in a family? How capable is a teenage parent at dealing with the stresses of motherhood or fatherhood? How skilled is a person in negotiating a job interview? Though practitioners make such assessments often, the danger is that they will be made unsystematically. The past 20 years have seen extensive development of systematic and, in some cases, quantitative assessment tools that can be used for both research and practice tasks. As one example, Mary Lou Balassone (1991) has developed quantitative tools for assessing the degree to which youngsters are at risk of various problematic outcomes, such as dropping out of school or getting pregnant. She has detailed, in particular, how these tools could be used by social work practitioners to assess the degree of risk of inconsistent contraceptive use and failed pregnancy prevention among their clients. These assessments can be compared at different times to see if any change or improvement has occurred. Additional examples of such client assessment tools can be found in Sheafor and Horejsi (2003).

Program Evaluation.

In the past few decades, we have seen the burgeoning of many large, ambitious, and expensive programs intended to cope with social problems and provide services to individuals. Along with the growth of these programs has emerged an increasing concern over their results: Do they achieve their intended goals? These programs are costly, and some evaluation is needed to assess whether resources are indeed being used effectively. Equally important, a program that fails to achieve its goals leaves a problem unsolved or a service undelivered. *Program evaluation* is the use of scientific research techniques to assess the results of a program and evaluate whether the program as currently designed achieves its stated goals (Rutman 1984). For example, one such evaluation project was part of an attempt in New York to replace foster care with a new method of providing services to children of families in need (Jones 1985). The innovation was a response to a dramatic increase in the number of children in foster care and rapidly rising costs per child of providing that care. A program was developed around the idea that, rather than using foster care, the family unit could be preserved by providing intensive services, such as family casework, homemaker services, and vocational and referral services. To assess whether the program was effective, authorities provided some families with the intensive family services, while other, comparable families were served as usual by the child welfare system (which, in most cases, meant foster care). The effectiveness of the program was then determined by comparing the two groups after one year in terms of the cost of providing services to each group, the amount of services provided, and the level of functioning of parents and children. The results of the program indicated that it was a success by all criteria. In a five-year follow-up, it was also found that the program led to fewer children going into foster care.

It is crucial that human service providers understand when program evaluation is called for and when it is possible to conduct an effective evaluation. In addition, many practitioners will likely find themselves participating in programs that include evaluation as one of their goals.

Practice Effectiveness Evaluation.

Whereas program evaluation focuses on the assessment of entire programs, the concern of human service professionals is often considerably more specific—namely, "Is what I am doing right now with this particular client working?" For this reason, practitioners have often been disenchanted with the utility of evaluation research as a direct aid to helping clients. However, in recent years, major advances have occurred in the ability of research to answer professionals' questions about the efficacy of intervention efforts on specific clients.

One form of such research is called *single-system design,* in which practitioners devise a way to repeatedly measure the occurrence of a problem and monitor the behavior of a single client, group, family, or larger system for a time period. Then intervention begins, and the behavior is again monitored. Comparison between the baseline and intervention periods permits the practitioner to make more accurate assessments of progress than the informal assessment on which human service professionals have traditionally relied. The procedures can be quite elaborate, but even a beginning staff member can readily apply the basic model. For example, an undergraduate student recently submitted a paper that described her work with a young mother who was trying to reduce the thumb-sucking behavior of her six-year-old daughter. Adapting a measurement scheme reported in a professional journal, the student designed a monitoring system involving observation of the child by means of a small piece of litmus paper taped to the child's thumb. This procedure allowed the student to determine how much time the child actually spent thumb sucking and to specify the conditions under which the behavior occurred. A behavior-modification procedure was implemented, and the amount of thumb sucking declined dramatically. (Single-system research is discussed at length in Chapter 11.) Through such careful monitoring of behavior and measuring of intervention effects, human service workers not only can enhance their own effectiveness but also can contribute to the development of an intervention technology that others can successfully apply.

Obvious similarities exist between program evaluation and practice effectiveness research. For example, both are concerned with the effectiveness of certain practices. The difference, however, is in the scope of the efforts. Program evaluation focuses on complete programs, whereas practice effectiveness research emphasizes the assessment of some particular aspect of a practice situation in a way that will not necessarily affect the entire program.

Special Issues: Research on Minorities and Women

The human services devote special attention to the problems of minority groups, whether their minority status is a function of race, ethnicity, gender, or something else. The reason for this special attention is twofold: First, minorities tend to suffer disproportionately from the problems that human service workers attempt to alleviate; second, many social conditions affect minorities very negatively and limit their opportunities and achievements. Because of the position of minorities in American society, conducting research that produces accurate and complete data on them can be a challenge. In fact, in certain circumstances, the standard research methods used in human service research result in misleading and in some cases outright false conclusions regarding a minority.

This problem is sufficiently important to human service research that we devote special attention to it throughout the book. In each chapter, where relevant, we point to particular ways in which problems or biases in research on minorities can occur and strategies for overcoming them. The goal is to create a sensitivity to the fact that research methods can have built-in biases when focused on particular minority groups and that care must be exercised to detect and avoid this.

Parallels and Linkages between Research and Practice

Although scientific research is different in many respects from human service practice, important parallels exist between the two. In fact, researchers and practitioners use many of the same strategies in approaching their problems. After reviewing the steps in conducting research, we will point out parallels that can be found in practice.

Steps in Conducting Research

Although each research project is unique in some fashion, some general steps characterize virtually every project. The research process can be divided into six identifiable stages: problem formulation, research design development, data collection, data analysis, drawing conclusions, and public dissemination of the results.

Problem Formulation.   The first step in conducting social research is to decide on the problem to research. When first encountering the issue of problem formulation, students commonly question its importance. So many problems exist that it would appear to be a simple matter to select one on which to conduct research. However, such a casual view of scientific problem formulation is erroneous. For example, some problems about which we might desire answers are not scientific questions at all, and no amount of research will answer them. Other problems, though possibly interesting and intriguing, might prove impractical from a methodological, ethical, or financial standpoint.

Another element of problem formulation is to shape a concern into a specific researchable question. Such global concerns as "the state of the modern family" are far too broad to be considered research problems. They need to be narrowed down to specific issues for which empirical data can be gathered, such as: What is the divorce rate? How does it compare with the divorce rate of previous years? Do children raised in single-parent families exhibit poorer social development than children raised in two-parent families? As the initial step in research, developing a researchable problem is highly important. In Chapter 4, we outline the many issues involved in this process.

Research Design Development. Having successfully established a researchable problem, we must develop a **research design,** a detailed plan outlining how observations will be made. The plan is followed by the researcher as the project is carried out. Research designs always address certain key issues, such as who will be studied, how these people will be selected, and what information will be gathered from or about them. In fact, the research design spells out in considerable detail what will occur in the following stages of the research process. Chapters 7 through 12 describe the different kinds of research designs and issues that must be considered in their development.

Data Collection. A part of any research design is a description of what kinds of data will be collected and how this will be done. The data collected at this stage constitute the basic information from which conclusions will be drawn, so great care must be ex-

ercised. Two aspects of data collection, *pretests* and *pilot studies,* illustrate just how careful scientists are about this. The **pretest,** as the name implies, is a preliminary application of the data-gathering technique for the purpose of determining its adequacy. It certainly would be risky and unwise to jump prematurely into data gathering without first knowing that all the data-collection procedures are sound. For example, if our study were a needs assessment of homemakers to determine how many would make use of occupational training services, we would choose a small group of homemakers and collect the same data from them that we plan to collect in the final project. A pretest is, in a sense, a trial run. And, unless we are very good or very lucky, some modifications in the data-collection technique are likely to be required based on the results of the pretest. After these modifications are made, the technique is pretested again. Additional pretests are always desirable after any modifications in the data-gathering technique to assess whether the modifications handle the problems encountered in the previous pretest.

In some cases, it may even be necessary to do a **pilot study,** which is a small-scale trial run of all the procedures planned for use in the main study. In addition to administering the data-gathering instrument, a pilot study might include such things as a test of the procedures for selecting the sample and an application of the statistical procedures to be used in the data analysis stage.

It is this kind of care in data collection that improves the validity of the data collected and bolsters confidence in the conclusions drawn.

Data Analysis. As with data collection, data analysis is spelled out in the research design and can be the most challenging and interesting aspect of a research project. It is challenging because data in raw form can be quite unrevealing. Data analysis is what unlocks the information hidden in the raw data and transforms it into something useful and meaningful. During data analysis, researchers learn whether their ideas are confirmed or refuted by empirical reality. During the course of data analysis, researchers often make use of statistical tools that can range from simple percentages to complex statistical tests that require much training to understand and master. These statistics aid in communicating the findings of research to others. Once a researcher has learned the special language and interpretations of statistics, he or she can be more effective at communicating research findings in a clear, concise manner than when using conventional English. In Chapters 14, 15, and 16, we review some of the basic data-analysis and data-manipulation techniques that are used in social research.

Drawing Conclusions.   The next step in conducting social research is to draw some conclusions from the data analysis. The form this takes depends partly on the goals of the research project. A descriptive study, for example, simply presents what was found, possibly in a summarized form to make it more easily understood. Predictive and explanatory research, on the other hand, usually have hypotheses, or statements of what the researchers expect to find, stated before the data are collected. In this case, a major element of drawing conclusions is to assess how much support exists for the hypotheses. The support that data provide for hypotheses can range from strong to weak to none, and researchers have an obligation to those who might use their research to accurately represent the strength of their findings. Finally, in evaluation research, drawing conclusions usually involves making a judgment about the adequacy and effectiveness of programs and changes that might improve conditions.

Often, research discovers some things that do not relate directly to any specific hypothesis or even things that are completely unanticipated. When drawing conclusions, the researchers should make note of the implications of any such findings that are of sufficient importance to warrant mention. When complete, the conclusions should clearly indicate what has been learned by conducting the research and the impact of this new knowledge.

Public Dissemination of Results.   Research findings are of little value if they remain the private property of the researchers who produce them. A crucial stage of social research is the public dissemination of the findings by publication in a book or professional journal or presentation to a professional

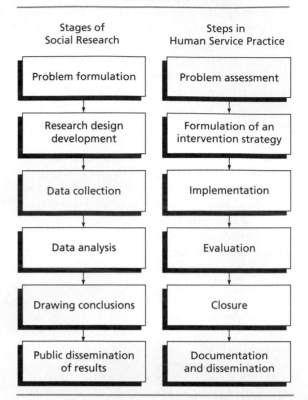

Figure 1.1   Parallels between Human Service Practice and Social Research

Stages of Social Research	Steps in Human Service Practice
Problem formulation	Problem assessment
Research design development	Formulation of an intervention strategy
Data collection	Implementation
Data analysis	Evaluation
Drawing conclusions	Closure
Public dissemination of results	Documentation and dissemination

organization. This shares the newly created knowledge with those who can put that knowledge to use or who can build on it in future research. In fact, public dissemination of knowledge is a major mechanism for scientific advancement. As we discuss further in Chapters 2 and 3, public dissemination makes it possible for others to reanalyze or replicate the research and to confirm the findings or identify cases of error-filled, biased, or fraudulent research.

Steps in Practice Intervention

Just as the research process can be organized as a series of steps, the process of human service practice is also often conceptualized as a series of stages. In fact, the stages of practice demonstrate the parallels and linkages between practice and research (see Figure 1.1). One development in the human services that shows great promise for linking practice and research is **evidence-based practice:** the conscientious, explicit, and judicious use of the best evidence in making decisions about human service assessment and intervention (Sackett, Richardson, Rosenberg, and Haynes 1997, p. 2). According to this approach, the best evidence is knowledge that has been gained via the research process. The steps of the evidence-based practice process outlined below are another example of the parallels between practice and research.

Problem Assessment. In much the same way that social researchers must decide on the problem to research, practitioners must specify the precise problem with which they are concerned, which factors might contribute to the problem, and which aspects of the problem will be given priority. In problem formulation, researchers make judgments concerning the feasibility of researching a particular phenomenon. Likewise, in problem assessment, practitioners must pose answerable questions. The initial step in evidence-based practice involves crafting questions for searching electronic databases so that the relevant information can be retrieved. A well-formed question describes the client, course of action, alternate courses of action, intended result, and whether effective intervention is possible.

Formulation of an Intervention Strategy. Just as researchers develop a research design, practitioners develop a strategy for intervention that will be effective in alleviating the problem specified in the assessment stage. Whereas researchers choose among a variety of research methods, practitioners choose among numerous intervention strategies, such as crisis intervention, behavior modification, or vocational training. Just as researchers may use more than one research technique over the course of a research project, practitioners may also use more than one intervention strategy in attacking a problem. Tracking down the research studies and other data that will help one evaluate intervention strategies requires electronic access to relevant databases and specialized skills in their efficient use. In addition to general Web-searching tools and library databases, databases specifically related to medicine and human

service practice are being developed to aid in the access and use of practice-related studies. As you will learn through the course of studying research methods, all research results are not of equal value. Some research designs generate more convincing evidence of causation than others. Determining how valid and useful the results of any given study are is approached in a systematic way so that so-called best evidence is given more weight than results of other studies. At this stage, the practitioner must organize the results, consider conflicting findings, and determine which practice interventions show the most promise.

Implementation. Following the development of the research design, researchers proceed to put it into practice. In similar fashion, practitioners implement the intervention strategies outlined in the preceding stage. Researchers' activities are normally limited to data collection; they do not attempt to change the people they are studying. Practitioners, on the other hand, may collect data as a part of the implementation stage, but they are primarily concerned with the effectiveness of the intervention strategy in creating some change in clients or in the systems that affect them.

Evaluation. Once researchers have collected their data, they analyze it to determine what their study has found. Similarly, evidence-based practice evaluates the effectiveness of the intervention strategy implemented during the preceding stage. Were the goals of the plan achieved? What were the costs of the strategy? Were any undesirable side effects brought about by the intervention? Which aspects of the intervention process seemed to be most important in producing the change that resulted? The evidence-based model emphasizes employing single-system designs and other systematic assessment strategies in contrast to the more casual observation associated with traditional practice. The results of these systematic assessments can help shape future research studies and may serve as evidence in their own right for guiding practice decisions.

Closure. Termination of intervention is an important part of the helping process. The extent to which the intervention has been effective must be determined, as well as the degree to which the goals of the intervention cannot be and possibly never will be achieved. Researchers may make suggestions for future research that might be helpful in further clarifying the relationships found in the study. Likewise, practitioners might suggest other sources of help that the client could use to cope with problems left unresolved by the intervention. In other words, for both researchers and practitioners, the conclusion is a time to review what has been accomplished and look forward to directions and alternatives for the future.

Documentation and Dissemination.   We have made the point that both the process and the results of research must be carefully documented; the same can be said for human service practice. At a minimum, this stage includes meeting agency requirements for record keeping and case documentation, such as preparing treatment plans and case-closing reports. Although such agency-mandated reporting may serve a useful quality control function, practitioners also have a responsibility to share with others the knowledge gained from practice. This may take the form of case conferences within the agency, workshop presentations, or formal articles published in appropriate journals. As a consequence of subjecting practice to the scrutiny of supervisors and peers, deficits are identified, intervention techniques are refined, and advances are made in the delivery of human services.

By this point, you should be gaining an appreciation for the parallels and linkages between social research and human service practice. The parallels involve the similarities between the activities of researchers and those of practitioners. The linkages involve the contributions that research can make to practice endeavors, and vice versa. In fact, Research in Practice 1.2 argues for making these parallels and linkages even more explicit and direct.

The Plan of the Book

This first chapter has discussed the extent to which research is fundamental to the delivery of human services. The remainder of the book discusses how

research is applied to the human services. Chapters 2 through 6 present some of the important issues that underlie research, including the role of hypotheses and theories, and ethical problems that researchers are likely to confront. We also address the issue of how to formulate a research problem and select a scientifically sound sample on which observations will be made.

With Chapter 7, we begin the first of five chapters on specific research methods. Chapter 7 covers *survey research,* which is a widely used data-collection technique based on obtaining people's responses to questions. In Chapter 8, we discuss the use of *available data* in research. Though not as common as surveys, available data can be useful to human service researchers. For example, the records kept by prisons, hospitals, or social service agencies would fall into the category of available data that could be used for research. Chapter 9 presents *field research* and *observational methods,* which involve the direct observation of people's behavior, often in the natural settings where people lead their everyday lives. This is also a common research technique in the human services because human service practitioners typically make observations of the everyday lives of clients in the course of intervention. In Chapter 10, we discuss *experiments,* which are research techniques designed to assess the effect of one factor on another. Although human service providers may only occasionally conduct conventional experiments, they are often in a position to carry out *single-system research,* the topic of Chapter 11. Single-system research involves assessing the impact of some factor on the feelings or actions of a client, and it derives its basic logic from the experimental designs discussed in Chapter 10.

The remaining five chapters focus on issues that may have to be addressed irrespective of which specific research method is used in a particular study. *Evaluation research,* discussed in Chapter 12, refers to assessing how well a particular program or practice achieves its goals. This has become an increasingly important element in the human services, and evaluation researchers often use some or all of the five research techniques discussed in the preceding chapters. In Chapter 13, we analyze how to develop *indexes* and *scales,* measuring devices that derive a

RESEARCH IN PRACTICE 1.2

PRACTICE EFFECTIVENESS:

Research–Practice Collaboration

Researchers and practitioners working together to improve human services, or research–practice collaboration, as it is known, is a current topic in the human services. Consider the following comment on the current status of addiction treatment.

> During the first years of the 21st century, few issues in the substance abuse field have captured as much attention as the efforts to link research and practice. (Rawson and Branch 2002, p. 769)

Although the label *collaboration* may be new, the goal of achieving effective integration of practice and research has long been desired. William Reid, a researcher and clinical practice theorist in social work, recognized the immense potential contribution to knowledge building of human service agencies (Reid 1978). He proposed that social agencies could be transformed into "research machines" if they would

- Build research questions into the routine collection of case information rather than simply attempt to devise research problems from the available data.
- Structure practice in such a way that goals and targets are clear and the intervention is well specified. This contributes to the utility of case records for research.

Today, the need that Reid saw for human service practice settings to actively engage in research activities is greater than ever, and specific steps are being taken within the human services to achieve that potential. Federal government organizations that fund both research and human service delivery are making collaboration a high priority in substance abuse treatment and across the human services. In 1998, a report entitled "Bridging the Gap between Practice and Research: Forging Partnerships with Community-Based Drug and Alcohol Treatment" was released by the Center for Substance Abuse Treatment (CSAT) and the National Institute on Drug Abuse (Lamb, Greenlick, and McCarty 1998). The report highlighted the importance of bringing down barriers between research and clinical practice. Subsequently, CSAT established the Practice Improvement Collaborative Program, which has provided several million dollars in grant funding. A key objective of the initial phase of the program was to develop partnerships between treatment providers and researchers. The Practice Improvement Program was designed as a two-phase program. During the initial phase (FY 1999–FY 2002), Practice Improvement Collaboratives were organized to demonstrate the benefits of engaging a broad range of community-based stakeholders in identifying service delivery needs and implementing evidence-based practices. These collaboratives developed practice–research networks, established researcher-in-residence programs, implemented practice improvement projects within their community treatment settings, and demonstrated the effectiveness of different implementation strategies.

The second stage, or implementation phase (FY 2003–FY2005), emphasizes the needs of treatment providers to institutionalize evidence-based practice improvements in their "real world," community-based treatment settings. The implementation phase of the Practice Improvement Program (PIP) addresses the organizational barriers that hinder the adoption of evidence-based practices. Treatment providers are to implement clinical and service delivery practices that have been demonstrated to improve client access, initiation, and engagement, for example, care management protocols, referral procedures, client assessment and placement protocols, and business and administrative practices.

The emphasis on collaboration that is highlighted in substance abuse programming reinforces a central theme of this first chapter, namely, the importance of research skills for all professionals in the human service field. Although the primary function of most human service professionals is service delivery, proficiency in research methods and familiarity with research are essential to practicing in the human services. Similarly, the researcher's capacity to operate within the human service arena is enhanced by knowledge of and appreciation for issues of service delivery.

COMPUTERS IN RESEARCH

Information Technology in the Human Services

The computer, probably more than any other single invention, stands as a symbol of technological progress at the beginning of the 21st century. Computers have entered all areas of society, including the human services. A few decades ago, computer applications in the human services were limited to accounting and bureaucratic record keeping. In fact, the impersonality and quantification that seem associated with computers were viewed by many as antithetical to the personal and qualitative approach of human service practitioners. By the 21st century, however, computers, or what are broadly called information technologies (IT), have become an integral part of virtually all human service activities (Coe and Menon 2000; Harlow and Webb 2003). This includes the Internet and the World Wide Web, which have increasingly become resources for research by human service professionals. In recognition of this, we have included in each chapter a section titled "Exploring the Internet." This feature follows the Important Terms for Review at the end of each chapter and contains exercises on how to use the Internet for research purposes related to the chapter.

The traditional use of computers in social research has been to assist in coding and analyzing data. In later chapters, we describe computer software that can run statistical tests, assist in interviewing respondents, help select a sample to use in data collection, and accomplish a host of other activities related directly to research fundamentals. However, computers today have many uses beyond these traditional ones. They can assist in the literature review process through computerized database searches available at most libraries (see Appendix A), they help in report preparation as word processors, and graphics programs have become essential in producing charts and figures to communicate the findings of research.

Computers are also rapidly entering use for human service practice tasks; with creativity, these service-delivery applications can be harnessed to make applied research easier and more feasible. This service base also increases the possibilities for making use of research in practice. Our discussion of computer applications illustrates the central theme of this book: Important linkages exist between social research and human service practice, and the imaginative application of computer technology is yet another way of forging this linkage.

For example, practitioners can perform assessments on a wide variety of problem areas by using such computer programs as Computer Assisted Social Services (CASS). CASS is a versatile software program that can adapt to a variety of human service tasks. It uses structured forms, questionnaires, case notes, measurement or assessment scales, and tests or examinations. CASS can provide clinicians with data to assist in diverse tasks from assessing marital interaction to making child placement decisions. Further information on CASS can be found in Nugent, Sieppert, and Hudson (2001) and at the publisher's Web site (wadsworth.com/social_work_d/index.html); the actual CASS software can be downloaded from that site.

Computers have also been used creatively in other practice situations, such as self-help therapies, biofeedback, patient education, and human service agency supervision tasks and training programs, and to create support networks. Good information about the uses of computers in human service research can be found in the journals *Journal of Technology in Human Services* (www2.uta.edu/cussn/jths/default.htm) and *Social Science Computer Review* (hcl.chass.ncsu.edu/sscore/sscore.htm).

A Computers in Research section will be included in most chapters of this book. The goal is not to teach you how to use computer software, as this depends on what kind of software and computers you have available at your school, home, or agency; instead, our purpose is to educate you regarding the range of computer uses in the field of social research today and to stimulate your thinking about ways of using this technology to link practice with research. This will enable you, when confronted with a research problem, to search for the computer tools that can assist in solving the problem.

single composite score from a number of other scores that measure something of interest. Chapters 14 through 16 offer an introduction to *data analysis,* or what to do with numerical and non-numerical data once they are collected. Chapter 17 is an introduction to the *grant-seeking process,* or how to find financial support for research, including how to write grant proposals and research reports.

Computers have now become an integral part of the research process. In recognition of this, we have included in most chapters an insert titled "Computers in Research." Each insert describes a particular research use of the computer that is relevant to the topic of the chapter. In addition, a feature titled "Exploring Infotrac® College Edition and the Internet" appears in each chapter; through exercises, this feature shows you how to use the Internet for a variety of research purposes.

The book ends with two appendices. The first is a guide to using the library for research in the human services. Effective use of library resources is an essential step in most research projects. The second appendix presents ways of generating and using tables of random numbers, which have many uses in research and are discussed in several chapters.

Main Points

■ The human services are those professions with the goal of enhancing the relations between people and societal institutions, to enable people to maximize their potential and alleviate distress.

■ While the primary goal of the human services is to deliver services to clients, research has become a fundamental part of such service delivery. In fact, a major theme of this book is the important parallels and linkages between research and human service practice.

■ A knowledge of research is necessary for both consumers of social research and those who produce it.

■ Social research is a systematic examination of empirical data, collected firsthand, concerning the social or psychological forces operating in a situation.

■ Social research seeks to achieve the goals of description, prediction, explanation, and evaluation.

■ Social research can also involve basic research or applied research.

■ The links between social research and human service practice can be identified in five focal areas: understanding human functioning in social environments, needs assessment, assessment of client functioning, program evaluation, and practice effectiveness evaluation.

■ Conducting accurate and unbiased research on members of minority groups confronts social researchers with special problems.

■ Research and practice follow similar, parallel paths in approaching a problem. Research, for example, follows a series of steps that have parallels to the steps in practice intervention.

Important Terms for Review

applied research
basic research
descriptive research
evaluation research
evidence-based practice
explanatory research
human services
pilot study
predictive research
pretest
pure research
research design
social research

Exploring InfoTrac® College Edition and the Internet

Wadsworth Publishing Company makes available an online library of hundreds of scholarly journals and popular periodicals for a variety of academic fields, including social research in the human services. It is called InfoTrac® College Edition, and it can be searched by entering appropriate search terms. In every Exploring InfoTrac® College Edition and the Internet section, we will present some suggested InfoTrac® College Edition search terms that will teach you how to use the Internet to enhance your understanding of social science research methods. We will also list some specific InfoTrac® College Edition articles, cited exactly as you will find them, that relate to chapter content. It can also be productive to enter "Important Terms for Review" as InfoTrac® College Edition search terms.

InfoTrac® College Edition search terms:

evidence-based practice
social research
practice effectiveness

InfoTrac® College Edition articles:

Evidence-Based Practice: An Alternative to Authority-Based Practice. (Knowledge Building) Eileen Gambrill. *Families in Society: The Journal of Contemporary Human Services* July–August 1999 v80 i4 p341(1) (6,848 words)

Knowledge for Direct Social Work Practice: An Analysis of Trends. William J. Reid. *Social Service Review* March 2002 v76 i1 p6(30) (12,572 words)

The sheer volume of material available on the Internet makes it a powerful resource, but at the same time it can seem overwhelming and chaotic. An important key to bringing order to the vast array of material is knowing where to look and how to search. Your reference librarian can be of great help in this regard. When using an Internet search engine, it is always a good idea to check out the "Help Page" for tips on refining your search. Also, once you locate one promising source, look for its own key terms. By substituting them in your search, you may locate additional sites. Save a record of interesting sites that you locate, or record the Internet addresses and share them with other students in the class. The class may wish to establish a discussion list on the university computer system to share information on research topics as you discover them.

One specific Web site to explore is Social Work Search.com (www.socialworksearch.com). This site is sufficiently broad-based that it can appeal to social

workers as well as other human service professionals. In addition to links to substantive areas in social work, such as mental health or child welfare, there are also links to research and statistics topics. Another comprehensive site with links to a virtual course on research methods is maintained by the School of Library, Archival and Information Studies at the University of British Columbia (www.slais.ubc.ca/resources/research_methods/index.htm).

These Internet exercises will mention some specific Internet addresses, but these addresses tend to change periodically and may have changed by the time you read this book. Therefore, many exercises will focus on how you can direct a search yourself.

For Further Reading

Agnew, Neil M., and Sandra W. Pyke. *The Science Game: An Introduction to Research in the Behavioral Sciences,* 6th ed. Englewood Cliffs, N.J.: Prentice-Hall, 1994. Presented as a "consumer's guide" to the products of science, *The Science Game* is much more than that. It is a compact and highly readable introduction to the research craft.

Brownson, Ross C., Elizabeth A. Baker, Terry L. Leet, and Kathleen N. Gillespie. *Evidence-Based Public Health.* New York: Oxford University Press, 2003. This text provides a case for evidence-based public health and practical guidance on how to choose, implement, and evaluate evidence-based programs and policies in public health settings. Extensive formal training in public health sciences is not required to grasp the presentation.

Frost, Peter J., and Ralph E. Stablein, eds. *Doing Exemplary Research.* Newbury Park, Calif.: Sage, 1992. This is a collection of the reflections of several researchers about their research experiences. Among other things, it illustrates a wide array of research topics and approaches.

Hayes, Steven C., David H. Barlow, and Rosemery O. Nelson-Gray. *The Scientist-Practitioner: Research and Accountability in the Age of Managed Care,* 2nd ed. Boston: Allyn & Bacon, 1999. This is an excellent book on the linkage of research and practice. Although it focuses on psychology, it will be of interest to any professional attempting to establish a scientist–practitioner model.

Hoover, Kenneth R., and Todd Donovan. *The Elements of Social Scientific Thinking,* 7th ed. Belmont, Calif.: Wadsworth, 2001. This book is an initiation to social science research intended for those who use the results of research or those just beginning as researchers. Through several editions it has remained to the point and up to date.

Kemeny, John G. *A Philosopher Looks at Science.* Princeton, N.J.: Van Nostrand, 1959. A discussion of the philosophical underpinnings of science and scientific research. To truly understand research, you need some knowledge of the basic logic of science, a field generally referred to as the "philosophy of science."

Kirk, Stuart A., and William J. Reid, *Science and Social Work: A Critical Appraisal.* New York: Columbia University Press, 2002. The authors analyze major efforts to integrate social work research and practice, including scientifically based practice, computer-assisted social work practice, research-based practice (evidence-based practice), and research dissemination and utilization.

Rossman, Gretchen B., and Sharon F. Rallis. *Learning in the Field: An Introduction to Qualitative Research,* 2nd ed. Thousand Oaks, Calif.: Sage, 2003. This text provides a comprehensive overview of qualitative research, discussing both when it is preferred over quantitative research and how it is conducted.

Rothman, Jack, and Edwin J. Thomas, eds. *Intervention Research: Design and Development for Human Service.* New York: Haworth, 1994. This book provides an extensive analysis of how research and practice activities can be fully integrated to enhance the effectiveness of practice intervention in the human services.

Stricker, George, and Robert H. Keisner, eds. *From Research to Clinical Practice: The Implications of Social and Developmental Research for Psychotherapy.* New York: Plenum, 1985. An excellent book of readings on the ways that research can be of value in human service practice. A number of authors address the issue of the tensions that can emerge between researchers and practitioners.

Exercises for Class Discussion

Use the case illustration presented below to do Exercise 1.1.

While out of the office on a home call, a teacher's aide for the first grade at a rural school called the Intermediate School District office where you serve as a school social worker. In addition to identifying information, the secretary left you a message that contains the following details: "Janet has been absent from school for eight days—illness, she says—and she is now back in school. Janet's mother and father are separating. The mother moved out; Janet, age six, remained with the father. Now the mother has returned, but the father moved out last week. Janet says that a 15-year-old girl is babysitting for her and her two-year-old brother all the time. She hates the sitter. Her mother works at a local supermarket and hasn't responded to attendance letters. Janet is really upset and isn't doing her schoolwork. She bursts into tears at the mention of her family. Janet's regular teacher is out for maternity leave."

The school district is asking you to look into Janet's situation.

1.1 We have emphasized the parallels between practice and research. With this in mind, do the following:
   a. Make a list of some problems in this referral that call for human service intervention. What additional information would you need to formulate an intervention plan?
   b. Make a list of research problems or questions that are suggested in this referral. How is this list similar to or different from your list of intervention problems?

1.2 Professional journals in the human services typically include a mixture of research articles, practice- and service-delivery descriptions, and policy issue discussions. Select recent issues of a major journal in your profession, such as *Social Work* or *The American Psychologist,* and identify those articles that qualify as research articles. Two or three students should independently review the same journal issue so that findings can be compared. What features distinguish a research article from other articles?

1.3 This chapter discusses several goals of research. For each of the research articles located for Exercise 1.2, determine whether it is primarily descriptive, predictive, explanatory, or evaluative. Explain why you classified each article as you did. If you are uncertain as to how an article should be classified, indicate why and state what additional information is needed to help you classify the study.

1.4 For each research study, state how it applies to human service practice in terms of the five focal areas discussed in the chapter.

Chapter 2

The Logic of Social Research

After dashing through the Looking-glass House to view its garden, Alice says,

> I should see the garden far better . . . if I could get to the top of that hill: and here's a path that leads straight to it—at least, no, it doesn't do *that* . . . but I suppose it will at last. But how curiously it twists! It's more like a corkscrew than a path! Well this turn goes to the hill, I suppose—no it doesn't! This goes straight back to the house! Well then, I'll try it the other way. (Carroll 1946, pp. 21–22)

Understanding the world—especially human behavior—sometimes bears a striking resemblance to Alice's convoluted and frustrating journey in Wonderland. People do what we least expect, without any apparent rhyme or reason. A prisoner on parole who appeared to be "making it on the outside" suddenly commits another offense and goes back to jail; a marriage of 25 years that seemed to be quite solid suddenly ends in divorce; a respected and successful business executive commits suicide. Human service providers, in particular, are familiar with experiences such as these, and the path to understanding often mirrors Alice's corkscrew.

Science, however, provides a method for mapping and understanding that corkscrew. In this chapter, we discuss the basic logic underlying scientific research, beginning with an assessment of how science differs from other ways of gaining knowledge. Then we analyze the importance of theories and their role in scientific research, drawing a parallel with the use of theories in human service practice. Following this, we discuss the role of concepts and hypotheses, showing how hypotheses serve to link theory and research. Finally, we analyze the nature of causality because research is at its core a search for cause-and-effect relationships among phenomena.

Sources of Knowledge

Human service practice is based on knowledge of human behavior and the social environment. There are numerous ways of gaining such knowledge, but all sources of knowledge have their pitfalls. We argued in Chapter 1 that practice knowledge should be grounded in scientific research. This does not mean that science is infallible, but science does have advantages as a source of knowledge that makes it superior to other ways of gaining knowledge.

To see why this is the case, we contrast science with four other common sources of knowledge: tradition, experience, common sense, and journalism. We then discuss how science can improve professional practice.

Tradition

Traditional knowledge is knowledge based on custom, habit, and repetition. It is founded on a belief in the sanctity of ancient wisdom and the ways of our forebears. People familiar with the musical *Fiddler on the Roof* will recall how the delightful character Tevye, a dairyman in the village of Anatevka, sang the praises of tradition:

> Because of our traditions, we've kept our balance for many, many years. Here in Anatevka we have traditions for everything—how to eat, how to sleep, how to wear clothes. . . . You may ask, how did this tradition start? I'll tell you—I don't know! But it's a tradition. Because of our traditions, everyone knows who he is and what God expects him to do. Tradition. Without our traditions, our lives would be as shaky as—as a fiddler on the roof! (Stein 1964, pp. 1, 6)

For Tevye and the villagers of Anatevka, where traditions come from is unimportant. Traditions provide guidance; they offer "truth"; they are the final word. Traditions tell us that something is correct because it has always been done that way.

Traditional knowledge is widespread in all societies. Many people, for example, believe that a two-parent family is preferable to a single-parent family because the former provides a more stable and effective socializing experience for children and reduces the likelihood of maladjustment. In some cases, these beliefs are grounded in religious traditions, whereas in other cases they are accepted because "everybody knows" how important two parents are to a child's development. In fact, some human service providers accept these beliefs about the traditional two-parent family despite the existence of considerable research suggesting that the two-parent family may not always be essential for high-quality adoption or foster care. For example, one review of research into this issue concluded, "In the studies reviewed here, single-parent families were found to be as nurturing and viable as dual-parent families. In fact, single-parent adoption emerged as a good plan for children" (Groze 1991). Human service providers can be affected in other ways by traditional beliefs. For example, the works of a Sigmund Freud or an Erik Erikson might be accepted without question, and emphasis might be placed on remaining true to their words rather than on assessing the accuracy or utility of their ideas.

Tradition can be an important source of knowledge, especially in such areas as moral judgments or value decisions, but it can have some major disadvantages. First, tradition is extremely resistant to change, even in those cases where change might be necessary because new information surfaces or new developments occur. Second, traditional knowledge easily confuses knowledge (an understanding of what *is*) with values (a preference for what *ought to be*). For many people, the traditional emphasis on the two-parent family is actually based on a value regarding the preferred family form rather than a knowledge of the effect such a family has on child development.

Experience

Experience as a source of knowledge refers to first-hand, personal observations of events. **Experiential knowledge** is based on the assumption that truth and understanding can be achieved through personal experience and that witnessing events will lead to an accurate comprehension of those events.

Experience is a common source of knowledge for human service workers, who have numerous opportunities to make firsthand observations of emotionally disturbed children, people with physical disabilities, foster children, and other service populations. From these contacts, practitioners can develop an understanding—not necessarily an accurate one—of what motivates their clients and what social or psychological processes have influenced them.

For example, a person working in a spouse abuse shelter will have considerable contact with women whose husbands have physically and psychologically abused them. Because of this, the worker likely is sensitive to the harm that can come to women from their husbands. After seeing women who have been so abused, this worker may conclude that marital counseling with such spouses cannot work in a climate of violence and anger and may even be dangerous. In fact, social worker Liane Davis (1984) found that shelter workers were much less likely to recommend marital counseling than were family court judges. Family court judges did not have the powerful experience of seeing women when the effects of their abuse were most visible; moreover, they have a mandate to maintain the integrity of the family. For them, marital counseling seems both a feasible and an appropriate way to keep the family intact. So we see that the experiences of shelter workers and judges in different settings can lead them to perceive problems and assess solutions differently.

This experiential knowledge about family dynamics and abuse may be reinforced by traditional knowledge about the importance of family life. Armed with this knowledge, a practitioner might shape an intervention effort that focuses on individual counseling or marital counseling.

However, experiential knowledge has some severe limitations that can lead to erroneous conclusions. First, human perceptions are notoriously unreliable. Perception is affected by many factors, including the cultural background and the mood of the observer, the conditions under which something is observed, and the nature of what is being observed. Even under the best conditions, some misperception is likely, and thus, knowledge based on experience is often inaccurate.

Second, human knowledge and understanding do not result from direct perception but rather from *inferences* made from those perceptions. The conclusion that marital counseling doesn't work is an inference—it is not directly observed. All that has been observed is that these women have been battered by their husbands. There is no observation of the effectiveness of any type of counseling. (We discuss in more detail this problem of making inferences from observations when we address the issue of causality later in this chapter.)

Third, the very people in positions to experience something directly frequently have vested interests in perceiving that thing in a certain way. Teachers, for example, observe that the students who do poorly are the ones who do not pay strict attention during class. However, teachers have a vested interest in showing that their teaching techniques are not the reason for poor performance among students. Teachers would probably be inclined to attribute students' failings to the students' lack of effort and attentiveness rather than to their own inadequacies as teachers.

A final limitation on experiential knowledge is that it is difficult to know if the people directly available to you are accurate representatives of all the people about whom you wish to draw conclusions. If they are not, any conclusions drawn from your observations may be in error. To use our earlier example, are the battered women who contact a spouse abuse shelter representative of all battered women? If the women who contact a shelter are different in some way, and these differences influence the effectiveness of counseling in the shelter, then you cannot generalize conclusions from their outcomes in counseling to the experiences of all battered women. Battered women who go to a shelter may be more affluent or less isolated and might therefore evidence different outcomes in counseling than would less affluent or more isolated women.

Common Sense

The accumulation of knowledge from tradition and experience often blends to form what people call **common sense:** practical judgments based on the experiences, wisdoms, and prejudices of a people. People with common sense are presumed to be able to make sound decisions even though they lack any specialized training and knowledge. Yet is common sense a very accurate source of knowledge? Consider the following contradictory examples. Common sense tells us that people with similar interests and inclinations will likely associate with one another. When we see a youngster who smokes marijuana as-

sociating with others who do the same, we may sagely comment, "Birds of a feather flock together." Then we see an athletic woman become involved with a bookish, cerebral man, and we say, "Opposites attract."

In other words, common sense often explains everything—even when those explanations contradict one another. This is not to say that common sense is unimportant or always useless. Common sense can be valuable and accurate, which is not surprising because people need sound information as a basis for interacting with others and functioning in society. However, common sense does not normally involve a rigorous and systematic attempt to distinguish reality from fiction. Rather, it tends to accept what "everyone knows" to be true and to reject contradictory information. Furthermore, common sense is often considered something people either have or don't have because it is not teachable. In fact, it is often contrasted with "book learning." This discourages people from critically assessing their commonsense knowledge and tempering it with knowledge acquired from other sources. For this reason, commonsense knowledge should be accepted and used cautiously. As a basis for human service practice, knowledge needs to be based on the rigorous and systematic methods used in scientific research. Common sense or a vague feeling of "helping" is not enough.

Journalism

The materials prepared by journalists for newspapers, magazines, television, or other media are another important source of knowledge about the world for most people. With the explosion of news sources available on cable television and the Internet, people now have access to vast amounts of journalistic information. Though some journalism consists of opinion pieces based on the speculations and inferences of the journalist, much of it, like science, is grounded in observation: Reporters interview people or observe events and write their reports based on those observations. In addition, with modern technology, journalists are often in a position to provide a video and/or audio record of what happened at a scene.

So it may seem, at first glance, that science and journalism have much in common as sources of knowledge, and significant similarities between the two endeavors can be identified. Both use observation to seek out accurate knowledge about the world. In fact, some journalism can at times take on many of the characteristics of social science research. Some journalistic output, for example, can look a lot like the in-depth interviews and case studies we will discuss in Chapter 9. However, although scientific standards require that scientists use the systematic procedures discussed in this book, journalism can and often does fall far short of meeting these standards.

A key difference between science and journalism is that the observations of scientists are much more systematic in nature. This means that scientists utilize far more careful procedures to reduce the chances that their conclusions will be inaccurate. For example, a journalist interested in the experiences of prison inmates will probably interview a few inmates who are made available to him by prison authorities and then use these interviews to draw conclusions, at least implicitly, about the experiences of all prisoners. Social scientists would recognize that the prisoners selected by the authorities are likely to differ in some important ways from other prisoners: They may have been selected because they committed less serious offenses or were model prisoners. Their experience of prison is likely to be very different from that of a more serious offender or from someone who has chronic confrontations with prison authorities. Recognizing this, social scientists would be very careful about how they selected inmates on whom to make observations and would usually not accept a sample selected by prison authorities. The best sampling procedures, which will be discussed in Chapter 6, would be those that ensure that all types of prisoners have a chance to appear in the sample. This could be done, for example, by interviewing all prisoners or, if that were not feasible, interviewing a randomly selected group of prisoners. If sampling procedures fall short of these standards, then social scientists have reduced confidence in the arrived-at conclusions. Journalists often do not use such rigorous sampling procedures.

A second key difference between science and journalism is that journalism is not concerned with theory building and theory verification as a way of developing an abstract explanation of people's behavior. Journalists are much more focused on, as the saying goes, "just the facts." Scientists, on the other hand, recognize that facts often don't speak for themselves—they need to be interpreted in the context of a theoretical understanding to fully comprehend what the facts mean.

Science

Winston Churchill, prime minister of Britain during World War II, is reported to have said that democracy is an imperfect form of government but that it is far superior to all other forms of government. Many scientists have a similar view of science: They realize that it is imperfect and limited, but they also recognize that it is far superior to other sources of knowledge for gaining an understanding of the world. **Science** is a method of obtaining objective knowledge about the world through systematic observation. (The term *science* is also sometimes used to refer to the accumulated body of knowledge that results from scientific inquiry.) Science has five distinguishing characteristics that, taken together, set it apart from the other sources of knowledge.

First, science is *empirical,* which simply means that science is based on direct observation of the world. Science is not, as some people mistakenly believe, founded in theorizing, philosophizing, or speculating. Though scientists at times do all these things, they must eventually observe the world to see whether their theories or speculations agree with the facts. Because of this, the topics that can be subjected to scientific scrutiny are limited; any issue that cannot be resolved through observation is not within the scope of science. For example, the questions of whether God exists or what values should underlie a human service profession are not scientific issues because to determine their truth (or lack thereof) through observation is impossible. These are matters of faith or preference, not of science.

Second, science is *systematic,* meaning that the procedures used by scientists are organized, methodical, public, and recognized by other scientists. One dimension of the systematic nature of science is that scientists report in detail all the procedures used in coming to a conclusion. This enables other scientists to assess whether inferences and conclusions drawn are warranted given the observations made. A second dimension of the systematic nature of science is *replication*—repeating studies numerous times to determine if the same results can be obtained. Scientists are very cautious about drawing hard-and-fast conclusions from a single observation or investigation. In fact, quite at variance with experiential knowledge, scientists assume that a single direct observation is as likely to be incorrect as correct. Only repeated observations can reduce the chance of error and misinterpretation (Rosenthal 1991).

Third, science is *the search for causes.* Scientists assume that there is order in the universe, that there are ascertainable reasons for the occurrence of all events, and that scientists can discover the orderly nature of the world. If we assumed that there was no order, no pattern, then there would be no need to search for it. We could write off events as due to chance or the intervention of some benevolent (or malevolent or indifferent) otherworldly force that we can never understand.

Fourth, science is *provisional,* which means that scientific conclusions are always accepted as tentative and subject to question and possible refutation. There are no ultimate, untouchable, irrevocable truths in science. There are no scientists whose work is held in such esteem that it cannot be criticized or rejected. As philosopher Jacob Bronowski (1978, pp. 121–122) put it, "Science is not a finished enterprise. . . . The truth is [not] a thing that you could find . . . the way you could find your hat or your umbrella." Science is a process of continuous movement toward a more accurate picture of the world, and scientists fully realize that we will never achieve the ultimate and final picture.

Finally, science strives for *objectivity,* which means that scientists try to avoid having their personal biases and values influence their scientific conclusions. This is a controversial and complicated characteristic of science because many social scientists would argue that true objectivity is impossible

for human beings to achieve. We will discuss this issue at a number of points in this volume, but it is sufficient to say here that all scientists are concerned that their scientific conclusions are not solely or merely a product of their own personal biases and values. This doesn't mean that scientists should be devoid of values. Quite the contrary—they can be as passionate, concerned, and involved as any other group of citizens. They realize, however, that their values and biases can and probably will lead to erroneous scientific conclusions. To address this problem, science incorporates mechanisms to reduce the likelihood of biased observations becoming an accepted part of the body of scientific knowledge. For example, publicizing all research procedures enables others to assess whether the research was conducted in a way that justifies the conclusions reached. Furthermore, such detailed reporting permits replication so that other researchers, with different values, can see if they come to the same conclusions regarding a set of observations.

Despite these checks, of course, values and biases will still be found in research. The very decision of what topics to investigate, for example, is often shaped by the researcher's values. One person studies family violence because a close friend was the victim of spousal abuse, and another studies factors contributing to job satisfaction because of a personal belief that work is central to identity. Values and biases also enter research through the interpretation of observations. For personal reasons, one researcher may desperately want to show that the criminal justice system rehabilitates (or does not rehabilitate). This may well influence how he or she goes about conducting research and interpreting the results. There are even a few cases (most common in biomedical research) of outright falsification of data to show a certain conclusion. The point is that values and biases commonly intrude on scientific research, but the overall scientific enterprise is organized to reduce their impact on the body of scientific knowledge.

The scientific method, then, with the characteristics just described, is viewed by scientists as preferable to other ways of gaining knowledge because it is more likely to lead to accurate knowledge of the world. To return to our earlier example of single-parent families and adoption, science views all knowledge regarding the family as provisional and open to question. And there have been many scientific investigations of the role of the family in these matters. Child adjustment and development in two-parent and single-parent families have been compared in both adoptive and biological as well as stepfamilies.

The conclusion from these various studies is that the traditional, two-parent family does not seem to play the indispensable role that much common sense knowledge would accord it or at least that the role of parents in families is more complicated than was once thought. For example, the research shows that adoption by a single parent is not always detrimental when compared with two-parent adoptive settings; some adoptees with one parent do quite well (Groze and Rosenthal 1991; Shireman and Johnson 1986). A related finding is that nontraditional family structure (having one rather than two parents) is probably less critical to children's development than is family process (such as warm relationships and low conflict between parents and children). The negative consequences often associated with single-parent families may arise from the conflict that often accompanies divorce, as divorce is how many single-parent families are produced (Amato and Booth 1997; Jekielek 1998; Lansford et al. 2001). Also, single-parent families often experience certain negative factors: low income, inadequate parental guidance, and less access to community resources. Single-parent families that overcome these difficulties do as well as other family forms in raising children (McLanahan and Sandefur 1994). Furthermore, children in one-parent families sometimes benefit from the experience (Amato 1987; Dowd 1997). For example, a single parent sometimes gives his or her teenage offspring more responsibility and a greater role in family decision making. So, the common sense or traditional view that the two-parent family is always superior to the single-parent setting is shown by research to be vastly oversimplified at best.

In this fashion, then, scientific knowledge overcomes many of the weaknesses of traditional, experiential, and commonsense knowledge. In particular, it enables us to accumulate accurate information despite the personal biases of individual researchers or practitioners. These positive attributes of science do not mean, however, that science is perfect. Scientists do make errors. But, as Jacob Bronowski (1978, p. 122) so aptly put it, "Science is essentially a self-correcting activity." If proper scientific procedures are followed, today's errors will be corrected by researchers in the future, whose errors in turn will be corrected by still more research.

Scientific Practice

We saw in Chapter 1 the parallels between the steps in the research process and the steps in practice intervention. Likewise, human service practice has characteristics, or at least it should have characteristics, that parallel those of science (Hayes, Barlow, and Nelson-Gray 1999; Rosen 1996). First of all, practice, like science, should be *empirical,* stressing problem assessment involving direct observation of client problems, actual counts of behaviors, and independent observations from multiple data sources. Such data are less subject to distortion and bias than self-reports, speculations, and philosophizing. Second, practice, like research, should be *systematic.* To the extent that practice procedures are well organized, clearly specified, and made public, they can be replicated and tested by others. In this manner, ineffective procedures can be eliminated, and promising ones can be refined and improved. One of the recurring criticisms of many human service interventions is that the intervention itself is not well specified. Consequently, research evaluating the intervention cannot clearly indicate what did or did not work. Practice models also involve *causality* in terms of specifying a clear link between cause and effect or explaining why a proposed intervention should work with the particular identified problem. Again, a criticism of human service projects in the past has been that many of them have consisted of a conglomeration of intervention efforts without a clearly articulated linkage between cause and effect.

Practice theory, like science, should be *provisional.* All practice models and techniques should be viewed as fair game for criticism and refutation. Through such a process of testing and challenging existing practices, healthy growth can occur in practice methodology.

Finally, human service professionals must deal with the problem of professional *objectivity*. The determination of the utility and effectiveness of practice procedures needs to be done under objective conditions. Just as the researcher must attempt to safeguard against the intrusion of values into the conduct of research, so practitioners must guard against the intrusion of values into practice. This issue of values and objectivity is particularly difficult for human service practitioners, who often approach problems with a strong set of values, both personal and professional. Personally, practitioners may have strong feelings about such matters as abortion, alcohol use, or domestic violence that may clash with those of groups with which they work. Furthermore, some human service providers are conventional and middle class in their personal lives, which may influence what they see as successful social functioning. In addition to these personal values, human service practice itself is heavily imbued with professional values. In fact, as one human service educator put it, "Social work is among the most value-based of all professions. . . . [It] is deeply rooted in a fundamental set of values that ultimately shapes the profession's mission and its practitioners' priorities" (Reamer 1995, p. 3).

At times, these values may emphasize a conservatism or a pressure to preserve the status quo, and at other times the values may reflect a commitment to support vulnerable or oppressed populations. In either event, the recommendation that human service providers not let their values intrude into the provision of services to clients is challenging to satisfy. In fact, it is probably impossible to mount an effective change effort without some imposition of values, either implicit or explicit. Even more, some therapeutic approaches, such as those of Carl Rogers, Albert Ellis, and Hobart Mowrer, include as one of their goals the acceptance by the client of new and more realistic values. In addition, many human services emphasize the value of alleviating deprivation and distress and of helping people achieve their aspirations.

As a means of controlling the imposition of practitioners' values on clients, the human services emphasize the importance of client self-determination, the notion that individuals have the right to freely make choices about their lives. This can confront practitioners with a dilemma: What if self-determination leads to client choices that run counter to the practitioner's personal or professional values? For example, should practitioners work in a child welfare agency that makes abortion referrals if they are morally opposed to this procedure? But the issue need not be this dramatic; indeed, it is often more subtle. Mental health has often been equated with a middle-class lifestyle. "Appropriate" behavior for women has been defined in terms of a male-dominated society, with one consequence being that there are now feminist therapists who target their services to clients with a feminist orientation.

So even though professional practice in the human services is clearly oriented toward the fulfillment of certain values, practicing in the profession requires that the worker establish checks on the intrusion of values into practice, much as the researcher does in the conduct of research. In later chapters, we will discuss research techniques that are less subject to biases in observation and measurement. Application of these principles in practice can also help restrict the unwanted intrusion of personal values into service delivery. Another way to control the influence of values is to do research on the role of values in practice and to design agency procedures that help provide services objectively. As Research in Practice 2.1 illustrates, the influence of values in the actual conduct of practice cannot be totally eliminated. However, by relying on a practice approach that is empirically based, employs procedures supported by research, and incorporates rigorous evaluation procedures, it is possible to sensitize professionals to the impact of their value positions and thus enhance the objectivity of service delivery.

Theories in Research and Practice

Theory is a word that is misunderstood by many people. To the neophyte, theories are often associated with the abstract, the impractical, or the unreal. In actuality, nothing could be farther from the truth. In

PRACTICE EFFECTIVENESS:
Providing Services to Gays and Lesbians

Human service practitioners often deal with clients or situations that involve value-laden controversies. One area where this is clearly the case is the issue of whether gays or lesbians should be permitted to have custody of their children or to adopt. Traditional, and in some cases religious, values lead some people to the conclusion that only intact, heterosexual, married couples provide a suitable environment for child rearing and that being raised by a gay or lesbian parent would be harmful to the children. The difficult problem for the human service provider is how to serve clients within the context of one's own personal and professional values.

The movement toward evidence-based practice in the human services suggests that it is possible to use scientific research to assess whether personal or professional values are unreasonably influencing the services provided to clients. One of the primary features of evidence-based practice involves identifying general trends gleaned from a review of studies that are applicable to practice. The example of providing child welfare services to gay and lesbian clients provides an excellent example of these features. A human service professional charged with making recommendations about child custody and adoption would approach this situation by systematically searching the literature and asking the question: How well do gays and lesbians perform in the role of parent?

Marcus Tye (2003) summarizes the theoretical and empirical evidence currently available to answer this question. Over the past quarter century, beginning with the work of Carol Lewis (1980), a considerable body of research has accumulated on the development and experiences of the children of lesbians and gay men (Stacey and Biblarz 2001). For the most part, this research does not support the negative developmental outcomes for the children that were predicted by much traditional and experiential knowledge and some people's personal values. Children raised by gay or lesbian families do not differ in sexual orientation or personal development from children raised in heterosexual families (Gottman 1990; McCandlish 1987).

A significant body of research has accumulated, but societal changes have continued to raise value issues that call for new topics for research. Christopher Alexander (1997) observes that by the 1990s there had been a shift. Rather than looking at the quality of family life after a parent had acknowledged his or her homosexuality, researchers began to examine gay men and lesbians who, often in the context of a committed homosexual relationship, were opting to have children by adoption, artificial insemination, or surrogate mothers. Articles appeared with such titles as "Gays and Lesbians Choosing to Be Parents" (Baum 1996) and "Families of the Lesbian Baby Boom" (Patterson 1995). These new studies reflect a twist on value issues surrounding gay and lesbian parenting, namely, the belief that marriage is the only appropriate context in which a child should be born and raised.

Thus, the empirical evidence that has accumulated to date suggests that children can be reared into healthy adults in families parented by homosexuals and that sexual orientation should not preclude individuals from serving as adoptive or foster parents. The general trends in the existing data help to provide direction for shaping agency policy. Science cannot inform human service workers regarding what their personal values ought to be, but it can point to practice situations in which personal values seem to intrude unreasonably on intervention decisions. Such research also safeguards against the danger that decisions based on personal values will masquerade as "the client's best interest" by providing an empirical knowledge base for decision making.

both research and practice settings, theories play a critical role in our understanding of reality and our ability to cope with problems. In fact, people commonly use theories in their daily lives without recognizing that they do so.

What Is a Theory?

A **theory** is a set of interrelated, abstract propositions or statements that offers an explanation of some phenomenon (Skidmore 1979). Three key elements in this definition are important to understanding theories. First, theories are made up of **propositions,** which are statements about the relationship between some elements in the theory. For example, a proposition from the differential association theory of crime is that "a person becomes criminal because of an excess of definitions favorable to the violation of the law over definitions unfavorable to the violation of the law." Elements in this proposition include "criminal" and "definitions favorable to the violation of the law" (Sutherland 1939). Behavior modification theory also contains numerous propositions, such as "behavior change can occur through a reorganization of the environmental cues that reward and punish behavior" (Sulzer-Azaroff and Mayer 1991). The elements in this proposition include "behavior change," "environmental cues," and "reward and punish behavior."

A second important part of our definition of theory is that theories are *abstract* systems, meaning they link general and abstract propositions to particular, testable events or phenomena. In many cases, these abstract systems are *deductive* systems, a general set of propositions that can be used to deduce further, more concrete relationships between the elements of the theory. Differential association theory is again illustrative. As noted, this theory relates definitions favorable to the violation of the law with the greater likelihood of criminal behavior. This means that the theory is supposed to apply to *all* specific types of crimes, such as robbery, larceny, and auto theft. So it would be logical to deduce from the theory that greater exposure to definitions favorable to the violation of the law would be associated with higher incidences of robbery, larceny, and auto theft.

Theories are abstract because they have this deductive power: The broader and more abstract the propositions and their related concepts, the more numerous the specific relationships that can be deduced from them.

The third key aspect of theories is that they provide *explanations* for the phenomena they address. Indeed, the ultimate purpose of a theory is to explain *why* something occurred. In differential association theory, the phenomenon to be explained is criminal behavior, and the explanation is that criminality is learned through much the same process as noncriminal behavior. The content of what is learned—definitions favorable to violation of the law—makes the difference. Thus, differential association provides an explanation for the development of criminal behavior.

In comprehending theories and the roles they play, it is helpful to realize that we all use theories in our everyday lives, although we may not call them theories or even be consciously aware of using them. Nonetheless, we base our decisions and behavior on our past experiences and what we have learned from others. From these experiences, we generalize that certain physical, psychological, and social processes are operative and will continue to be important in the future, with predictable consequences. This is our "commonsense theory" about how the world operates and forms the basis for our decisions. For example, most people have certain general notions—personal theories—about what causes poverty. Some personal theories emphasize poverty as an individual problem: People are poor because of their individual characteristics, such as laziness, low intelligence, poor education, or lack of marketable skills. Others' theories of poverty emphasize structural features of the American economy that dictate that even in times of economic expansion some people will be left impoverished through no fault of their own. Which of these theories people identify with most closely determines, in part, how they react to poor people and which public policy provisions toward poverty they support. Advocates of the individualistic theory might be hostile toward the poor and programs to aid them because they believe the poor are undeserving people who suffer only from their own shortcomings. Supporters of the structural theory may view the poor as victims and tend to be more benevolent toward them.

Personal theories like these concerning poverty may be extreme and misleading because they are based on casual observations, personal experience, or other information lacking the rigorous concern for accuracy of scientific investigations. Unlike commonsense theories, theories in research and practice are precise, detailed, and explicit. It is, however, important to recognize that a theory is always tentative in nature. That is, any theory is best viewed as a *possible* explanation for the phenomenon under investigation. By conducting research, scientists gather evidence that either supports or fails to support a theoretical explanation or practice intervention. No theory stands or falls on the basis of one trial. Theories are tested over a long period of time by many investigations. Only with the accumulation of research outcomes can one begin to have confidence concerning the validity of a theory.

The Functions of Theories

We have all heard the refrain "It's only a theory" or "That's your theory." Such phrases are often used in the context of deflating an argument. Actually, these comments, though often intended in a disparaging sense, convey some truth regarding theories. In particular, they point out that theories are sometimes *untested* (but testable) assertions about reality and that theories are not the end product of scientific investigation but rather a part of the process of science. Theories have particular purposes in both research and practice settings. In fact, the same theories are often used in both research and practice because both researchers and practitioners turn to them for similar reasons. We can identify three major functions of theories in research and practice.

Explanation of Phenomena.   As we have seen, theories provide an explanation for phenomena. They say not only what will happen under certain conditions (which is what hypotheses also do, but more concretely) but also why it will happen. This provides a much more powerful understanding of

human behavior. In differential association theory, for example, the phenomenon to be explained is criminal behavior, and the explanation is that criminal behavior is a product of learning appropriate behaviors from others who are important to us. Thus, differential association theory provides a broad, abstract explanation for the development of criminal behavior that links such behavior with general processes of conformity and group process. People learn to be criminals in the same way they learn to be doctors, nurses, or lawyers—by learning through association with other people.

Guide for Research and Practice.   Theories serve to guide and direct research and practice. They focus attention on certain phenomena as relevant to the issues of concern. If we were to dispense with theories altogether, as some would suggest, then what would we study? What data would be collected? What intervention strategy would be adopted? Theories help us to find answers to these questions.

Imagine that a counseling center wants to attack the problem of teenage alcohol consumption in a particular high school and that the staff decides to study the problem. Where to begin? What variables are important? As a first step, it is essential to fall back on some theory related to these issues. We might, for example, use the theory of differential association, which posits that alcohol consumption results from attitudes and patterns of behavior that are learned in association with other people, particularly peers. To test this theory, we could determine whether alcohol consumption is more common when it is viewed as an acceptable form of behavior among peers. We are then in a position to collect data on attitudes toward alcohol and patterns of alcohol consumption in peer groups. If the theory is confirmed, then it supports the idea that effective intervention will need to focus on attitudes toward alcohol consumption in peer groups.

We could have selected a different theory regarding alcohol consumption. For example, some theories posit an inherited predisposition toward alcoholism. Other theories suggest that alcoholism results from a nutritional deficiency that is satiated by alcohol consumption. We do not presume to suggest which theory is more accurate—future research will settle that issue, one hopes. The same thing occurs in practice intervention. If a practitioner used crisis intervention theory to deal with the disruption caused by an alcoholic parent, the theory would direct attention to such factors as family coping strengths and emotional adaptation. Community-organization practice theory, on the other hand, would focus on community resources available to recovering alcoholics and community services for families of alcoholics. The point is that the theories used by researchers and practitioners serve to guide their approaches and focus their attention on particular phenomena.

Integration of Multiple Observations.   Theories help integrate and explain the many observations made in diverse settings by researchers and practitioners. They tell us *why* something happened, and they enable us to link the outcomes of numerous studies and interventions made in a variety of settings. As long as the findings of these efforts remain individual and isolated, they are not particularly valuable to science. Recall that a single observation is viewed with considerable skepticism. Single research findings may be in error, they may be passed over and forgotten, or their broader implications may be missed entirely. Theories enable us to organize these dispersed findings into a larger explanatory scheme. For example, someone investigating problem pregnancies among teenagers might observe that the groups of teenagers among whom such pregnancies are common tend to view parenthood out of wedlock in a positive fashion. A familiarity with differential association theory would suggest that the social learning

processes important in teenage drinking may also be relevant in problem pregnancies among teenagers. If this is the case, then practitioners working in one area may be able to borrow strategies for intervention from the other area. Thus, theories integrate the findings from independent research endeavors and provide implications for intervention strategies.

Theories, then, play an important part in both research and practice. But one point needs to be reiterated: The utility of theories must be based on their *demonstrated* effectiveness. Theories should never be allowed to become "sacred cows" whose use is based on tradition or custom. Authorities on human service practice report that the proliferation of theories in the social sciences and the human services has made using theories as guides for practice a major challenge for today's practitioners. These theories differ widely in terms of what they specify as the cause of problems, the targets of change, and the most effective intervention techniques. Yet, when selecting among competing theories and integrating multiple theories into a change effort, most authorities would agree with this conclusion: "The most important criterion to consider is the extent to which a given theory has been supported by empirical research" (Hepworth and Larsen 1990, p. 18). In other words, has the intervention been shown to produce the desired results? In scientific research, this is called the **verification** of theories. Researchers approach the problem of verification by developing and testing hypotheses. This process of verification is diagrammed in Figure 2.1, which also shows a parallel process as it occurs in human service practice.

Figure 2.1   The Process of Theory Verification in Research Compared with Practice Intervention

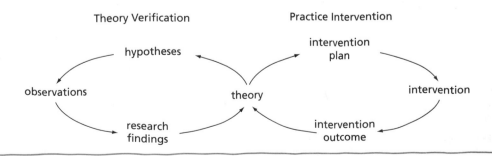

Concepts and Hypotheses
Defining Concepts

An important part of theories is **concepts:** mental constructs or images developed to symbolize ideas, persons, things, or events. Concepts are the elements of theories discussed earlier; they are the building blocks that are interrelated in propositions to form the explanatory statements of a theory (Alford 1998). Some of the concepts in behavior modification theory, for example, are reinforcement, conditioning, learning, and behavior change.

Concepts are similar in function to the words we use in everyday communication. The word "automobile," for example, is the agreed-on symbol for a particular object that is used as a mode of transportation. The symbol or word is not the object itself but something that stands for or represents that object. Scientific concepts, like words in everyday language, are also symbols that can refer to an extremely broad range of referents. They may refer to something fairly concrete, like leadership, or something highly abstract, like reinforcement or cohesion.

Despite the similarities between scientific concepts and ordinary words, some differences are critical to the scientific endeavor. In particular, concepts used in scientific research must be defined very carefully. With the words we use for everyday communication, we can get along quite well with only a general idea of how these words are defined. In fact, it is doubtful whether most people could give a dictionary-perfect definition of even the most commonly used words. Such imprecision in the use of scientific concepts, however, is totally inadequate. Scientists, widely scattered both geographically and temporally, carry on research that tests various aspects of theories. For these disconnected research projects to produce information of maximum utility, all the bits of knowledge need to be integrated into an explanatory scheme: a theory. This accumulation of knowledge is severely hampered—in fact, becomes practically impossible—if these isolated scientists use different definitions of the same concepts.

For example, many studies of the relationship between reinforcement and learning have been conducted. If the results of different studies are to be comparable, the concepts of reinforcement and learning should be defined the same way. Learning, for instance, can be defined in *behavioral* terms as the performance of a new behavior or in *cognitive* terms as the understanding of how a particular behavior might be performed. When defined in these two different ways, the concept refers to something quite different in the world, and results from two investigations using the different definitions would not be directly comparable. Perhaps, for example, behavioral learning occurs under quite different conditions than cognitive learning.

Scientific analysis involves two types of definitions of concepts, each functioning at a different level of analysis and serving a different purpose. At the theoretical or abstract level, concepts are given **nominal definitions:** verbal definitions in which scientists agree that one set of words or symbols will be used to stand for another set of words or symbols. Nominal definitions are directly analogous to the dictionary definitions of ordinary words in which a phrase is designed to give meaning to the word or concept being defined (Cohen and Nagel 1934). For example, a nominal definition of "poverty" might be a deficiency in resources to the extent that people are not able to maintain a lifestyle considered minimally acceptable in a particular society (Sullivan 2003, p. 155).

An important step in moving from the abstract level of theory to the concrete level of research is to give concepts **operational definitions:** definitions that indicate the precise procedures or operations to be followed in measuring a concept. For example, Mollie Orshansky developed one of the most widely used operational definitions of poverty for the Social Security Administration (Ruggles 1990). Her measure, still used by the government as a basis for policy decisions, is based on what it costs to purchase a low-budget, nutritious diet for a family. If we use U.S. Department of Agriculture figures, the poverty line is determined by the cost of food, the size of the family, the age of the head of the household, and other factors. This operational definition of poverty yields a series of income cutoffs below which families are defined as poor. This is a precise definition that lists the exact operations (in this case, mathematical operations) to follow in defining poverty. Anyone using this definition measures the same thing in the same way.

The process of moving from nominal to operational definitions can be complex because concepts are very general and abstract, and controversy often arises over exactly what they refer to. Some concepts that have been a part of the literature for decades have yet to be operationalized in a way that is fully satisfactory. For example, "alcoholism" has proved extremely difficult to operationalize, especially establishing where alcoholism begins and social drinking leaves off (Schuckit 1989). Owing to substantial individual and cultural differences, simple measures relying on amount and frequency of consumption are inadequate. Researchers have been forced to operationalize alcoholism on the basis of such symptoms as family or work problems, morning drinking, poor eating, and recurrent blackouts. Whereas symptom-based measures of alcoholism avoid the errors inherent in consumption measures, substantial controversy remains concerning which symptoms are the best indicators, how many symptoms must be evident, and how serious they must be before the label of "alcoholic" may be meaningfully applied.

Even the concept of poverty, which may seem straightforward and easy to operationalize, has proven controversial. There is, of course, the issue of where to set the income cutoffs. Orshansky's cutoffs are based on the assumption that the average American family spends one third of its income on food; some critics have argued that this results in poverty thresholds that are too low. Furthermore, Orshansky's definition sets a fixed income level as the poverty level, and thus it is unaffected by changing levels of affluence within society as a whole. Some have argued for a relative definition of poverty that defines as poor those who earn one third or one half of the median family income (Bell 1987). With such a definition, the poverty thresholds would rise automatically if the affluence of society as a whole increased. So it should be evident that operationalizing concepts can be difficult, complex, and sometimes controversial. The process of moving from the nominal to the operational level is called *measurement,* and it is treated extensively in Chapters 5 and 13.

Developing Hypotheses

A common strategy in scientific investigations is to move from a general theory to a specific, researchable problem. A part of this strategy is to develop **hypotheses,** which are testable statements of presumed relationships between two or more concepts. Hypotheses state what we expect to find rather than what has already been determined to exist. A major purpose of developing hypotheses in research is to test the accuracy of a theory (see Figure 2.1). The concepts and propositions of which theories are composed are usually too broad and too abstract to be directly tested. Such concepts as *reinforcement* and *learning,* for example, need to be specified empirically through operational definitions before they are amenable to testing. Once operationally defined, these concepts are generally referred to as **variables,** or things that are capable of taking on more than one value. If hypotheses are supported, then this supplies evidence for the accuracy of the theory on which they are based.

In the construction of hypotheses, the relationship between variables is stated in one of two possible directions: a positive relationship or a negative (also called inverse) relationship. In a *positive relationship,* the values of the variables change in the *same* direction, both increasing or both decreasing. For example, we might hypothesize that the acceptance of the use of alcohol among an adolescent's peers will lead to increased likelihood that the adolescent will consume alcohol. In other words, as acceptance of the use of alcohol by one's peers increases, so does the adolescent's own use of alcohol. In a *negative* or *inverse relationship,* the values of variables change in *opposite* directions. We might hypothesize, for example, that, among adolescents, reduced parental supervision will lead to an increase in the likelihood of substance abuse. In this case, as the value of one variable (parental supervision) declines, the value of the other (substance abuse) is predicted to increase.

Useful guidelines to keep in mind for developing hypotheses include the following:

1. *Hypotheses are linked to more abstract theories.* Although generating hypotheses without deriving them from theories is possible, hypotheses are

always linked to theories because the theories provide explanations for why things happen.

2. *It is important that the independent and dependent variables in hypotheses be clearly specified.* The **independent variable** is the presumed active or causal variable—it is the one believed to be producing changes in the dependent variable. The **dependent variable** is the passive variable or the one that is affected. In the previous examples, peer acceptance of alcohol and parental supervision are the independent variables, and alcohol use and substance abuse are the dependent variables.

3. *It is important that the precise nature and direction of the relationship between variables be specified in the hypothesis.* Students are sometimes tempted to state hypotheses like this: "Parental supervision will have an effect on teenage alcohol use." However, although this statement says that there *is* a relationship, it doesn't say exactly *what the nature or direction of the relationship is.* A proper hypothesis, as above, would state how changes in one variable will be associated with particular changes in the other: "As parental supervision decreases, teenage alcohol use increases."

4. *Hypotheses should be so stated that they can be verified or refuted.* Otherwise, they are not hypotheses. Hypotheses, after all, are statements about which we can gather empirical evidence to determine whether they are correct or false. A common pitfall is to make statements that involve judgments or values rather than issues of empirical observation. For example, we might hypothesize that investigations should be increased to reduce the incidence of welfare fraud. On the surface, this statement might appear to be a hypothesis because it relates investigations and welfare fraud in a negative direction. But note that, as stated, it is not a testable hypothesis. The problem is the evaluative "should be." What should or should not be social policy has no place in hypotheses. However, the statement can be modified so that it qualifies as a testable hypothesis: "Increased levels of investigation tend to reduce the incidence of welfare fraud." The hypothesis now makes an empirical assertion that can be checked against fact.

5. *All the concepts and comparisons in hypotheses must be clearly stated.* For example, consider the hypothesis, "Southern Baptists have superior moral standards." The concept of "moral standards" is so abstract and vague that it is impossible to know what it means. This would have to be clearly specified in terms of what is considered a moral standard. In addition, to say that someone's standards are superior requires a referent for comparison: superior to whom or what? It could mean higher than some other religious group, or it could mean above some chosen, absolute standard.

Developing hypotheses from theories is a *creative* process that depends in part on the insight of the investigator. Because hypotheses link theories to particular concrete settings, the researcher's insight is often the trigger to making such connections. In addition, researchers at times combine two or more theories to develop hypotheses that neither theory alone is capable of generating.

Concepts and Operational Definitions among Minority Populations

When conducting research on minority populations, considerable opportunity for bias exists if concepts and operational definitions are not carefully developed. This has been a chronic problem with research on crime. For example, many people believe that nonwhites commit crimes at a higher rate than we would expect, given their numbers in the population. Although this is partly true, it greatly oversimplifies a complex reality, and it reflects how crime is typically operationalized. Official crime statistics from the Federal Bureau of Investigation (FBI 1992) are an important source of data on crime. The FBI operationalizes some crimes as "offenses cleared by arrest" and others as "offenses known to the police." In other words, an occurrence is not officially considered a crime until it is "known to the police" or "cleared by arrest." These official crime statistics show that nonwhites commit more crimes proportionate to their numbers in the population than do whites. However, this is in part a function of how the official statistics operationalize the concept of crime. We know that nonwhites are more likely to be arrested for a given offense, suggesting that it may be arrest that is more common among them rather than the actual commission of crimes. It has been proposed that nonwhites are also more likely to commit highly visible crimes, such as armed robbery or assault, that are more frequently reported to the police and result in an arrest. Some suggest that whites, on the other hand, commit more "hidden" crimes, like embezzlement or fraud, that are less likely to come to the attention of the police. Research suggests that there may be no class difference in the amount of hidden crimes that are committed (Elliott and Huizinga 1983). There are other ways to operationalize crime, such as through victimization studies (asking people if they have been a victim of a crime) and self-reports (having people anonymously report their own involvement in crime). Studies based on these operational definitions tend to show much smaller differences between white and nonwhite crime rates.

Another area in which poorly constructed operational definitions have produced misleading conclusions is that of spousal abuse (Lockhart 1991). Most studies have found rates of spouse abuse to be considerably higher among African Americans than among whites. Typically, these studies have used one of the following as an operational definition of the occurrence of wife abuse: a homicide involving a domestic killing, a battered woman seeking care in an emergency room or social service setting, a wife-abuse claim handled by a domestic court, or a domestic dispute call to a police department. It is well known, however, that African Americans are overrepresented among people who come to the attention of the police, emergency room personnel, or social service workers. Because they are generally overrepresented among these populations, they will appear to have higher rates of abuse than will whites when abuse is operationalized in this fashion. These problems can be reduced by selecting a sample of people from a community and having them answer questions about the amount of conflict and violence that occurs in their own families. This avoids the biased effect of looking only at certain locales. The National Family Violence Resurvey, for example, employed a sampling strategy

that selected about 6,000 cases representing all racial and ethnic groups (Straus and Gelles 1988).

The Committee on the Status of Women in Sociology (1986) has indicated another area in which operational definitions have led to misleading results: studies of work and social contribution. Work is often operationalized in terms of paid employment, but this excludes many types of work from consideration, such as community service or home-based work. With this kind of operational definition, if an employee of a carpet-cleaning firm shampoos the carpets in a home for a fee, that is counted as work, but if a woman does the same activity on her own time in her own home, it is not be classified as work. Such an operationalization of work tends to underestimate the extent of productive activity engaged in by women because women are less likely than men to be paid for their social contributions.

So in developing operational definitions, care must be taken to assess whether these definitions might lead to a distorted view of minorities. In some cases, this calls for careful consideration of what a concept is intended to mean. For example, is the focus of the research on paid employment, or is it on social contribution? In other cases, it calls for careful assessment of whether a definition will lead to an inaccurate over- or under-representation of minorities.

Perspectives on Science

Up to this point in these first two chapters, we have presented science as if it is a coherent, unified activity about which all scientists are in agreement. It isn't. Or, more accurately, we should say that some people believe it is a coherent and unified activity, whereas others are critical of that claim. Scientists debate vigorously over a number of issues concerning the best ways to engage in scientific work. One such debate is over whether science should be deductive or inductive in nature.

Deduction versus Induction

We mentioned earlier that theories are often deductive systems. This means that hypotheses can be logically derived from the propositions that make up a theory. So **deductive reasoning** involves deducing or inferring a conclusion from some premises or propositions. If the propositions—or the theory—are correct, then hypotheses logically derived from them will also be correct. In Figure 2.1, deduction involves moving from the level of theory to that of hypotheses or an intervention plan. Deductive reasoning is central to the scientific process.

However, inductive reasoning enables us to assess the validity of the hypotheses and the theory. **Inductive reasoning** involves inferring something about a whole group or class of objects from our knowledge of one or a few members of that group or class. We test one or a few hypotheses derived from a theory and then infer something about the validity of the theory as a whole. Thus, inductive reasoning carries us from the observations or interventions in Figure 2.1 to some assessment regarding the validity of the theory. The logic of scientific analysis involves an interplay between deduction, or deriving testable hypotheses, and induction, or assessing theories based on tests of hypotheses derived from the theories.

At times, inductive research is conducted without benefit of prior deductive reasoning. This occurs in descriptive or exploratory research where no theory exists from which to deduce hypotheses. In the absence of theory, we begin to make observations and then develop some theoretical propositions that would be plausible given those observations. For example, practitioners may observe that clients with problem pregnancies tend to come from families with low socioeconomic status. Based on the assumption that the parent–child bond is weaker in low socioeconomic families and that such parents therefore have less control over their children, the practitioners could inductively conclude that a weak parent–child bond leads to an increased risk of unwanted pregnancy. In other words, the observations are used to infer a proposition regarding the causes of unwanted pregnancies. In fact, as we will explore in more detail in Chapter 9, some researchers claim that such inductive approaches can be superior to deductive approaches because the former can involve fewer hidden assumptions or preconceived notions on the

part of the scientist. Some of these inductive approaches permit the data to shape the theory rather than having a preconceived theory impose meaning on the data. Inductive research of this sort can serve as a foundation for building a theory, and the theory, in turn, can serve as a source of testable hypotheses through deductive reasoning. Thus, induction and deduction are key links in the chain of scientific reasoning, and they parallel the reasoning process that is found in practice intervention.

Research in Practice 2.2 describes research projects that highlight many of the issues discussed in the previous two sections regarding the use of theories and hypotheses in research and the importance of inductive and deductive reasoning.

Types of Explanation

Beyond deciding whether to use deductive or inductive approaches, scientists also need to decide what type of explanation will be contained in the theory. Earlier in this chapter, we defined theories as involving explanations of some phenomena. An explanation is one way of gaining knowledge of something; it tells why something happens or specifies the conditions under which something occurs. Theories can focus on two different types of explanations (Miller 1987; Nagel 1961).

Nomothetic Explanations.   **Nomothetic explanations** focus on a class of events and attempt to specify the conditions that seem common to all those events. We will use the social control theory of deviant behavior as an illustration. Social control theory argues, in part, that delinquent behaviors, such as shoplifting, are produced by weak attachments to parents. A nomothetic explanation, then, might attempt to prove that all juveniles who shoplift have weak attachments to their parents. The focus of the explanation is on understanding the entire category of youth who shoplift. These explanations do not focus on understanding all of the causes of a phenomenon. In fact, control theory would recognize that a complex behavior such as shoplifting probably has many causes other than weak social bonds and that other theories would be necessary to locate and iden-

RESEARCH IN PRACTICE 2.2

PRACTICE EFFECTIVENESS:

Social Theory and Burnout among Social Workers

A Social Worker: I began to despise everyone and could not conceal my contempt.

A Psychiatric Nurse: Sometimes you can't help but feel "Damn it, they want to be there, and they're fuckers, so let them stay there." You really put them down . . .

A Social Worker: I find myself caring less and possessing an extremely negative attitude.

[Quoted in Maslach 1979, p. 217]

These are hardly the caring, empathic reactions one would expect from human service workers. Yet negative attitudes toward clients are expressed at some point by many social workers, nurses, psychologists, and others. The problem of burnout is of considerable concern to human service professionals because it can impair their ability to deal with client problems. *Burnout* refers to a service worker's emotional disengagement from clients, dissatisfaction with his or her job, feelings of worthlessness, and physical and interpersonal problems (Arches 1991). Commonsense approaches often focus on the personal abilities of human service workers to explain why they suffer burnout: They lack sufficient emotional strength or distance from clients, or they over-identify or over-empathize with their clients. Rather than relying on such intuition, scientific researchers turn to theories for direction in identifying variables that might play a part.

When social work researcher W. David Harrison (1980) approached these issues, he turned to *role theory*, which views human behavior as resulting from conformity to expectations that are associated with particular roles. One of the tenets of role theory is that role expectations should be clear, unambiguous, and achievable. Furthermore, the various expectations associated with a role should not conflict with one another. Previous research suggests that situations in which role expectations are conflicting, incompatible, or unclear lead to personal stress and dissatisfaction. Role theory enabled Harrison to identify two different kinds of role difficulty; *role conflict* refers to a situation in which conflicting and incompatible demands are

placed on a person in a role; *role ambiguity* refers to a lack of clarity in terms of what is expected of a person in a particular role. Harrison's research on child protective service workers showed that role difficulties, especially role ambiguity, produced job dissatisfaction and burnout among these social workers.

In contrast, Joan Arches (1991) turned to *theories of organizational structure and change*, reasoning that recent developments in social service organizations might have an impact on burnout. The theories suggest that increasing bureaucratization and centralization in organizations can reduce workers' feelings of autonomy, and this in turn can contribute to the job dissatisfaction that is often a part of burnout. Arches's research then provided evidence that this was the case, offering further verification for those organizational theories.

Burnout continues to be a topic of interest to social scientists and human service practitioners throughout the world. Peter Janssen and his colleagues at Utrecht University in The Netherlands reviewed the extensive body of research on burnout that has accumulated over the past few decades and designed a study of Dutch nurses (Janssen, Schaufeli, and Houkes 1999). Their research examined work-related and individual determinants of burnout by using *conservation of resources theory* as a framework. This theory focuses on the impact of work-related demands and resources on different dimensions of burnout. They found that a scarcity of resources, in the form of excess job demands and work overload, increased emotional exhaustion (one dimension of burnout) but not depersonalization (another dimension of burnout).

Thus, the theoretical considerations of role theory, organizational theory, and conservation of resources theory do not point to excessive empathy or emotional weakness as the culprits in burnout among human service workers. Rather, the organizational and role structures that surround them are important. These investigations illustrate

continued on next page

the importance of grounding research in theory. It is theory that suggests which variables might be important and how they might relate to one another. Theory also shows how hypotheses can be developed through deductive reasoning. Once confirmed, the hypotheses of these researchers provide support, through inductive reasoning, for the interpretations of these theories in regard to the causes of burnout in the human services. Based on this slow, methodical accumulation of knowledge, we should eventually establish a solid foundation from which to develop programs to alleviate the problem of burnout among human service workers.

tify those factors. For nomothetic explanations, knowledge results from an understanding of a particular cause in relation to a class of events.

Nomothetic explanations attempt to develop knowledge that can be generalized beyond a single study or set of circumstances. In a sense, a nomothetic explanation is designed to produce the conclusion that weak attachment to parents in all cases increases the likelihood that shoplifting will result. This doesn't mean that every person who experiences weak attachment will shoplift. However, it does mean that those people have a higher probability of engaging in shoplifting. To put it another way, a randomly selected group of teens with weak parental attachments will have a higher rate of shoplifting than a randomly selected group with strong attachments. The explanation or knowledge that is gained is probabilistic in nature: It tells us something about the probability of events occurring. The knowledge gained is about the aggregate, or the whole group, rather than about specific individuals in the group.

Once you understand what nomothetic explanations consist of, you can begin to see their weaknesses. One weakness is that you can't say for sure what will happen in any particular case or to any specific person. You can't say whether Joe Smith, who has experienced weak parental attachment, will become a shoplifter. A second weakness is that you can't make any claims to knowing the totality of causes that produced some event or phenomenon. So, the knowledge, though valuable, is incomplete. There may be, for example, some key factors that must occur in combination with weak parental attachments to produce shoplifting.

Idiographic Explanations.

Idiographic explanations focus on a single person, event, or situation and attempt to specify all of the conditions that helped produce it. An idiographic explanation of shoplifting might focus on one juvenile who shoplifts and attempt to understand the multiple factors that contributed to bringing about shoplifting behavior in that person. The focus of the explanation is on a particular unique individual or situation. These explanations do not attempt to understand all instances of shoplifting; in fact, they recognize that other shoplifters may be propelled by a different combination of causes. For idiographic explanations, knowledge results from a thorough understanding of the particular.

Idiographic explanations see causality in terms of a complex pattern of factors combining over a period of time to produce an outcome. To truly understand something, researchers need to comprehend that whole patterned sequence, the whole complex context in which something occurs. When the nomothetic approach isolates particular variables for study, knowledge is incomplete for two reasons: One reason is that some factors or variables have not been included in the investigation; the second reason is that the isolating approach cannot see how the combination of or interaction among the various elements plays a critical role in producing an outcome. It may be, for example, that weak parental bonds produce shoplifting only when they combine with or interact with a host of other factors. In fact, it may be that the particular combination of factors that produces shoplifting in one person may be unique and not occur in other cases. It may be that each distinct case of shoplifting is produced by a unique combination of factors. In other words, the explanation or knowledge that we gain is idiosyncratic. Though nomothetic explanations are probabilistic in nature, idiographic explanations are deterministic in that the event being studied (such as shoplifting) did actually occur in the case being studied, and the idiographic explanation identifies the causes that determined that outcome.

As with nomothetic explanations, idiographic explanations have weaknesses. One major fault is their limited generalizability. With such explanations, it is difficult to determine whether knowledge can be extended beyond the particular case or situation being studied.

Combining Explanations. Because each type of explanation has its strengths and its limitations, you might have guessed that our conclusion is going to be that neither is inherently better than the other. As we alluded to in the beginning of this chapter with the excerpt from *Through the Looking-Glass,* numerous routes to gaining knowledge about the world exist, and each of these types of explanations provides us with a valuable though incomplete route. In later chapters, we will see that some research methodologies, such as surveys and experiments, tend to be used to develop nomothetic explanations, and other methodologies, such as field research, in-depth interviewing, and historical-comparative research, are often used to develop idiographic explanations. The point is to understand the logic of each type of explanation and to be aware that conclusions supported by research that uses both types of explanation are more complete than if the research only uses one type.

Paradigms in Science

Over the centuries, philosophers and scientists have debated the nature of reality and how people can know that reality (Couvalis 1997; Miller 1987). These have been controversial issues for scientists who study the physical world, but they are even more contentious among social scientists, who study human beings and their psychological and social reality. Part of the reason for this heightened con-

tention is the belief that human beings are different from the natural world of physical objects and events. People emote, remember, speculate, love, hate—they think about what is happening to them and have feelings about it. People refuse to behave the way a scientist hypothesizes that they might. People do the unexpected or unpredictable. Atoms, molecules, and chemical compounds do not have these elusive properties. This is one of the reasons why natural scientists can often make certain, non-probabilistic predictions about what will happen: Under a certain set of conditions, all water molecules will freeze when the temperature drops below zero degrees centigrade. Social scientists have been unable, thus far, to make such statements about social reality.

Another reason that the issue of how we know the world has been controversial among social scientists is that the scientists who study social reality are people themselves, with personal values, goals, desires, and reactions to what they observe. These personal matters may interfere with their ability to comprehend the world accurately. Going a step further, the scientific endeavor is itself a social process, part of the social world that social scientists attempt to understand. After all, scientific work can advance one's career, help one make a living, and move one up (or down) in the stratification system. In doing their scientific work, scientists may be influenced by a variety of social and psychological factors that routinely influence other human beings in their social endeavors.

What does all this mean? For one thing, science is a much more complicated—and in many respects, a much messier—enterprise than many people recognize. For another, a number of competing perspectives exist concerning the issues of how society works and what implications this has for how the scientific endeavor works. In fact, historian Thomas Kuhn (1970), in a ground-breaking study of scientific work over many centuries, concluded that scientific activity is shaped by **paradigms,** which are general ways of thinking about how the world works and how we gain knowledge about the world. Paradigms are fundamental orientations, perspectives, or world views that are often not questioned or subject to empirical test. People may not even be aware that their thinking about the world is shaped by an orientation or world view. In his study of the history of science, Kuhn discovered that, although paradigms change over time, at any given moment scientific research was shaped by the paradigm that was dominant at that time. Research that fell outside of that paradigm was considered inappropriate, irrelevant, oddball, or just plain wrong. In a sense, the world of paradigms falls outside the scientific realm in that issues are not accepted or rejected on the basis of empirical evidence; instead, some things are considered true and others false because it is obvious that that is how things work. Evidence that supports the paradigm will be accepted and competing evidence ignored or rejected.

At the risk of oversimplification, we can classify the paradigms in the social sciences into two general categories: *positivism* and a number of different approaches that we will call *nonpositivist* (Alford 1998; Benton 1977; Smart 1976). Keep in mind that these viewpoints are not necessarily mutually exclusive; people may adopt ideas from more than one of them at the same time. In addition, one could agree with some parts of a paradigm but disagree with other parts of the same paradigm. We address this issue early in this book because it is a debate that arises repeatedly as we discuss different research methodologies.

Positivist Approaches. **Positivism** (sometimes also called **logical empiricism**) argues that the world exists independently of people's perceptions of it and that science uses objective techniques to discover what exists in the world (Blaikie 1993; Durkheim 1938; Halfpenny 1982). Astronomers, for example, use telescopes to discover stars and galaxies, which exist regardless of whether we are aware of them. So, too, scientists can study human beings in terms of observable behaviors that can be recorded using objective techniques. Recording people's gender, age, height, weight, or socioeconomic position are legitimate and objective measurement techniques—the equivalent of the physicist measuring the temperature, volume, or mass of some liquid or solid. For the positivist, quantifying these measurements—assessing the average age of a group or looking at the percentage of a group that is male—is merely a precise way of describing and summarizing an objective reality. Such measurement provides a solid, objective foundation for understanding human social behavior. Limiting study to observable behaviors and using objective techniques, positivists argue, is most likely to produce systematic and repeatable research results that are open to refutation by other scientists.

The natural and social world is governed by natural and social rules and regularities that give it pattern, order, and predictability. The goal of research in the natural and social sciences is to discover laws about how the world works and to express those discovered regularities in the deductive theories and propositions discussed in this chapter. As scientists conduct research, they move progressively closer to the truth, which involves uncovering the laws and patterns that underlie objective reality. So science is, at least in its ideal, an objective search for the truth, in which human values are a hindrance whose impact should be limited if not eliminated. Values can only interfere with the objective search for truth. For example, Emile Durkheim, an early sociologist, was a strong believer that sociologists could study the social world in much the same way that physical scientists could study the physical world. Durkheim believed that there were "social facts" that social scientists could observe and then use those observations to discover the social laws that govern the social world. He believed that once we have discovered these social laws, we will be able to both explain and predict human social behavior.

Of the various paradigms that we will review, positivism is clearly the most widely held view among natural scientists and, to a lesser degree, among social scientists. Among social scientists, those who adopt the positivist stance often tend to use certain kinds of research methodologies. For example, they tend toward **quantitative research,** which involves measurement of phenomena using numbers and counts. They also tend to use deductive and nomothetic explanations, experimental designs, and survey research. However, it is important not to oversimplify the link between a paradigm and the preferred research methodology because positivists at times use **qualitative research,** which involves data in the form of words, pictures, descriptions, or narratives rather than numbers and counts. They also use inductive or idiographic explanations and field observations when these are appropriate to a research question.

Despite the popularity and dominance of the positivist paradigm, it has been subject to considerable criticism over the years. Some of this criticism arises out of empirical studies by social scientists of exactly how science operates (Galison and Stump 1996; Lynch and Bogen 1997; Shapin 1995). What many of these researchers find is that what scientists actually do looks quite different from what the positivist paradigm says science should look like. This has led some critics to conclude that the positivist model is an idealized conception of science rather than an accurate description of it. Based on these and other concerns, alternative paradigms have emerged.

Nonpositivist Approaches. One prominent nonpositivist approach to science is what is called the interpretive approach. **Interpretive approaches** (also called interactionist or *verstehen* approaches) perceive social reality as having a subjective component and as arising out of the creation and exchange of social meanings during the process of social interaction. Social science must have ways to understand that subjective reality, and to an extent science is a part of that process of meaning creation (Holstein and Gubrium 1994; Smith 1989; Wilson 1970). Interpretivists argue that the objective, quantitative approaches of positivism miss a very important part of the human experience: the subjective and personal meanings that people attach to themselves and what they do. Reality is seen as something emergent and in constant flux that arises out of the creation and exchange of social meanings during the process of social interaction. Rather than seeing reality as apart from human perceptions, interpretive social science sees reality, at least social reality, as created out of human perception and the interpretation of meaning. These kinds of ideas led many 19th-century and early 20th-century theorists, such as Wilhelm Dilthey, Ernst Troeltsch, and Max Weber, to conclude that so-

cial life cannot be understood by the same method used to study the natural world (Barnes 1948).

Weber, for example, argued that we need to look not only at what people do but also at what they think and feel about what is happening to them (Weber 1957, orig. pub. 1925). This "meaning" or "feeling" or "interpretive" dimension cannot be adequately captured through objective, quantitative measurement techniques. Researchers need to gain what Weber called **verstehen,** or a subjective understanding. They need to view and experience the situation from the perspective of the people themselves, "to walk a mile in their shoes." They need to talk to the people at length and to immerse themselves in their lives so they can experience the highs and lows, the joys and sorrows, the triumphs and the tragedies as seen from the perspective of the people being studied. Researchers need to see how individuals experience and give meaning to what is happening to them. Interpretive research methods provide an understanding through empathy or fellow feeling, whereas positivist methods provide understanding through abstract explanation. Yet the important point is that both methods provide an understanding of the world, and both are a part of the scientific enterprise.

Qualitative research methods attempt to gain access to that personal, subjective experience; for interpretivists, quantitative research by its very nature misses this important dimension of social reality. Positivists, for their part, do not necessarily deny the existence or importance of subjective experiences, but they do question whether the subjective interpretations of the *verstehen* method have scientific validity.

According to the interpretivist approach, regularity and pattern in social life does not result from objective social laws that exist apart from the human experience and are discovered by scientists. Instead, pattern and predictability arise out of mutually created systems of meaning that emerge from social interaction (Rabinow and Sullivan 1987; Roscoe 1995). Regularity and pattern are created and maintained by people, not imposed by external force. Proponents of interpretive approaches argue that qualitative research methods enable the researcher to approximate *verstehen,* an understanding of the subjective experiences of people. Of course, actual access to such experience is impossible; thoughts and feelings, by their very nature, are private. Even when someone says how he or she feels, the speaker has objectified that subjective experience into words and thus changed it. Researchers, however, can gain some insight into subjective experiences by immersing themselves in the lives and daily experiences of the people they study. By experiencing the same culture, the same values, the same hopes and fears, researchers are in a better position to take on the point of view of these people. However, despite its focus on subjective experiences, such research is still empirical in the sense that it is grounded in observation. Qualitative researchers consider their qualitative observations and conclusions no less systematic or scientific than the more positivistic quantitative research techniques. Although positivists would argue that subjective meaning is difficult to quantify and study objectively, interpretive researchers would argue that it is nonetheless a key part of human social reality.

Another important difference between positivists and interpretivists has to do with the role of science: While positivists argue that scientists merely discover what exists in the world, some interpretivists claim that scientists actually help create social reality through their scientific work (Knorr 1981). As researchers make observations, gather data, and draw conclusions, their activities contribute to the construction of patterns of meaning. Scientific principles and laws about social behavior become another aspect of reality that can influence people's behavior. Even something as simple as computing the average age of a group creates a new reality: Instead of recognizing that some people in the group are 22 years old, others 34 years old, and still others 43 years old, we now say that the "average age of the group is 36.7 years." This summary statement gives the impression—and creates the reality—that the group members share something in common in terms of age and that we know something very precise about their ages. But that sense of commonality or precision comes from the numbers created by the scientist, not from reality. In addition, though the average appears very precise, it is actually less precise than listing all the ages of the group members.

The interpretive approach focuses more on inductive and idiographic theory construction than on deductive and nomothetic approaches, seeing the theories emerge out of people's experiences rather than viewing them as abstractions developed by scientists. Understanding and truth come from an empathic grasp of the social meanings of a setting rather than from statistical analysis and abstract generalization to large numbers of cases. Once again, however, the link between paradigms and research approaches is not mutually exclusive. Interpretive social scientists at times do deductive and nomothetic theory construction, and they have even been known to use quantitative methods when appropriate.

Other nonpositivist characterizations of science exist as well. For example, critical and feminist approaches to research argue that science is inevitably linked to inequitable distributions of power and resources. These approaches posit that groups can and do use science to enhance their position in society and that patterns of dominance and subordination may exist between researchers and those on whom they conduct research. Other nonpositivist critiques will be addressed in later chapters. At this point, we simply want to raise the controversy regarding positivist and nonpositivist views of science to stress the point that science and scientific research are more complicated than you might have originally thought. The goal for the student should not be to attempt to resolve the disputes or to choose among the paradigms. Instead, the goal should be to understand the dimensions of the debate, to recognize how the paradigms are similar to or different from one another, and to comprehend the implications of each paradigm for the research process. In addition, the paradigms are not completely exclusionary of one another. All the paradigms agree with much of what will be covered in this book. For example, all the paradigms base their search for knowledge on systematic observation, and all agree that scientific work should be open and public. Of course, they may not always agree on what makes observations systematic, but there is not total agreement within each paradigm about that issue, either.

Another reason why the student need not adopt a preferred paradigm is that many researchers do not choose a particular perspective to follow exclusively (Alford 1998). Many researchers find that each of the approaches offers some insights into social life and the scientific process that the others ignore. They move back and forth among the paradigms, using the best that each has to offer in understanding a particular aspect of human social life.

Cause-and-Effect Relationships

One of the more important yet difficult tasks in scientific research is the search for causes—the reasons *why* particular forms of behavior occur. Why do child abuse and spouse abuse occur? Why do some juveniles become delinquent, whereas others present no behavior problems? Why do some people exhibit symptoms of mental illness and others appear psychologically stable?

Discovering causal relationships is a difficult task because causality cannot be directly observed. Rather, it must be inferred from the observation of other factors. Because of this, the philosopher John Kemeny has labeled causality "the mysterious force" (1959, p. 49). We cannot see it, feel it, or hear it; but we often assume it is there, and many scientists search for causality with hopefulness and tenacity. This search is a controversial task because some philosophers, notably Bertrand Russell (1953), have argued for excluding the notion of causality from scientific investigation altogether. These people opt for restricting ourselves to description and the analysis of "associations" without the implication that a "mysterious force" called causality lurks behind the scene and orchestrates the actions of people and things. This controversy is long-standing; we do not presume to resolve it here. Nonetheless, it is important to understand the criteria that need to be satisfied if one wants to infer that one event caused another.

By **causality,** we mean that some independent variable (X) is the factor, or one of several factors, whose change produces variation in a dependent variable (Y). As noted, causality can only be inferred. We can observe the relationships among things in the world, and from that we infer or deduce that changes in one factor are causing changes in another. However, it is always an inference. To infer the existence of a causal relationship, one must demonstrate the following:

1. A statistical association between the independent and dependent variables must exist.
2. The independent variable must occur prior in time to the dependent variable.
3. The relationship between independent and dependent variables must not be spurious; that is, the relationship must not disappear when the effects of other variables are taken into account.

We will consider each requirement of causal inference in the context of an issue that is much in the news today—the campaign to reduce cigarette smoking. Over the years the media has reported heavily on the negative impact of cigarette smoking on people's health. Some argue that making these reports public as part of a health campaign can motivate people to quit smoking. Table 2.1 presents hypothetical data that seems to show a link between reading such reports about smoking and actually quitting smoking: 50 percent of those who read the reports quit smoking as compared to only 27 percent of those who do not read the reports. Finding such a statistical relationship satisfies the first criterion for establishing a causal relationship.

The second requirement, that the independent variable occur prior in time to the dependent, is often not as easy to establish. A major factor in this is the nature of the study. Some research techniques,

Table 2.1 Effectiveness of Reading Media Reports on Smoking Cessation

		Person Reads Report	
		Yes	No
Person Quits Smoking	Yes	200 (50%)	135 (27%)
	No	200 (50%)	365 (73%)
	Totals	400 (100%)	500 (100%)

such as the experiment or participant observation, are inherently *longitudinal,* which means that the researcher is in a position to trace the development of behavior as it unfolds over time. In these cases, establishing the time sequence of events is generally simple. Questions of temporal order are more difficult to resolve when dealing with *cross-sectional* data, such as surveys, in which measurements of the independent and dependent variables occur at the same time. This is especially true if the question of temporal sequence is not addressed until after the data have been collected. It is sometimes possible to sort out the time sequence of variables in survey data by asking additional questions. However, if the researcher does not gather the necessary information at the time of the survey, establishing the appropriate time order of the variables may be impossible—hence the emphasis on the importance of carefully considering issues of data analysis when originally developing a research design.

The data in our illustration may suffer from this problem. One interpretation is that reading reports is the independent variable that has an influence on whether people quit smoking, the dependent variable. For this interpretation to be correct, the reports would have to have been publicized before the people quit smoking. If the respondents were not asked when they quit smoking, it would be impossible to say whether they quit smoking before or after reading the reports. Obviously, if they quit smoking before reading the reports, then such health campaigns could not have caused their quitting. In our example, without knowing the temporal sequence, one could argue logically for either factor being the cause of the other. Obviously, the health campaign could encourage people to quit smoking if they become frightened by learning the dire consequences of their habit. However, it could also be that those who quit smoking are happy with and proud of their victory and enjoy reading reports on what could have happened to them had they not quit smoking. In this second scenario, quitting smoking would be the independent variable that increases the likelihood that people will read reports about the health threat of smoking, the dependent variable.

Figure 2.2   Causal and Spurious Relationships

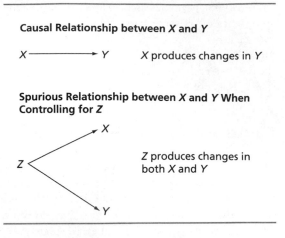

The final criterion necessary for inferring causality is that the relationship between the independent and dependent variables not be *spurious,* or disappear when the effects of other variables are considered. The logic of causal and spurious relationships is compared in Figure 2.2. This is often the most difficult of the three criteria to satisfy. In fact, one is never *totally* sure that some other variable—one you have not even considered—might not confound an apparent causal relationship. All that can be accomplished is to rule out as many extraneous variables as we can, to the point where it is unlikely that a variable exists that could render a given relationship spurious or noncausal.

Considerable effort is expended during the design stage of research to control as many potentially troublesome extraneous variables as possible. Experiments, for example, are particularly good for avoiding spurious relationships, owing to the high degree of control the experimental situation affords the researcher. Surveys, on the other hand, provide far less control, such that several variables capable of producing spuriousness typically have to be considered during data analysis. Several statistical techniques exist to control extraneous variables when the data are analyzed.

Returning to our example of smoking cessation, suppose we had solved the time sequence problem

Figure 2.3 Causal and Spurious Relationships between Reading a Report and Quitting Smoking

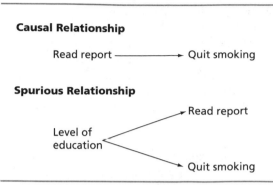

Causal Relationship

Read report ⟶ Quit smoking

Spurious Relationship

Level of education → Read report

Level of education → Quit smoking

Table 2.2 Effectiveness of Reading Media Reports on Smoking Cessation, Controlling for Education

Less Than High School Education

		Person Reads Report		
		Yes	No	Totals
Person Quits Smoking	Yes	20 (20%)	75 (19%)	95 (19%)
	No	80 (80%)	325 (81%)	405 (81%)
	Totals	100 (100%)	400 (100%)	500

High School Education or More

		Person Reads Report		
		Yes	No	Totals
Person Quits Smoking	Yes	180 (60%)	60 (60%)	240 (60%)
	No	120 (40%)	40 (40%)	160 (40%)
	Totals	300 (100%)	100 (100%)	400

and thus had satisfied the first two requirements for establishing a causal relationship. We would now begin to consider variables that might render the relationship spurious. One variable that might do this is the level of education of the people studied. (The logic of this is outlined in Figure 2.3.) Considerable research links education with health behavior. Generally, people with higher levels of education engage in more health-promoting activities, such as quitting smoking or getting regular exercise. How do we determine whether the link between report reading and smoking cessation is spurious? We introduce the level of education as a control variable, which is illustrated with our hypothetical data in Table 2.2. We have divided the respondents in Table 2.1 into those with at least a high school education and those with less than a high school education. First, we can see by examining the row totals in each table that education is related to health behavior: 60 percent of the better-educated group have quit smoking, compared to only 19 percent of the less-educated group. However, we are really interested in what happens to the link between report reading and smoking cessation. Table 2.2 shows that the relationship largely disappears: Within each educational group, the same percentage of people quit smoking among those who read the report as among those who did not. So educational level, not whether one has read the report, influences a person's likelihood of quitting

smoking. Furthermore, in our hypothetical example, educational level also influences whether one reads the report: 300 out of 400, or 75 percent, of those with a high school education read the report, compared with only 100 of 500, or 20 percent, of the others. So in our example, the link between reading the report and quitting smoking is spurious; it occurs only because each of those two variables is affected by the same third variable.

If we had found the link between report reading and smoking cessation to be nonspurious when we controlled for education, could we conclude that the relationship was causal? The answer is no. We could not come to that conclusion—at least not yet. All that would show was that the relationship remained when *one* alternative explanation was ruled out. Any other variables that could render the relationship spurious would also have to be investigated and the relationship still hold before we could argue with any confidence that it was in fact causal.

(More intricacies of this sort of analysis are addressed in Chapter 15.)

We said at the outset that establishing the existence of causal relationships is difficult. Statistical relationships are easy to find but on further investigation all too frequently turn out to be spurious. The appropriate time sequence can also be problematic, especially with survey data. All in all, establishing causal relationships is a difficult but important and challenging task.

Main Points

- Science is one source of knowledge, along with tradition, experience, common sense, and journalism; but it is a superior source of objective and accurate knowledge about the world.

- The five key characteristics of science are that it is empirical, systematic, provisional, and objective and searches for the causes of events. These crucial characteristics are also central features of scientifically based practice.

- Theories are sets of interrelated, abstract propositions that explain phenomena. Theories perform three major functions: They provide explanations, they guide research and practice, and they integrate observations from research.

- Concepts are mental constructs that symbolize ideas, persons, things, or events and form the basis for propositions and theories.

- Concepts are given both nominal definitions that explain their meaning, and operational definitions that indicate how they are measured. Care must be taken in developing operational definitions in research on minorities to ensure that such definitions do not lead to a distorted view of these populations.

- Hypotheses are statements that predict relationships between two or more variables and are tested through research.

- Theories are developed and elaborated by going back and forth between the abstract, conceptual level and the concrete, empirical level, using either deductive reasoning or inductive reasoning.

Theories also differ in the types of explanations they seek, some nomothetic and others idiographic.

- Two paradigms, or ways of understanding how we know the world, are predominant in the social sciences today: positivism and nonpositivism. Each tends to be associated with particular research methodologies. The goal for the student in this debate should be to understand the dimensions of the debate, to recognize how the paradigms are similar to or different from one another, and to comprehend the implications of each paradigm for the research process.

- Causality means that some independent variable produces variation in a dependent variable.

- To demonstrate a causal relationship, one must establish a statistical association between two variables, show that the independent variable occurs temporally first, and demonstrate that the relationship is not spurious.

Important Terms for Review

causality
common sense
concepts
deductive reasoning
dependent variable
experiential knowledge
hypotheses
idiographic explanations
independent variable
inductive reasoning
interpretive approaches
logical empiricism
nominal definitions
nomothetic explanations
operational definitions
paradigms
positivism
propositions
qualitative research
quantitative research
science

theory
traditional knowledge
variables
verification
verstehen

Exploring InfoTrac® College Edition and the Internet

InfoTrac® College Edition search terms:

operational definition
paradigm* AND science
theory AND social research

See Infotrac® College Edition Help-Search for using wildcard characters " * , ? , and ! ".

InfoTrac® College Edition articles:

The Role of Theory in Social Work Research: A Further Contribution to the Debate. Eileen Munro. *Journal of Social Work Education* Fall 2002 v38 i3 p461(10) (4,928 words)

Social Work Method: Karl Popper "Justified," Induction (Justification) Falsified—a Response to Eileen Munro. Tomi Gomory. *Journal of Social Work Education* Fall 2002 v38 i3 p475(7) (3,077 words)

Researchers Offer an Operational Definition of Emotional Abuse. Stephanie Hamarman, William Bernet. *The Brown University Child and Adolescent Behavior Letter* Dec 2000 v16 i12 p1 (1,192 words)

One of the central themes of this book is how research can inform practice. For Internet resources on applying research to human service practice, we suggest you use a search engine and search for such phrases as "children's mental health" or "evaluation outcomes." A site we found from such a search was the home page of the Office of Alcoholism and Substance Abuse Services (OASAS) of New York state (www.oasas.state.ny.us/). At this location, you can find other Web pages that report research conducted on the effectiveness of substance abuse services. In this chapter, we discussed the development of hypotheses and introduced the ideas of operational definition, dependent variable, and independent variable. As a way of applying these concepts to actual research, select several of the research studies reported at the OASAS site. For each study you find, identify one or more hypotheses that the study addressed. Determine if the review identifies how the dependent and independent variables were operationally defined. Finally, if the review describes how the independent and dependent variables are measured, state whether success in the program would be expected to show an inverse or direct relationship between the dependent and independent variables.

We covered some fairly core and controversial issues in social research in this chapter, especially in relation to the positivist and nonpositivist paradigms. Suppose that you work for a research organization and your boss wants you to create an online discussion of these paradigms. You need to locate people, organizations, or resources on the Web that espouse one position or another on these issues. Use a search engine and enter one or more of the terms used to identify the paradigms or that have some relationship to the paradigms: "positivism," "logical positivism," "subjectivism," "relativism," "postmodernism," "feminism," and so on. These terms alone may generate an excess number of relevant pages, so combine some of the terms or link them with other qualifiers, such as "social science," "natural science," "research," or others. From your search, discuss how many different social sciences address issues having to do with these paradigms. Do some social sciences address different issues than do others? Do the same kind of analysis for the natural sciences. Also address whether fields that are nonscientific, such as the humanities, address these issues. Can you put together the online discussion your boss has requested?

For Further Reading

Glaser, Barney G., and Anselm L. Strauss. *The Discovery of Grounded Theory.* New York: Aldine, 1967. An excellent book about the virtues and procedures of developing theoretical propositions from data. This approach emphasizes qualitative research and induction.

Goldenberg, Sheldon. *Thinking Methodologically.* New York: HarperCollins, 1992. Although it contains additional topics, this book presents detailed and in-depth coverage of many of the issues that we touch on in this chapter.

Hoover, Kenneth R. and Todd Donovan. *The Elements of Social Scientific Thinking,* 7th ed. Belmont, Calif.: Wadsworth, 2001. A brief and readable initiation into social science thinking and research. It is intended for those who use the results of research and those just getting into the field.

Kaplan, Abraham. *The Conduct of Inquiry.* New York: Harper & Row, 1963. A very good discussion of the logic of scientific analysis in the behavioral sciences. It covers such topics as concepts, theories, and values.

Merton, Robert K. *Social Theory and Social Structure,* 2nd ed. New York: Free Press, 1968. A classic statement by a sociologist of the relationship between theory and research.

Phillips, D. C. *Philosophy, Science, and Social Inquiry: Contemporary Methodological Controversies in Social Science and Related Applied Fields of Research.* Elmsford, N.Y.: Pergamon, 1987. An excellent philosophical analysis of issues in applied social research in such areas as social work and nursing. It addresses the issue of whether applied social research can or should emulate the positivist model found in the natural sciences.

Root, Michael. *Philosophy of Social Science: The Methods, Ideals, and Politics of Social Inquiry.* Oxford, U.K., and Cambridge, Mass.: Blackwell, 1993. This book provides an overview of the philosophical underpinnings of social science research. The author examines the position that social science should be objective and value-free but concludes that this is not possible.

Sagan, Carl. *The Demon-Haunted World.* New York: Random House, 1996. In this controversial book, the noted astronomer and author makes the case that science is a kind of savior of humankind: It can save us from believing in the unproven. In making his argument for science, Sagan pillories many other ways of trying to understand the world, such as astrology, turning to psychics, mysticism, faith healing, and even conventional religion.

Turner, Jonathan H., ed. *Theory Building in Sociology: Assessing Theoretical Accumulation.* Newbury Park, Calif.: Sage, 1989. One of the foremost theoreticians in sociology in the United States addresses in this collection of essays a key assertion of the positivist approach: Does knowledge accumulate through the deductive approach of theory building and hypothesis testing?

Exercises for Class Discussion

2.1 Many commonsense beliefs relate to child development, such as "spare the rod and spoil the child" or the belief that age-graded schools enhance learning. Through class discussion, develop a list of such "known" principles of child development. For each such principle, decide whether it is based on traditional knowledge, experiential knowledge, or a combination of these. How might you conduct systematic observations to determine the worth of these statements as scientific knowledge?

2.2 A mental health worker assigned to a large residential facility for senior citizens receives a request from staff members to "do something" about a new resident, a 72-year-old woman. From the information provided, the woman has apparently been assigned to an eighth-floor room, but she refuses to take the elevator alone or if it is crowded. The woman becomes terrified of the enclosed space and uses the stairs unless she can ride the elevator with a staff member. The woman's husband died about six months ago, and she is now living alone for the first time.

   a. Consider this case from the alternative theoretical positions of behavior modification versus traditional Freudian psychology. (You may substitute some other relevant theories of human behavior with which you are familiar.) What are some major theoretical concepts from each theory that apply to this case?

   b. For the concepts that you identified in part a, use the illustrative case to develop operational definitions for each concept.

2.3 Using each theory from Exercise 2.2, construct a possible explanation for the woman's behavior. Now try to state your explanations in terms of testable hypotheses. Can you foresee any problems in assessing causality when testing these hypotheses? Compare the hypotheses you developed with those of other students in terms of the theory used, the concepts selected, and the variables identified. How are the concepts and variables that are derived from the same theory alike? How do they differ from those derived from the other theory?

2.4 We have made the point that the same theories can be useful to both practitioner and researcher. Using the hypotheses developed in Exercise 2.3, explain how they could be used either to help the worker change behavior or to conduct a study. How might the hypotheses need to be changed to be useful to both practice and research?

2.5 A clinician in a treatment program for woman batterers notices that about 75 percent of the individuals who are mandated by the court to participate in group therapy also have a history of substance abuse problems, such as arrests for drunk driving. Furthermore, a large proportion of the clients had been drinking prior to committing assault. Can the clinician conclude that substance abuse causes woman battering? Identify what conditions would need to be met to support this contention. Prepare a diagram involving a third variable that might show that the relation between substance abuse and woman battering is spurious.

Chapter 3

Ethical Issues in Social Research

People are the subjects of social research, and, because people have rights and feelings, special considerations apply in social research that do not confront the chemist studying molecules or the physicist investigating gravity. Consider, for example, the area of substance-abuse control and treatment. In recent years, considerable controversy has arisen over the use of drug testing to deal with the problem. Some employers have instituted random drug testing of their employees as a condition of gaining employment or remaining employed. Some college athletes are randomly tested, as are prison inmates. In the context of social research, drug testing of a population would be a useful method for assessing the effectiveness of drug interdiction programs or substance-abuse counseling programs. To be most effective, such testing should be required of all people affected by a program. So if new security procedures to control the entrance of drugs into a prison are established, their effectiveness can be measured by random testing of a sample of inmates. Likewise, if a drug education program is established in a college, random testing of a sample of students at the college could assess its effectiveness.

Would such involuntary drug testing of inmates or students be proper? This question can be answered only by referring to some cultural, professional, or personal values that help us decide what is right and proper behavior. In the U.S., three such values have been articulated in the Belmont Report (National Commission 1978), a document that is considered a pillar of human research ethics. The principles are:

1. Respect for persons: We recognize the personal dignity and autonomy of individuals, and we should provide special protection of those persons with diminished autonomy.
2. Beneficence: We have an obligation to protect persons from harm by maximizing anticipated benefits and minimizing possible risks of harm.
3. Justice: The benefits and burdens of research should be distributed fairly.

Viewing drug testing in this context, some would argue that people's rights to autonomy and privacy preclude taking bodily fluids against their will to find out something about them. Is such an invasion of the privacy of college students proper or acceptable? What about prison inmates? Involuntary testing of a whole population would also seem to violate self-determination: The subjects have no choice about participating in the research. Because a person who tests positive for drugs might be subject to criminal prosecution or stigmatization, it raises the question of whether the research could bring harm to the person. Finally, who bears the cost and who benefits from such research? Some would be quick to employ drug testing to evaluate a treatment program with prison inmates but would be reluctant to subject participants in a middle-class community program to such scrutiny, even though the program may be implemented there once it is proven to be effective.

These are complicated issues. We do not presume that our statement of values is the final word or that the application of these values to particular cases is easy or straightforward. They do serve as an introduction, however, to the discussion of ethical issues in social research.

Ethics is the study of what is proper and improper behavior, of moral duty and obligation (Reese and Fremouw 1984). Moral principles can be grounded in philosophy, theology, or both. For social researchers, ethics involves the responsibilities that researchers bear toward those who participate in research, those who sponsor research, and those who are potential beneficiaries of research. It covers many specific issues. For example, is it ever permissible to harm people during the course of a research project? Should people who participate in a research project ever be deceived? Is it appropriate to suppress research findings that cast a sponsor's program in a negative light? Should researchers report to the police crimes they uncover while conducting their research? The ethics of a given action depends on the standards used to assess the action, and those standards are grounded in human values. Because of this, ethical questions have few simple or final answers and no scientific tests that can show us whether actions are ethical. In fact, debate continues among scientists about ethical issues because such issues involve matters of judgment and assessment.

Our purpose in this chapter is to identify the basic ethical issues in social research and to suggest some strategies for making sure that ethical considerations are attended to in the conduct and use of research.

The Minority Experience: The Need for Ethical Standards

Ethical issues do not exist in a vacuum but rather within the context of a particular society and its historical development. Two events in the 20th century—one abroad and the other in the United States—served as major catalysts for efforts to codify a set of ethical standards for research.

The first event occurred in Europe during World War II: the heinous series of medical experiments conducted by the Nazis on Jews and others in concentration camps (Beauchamp et al. 1982). Prior to this, there had been no codification of scientific ethics, and researchers had been left largely to their own devices in deciding how to conduct their studies. The revelation of the German atrocities, exposed during the Nuremberg trials in 1945 and 1946, shocked the sensibilities of the world and left an indelible imprint on research ethics. The cruelty of the experiments is almost inconceivable. Healthy people were intentionally infected with such serious diseases as spotted fever or malaria to observe the course of the disease with and without medication. Others were used as subjects to test the effects of various poisons. Some had parts of their bodies frozen to test new treatments. Still others were deliberately wounded to study new antibiotics and other treatments. Perhaps most evil of all were the excruciating decompression studies designed to test reactions to high-altitude flight (Katz 1972). These gruesome experiments brought home exactly how far people would go in using research to further their own ends. They also brought home the vulnerability of minorities to exploitation in research, especially when the resources and authority of powerful groups support researchers with few ethical standards. Public outrage afterward led to heightened concern for establishing codified standards for the ethical conduct of medical research on human subjects.

The second event that influenced the development of a codified set of ethical standards was an infamous study of syphilis conducted by the U.S. Public Health Service (PHS). The study began with black males from Tuskegee, Alabama, in 1932, 425 with syphilis and 200 without syphilis. All were poor and only semiliterate. None was told he had syphilis. The intent was to observe the men over a span of years to learn how the disease progressed. When the study began, there was no cure for syphilis. Fifteen years later, penicillin was discovered to be an effective cure for this affliction. Despite this discovery, the PHS continued the syphilis study for an additional 25 years, withholding treatment from all but a fortunate few who discovered its existence on their own and requested it. The justification for deceiving the men was that, because they were poor and semiliterate, they would in all likelihood not seek treatment even if they knew of it. If syphilis is untreated, it can cause paralysis, insanity, blindness, and heart disease. Ultimately, it can be fatal. Yet the men were allowed to spread the disease to their wives and lovers. Many of the afflicted participants in the Tuskegee study suffered serious physical disorders or died as a result of not receiving treatment for the disease (Jones 1992; Reverby 2000).

Most Americans today—and especially those in the human services—would agree that the actions of the PHS were repugnant, racist, and unethical in the extreme. In fact, as perhaps the final chapter of this tragic saga, President Bill Clinton issued an apology on behalf of the nation for the Tuskegee Syphilis Study in a White House ceremony in 1997 (Eckenwiler 1999). When the study began, however—and even when effective treatment for syphilis became available—the subordinate position of blacks and poor people in American society resulted in their receiving fewer of the political, economic, and even medical rights than whites and more affluent citizens receive. It is unlikely that well-to-do whites would have been treated in the same arrogant fashion, and one would hope that no such debacle would be seriously contemplated today. Yet, we should keep in mind that the PHS study continued into the 1970s—an era we like to consider as more enlightened regarding human rights—and ended only when it received public notoriety. This further documents the extent to which minorities (and others) can be at risk of dangerous and inhumane treatment by researchers who are not governed by clear and enforceable ethical standards.

The immoral treatment of some minorities in research in this century, especially the Nazi and PHS episodes, brought home to people the need to codify standards for ethical conduct so that researchers would have guidelines available and research subjects would be afforded some protection. The first effort along these lines was the Nuremberg Code, developed in 1946 in direct response to the atrocities committed during World War II. The Nuremberg Code was limited to issues of ethics in medical research. In 1966, the PHS established ethical regulations for medical research that emphasized the following: (1) Full disclosure of relevant information should be made to the participants; (2) the decision to participate must be completely voluntary; and (3) researchers must obtain documented, informed consent from participants (Gray 1982; Reynolds 1979). In 1974, the Department of Health, Education, and Welfare (DHEW, now the Department of Health and Human Services, or DHHS) decreed that the PHS guidelines would apply to social science research. Furthermore, DHEW recognized that codes of conduct alone would not ensure ethical research without some oversight procedures in place. To this end, DHEW required research institutions, such as universities, to establish institutional review boards, or IRBs, that would review research proposals and ensure that the guidelines were followed. These regulations have been broadened to apply not only to those projects directly funded by that agency but also to any research carried on in organizations that obtain DHHS funding.

The DHHS regulations are codified at Title 45, Part 46 of the Code of Federal Regulations. Those basic regulations became final in 1981 and were subsequently revised in 1983 and again in 1991. The 1991 revision was especially important because it involved the adoption of the Federal Policy for the Protection of Human Subjects that had been set forth in the Belmont Report. Those principles of respect, beneficence, and justice are now accepted as the three quintessential requirements for the ethical conduct of research involving human subjects. Although few would take issue with the basic ethical principles that had been expressed in the 1974 DHEW policy, the fact that the regulations had initially originated in the context of medical research did cause concern for social scientists. A common feeling is that risks to participants in most social science research are minimal and different from risks in medical research (Murray et al. 1980). Breach of confidentiality, not direct harm, is the most likely ethical problem. There was concern that the original regulations would obstruct important research, hinder response rates, and reduce the validity and generalizability of findings.

In response to these concerns the DHHS, under a policy issued in 1981, exempted the following research methodologies from IRB review: evaluation of teaching procedures or courses, educational testing, survey or interview techniques, observation of public behavior, and documentary research (Huber 1981). The only exceptions are research dealing with "sensitive" behavior, such as drug and alcohol use, illegal behavior, or sexual conduct. In assessing social science research not exempt from IRB review, the IRBs have tended to subscribe to a risk-benefit doctrine (Smith 1981). This means that questionable practices, such as deception or disguised observation, may be utilized if the purpose of the study is viewed as sufficiently important to justify them.

Although the DHHS regulations exempt much social science research from IRB review, many universities and other research institutions require that *all* research projects be reviewed to determine whether they are legitimately exempt. Furthermore, it has become increasingly common for private foundations to require IRB review as a prerequisite for funding (Ceci, Peters, and Plotkin 1985). When planning research, an application to conduct the research should routinely be submitted to the appropriate IRB to determine whether the research is exempt and, if it is not, gain permission to conduct the research. Table 3.1 lists the content that the DHHS expects to find on an IRB application form. As you read the rest of this chapter, you will see that many of the ethical issues discussed are addressed by the criteria listed for

Table 3.1 Criteria for IRB Approval of Research

In order to approve research covered by this policy, the IRB shall determine that all of the following requirements are satisfied:

1. Risks to subjects are minimized:

    (i) by using procedures which are consistent with sound research design and which do not unnecessarily expose subjects to risk, and

    (ii) whenever appropriate, by using procedures already being performed on the subjects for diagnostic or treatment purposes

2. Risks to subjects are reasonable in relation to anticipated benefits, if any, to subjects, and the importance of the knowledge that may reasonably be expected to result. In evaluating risks and benefits, the IRB should consider only those risks and benefits that may result from the research (as distinguished from risks and benefits of therapies subjects would receive even if not participating in the research). The IRB should not consider possible long-range effects of applying knowledge gained in the research (for example, the possible effects of the research on public policy) as among those research risks that fall within the purview of its responsibility.

3. Selection of subjects is equitable. In making this assessment the IRB should take into account the purposes of the research and the setting in which the research will be conducted and should be particularly cognizant of the special problems of research involving vulnerable populations, such as children, prisoners, pregnant women, mentally disabled persons, or economically or educationally disadvantaged persons.

4. Informed consent will be sought from each prospective subject or the subject's legally authorized representative, in accordance with, and to the extent required by §46.116.

5. Informed consent will be appropriately documented, in accordance with, and to the extent required by §46.117.

6. When appropriate, the research plan makes adequate provision for monitoring the data collected to ensure the safety of subjects.

7. When appropriate, there are adequate provisions to protect the privacy of subjects and to maintain the confidentiality of data.

Source Adapted from Part 46.111, Protection of Human Subjects Code of Federal Regulations, Title 45, Public Welfare, DHHS National Institutes of Health Office for Protection from Research Risks, 2001.

such applications. Even if a project is exempt from IRB review, researchers are not exempt from ethical concerns. Whether one's research will be reviewed or not, one still has the responsibility of considering the impact of the research on those who participate and on those who might benefit from it. As we will see, ethical guidelines do not eliminate the controversy that surrounds ethical issues because guidelines need to be interpreted and applied to specific contexts. Much debate surrounds such interpretation and application.

The debate over the Nazi experiments is not over. Controversy persists in terms of whether the data from that research are valid and reliable and, if so,

whether those data should be used today (Moe 1984; Schafer 1986). Some have argued that use of the data is justified if the data are scientifically valid and no other source of such data exists. If the data are used, it is argued, one should feel compelled to express horror and regret at the manner of collection. On the other side, some argue that our collective outrage at the treatment of minorities by the Nazis should be so great that use of the data is repulsive. In this view, refusing to use the data is a symbolic denunciation of such atrocities, and using the data might be interpreted as an acceptance of their methods or at least a willingness to let the importance of the Holocaust diminish with the passage of time. Between these two extremes, some researchers argue that the data should be used only if some overriding need demands it and the objective of using the data overrides our symbolic rejection of the manner in which the data were collected. Recent assessments suggest that the data from the Nazi experiments are seriously flawed—even fraudulent in some cases—and therefore should not be used, regardless of the ethical issues surrounding how the data were obtained (Berger 1994). This controversy remains long-lasting and deeply rooted in ethical research issues.

Ethical Issues

Six basic ethical issues arise in social science research: informed consent, deception, privacy (including confidentiality and anonymity), physical or mental distress, problems in sponsored research, scientific misconduct or fraud, and scientific advocacy. The unique situation confronting the human service researcher raises two additional considerations: protecting vulnerable clients and withholding treatment for research purposes.

Informed Consent

Informed consent refers to telling potential research participants about all aspects of the research that might reasonably influence the decision to participate. Very often people are asked to sign a *consent form,* which describes the elements of the research that might influence a person's decision to participate (see Table 3.2). General agreement exists today on the desirability of informed consent in behavioral science research, primarily because in the United States, cultural values place great emphasis on freedom and self-determination. Whether the issue is who to marry, what career to pursue, or whether to participate in a research project, we value the right of individuals to assess information and weigh alternatives before making their own judgments. To deceive potential

Table 3.2   Basic Elements of an Informed Consent Form

The Following Information Shall Be Provided to Each Subject:
(1) A statement that the study involves research, an explanation of the purposes of the research and the expected duration of the subject's participation, a description of the procedures to be followed, and identification of any procedures which are experimental;
(2) A description of any reasonably foreseeable risks or discomforts to the subject;
(3) A description of any benefits to the subject or to others which may reasonably be expected from the research;
(4) A disclosure of appropriate alternative procedures or courses of treatment, if any, that might be advantageous to the subject;
(5) A statement describing the extent, if any, to which confidentiality of records identifying the subject will be maintained;
(6) For research involving more than minimal risk, an explanation as to whether any compensation and an explanation as to whether any medical treatments are available if injury occurs and, if so, what they consist of, or where further information may be obtained;
(7) An explanation of whom to contact for answers to pertinent questions about the research and research subjects' rights, and whom to contact in the event of a research-related injury to the subject; and
(8) A statement that participation is voluntary, refusal to participate will involve no penalty or loss of benefits to which the subject is otherwise entitled, and the subject may discontinue participation at any time without penalty or loss of benefits to which the subject is otherwise entitled.

Source   Part 46, Protection of Human Subjects. Code of Federal Regulations, Title 45, Public Welfare. DHHS National Institutes of Health Office for Protection from Research Risks, 2001.

research participants is to deny them the ability to determine their own destinies.

Although there is consensus about the general principle of informed consent, the debate regarding exactly how far researchers' obligations extend in this realm is still a hot issue. At one extreme, researchers known as *ethical absolutists* argue that people should be fully informed of all aspects of the research in which they might play a part (Baumrind 1985; Elms 1982; Kimmel 1988). Even when research is based on the public record, such as agency documents, or on observations of behavior in public, some absolutists argue that people about whom observations have been made should be informed of the research. Otherwise, they do not have the full right to decide whether to participate.

However, rigid adherence to the absolutist position makes social research much more difficult to conduct. First, such adherence rules out many practices that some researchers consider important or essential. Many experiments, for example, rely on some degree of deception, at least to the extent of not telling participants the true research hypotheses. The reason for this is that people might respond differently if they knew of these hypotheses. However, all such studies would be unacceptable to the absolutists and could not be conducted. Absolutists would also disallow disguised observation, in which people in public settings are not aware they are being observed. No longer could researchers engage in such effective strategies as infiltrating organizations—unless, of course, they told all employees what they were doing. The net result would be to make social science research highly conservative and very limited. It would become the study of people who volunteer to be studied, and research shows that volunteers are different in many ways from people who do not volunteer. This would have the effect of seriously reducing the generalizability of research findings.

Second, the absolutist approach would call for obtaining informed consent in all research projects, and research has shown that obtaining written consent can reduce people's willingness to participate in research. One study found that formally requesting informed consent prior to conducting an interview reduced the rate of cooperation by 7 percent in comparison to cases in which a formal request was not made (Singer, VonThurn, and Miller 1995). Because any reduction in response rate reduces the generalizability of the findings, as we will explain in Chapter 7, obtaining informed consent in survey research can have serious negative consequences in terms of the validity of the research.

Written informed consent probably reduces people's willingness to participate because it appears to some respondents to contradict the researcher's assurance of confidentiality. One minute people are being told that their answers will remain confidential, and the next they are asked to put their names on a consent form! Even though signing a consent form need not impede the maintenance of confidentiality, it is not surprising that respondents may not perceive it that way. Anything that undermines respondents' beliefs in the confidentiality of the answers will reduce response rates. Signing a consent form may also affect the quality of the data obtained because those who do give consent may be less candid in their responses than they otherwise might have been. It is ironic that an attempt to enhance one aspect of ethical research—informed consent—is potentially a threat to another aspect—confidentiality.

Because of these problems with the absolutist approach to informed consent, many researchers take a less extreme position. They argue, first of all, that people should be informed of factors that might reasonably be expected to influence their decision to participate, such as any harm that might occur or how much time and effort will be involved. However, they also use a risk-benefit approach: Questionable research strategies, such as deception, are appropriate if they are essential to conduct the research, they will bring no harm to participants, and the outcome is sufficiently important to warrant the research. Lively debate continues concerning the use of questionable practices and their routine approval by IRBs (Baumrind 1985).

A final issue regarding informed consent has to do with the possibility that a person might feel pressured to agree or might not understand precisely what he or she is agreeing to. After all, asking a person to participate in a study can involve social pressures not unlike those in other settings. We often feel pressured to help others when they ask for our assistance, and some people find it difficult to say no to a face-to-face request. In addition, scientific researchers represent figures of some authority and status, and people are often disinclined to refuse their requests. In other cases, people may be temporarily confused about what is being asked of them.

To resolve these problems, a study involving institutionalized elderly people used a two-step consent procedure (Ratzan 1981). In the first step, people were told what their participation would involve, what risks were entailed, and that several days later they would be asked whether they were willing to participate. This was meant to reduce any immediate pressures to agree and to enable people to talk with others and clarify any confusing issues. The second step, occurring a few days later, involved obtaining the actual consent. In this study, all those who were asked refused to participate. This was probably due to the fact that a part of the study involved having a needle inserted in a vein continuously for eight days in order to take blood samples. However, some of the people might have agreed to participate had they been asked to sign a consent form during the first interview. Yet it is questionable whether consent obtained at that time would have been as informed and considered as it should be. The goal of obtaining informed consent is not to pressure people into participating in the research, but to gain participation that is truly informed.

Deception

Despite its status as a controversial strategy, deception is still fairly common in some areas of social science research, such as social psychology (Korn 1997). One reason for this is that some research would be difficult or impossible to conduct without some level of deception. At a minimum, many experiments necessitate not telling the participants the true research hypotheses; this withholding of information is a form of deception. As another example, field research sometimes uses disguised observation, where people in public settings are observed but are not aware that such observation is occurring. Some

would argue that this involves an implicit deception of those being observed. Other types of field research can involve more explicit deception to gain the cooperation of those who are being observed.

Richard Leo (1996), in his field study of police interrogators, withheld or concealed information on his own views of crime, punishment, homosexuality, and other issues from the police that he was observing. In fact, he dubbed what he did the "chameleon strategy": "I consciously reinvented my persona to fit the attributes, biases, and worldview of my subjects" (Leo 1995, p. 120). Before the detectives he feigned opposition to abortion, support for the death penalty, and antipathy toward gays. He created this persona to gain their cooperation and to encourage them to act openly and naturally in front of him. If the police interrogators had known his true views on these issues, Leo claims, they might have distrusted him and not acted openly in front of him. Because his observations produced groundbreaking sociological research on this topic, he felt that the deception was warranted, given that little harm came to the police officers.

Ethical absolutists would rule out all such deception on the grounds that it is unethical to deceive other human beings deliberately (Erikson 1967). However, Leo argues that the situation is more complicated: "Fieldwork is a morally ambiguous enterprise that is fraught with moral hazards, contingencies, and uncertainties" (Leo 1996, p. 125). There are trade-offs and compromises to be taken into account. Furthermore, Leo makes the distinction between "acts of commission," where the researcher intentionally falsifies information, and "acts of omission," where information is withheld. Some would argue that Leo did the former when he "reinvented" his persona, but he himself claims that his research strategy involved only omission and was thus ethically justifiable. In addition, he argued that his use of deception passed the test of the three major criteria that are applied: (1) the research is important, (2) no other way to conduct the research is available, and (3) no harm came to those studied.

When deception is used, it is a sound practice to conclude the period of observations with a debriefing, during which people are told the true purposes of the research and informed of any deceptions that were utilized. This should be done in a positive and supportive way, so that the participants feel they were joint partners in a worthwhile enterprise rather than dupes of the researchers. This can usually be achieved by explaining the reasons for the deception and for the impossibility that anyone could have detected the deceptions before being informed of them. In some research, of course, debriefings are not possible, such as in disguised observations in field settings where the researcher never has a chance to contact the participants after observations are made.

The Right to Privacy: Anonymity and Confidentiality

The right to privacy is one of the key values and ethical obligations mentioned at the beginning of this chapter. **Privacy** refers to the ability to control when and under what conditions others will have access to your beliefs, values, or behavior. Intrusions on our privacy have become endemic in modern society; with the growth of social research in the past century the danger of even greater intrusion arises. Virtually any attempt to collect data from people raises the issue of privacy and confronts the investigator with the dilemma of whether threats to privacy are warranted by the research. Two well-known research projects illustrate the complexity of this issue.

Two Case Studies.   The sociologist Laud Humphreys (1970), in an effort to understand a particular type of sexual behavior, made observations of men having quick and impersonal sexual encounters with other men in public restrooms. To gather his data without arousing suspicion, Humphreys played the role of the "watch queen," who keeps watch and warns participants of approaching police or "straight" males who might disrupt the activities. None of the men who went to the restrooms to engage in sex was aware that a researcher was recording his behavior. Humphreys also noted the license plates on the cars of these men and was able to find their home addresses through public motor vehicle records. He then interviewed them in their homes but did not inform them of the real reason for the interviews or that he had earlier observed them in the restrooms.

Humphreys was heavily criticized for using deception, for not obtaining informed consent, and for violating the privacy of these men engaging in highly stigmatized actions that, were they made public, might disrupt their family lives or threaten their jobs. Many sociologists believe that research on such sensitive topics is not simply a matter of confidentiality—that is, not letting people's identities become known. Rather, such data should not even be collected because these men were obviously trying to conceal their actions. Social science researchers, it is argued, should respect that privacy.

Humphreys defended his research on the grounds that the confidentiality of his subjects was maintained and the results of the study were of significant scientific value. In fact, no one else has devised another method to study such sexual behavior. Humphreys discovered that the men who engage in this type of sexual activity are not unusual or deviant in the rest of their lives and for the most part were normal, respectable citizens with a rather unusual sexual outlet. Humphreys believes that the greater understanding of what had been considered deviant sexual conduct justifies the threat to privacy these men experienced. In addition, the public setting in which they performed their acts, he argues, reduced their right to claim privacy.

Another field study illustrates further difficulties in protecting people's privacy. When research describes an actual group or community of people, a common practice is to report results by giving fictitious names to the people and places to protect privacy. This procedure works fairly well as long as researchers do not become so detailed in their descriptions of places, events, and people that the protection afforded by the fictitious names is undermined. A now infamous example of this was *Small Town in Mass Society,* by Arthur Vidich and Joseph Bensman. First published in 1958, this observational community study described the power relationships and local governmental operations in a small town the authors called Springdale. The authors had assured all people they interviewed that confidentiality would be maintained. Even though no identities were directly revealed, it was easy for the residents of the small community to recognize the people and events described in the highly detailed report. Because the study was critical of some residents of Springdale, these people understandably became outraged. Local newspapers vociferously attacked the researchers for betraying the community. The townspeople even held a Fourth of July parade that featured a full manure spreader carrying mired effigies of the authors (Whyte 1958). To avoid such breaches of confidentiality, one must balance enthusiasm for producing a highly detailed account against the ethical obligation to fully protect the identities of those observed.

Single-system research requires particular caution in this regard. As we will explain in Chapter 11, single-system research involves observing the changes in feelings or behavior of an individual over a period of time. Furthermore, the clients in these studies often suffer from some condition, such as a mental disorder, that might lead to stigmatization should others find out about it. Therefore, great care must be taken to ensure that people's identities are not unintentionally revealed in the process of providing a description of the case. Researchers must often tread a fine line between providing sufficient case detail and minimizing the risk of identifying a client. Final reports should always be written with sensitivity to this issue.

As these two case studies show, the right to privacy is often a difficult ethical issue to resolve. Researchers have come up with three major ways to deal with the problem of protecting people's privacy: let subjects edit their data, keep the data anonymous, and keep the data confidential.

Editing the Data.

One very effective way to protect privacy is to offer participants the opportunity, after the data has been collected, to destroy any data they wish to remain private. This was done in a study of family interaction that utilized videotape cameras installed in apartments to record all interchanges between family members (Ashcraft and Scheflen 1976). Even though the families consented to the taping, the investigators, sensitive to the issue of privacy, offered them the opportunity to review the tapes and edit out anything they wished. The assumption was that, despite agreeing to participate, family members might do something on the spur of the moment that

they would prefer not be made public. Surprisingly, not one family exercised the option to edit the tapes. This and other research suggests that people can be more tolerant of invasions of privacy than researchers might expect. Nonetheless, it should always be the research subject's decision; the researcher should never assume for people that they will be tolerant of invasions or breaches of privacy.

Anonymity.

A second means of ensuring privacy is to accord the participants **anonymity,** which means that *no one,* including the researcher, can link any data to a particular respondent. This can be accomplished by not including any identifying names or numbers with the data collected. True anonymity means that even the researcher can never link data to a particular respondent. This method of protecting privacy is the ideal because the data are collected in such a way that it is impossible for anyone to determine which data comes from which individual. However, in many research situations, it is not possible or feasible to collect data in this fashion, so researchers turn to confidentiality.

Confidentiality.

A third way of protecting privacy is through **confidentiality:** ensuring that information about or data collected from those who participate in a study are not made public in a way that can be linked to an individual. Researchers, of course, commonly release their data to the public, but usually only in aggregate forms, which means reporting on how a whole group responded rather than how individuals responded. In many studies, the data are not of a sensitive nature, and thus confidentiality would seem less important, but it is impossible to predict what bits of data all participants will want kept confidential. Because aggregate and anonymous reporting of results is all that is necessary in most research studies, confidentiality is routinely extended to encourage people's participation and honest responses.

It is worth pointing out that anonymity and confidentiality are quite distinct. With confidentiality, the researcher can link responses to particular respondents but does not release this information publicly; with anonymity, even the researchers can't link responses to particular respondents. So, if a researcher sends out mailed questionnaires and they are returned with no names or other identifiers on them, then the respondents have true anonymity. If the same questionnaires are mailed back with a name or other identifier on them, then only confidentiality is possible because the researcher can link responses to respondents. Even if the identifiers are removed as soon as the questionnaire is received, it would still be ethical to make promises only of confidentiality because the researcher could link responses to respondents at the point at which the questionnaires are received. Obviously, it is unethical to tell respondents that they will have confidentiality when they won't, but it is also wrong to claim that responses will be anonymous when all that will actually be protected is confidentiality.

In some cases, confidentiality can be breached merely by a person's involvement in a research project becoming known. If it becomes known, for example, that an individual was a part of a study of drug users, then knowledge that the individual is a drug user has become public even if none of the data collected from that individual have been made public. So, one aspect of confidentiality is to ensure that the identities of those who are subjects in the research, especially when it is sensitive, are kept hidden.

Confidentiality can also be threatened when third parties, such as the people sponsoring the research or the courts, seek to identify research participants. Intrusion by a sponsor is relatively easy to avoid. When establishing a research agreement with a sponsoring agency or organization, one should make clear in the agreement that identities will not be revealed under any circumstances. If the sponsor objects, researchers should refuse to accept the agreement. We have more to say about sponsors and ethics later in this chapter.

Court and Legislative Challenges to Confidentiality.   The courts and some laws and statutes pose a more complicated threat to confidentiality. Most communication that physicians, lawyers, and clergy have with their clients is protected from judicial subpoena. Social workers in their clinical capacity also are afforded such protection in many instances, although the degree of protection varies with agency settings and jurisdictions. Social researchers, however, do not have a legal protection of privileged communication with the people from whom they gather data (Kimmel 1988; Reece and Siegal 1986). In addition, physicians, most human service professionals, and in some cases researchers are required by many state laws to report to public agencies when they observe evidence of mistreatment of children or the elderly. Thus, courts or public agencies may subpoena research data that reveal participants' identities; failure to comply with such a subpoena renders researchers open to charges of contempt of court. Actually, social science researchers have been treated somewhat inconsistently by the courts in civil cases. In a civil suit in California, for example, the court refused to force a researcher to reveal the identities of respondents in confidential interviews (Smith 1981).

In criminal cases, however, the courts have generally held that the right of the public to be protected from criminal activity or the right of suspects to a fair trial supersedes any assurance of confidentiality in research. In one case, for example, the researcher had been making field observations in a restaurant when it was heavily damaged in a suspicious fire (Brajuha and Hallowell 1986). Police wanted the researcher's field notes to determine whether any evidence of arson could be substantiated. One court squashed a subpoena for the field notes, but another upheld it. Eventually a compromise was reached: The researcher's field notes were considered subject to subpoena, but the researcher was allowed to remove material that would have violated confidentiality. With rulings like this, the courts seem to recognize that the confidentiality a legitimate social researcher establishes in a relationship should be protected, if that can be done while still protecting the rights of the public and criminal suspects.

In another case, a sociologist actually spent time in jail because he refused to give information in court that he believed violated his promise of confidentiality to his research subjects. Rik Scarce (1994) conducted research on activists in the animal liberation movement in the 1990s. A federal grand jury was investigating break-ins by such activists at university laboratories, and some of the activists in whom the grand jury was interested had been interviewed by Scarce as part of his research. He refused to answer certain questions about these activists put to him by the grand jury because he thought it would violate the confidentiality he had extended to the people he interviewed. He was jailed for four months on contempt-of-court charges. Leo, in his study of police interrogators, was compelled to testify in court under threat of contempt-of-court charges. As these cases illustrate, the courts have generally held that confidential communication between a researcher and a research participant is not protected in criminal cases; however, some courts also recognize that the confidential relationship is an important and special one and that efforts should be made not to violate it. Because of cases like these, some researchers have called for federal legislation that would give social science researchers protection, even if limited, from being compelled to violate their confidential relationship (Leo 1995; Scarce 1994).

Concern over possible subpoena of their research data has led some researchers to adopt elaborate measures to protect the data. For example, it is common to establish computer files with the data identified only by numbers rather than by names. Often, it is unnecessary to retain name identification for research purposes once the data have been collected. In such cases, the names should be destroyed. If name identification is required—say, because you want to interview the same people at a later time—the names should be stored in a separate computer file. This procedure reduces the possibility of unauthorized persons linking names with data.

One of the best means of securing confidentiality for sensitive research, such as that dealing with AIDS, substance abuse, or criminal behavior, is to use *certificates of confidentiality,* which were made available by the Public Health Service Act Amendments of 1974 (Bonnie and Wallace 2003; Melton and Gray 1988). Certificates of Confidentiality are issued by the National Institutes of Health (NIH) and other Health and Human Service offices to protect identifiable research information from forced disclosure. They allow the investigator and others who have access to research records to refuse to disclose identifying in-

formation on research participants in any civil, criminal, administrative, legislative, or other proceeding, whether at the federal, state, or local level. By some interpretations, the certificates of confidentiality supersede even laws that require mandatory reporting of instances of child and elderly mistreatment. Certificates are generally awarded only for research on sensitive topics, such as illegal drug use or sexual behavior, and regardless of whether the research receives federal funding. However, the certificates are discretionary, so a researcher must make application to receive one, and they are given out sparingly. Certificates of confidentiality were first issued by the DHHS as a means of assisting drug abuse–related research projects where, in the course of research, the study participants may provide legally incriminating or sensitive personal information. Legal authority was granted under the Comprehensive Drug Abuse Prevention and Control Act of 1970. Courts have challenged the confidentiality protections afforded by the certificates. In 1973 the New York Court of Appeals upheld the certificate's authority. The U.S. Supreme Court declined to hear the case (National Cancer Institute 1998). Despite the fact that intrusion by the courts is a real danger with research on some topics, the reality is that court involvement is extremely rare. Although more than 200 cases have involved courts seeking journalists' information, in only a dozen or so cases have courts sought research data (Reynolds 1979; Smith 1981). Thus, the odds of a researcher's becoming embroiled in this kind of situation are remote. Nonetheless, researchers have an obligation to inform potential subjects accurately of any possible threats to confidentiality that might arise, including what would be likely to happen should their data be subpoenaed by the courts. The lengths to which investigators will go to protect privacy indicate the importance of this ethical issue. The bottom line is that no one should be threatened with harm to themselves or their reputation as a result of participating in a scientific study.

Harm, Distress, and Benefit

Researchers should avoid exposing participants to physical or mental distress or danger. If the potential for such distress exists in a research investigation, the participants should be fully informed, the potential research findings should be of sufficient importance to warrant the risk, and no possibility should exist of achieving the results without the risk. People should never be exposed to situations that might cause serious or lasting harm.

Research in the human services rarely involves physical danger, but there are research settings in which psychological distress may be an element. Some studies, for example, have asked people to view such things as pornographic pictures, victims of automobile accidents, and the emaciated inmates of Nazi concentration camps. Certainly, these stimuli can induce powerful reactions, in some cases emotions that the participants had not expected to experience. A strong emotional reaction, especially an unexpected one, can be very distressful. In some studies, people have been given false feedback about themselves to observe how they respond. People have been told, for example, that they failed an examination or that tests show that they have some negative personality characteristics. Any situation in which people might learn something about themselves of which they were unaware can be distressing. Even the minor deceptions that are a part of much research can be distressful to people who thought they could not so easily be deceived.

Another area in which social science research contains the potential for harm to those studied is in field research of people engaging in stigmatized, deviant, or illegal behavior. The potential harm comes if the researcher says or does anything that might lead the research subjects to be sanctioned for the deviant or illegal behaviors they displayed in front of the researcher (Klockars 1979). This is a complex topic that will be explored in more detail in Chapter 10, but the problem can arise because field research often involves an implicit or explicit agreement between the researcher and those being observed. In this agreement, the observed consent to letting the researcher join them and make observations on them; in return they expect the researcher will support their illegal or deviant behavior, or at least not do anything to get them in trouble for it. For example, if police interrogations of suspects are

likely to include some harsh or even illegal treatment of the suspects, police officers would be unlikely to let a researcher observe the interrogations unless they believed the researcher would support their actions or not report them to authorities or testify against them in court. In other words, the police would likely expect the researcher, in return for being permitted to observe them, to act like fellow officers and support them in their actions. In developing a relationship with the police, the researcher may give the impression that he or she understands this or the police may just assume the researcher understands. This actually creates a moral dilemma for the researcher because either choice is morally compromised. If the researcher supports the police and doesn't report the harsh treatment of the suspect, the suspect is harmed by the researcher's actions; if the researcher supports the suspect and reports the actions, the police are harmed both by having their implicit agreement with the researcher violated and by being sanctioned by authorities for their behavior. This kind of ambiguous dilemma is inherent in some field research on deviant lifestyles and is part of what Leo meant by his comment that field work is "a morally ambiguous enterprise" (Leo 1996, p. 125).

Assuming that the scientific benefits warrant the risk of distress and that the participants are fully informed, it is then the researcher's obligation to alleviate the impact of whatever distress actually does occur. As with problems created by deception, alleviating problems related to harm or distress is often accomplished through a debriefing that assesses people's psychological and emotional reactions to the research.

For some social scientists, an ethical standard that rests only on avoiding harm is far too limited. They would also argue that those on whom we conduct research should also gain some positive benefit from the research. This stance has been put forth most clearly by feminist researchers, as discussed in Chapter 2, and collaborative researchers (Nyden et al. 1997; Reinharz 1992). Viewing research as a two-way street, they argue that both researcher and research subject should gain something positive from the research. Researchers, of course, get data from the research that enable them to publish books and articles, which advance their careers. But what do the research subjects get? This raises the ethical issue of what the research community owes to research subjects. The subjects could be paid for their time and effort, or the research results could be translated into social policies or practices that benefit the community from which the research subjects come. Or, by participating in the research, the subjects might develop knowledge or skills that will enable them to make their own lives better. The point is that, from this perspective, researchers have an ethical obligation not only to not leave research participants worse off but also to compensate them for their time and effort and leave them better off in some way for having participated in the research.

Research in Practice 3.1 explores some of the difficulties surrounding such issues as privacy, confidentiality, harm, and informed consent, especially when the research topic is sensitive.

RESEARCH IN PRACTICE 3.1

PRACTICE EFFECTIVENESS:

Sex Offenders as Participants

Applied social researchers often find themselves doing socially sensitive research, research on people who arouse intense and sometimes negative emotions in others—murderers, rapists, prostitutes, or illegal drug users, to name only a few. Such research often involves evaluation research or program evaluations (discussed in Chapters 1 and 12) and can be very challenging, especially in terms of maintaining ethical standards.

One example of such research is a program evaluation assessing two methods of treating people convicted of child molestation (Jenkins-Hall and Osborn 1994). The goal of the research was to provide observational evidence regarding which treatment approach is more effective. In conducting the research, the researchers had to consider the rights of the child-molester participants as well as the safety of staff. There were potential negative consequences for each group in participating in the research. The researchers identified three general areas of concern: (1) informed consent and voluntary participation, (2) confidentiality of data and privacy, and (3) protection against dangers that a participant may pose to himself or others.

Informed consent was considered so important by the researchers that they incorporated a multi-phase consent process, requiring participants to give consent at each stage of the process. All clients completed a general consent form that covered the basic requirements of the DHHS. Prior to a comprehensive psychological and social assessment that was a necessary part of the research, the clients completed an evaluation consent form that spelled out the assessment process. Additional consent forms were completed in conjunction with each subsequent treatment component. Given the complexity of the intervention, this multi-phase consent process, though unusual, ensured that participants understood the program and were freely consenting to participation throughout the project.

Confidentiality and privacy were also considered very important because of the negative consequences that might occur to the molesters if information about their participation in the program were to be released. One protection of privacy was the use of federal certificates of confidentiality. Additional steps were also taken. The project was located in a public office building suite and was not identified as a sex offender treatment site. Each participant was given a six-digit ID number that appeared on all documents. Names and other identifying information were removed from all correspondence, consents, and records from referral sources. Staff addressed participants by first name only, and information was never released without signed waivers of confidentiality that specified what information could be released and to whom. Because the program involved the delivery of treatment services, each participant was provided with a

continued on next page

client advocate who was a volunteer clinician not affiliated with the project. This advocate's sole responsibility was to protect the rights of the clients.

In addressing the issue of harm or distress, the researchers considered not only harm to the participants but also, given that the participants were convicted sex offenders, potential danger to the staff or members of the local community. Several measures were employed to reduce such risks. One concern for the project was quick detection if a participant were in danger of committing another sex offense. Researchers argued that the project had an ethical and perhaps legal duty to protect potential victims. The project provided each participant with a 24-hour crisis call service, as well as therapists to deal with minor crises such as loss of employment or a breakup with a significant other. Over a two-year period, three cases required involuntary commitment of participants due to deterioration in their mental health status. In several cases where the participant was exhibiting negative

signs, he was temporarily removed from the project and offered alternative treatment. If a participant who was at risk of relapse failed to follow the terms of a crisis intervention plan, the director of the project was notified and authorities were alerted. Failure to comply would result in termination from the project.

To assure the safety of the staff, the program employed a variety of procedures. Staff were directed to have unlisted personal phone numbers, never reveal home addresses, never be alone with clients in the suite, and never enter with a client a room lockable from the inside. Each office and work area contained a "panic button" that sounded an alarm in the office and at the university police office. Entry to the project was strictly controlled so that client interaction with other office-building occupants was minimal. Participants were routinely debriefed after treatment sessions to ensure that they would not leave the center in a distressed, agitated, or aroused state.

Sponsored Research

Because much social research is conducted under the auspices of a third-party sponsor, certain ethical considerations arise from that relationship. When research is sponsored, some type of research agreement, essentially a contract, is developed. Researchers and sponsors alike should exercise great care in drafting this agreement. The potential for ethical problems arising later is reduced when the research agreement clearly specifies the rights and obligations of the parties involved.

Three areas are of particular concern in sponsored research (King, Henderson, and Stein 1999). First, it is common for sponsors to want to retain control over the release of the collected data. The precise conditions of release should be specified in the research agreement to avoid conflicts. One limitation that should not be tolerated, however, is the conditional publication of results—that is, agreeing to publish results only if they turn out a certain way (usually so they support the preconceived notions of

the sponsor). Such conditional publication violates the integrity of the research process and the autonomy of the researcher (Wolfgang 1981). If the researcher agrees to some other type of limitation on release, however, it must be honored. To do otherwise would be a breach of the agreement and therefore unethical.

The second major concern in sponsored research is the nature of the research project itself. The precise purpose and procedures of the study should be specified in the agreement. Ethical questions arise if the researcher heavily modifies the study to cover matters not in the agreement. Often, sponsors will allow researchers to use the data gathered for scientific purposes beyond the needs of the sponsor, but it is unethical to agree to do a study that a sponsor wants and then change it for personal reasons so that it no longer meets the expectations of the sponsor.

A third area of ethical concern in sponsored research relates to the issue of informed consent, namely, revealing the sponsor's identity to participants. Although controversy exists in this regard, some researchers take the stance that truly informed consent can be given only if one knows who is sponsoring the study and for what purpose. Some people might object, for example, to providing data that would help a company better market a product, a political party to present a candidate, or the government to propagandize its citizens. In fact, studies show that people are less likely to participate in research they know to be sponsored by commercial organizations, which suggests that information about sponsorship can influence the decision of whether to participate (Fox, Crask, and Kim 1988). Each researcher, then, must carefully consider whether to make the sponsorship of a research project explicit. At a minimum, to deceive people regarding the sponsorship of a study to gain their participation is certainly unethical.

Scientific Misconduct and Fraud

When a research project reaches the final stage—dissemination of results—the primary consideration regarding ethical conduct shifts from avoiding harming the participants in research to making sure the consumers of the research are not adversely affected. Results of a study are typically communicated in the form of a report to a sponsoring organization, publication in a professional journal, or possibly a news release to the media. The preeminent ethical obligation in this regard is not to disclose inaccurate, deceptive, or fraudulent research results. To do so risks misleading scientists who depend on previous research to guide their own work. Ethical violations concerning disclosure of results undermine the very nature of the scientific process, which, as we have seen in Chapter 2, depends upon building future knowledge on the foundation of existing knowledge. If we cannot depend on the accuracy of existing knowledge, then the scientific endeavor is threatened. In that case, the credibility of all research is damaged by such violations. Furthermore, deceptive or fraudulent disclosures of research results can cause human service practitioners to design useless—even dangerous—interventions based on faulty studies.

Many ethical violations can occur in the process of reporting research (Gibelman and Gelman 2001).

Fraud is the deliberate falsification, misrepresentation, or plagiarizing of data, findings, or the ideas of others. This includes such things as falsifying data, embellishing research reports, reporting research that has not been conducted, or manipulating data in a deceptive way. **Misconduct** is a broader concept that includes not only fraud but also carelessness or bias in recording and reporting data, mishandling data, and incomplete reporting of results. Other questionable practices are irresponsible claims of authorship (listing coauthors who did not really make contributions to the research) and premature release of results to the public without peer review.

Estimates of the actual amount of scientific misconduct suggest that the problem is relatively small. The Office of Research Integrity of the DHHS, which keeps track of such matters, reports that only an average of 63 new cases of alleged misconduct are brought to their attention each year, and many of these allegations prove to be unfounded (Office of Research Integrity 2002). Of course, underreporting could hide a larger problem. But even if the number of cases is small, any misconduct in research can still damage the credibility of all research and place human service clients—and, by extension, human service providers—at risk.

The issue of who has responsibility for detecting scientific misconduct is still very controversial (Gibelman and Gelman 2001). For many years, government agencies that fund research pushed this responsibility onto the shoulders of the universities and other institutions where research was actually conducted. By the late 1980s, however, the National Institutes of Health (NIH) and the DHHS both had established their own offices to watch for misconduct. Yet most scientists still consider protection against misconduct to be primarily a responsibility of the scientific community, which uses two major mechanisms to detect fraud: *peer review* and *replication.* There are, however, limitations to each of these mechanisms, as illustrated by a case of fraud in medical research involving Dr. Robert Slutsky (Engler et al. 1987).

The prolific Dr. Slutsky had authored or coauthored 137 articles on cardiological and radiological research over a seven-year period. During evaluation of his appointment as a researcher at a university, questions were raised about duplicate data in two of his papers. In the ensuing investigation, 12 articles were deemed fraudulent and 48 were considered questionable. In some cases, articles described experiments that had never been conducted. How is it that these articles eluded the net of peer review by respected medical journals? There seem to have been two problems. First, peer review of article submissions cannot detect plausible, internally consistent fabrications. Second, the sheer number of research articles submitted to publications for review requires a large number of qualified reviewers who understand both the methodology and the content of the article.

If peer review does not detect and deter fraud, then will replication solve the problem? It might, but the effectiveness of replication has been severely crippled by the modern research system because research funds are not often appropriated for replication. Funding agencies prefer to fund research efforts that delve into new areas. Furthermore, where replication does occur, it tends to be reserved for projects that have produced unusual results. Fraudulent studies that enhance the prestige of researchers but that do not run counter to accepted findings in a field are not likely to arouse enough attention to warrant replication (Engler et al. 1987).

Beyond peer review and replication, there are several ways of reducing the chances of fraud or detecting it if it occurs. One is to supervise novice researchers until they demonstrate good practices, ethical conduct, and technical competency. Second, organizations need to guard against overly prolific researchers. Senior researchers and coauthors should not simply allow their names to be associated with research reports without carefully examining the work. Third, journals can reduce fraud by requiring more complete data to be submitted to reviewers, even if all data cannot be included in the published article. When fraud is detected, journals have a responsibility to make the fraud public so that others will not unsuspectingly base research or treatments on the fraudulent material. Despite agreement on this responsibility, however, some question remains concerning the capacity or willingness of journals to

deliver (Anderson 1989). It seems that journals fear legal action against them by those accused of fraud, even when protected by the truth of factual statements. Legislation that would provide immunity for good-faith reporting of scientific misconduct by academic institutions and scientific journals has been requested to bolster the watchdog function of journals. Fourth, professionals in the field can also help reduce fraud by considering it their ethical obligation to report suspected cases to appropriate authorities. Finally, organizations can reduce fraud by establishing standards and developing facilities to retain data from research projects.

Though not as unethical as purposeful deception, careless errors in research have the same effect of creating misinformation. Social researchers owe the scientific community carefully conducted research that is as free of error as possible. As with fraud, errors are discovered and corrected through critical review of research and reanalysis of data or through replication. For example, Research in Practice 4.1 in the next chapter describes a study done in the 1980s that claimed to document substantial negative economic consequences of divorce for women; the study was an important foundation for developing social policy. Partly because these findings were somewhat at variance with the results of other studies, a reanalysis of the data was undertaken (Peterson 1996). The reanalysis showed that the original conclusions were partly due to errors in the original analysis. The reanalysis showed that women do suffer economically after divorce but not nearly as severely as the original analysis had suggested. Had the original research conclusions not been based on an inaccurate analysis, the subsequent policy development might have been different. Scientists are human, and human beings make mistakes. But researchers must maximize safeguards to keep mistakes to the absolute minimum.

Beyond the problems of fraud and carelessness, researchers also have an obligation to report their results thoroughly. Researchers must take care to ensure that what they report does not give a distorted picture of the overall results. In addition, researchers should point out any limitations that might qualify the findings. Researchers must also be concerned with how the findings are applied to human service practice and policy decisions. The research projects on the effectiveness of arrest as a deterrent to intimate partner violence (see Chapter 10 for a detailed discussion) are an excellent example. A study conducted in Minneapolis has been singled out as a primary catalyst for widespread adoption of pro-arrest policies. Critics have argued that propaganda generated by some of the participating agencies was a key factor in the study's impact on policy, an impact that they say was unjustified by a single study. Subsequent replications in several cities failed to support the findings of the Minneapolis study and have underscored the call for caution in rushing to apply findings to practice (Sherman 1992). This was not a case of publishing fraudulent results or misrepresenting data but rather an issue of the researcher's role in applying research findings.

Scientific Advocacy

Scientific knowledge rarely remains the exclusive domain of the scientific community but typically finds its way into public life in the form of inventions, technological developments, or social policy. This raises potential ethical dilemmas in terms of the role of researchers as advocates of particular uses of their research results. What responsibility, if any, do scientists have for overseeing the use to which their results are put? To what extent should scientists become advocates for applying knowledge in a particular way? Quite naturally, disagreements arise on how to resolve these issues. The controversy is compounded in the case of human service researchers because their research is normally initiated with some explicit clinical application in mind. The classic approach to these issues derives from the exhortations of sociologist Max Weber (1946) that science should be "value-free." Social scientists, according to Weber, should create knowledge, not apply it. Therefore, they have no special responsibility for the ultimate use to which that knowledge is put. Furthermore, according to Weber, they are under no obligation to advocate particular uses of scientific knowledge. Indeed, advocacy is frowned on as threatening objectivity, which is a central concern of

science. So although remaining value-free is difficult, many argue that abandoning the effort would be disastrous in that it would prevent us from acquiring an accurate body of knowledge about human social behavior and might threaten the researcher's credibility as a disinterested expert (Gibbs 1983; Gordon 1988; Halfpenny 1982).

Karl Marx (1964, orig. pub. 1848) originally developed the opposite stance in this controversy. Marx championed the cause of the poor and downtrodden; he believed that social researchers should bring strong moral commitments to their work and strive to change unfair or immoral conditions. Following Marx, some modern researchers believe that social research should be guided by personal and political values and directed toward alleviating social ills (Brunswick-Heinemann 1981; Fay 1987). Furthermore, scientists should advocate for uses of their research by others that would help accomplish those personal goals.

Sociologist Alvin Gouldner (1976) developed a compromise position on the value-free controversy. Gouldner pointed to the obvious, namely, that scientists have values just as do other human beings. Furthermore, he noted, those values can influence research in so many subtle ways that their effects can never be totally eliminated. Instead of denying or ignoring the existence or impact of these personal values, scientists need to be acutely aware of them and up front about them in research reports. Being thus forewarned, consumers of their research are then better able to assess whether the findings have been influenced by personal bias. In addition, Gouldner argued that social scientists have not only the right but also the duty to promote the constructive use of scientific knowledge (Becker 1967; Gouldner 1976). Because someone will make decisions concerning the use of scientific knowledge, scientists themselves are best equipped to make those judgments. As Gouldner states, technical competence would seem to provide a person with some warrant for making value judgments. People who take this position view the value-free stance as a potentially dangerous dereliction of a responsibility that accrues to scientists by virtue of their role in developing new knowledge and their expertise.

Clinician–researchers, in particular, may be attracted by this stance. Because their research is conducted, in part, to advance the practice goals of the profession, they would probably view as one of their duties ensuring that any clinical application of the results be faithful to the outcome of the research. Thus, human service researchers are more likely than many other behavioral scientists to take a strong stand in favor of advocacy.

Nothing is wrong with researchers openly pressing for the application of scientific knowledge in ways they deem desirable, so long as their advocacy is tempered with respect for objectivity. The danger of advocacy is that scientists can come to feel so strongly about issues they promote that those feelings hamper the objective collection and analysis of data.

Protecting Vulnerable Clients

Human service clients, because they are often involuntary recipients of services, may find themselves vulnerable to pressures to cooperate in research projects conducted by the organizations that provide them with services. Such clients are likely to be sought out as research subjects because they are often viewed as deviant in some way and therefore interesting to study or because they may be easier than other groups to locate and keep track of during a research project.

Welfare recipients, children in day care settings, patients in public mental hospitals, and participants in job-training programs, to name only a few, are likely candidates for participation in social research projects. In fact, it is common for operators of new or special programs to be required by their funding sources to do research on the effects of their programs as a condition for receiving funds. Although such safeguards as codes of ethics and governmental regulations may serve as useful guides, special obligations fall on human service practitioners to safeguard their clients from unreasonable pressures to participate in research.

A crucial issue in this regard is the matter of voluntary and informed consent. Can clients actually give consent freely? This is one of the reasons that much research using prison inmates as subjects has been discontinued: It is debatable how free inmates really are to give consent. If participation in the research brings significant rewards in the form of separate living quarters or greater privacy, these rewards may be almost coercive in the Spartan, degrading, and often dangerous world of the prison inmate. Although participation in the research is on the face of it voluntary, inmates may not seriously weigh the disadvantages or dangers of the research when participation is perceived as a means of avoiding assault or rape.

Similar ethical questions arise with research on people with significant psychopathologies. If the psychopathology involves defective comprehension or impaired insight, then the subjects may be unable to give truly informed consent. Research on such a population would have to be approached very carefully and could be justified only if it could not be done on a less vulnerable group. If the same research goals could be accomplished with a less vulnerable group, then that would be the route to follow. If it were decided to do research on a group with significant psychopathology, then informed consent should be approached in ways that protect potential participants from even covert coercion; for example, consent could be sought by some party other than the researchers (to avoid the force of authority) or it could be sought in the presence of a relative, friend, or other advocate for the individual (to provide the social support for a refusal). If the psychopathology completely impairs the ability to consent, then most forms of research would be unethical unless it could be shown that either the patient or society would benefit significantly and that the research could be done in no other way (Fulford and Howse 1993).

The problem of voluntary consent may be somewhat more subtle among other recipients of human services. Even though refusal to participate was not linked to termination of benefits, clients might not be sure of this and thus might be disinclined to take the risk of finding out. The reading level of clients receiving public assistance is often less than that of the eighth grade, yet the reading level necessary to comprehend many welfare documents is above 13 years of education. Thus, it is not unreasonable to suspect that clients who are accustomed to being confused by welfare requirements might not aggressively seek to determine their right to refuse participation in a research project presented by official-looking people with official-looking forms. We are not suggesting that research never be conducted on prisoners or public welfare recipients. Rather, clinician–researchers need to exercise additional caution—and in some cases possibly forgo valuable research projects—in the interests of ensuring truly voluntary informed consent.

Research in Practice 3.2 discusses ethical issues involving harm, misconduct, and protecting vulnerable clients and what can be done to protect clients who might be negatively impacted.

RESEARCH IN PRACTICE 3.2

PROGRAM EVALUATION:

Vulnerable Clients at Risk

Science must maintain constant vigilance against research that harms people or is a product of fraud and misconduct. This is especially true in applied research where social or medical interventions that impact people's lives may be implemented. Several recent cases of such ethical violation demonstrate this point. In 1996, the internationally respected researcher Dr. Francis Collins, famous for his work on the government's project to map all human genes, retracted five research papers because a junior colleague had fabricated data. The studies, which were on leukemia, had been published in leading scientific journals (Altman 1996). Another case involved cell biologist Robert P. Liburdy, who published studies purporting to demonstrate a link between exposure to electromagnetic fields and cancer. Eventually, the Office of Research Integrity of the DHHS concluded that much of his data was fictitious, but not before several multimillion-dollar liability suits had been initiated against power companies (*Federal Register* 1999).

When such fraud occurs in the context of human service research, the consequences can be especially chilling. The case of Dr. Stephen Breuning came to light in the 1980s. He had published research alleging beneficial effects of certain drugs for the control of behavior in severely developmentally disabled individuals. Social interventions were implemented to help many developmentally disabled children based on the results of his research. Yet Breuning's results were based, in part, on falsified data. Eventually, the case led to a criminal indictment, and Dr. Breuning was sentenced to 60 days in a halfway house and five years of probation. However, detecting, documenting, and acting on this fraud was a long, protracted battle (Garfield and Welljams-Dorof 1990).

A recent example of ethical violations in the protection of human subjects in applied research comes from the University of Oklahoma, where it was alleged that the principal researcher and an oversight official repeatedly violated federal regulations meant to protect human subjects in cancer research (Pound 2000). The researchers reportedly were unqualified to conduct the research, the vaccine injected hadn't been properly tested, and the IRB had failed to monitor the tests. What makes this case especially significant for this illustration is not only the nature of the violations but the manner in which the ethical violations came to light. It was not a high-level scientist or an IRB that detected the ethical problems but a registered nurse with a limited background in clinical research who had been recently hired at the project and was troubled by what she saw as violations of safety rules, suppression of information, and lying to patients and federal regulators. When her university superiors failed to address her concerns, she didn't give up; instead, she advocated for the patients by writing federal health regulators. As a consequence, government regulators shut down all government-funded research at the Tulsa campus and directed the university to address the problems. The case emphasizes the importance of all human service professionals, not just scientists, understanding the

continued on next page

principles of research ethics. Although cases of ethical violation in social and medical research may be rare, detection and prevention of such conduct may well depend on the vigilance of the human service practitioner who encounters the subjects of research.

These cases highlight several disturbing issues in ethics, research, and human service practice. First, some of this research managed to pass through the filters of review panels and institutional procedures without question. How well can the institutionalized research system prevent fraudulent work? Second, when unethical practices are discovered, who bears the responsibility for alerting practitioners and the public to potential harmful implications? In manufacturing, the government can require product recalls, but how do we protect the public from implementation of fraudulent research? Third, how do we safeguard those who detect potential fraud? In many cases, the people most likely to discover such fraud are colleagues, assistants, students, and others close to the research. To the extent that these people perceive disclosure as risking unpleasant consequences for themselves, they will be reluctant to come forward. Finally, the slow, plodding nature of the bureaucratic process raises the question of what can be done to process cases efficiently while also protecting the rights of individuals accused of fraud.

A close study of the Breuning case suggests that the procedures of the scientific process do afford some protection against the widespread impact of fraudulent data on both science and practice. Based on the assumption that influential research will be widely cited in other research studies, an ingenious study used the *Science Citation Index* and the *Social Science Citation Index* to examine the number of citations made by other researchers to Breuning's 20 publications between 1980 and 1988 (Garfield and Welljams-Dorof 1990). The 200 citations found suggested that his work was influential. However, when the researchers evaluated who made the citations and the *context* of the citations to better understand the effects of the Breuning studies, things looked a little different. For example, of the 200 citations, 40 percent were self-citations by Breuning or his coauthors. In addition, following the publication of a critical review of Breuning's work, citations to his work by others declined sharply. Finally, of 38 studies judged to be materially affected by Breuning's publications, 21 led to negative conclusions, disagreeing with his findings or criticizing his methods. The authors conclude that the pattern of citations suggests that the process of scientific publication and critique is capable of purging science, to a degree, of fraudulent studies.

Withholding Treatment for Research Purposes

An issue of particular concern to human service providers is the research practice of withholding treatment from a control group to assess whether a given treatment is effective. The **control group** serves as a comparison group. If a group receiving the treatment shows more improvement than the control group over a certain span of time, we can feel justified in claiming that the treatment brought about the improvement. With no control group, when the treatment group shows improvement, we cannot say with confidence that the improvement was due to the treatment. It could be that the improvement would have occurred even in the absence of the treatment. The control group, which is comparable to the treatment group in all ways except that it does not receive the treatment, makes it possible to rule out this possibility. Control groups are thus very important to the ability to state whether an independent variable causes change in a dependent variable (see Chapters 2 and 10).

Presumably, research is being conducted on some treatment because the treatment is believed to be effective. Herein lies the ethical dilemma: Some service providers believe it is unethical to withhold a treatment that might help people. They believe withholding treatment deprives people in the control group of the possibility of improvement. This is a serious problem that is not easy to resolve, but there are a number of issues to consider. First, we might ask whether it is ethical to proffer untested treatments. We pointed out in Chapter 1 that many contemporary approaches to human service professions explicitly caution against the use of treatments without proven effectiveness. Providing services is expensive and time-consuming, and it also raises clients' expectations for improvement. Is it ethical to do this when there is no evidence to document that the treatment will be beneficial? For the most part, we would not think of marketing new medicines without a thorough test of their effects, both positive and negative. We should expect no less from the human services we offer.

There may be, in some cases, alternatives to withholding treatment. One alternative would be to offer the control group a treatment that is known to be effective and then see whether the new treatment provides more or less improvement. In this way, all clients are receiving a treatment that is either known to be or suspected of being effective. In the study of the effectiveness of suicide intervention programs, for example, one would certainly be reluctant to evaluate a new intervention by using a control group that received no intervention at all. One recent study of outpatient interventions targeting suicidal young adults used a randomized experiment in which subjects were assigned to either a new experimental treatment or a control group that received a treatment that had been commonly used for these interventions. Although both groups showed improvement, the experimental treatment was more effective in retaining the highest-risk participants (Rudd, Rajab, and Orman 1996).

Another alternative to withholding treatment would be to delay giving the treatment to the control group for a period of time and make the comparisons between those receiving treatment and the control group over this time period. For example, in a study of two different approaches to controlling people's smoking, all participants in the study were told that, if they were randomly placed in the group that would not receive immediate treatment, they would receive treatment when the study was over and would receive whichever treatment the study showed to be most effective (Coelho 1983). This re-

solves the ethical problem by ensuring that all participants will receive treatment at some point. In fact, clients often confront a delay in receiving services when the resources of an agency are taxed.

In cases without such alternatives, however, clinician–researchers must use the risk-benefit approach: Does the benefit to be gained from the research outweigh the risks of withholding treatment from the people in the control group? If we were studying people at high risk of suicide, we would be cautious about withholding treatment. In the treatment of nonassertiveness, on the other hand, we might decide that a delay of a few weeks in treatment would not be terribly detrimental, and whatever damage occurred could be undone once treatment was initiated. As with so many other ethical issues, this is ultimately a judgmental one over which clinician-researchers will continue to agonize.

The ethical issues involved in withholding treatment can also arise in a more subtle fashion, namely, the extent to which research activities might interfere with the delivery of services to clients. Research activities might include, for example, administering questionnaires, making observations in clients' homes, or gathering data from agency records. If these activities take much of a client's time, the client may be reluctant to ask for services or cooperate with treatment. Likewise, the time necessary to interview a client for purposes of data collection might reduce the amount of time available to provide treatment. Given that a major concern of practitioners is to provide services, practitioners would have to weigh the costs of any interference with service delivery against the benefits of conducting research. And they would also need to consider the costs of not carrying out the research in their assessment of whether the interference is unethically impairing service delivery.

Codes of Ethics

A point emphasized in this chapter is that ethical judgments are difficult and often controversial because they involve interpretation and assessment. Most professional organizations establish written

COMPUTERS IN RESEARCH

Ethical Challenges in Computer-Based Research

"When I joined this, I thought it would be a support group, not a fishbowl for a bunch of guinea pigs. I certainly don't feel at this point that it is a safe environment, as a support group is supposed to be, and I will not open myself up to be dissected by students or scientists."

—Comment by a group member upon realizing that a researcher was monitoring a listserv (King 1996, p. 122)

The Internet offers a vast new arena in which to conduct social science research. After all, the online interactions of people represent yet another setting in which human beings engage one another, and these interactions are often readily accessible and convenient to researchers. However, as the above comment by a listserv participant indicates, not all people warmly welcome scientific scrutiny in this venue. Although it has great promise, use of the Internet as a vehicle for research raises new questions about the application of ethical principles such as informed consent and privacy.

Eysenbach and Till (2001) use the term "Internet communities" to refer to the various ways people now communicate using the Web. Included are discussion boards on Web sites, mailing lists, chat rooms, and newsgroups. All of these venues could be settings in which social researchers gather data. Some of these communities address sensitive issues, such as dealing with breast cancer or surviving childhood sexual abuse. Eysenbach and Till argue that there is increasing evidence that researchers posting on or monitoring such communities may be damaging to the community. To back up their assertion, Eysenbach and Till actually used a search engine to locate comments by newsgroup members in response to researcher's requests. The comments were often negative.

A fundamental issue here has to do with privacy. Are Internet communities public spaces or are they private? According to the Code of Ethics of the American Sociological Association, Section 12 (c):

Sociologists may conduct research in public places or use publicly available information about individuals (e.g., naturalistic observations in public places, analysis of public records, or archival research) without obtaining consent. If, under such circumstances, sociologists have any doubt whatsoever about the need for informed consent, they consult with institutional review boards or, in the absence of such boards, with another authoritative body with expertise on the ethics of research before proceeding with such research. (American Sociological Association 1997)

An Internet study of hate crimes illustrates some of the complexities of issues of privacy and informed consent (Glaser, Dixit, and Green 2002).

codes of ethics to serve as guides for their members to follow. Though these codes by no means settle all debate, they do stand as a foundation from which professionals can begin to formulate ethical decisions. These codes of ethics can be found at the Web sites and in publications of the major organizations of professionals who conduct research in the social sciences and human services. See, for example, the Web pages of these organizations:

- American Sociological Association (www.asanet.org/ecoderev.htm)
- National Association of Social Workers (www.naswdc.org/code.htm)
- Society for Applied Sociology (www.appliedsoc.org/m_govstructre_ethics.htm)
- American Association for Public Opinion Research (www.aapor.org/ethics/).

The codes of ethics of other social science and human service professions would be similar to these.

A team of researchers conducted semi-structured interviews with participants in white racist Internet chat rooms. To do the interviews, the researchers went online to the chat rooms and posed as people who were interested in joining the discussion. From a methodological standpoint, the chat room venue was ideal in that the anonymity and candor of chat rooms reduced the reactivity that might have occurred with other approaches. From an ethical standpoint, does this research require informed consent? The researchers consulted with the IRB at their university, which concluded that informed consent was not necessary because (1) participants were involved without coercion in a public forum, discussing topics that were common subjects at the chat room, and (2) respondent identities were protected through use of pseudonyms and separation in the data of the identifiers from the responses. So, the white racist Internet forum was deemed to be a public place.

A more complicated question was whether informed consent could be dispensed with because it might reduce participation and produce a less representative sample. Both the researchers and the IRB gave this justification. However, in the absence of other rationales for not obtaining informed consent (i.e., the research is in a public place), the effect on the sample would be a weak argument.

In cases where the researcher does desire to obtain informed consent in such online research, how does one go about doing so? One suggestion is to send a message to the mailing list describing the research and giving participants the opportunity to withdraw. A second option is to retrospectively ask persons whose postings will be used to give permission. In terms of privacy, Eysenbach and Till point out a special wrinkle that can thwart privacy. A researcher may judiciously separate identifiers from comments, but if the report includes verbatim quotes, the original participant comments can sometimes be located on the Internet by using a search engine.

Eysenbach and Till suggest some other considerations in deciding whether to conduct research online or whether informed consent is called for:

- *Intrusiveness*—Will the research involve passive analysis of Internet postings versus active involvement of the researcher in the community by participating in communications?
- *Perceived privacy*—Do participants perceive their community as private, possibly because is it a closed group requiring registration or because group norms define what transpires there as private?
- *Vulnerability and harm*—Will the intrusion of the researcher or publication of results potentially be upsetting or bring harm to individuals or the community as a whole?
- *Confidentiality and anonymity*—Can confidentiality or anonymity truly be protected, given the search potential of online technology (if verbatim quotes are used in a research report, search engines may be able to locate the source of the quote)?

Thus, research via the Internet is a new field where social scientists, IRBs, and funding agencies confront new challenges related to ethics and are finding ways to address basic ethical issues in this rapidly changing medium.

Main Points

- What is ethical in research and practice is based on human values and varies as those values change.
- The mistreatment of minority peoples in research has been a major impetus to the development of ethical standards for research in the United States and abroad.
- Social research is typically evaluated in terms of risks versus benefits, with some "questionable practices" allowed if the research promises sufficient benefits.
- Informed consent assures participants the ability to determine their own destiny but may prevent the use of some research methods and force the study of only those persons who volunteer.

- Some level of deception is sometimes used in research, but whether or under what conditions deception is acceptable has been highly controversial.
- Research subjects have a right to privacy, which can be protected by letting them edit data about themselves from a data set, keeping the data anonymous, or keeping the data confidential.
- Confidentiality and anonymity are not the same thing. Intrusion by third parties, such as courts of law, can occasionally be a threat to the guarantee of confidentiality.
- Exposing subjects to physical or mental distress should be kept to a minimum and should never be done without fully informed consent. Subjects should be thoroughly debriefed at the conclusion of the research.
- When conducting research for a sponsor, many ethical difficulties can be avoided by a detailed research agreement that covers such topics as the purpose and nature of the research, rights of publication, and revealing to participants the sponsor of the research.
- Researchers have an obligation to report their results fully and honestly and to avoid any kind of scientific misconduct or fraud. Replication is a major tool of science for correcting research errors and fraudulent reports.
- It is the researcher's own decision regarding the degree to which he or she will become an advocate; however, caution is required so that objectivity is not undermined.
- Because of their disadvantaged status, human service clients are often vulnerable to coercion to participate in research projects and therefore require special protection.
- Withholding treatment from control groups raises an ethical dilemma, but it is often justified when testing unproved approaches.
- Most professional organizations have established codes of ethics that provide useful guidelines for making ethical decisions.

Important Terms for Review

anonymity
confidentiality
control group
ethics
fraud (scientific)
informed consent
misconduct (scientific)
privacy

Exploring InfoTrac® College Edition and the Internet

InfoTrac® College Edition search terms:

code of ethics AND research
confidentiality AND research
research AND human subjects
research ethics
scientific misconduct

InfoTrac® College Edition articles:

Updating Protections for Human Subjects Involved in Research. (Policy Perspectives). Jonathan Moreno, Arthur L. Caplan, Paul R. Wolpe. *JAMA, The Journal of the American Medical Association* Dec 9, 1998 v280 i22 p1951(1) (8,440 words)

Is It Research or Quality Improvement? (clinical practice problems) Suzanne C. Beyea, Leslie H. Nicoll. *AORN Journal* July 1998 v68 n1 p117(3) (1,799 words)

Use the search engines on the Internet (we find google.com to be especially effective) to locate professional organizations' Web pages other than those already mentioned in the text—research organizations, such as the American Psychological Association or the American Criminological Society, or practitioner organizations, such as the American Medical Association or the American Nurses Association. Explore those sites for topics related to ethics. Also use the search engine to look for a variety of key words, such as "ethics," "science," "research fraud," "IRB," or some combination of these.

A site that is especially informative about IRBs is www.mcwirb.org, which is the IRB Discussion Forum, maintained by a research institute at a hospital in Pennsylvania. It has links to wide-ranging resources on IRBs. An invaluable source for ethics information is the Office of Research Integrity

(ORI), which is located in the Office of Public Health and Science in the DHHS. ORI's mission is to promote integrity in biomedical and behavioral research supported by the Public Health Service. ORI monitors institutional investigations of research misconduct and facilitates the responsible conduct of research through educational, preventive, and regulatory activities. You can access the full text of the Belmont Report, the Nuremburg Code, and other major documents. ORI can be accessed on the Web at ori.dhhs.gov.

The NIH has an extremely useful Web site where ethics materials can be downloaded: ohrp. osophs.dhhs.gov/irb/irb_guidebook.htm. The guidebooks at this site cover practically all the issues discussed in this chapter, including certificates of confidentiality. Of particular note is a NIH policy that became effective in 2000, whereby the NIH requires education on the protection of human research participants for all investigators submitting NIH applications for grants or proposals for contracts or receiving new or non-competing awards for research involving human subjects.

Many universities are developing online courses to meet this requirement. (See, for example, the University of Michigan's online course at: www. irb.research.umich.edu.) Universities often put their guidelines for research on their Web sites, so you can learn how their IRBs operate and how they protect human subjects. If you go to a university's Web page, you may find a link such as "Guidelines for Researchers" or "Research Policies and Procedures," with issues related to the ethical conduct of research. Visit several sites and compare them with your own university's policies.

Another Web site is one called Ethics in Science: www.chem.vt.edu/chem-ed/ethics/. This has links to many resources and sites related to ethical issues in research. Many of the links relate to the physical and natural sciences, but some apply to the social sciences, and many ethical issues span disciplines. A highly recommended Canadian site that does an especially nice job of explaining key ethics terms is the National Council on Ethics in Human Research (www.ncehr-cnerh.org/english/consent/consente.htm). Another Canadian site especially useful for ethics information

related to research on children and families is the Centre for Children and Families in the Justice System (www.lfcc.on.ca/ethical.html). Information relevant to research on the mentally ill can be found at the Onlineethics.org site (onlineethics.org/reseth/mod/mentres.html).

For Further Reading

Beauchamp, Tom L., et al., eds. *Ethical Issues in Social Science Research*. Baltimore, Md.: Johns Hopkins University Press, 1982. A volume of readings that covers the range of ethical issues one is likely to face in human service research.

Caplan, A. L., ed. *When Medicine Went Mad.* Totowa, N.J.: Humana Press, 1992. This volume contains articles relating to the research conducted by the Nazis during World War II. Although it deals with an extreme situation that many hope will never occur again, it does provide an illustration of what can happen when science "goes mad."

Corey, Gerald, Marianne Schneider Corey, and Patrick Callanan. *Issues and Ethics in the Helping Professions,* 6th ed. Pacific Grove, Calif.: Brooks/Cole, 2003. This is a comprehensive review of ethical issues in the many realms of human service practice. Given the linkage between research and practice, the analysis of practice ethics is relevant to clinician–researchers in the human services.

Crossen, Cynthia. *Tainted Truth: The Manipulation of Fact in America.* New York: Simon & Schuster, 1994. An enlightening book by a journalist about the many frauds that can be perpetrated by scientists. The author shows how frauds can be artfully crafted and how they can adversely affect us all.

Gubrium, Jaber F., and David Silverman, eds. *The Politics of Field Research.* Newbury Park, Calif.: Sage, 1989. This collection of articles by experienced researchers focuses on the special ethical issues surrounding the conduct of field research.

Kimmel, Allan J. *Ethics and Values in Applied Social Research.* Beverly Hills, Calif.: Sage, 1988. An excellent overview of the ethical dilemmas that confront applied researchers.

Lee, Raymond. *Doing Research on Sensitive Topics.* Newbury Park, Calif.: Sage, 1993. Ethical issues become especially important and complicated when doing research on sensitive topics, and this author suggests ethical guidelines for navigating such treacherous waters.

Miller, Arthur G. *The Obedience Experiments: A Case Study of Controversy in Social Science.* New York: Praeger, 1986. An exhaustive discussion of the controversial Milgram experiments on obedience to authority and their ethical implications, especially in terms of the psychological harm done to the participants. Other experiments involving deception and stressful conditions are also presented.

Penslar, Robin Levin, ed. *Research Ethics: Cases and Materials.* Bloomington and Indianapolis: Indiana University Press, 1995. This book covers ethical dilemmas in psychology, history, and biology, but the issues are relevant to all social sciences and human service research. Issues are explored by the case-study method.

Sieber, Joan E. *Planning Ethically Responsible Research: A Guide for Students and Internal Review Boards.* Newbury Park, Calif.: Sage, 1992. This short volume offers a lot of practical information on how to translate ethical principles and federal regulations into valid applied research methods.

Exercises for Class Discussion

3.1 A student majoring in criminal justice needs to do a research project as a course requirement. He is working part-time as an undercover store detective in a large discount department store. His idea is to do observational research on the shoplifting behavior that he encounters as a part of his job. In addition, he has access to store records on suspects apprehended for shoplifting in the past. He also plans to interview a sample of shoppers about shoplifting without disclosing that he is also a store detective. Discuss how the issues of informed consent, confidentiality, and disclosure of results apply to this case.

3.2 What recommendations could you make to the student in Exercise 3.1 to safeguard the ethical standards for research in this case? Consider each of the ethical issues discussed in this chapter. Do you think the study could be done ethically at all? Support your conclusion.

3.3 Suppose you are working in an alcoholism treatment unit, and a proposal is made to initiate a new treatment program that looks promising but is largely untested. Under what conditions do you think it would be acceptable to utilize a control group as a comparison group that does not receive any treatment? Under what conditions would it be ethically unacceptable? How might you avoid some of the ethical dilemmas that come from withholding treatment but still have some form of control group to use for comparison?

3.4 Consider the codes of ethics of the various professional organizations mentioned toward the end of the chapter. What changes in the codes would you recommend making to improve them? Why do you think these would be improvements?

3.5 Invite a representative of the IRB at your college or university to address your class on the kinds of ethical issues that arise in research done by faculty or students at the university. Explore with this person the safeguards that can be built into research designs to protect against such ethical problems.

Chapter 4

Issues in Problem Formulation

Suppose you were required, as many students in social research courses are, to design and conduct a research project. Our experience teaching research courses in the social sciences and human services is that some students respond to this assignment by drawing a total blank. Others grasp eagerly onto a topic, such as "the cause of drug addiction," and rush off with total confidence that they are about to solve this enduring problem. In each case, the student is having difficulty adequately formulating a research problem. In the first case, the difficulty is in locating a problem to investigate, whereas in the second, the trouble lies in formulating a problem sufficiently specific that it is amenable to scientific research.

We assure you this problem is not unique to students. Every researcher must grapple with problem formulation. Because it is the initial step and provides the basis for the complete research project, problem formulation is of crucial importance. Many potentially serious difficulties can be avoided—or at least minimized—by careful problem formulation. In this chapter, we present the major issues to be considered in problem formulation, beginning with how to select a problem on which to conduct research. Then we analyze how to refine the research question so that it can be answered through research. Finally, we discuss factors relating to the feasibility of research.

Selecting a Research Problem

The first hurdle confronting a researcher is to select an appropriate topic for scientific investigation. Actually, this is not as difficult as it may first appear because the social world around us is teeming with unanswered questions. Selecting a problem calls for some creativity and imagination, but researchers can turn to a number of places for inspiration.

Personal Interest

Research topics are often selected because a researcher has an interest in some aspect of human behavior, possibly owing to some personal experience.

One social scientist, for example, conducted research on battered women and women's shelters in part because of her own earlier experience of being abused by her husband; another researcher, who had grown up in the only African American family in a small rural town, did research on prejudice, discrimination, and the experience of minorities (Higgins and Johnson 1988). Research sometimes focuses on behavior that is unique or bizarre and thus compelling to some. Examples of such research abound, including studies of nudist colonies, pool hustlers, juvenile gangs, striptease dancers, burglars, homeless heroin addicts, and body piercers (Bourgois, Lettiere, and Quesada 1997; Miller and Tewksbury 2001; Polsky 1967; Weinberg 1968).

Researchers who select topics from their personal interests must be careful to demonstrate the scientific worth of their projects. Recall from Chapter 1 that the goals of scientific research are to describe, explain, predict, and evaluate. The purpose of research is to advance our knowledge, not just satisfy personal curiosity. For example, in her study of female strippers, psychologist Tania Israel (2002) was interested in learning how people adapt to a job many consider deviant. Such a focus placed her research firmly in an established area of study and amplified its scientific contribution. A researcher who chooses a topic based on personal interest—especially if it deals with some unusual or bizarre aspect of human behavior—should be prepared for the possibility that others will fail to see the worth of that research. Even though Israel, as noted, established a legitimate scientific rationale for her study of strippers, she was subjected to considerable criticism by those who failed to appreciate its scientific value; the critics derided her research as lacking in rigor, illegitimate, and embarrassing.

Social Problems

In selecting a topic for research, researchers often need look no farther than the daily newspaper, full of the many social problems that our society faces. Such problems as crime, delinquency, poverty, pollution, overpopulation, drug abuse, alcoholism, mental illness, sexual deviance, discrimination, and political oppression have all been popular sources of topics for social research. The Society for the Study of Social Problems—a professional organization to which many social scientists and human service providers belong—publishes a journal titled *Social Problems,* whose sole purpose is to communicate the results of scientific investigations into current social problems.

Each of these general categories of social problems encompasses a range of issues for study. Many studies, for example, focus on the sources of a problem. Others are concerned with the consequences these problems have for individuals or for society. Still others deal with the outcomes of social programs and other intervention efforts intended to ameliorate these problems. People in the human services, who are routinely involved with many of these problems, can find opportunities for research that are directly related to their professional activities.

Testing Theory

Some researchers select problems on the basis of their use in testing and verifying a particular theory. We noted in Chapter 2 that theoretical concerns should be at issue to some degree in all research. Nearly all research has some implications for existing theory. Certain research topics, however, are selected specifically for the purpose of testing some aspect of a given theory. Many theories relevant to the human services have not been thoroughly tested. In some cases, this means we do not know how valid the theories are; in other cases, it means that we do not know how wide the range of human behavior is to which the theory can be applied.

Prior Research

One of the most fruitful sources of research problems is prior research because the findings of all research projects have limitations. Though some questions are answered, others always remain. In addition, new questions may be raised by the findings. It is, in fact, common for investigators to conclude research reports with a discussion of the weaknesses and limitations of the research, including suggestions for future research that follow from the findings that have been presented. Focusing on these unanswered questions or expanding on previous research is a good way to find research problems.

Prior research can also lead to new research problems if we have reason to question the findings of the original research. Research in Practice 4.1 provides an example of this. As emphasized in Chapter 2, it is imperative that we not complacently accept research findings, especially when conclusions are based on a single study, because opportunities exist for error or bias to influence results. If we have reason to suspect research findings, we have a ready-made problem on which to conduct research ourselves. One of our own students, in fact, found his problem in just this way when faced with the course assignment of conducting a research project. The student had read a research article suggesting a number of differences between the social settings in which marijuana is used and those in which alcohol is used. The student disagreed, partly because of his own experiences, believing instead that the social environments in which the two substances were used were quite similar. He designed a study that allowed him to determine whether his hypotheses—or those presumably verified by the previous investigation—would better predict what he would observe. As it turned out, many of his hypotheses were supported by his findings.

Program Evaluation

Program evaluation focuses on assessing the effectiveness or efficiency of some program or practice. As noted in Chapter 1, program and practice effectiveness evaluations have become increasingly important activities for human service professionals. Agencies or organizations that fund the human services today typically demand that evaluation research be conducted if funding is to be granted or continued. Such research, developed for practical reasons, can take many forms. A social agency, for example, may require some needs-assessment research to gather information about its clients if it is to efficiently deliver services to them. Or a practitioner may need to know which intervention strategy—

RESEARCH IN PRACTICE 4.1

NEEDS ASSESSMENT:

Reevaluating the Economic Consequences of Divorce

As legal and administrative restrictions on obtaining a divorce have eased over the decades, the question arises of just how well women and children fare under the new divorce codes. This concern was the subject of a study by Lenore Weitzman (1985), who analyzed data on 228 cases drawn from the Los Angeles County Court docket in 1977. The shocking conclusion was that, in the first year following divorce, the average standard of living of women who divorced declined by 73 percent, while men's standard of living actually rose by 42 percent. Weitzman's study became widely used in policy debates. From 1986 to 1993, it was cited in 348 social science articles and in more than 250 law review articles. It was also cited by at least 24 legal cases in state appellate and supreme courts and even once by the U.S. Supreme Court. In other words, the study had a significant impact on policies developed by courts and others.

When research findings are as extreme as these, and when they are so influential in social policy debates, other researchers often replicate the research to ensure that the results are not due to some bias or error. Such replications involve using prior research as the source of the research problem. In fact, in the decade after publication of the Weitzman research results, many researchers conducted replications of it, often based on much broader-based national samples. These studies also showed that disparities existed between the financial experiences of women

and men after divorce. However, these replications also consistently showed a much smaller disparity than had Weitzman: Women's standard of living declined by 13 percent to 35 percent (depending on the particular study), whereas men's standard of living increased by 11 percent to 13 percent. As noted in Chapter 2, replications of this sort are one of the self-correcting mechanisms in science for rooting out error and providing the most accurate findings.

When replications produce results that are widely at variance with the original research, an effort is sometimes made to reanalyze the original data to determine the source of the disparity, and so it was in the case of the Weitzman data (Peterson 1996). However, the task of reanalysis proved difficult from the beginning. First, Weitzman was reluctant to turn over the data for reanalysis. She alleged that there were errors in the master computer file that she wanted to correct first (Weitzman 1996). In the course of various moves between universities, the original, cleaned master data file had disappeared. What data did remain had been cobbled together from various subanalyses and were likely to contain many errors. Eventually, the data were deposited in a university data archive, a common practice with data sets after the original researcher is done with them. However, only after the National Science Foundation, which had funded the original research, threatened to withhold future grant

---

group work, psychotherapy, behavior therapy, or some other—will be most effective with a particular problem. Prison officials need to know which criminal offenders are the riskiest to parole. Home health care workers need information about how to ensure that people will take medications as prescribed. In all these cases, the practical information required by an agency or practitioner determines the focus of the research effort.

The ability to find problems in practice settings that could be the focus of program evaluation research is limited only by the creativity and

imagination of the practitioner. This was brought home to us by two of our students in a recent social research course. They were doing a field placement in a community mental health clinic while taking our research course, so they decided to search for some problem at the clinic to serve as the focus of their research paper. They noticed that one problem the clinic faced was the failure of clients to show up for appointments. In addition to creating difficulties in achieving effective intervention, this also resulted in an inefficient use of staff resources because counselors were left idle by money from Weitzman did she reluctantly allow other researchers access to the data.

Once he obtained the data, social scientist Richard Peterson still faced a number of challenges. One was detecting and eliminating (or at least reducing) the errors in the data file. By painstaking comparison of computer files with paper records, he was able to prepare a final computer file suitable for analysis. In the process, he detected errors in important income variables for 27 of the 228 cases and had questions about how certain concepts were measured. One criticism Peterson made of the original measures was that new spouses, cohabitators, and other adults were included in calculation of economic need but not in calculation of income. The fact that the original researcher had not thoroughly documented how she had handled a number of measurement problems complicated Peterson's task. Consequently, he could not be certain that he was duplicating Weitzman's procedures exactly. Without such duplication, the researcher could not pinpoint where errors occurred in the original study. To compensate for lack of documentation on the original procedures, the new study also included reanalyses using a variety of reasonable alternative approaches in an effort to discover how the estimates of a 73 percent decline in women's standard of living and a 42 percent increase for men might have been obtained. Peterson's final conclusion was that errors in the original analysis of the data were responsible for the results. Based on the corrected data files, his analysis showed that women's standard of living declined by 27 percent and men's increased by 10 percent. Even with testing various alternative assumptions, the results came out about the same. The results of the reanalysis are generally consistent with those of other studies that have since looked at the consequences of divorce.

We can draw a number of lessons from examining the reanalysis of Weitzman's data. First, in spite of the wide difference in findings, both Weitzman's original analysis and Peterson's reanalysis found a significant gender gap in the economic consequences of divorce and documented that this gap produces hardships for many divorced women and children. Second, the errors in the original research underscore the need to scrupulously check analysis to prevent errors in the first place, particularly when a study has the potential to influence policy decisions. The experience also reinforces the importance of carefully and fully documenting the procedures that one uses in the course of conducting a study. Third, Peterson's work also clearly illustrates the value of replication to science, especially applied research. Simply because a study is published in a book or respectable journal and is widely cited by researchers and policymakers does not prove that it is completely accurate; certainly no single study is the definitive answer. In this case, replications by other scholars with other data raised suspicion about the original analysis, and the reanalysis of the actual data confirmed those suspicions. The self-correcting process of science did occur, albeit in a more ponderous than exemplary fashion given the problems that we have described.

missed appointments. The students designed a very simple investigation in which some clients were given a reminder phone call a day or so before their appointment and other clients were not contacted, as had been previous practice. The researchers' concern was to establish whether the reminder call increased the rate at which people showed up for their appointments. After implementing this procedure for a while, the students concluded that the phone call did help and would be a useful and efficient addition to the functioning of the agency.

Human Service Practice

The linkage between human service practice and evaluation research is obvious, but service delivery can serve as the catalyst for basic research as well. In the course of working in human service programs, practitioners confront social problems and human diversity daily as they interact with clients who are struggling with life problems. Often, human service workers encounter client behavior that is unusual or even dramatic, and it stimulates questions about human behavior and society. The protective service worker who faces child abuse and neglect may derive research questions about parent–child bonding or human development. Hospice staff may generate questions about the dying process and grieving. Although answers to these questions may have practice implications, research that addresses issues like these also has important implications for social science theory.

It is not only the behavior or characteristics of clients that generate research questions in practice settings; the mode and process of human service practice itself may even be the topic of research. For example, the mechanisms by which some human service agencies differentially allocate services according to social class or race might be a research issue. In fact, study of the human service delivery system has generated many of the major theoretical advances in our understanding of human behavior and social environments. For instance, Glaser and Strauss (1965) based their classic studies concerning death and social worth on observations of hospital patient care. More recently, controversy has surfaced in the human services over what appears to be the intergenerational transmission of family violence, suggesting that experiencing or observing violence in childhood results in subsequent violent behavior as a parent or spouse. Not only does research into this issue have practical implications for intervention programs; it is also directly relevant to developing our understanding of learning, human development, the family, and society as well (Burgess and Youngblade 1988).

Minorities in Research: The Political Context of Problem Selection

From the preceding discussion of how to select a research problem, one could get the impression that the problem selection process is largely a matter of personal preference. Guided by personal interest or experience, the prospective researcher identifies a worthy problem and sallies forth in the pursuit of knowledge. But problem selection, like most other types of human activity, cannot be explained solely in such individual terms. In fact, if we asked students in research courses why they chose the term paper topics they did, we might find that, in addition to

personal interest, theoretical orientation, or practice interest, they governed their choices by such factors as these: "My instructor had a data set available on this problem." "I got financial aid to work as a research assistant." "I knew my prof was interested in this topic, so I hoped studying it might help me get a better grade." In other words, issues of political efficacy can influence problem selection as well.

In the world of professional research, the situation is not unlike that of the student. But the stakes are much higher and the consequences much greater. Although the number of possible research problems may be infinite, the resources society can allocate to research them are not. Research is a major societal enterprise in which universities, governmental organizations, private research corporations, and independent researchers compete with each other for limited resources. At the same time, societal forces are working to make sure that the concerns of vested interest groups receive attention from the research community. Thus, problem selection is very much a political issue, and the problems that affect minorities and other groups with little clout may not receive the research attention they deserve.

Consider the example of spouse abuse. Men have been assaulting their wives since long before there was social research. Prior to the 1970s, however, one would have been hard pressed to find much research on the topic. Today the social science and human service literature is replete with studies on spouse abuse, and the research endeavor in this area has expanded into a focus on intimate-partner violence. What explains the change? There is no single answer, but a major factor has been the rise of the women's movement. Before the 1960s, women as a group had considerably less political power than they have today, and the special problems of this minority often received little research attention. Woman battering is now an important issue to the women's movement, and this politically powerful group has been able to translate its concerns into public policy. Partly because of its pressure, the government has allocated money specifically for intimate-partner violence research. In addition, with the changing roles of women in society, more women in the past three decades have chosen to pursue careers as researchers in the social sciences. One consequence of more women in research positions is that, given the role of personal interest in the selection of research topics, women are more likely to identify woman battering as a problem warranting research investigation. As the topic gained more prominence in the social science and human service fields, editors of journals became more receptive to publishing research articles on the topic. All these factors, over time, had a snowball effect. The availability of funds, the potential for publication, and the desire to contribute knowledge to an area of public concern attracted researchers seeking problems to study to the area.

So one major factor influencing the allocation of research funds is the existence of a powerful, articulate, and effective interest group that can push for research on a particular problem (Lally 1977; Varmus 1999). Other factors include the following:

- Support for research by influentials at the national policymaking levels
- Definition of a condition as a social problem by national influentials
- Public awareness of and concern about the condition
- Severity, extent, and economic costs of the condition
- Amount of publicity about the condition
- Amount of support for research on the condition in the major funding agencies

On this last point, it is important to recognize that major agencies of the government, such as the Department of Health and Human Services (DHHS) and the National Science Foundation (NSF), dispense millions of dollars for research each year. Support of congressional leaders and key personnel in these major departments is essential for problem areas to be deemed worthy of financial backing for research. Typically, funding sources publish *requests for proposals* (RFPs), which outline the organization's funding priorities and requirements. Researchers are invited to submit proposals for competitive consideration with other researchers. Proposals may be for millions of research dollars, and the competition for funding is as intense and high-pressure as any major business deal.

Given that the political process plays a major role in determining which problems are sufficiently important to warrant research attention, it is not surprising that those people who lack access to social power in our society are also those whose interests are least likely to be served by the research conducted. Children, for example, are among the least powerful groups in our society, and where their interests conflict with those of adults, children are typically the losers. Child abuse has been around for centuries, but it was not until recently that the research and practice communities began to pay attention to the needs of abused children (Gelles 1987; Radbill 1980). As another example, problem pregnancies have traditionally been viewed as a problem of women only, despite the fact that it doesn't take a researcher to surmise that males were involved somewhere. Only recently, possibly because more women are now conducting research, have researchers begun, when studying problem pregnancies, to use the couple as the unit of analysis rather than the teenage mother (Brown 1983).

One recent and particularly disturbing example of minority status influencing funding was with Acquired Immune Deficiency Syndrome, or AIDS, research. In the early years of the spread of AIDS in the United States, almost all people contracting the virus were men who had sex with other men. This has changed: Currently, only 40 percent of new HIV infections involve male-to-male sexual contact; 30 percent are due to intravenous drug use, and another 30 percent result from heterosexual contact (Centers for Disease Control and Prevention 2002). However, in the earlier years, AIDS was associated in many people's minds with two groups of people—homosexuals and IV drug users—who were seen as marginal and highly stigmatized by many Americans, especially those in positions of power. In fact, people widely defined AIDS for a number of years as a "gay disease" and thus something that most Americans need not worry about. The attitude of many was summed up by the comment of a person who was later to be a staff member at the White House: "Those poor homosexuals. They have declared war on nature, and nature is exacting an awful retribution" (quoted in Shilts 1987, p. 311). As long as

AIDS was defined as a disease of deviants, funds for research on its cause and prevention were slow in coming.

Other reasons for the delayed response to the AIDS crisis existed beyond the marginality and stigma the early victims suffered (Shilts 1987). For instance, the Reagan administration, which entered office in 1981, expressed as policy the emphasis on smaller government and austerity in social and health programs. The first AIDS victims in the United States appeared in 1980. The competition for government funds in the early 1980s was fierce, and AIDS researchers typically lost the battle, partly because those suffering from AIDS had less clout in the policy process than other groups competing for dwindling funds. Another reason the fight against AIDS was slow to start was urban politics. New York City had the largest number of AIDS cases in the early 1980s, yet New York Mayor Edward Koch refused to do anything about it for a number of years, apparently because of the belief that support for gay causes would link him with the gay rights movement and hurt his chances for reelection.

In short, society's response to the minority status of those afflicted with AIDS, along with other political factors, contributed to a significant delay in attacking the problem. It wasn't until AIDS began to threaten the supply of blood available for transfusions and fear arose that AIDS was entering the heterosexual population that considerable research support was forthcoming. Even though gays have become a fairly powerful minority group in some cities—as a group, they are well-educated and affluent—they did not have clout in the domains where decisions were made about the funding of research.

The selection of research problems is thus a highly political process. Although powerful interest groups will always play a role in this process, researchers need to avoid the perceptual blinders that often hinder the ability of the powerful to see which problems are sufficiently important or serious to warrant attention. Human service professionals can play an important role in the political issues surrounding problem selection, whether they actually conduct research or not. In the course of practice, human service providers deal directly with the poor,

with those labeled as deviant, with minorities, and with the powerless. This puts these providers in a position to serve as advocates for inclusion on the societal research agenda of problems relevant to their clientele.

We have discussed numerous sources of research topics for practitioner–researchers. Although we have discussed them separately, more than one of these factors at the same time often influences choice of a research topic. Finding a research topic, however, is only the first step in problem formulation. The next step is to shape it into a problem that empirical research can solve.

Shaping and Refining the Problem

As we mentioned, a frustrating trap in which novice researchers often become ensnarled is choosing a topic that is so broad and encompassing that, by itself, it offers little guidance in terms of how to proceed. Finding the "causes of juvenile delinquency" or the "weaknesses of the modern family" sounds intriguing, but these topics provide little direction concerning specifically where to begin to look. The next step in the research process, then, is to begin translating a general topical interest into a precise, researchable problem by narrowing the scope of the problem to manageable proportions. A single investigation is unlikely to uncover "the causes of juvenile delinquency," but it might provide some insight into the influence of particular variables on the emergence of particular delinquencies. Refining, narrowing, and focusing a research problem do not occur at once but rather form a continuous process involving a number of procedures.

Conceptual Development

In Chapter 2, we discussed the role of theories and hypotheses in the research process, pointing out that concepts are one of the central components of theories. In the refining of a research problem, one of the key steps is *conceptual development:* identifying and properly defining the concepts that the study will focus on. In exploratory studies, of course, we are entering areas where there is little conceptual development, and a major purpose of the research itself may be to identify and define concepts. In cases where theory and research already exist to rely on, however, some conceptual development occurs as a part of formulating a research problem. One part of this process, already discussed in Chapter 2, is to clearly define the meaning of concepts. Another part of the process is to narrow the focus of the concept so that it encompasses a topic that is feasible to research in a single study. For example, practitioners in a youth home who had an interest in juvenile delinquency might ask themselves, "Are we interested in all forms of delinquent behavior or only in some types?" In reality, the concept of delinquency is an extremely broad category that includes all actions by juveniles that violate criminal or juvenile codes. We have no reason to assume that a single cause can explain all types of delinquency. The focus of the research, therefore, might narrow to include only certain behaviors, such as violence or truancy. The goal of this specification process, then, is to make clear exactly the focus of the research effort.

Once key concepts are clearly defined, the next consideration is their measurability. Only concepts that are in some way measurable can be used in the research process. Eventually, of course, concepts will have to be operationalized, as discussed in Chapter 2, so any that are not readily measurable will have to be dropped. Measuring concepts can sometimes be difficult, as we note in more detail in Chapter 5. In fact, theories at times include concepts that are difficult to operationalize. Theorists are sometimes criticized for this practice, although the criticism is misdirected. Theorists, of necessity, must be free to create and utilize whatever concepts are deemed necessary, without regard to their immediate measurability. To do otherwise would limit theoretical development to those concepts we currently have the skill to measure (Denzin 1989; Shearing 1973). Theorists' use of concepts that are not immediately measurable allows for theoretical advances, but it also presents researchers with the task of creating ways to measure the concepts. However, if concepts in a proposed study cannot be measured, then some

modification in the project—and possibly in the theory—is necessary. This process of refining and developing concepts as a part of the research process illustrates a point made in Chapter 2 regarding the interplay between theory and research: Theories provide concepts and hypotheses for research, whereas research modifies theories through conceptual development.

Review of the Literature

With concepts clarified and deemed measurable, we are ready to conduct a review of previous research that relates to our research problem. This "review of the literature" is a necessary and important part of the research process (Locke, Silverman, and Spirduso 1998). We do it to familiarize ourselves with the current state of knowledge regarding the research problem and to learn how others have delineated similar problems. Unless we are planning a replication, it is unlikely that we will formulate our problem precisely like any one of these previous studies. Rather, we are likely to pick up ideas from several that we can integrate to improve our own. Through reviewing the relevant literature, we can further narrow the focus of the research project and ensure that we do not unnecessarily duplicate what others have already done. Researchers will undoubtedly find that pitfalls can be avoided by learning from others' experiences. For example, one or more specific approaches to a topic have proven unproductive. That is, several studies have failed to find significant results or strong relationships. Unless there is good reason to believe these earlier studies contained methodological weaknesses, the same approach is likely to lead to failure once again. Research is likely to be more productive if it focuses on studies that have achieved some positive results.

A thorough literature review calls for familiarity with basic library utilization skills, including how to locate books, professional journals, and public documents. To help with this important aspect of doing research, we have included Appendix A in this book on the use of a library. This appendix shows how to find the books, journals, government documents, and other sources for finding reports of research.

Even those with some experience using a library will likely find some helpful new information in this appendix.

In a literature review, we conduct a systematic search of each research report for certain kinds of information. First, the reviewer pays attention to *theoretical and conceptual issues:* What concepts and theories are used, how well developed are they, and have they been subject to empirical test before? If the theories and concepts are well developed, they can serve as an important guide in designing the planned research and explaining the relationships between variables. If they are not well developed, one will have to rely more on personal insight and creativity. In this case, researchers sometimes consider doing exploratory research, which may involve loosely structured interviews and less quantitative measuring devices, as a way of advancing conceptual and theoretical development.

The *research hypotheses,* including identification of the *independent and dependent variables,* is a second component of a literature review. Are the hypotheses clearly stated and testable? Are they related to the variables and hypotheses being considered in the planned study? Existing research can provide some fairly specific direction in terms of already tested relationships between independent and dependent variables.

The *measurement* and the *operational definitions* used in previous research are a third focus of a literature review. As noted, successful operationalization of concepts is often difficult. Previous work in this area is invaluable in finding workable measures for concepts. Past measures may require modification to meet current needs, of course, but making these modifications is probably easier than developing completely new measures, which is a difficult and time-consuming process.

A literature review also informs us about a fourth important element of research—the most appropriate *research technique* for a particular research problem. Successful approaches by others should be noted and unsuccessful approaches avoided. It is of the utmost importance that the problem determine the research technique used, and not the other way around. A variety of data-gathering techniques ex-

ists because no single method is always best. As we note in subsequent chapters, each technique has strengths and weaknesses, and each is suitable for answering some questions but not others.

The *sampling strategy* is a fifth element of a literature review. Previous research can be useful in determining the sampling strategy to use and in avoiding sampling problems others have encountered. For example, suppose that the study we propose calls for the use of mailed questionnaires. An ever-present problem with mailed questionnaires is making sure that a sufficient number of people complete and return them. It would be useful for us to know what other investigators have experienced with people like those we plan to survey. Not all groups respond to mailed questionnaires with the same degree of enthusiasm. If the group we are proposing to sample has exhibited notoriously low return rates in the previous studies, we have to plan accordingly. We would probably increase the number of questionnaires mailed and would certainly use all available means of obtaining the highest response rate possible. Or, if we anticipate very low return rates, we may want to search for another group to study or even consider whether this particular project is feasible at all.

Statistical technique is a sixth element of a literature review. In Chapters 5, 14, and 15, we discuss issues relating to appropriate use of statistics. In a literature review, we must be aware of whether the appropriate procedures were used, if any inappropriate ones were used, and what constraints the concepts, variables, and hypotheses placed on the kind of statistics that would be appropriate.

Finally, a literature review notes the *findings and conclusions* of the study. Which hypotheses were confirmed, and what guidelines for future research were presented? One aspect of the findings to watch for is the *effect size,* which refers to how big an effect an independent variable has on a dependent variable. Although we discuss this concept more in Chapter 15, we need to assess whether a dependent variable is affected in only a small but measurable way or whether the impact is dramatic (Gibbs 1991).

A thorough literature review involves evaluating and comparing many research reports, identifying

Table 4.1 A Summary Table of a Literature Review of Research on Interventions with Abusive and Neglectful Parents

Author/Model	Design/Sample	Measures	Results	Limitations
Acran & Doring (1992) 13-week, 90 minute session cognitive-behavioral group treatment focused on: 1. anger management training to reduce physiological arousal; 2. training in communication and problem-solving; 3. training in empathic understanding	Pretest/posttest N = 29 (out of 47 who started program) referred from child protective services because of physical abuse or by child abuse program within a pediatric medical center (Canada) 69% married or common-law; 55% unemployed; 69% females	Parenting Stress Index; State-Trait Anger Scale; Index of Parenting Attitudes; Child Abuse Potential Inventory; Eyberg Child Behavior Inventory	Statistical and clinical significant positive improvements on Child Abuse Potential Inventory, Parenting Stress Index, and Index of Parenting Attitudes; State-Trait Anger Scale showed statistically but not clinically significant positive improvements; although parents reported their children's behavior as just as disruptive, they were less distressed by it	No comparison/control group; no behavioral measures of changes; no follow-up
Koiko (1996) Cognitive-behavioral treatment or family therapy 12 one-hour weekly clinic sessions; home visits after every 1–2 clinic visits; average length of treatment = 19.1 weeks for cognitive-behavioral, 19.2 weeks for family therapy	Quasi-experimental random assignment based on stratification in terms of child age (6–9 vs. 10–13), gender, and family constellation to cognitive-behavioral treatment (parent and child separately) or family therapy, pretest, posttest	Likert scales on severity of child/family problems, severity of anger arousal displayed by parents toward children and use of physical discipline administered weekly to both child and parent Conflict Tactics Scales; Family Environment Scale; Child Abuse Potential Inventory	Parents in cognitive-behavioral treatment improved over family therapy group in overall levels of anger and use of physical discipline; parents of children diagnosed with a psychiatric disorder and longer duration of problems more likely to report heightened anger and use of physical force	Standardized measures were not administered pretest and post-test—they were just used as criterion validity measures; self-report bias; family therapy orientation not specifically named; small sample size.

Source Adapted from Jacqueline Corcoran, *Evidence-Based Social Work Practice With Families: A Lifespan Approach.* pp. 9–16. copyright © 2000 by Springer Publishing Co., Inc., New York, 10012. Used by permission of Springer Publishing Co.

where they used similar procedures and reached similar outcomes, and where there were discrepancies between studies. This can be a complicated process, especially when hundreds of studies may be involved.

It is sometimes helpful to produce a summary table such as Table 4.1 to make comparisons. This table summarizes research studies on the effectiveness of various interventions with abusive and neglectful

Table 4.2 Possible Units of Analysis in Research on Juvenile Delinquency

Unit of Analysis	Example	Appropriate Variables	Research Problem
Individuals	Adolescents arrested for larceny	Age, sex, prior arrests	Do males receive different penalties from females for similar offenses?
Groups	Delinquent gangs	Size, norms on drug usage	Are gangs involved in drug trafficking more violent than other gangs?
Organizations	Adolescent treatment agencies	Size, auspices, funding level	Do private agencies serve fewer minority and lower-class delinquents than public agencies?
Programs	Delinquency prevention programs	Theoretical model, type of host setting	What services are most frequently included in prevention programs?
Social artifacts	Transcripts of adjudication hearings	Number of references to victim injury	To what extent does the level of violence in the offense affect the kind of penalty imposed?

parents. Notice that the table cites each separate study in the left-hand column, along with a brief description of the intervention model used in the study. The next two columns give information about the research design, sampling procedures, and measurement devices. Then a column contains a summary of the results of each study. The final column on the right addresses any limitations found in the research. A systematic literature review of this sort provides the most useful information from previous studies. One can see at a glance how many studies came to similar conclusions and how commonly certain measuring devices were used. The ability to compile and summarize succinctly the features of studies in this fashion is essential to formulating a research problem and refining it into a research question that can be empirically investigated.

Units of Analysis

An important element in the process of shaping and refining a research problem is the decision regarding the unit of analysis to be investigated. **Units of analysis** are the specific objects or elements whose characteristics we wish to describe or explain and about which we will collect data. Although there are many units of analysis, five commonly used in human service research are individuals, groups, organizations, programs, and social artifacts (see Table 4.2). Different units of analysis are used in studying documents; these are discussed in Chapter 8.

Much social research focuses on the *individual* as the unit of analysis. The typical survey, for example, obtains information from individuals about their attitudes or behavior. Any time we define a population of inquiry with reference to some personal status, we are operating at the individual level of analysis. For example, unwed mothers, welfare recipients, mental patients, retarded children, and similar categories all identify individuals with reference to a status they occupy.

If we identify our unit of analysis as individuals, it is important to recognize that the entire analysis will remain at that level. For the sake of describing large numbers of individuals, it is necessary to utilize summarizing statistics, such as averages. For example, we might, as a part of a study of unwed mothers, note that their average age when giving birth was 16.8 years. Aggregating data in this fashion in no way changes the unit of analysis. We are still collecting our data about individuals.

Social scientists sometimes focus on social *groups* as their unit of analysis and collect data on some group characteristic or behavior. Some groups consist of individuals who share some social relationship with the other group members. For example, in families, peer groups, occupational groups, or juvenile gangs, the members have some sense of membership or belonging to the group. If we study families in terms of whether they are intact or not, we are investigating the characteristics of a group—the family—not of individuals. Other groups of interest to social scientists are merely aggregates of individuals with no necessary sense of membership, such as census tracts, cities, states, or members of a particular social class. For example, we might study the relationship between poverty and delinquency by comparing rates of delinquency in census tracts with low income and those with high income. In this case, we have collected data regarding the characteristics of census tracts rather than individuals.

Social scientists also deal with *organizations* as the unit of analysis. Formal organizations are deliberately constructed groups organized for the achievement of some specific goals. Examples of formal organizations include corporations, schools, prisons, unions, government bureaus, and human service agencies. For example, our experience may lead us to suspect that organizations providing substance-abuse services can more effectively serve their clients if they have an open and democratic communication structure rather than a closed and rigidly stratified one. If we compare the success rates of organizations with different communication structures, our study would use organizations, not individuals or groups, as the unit of analysis. Although individuals may experience success at overcoming substance abuse, only organizations can have a *success rate.*

Research in the human services can also focus on *programs* as the basic unit of analysis. The program may provide services for individuals, and it may exist as part of an organization, but it is still a separate unit of analysis about which data can be collected. Like organizations, programs can have success rates or be assessed in terms of overall costs. For example, one research project investigated 25 programs that provided services for pregnant and parenting teenagers (Fernandez and Ruch-Ross 1998). The research assessed each program according to its overall success rate: A successful program was one in which the clients were more likely to stay in school or stay employed and less likely to get pregnant than were clients in the other programs. Note that a program can have a success rate (in other words, a certain proportion of their clients succeeding) but an individual can only succeed or fail (rather than showing a rate of success). The researchers compared the programs to determine the characteristics of successful and unsuccessful programs. Programs might cut across a number of different organizations, such as social service agencies, in which case the unit under observation is the effectiveness of the combination of services provided by these organizations.

Finally, the unit of analysis may be *social artifacts,* which are simply any material products people produce. Examples are virtually endless: newspapers, buildings, movies, books, magazines, automobiles, songs, graffiti, and so on. Of all the units of analysis, social artifacts are the least frequent focus of human service research, but as reflections of people and the society that produces them, analysis of social artifacts is useful. Books and magazines, for example, can be used as artifacts in the assessment of sex-role stereotyping. Children's books have been attacked for allegedly reinforcing traditional gender roles through their presentations of men and women (Peterson and Lach 1990; Purcell and Stewart 1990). Any kind of legal or administrative statute also is an artifact worthy of study. One effort, for instance, used state juvenile codes as the independent variable in a study of whether legal statutes made a difference in how courts handled juvenile cases (Grichting 1979).

Clearly specifying the unit of analysis in research is important in avoiding a serious problem: an illegitimate shift in the analysis from one unit to another. Careless jumping from one level to another can result in drawing erroneous conclusions. One way this can happen is called the **ecological fallacy,** inferring something about individuals based on data collected at higher units of analysis, such as groups. A mismatch occurs between the unit of analysis about which data are collected and about which conclusions are drawn. Suppose, for example, a study found that census tracts with high rates of teenage drug abuse also had a large percentage of single-parent families. We might be tempted to conclude that single-parent families are a factor promoting teenage drug abuse. Such a conclusion, however, represents an illegitimate shift in the unit of analysis. The data have been collected about census tracts, which are at the group level. The conclusion drawn, however, is at the individual level, namely, that teenage drug abusers live in single-parent families. But the data do not show this. The data only show the association of two rates—substance abuse and single parenthood—in census tracts. (Perhaps two-parent families are a minority in a census tract, but a high proportion of children in these families abuse drugs.) It is, of course, possible that relationships found at the group level will hold at the individual level, but they may not. In our hypothetical study, some other characteristic of census tracts may lead to both high rates of drug abuse *and* single-parent families. The error comes in the automatic assumption that correlations at the group level necessarily reflect relationships at the individual level.

Fallacious reasoning can occur in the opposite direction and is called the **reductionist fallacy,** inferring something about groups, or other higher levels of analysis, based on data collected from individuals. Suppose we collected data from individual teenagers about their drug use and family environments and found an association, namely, that teens from single-parent families are more likely to abuse drugs. Could we then conclude that communities with high rates of single-parent families would have high rates of teen drug abuse? The answer once again is that we could not draw that conclusion about the group level (communities) with any certainty because the data we have is about social process at the individual level (what happens in the lives of individual teens). It well may be that the social process that produces high rates of drug abuse in communities is different from the social process that leads individuals to use drugs. When data is collected at one

level of analysis, it is always an empirical question as to whether conclusions can be drawn from that data about other levels of analysis. A clear awareness of the unit of analysis can help ensure that we do not make such illegitimate shifts.

A final point needs to be made about the unit of analysis in contrast to the source of data. The unit of analysis refers to the element *about which* data are collected and inferences made, but it is not necessarily the source *from which* data are collected. A common example is the U.S. Census, which reports data on *households.* We speak of household size and income, but households don't fill out questionnaires; people do. In this case, individuals, such as the heads of households, are the *source* of the data, but the household is the unit of analysis *about which* data are collected. When the unit of analysis is something other than the individual, attention must be paid to the source of the data because this might introduce bias into the data analysis. For example, when the household is the unit of analysis, we often collect data from one member of the household. In single-parent families, headed primarily by women, we would be gathering data mostly from women. In two-parent families we would be obtaining data from both men and women because either could be the head of the household, and in some cases men might be the majority of those we collect data from. If men tend to give answers to some questions that are different from those women give, there could be a sex bias in the results even though our unit of analysis was not linked to sex. A difference that we attribute to single-parent as compared to two-parent families may be due to the fact that the former involves mostly women answering questions, whereas the latter involves mostly men.

Reactivity

The issue of reactivity is another consideration in refining a research problem. The term **reactivity** refers to the fact that people can react to being studied and may behave differently than when they don't think they are being studied. In other words, the data we collected from people who know they are the objects of study might be different from data we collected from the same people if they did not know. So a reactive research technique changes the very thing that is being studied. Suppose, for example, that you are a parent. A researcher enters your home and sets up videotaping equipment to observe your interactions with your children. Would you behave in the same way that you would if the observer were not present? You might, but most people would feel strong pressures to be "on their toes" and present themselves as good parents. You might be more forgiving of your child, for instance, or give fewer negative sanctions.

Reactivity in research can take many forms, and it is a problem for virtually all sciences. However, it is especially acute in social research because human beings are self-conscious and aware of what is happening to them. Refining a research problem and choosing a research design are done with an eye toward reducing as much as possible the extensiveness of reactivity. We consider this in assessing the various research strategies in later chapters.

Qualitative versus Quantitative Research

Another aspect of refining a research problem is to decide whether to use one of two broad strategies toward research: qualitative or quantitative. **Qualitative research** involves data in the form of words, pictures, descriptions, or narratives. **Quantitative research** uses numbers, counts, and measures of things (Berg 2004; Wakefield 1995). In general, two factors come into play in deciding whether to conduct qualitative or quantitative research: the state of our knowledge on a particular research topic and the individual researcher's position regarding the nature of human social behavior. Regarding the first factor, when knowledge is sketchy or when there is little theoretical understanding of a phenomenon, it may be impossible to develop precise hypotheses or operational definitions. In such cases, researchers often turn to qualitative research because it can be more exploratory in nature. The research can be descriptive, possibly resulting in the formulation of hypotheses rather than the verification of them. When enough previous research exists on a topic, it may be

more feasible to state precisely concepts, variables, and hypotheses. It also may be possible to develop quantifiable operational definitions of what the researcher is interested in, which then allows research to take on a more quantitative nature.

The second consideration in choosing between quantitative and qualitative research stems from a more fundamental controversy over the nature of human social behavior. We saw in Chapter 2 that the choice between qualitative and quantitative research is related to whether one follows positivist or nonpositivist paradigms toward science. This complicated issue (we discuss it in more detail in Chapters 1 and 9) basically involves debate over whether we can meaningfully reduce the human experience to numbers and measures. Some social scientists argue that the human experience has a subjective dimension—the personal meanings and feelings that people have about themselves and what they do. These meanings or feelings cannot be captured very well through numbers or measures. Narrative descriptions of people going about their daily routines or through lengthy and broad-ranging interviews with them better express those meanings and feelings. Such techniques are better able to capture the critical subjective meanings that are an essential element of understanding human behavior. Quantitative research, on the other hand, provides us with much more precise statements about human behavior.

The line between qualitative and quantitative approaches is not always completely clear, and the choice between the two can be difficult. Many research projects incorporate both approaches in order to gain the most benefit. Research in Practice 4.2 presents some additional elaboration on this issue.

Cross-Sectional versus Longitudinal Research

In addition to deciding on the unit of analysis to investigate, refining a research problem also requires a decision about the time dimension. The basic issue is whether the researcher wants a single snapshot in time of some phenomenon or an ongoing series of photographs over time. The former is called **cross-sectional research,** and it focuses on a cross section

RESEARCH IN PRACTICE 4.2

BEHAVIOR AND SOCIAL ENVIRONMENTS:

Feminist Research Methods: Do Males and Females Have Different "Voices"?

Positivism assumes that "one size fits all"—that there is one way to know the world, and the diversity of people in the world is irrelevant to how we gain knowledge. One of the areas in which the debates over the scientific paradigms discussed in Chapter 2 have probably been most intense is feminist research. Feminist researchers have argued that one size does *not* fit all—the diversity in the world also produces diverse ways of gaining knowledge of the world. This has led some feminist researchers to explore the non-positivist paradigms for a more complete and complex methodology for understanding human behavior (Olsen 1994; Reinharz 1992; Schiebinger 1999). One profound question feminists have raised is whether ways of knowing are gendered: Are males and females socialized to perceive the world and acquire knowledge in fundamentally different ways? Furthermore, is positivism merely one of the ways of knowing rather than the only way of knowing?

The basic argument is that, because of differences between the genders—due either to biology or to socialization—there is a male model of knowledge development and a female one and that the two are, to an extent, alien to each other (DeVault 1999; Nielson 1989). In developing some of these ideas, Carol Gilligan (1982) used the term "voice" to mean modes of thinking about the world and tried to describe the differences between male and female "voices." Women emphasize the importance of relationships and the danger of being separated from others. Women see connectedness between people and feel obliged to protect and

nurture those to whom they feel connected. This leads to a concern about the needs of others, but the needs of self and others exist primarily in the context of relationships with other people. So women's voices focus on the individual embedded in a social network. This emphasis on connectedness and relationships means that problems and people are inextricably intertwined. Neither problems nor the people they affect can be fully understood if they are separated from one another.

By contrast, men's voices speak of separation and autonomy. They emphasize independence and, to an extent, alienation, at least in the sense that people can be abstracted from their relationships, from their context, and even from their own uniqueness. For men, the separate individual has some meaning and importance and possibly even more value than a person encumbered by relationships and connections. This view treats these abstracted individuals the same, ignoring the unique needs or contexts of each person. To this extent, men's voices are abstract and formal. People and their problems can be separated.

Proponents of the male-female distinction argue that these male and female voices are fundamentally contrasting ways of perceiving and developing knowledge about the world. The distinction suggests a paradigm different from the positivist one, with some affinities to a variety of nonpositivist paradigms. The male voice tends to be logical and objective and to avoid or downplay feelings, while focusing on accomplishing practical goals. It

of a population at one point in time. Many surveys, for example, are cross-sectional in nature.

Although researchers collect all the data in cross-sectional research at one time, we can use such studies to investigate the development of some phenomenon over time. For example, to study the developmental problems of children of alcoholic parents, one could select groups of children of varying ages, say, one group at age 5, another at 10, and

a third group at age 15. By observing differences in developmental problems among these groups, we may infer that a single youngster would experience changes as he or she grew up similar to the differences observed among these three groups. Yet one of the major weaknesses of such cross-sectional studies is that we have not actually observed the changes an individual goes through; rather, we have observed three different groups of individuals at one point in tends to view the world in terms of separation: The researcher extracts data from the "subject" or "respondent" and avoids any personal relationship (or connectedness) between them in the interests of objectivity. All contact except that necessary to collect data is avoided. The researcher prefers a more quantitative approach, with standardized measuring instruments and procedures, on the assumption that treating all people alike will produce the most valid and objective data. A number of procedures commonly used in positivist research can be seen as efforts to strip away the context from the individual: placing them in laboratory settings, using random assignment to conditions, using aggregate responses from large-scale surveys, and isolating variables for study. All these procedures assume that the context in which a person lives is merely interfering "noise" and that more meaningful information can be obtained without it. Through quantification, the male voice minimizes the uniqueness and subjectivity of experiences by providing summary responses of the aggregate; so the fact that Jane Doe got pregnant at age 13 under a certain set of unique and meaningful circumstances gets lost when we conclude that the average teenage pregnancy in a high school occurs at age 14.7 years.

The female voice, on the other hand, stresses feeling, empathy, and the subjective side of life and places emphasis on connectedness: Researcher and respondent are tied together in a relationship that influences the data produced. Objectivity, in the positivist sense, is impossible because the meaning and importance of data relate to specific individuals and their relationships with one another. The researcher and subject are partners in the relationship of producing research. Subjects are collaborators. The feminist researcher also disdains the notion of the objec-

tive, impartial researcher in favor of involvement with the topics of their research. In the feminist view of gaining truth, researcher and subject work together, although in different ways, to develop understanding; truth-seeking is a mutual, cooperative effort on their part. Research questions emphasize connectedness: keeping people in their social contexts and studying the complexity of the whole. In short, qualitative approaches are preferred. People can be studied in their homes or where they work and play. Some research methods (such as the field methods we will discuss in Chapter 9) are better suited to emphasizing this connectedness. Feminist research also emphasizes in-depth interviews, where people have an opportunity to express the fullness and complexity of their lives in their own words.

Obviously, it is possible for men to speak with a "female" voice and for women to speak with a "male" voice. The point is that these are fundamentally different ways of knowing the world. Feminist researchers do not reject positivism; they recognize that it is different but not superior. In fact, some critics argue that researchers in the social sciences, whether male or female, have generally been trained in graduate schools with a male voice because that is what has dominated over the years among graduate faculty. Yet neither voice is inherently superior, and neither is complete or totally objective. Each is a valid way of gaining knowledge about the world. Each involves a perspective that has some limitations. The basic insight of feminist researchers is that all people, including researchers, are fundamentally gendered beings, and this shapes—whether we admit it or not— how we perceive and think about the world, how we do research, and the research results that are produced.

time. Differences among these groups may reflect something other than the developmental changes that individuals experience. Because of this disadvantage, researchers sometimes resort to the other way of handling the time issue: longitudinal studies.

Longitudinal research involves gathering data over an extended period, which might span months, years, or, in a few cases, decades. One type of longi-

tudinal approach is the **panel study,** in which the same people are studied at different times. This allows us to observe the actual changes these individuals go through over time. For example, a study of the social, psychological, and familial characteristics that influence whether drug addicts can successfully remain free of drugs followed the same 354 narcotics addicts for more than 24 years, collecting data on their family experiences, employment records, and a host of other factors (Bailey et al. 1994). Another longitudinal approach is the **trend study,** in which different people are observed at different times. Public opinion polling and research on political attitudes are often trend studies.

Both the nature of the research problem and practical considerations typically determine the decision about whether to use a longitudinal or cross-sectional approach. Longitudinal studies, especially panel studies, have the advantage of providing the most accurate information regarding changes over time. A research question regarding such changes, then, would probably benefit from this approach. A disadvantage of panel studies is that they can be reactive: People's responses or behavior at one time may be influenced by the fact that they have been observed earlier. For example, a person who stated opposition to abortion in one survey may be inclined to respond the same way six months later so as not to appear inconsistent or vacillating, even if those attitudes had changed in the interim. Another disadvantage of panel studies is that people who participated early in a panel study may not want to or may be unable to participate later. People die, move away, become uninterested, or in other ways become unavailable as panel studies progress. This loss of participants can adversely affect the validity of the research findings. The disadvantages of all longitudinal studies are that they can be difficult and expensive to conduct, especially if they span a very long period of time.

Cross-sectional research is cheaper and faster to conduct, and one need not worry about the loss of participants. However, cross-sectional research may not provide the most useful data for some research questions. Thus, the decision on the issue of time dimension should be based on considerations of both the nature of the research problem and practical issues. There are times, of course, when practical feasibility plays a large part in the decision.

Feasibility of a Research Project

By the time researchers have selected, shaped, and refined a research problem, the problem should be suffi-

ciently clear that a consideration of practical issues involving the feasibility of the project is in order. Practical considerations of what the research can reasonably accomplish given the time and resources available can force researchers—sometimes painfully—to reduce the scale of a project. A careful and honest appraisal of the time and money required to accomplish a project is useful in determining the feasibility of the project as envisioned and can reveal if a change in goals is called for. In making a feasibility assessment, one should keep in mind a couple of axioms that apply to research projects: "Anything that can go wrong will" (Murphy's law), and "Everything will take longer than possibly imagined."

The practical aspects of a project's feasibility center primarily on two related concerns: time and money (Kelly and McGrath 1988).

Time Constraints

In developing a research project, one of the major considerations is whether there will be sufficient time to complete adequately what you hope to do. In later chapters, as we consider specific research techniques, we will see how different techniques vary in terms of how much time they take. Here, we want to mention some of the major factors related to time considerations. One factor concerns the population that is the focus of the research. If that population has characteristics that are fairly widespread, then a sufficient number of people will be readily available from which to collect data. For instance, if we were studying the differing attitudes of men and women toward work-release programs for prison inmates, we could select a sample of men and women from whatever city or state we happened to be in. If, however, our study focuses on people with special characteristics that are somewhat rare, problems may arise. In general, the smaller the number of people who have the characteristics needed for inclusion in a study, the more difficult and time-consuming it will be to contact a sufficiently large number necessary to make scientifically valid conclusions. For example, a study of incestuous fathers, even in a large city, may encounter problems obtaining enough cases because relatively few such people will be openly known.

A second problem relating to time constraints involves the proper development of measuring devices. Researchers should test all techniques used for gathering data before the actual study is conducted, and this can be very time-consuming in itself. A pretest, as we saw in Chapter 1, refers to the preliminary application of the data-gathering techniques for purposes of assessing their adequacy. A pilot study is a small-scale "trial run" of all the procedures planned for use in the main study. In some studies, we may need to conduct several pretests as we modify data-collection devices based on the results of previous pretests. All in all, refining of data-gathering procedures can consume a lot of time. A third major factor related to time considerations is the amount of time required for actual data collection, which can range from a few hours for a questionnaire administered to a group of "captive" students to the years that are necessary in many longitudinal studies. Because the amount of time required for data collection is so variable, time requires close scrutiny when addressing the question of the feasibility of a particular research design.

A fourth consideration related to the time issue is the amount of time necessary to complete the analysis of the data. In general, the less structured the data, the more time will be required for analysis. The field notes that serve as the data for some observational studies, for example, can be very time-consuming to analyze (see Chapter 9). Likewise, videotapes collected during an experiment or during single-subject research may take many viewings before they are adequately understood (see Chapters 10 and 11). However, highly structured data in quantified form can also be time-consuming to analyze, as we will see in Chapters 14 and 15. Although computers can manipulate the data rapidly, it takes considerable time to prepare the data for entry into the computer, and the amount of time needed increases as the number of cases increases. So, as with the time required for data collection, the time needed for analysis requires careful consideration owing to wide variation in the amount that may be necessary.

The fifth area in which time becomes a factor is writing the report itself. The amount of time this consumes depends on the length and complexity of the report and the skills of the investigator. Each researcher is in the best position, based on past writing experiences, to assess the amount of time he or she requires. As a final reminder, it will likely take longer than you expect.

Financial Considerations

The financial expenditures associated with a research project are another constraint on feasibility. Good research is not always expensive. In many instances, students and human service practitioners are able to get by with only modest costs because data are easy to obtain, analysis procedures are simple, and the labor is voluntary or provided at no additional charge. But even small projects are likely to require money for long-distance telephone calls, typing and duplicating questionnaires, and other services that can quickly stress the tight resources of a small human service agency. At the other extreme, it is not unusual for the price tag of major research and demonstration projects in the human services to run into six figures or more. For example, between 1997 and 2003, the National Institute of Justice (2003) provided annual grants of about $1 million for the development and evaluation of educational programs to assist teenagers in developing skills to avoid drug use or other forms of delinquency and to avoid becoming crime victims. Table 4.3 shows the budget for a survey research project of a modest scale and indicates some of the general expenditure categories to consider in assessing the feasibility of any project.

The salaries of those who conduct the study are potentially the most expensive item, especially for studies that require large interviewer staffs. Such expenses include not only the interviewers' wages but transportation costs and living expenses, which can be sizable. Interviewers may require hours of training before they can begin to collect data. If respondents are not available, callbacks may be necessary, which further increases the cost of each interview. To get the work done in a timely fashion and to ensure reliability, investigators may need to hire people or contract with an organization to code the raw data into an analyzable format.

Table 4.3 A Budget for a Study Involving Face-to-Face Interviews of 520 People

	Total Cost (Dollars)	Percent of Total*
Prepare for survey		
Purchase map for area frame	200	1.0
Print interviewer manuals	29	<1.0
Print questionnaires (690)	379	1.9
Train interviewers (20-hour training session)	1,134	5.7
Miscellaneous	25	<1.0
Conduct the survey		
Locate residences: contact respondents; conduct interviews; field edit questionnaires; 3.5 completed interviews per 8-hour day	9,655	48.8
Travel cost ($8.50 per completed interview; interviewers use own car)	4,420	22.3
Office edit and general clerical		
(6 completed questionnaires per hour)	728	3.8
Total, excluding professional time	16,570	
Professional time (160 hrs @ $35,000 annual salary plus 20% fringe benefits)	3,231	16.3
Total, including professional time	19,801	100.0

*Totals more than 100% because of rounding.
Source Adapted from *How to Conduct Your Own Survey* by Priscilla Salant and Don A. Dillman, pp. 46–49. Copyright © 1994 by John Wiley & Sons, Inc. Used by permission of John Wiley & Sons, Inc.

Computer expenses can also be formidable. A few decades ago, data analysis comprised the bulk of computer costs, but now personal computers are also used for questionnaire design, project management, data collection, literature searches, and report preparation. A significant cost here is for the software packages that actually perform the procedures, in addition to the cost of the computer itself and peripherals like printers, scanners, zip drives, and so on.

Another major cost consideration is expenditures for office supplies and equipment. Under this category are such items as paper, envelopes, postage, tape, printing, and the like. Paper products might seem inexpensive at first glance, but given the large samples used for some surveys, the cost can be substantial. For example, suppose we conducted a survey of approximately 500 people. Each person receives a large envelope containing a letter of introduction, a professionally printed four-page questionnaire, and a postage-paid return envelope. In addition, all members of the sample receive a reminder letter urging them to respond, and about 250 nonrespondents receive a second questionnaire. Cost for printing, envelopes, and postage could easily exceed $1,200. Different kinds of studies present different cost issues. For example, studies based on direct observation of behavior may necessitate high-cost equipment items, such as video cameras, recorders, and videotape. Unless these are already available, the project will require substantial outlays.

Providing incentives to ensure cooperation of people in the study may also be a cost factor. This may range from giving stickers or balloons to schoolchildren for completing a questionnaire to paying respondents in recognition of the large time commitment required for a longitudinal study. A study evaluating the effectiveness of advocacy services to women leaving their abusive partners illustrates participant incentive costs. Women were interviewed before the program and at 5, 10, and 20 weeks following the program. Not only was it difficult to maintain contact with this highly mobile population, but completing a survey form was a low priority for them, given the stress and disruption in their lives. To encourage the women to participate, the 46 participants were paid $10, $20, $30, and $40, respectively, for the four interviews, a total cost of $4,600 (Sullivan 1991). Payment of subjects is more of an issue in experiments that require more time investment and greater commitment from participants than is usually required in most surveys or observational studies.

Dissemination of research findings also generates costs. Besides the additional printing and office supplies for preparing reports, this expense category may include travel to professional meetings to present papers. Program evaluation studies may also entail hosting workshops or conferences with sponsors and other interested parties to ensure that the findings are incorporated into the policy and intervention planning process.

Finally, some costs associated with a research project are difficult to specify. When research is conducted under the auspices of a university, a human service agency, or a research center, some organizational resources will partially or indirectly support the research. For example, money will be spent to heat and light the building where the research project is housed, but this cost is difficult to assess precisely. A major factor in awarding a research project to a particular organization may be the fact that the organization has an extensive research library, sophisticated computer facilities, or an extensive research laboratory. The organization maintains these facilities for general use, not just for a particular research project, so it is difficult to ascertain how much of the overall cost of supporting the facilities should be assigned to a given project. Consequently, the concept of "indirect cost," typically a percentage of the total grant request, is employed to cover these real but hard to specify costs. Each organization negotiates its rate with the granting agency on the basis of the facilities and equipment the organization has for research. The amount charged to indirect costs varies from 15 percent to well in excess of 100 percent of the basic grant.

Anticipating and Avoiding Problems

Problems related to time and financial considerations arise during virtually all research projects, but their impact on the outcome of the research can be minimized if they are anticipated as much as possible, especially during the planning stage, when the details of the project are easier to change. A number of steps can be taken to anticipate problems. First, learn as much as possible from the experiences of others through the studies consulted during the literature review. We mentioned earlier that finding problems other researchers encountered is one purpose of the literature review. Solicit personal advice from expe-

rienced researchers who might be available for consultation. A knowledgeable researcher may be able to identify potential trouble spots in the plans and suggest modifications to avoid them.

Second, obtain whatever permissions or consents may be needed early in the planning stages of the project. Depending on the people the researcher wishes to study, it may be necessary to obtain permission from them to collect data. For example, some studies are aimed at school-age children and seek to gather data while the children are in school. To protect students from undue harassment and themselves from parental complaints, school administrators are frequently cool to allowing researchers into their schools. It may take considerable time to persuade whatever authorities are involved to grant the permissions needed—if they are granted at all. It is certainly wise to obtain any needed permissions before expending effort on other phases of the project, which might be wasted if permissions cannot be obtained.

The final—and perhaps most important—suggestion for avoiding problems is to conduct a pilot study. As noted, a pilot study is a preliminary run-through on a small scale of all the procedures planned for the main study. For surveys, contact and interview a small part of the sample, say, 20 people. Then analyze the data as for the complete project. In experiments, the researcher should run a few groups through all procedures, looking for any unexpected reactions from participants. Observational researchers should visit the observation sites and make observations as planned for the larger study. The focus is again on problems that might force modifications in research plans. Deal with any problems that surface during the pilot study before the main project is launched.

Given all the pitfalls that a project might encounter, it is quite possible that at some point the researcher may conclude that the project is not feasible as planned. Before calling it quits, however, give careful consideration to possible modifications that would enhance the project's feasibility. If inadequate time or money is the problem, perhaps the project can be scaled down. It might be possible to reduce the sample size or reduce the number of hypotheses tested to make the experiment manageable. If interviewing were originally planned, consider a mailed questionnaire or even a telephone survey as cost-cutting and time-reducing measures. If the problem is with procedures, such as may occur in an experiment, consider how they might be changed so that the project can proceed. The point is that a project should not be abandoned until all efforts to make it feasible have been investigated.

COMPUTERS IN RESEARCH

Searching the Literature: Lessons from Evidence-Based Practice

Whether one is a researcher seeking to hone a research idea into a feasible project or a human service practitioner seeking the best means to help a client, efficient access to the literature is essential. In fact, literature access represents one of the linkages between practice and research, and developments along these lines in evidence-based practice serve the needs of researchers and practitioners alike.

Evidence-based practice means integrating individual human service expertise with the best available external evidence from systematic research. The challenge for evidence-based practice is to provide a means whereby practitioners and researchers can find the evidence in a readily useable form. Access to evidence is the mission of such organizations as the Cochrane Library (www.cochrane.org). Although the Library is designed for both practitioners and researchers, each may use it for different purposes. The attraction for practitioners is that the Library provides rapid access to the latest research to help answer questions such as "How well does the intervention I'm considering work with patients who have symptoms of depression like those of my client?" The researcher might want to know "How well defined is the knowledge about depression? What measurement tools have been used? What recommendations for further research have previous studies identified?"

The Cochrane Collaboration (2003) points out that the major bibliographic databases cover less than half the world's literature for health care and are biased toward English language publications. Furthermore, of the evidence available in the major databases, the average searcher can find only a fraction, and reliance on this more easily accessible research tends to exaggerate the benefits of interventions. While common online literature databases such as Sociological Abstracts or Social Work Abstracts enable the user to locate studies, the user must sort through all the studies and draw relevant conclusions. A central feature of the Cochrane Library is the Cochrane Database of Systematic Reviews, which consists of full-text articles reviewing the research available on health care topics. Each review follows a highly structured and systematic format and covers particular content areas, such as the methodologies used on a particular area of research, the criteria for including studies in the review, and the conclusions from the research. Data from numerous small studies are often combined statistically in a review using a procedure known as "meta-analysis" to increase the power of the findings and to improve the reliability over that of the individual studies alone (Siwek, Gourlay and Slawson 2002). Although primarily designed for medicine, other human services are adopting the general Cochrane review model, including mental health (Lyddon and Jones 2001), alcohol abuse (O'Farrell and Fals-Stewart 2003), geriatric care (Kennet, Burgio, and Schulz 2000), developmental disabilities (Tuffrey-Wijne 2003), and vocational rehabilitation (Loisel et al. 2003).

Of course, having the empirical data available in readily useable form is still only one part of the equation. The other part is accessing the data, and the key to access is asking the right questions for the database search. In addition to the Cochrane review, practitioners and researchers may also need to locate actual studies. Whether searching for a review or for individual research studies, evidence-based practice experts point out that a good question for a systematic search must be clear and describe exactly what is being sought—just as a good research hypothesis clearly specifies the independent and dependent variables (Sackett et al. 2000). A widely accepted evidence-based practice principle for framing search questions is the acronym "PICO," which stands for:

- P—People or patient population of interest. The demographic characteristics, the problem or condition, and the particular setting (such as community or institution) should be specified.
- I—Intervention. The intervention should be specified as clearly as possible, such as cognitive-behavioral therapy, couples counseling, or bi-polar support group.
- C—Comparisons which will be made. This category would be included if the reviewer wishes to specifically limit inclusion of studies to those using control groups, placebos, or alternate treatments in the research design.
- O—Outcomes. Here the reviewer specifies the kinds of outcomes such as behavior change, prevention, reduced cost, etc., that are of interest.

For example, an evidence-based literature search related to unintended pregnancy included the following key questions (identify the PICO elements in each of these questions):

1. How effective is counseling in a clinical setting to prevent unintended pregnancy in changing knowledge, skills and attitudes?
2. What is the association between behaviors that support fertility desires and the prevention of unintended conceptions?
3. What are the potential harms of contraception counseling?
4. What is the cost-effectiveness of counseling in the clinical setting to prevent unintended pregnancy?
   (Moos, Bartholomew, and Lohr 2003, p. 116)

The questions provide the road map for navigating through the various databases appropriate to the practitioner's interest. In addition to helping identify search terms, the questions provide guidance for including and excluding studies from the plethora of articles that one is likely to encounter. (See Appendix A for databases useful to the human services that are widely available online.)

Main Points

- Suitable topics for research come from a variety of sources, including personal interest, social problems, theory testing, prior research, program evaluation, and human service practice.
- Political factors also influence problem selection: Powerful interest groups encourage the expenditure of research resources on issues that are of interest to them and that may not serve the interests of less advantaged and minority groups.
- A general topic for research must be narrowed and focused into a precise, researchable problem.
- An important part of refining a research problem is conceptual development: identifying and defining the concepts that the study will focus on.
- Reviewing previous research related to the selected topic is a crucial step in problem development and preparing to conduct a research project. This review should produce information about theoretical and conceptual issues, research

hypotheses and variables, measurement and operational definitions, research technique, sampling strategies, statistical techniques, and findings and conclusions.
- The units of analysis must be clearly specified as individuals, groups, organizations, programs, or social artifacts.
- Continual awareness of the operative unit of analysis ensures avoidance of such errors as the ecological fallacy or the reductionist fallacy.
- Reactivity refers to the fact that people may behave differently when they are being watched than when they are not being watched, and the effects of reactivity must be considered when shaping a research problem.
- Qualitative research emphasizes the description of how people experience the world; it relies on data in the form of words, pictures, descriptions, and narratives. Quantitative research uses numbers, counts, and measures to assess statistical relationships between variables.

■ Cross-sectional research is based on data collected at one point in time, making accurate conclusions about trends or behavioral changes difficult. Longitudinal studies are based on data collected over a period of time and are particularly useful for studying trends or behavioral changes.

■ Once fully refined, the practical feasibility of a proposed research project requires realistic assessment.

Important Terms for Review

cross-sectional research
ecological fallacy
longitudinal research
panel study
qualitative research
quantitative research
reactivity
reductionist fallacy
trend study
units of analysis

Exploring InfoTrac® College Edition and the Internet

InfoTrac® College Edition search terms:

ecological fallacy
qualitative research
longitudinal research
cross-sectional research

InfoTrac® College Edition articles:

IOM: Let Science, Not Politics Drive NIH Research Funding. Stephanie Stapleton. *American Medical News* July 27, 1998 v41 n28 p22 (1) (589 words)

Methodological Issues in Research on Sexual Behavior with Latino Gay and Bisexual Men. Maria Cecilia Zea, Carol A. Reisen, Rafael M. Diaz. *American Journal of Community Psychology* June 2003 v31 i3-4 p281 (11) (7,699 words)

Practice-Based Evidence: Towards Collaborative and Transgressive Research. (Articles). Nick J. Fox. *Sociology* Feb 2003 v37 i1 p81 (22) (9,181 words)

The Internet can be a valuable resource throughout the problem formulation process, from selecting a research problem through shaping and refining the problem to ascertaining its feasibility. When selecting a problem based on personal interest, a social problem, or testing a theory, begin by using some of the search engines on the Web to locate information on that general topic. For example, if you were interested in conducting research on such topics as self-esteem, drug use, or depression, you could use a search engine, such as Lycos or Yahoo, or a meta-search engine, such as dogpile.com or savvysearch.com, to locate a wide array of sites devoted to those topics. An initial perusal of such sites can help identify important issues for developing the research problem, such as these: "How is the concept defined? Does there appear to be consensus on what the concept is? What controversies or issues are being debated about the topic?" Exploring such questions can help you focus on potentially interesting research problems. You may also find organizations and resources that may prove useful in later steps in the research process, such as measurement tools. Select a topic to research and explore some of the Web sites that the search engine locates.

The Internet can prove extremely useful in discovering prior research. Many Web sites consist of bibliographies or include them as a special section. One example is the National Criminal Justice Reference Service. Access this site at www.ncjrs.org and select "victims of crime." This will lead to a diverse listing of sources on victims of crime. Select one of the victim categories, such as "domestic violence," and peruse some of the available sources. Note that Web sites like this may also contain links to other sites specifically devoted to your topic of interest. For example, the National Clearinghouse for Alcohol and Drug Information (www.health.org/newsroom) provides immediate access to a wealth of articles related to substance abuse. Try out this site by entering a combination of terms such as "alcohol" and "violence." By beginning with a basic search engine, such as Google.com, and using a general term, such as "crime," "health," or "education," you can locate a major center or clearinghouse for that topic, as illustrated for domestic violence and alcohol. These sites will then lead you to the specific articles and bibliographies.

For those seeking to develop research questions around program evaluation, the Internet can be an excellent source of information. Sites associated with organizations that sponsor program evaluations often include descriptions of previous evaluations, projects that are currently under way, and information on future funding opportunities. As an example, explore "Research and Evaluation" from the Justice Information Center home page (www.ncjrs.org/homepage.htm).

For Further Reading

Berg, Bruce L. *Qualitative Research Methods for the Social Sciences.* 5th ed. Boston: Allyn & Bacon, 2004. Although this book focuses primarily on how to conduct good qualitative research, it also contains a good comparison of qualitative and quantitative research and assesses when each is the most appropriate design.

Bransford, John D., and Barry S. Stein. *The Ideal Problem Solver: A Guide for Improving Thinking, Learning, and Creativity.* 2nd ed. New York: Freeman, 1995. Sound thinking combined with creativity are clearly important to formulating research problems. This guide assists in improving thought processes, drawing logical deductions, enhancing creativity, and even improving communication skills.

Gross, Ronald. *The Independent Scholar's Handbook.* Berkeley, Calif.: Ten Speed Press, 1993. This book contains many examples of how successful scholars developed personal hunches and notions into serious research inquiries. It is also filled with practical advice about such things as obtaining resources and communicating with other researchers who share similar research interests.

Higgins, P. C., and J. M. Johnson. *Personal Sociology.* New York: Praeger, 1988. This book includes many illustrations of how personal life events and experiences shaped the research interests of a variety of sociologists.

Hunt, Morton. *Profiles of Social Research: The Scientific Study of Human Interactions.* New York: Basic Books, 1985. As its title implies, this book presents a series of descriptions of major research projects. Follow these projects from inception to completion and see successful social scientists at work.

Locke, Lawrence F., Stephen J. Silverman, and Waneen Wyrick Spirduso. *Reading and Understanding Research.*
Thousand Oaks, Calif.: Sage, 1998. This is an excellent and thorough overview of how to do a good literature review and extract the appropriate information from it in an organized fashion.

Menard, Scott. *Longitudinal Research,* 2nd ed. Newbury Park, Calif.: Sage, 2002. This book provides a readable overview of both longitudinal and cross-sectional research. It discusses when each is an appropriate design and some of the problems confronted in doing good longitudinal research.

Reinharz, Shulamit. *Feminist Methods in Social Research.* New York: Oxford University Press, 1992. This book is a massive compilation of examples of all types of research conducted by researchers identified as feminists. Anyone interested in conducting research from this perspective is well advised to consult this impressive work.

Exercises for Class Discussion

In working through the exercises in this chapter, we suggest that you review Appendix A in the back of this book, which covers the basic issues involved in conducting research in a library. We have also found it helpful for students in our research classes to schedule a one- or two-hour workshop with the reference personnel in the library to help familiarize you with the materials available in their library, especially human service resource material.

4.1 Following are several broad topic areas relevant to the human services. Select one that has the greatest personal appeal to you. Identify why this topic interests you. How do your selection and the reasons for it compare with those of other students?
   a. child abuse
   b. nursing home care of the elderly
   c. emotionally disturbed children
   d. victims of crime
   e. violence in the family
   f. alcoholism
   g. discrimination against minorities
   h. adaptation to stress
   i. community living for the developmentally disabled
   j. effects of unemployment

4.2 Use your library's resources to locate at least five research studies published in the professional literature on the topic you selected. Your search efforts should include but need not be limited to the following: *Social Science Index, Social Work Abstracts, Monthly Catalog of Government Publications,* and the library's public catalog. Be prepared to discuss with the class how you located your studies.

4.3 For each research study you locate, do the following:

a. Indicate which factors seemed to influence the selection of topic in this study (that is, personal interest, social problems, theory testing, program evaluation, prior research, or practice experience).

b. What was the unit of analysis for each study? Was it the same as or different from the source of the data? If different, indicate the source. Can you think of any reasons for selecting a different unit of analysis?

c. What specific problem did the study address? From the presentation of the study, what factors influenced the final, actual problem formulation? In particular, were there issues of cost, time, or feasibility that necessitated a modification of the problem from the initial proposal?

d. Chapter 3 presented a discussion of ethical issues in research. What ethical issues confronted the researchers in studying each problem? Did a concern for ethics impact on what specific research problem emerged from an interest in studying the general topic?

4.4 We have made the point that problem selection in research is a social process in which power, interest groups, and other factors play significant roles. One practice issue that has received considerable attention in recent years is the placement of minority children, especially Native American children, in foster and adoptive homes with white families.

a. Have one group of students imagine that they are members of an adoptive/foster parent association that has been asked to provide suggestions to the DHHS for research priorities. What research problems would this group want to have studied?

b. Have a second group of students imagine that they are tribal leaders representing Native American interests. What priorities would they have, and what questions might this group suggest? Contrast the problems suggested by each group.

Chapter 5

The Process of Measurement

A crisis counselor working with a mental health agency receives a call from the county jail. The deputy there is concerned about an inmate he describes as severely depressed. The counselor responds by asking a number of questions, attempting to make an initial assessment of the severity of the inmate's depression. Has the inmate been eating his meals? Is he sleeping too much or too little? Is his affect flat when he responds to questions? Has he made any remarks about committing suicide? Later, the counselor may interview the inmate directly, request psychological testing, or refer him to a psychiatrist for further evaluation. Such assessments are analogous to a process in research called *measurement*. Just as the clinician used a variety of observations by the deputy as indicators of the inmate's condition, so researchers use various observations as indicators of the concepts of interest in a research project. **Measurement** refers to the process of describing abstract concepts in terms of specific indicators by assigning numbers or other symbols to these indicants in accordance with rules. At the very minimum, one must have some means of determining whether a variable is either present or absent, just as the counselor needs to know whether or not the inmate is eating. In many cases, however, measurement is more complex and involves assessing how much or to what degree a variable is present. An example of this is the counselor's question about how much the inmate is sleeping, "amount of sleep" being a variable that can take on many values.

Measurement is a part of the process of moving from the abstract or theoretical level to the concrete. Recall from Chapter 2 that scientific concepts have two types of definitions—nominal and operational. Before research can proceed, researchers have to translate nominal definitions into operational ones. The operational definitions indicate the exact procedures, or operations, that the researchers will use to measure the concepts. Measurement is essentially the process of operationalizing concepts. Figure 5.1 illustrates the place of measurement in the research process.

In this chapter, we discuss the general issues that relate to all measurement, beginning with some of the different ways we can make measurements. We then analyze how measurements made at different levels affect the mathematical operations that can be performed on them. Finally, we present ways of evaluating measures and determining the errors that can occur in the measurement process.

Ways of Measuring
From Concepts to Indicators

We cannot normally observe directly the concepts and variables that are the focus of both research and practice. We cannot see such things as poverty, social class, mental retardation, and the like but only infer them from something else. Take something as seemingly obvious as child abuse. Can you directly ob-

Figure 5.1   The Measurement Process

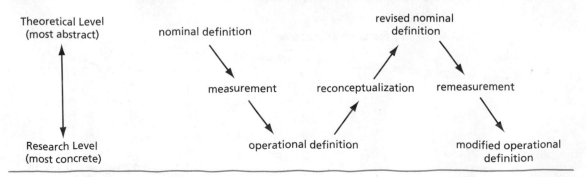

serve child abuse? Not really. What you directly observe is a bruise on a child's back, an infant's broken leg, or a father slapping his daughter. Even the slap may not relate to child abuse because parents sometimes slap their children without its being a case of child abuse. However, all these things—the bruise, the broken leg, the slap—may be used as *indicators* of child abuse. In research and in practice, an **indicator** is an observation that we assume is evidence of the attributes or properties of some phenomenon. What we observe are the indicators of a variable, not the actual properties of the variable itself. Emergency room personnel may assume a child's broken leg is an indicator of child abuse even though they have not observed the actual abuse.

Child abuse represents a good illustration of the difficulties of moving from nominal to operational definitions with variables involving social and psychological events. At the nominal level, we might define child abuse as an occurrence in which a parent or caretaker injures a child, not by accident but in anger or with deliberate intent (Gelles 1987; Korbin 1987). But what indicators would we use to operationalize this definition? Some things would obviously seem to indicate child abuse, such as a cigarette burn on a child's buttock. What about a bruise on the arm? Some subcultures in our own society view hitting children, even to the point of bruising, as an appropriate way to train or discipline them. Furthermore, some people would argue that a serious psychological disorder a child suffers is an indicator of child abuse because it shows the parents did not provide the proper love and affection for stable development. In short, one of the problems in operationalizing child abuse, as is true with many other variables in human service research, is that its definition is culture-bound and involves subjective judgments. This illustrates the importance of good conceptual development and precise nominal definitions for research. It also shows how the theoretical and research levels can mutually influence one another: As we shape nominal definitions into operational ones, the difficulties that arise often lead to a reconceptualization, or change, in the nominal definition at the theoretical level (see Figure 5.1).

The example of child abuse also illustrates another point about measurement, namely, that more than one indicator of a variable may exist. The term **item** is used to refer to a single indicator of a variable. Items can take numerous forms, such as an answer to a question or an observation of a behavior or characteristic. Asking a person her age or noting her sex, for example, would both produce items of measurement. In many cases, however, operationalizing variables involves combining a number of items into a composite score called an **index** or **scale.** (Although scales involve more rigor in their construction than do indexes, we can use the terms interchangeably at this point; Chapter 13 presents some distinctions between them.) Attitude scales, for example, commonly involve asking people a series of questions, or items, and then summarizing their responses into a single score that represents their attitude on an issue. A major reason for using scales or indexes rather than single items is that scales enable us to measure variables in a more precise and usually more accurate fashion. To illustrate the value of scales over items, consider your grade in this course. In all likelihood, your final grade will be an index, or composite score, of your answers to many questions on many tests throughout the semester. Would you prefer that your final grade be determined by a one-item measure, such as a single multiple-choice or essay question? Probably not, because that item would not measure the full range of what you learned. Furthermore, an error on that item would indicate that you had not learned much in the course, even if the error were due to ill health or personal problems on the day of the exam. For these reasons, then, researchers usually prefer multiple-item measures to single-item indicators.

We began this discussion by noting that because variables are abstract, we cannot normally observe them directly. Actually, variables differ in their degree of abstraction, and this affects the ease with which we can accomplish measurement. In general, the more abstract the variable, the more difficult it is to measure. For example, a study of child abuse might include the variable "number of children in family," on the theoretical presumption that large families create more stress for parents and are therefore more likely to precipitate abusive attacks on children. This is a rather easy variable to measure because the concepts of "children" and "family" have readily identifiable empirical referents and are relatively easy and unambiguous to observe and count. Suppose, however, that the child abuse study also included as a dependent variable "positiveness of child's self-concept." "Self-concept" is a difficult notion to measure because it can take many different forms. Although we have narrowed it to the "positive–negative" dimension, it is still more difficult to measure than "number of children in family" because we could ask a whole variety of questions to explore how positively people feel about themselves. We can also measure self-concept by behaviors, on the theoretical presumption that people who feel positively about themselves behave differently from those who do not. The point is that highly abstract concepts usually have no single empirical indicator that is clearly and obviously preferable to others as a measure of the concept.

We have emphasized the point that measurement involves transition from the abstract and conceptual level to the concrete and observable level, and this is what most typically occurs in research. However, exploratory studies can involve measurement in the opposite direction: First, we observe empirical indicators and then formulate theoretical concepts that those indicators presumably represent. In Chapter 2, we called this inductive reasoning. In a sense, you might think of Sigmund Freud or Jean Piaget as having done this when they developed their theories of personality and cognitive development, respectively. Piaget, for example, observed the behavior of children for many years as he gradually developed his theory of the stages of cognitive development, including concepts like egocentrism, object permanence, and reversibility (Ginsburg and Opper 1988). Piaget recognized that what he observed could be understood only if placed in a more abstract theoretical context. In a sense, he measured something before he knew what it was he had measured. Once his theories began to develop, he then developed new concepts and hypotheses and formulated different measuring devices to test them deductively. The point is that whether one shifts from the abstract to the concrete, or vice versa, the logic

is the same, involving the relationship between theoretical concepts and empirical indicators.

Techniques of Measuring

We will discuss specific techniques for measuring variables in other chapters in this book, but we find that discussing these techniques briefly at this point helps make clear the issues surrounding measurement. Measurement techniques in the social sciences and human services vary widely because the concepts we measure are so diverse, but these techniques mostly fall into one of three categories (see Figure 5.2).

1. *Verbal reports.* This is undoubtedly the most common measurement technique in social research. It involves people answering questions, being interviewed, or responding to verbal statements (see Chapters 7 and 9). For example, research on people's attitudes typically uses the verbal reports technique by asking people how they feel about commercial products, political candidates, or social policies. In a study of school performance, to mention another example, we could measure how well students do in school by asking them what their grades are or asking them how much they know about a particular subject.

2. *Observation.* Social researchers also measure concepts by making direct observations of some phenomena (see Chapter 9). We watch people at school or at work and make notes of what they say and do. We may even make an audio or video recording as a way of preserving the observations. In a study of school performance, we could measure how well students do in school by directly observing their behavior in the classroom, noting how often they answer questions posed by teachers, how often their answers are correct, and how they get along with teachers and students.

3. *Archival records.* Researchers also use a variety of available recorded information to measure variables (see Chapter 8). These records might take the form of statistical records, governmental or organizational documents, personal letters and

Figure 5.2   The Major Strategies Used by Social Scientists to Measure Variables

**Verbal Reports**

People answering questions, being interviewed, or responding to verbal statements

Measuring School Performance:

Ask students to tell us what their grades are or how much they know about a particular subject

Researcher

Observation

Directly watch people at school, work, or other setting and make note of what they say and do

Measuring School Performance:

Directly observe their behavior in the classroom, noting how often they answer questions posed by teachers, how often their answers are correct, and how they get along with teachers and students

Researcher

Archival Reports

Review available recorded information

Measuring School Performance:

Use the school records to locate students' grades, performance on exams, attendance records, and disciplinary problems

Researcher

diaries, newspapers and magazines, or movies and musical lyrics. All of these archival records are the products of human social behavior and can serve as indicators of concepts in the social sciences. In the study of school performance, for example, a researcher could use school records to locate students' grades, performance on exams, attendance records, and disciplinary problems as measures of how well they are doing in school.

These are the major ways that social scientists measure concepts. Researchers must specify exactly what aspects of verbal reports, observations, or available data will serve as indicators of the concepts they want to measure. In addition, researchers use some key criteria to help them decide whether a particular indicator is a good measure of some concept. These criteria will be discussed later in this chapter.

Positivist and Nonpositivist Views of Measurement

Much of the foundation for measurement and operationalization in the social sciences derives from the

Table 5.1 Elements in the Process of Measurement

X **Observation**	**=**	*T* **True Phenomenon**	**+**	*E* **Error**
Reading on a weight scale	=	Your actual weight	+	Clothing you are wearing Heavy object in your pocket
Grade on an examination in social research class	=	Actual knowledge you acquired in social research class	+	Heat and humidity in test room Distraction due to fight with partner
Score on a scale measuring self-esteem	=	Your actual level of self-esteem	+	Incorrectly marking a self-esteem scale Questions on self-esteem scale that are difficult to understand

work of statisticians, mathematicians, philosophers, and scientists in a field called classical test theory or measurement theory (Bohrnstedt 1983; Stevens 1951), which provides the logical foundation for issues discussed in this chapter and derives largely from the positivist view of science discussed in Chapter 2. The logic of measurement can be described by the following formula:

$$X = T + E$$

In the formula, X represents our observation or measurement of some phenomenon; it is our indicator. X might be the grade in an exam in a social research class, for example, or responses to a self-esteem scale (see Table 5.1). T represents the true, actual phenomenon that we are attempting to measure with X. T would be what a student actually learned in a social research class or what his or her true self-esteem is. The third symbol in the formula, E, represents any measurement error that occurs, or anything that influences X other than T. E might be the heat and humidity in the classroom on the day of the social research exam that made it difficult to concentrate during the exam; or E could reflect the fact that a subject incorrectly marked a choice on the self-esteem scale, inadvertently circling a response that indicated higher or lower self-esteem than he or she actually possessed.

The formula is very simple but also very profound and important: Our measurement of any phenomenon is a product of the characteristics or qualities of the phenomenon itself and any errors that occur in the measurement process. What we strive for is measurement with no error:

$$E = 0$$

and therefore:

$$X = T$$

The ideal to strive for is measurement of the phenomenon determined only by the true state of the phenomenon itself. However, scientists recognize that they cannot normally achieve this ideal state in its entirety. In reality, we attempt to reduce E as much as possible. Later in this chapter we will complicate this measurement formula a bit, but for now it can stand as a shorthand way of understanding the process of measurement.

Before going more into the process of measurement, it is important to consider the nonpositivists' critique of classical measurement theory. Many nonpositivists argue that we haven't examined a huge assumption in this at all, one that may render the entire topic somewhat problematic. The assumption is that the phenomenon being measured (T) exists objectively in the world and that our measurement device is merely discovering it and its properties. Some things do exist in the world independently of our perceptions and judgments about them. The computer monitor on which these words are being written has a screen that is nine inches tall—we just measured it with a ruler. Our measurement of it was a discovery of its properties; the measurement process did not create or change those properties. However, think about a social science concept, such as self-esteem. We measure it by asking subjects to agree or disagree with a series of statements; we score a "strongly agree" response as "4" and a "strongly disagree" response as "1"; then we sum up those responses to all the separate items in the scale and give a self-esteem score that ranges from 10 to 40. But what is the objective reality behind this measurement? If a subject receives a score of 32 on our measurement device, what does that 32 correspond to in his or her subjective world, or mind, or consciousness? The 32 is the X in our measurement formula; what is the T that it corresponds to? Is the link between the measurement of a computer screen and its actual length as direct as the link between the 32 score on the self-esteem measure and actual subjective experience of self?

The nonpositivists argue that many social science concepts do not have such clear and objective referents in the world. Our concepts are based on an intuitive and theoretical understanding of what parts of the world are like. In other words, we are *constructing* the world, not just discovering it. We believe that something like self-esteem exists, but it is our construction of it that we measure with the self-esteem scale, not the thing itself (if the thing itself even exists). This does not make measurement theory useless, but it does suggest that the whole process is more complicated and not nearly as objective as the positivists suggest. Nonetheless, many nonpositivists agree that some social science measurement can follow the model of measurement theory. Some social phenomena, such as age and sex, do have some objective existence in the world. Age has something to do with how many times the earth has circled the sun since birth, and sex has something to do with physical genitalia. The social significance of these characteristics is another matter, of course, but the measurements of age and sex in many cases can follow classical measurement theory. Research in Practice 5.1 addresses

RESEARCH IN PRACTICE 5.1

BEHAVIOR AND SOCIAL ENVIRONMENT:

Controversies in Measuring Violence against Women

An extensive body of literature has accumulated on the topic of violence against women. In the process of building this knowledge base, considerable disagreement has arisen about what harmful behaviors to include in a definition of nonlethal violence and how best to go about measuring this violence. Consider the two following excerpts, the first from a qualitative study and the second from a summary of a national, randomized survey.

> I was raped by my uncle when I was 12 and my husband has beat me for years. For my whole life, when I have gone to a doctor, to my priest, or to a friend to have my wounds patched up, or for a shoulder to cry on, they dwell on my bruises, my cuts, my broken bones. The abuse in my life has taken away my trust in people and in life.

> It's taken away the laughter in my life. I don't trust myself to be able to take care of my kids, to take care of myself, to do anything to make a difference in my own life or anyone else's. That's the hurt I would like to fix. I can live with the physical scars.

> It's these emotional scars that drive me near suicide sometimes.
> —A respondent interviewed by DeKeseredy and MacLeod (1997, p. 5)

Women experience significantly more partner violence than men do: 25 percent of surveyed women, compared with 8 percent

continued on next page

of surveyed men, said they were raped and/or physically assaulted by a current or former spouse, cohabiting partner, or date in their lifetime; 1.5 percent of surveyed women and 0.9 percent of surveyed men said they were raped and/or physically assaulted by such a perpetrator in the previous 12 months. According to survey estimates, approximately 1.5 million women and 834,700 men are raped and/or physically assaulted by an intimate partner annually in the United States.

—Tjaden and Thoennes (1998, p. 2)

The gut-wrenching words of a violence survivor or the decimal precision of an executive summary: Which approach is the better measure of domestic violence? The qualitative study vividly portrays one person's experience, an experience with which many victims can identify. The survey lacks the rich description but appears to capture the immensity of the problem in terms of numbers of victims. The two approaches have fueled a debate over what focus to use when we attempt to measure violence against women.

Traditionally, many survey researchers have used operational definitions that include physical abuse indicators, such as beatings or kicks, or sexual assault features, such as forced penetration. For example, the Conflict Tactics Scale asks people to indicate how often a partner has "used a knife or gun on them" or "beat them up" (Straus, Hamby, Boney-McCoy, and Sugarman 1996). An argument in favor of such an approach is that it lends itself to readily quantifiable measures. One can count the number of times a victim was beaten, the number of visits to the emergency room, or the number of workdays lost due to injury. Standardized instruments such as the Conflict Tactics Scale permit researchers to make comparisons across studies and with different populations. So, in the case of the survey quoted above, the researchers can estimate the number of women who were raped or physically assaulted and the results used in conjunction with other surveys to estimate the extent of the problem.

But is this really what is most important? The victim who is quoted in the qualitative study makes an eloquent plea to focus on the psychological hurt that she endures forever as a consequence of living with an abusive partner rather than counting the number of assaults or physical injuries that happened. In an article discussing definition and measurement issues, Walter DeKeseredy (2000) points out that many North American surveys have followed a narrow definition, based in part on the argument that grouping physical assault with psychological, spiritual, and economic abuse muddies the water and makes causal determination impossible. Another argument is that to include "soft" abuse, such as verbal aggression and psychological damage, trivializes what most people agree is seriously abusive. In contrast, many researchers, especially those using qualitative methods, contend that violence against women is much more than just physical blows; it is multidimensional, and such actions as harming pets, threatening children, and verbal degradation are essential elements, too. The qualitative data presented above can be part of a convincing argument that the psychological damage resulting from abuse is far from trivial.

In fact, when it comes to estimating the amount of violence, DeKeseredy argues that narrow definitions generate low incidence and prevalence rates and that these constitute a significant problem. He points out that policymakers react only to large numbers, and thus underestimating the amount of abuse may have important policy implications. Furthermore, narrow definitions create a ranking of abuse based on what is defined as crime rather than on women's true feelings. Finally, narrow definitions increase the problem of underreporting because research participants would only disclose abuse that fits the narrow definition rather than include other experiences that hurt them deeply. Although it may be problematic to include a wide array of abusive experiences, DeKeseredy points out that qualitative research, such as that quoted above, emphasizes the need to incorporate into survey research the features of violence that women find so devastating. As the debate developed, qualitative research served as the catalyst for forcing the violence research community to broaden its definition of abuse. Several measurement tools, created in part in response to the work of qualitative researchers, now tap nonphysical and nonsexual abuse. These include Tolman's (1989) Psychological Maltreatment of Women Inventory and psychologically/emotionally abusive and controlling behaviors data elements developed by the National Center for Injury Prevention and Control, Centers for Disease Control and Prevention (Saltzman et al. 1999).

This debate over how to measure domestic violence shows the benefits of utilizing both qualitative and quantitative research approaches and considering both positivist and nonpositivist arguments about measurement. DeKeseredy, for example, makes a case for the use of multiple measures to further enhance measurement. He argues that using open-ended, supplemental questions in addition to such quantitative measures as the Conflict Tactics Scale increases the chance that silent or forgetful participants may reveal abuse not reported in the context of the structured, closed-ended instrument. In summary, we see that careful definition of terms, inclusion of both qualitative and quantitative research, improvement of measurement instruments, and the use of multiple forms of measurement all advance our understanding of the dynamics of important social issues, such as violence against women.

some of these measurement issues in regard to the significant social issue of domestic violence.

A major problem in most measurement has to do with which indicators to use in a particular research project. This partly depends, of course, on theoretical concerns, but there are other matters to consider as well. One such matter has to do with whether a particular measure permits one to perform mathematical operations on it; we turn to this issue next.

Levels of Measurement

We have seen just a few of the many ways of measuring phenomena, such as asking questions or noting observations. Measures differ from one another in terms of what is called their **level of measurement,** or the rules that define permissible mathematical operations that can be performed on a set of numbers produced by a measure. There are four levels of measurement: nominal, ordinal, interval, and ratio. If we keep in mind that variables can take on different values, measurement basically involves assessing the value or category into which a particular entity falls. Measuring age, for example, is the process of placing each person into a particular age category.

Nominal Measures

Nominal measures classify observations into mutually exclusive categories that represent nominal variables at the theoretical level. Variables such as sex, ethnicity, religion, or political party preference are examples. Thus, we might classify people according to their religious affiliation by placing them into one of five categories: Protestant, Catholic, Jewish, other, or no religious affiliation. These are mutually exclusive categories because membership in one precludes membership in another. For purposes of data analysis, we might assign numbers to represent each of the categories. We could label Protestant as 1, Catholic as 2, Jewish as 3, other as 4, and none as 5. It is important to recognize, however, that the assignment of numbers is purely arbitrary; the numbers making up a nominal measure have none of the properties—such as ranking, ordering, and magnitude—that we usually associate with numbers. None of the usual arithmetic operations, such as adding, subtracting, multiplying, or dividing, can legitimately be performed on numbers in a nominal scale. The reason for this is that the numbers in a nominal scale are merely symbols or labels used to identify a category of the nominal variable. We could just as easily have labeled Protestant 2 as 1.

Table 5.2 Ordinal Ranking of Socioeconomic Status

Category	Rank
Upper-upper	7
Lower-upper	6
Upper-middle	5
Middle	4
Lower-middle	3
Upper-lower	2
Lower-lower	1

Ordinal Measures

When variables can be conceptualized as having an inherent order at the theoretical level, we have an ordinal variable and, when operationalized, an ordinal measure. **Ordinal measures** are of a higher level than nominal measures because, in addition to mutual exclusivity, the categories have a fixed order. Socioeconomic status, for example, constitutes an ordinal variable, and measures of socioeconomic status are ordinal scales. Table 5.2 illustrates how we might divide socioeconomic status into ordinal categories. With ordinal measurement, we can speak of a given category as ranking higher or lower than some other category; lower-upper class, for example, is higher than middle class but not as high as upper-upper class. It is important to recognize that ordinal measurement does not assume that the categories are equally spaced. For example, the distance between lower-upper and upper-upper is not necessarily the same as between lower-middle and middle, even though in both cases the classes are one rank apart. This lack of equal spacing means that the numbers assigned to ordinal categories do not have the numerical properties necessary for arithmetic operations. Like nominal scales, we cannot add, subtract, multiply, or divide ordinal scales. The only characteristic they have that nominal scales do not is the fixed order of the categories.

Interval Measures

The next highest level of measurement is interval. **Interval measures** share the characteristics of ordinal scales—mutually exclusive categories and an inherent order—but have equal spacing between the categories. Equal spacing comes about because some specific unit of measurement, such as a degree on a temperature scale, is a part of the measure. Each of these units has the same value that results in the equal spacing. We have an interval scale if the difference between scores of, say, 30 and 40 was the same as the difference between scores of 70 and 80. A 10-point difference is a 10-point difference regardless of where on the scale it occurs.

The common temperature scales, Fahrenheit and Celsius, are true interval scales. Both of these temperature scales have, as units of measurement, degrees and the equal spacing characteristic of interval scales. A difference of 10 degrees is always the same, no matter where it occurs on the scale. These temperature scales illustrate another characteristic of true interval scales: The point on the scale labeled zero is arbitrarily selected. Neither 0°C nor 0°F is absolute zero, the complete absence of heat. Because the zero point is arbitrary in true interval scales, we cannot make statements concerning ratios. That is, we cannot say that a given score is twice or three times as high as some other score. For example, a temperature of 80°F is not twice as hot as a temperature of 40°F. Despite not having this ratio characteristic, interval scales have numbers with all the other arithmetic properties. If we have achieved interval level measurement, we can legitimately perform all the common arithmetic operations on the numbers.

Considerable controversy exists over which measures used in behavioral science research are true interval measures, with only a few measures clearly of interval level. For example, one that is relevant to the human services is intelligence as measured by IQ tests. IQ tests have specific units of measurement—points on the IQ scale—and each point on the scale is mutually exclusive. Furthermore, the distance between IQs of 80 and 90 is equivalent to the distance between IQs of 110 and

Table 5.3 The Characteristics of the Four Levels of Measurement

Level of Measurement	Characteristics of Categories			
	Mutually Exclusive	Possesses a Fixed Order	Equal Spacing between Ranks[a]	True Zero Point[a,b]
Nominal	y			
Ordinal	y	y		
Interval	y	y	y	
Ratio	y	y	y	y

y = possesses that characteristic

[a]Permits standard mathematical operations of addition, subtraction, multiplication, and division.

[b]Permits statements about proportions and ratios.

120. However, an IQ scale has no absolute zero point, so we cannot say that a person with an IQ of 150 is twice as intelligent as a person with an IQ of 75. As with temperature scales, the IQ scale is in part an arbitrary construction that allows us to make some comparisons but not others.

Beyond a few measures such as intelligence, however, the debate ensues. Some researchers argue, for example, that we can treat attitude scales as interval scales (Kenny 1986). The questions that make up attitude scales commonly involve choosing one of five responses: strongly agree, agree, uncertain, disagree, or strongly disagree. The argument is that people see the difference between "strongly agree" and "agree" as roughly equivalent to the distance between "disagree" and "strongly disagree." This perceived equidistance, some argue, makes it possible to treat these scales as interval measures. Other researchers argue that there is no logical or empirical reason to assume that such perceived equidistance exists and, therefore, we should always consider attitude scales ordinal rather than interval measures.

We do not presume to settle this debate here. Rather, we raise the issue because level of measurement influences which statistical procedures to use at the data analysis stage of research. (This matter is discussed in Chapters 14 and 15.) The results of research in which the researcher used a statistical procedure inappropriate for a given level of measurement should be viewed with caution.

Ratio Measures

The highest level of measurement is ratio. **Ratio measures** have all the characteristics of interval measures, but the zero point is absolute and meaningful rather than arbitrary. As the name implies, with ratio measures we can make statements to the effect that some score is a given ratio of another score. For example, one ratio variable with which human service workers are likely to deal is income. With income, the dollar is the unit of measurement. Also, as many are all too well aware, there is such a thing as no income at all, so the zero point is absolute, and thus it is perfectly legitimate to make these kinds of statements about income: An income of $20,000 is twice as much as $10,000 but only one third as much as $60,000. (We recognize, of course, that income is a ratio measure only as an indicator of the *amount* of money available to a person; if income is used as a measure of a person's *social status,* for example, then a difference between $110,000 and $120,000 does not necessarily represent a shift in status equivalent to that between $10,000 and $20,000.) Given that ratio scales have all the characteristics of interval scales, we can, of course, perform all arithmetic operations on them.

We summarize the characteristics of the four levels of measurement in Table 5.3. Keep in mind that although researchers have no control over the nature of a variable, they do have some control over how they define variables, at both the nominal and operational levels, and this affects the level of measurement. It is sometimes possible to change the level of measurement of a variable by redefining it at the nominal or operational level. This is important because researchers generally strive for the highest level of measurement possible because higher levels of measurement generally enable us to measure variables more precisely and use more powerful statistical procedures (see Chapters 14 and 15). It is also desirable to measure at the highest possible level of measurement because it gives the researcher the most options: The level of measurement can be reduced during the data analysis, but it cannot be increased. Thus, choosing a level of measurement that is too low introduces a permanent limitation into the data analysis.

However, the primary determinant of the level of measurement is the nature of the variable we want to measure. The major concern is an accurate measure of a variable (a topic we will discuss at length in the next section). Religious affiliation, for example, is a nominal variable because that is the nature of the theoretical concept of "religious affiliation." There is no way to treat religious affiliation as anything other than merely nominal classification. However, by changing the theoretical variable somewhat, we may open up higher levels of measurement. If, instead of religious *affiliation,* we were to measure *religiosity,* or the strength of religious beliefs, we would have a variable we could conceptualize and measure as ordinal and perhaps even as interval. On the basis of certain responses, we could easily rank people into ordered categories of greater or lesser religiosity. Thus, the theoretical nature of the variable plays a large part in determining the level of measurement. This illustrates once again the constant interplay between theoretical and research levels (see Figure 5.1). The decision regarding level of measurement at the research level might affect the conceptualization of variables at the theoretical level.

Finally, note that nominal variables are not inherently undesirable. The impression that variables capable of measurement at higher levels are always better than nominal variables is wrong. The first consideration is to select variables on theoretical grounds and not on the basis of their possible level of measurement. Thus, if a research study really is concerned with religious affiliation and not religiosity, the nominal measure is the correct one to use, and not a measure of religiosity even though it is ordinal or possibly interval. On the other hand, researchers do strive for more accurate and powerful measurement. Other things being equal, a researcher who has two measures available, one ordinal and the other interval, generally prefers the interval measure.

Discrete versus Continuous Variables

In addition to considering the level of measurement of a variable, researchers also distinguish between variables that are *discrete* or *continuous*. **Discrete variables** have a finite number of distinct and separate values. A perusal of a typical client fact sheet from a human service agency reveals many examples of discrete variables, such as sex, race, household size, number of days absent, or number of arrests. Household size is a discrete variable because households can be measured only in a discrete set of units, such as having one member, two members, and so on. No meaningful measurement values lie between these distinct and separate values. **Continuous variables,** at least theoretically, can take on an infinite number of values. Age is a continuous variable because we can measure age by an infinite array of values. We normally measure age in terms of years, but theoretically we could measure it in terms of months, weeks, days, minutes, seconds, even nanoseconds! There is no theoretical limit to how precise the measurement of age might be. For most social science purposes, the measurement of age in terms of years is quite satisfactory, but age is nonetheless a continuous variable.

Nominal variables are, by definition, discrete in that they consist of mutually exclusive or discrete categories. Ordinal variables are also discrete. The mutually exclusive categories of an ordinal variable may be ranked from low to high, but there cannot be a partial rank. For example, in a study of the military, rank might be ordered 1 = private, 2 = corporal, and so on, but it would be nonsensical to speak of a rank of 1.3. In some cases, interval and ratio variables are discrete. For example, family size or number of arrests are whole numbers or discrete intervals. (We can summarize discrete interval and ratio data by saying, for example, that the average family size is 1.8 people, but this is a summary statistic, not a measurement of a particular household.) Many variables at the interval and ratio level are continuous, at least at the theoretical level. A researcher may settle for discrete indicators because the study does not demand greater precision or because no tools exist that can measure the continuous variable with sufficient reliability. In some cases, researchers debate over whether a particular variable is discrete or continuous in nature. For example, we used social class as an illustration of an ordinal variable, suggesting that several distinct classes exist. Some argue that social class is inherently a continuous interval variable and that we only treat it as ordinal because of the lack of instruments that would permit researchers to measure it reliably as a true continuous, interval variable (Borgatta and Bohrnstedt 1981).

A variable, then, is continuous or discrete by its very nature, and the researcher cannot change that. It is possible to measure a continuous variable by specifying a number of discrete categories, as we typically do with age, but this does not change the nature of the variable itself. Whether variables are discrete or continuous may influence how we use them in data analysis. Knowing the level of measurement and whether variables are discrete or continuous has implications for selecting the best procedures for analyzing the data.

Evaluating Measures

We have seen that there are normally a number of indicators, sometimes a large number and at different levels of measurement, that we can use to measure a variable. How do we choose the best of these measures for a particular study? A number of factors come into play in making this decision, including matters of feasibility discussed in Chapter 4. Here we want to discuss two additional and very important considerations in this regard: the validity and reliability of measures.

Validity

Validity refers to the accuracy of a measure: Does it accurately measure the variable it is intended to measure? If we were developing a measure of self-concept, a major concern would be whether our measuring device measures the concept as it is theoretically defined. There must be a fairly clear and logical relationship between the way a variable is nominally defined and the way it is operationalized. For example, if we propose to measure self-concept on the basis of how stylishly people dress, we would probably have an invalid measure. Many factors influence the way people dress at any given time. The slight possibility that one of these factors might have something to do with self-concept is not sufficient to make the suggested measure valid. The validity of measures is very difficult to demonstrate with any finality. However, several approaches to the question of validity exist, and they can offer evidence regarding the validity of a measure.

Face validity involves assessing whether a logical relationship exists between the variable and the proposed measure. It essentially amounts to a rather commonsense comparison of what makes up the measure and the theoretical definition of the variable: Does it seem logical to use this measure to reflect that variable? We might measure child abuse in terms of the reports physicians or emergency room personnel make concerning injuries suffered by children. Although this is not a perfect measure because health personnel might be wrong, it does seem logical that an injury such people report might reflect actual abuse.

No matter how carefully done, face validity is clearly subjective in nature. All we have is logic and common sense as arguments for the validity of a measure. This serves to make face validity the weakest demonstration of validity, and it should usually be considered no more than a starting point. All measures must pass the test of face validity. If they do, we should attempt one of the more stringent methods of assessing validity.

An extension of face validity is called **content validity** or **sampling validity,** which has to do with whether a measuring device covers the full range of meanings or forms included in a variable to measure. In other words, a valid measuring device provides an adequate, or representative, *sample* of all *content,* or elements or instances, of the phenomenon being measured. For example, if one were measuring general self-esteem, it would be important to recognize that self-esteem can relate to many realms of people's lives, such as at work, at school, or in the family. Self-esteem might get expressed or come into play in all those settings. A valid measure of self-esteem would take that variability into account. If a measure of self-esteem consisted of a series of statements to which people expressed degrees of agreement, then a valid measure would include statements that relate to those many settings in which self-esteem might be expressed. If all the statements in the measuring device had to do, say, with school, then it would be a less valid measure of general self-esteem.

Content validity is a more extensive assessment of validity than is face validity because it involves a detailed analysis of the breadth of the measured concept and its relationship to the measuring device. Content validity involves two distinct steps: (1) determining the full range or domain of the content of a variable and (2) determining whether all those domains are represented among the items that constitute the measuring device. It is still a somewhat subjective assessment, however, in that someone has to judge what the full domain of the variable is and whether a particular aspect of a concept is adequately represented in the measuring device. There are no agreed-on criteria that determine whether a measure has content validity. It is ultimately a judgment, albeit a more carefully considered judgment than with face validity.

One way to strengthen confidence in face or content validity is to gather the opinions of other investigators, especially those knowledgeable about the variables involved, regarding whether particular operational definitions are logical measures of the variables. This extension of face or content validity, sometimes referred to as **jury opinion,** is still subjective, of course. However, because more people serve as a check on bias or misinterpretation, jury opinion is superior to individual tests of face or content validity.

Criterion validity establishes validity by showing a correlation between a measurement device and some other criterion or standard that we know or believe accurately measures the variable under consideration. Or we might correlate the results of the measuring device with some properties or characteristics of the variable the measuring device is intended to measure. For example, a scale intended to measure risk of suicide should correlate with the occurrence of self-destructive behavior if it is to be considered valid. The key to criterion validity is to find a criterion variable against which to compare the results of the measuring device.

Criterion validity moves away from the subjective assessments of face validity and provides more objective evidence of validity. One type of criterion validity is **concurrent validity,** which compares the instrument under evaluation to some already existing criterion, such as the results of another measuring device. (Presumably, any other measuring devices in this assessment have already been tested for validity.) Lawrence Shulman (1978), for example, used a form of concurrent validity to test an instrument intended to measure the practice skills of human service practitioners. The instrument consisted of questions on a questionnaire in which clients rated the skills of practitioners. Shulman reasoned that clients would view more skilled practitioners as more helpful, and those practitioners would have more satisfied clients. Thus, Shulman looked for correlations between how positively clients rated a practitioner's skills and the perceived helpfulness of practitioners or satisfaction of clients. These correlations offered evidence for the validity of the measure of practitioners' skills.

Numerous existing measures can help establish the concurrent validity of a newly developed measure. (Following are only some of the compilations of such measures available in the social sciences and the human services: Bloom, Fischer, and Orme 1999; Corcoran and Fischer 2000; Fredman and Sherman, 1987; Magura and Moses 1986; McDowell and Newell 1996; Miller and Salkind 2002; Robinson, Shaver, and Wrightsman 1991; Schutte and Malouff 1995; Touliatos, Perlmutter, Strauss, and Holden 2000.) More measures can be found in research articles in professional journals. In addition, the Consulting Psychologists Press and other organizations publish catalogs of measures they make available to assess a wide array of skills, behaviors, attitudes, and other variables. (This also suggests, as pointed out in Chapter 4, that a thorough review of existing literature, undertaken before going through all the work of creating a new measure, may unearth an existing measure that meets one's needs and has already demonstrated adequate validity and reliability.) Then it is a matter of applying both measures to the same sample and comparing the results. If a substantial correlation is found between the measures, we have reason to believe that our measure has concurrent validity. As a matter of convention, a correlation of $r = .50$ is considered the minimum required for establishing concurrent validity.

The inherent weakness of concurrent validity is the validity of the existing measure that is used for comparison. All we can conclude is that our measure is about as valid as the other one. If the measure we select for comparison is not valid, the fact that ours correlates with it hardly makes our measure valid. For this reason, researchers should use only those measures established as valid by research for comparison purposes in concurrent validity.

A second form of criterion validity is **predictive validity,** in which an instrument predicts some future state of affairs. In this case, the criteria used to assess the instrument are certain future events. The Scholastic Assessment Test (SAT), for example, can be subjected to predictive validity by comparing performance on the test with how people perform in college. If people who score high on the SAT do better in college than those who score low, then the SAT is presumably a valid measure of scholastic ability. Some measures are created for the specific purpose of predicting a given behavior, and these measures are obvious candidates for assessment by predictive validity. For example, researchers have attempted to develop a measure that can predict which convicted criminals are likely to revert to high involvement with crime when released from prison (Chaiken and Chaiken 1984). Information about the number and types of crimes people commit, the age at which they commit their first crime, and in-volvement with hard drugs serve as the basis for these predictions. Ultimately, a measure's ability to make accurate predictions about who actually experiences high crime involvement after release validates it.

Because this may require numerous applications and many years, the scales can be initially assessed for validity on their ability to differentiate between high and low crime involvement among current criminals. We expect that if a measure can make this differentiation, it can also predict future involvement in crime. This variation on predictive validity is the *known groups* approach to validity. If we know that certain groups are likely to differ substantially on a given variable, we can use a measure's ability to discriminate between these groups as an indicator of validity. Suppose, for example, we were working on a measure of prejudice. We might apply the measure to a group of ministers, whom we would expect to be low in prejudice, and to a group of people affiliated with the group Aryan Nation, whom we would expect to be high in prejudice. If these groups differed significantly in how they responded to the instrument, then we would have reason to believe that the measure is valid. If it failed to show a substantial difference, we would certainly have doubt about its validity.

Despite the apparent potential of the known groups approach, it does have its limitations. Frequently, there are no groups known to differ on the variable we are attempting to measure. In fact, the purpose of developing a measure is often to allow the identification of groups who do differ on some variable. Thus, we cannot always use the known groups technique. When we do, we have to consider a further limitation, namely, that it cannot tell us whether a measure can make finer distinctions between less extreme groups than those used in the validation. Perhaps the measure of prejudice just described shows the members of Aryan Nation to be high in prejudice and the ministers low. With a broader sample, though, the measure may show that *only* the Aryan Nation members score high and *everyone else,* not just ministers, scores low. Thus, the measure can distinguish between groups only in a very crude fashion.

Construct validity, the most complex of the types of validity we discuss here, involves relating an instrument to an overall theoretical framework to determine whether the instrument is correlated with all the concepts and propositions that comprise the theory (Cronbach and Meehl 1955). In this case, instruments are assessed in terms of how they relate not to one criterion but rather to the numerous criteria derivable from some theory. For example, if we develop a new measure of socioeconomic status, we can assess construct validity by showing that the new measure accurately predicts the many hypotheses that can be derived from a theory of occupational attainment. In the theory, numerous propositions would relate occupational attainment and socioeconomic status to a variety of other concepts. If we do not find some or all of the predicted relationships, then we may question the validity of the new measuring instrument. (Of course, it may be that the theory itself is flawed; this possibility must always be considered in assessing construct validity.)

Construct validity takes some very complex forms. One is the **multitrait–multimethod approach** (Campbell and Fiske 1959). This is based on two ideas. The first is that two instruments that are valid measures of the same concept should correlate rather highly with each other even though they are different instruments. Second, two instruments, although similar to each other, should not correlate highly if they measure different concepts. This approach to validity involves the simultaneous assessment of numerous instruments (multimethod) and numerous concepts (multitrait) through the computation of intercorrelations. Wolfe and colleagues (1987) used this technique to assess the validity of children's self-reports about negative emotions, such as aggressiveness and depression. The point is that assessing construct validity can become highly complex, but the complexity offers greater evidence of the validity of the measures.

The types of validity we have discussed—face, content, criterion, and construct—involve a progression in which each builds on the previous one. Each requires more information than prior ones but provides a better assessment of validity. Unfortunately, many studies limit their assessment to content validity, with its heavy reliance on the subjective judgments of individuals or juries. Although sometimes this is necessary, measures subjected only to content validity should be used with caution.

Reliability

In addition to validity, measures are also evaluated in terms of their **reliability.** Reliability refers to a measure's ability to yield consistent results each time it is applied. In other words, reliable measures only fluctuate due to variations in the variable being measured. An illustration of reliability can be found at any carnival. At carnivals, there is usually a booth with a person guessing people's weights within a certain range of accuracy, say, plus or minus three pounds. The customer essentially bets that the carnie's ability to guess weights is sufficiently unreliable, that his or her estimate will fall outside the prescribed range, and that the customer will win a prize. A weight scale, of course, is a reliable indicator of a person's weight because it records roughly the same weight each time the same person stands on it, and the carnie provides such a scale to assess his or her guess of the customer's weight. Despite the fact that carnies who operate such booths become quite good at guessing weights, they do occasionally guess wrong—influenced, perhaps, by aspects of the customer other than actual weight, such as loose clothing that obscures the customer's physique.

In general, a valid measure is reliable. So if we were certain of the validity of a measure, we would not need to concern ourselves with its reliability. However, evidence of validity is always less than perfect, and that is why we turn to other ways of evaluating measures, including reliability. Reliability gives us more evidence for validity because a reliable measure may be valid. Fortunately, we can demonstrate reliability in a more straightforward manner than validity. Many specific techniques exist for estimating the reliability of a measure, but they are all based on one of two principles: stability and equivalence. *Stability* is the idea that a reliable measure should not change from one application to the next, assuming the concept being measured has not changed. *Equivalence* is the idea that all items that

Table 5.4 Hypothetical Test–Retest Data

Subjects	Initial Test	Retest
1	12	15
2	15	20
3	22	30
4	38	35
5	40	35
6	40	38
7	40	41
8	60	55
9	70	65
10	75	77

$r = .98$

Table 5.5 Design for Test–Retest

	Initial Test	Retest
Experimental group	Yes	Yes
Control group	No	Yes

make up a measuring instrument should measure the same thing and thus be consistent with one another. The first technique for estimating reliability, test–retest reliability, uses the stability approach. The others discussed use the equivalence principle.

Test–Retest. The first and most generally applicable assessment of reliability is called test–retest. As the name implies, this technique involves applying a measure to a sample of people and then, somewhat later, applying the same measure to the same people again. After the retest, we have two scores on the same measure for each person, as illustrated in Table 5.4. We then correlate these two sets of scores with an appropriate statistical measure of association (see Chapter 15). Because the association in test–retest reliability involves scores obtained from two identical questionnaires, we fully expect a high degree of association. As a matter of convention, a correlation coefficient of .80 or better is normally necessary for a measure to be considered reliable. In Table 5.4, the r means that the particular statistic used was Pearson's correlation coefficient, and the value of .98 indicates that the measurement instrument is highly reliable according to the test–retest method.

Lawrence Shulman (1978), in addition to subjecting his measure of practice skills to the tests of va-

lidity mentioned earlier, also tested its reliability. He did so by sending versions of the questionnaire to a set of clients and then sending an identical questionnaire two weeks later to the same clients. This provided him with a test–retest assessment of reliability, and he obtained a correlation coefficient of .75. When a reliability coefficient is close to the conventional level, such as in this case, the researcher must make a judgment about whether to assume that the instrument is reliable (and the low coefficient is due to factors other than the unreliability of the instrument) or to rework the instrument to obtain higher levels of association.

In actual practice, we cannot simply use the test–retest method as suggested because exposing people to the same measure twice creates a problem known as multiple-testing effects (Campbell and Stanley 1963). Whenever we apply a measure to a group of people a second time, they may not react to it the same as they did at first. They may, for example, recall their previous answers, and that could influence their second response. People might respond as they recall doing the first time to maintain consistency or purposely change responses for the sake of variety. Either case can have a confounding effect on testing reliability. If people strive for consistency, their efforts can mask actual unreliability in the instrument. If they deliberately change responses, a reliable measure can appear less reliable.

A solution to this dilemma is to divide the test group randomly into two groups: an experimental group to test twice and a control group to test only once. Table 5.5 illustrates the design for such an experiment. Ideally, the measure will yield consistent results in all three testing sessions; if it does, we have solid reason to believe the measure is reliable. On the other hand, substantial differences among the groups may indicate unreliability. If, for example, the experimental group shows consistency in both responses to the measurement instrument but the control group differs, the measure may be unreliable, and the consistency of the experimental group might result from the multiple-testing effects. On the other hand, if the experimental group yields inconsistent results but the control group is similar to the results of the experimental group's initial test, this outcome may also be due to multiple-testing effects and result from the experimental group's changing answers during the retest. Despite the inconsistency in the experimental group, the measure still might be reliable if we observe this outcome. Finally, we may see that the results of all three testing sessions appear inconsistent. Such an outcome would suggest that the measure is not reliable. If either of the outcomes that leaves the reliability of the measure in doubt occurs, researchers should conduct a second test–retest experiment with the hope of obtaining clearer results. If the same result occurs, we should redesign the instrument.

The test–retest method of assessing reliability has both advantages and disadvantages. Its major advantage is that we can use it with many measures, which is not true of alternative tests of reliability. However, its disadvantage is that it is slow and cumbersome to use, with two required testing sessions and the desirability of a control group. In addition, as we have seen, the outcome may not be clear, leading to the necessity of repeating the whole procedure. Finally, we cannot use the test–retest method on measures of variables whose value might have changed in the interval between tests. For example, people's attitudes can change for reasons that have nothing to do with the testing, and a measure of attitudes might appear unreliable when it is not.

Multiple Forms.   If our measuring device is a multiple-item scale, as is often the case, we can approach the question of reliability through the technique of multiple forms. When developing the scale, we create two separate but equivalent versions made up of different items, such as different questions. We then administer these two forms successively to the same people at a single testing session. We correlate the results from the forms, as in test–retest, using an appropriate statistical measure of association, with the same convention of $r = .80$ or better required for

establishing reliability. If the correlation between the two forms is sufficiently high, we can assume that each scale is reliable.

Multiple forms have the advantage of requiring only one testing session and needing no control group. This may be a significant advantage if using either multiple-testing sessions or a control group is impractical. In addition, we need not worry about changes in a variable over time because both forms are administered at the same time.

The multiple-forms technique relies on the two forms' appearing to the respondents as though they were only one long measure, so the respondents do not realize they are really taking the same test twice. This necessity of deluding people points to one of the disadvantages of multiple forms. To maintain the equivalence of the forms, the items in the two forms will probably be quite similar—so similar that people may realize that they are responding to essentially the same items twice. If this occurs, it raises the specter of multiple-testing effects and casts doubt on the accuracy of the reliability test. Another disadvantage of multiple forms is the difficulty of developing two measures with different items that are really equivalent. If we obtain inconsistent results from the two forms, it may be due to differences in the forms rather than the unreliability of either one. In a way, it is questionable whether multiple forms really test reliability and not just our ability to create equivalent versions of the measure.

Internal Consistency Approaches.   Internal consistency approaches to reliability use a single scale administered to one group of people to develop an estimate of reliability. For example, in the split-half approach to reliability, the test group responds to the complete measuring instrument. We then randomly divide the responses to the instrument into halves, treating each half as though it were a separate scale. We correlate the two halves by using an appropriate measure of association. Once again, we need a coefficient of $r = .80$ or better to demonstrate reliability. In his study of practice skills mentioned earlier, Shulman utilized a split-half reliability test on his instrument in addition to the test–retest method. He divided each respondent's answers to his questions about practitioners' skills into two roughly equivalent sets, correlated the two sets of answers, and found a correlation (following a correction, to be mentioned shortly) of .79. This is an improvement over the reliability he found with the test–retest method and comes very close to the conventional level of .80.

One complication in using the split-half reliability test is that the correlation coefficient may understate the reliability of the measure because, other things being equal, a longer measuring scale is more reliable than a shorter one. Because the split-half approach divides the scale in two, each half is shorter than the whole scale and will appear less reliable than the whole scale. To correct for this, we can adjust the correlation coefficient by applying the Spearman-Brown formula, which Shulman did:

$$r = \frac{2r_i}{1 + r_i}$$

where:

r_i = uncorrected correlation coefficient
r = corrected correlation coefficient
  (reliability coefficient)

To illustrate the effect of the Spearman-Brown formula, suppose we have a 20-item scale with a correlation between the two halves of r_i = .70, which is smaller than the minimum needed to demonstrate reliability. The Spearman-Brown formula corrects as follows:

$$r = \frac{(2)(.70)}{1 + .70} = \frac{1.40}{1.70} = .82$$

It can be seen that the Spearman-Brown formula has a substantial effect, increasing the uncorrected coefficient from well below .80 to just over it. If we had obtained these results with an actual scale, we would conclude that its reliability was now adequate.

Using the split-half technique requires two preconditions that can limit its applicability. First, all the items in the scale must measure the same variable. If the scale in question is a jumble of items measuring several different variables, it is meaningless to divide it and compare the halves. Second, the scale must contain a sufficient number of items so that, when it is divided, the halves do not become too short to be

considered scales in themselves. A suggested minimum is 8 to 10 items per half (Goode and Hatt 1952, p. 236). As many measures are shorter than these minimums, it may not be possible to assess their reliability with the split-half technique.

A number of other approaches to internal consistency reliability are sometimes used to overcome the weaknesses of the split-half approach. After all, the split-half approach only uses one random separation of the scale into two halves; randomly dividing the items in a scale into halves could result in many different arrangements of items, and each would yield a slightly different correlation between the halves. One common approach to this problem is to use Cronbach's alpha, which may be thought of as the average of all possible split-half correlations. Theoretically, the scale is divided into all possible configurations of two halves; a correlation is computed for each possibility, and the average of those correlations is computed to derive alpha (Cronbach 1951). This is not actually how Cronbach's alpha is calculated, but it does describe the logic of the procedure. Another approach to internal consistency reliability is to correlate each item in the scale with every other item and then use the average of these correlations as the measure of reliability. This is also done by correlating each item with the overall scale score. (Statistical packages such as SPSS contain procedures that will produce Cronbach's alpha, as well as other reliability tests based on inter-item correlations.)

Internal consistency reliability tests have several advantages. They require only one testing session and no control group. They also give the clearest indication of reliability. For these reasons, researchers prefer these methods of assessing reliability whenever possible. The only disadvantage, as we noted, is that we cannot always use them. Shulman's approach teaches a lesson, however: use more than one test, if possible, to assess both reliability and validity. The issues are sufficiently important that the expenditure of time is justified.

Measurement with Minority Populations

Researchers often first assess the validity and reliability of measuring instruments by applying them to white, non-Hispanic respondents because they find such people the most accessible. However, we should almost never be assumed that such assessments can be generalized to minority populations (Becerra and Zambrana 1985; Tran and Williams 1994). The development of such instruments typically does not consider the unique cultural characteristics and attitudes of minorities. For some minorities, such as Asians and Hispanics, language differences mean that an English-language interview would have some respondents answering in a second language. Researchers cannot assume that such a respondent will understand words and phrases as well as—or in the same way as—a person for whom English is his or her first language. In addition, some concepts in English do not have a precise equivalent in another language.

Therefore, it is important to refine measuring instruments to assure that they are valid and reliable measures among minorities. A study of mental health among Native Americans, for example, had to drop the word "blue" as a descriptor of depression because that word had no equivalent meaning among the Native Americans (Manson 1986). Researchers also had to add a category of "traditional healer" to a list of professionals to whom a Native American might turn for help. A study of Eskimos found that cultural context often caused different interpretation of questions. Because Eskimo culture emphasizes tolerance and endurance, Eskimos are less likely than Anglo-Americans to give in to pain by not working. A positive response from an Eskimo to a question like "Does sickness often keep you from doing your work?" is thus considered a much more potent indicator of distress than the same answer by Anglo-Americans.

These illustrations should make clear that measurement in social research must be culturally sensitive. When conducting research on a group with a culture different from that of the researchers, researchers can take a number of steps to produce more valid and reliable measurement instruments (Marin and Marin 1991; Tran and Williams 1994):

1. Researchers can immerse themselves in the culture of the group under study, experiencing the daily activities of life and the cultural products as the natives do.
2. Researchers should use key informants, people who participate routinely in the culture of the group under study, to help develop and assess the measurement instruments.
3. When translating an instrument from English into another language, researchers should use the most effective translation methods, usually *double translation* (translate from English into the target language and back into English by an independent person), to check for errors or inconsistencies.
4. After developing or translating measurement instruments for use with minority populations, researchers should test the instruments for validity and reliability on the population they intend to study.

Errors in Measurement

The range of precision in measurement is quite broad: from the cook who measures in terms of pinches, dashes, and smidgens to the physicist who measures in angstroms (0.003937 millionths of an inch). No matter whether a measurement is crude or precise, it is important to recognize that *all* measurement involves some component of error. There is no such thing as an exact measurement. Although some measurement devices in the social sciences are fairly precise, others contain substantial error components because most of our measures deal with abstract and shifting phenomena, such as attitudes, values, or opinions, which are difficult to measure with a high degree of precision. The large error component in many of our measurements means that researchers must pay close attention to the different types and sources of error. In measurement, researchers confront two basic types of error: *random* and *systematic*. In fact, we can modify the formula from the measurement theory introduced earlier in this chapter with the recognition that the error term in that formula, E, is actually made up of two components:

$$E = R + S$$

where the term R refers to random error and the term S refers to systematic error. Now our measurement formula looks like this:

$$X = T + R + S$$

Our measurement or observation of a phenomenon is a function of the true nature of the phenomenon along with any random and systematic error that occurs in the measurement process.

Random Errors

Random errors are those that are neither consistent nor patterned; the error is as likely to be in one direction as another. Essentially, random errors are chance errors that in the long run tend to cancel themselves out. In fact, in measurement theory, mathematicians often assume that $R = 0$ in the long run. For example, a respondent may misread or mismark an item on a questionnaire; a counselor may misunderstand and thus record incorrectly something said during an interview; a computer operator may enter incorrect data into a computerized data file. All these are random sources of error and can occur at virtually every point in a research project. Cognizant of the numerous sources of random error, researchers take steps to minimize them. Careful wording of questions, convenient response formats, and "cleaning" of computerized data all keep random error down. Despite researchers' best efforts, however, the final data may contain some component of random error.

Because of their unpatterned nature, it is assumed that random errors tend to cancel each other out. For example, the careless computer operator mentioned earlier would be just as likely to enter a score lower than the actual one as to enter a higher score. The net effect is that the random errors at least partly offset each other. The major problem with random error is that it weakens the precision with which a researcher can measure variables, thus reducing the ability to detect a relationship between variables when in fact one is present. For example, consider a hypothetical study on the relationship between empathy on the part of human service workers and client satisfaction with treatment. Assume that higher levels of client satisfaction actually are associated with higher levels of empathy. For such a study, measurements would be taken of the level of empathy that a worker expressed and of client satisfaction. Suppose we monitor five client interviews by each of five workers—a total sample of 25 cases—for level of worker empathy and client satisfaction. To the extent that random error is present in our measures, some interviews will be scored too high and some too low, even though the overall mean empathy and satisfaction scores can be expected to be quite close to the true averages. However, in terms of individual cases, random measurement will produce some empathy scores that are erroneously low for their associated satisfaction scores. Conversely, random error will produce some empathy scores that are high for their associated satisfaction scores. Thus, the random error tends to mask the true correlation between empathy and satisfaction. Despite the fact that worker empathy and client satisfaction really are correlated, too much of this type of random measurement error may result in concluding that the relationship between the variables does not exist.

Fortunately, researchers can combat random error with a variety of strategies. One is to increase sample size. Instead of using five workers and five interviews per worker, the researcher might use 10 workers and 10 interviews per worker, for a total sample of 100. A second strategy is to increase the "dose" or contrast between levels of the independent variable. For example, researchers might select workers for the study according to their empathy skills to assure some cases with low expression of empathy and some with high expression. Finally, the researcher might increase the number of items on the measurement scales or in other ways more precisely refine the tools. Although such strategies can reduce the impact of random error, the same is not true for systematic error.

Systematic Errors

Systematic error is consistent and patterned. Unlike random errors, systematic errors may not cancel themselves out. If there is a consistent over- or understatement of the value of a given variable, then the errors will accumulate. For example, we know that systematic error occurs when measuring crime with official reports of crimes known to the police; the Uniform Crime Reports (UCR) of the Federal Bureau of Investigation count only crimes that are reported to the police. The Department of Justice supplements these statistics with the National Crime Victimization Survey (NCVS), which measures the number of people who claim to be the victims of crime. Comparisons of these two measures consistently reveal a substantial amount of hidden crime: crimes reported by victims but never brought to the attention of the police. For example, NCVS data indicate that approximately 40 percent of all personal and household crimes are not reported to the police (Rennison and Rand 2003). So there is a large systematic error when measuring the amount of crime the way the UCR does because of the underreporting of most crimes (see Research in Practice 8.2 for a more detailed discussion of this issue).

Systematic errors are more troublesome to researchers than random errors because they are more likely to lead to false conclusions. For example, official juvenile delinquency statistics consistently show higher rates of delinquency among children of lower socioeconomic status families. Self-report studies of delinquency involvement suggest, however, that the official data systematically overstate the relationship between delinquency and socioeconomic status (Binder, Geis, and Bruce 1988). How the systematic error in delinquency data could lead to erroneous conclusions as to possible causes of delinquency as well as to inappropriate prevention or treatment strategies is easy to see.

In Research in Practice 5.2, we suggest ways that concerns about measurement—problems of reliability, validity, and error—have direct parallels in practice intervention.

Improving Validity and Reliability

When a measurement device does not achieve acceptable levels of validity and reliability—when much error occurs—researchers often attempt to redesign the device so that it is more valid and reliable.

We will discuss how to develop valid and reliable measuring devices at length in other chapters, where we discuss how to design good measurement tools. However, we mention a few techniques here as a preview of what happens when a measurement device does not yield adequate validity and reliability.

1. *More extensive conceptual development.* Often validity and reliability are compromised because the researcher is not sufficiently clear and precise about the nature of the concepts measured and their possible indicators. Rethinking the concepts often helps in revising the measuring instrument to make it more valid.

2. *Better training of those who will be applying the measuring devices.* This is especially useful when a measuring device is based on someone's subjective assessment of an attitude or state. Researchers show the people applying the device how their judgments can be biased or produce error and how they can guard against it in their assessments.

3. *Interview the subjects of the research about the measurement devices.* Those under study may have some insight into why the verbal reports, observations, or archival reports are not producing accurate measures of their behavior. They may, for example, comment that the wording of questions is ambiguous or that members of their subculture interpret some words differently than the researcher intended.

4. *Higher level of measurement.* This does not guarantee greater validity and reliability, but a higher level of measurement can produce a more reliable measuring device in some cases. So, when the researcher has some options in terms of how to measure a variable, it is worth considering a higher level of measurement.

5. *Use more indicators of a variable.* This also does not guarantee enhanced reliability and validity, but a multiple-item measuring device can in some cases produce a more valid measure than does a measuring device with fewer items.

6. *Conduct an item-by-item assessment of multiple-item measures.* If the measuring device consists of a number of questions or items, perhaps only one or a few items are the problem: They are the in-

ASSESSMENT OF CLIENT FUNCTIONING:

Valid and Reliable Practice Measurement

At the beginning of this chapter, we emphasized the point that practitioners as well as researchers engage in a process of measurement, although for different purposes. We have discussed the evaluation of measurement primarily as it applies to research settings. Yet practitioners also need to concern themselves about such measurement issues to ensure that instruments used in practice are valid and reliable. D. L. Rosenhan (1973) brought this problem dramatically to light in a now well-known study.

Rosenhan was concerned with the ability of mental health practitioners to diagnose, or measure accurately, the presence of various mental disorders in people. To evaluate these abilities, he and a few other people attempted to gain admission to mental hospitals as patients. All these people, whom Rosenhan called "pseudopatients," had taken a variety of psychological tests that judged them to have no serious mental disorders. Yet every pseudopatient gained entrance to the hospital he or she approached—and with surprising ease! All were diagnosed as schizophrenic based on their intake interview, in which they claimed they heard voices saying things like "thud" and "hollow." All were later released as "schizophrenia in remission."

It seems clear that the assessment tools these mental health practitioners used were not completely valid measures of psychological disorder. (The diagnostic tool used here was the *Diagnostic and Statistical Manual,* or DSM, of the American Psychiatric Association.) It is possible, of course, that the psychological tests Rosenhan administered to the pseudopatients were invalid, and the pseudopatients (including Rosenhan) were, in fact, schizophrenic. Yet we know from a host of research studies that the reliability of psychiatric diagnoses are variable (Kirk and Kutchins 1992; Teitelbaum and Mullen 2000; Wood, Lilienfeld, and Garb 2000). In some cases, diagnoses vary little from one practitioner to another, whereas in other settings there is great variation. The reliability of psychiatric diagnoses is affected by the nature of the disorder, the characteristics of the patient, the skill of the practitioner, the circumstances that surround the assessments, and the kinds of efforts that are made to reach agreement. This fluctuation in reliability certainly suggests that the assessments practitioners made at the hospitals were unreliable and probably invalid as well.

The point is that measurement issues should concern practitioners as much as they do researchers. Problems of validity, reliability, and error can result in ineffective and possibly harmful practice intervention. By observing how researchers deal with such problems, practitioners can learn systematic ways of evaluating measurement instruments.

In addition, researchers often use measures developed for practice to measure the independent or dependent variable in research. Research on mental illness, for example, sometimes uses the DSM as a measurement tool for assessing the extent and type of mental illness. Corcoran and Fischer (1987) describe a host of practice measures useful in research. They also assess what reliability and validity information exists about each measure.

---

valid ones that are reducing the validity and reliability of the instrument. Deleting them may improve validity and reliability.

After revising a measuring device based on these ideas, researchers must, of course, subject the revised version to tests of validity and reliability.

Choosing a Measurement Device

We have seen that we can use a number of indicators, sometimes a large number and at different levels of measurement, to measure a variable. How do we choose the best of these measures to use in a particular study? If we are developing a new measuring device, how do we decide whether it is good or not? It is a complicated and sometimes difficult decision for researchers, but a number of factors, discussed in this or earlier chapters, can serve as guidelines in making this decision:

1. Choose indicators that measure the variables in ways that are theoretically important in the research, as discussed in Chapter 2.

2. Choose indicators based on their proven validity and reliability.

3. If two measuring instruments are equivalent in all other ways except for level of measurement, then choose the indicator at the higher level of measurement.

4. Choose indicators that produce the least amount of systematic and random error.

5. Choose indicators with matters of feasibility, as discussed in Chapter 4, in mind.

COMPUTERS IN RESEARCH

Computerized Data Collection: Enhancing Researcher–Practitioner Collaboration

Both practitioners and researchers need data, and both want better ways to ameliorate the social problems that impact people's lives. The practitioner assesses the problems facing each client, as well as the strengths and coping skills for dealing with those problems. In addition to gathering data for the intervention process, the practitioner also needs to satisfy agency and monitoring organization demands for documentation of progress and intervention outcome. The motivation for research is often to find solutions to social problems by collecting data on the causes of those problems, the characteristics of those afflicted, and the features of interventions that bring about change. In spite of this common need for information, a widely recognized gap exists between research and practice (Clark 2002). Practitioners may see participating in research as an interference with practice and complain that the results of research are not helpful to guiding practice. Conversely, researchers may complain that practitioners are uncooperative and fail to provide the structured, controlled data collection valued for research.

The field of substance abuse provides an exciting example of a collaboration between addiction treatment practitioners and researchers, a collaboration that helped to bridge that gap through the design and implementation of a computer-assisted method of data collection (Carise, Cornely, and Gurel 2002). The project involved the Treatment Research Institute, an organization specializing in substance-abuse treatment research, and a treatment provider, Fresh Start, which operates recovery houses. The implementation of a computerized data collection system known as the Drug Evaluation Network System (DENS) proved both valuable to practitioners in delivering services and an excellent source of data for research.

DENS features the Addiction Severity Index (ASI), a well-accepted instrument for measurement, as its primary data source. The ASI has been a popular assessment tool in substance abuse for over two decades. Designed as a semistructured, 200-item interview, the index addresses seven potential problem areas in substance-abusing patients: medical status, employment and support, drug use, alcohol use, legal status, family/social status, and psychiatric status (McLellan et al. 1992) In its original paper-and-pencil format, a skilled interviewer requires about an hour to gather information on recent (past 30 days) and lifetime problems in all of the problem areas. Practitioners have used the ASI with psychiatrically ill, homeless, pregnant, and prisoner populations, but mostly with adults seeking treatment for substance abuse problems.

Because treatment personnel use the ASI as an intake or assessment instrument, incorporating it into the DENS software system makes DENS potentially useful to the treatment staff. The ASI is also widely used in clinical and health service research projects, so the DENS is of value to researchers who need scientifically valid information. Research cooperation in adopting the DENS program is especially attractive to the practitioner for two reasons. First, the computer form can be completed in less time than the paper-and-pencil version of the ASI and with fewer errors, thanks to an automatic error-checking feature. Second, the software generates an admissions narrative report for clinical staff that serves as the basis for mandatory third-party reports to state regulatory agencies and insurance providers. The software also provides program administrators with aggregate comparison reports of their patients on all intake variables. In short, the DENS helps the practitioner cope with that most dreaded feature of the job—paperwork. In the long term, research results should prove helpful to guiding practice, but the real selling point for the practitioner is this immediate timesaving benefit.

For the researcher's purposes, treatment program staff collect ASI data, which is then transferred electronically to the Treatment Research Institute's computer server so that the researchers have immediate access to the data. In addition, it is possible to add new questions to the data collection instrument so that the researchers can follow emerging trends as they happen. At the time of reporting on the project, 72 treatment programs in five major cities were participating in the program.

A major factor in the success of this collaborative effort between researchers and practitioners was the fact that both parties clearly stood to benefit. Besides greater efficiency and reduced paperwork, the collaboration helped practitioners modify service delivery of the program to meet client needs. For example, when the data showed a high percentage of female clients reporting a history of sexual abuse, Fresh Start added a female staff member to provide group sessions aimed at the needs of women survivors of sexual abuse. Such benefits for practice motivated the clinicians to provide the best quality data that the researchers required for valid, reliable measurement.

Main Points

- Measurement is the process of describing abstract concepts in terms of specific indicators by assigning numbers or other symbols to them.
- An indicator is an observation that we assume to be evidence of the attributes or properties of some phenomenon. Social research measures most variables through either verbal reports, observation, or archival records. Positivists and nonpositivists disagree about the nature of measurement.
- The four levels of measurement are nominal, ordinal, interval, and ratio.
- The nature of the variable itself and the way it is measured determines the level of measurement achieved with a given variable.
- Discrete variables have a limited number of distinct and separate values. Continuous variables theoretically have an infinite number of possible values.

- Validity refers to a measure's ability to measure accurately the variable i measures.
- Face validity, content or sampling validity, jury opinion, criterion validity, and construct validity are techniques of assessing the validity of measures.
- Reliability refers to a measure's ability to yield consistent results each time it is applied.
- Test–retest, multiple forms, and internal consistency (such as split-half) are techniques for assessing the reliability of measures.
- Measurement in social research must be culturally sensitive; researchers should never assume that a measurement instrument that is valid and reliable for a majority group will be so for minorities.
- Random errors are neither consistent nor patterned and can reduce the precision with which variables are measured.
- Systematic errors are consistent and patterned and, unless noted, can potentially lead to erroneous conclusions.

■ Researchers can take a number of steps to improve the validity and reliability of measurement devices.
■ Measurement devices are chosen on the basis of theoretical considerations, their validity and reliability, their level of measurement, the amount of systematic and random errors, and feasibility.

Important Terms for Review

concurrent validity
construct validity
content validity
continuous variables
criterion validity
discrete variables
face validity
index
indicator
interval measures
item
jury opinion
level of measurement
measurement
multitrait–multimethod approach
nominal measures
ordinal measures
predictive validity
random errors
ratio measures
reliability
sampling validity
scale
systematic error
validity

Exploring InfoTrac® College Edition and the Internet

InfoTrac® College Edition search terms:

measurement AND concept*
measurement AND social research
measuring _____ (insert concept of interest, e.g. "violence," "self concept," etc.)

InfoTrac® College Edition articles:

Intimate Partner Violence Against Immigrant Women: Measuring the Effectiveness of Protection Orders. Judith McFarlane, Ann Malecha, Julia Gist, Kathy Watson, Elizabeth Batten, Iva Hall, Sheila Smith. *American Journal of Family Law* Winter 2002 v16 i4 p244(9) (4,686 words)

The Development of a Measure of Prosocial Behaviors for Late Adolescents. (Statistical Data Included) Gustavo Carlo, Brandy A. Randall. *Journal of Youth and Adolescence* Feb 2002 v31 i1 p31(14) (9,682 words)

United States Poverty Studies and Poverty Measurement: The Past Twenty-Five Years. Howard Glennerster. *Social Service Review* March 2002 v76 i1 p83 (26) (11,728 words)

Many Web sites can help you find existing measurement tools, such as scales and indexes. An excellent example is the Web site of the Buros Institute of Mental Measurements. The institute monitors the quality of commercially published tests and encourages improved test development by providing critical analysis of individual instruments. Buros publishes the Mental Measurements Yearbook, and its Web site (www.unl.edu/buros/index.html) lists thousands of instruments and provides access to critical reviews of the various scales.

Another site worth visiting is the WALMYR Publishing Co. home page (www.walmyr.com). This site includes information on specific scales and measurement tools. We suggest that you review the list of scales and examine the samples.

Another approach to finding Internet resources on measurement is to use a search engine and search for such terms as "measurement group" or "social work measurement." The former term produced the Web site of The Measurement Group, which is a private consulting firm that focuses on evaluation research and policy development, primarily in the health area. At this Web site, you will find much information about measurement with standardized tests and instruments, as well as links to numerous other Web sites, journals, and professional associations relevant to measurement issues. You can also search for such terms as "measurement error," "validity," "reliability," and so on. Many of these Web sites are not specifically related to the social sciences, but you will see that many of the measurement issues are the same in any field that uses a scientific approach. You should use this opportunity to identify the commonalities across scientific disciplines.

One specific area that you might find valuable to search through is psychometrics, which is the study of personality and mental states and attributes, often used for diagnostic and clinical (rather than research) purposes. However, psychometrics is a highly quantitative field and thus is a good area in which to explore measurement issues. You might try the home page of the American Psychological Association (www.apa.org) by using its search feature or clicking on the Quick Links button "Testing and Assessment."

For Further Reading

Blythe, Betty J., and Tony Tripodi. *Measurement in Direct Practice.* Newbury Park, Calif.: Sage, 1989. This book looks at measurement issues from the standpoint of day-to-day efforts to apply successful interventions to help clients. It should be particularly useful for those who are currently in or those planning to enter direct practice.

Campbell, Donald T. and M. Jean Russo. *Social Measurement.* Thousand Oaks, Calif.: Sage, 2001. This book provides a user-friendly presentation of Campbell's essential work in social measurement. The book includes his arguments as to why qualitative approaches belong with quantitative ones, as well as his debate with deconstructionists and social constructionists on measurement validity.

Geismar, Ludwig L., and Michael Camasso. *The Family Functioning Scale: A Guide to Research and Practice.* New York: Springer, 1993. This book provides an excellent illustration of measurement in both research and practice as it explores development of a family functioning scale for use in both realms. It is a good example of both the parallels and linkages between research and practice.

Hersen, Michel, editor-in-chief. *Comprehensive Handbook of Psychological Assessment,* Volumes 1-4. New York: Wiley, 2003. These volumes provide essential information on developing and using the major types of psychological assessment instruments. These assessment instruments address the same kinds of measurement issues as do instruments used in research.

Hindelang, Michael J., Travis Hirschi, and Joseph G. Weis. *Measuring Delinquency.* Beverly Hills, Calif.: Sage, 1980. A good description of the development of a measuring device related to a human service issue. The volume covers all the issues related to problems of measurement.

Kirk, Jerome, and Marc L. Miller. *Reliability and Validity in Qualitative Research.* Beverly Hills, Calif.: Sage, 1986. This work presents the measurement issues of reliability and validity as they apply to qualitative research, such as field research (see Chapter 9). Unfortunately, reliability and validity are often only presented in the context of quantitative research.

Martin, Lawrence L., and Peter M. Kettner. *Measuring the Performance of Human Service Programs.* Thousand Oaks, Calif.: Sage, 1996. This short book explains in detail how to measure and assess human service programs, especially with outcome measures. It includes such measures as levels of functioning scales and client satisfaction.

Miller, Delbert C., and Neil J. Salkind. *Handbook of Research Design and Social Measurement,* 6th ed. Thousand Oaks, Calif.: Sage, 2002. A good resource work for scales and indexes focusing on specific human service concerns.

Exercises for Class Discussion

5.1 Here is an interesting way to illustrate measurement issues. Imagine that a new student at your college is blind. He is trying to become independent of others and asks some students to help him measure the distance to such places as the nearest drinking fountain, the restroom, and the student lounge. Select a destination at least 50 feet from the classroom and preferably around a corner or two. Have four or five students independently count the number of steps to the destination and write their count on the board. Compare the counts. How does this exercise illustrate the definition of measurement presented in this chapter? Given the responses of the volunteers, would the blind student be able to find the destination? Was this a valid and reliable measurement procedure?

5.2 What modifications could you make in the rules of measurement presented in Exercise 5.1

that would improve the validity and reliability of the measure?

5.3 The following list contains variables that researchers and practitioners in the human services commonly encounter:

race
income
health
drug use
school achievement
number of arrests
depression
marital satisfaction
employment status
assertiveness
parenting skill
client satisfaction

How could each variable be measured? Which level of measurement is applicable to each of these variables? Which of these variables are discrete and which are continuous? Which of these variables could be measured at more than one level of measurement? Which level is best?

5.4 Understanding levels of measurement can be challenging, and it helps to examine some actual variables in research. The Computers in Research insert describes the Addiction Severity Index. This assessment tool is considered public domain and is readily available in printed form or can be accessed on the Internet by using a search engine. The class can divide up the instrument, examine the various items in the ASI, and classify the variables as nominal, ordinal, interval, or ratio.

5.5 Working independently or in teams of two or three students, locate in your library some studies that have used one of the variables from the list in Exercise 5.3. Describe how the variable was operationalized in each study. Do you see any weaknesses in using this operational definition given the nominal definition of the variable? What problems might there be in obtaining valid and reliable measures of these variables based on the studies that you have reviewed?

Chapter 6

Sampling

number of correctional systems have established programs that use behavior-modification techniques to shape inmate behavior by rewarding sought-after behavior and withholding privileges from those who are recalcitrant or hostile. Each inmate placed in such a program becomes, in a sense, a test of the hypotheses about behavior change derived from behavioral theory. What can we conclude, however, if one inmate's behavior changes in a way that supports these hypotheses? Will the program work with other inmates?

This is the issue at the core of this chapter. Can knowledge gained from one or a few cases be considered knowledge about a whole group of people? The answer to this question depends on whether the inmate is *representative* of some larger group of which the inmate is a "sample." Does he or she represent all inmates? Only inmates in a particular prison? Just inmates who have committed certain offenses? Or is this inmate not representative of any larger group? These issues are at the center of the problem of *sampling,* or selecting a few cases out of some larger grouping for study. All of us have had experience with sampling. Cautiously tasting a spoonful of soup is a process of sampling to see how hot it is; taking a bite of a new brand of pizza is sampling to see if we like it. All sampling involves attempting to make a judgment about a whole something—a bowl of soup, a brand of pizza, an inmate population—based on an analysis of a part of the whole. Scientific sampling, however, is considerably more careful and systematic than casual, everyday sampling. In this chapter, we discuss the fundamentals of sampling along with the benefits and disadvantages of various sampling techniques.

The Purpose of Sampling

When we first encounter the subject of sampling, a common question is this: Why bother? Why not just study the whole group? A major reason for studying samples rather than whole groups is that the whole group is sometimes so large that studying it is not feasible. For example, human service workers might want to learn about welfare recipients, the mentally ill, prison inmates, or some other large group of people. It would be difficult—often impossible—to study all members of these groups. Sampling allows us to study a workable number of cases from the large group to derive findings that are relevant for all members of the group.

A second reason for sampling is that, surprising as it may seem, we can get better information from carefully drawn samples than from an entire group. This is especially true when the group under study is extremely large. For example, the United States takes a census of all residents at the beginning of each decade. Despite the vast resources the federal government puts into the census, substantial undercounts and other errors occur. In fact, after recent censuses, numerous cities filed lawsuits complaining of alleged undercounts. Between the decennial censuses, the Census Bureau conducts *sample* surveys to update population statistics and collect data on other matters. The quality of the data gathered in these sample surveys is actually superior to that of the census itself. The reason is that, with only a few thousand people to contact the task is more manageable, involving better-trained interviewers, greater control over the interviewers, and fewer hard-to-find respondents. In fact, the Census Bureau even conducts a sample survey after each census as a check on the accuracy of that census. Indeed, were it not a constitutional requirement, the complete census might well be dropped and replaced by sample surveys.

Much research, then, is based on samples of people. Samples make possible a glimpse at the behavior and attitudes of whole groups of people, and the validity and accuracy of research results depend heavily on how samples are drawn. An improperly drawn sample renders the collected data virtually useless. So an important consideration regarding samples is how *representative* they are of the population from which we draw them. A **representative sample** is one that accurately reflects the distribution of relevant variables in the target population. In a sense, the sample should be considered a small reproduction of the population. Imagine, for example, that a researcher wants to study the success of unmarried teenage mothers in raising their children, with the goal of improving the provision of services to these adolescents.

The research sample should reflect the relevant characteristics of unmarried teenage mothers in the community. Such characteristics might include age, years of education, and socioeconomic status. To be representative, the sample would have to contain the same proportion of unmarried teenage mothers at each age level, educational level, and socioeconomic status that exists in the community. In short, a representative sample should have all the same characteristics as the population. The representative character of samples allows the conclusions based on them to be legitimately generalized to the populations from which they are drawn. As we will see later in this chapter, nonrepresentative samples are useful for some research purposes, but researchers must always assess the representativeness of their samples to make accurate conclusions. Before comparing the various techniques for drawing samples, we will define some of the major terms used in the field of sampling.

Sampling Terminology
Populations and Samples

A sample is drawn from a **population,** which refers to all possible cases of what we are interested in studying. In the human services, the target population is often people who have some particular characteristic in common, such as all Americans, all eligible voters, all school-age children, and so on. A population need not, however, be composed of people. Recall from Chapter 4 that the unit of analysis can be something other than individuals, such as groups or programs. Then the target population is all possible cases of whatever our unit of analysis is. A **sample** consists of one or more elements selected from a population. The manner in which we select elements for the sample has enormous implications for the scientific utility of the research based on that sample. To select a good sample, we need to clearly define the population from which to draw the sample. Failure to do so can make generalizing from the sample observations highly ambiguous and result in inaccurate conclusions.

The definition of a population should specify four things: content, units, extent, and time (Kish

1965, p. 7). Consider the sample James Greenley and Richard Schoenherr (1981) used to study the effects of agency characteristics on the delivery of social services. First, the *content* of the population refers to the particular characteristic that the members of the population have in common. For Greenley and Schoenherr, the characteristic that was common to the members of their population was that they were health or social service agencies. Second, the *unit* indicates the unit of analysis, which in our illustration is organizations rather than individuals or groups. Although Greenley and Schoenherr collected data from practitioners and clients in the organizations, their focus was on comparing the performance of agencies. Third, the *extent* of the population refers to its spatial or geographic coverage. For practical reasons, Greenley and Schoenherr limited the extent of their population to health and social agencies serving one county in Wisconsin. It was not financially feasible for them to define the extent of their population as all agencies in Wisconsin or in the United States. Finally, the *time* factor refers to the temporal period during which a unit must possess the appropriate characteristic to qualify for the sample. Greenley and Schoenherr conducted a cross-sectional study, and only agencies that were in operation at the time they collected their data qualified. A longitudinal study might include agencies that came into existence during the course of the study.

With these four factors clearly defined, a population normally is adequately delimited, and we can construct what is called a sampling frame.

Sampling Frames

A **sampling frame** is a listing of all the elements in a population. In many studies, we draw the actual sample from this listing. The adequacy of the sampling frame is crucial in determining the quality of the sample, and the degree to which the sampling frame includes *all* members of the population is of major importance. Although an endless number of possible sampling frames exist, a few illustrations will describe some of the intricacies of developing good sampling frames.

In human service research, some of the most adequate sampling frames consist of lists of members of organizations. For example, if we wanted to expand the study mentioned at the beginning of this chapter of the impact of behavior modification on inmates, we could draw a larger sample of inmates in that prison using a straightforward sampling frame, consisting of all inmates currently listed as residents of that institution. Given the care with which correctional facilities maintain accurate records of inmates, the sampling frame would undoubtedly be complete and accurate. Other examples of sampling frames based on organizational affiliation would be the membership rosters of professional groups, such as the National Association of Social Workers (NASW), the American Psychological Association, or the American Society of Criminology. These lists are not quite as accurate as an inmate roster because people who had very recently joined the organization might not appear on the official lists; also, clerical errors might lead to a few missing names. These errors, however, would have little effect on the adequacy of the sampling frame.

When using organizational lists as a sampling frame, we must exercise caution about what we define as the population and about whom we make generalizations. The population consists of the sampling frame, and we can make legitimate generalizations only about the sampling frame. Many social workers, for example, do not belong to the NASW. Thus, a sample taken from the NASW membership roster represents only NASW members and not all social workers. When using organizational lists as sampling frames, then, it is important to assess carefully who the list includes and who it excludes. Sometimes research focuses on a theoretical concept that is operationalized in terms of an organizational list that does not include all actual instances of what the concept intends. For example, a study of poverty could operationalize the concept "poor" as those receiving some form of public assistance. Yet many people with little or no income do not receive public assistance. In this case, the sampling frame would not completely reflect the population the theoretical concept intended.

Some research focuses on populations that are quite large, such as residents of a city or state. This is particularly true of needs assessment research and often of evaluation research. We commonly use three types of listings to develop sampling frames for these populations: telephone numbers, utility subscribers, and city directories (Lavrakas 1987). Telephone books provide a listing of telephone numbers in an area, but they have a number of problems as sampling frames. Even today some people do not have telephone service, and many others have unlisted numbers. The number of households that lack telephone service has diminished over the past few decades. As recently as 1970, 13 percent of American households were without telephone service; today, 6 percent lack such service (U.S. Census Bureau 2002). Those without telephones, however, are concentrated among the poor, those living in rural areas, and transient groups, such as the young. So for a research project in which these groups are important, sampling based on telephone books could be unrepresentative. As for unlisted numbers, the extent varies from one locale to another and by as much as 50 percent in some areas. Because of these problems, we typically do not use telephone book listings (at least by themselves) for drawing samples. Instead, we turn to other techniques, such as *random-digit dialing* (or RDD), to ensure that every household with telephone service has an equal chance of appearing in the sample. With RDD, we select telephone numbers for the sample from a table of random numbers or a computer-generated random numbers list (see Appendix B). If the researcher knows the telephone prefixes of the areas to be sampled, then only the last four numbers need be randomly chosen. By randomly determining phone numbers, RDD gives all telephone numbers an equal chance of selection, regardless of whether they appear in the directory, and therefore removes the problem of unlisted numbers. RDD, of course, does nothing about noncoverage due to the lack of telephone service in some households.

Another population listing we use for sampling is a list of customers from the local electric utility. Although some households do not have telephone service, relatively few households lack electricity, and the problem of noncoverage, therefore, is less significant. Utility listings do, however, have their own problems that we must handle in order to draw a satisfactory sample. The major problem comes from multiple-family dwellings, which often list utilities only in the name of the building's owner rather than all the individual residents. The young, the old, and the unmarried are more likely to inhabit multiple-family dwellings. Unless we supplement the utility listings, samples will systematically underrepresent people in these groups. Visiting the dwellings and adding the residents to the list of utility subscribers can overcome this problem, but this is a time-consuming task. Beyond the problem of multiple dwellings, the old, the poor, and those living in rural areas are more likely to be without utilities and thus may not appear in such a sampling frame.

As a source of population listings, city directories are quite useful. Available in most libraries, city directories are generally divided into four sections. The first is a listing of commercial firms, analogous to the yellow pages of a phone book. The second section is an alphabetical listing of residents, with their addresses, phone numbers, and the head of household's occupation. This section of the directory is useful if the research problem calls for a sample of people or households with particular occupational characteristics. Next comes an alphabetical listing of streets and addresses with residents' names. For sampling purposes, this is often the most useful section of the directory. The other sections can become outdated, but the address listing excludes only new construction. The last section is a listing of telephone numbers in numerical order, together with the name of the person to whom the number is assigned. The accuracy of city directories is quite high, certainly as good a sampling frame as a researcher could compile starting from scratch (Sudman 1976). In addition, city directories are the least likely to exclude people with low incomes.

A Classic Sampling Disaster

Some disastrous mistakes have occurred in sampling in past investigations, often because of inadequate sampling frames. These mistakes result in special chagrin when the investigator makes some precise—and easily refutable—predictions based on the sample. A classic example of this was the attempt *Literary Digest* magazine made to predict the outcome of the 1936 presidential race between Alfred Landon and Franklin Roosevelt. In election predicting, the target population is all likely voters. The *Literary Digest,* however, did not utilize a sampling frame that listed all likely voters. Rather, they drew their sample from lists of automobile owners and from telephone directories. On the basis of their sample results, they predicted Landon would win by a substantial margin. But of course Roosevelt won the election easily. Why the error in prediction? This question continues to generate debate in the professional literature, but the evidence points to two possible factors, each serious in itself but deadly in combination (Bryson 1976; Cahalan 1989; Squire 1988). The first problem was a flawed sampling frame. In 1936, with the Great Depression at its peak, a substantial proportion of eligible voters, especially poorer ones, did not own cars or have telephones. In short, the sample was drawn from an inadequate sampling frame and did not represent the target population. Because the poor are more likely to vote Democratic, most of the eligible voters excluded from the sampling frame voted for the Democratic candidate, Roosevelt. The second problem in the *Literary Digest* poll was a poor response rate. Although employing a massive sample size, the pollsters used a mailed survey, and the percentage of respondents who returned the surveys was very low, about 23 percent. An independent follow-up investigation in a city where half the voters voted for Roosevelt and half for Landon found that only 15 percent of the Roosevelt supporters returned their surveys, whereas 33 percent of the Landon supporters did (Cahalan 1989). So if a bias existed in the sampling frame against Roosevelt supporters, the nonresponse bias compounded it: Landon supporters were much more likely to return their surveys to the *Literary Digest.* The result was the magazine's embarrassingly inaccurate prediction. Although the *Literary Digest* was a popular and respected magazine before the election, it never recovered from its prediction and went out of business a short time later.

We can construct adequate sampling frames for many human service projects from existing listings (such as those already mentioned) already available or readily made. Still, we must exercise caution in using such lists because they may inadvertently exclude some people. In fact, human service research is especially vulnerable to this because we often study populations that are difficult to enumerate. For example, undocumented aliens are by definition not listed anywhere. We know they comprise a large segment of the population in such urban centers as Los Angeles, but a study of the poor in these areas that relied on a city directory would obviously miss large numbers of such people. Early studies of gay men also fell prey to this problem (Bell and Weinberg 1978; Hooker 1957). In some of these studies, the sampling frame was homosexuals who were listed as patients by psychotherapists who participated in the research. The studies concluded that homosexuality was associated with personality disturbance. Yet it does not take great insight to recognize that the sampling frames did not list many gay men—those feeling no need to see therapists—and were thus strongly biased toward finding personality disorders among gays.

We must assess sampling frames carefully to ensure that they include all elements of the population of interest. The remainder of this chapter is a discussion of the different ways in which to select samples. First, we discuss probability samples, for which we are most likely to have a sampling frame from which to draw the sample. Researchers use probability samples in some types of human service research, such as needs assessment and evaluation research. Then we discuss nonprobability samples, which researchers use in assessing client functioning and evaluating the effectiveness of intervention strategies.

Probability Samples

With luck, almost any sampling procedure could produce a representative sample. But that is little comfort to the researcher who wants to be as certain as possible that his or her sample is representative. Techniques that make use of probability theory can both greatly reduce the chances of getting a nonrepresentative sample and, more important, permit the researcher to estimate precisely the likelihood that a sample differs from the true population by a given amount. In these samples, known as **probability samples,** each element in the population has some chance of inclusion in the sample, and the investigator can determine the chances or probability of each element's inclusion (Scheaffer, Mendenhall, and Ott 1996). In their simpler versions, probability-sampling techniques ensure that each element has an *equal* chance of inclusion. In more elaborate versions, the researcher takes advantage of knowledge about the population to select elements with differing probabilities. The key point is that, whether the probabilities are equal or different, each element's probability of inclusion in a probability sample is nonzero and known. Furthermore, probability sampling enables us to calculate **sampling error,** which is an estimate of the extent to which the values of the sample differ from those of the population from which it was drawn.

Simple Random Sampling

The simplest technique for drawing probability samples is **simple random sampling** (SRS), in which each element in the population has an equal probability of inclusion in the sample. Simple random sampling treats the target population as a unitary whole. We might begin with a sampling frame containing a list of the entire population or as complete a list as we can obtain. We would then number the elements in the sampling frame sequentially and select elements from the list using a procedure known to be random. If we computerized the sampling frame, we could accomplish random selection merely by programming the computer to select randomly a sample of whatever size we desired. (Appendix B describes how to generate random samples both with the computer and by hand, using a table of random numbers.)

Although simple random samples have the desirable feature of giving each element in the sampling frame an equal chance of appearing in the sample, SRS is often impractical. A major reason for this is cost. Imagine doing a research project that calls for a national sample of 2,000 households. Even if one could obtain such a sample using SRS, which is unlikely, it would be prohibitively expensive to send interviewers all over the country to obtain the data. Furthermore, alternatives to SRS might prove more efficient in terms of providing a high degree of representativeness with a smaller sample. Simple random sampling is normally limited to fairly small-scale projects that deal with populations of modest size for which we can obtain adequate sampling frames. The importance of SRS lies not in its wide application. Rather, SRS is the basic sampling procedure on which statistical theory is based, and it is the standard against which other sampling procedures are measured.

Systematic Sampling

A variation on SRS is called **systematic sampling,** which involves taking every *k*th element listed in a sampling frame. Systematic sampling uses the table of random numbers to determine a random starting point in the sampling frame. From that random start, we select every *k*th element into the sample. The value of *k* is called the *sampling interval,* and it is determined by dividing the population size by the desired sample size. For example, if we wanted a sample of 100 from a population of 1,000, the sampling interval would be 10. From the random starting point, we would select every 10th element from the sampling frame for the sample. If the starting point is in the middle of the list, we proceed to the end, jump to the beginning, and end up at the middle again.

In actual practice, dividing the population by the sample size usually does not produce a whole number, so the decimal is rounded upward to the next largest whole number. This provides a sampling interval that takes us completely through the sampling frame. If we round downward, the sampling interval becomes slightly too narrow, and we reach the desired sample size before we exhaust the sampling frame, which would mean that those elements farthest from the starting point have no chance of selection.

We commonly use systematic sampling when we draw samples by hand rather than by computer. The only advantage of systematic sampling over SRS is in clerical efficiency. In SRS, the random numbers will select elements scattered throughout the sampling frame. It is time-consuming to search all over the sampling frame to identify the elements that correspond with the random numbers. In systematic sampling, we proceed in an orderly fashion through the sampling frame from the random starting point.

Unfortunately, systematic sampling can produce biased samples, although this is rare. The difficulty occurs when the sampling frame consists of a population list that has a cyclical or recurring pattern, called *periodicity.* If the sampling interval happens to be the same as that of the cycle in the list, it is possible to draw a seriously biased sample. For example, suppose we were sampling households in a large apartment building. The apartments are listed in the sampling frame by floor and apartment number (2A, 2B, 2C, 2D, 2E, 2F, 3A, 3B, and so on). Furthermore, suppose that, on each floor, apartment F is a corner apartment with an extra bedroom and correspondingly higher rent than the other apartments on the floor. If we had a sampling interval of 3 and randomly chose to begin counting with apartment 2D, every F apartment would appear in the sample, which would mean that the sample is biased in favor of the more expensive apartments and thus in favor of the more affluent residents of the apartment building. So when we use systematic sampling techniques, we need to assess the sampling frame carefully for any cyclical pattern that might confound the sample and rearrange the list to eliminate the pattern. Or we could use SRS instead of systematic sampling.

Stratified Sampling

With SRS and systematic sampling methods, we treat the target population as a unitary whole when sampling from it. **Stratified sampling** changes this by dividing the population into smaller subgroups, called *strata,* prior to drawing the sample, and then drawing separate random samples from each of the strata.

Reduction in Sampling Error.   One of the major reasons for using a stratified sample is that stratifying has the effect of reducing sampling error for a given sample size to a level lower than that of an SRS of the same size. This is so because of a very simple principle: The more homogeneous a population on the variables under study, the smaller the sample size needed to represent it accurately. Stratifying makes each subsample more homogeneous by eliminating the variation on the variable used for stratifying. Perhaps a gastronomic example will help illustrate this point. Imagine two large, commercial-size cans of nuts: one labeled "peanuts" and the other labeled "mixed nuts." Because the can of peanuts is highly homogeneous, only a small handful from it gives a fairly accurate indication of the remainder of its contents. The can of mixed nuts, however, is quite heterogeneous, containing several kinds of nuts in different proportions. A small handful of nuts from the top of the can cannot be relied on to represent the contents of the entire can. However, if the mixed nuts were stratified by type of nut into homogeneous piles, a few nuts from each pile could constitute a representative sample of the entire can.

Although stratifying does reduce sampling error, it is important to recognize that the effects are modest. We expect approximately 10 to 20 percent or less reduction in comparison to an SRS of equal size (Henry 1990; Sudman 1976). Essentially, the decision to stratify depends on two issues: the difficulty of stratifying and the cost of each additional element in the sample. It can be difficult to stratify a sample on a particular variable if it is hard to get access to data on that variable. For example, we would find it relatively easy to stratify a sample of university students according to class level because universities typically include class status as part of a database on all registered students. In contrast, we would find it difficult to stratify the same sample on the basis of whether they had been victims of sexual abuse during childhood because these data are not readily available and getting them would require a major study in itself. So stratification requires either that the sampling frame include information on the stratification variable or that the stratification variable is easily determined. Telephone surveys and stratification by gender of respondent illustrate the latter sit-

uation. Telephone interviewers can simply ask to speak to the man of the house to obtain the male stratum and request to speak to the woman of the house for the female stratum. If no one of the desired gender is available, the interviewer drops that household and substitutes another. The process may require some extra phone calls, but the time and cost of doing this can pay for itself in the quality of the sample. As for the effect of cost issues on the decision of whether to stratify, if the cost of obtaining data on each case is high, as in an interview survey, stratifying to minimize sample size is probably warranted. If each case is inexpensive, however, stratifying to reduce cost may not be worth the effort unless it can be easily accomplished.

Proportionate Sampling.   When we use stratification to reduce sampling error, we normally use *proportionate* stratified sampling, in which the size of the sample taken from each stratum is proportionate to the stratum's presence in the population. Consider a sample of the undergraduates at a college or university. Although students differ on many characteristics, an obvious difference is their class standing. Any representative sample of the student body should reflect the relative proportions of the various classes as they exist in the college as a whole. If we drew an SRS, the sample size would have to be quite large for the sample to reflect accurately the distribution of class levels. Small samples would have a greater likelihood of being disproportionate. If we stratify on class level, however, we can easily make the sample match the actual class distribution, regardless of sample size. Table 6.1 contains the hypothetical class distribution of a university student body. If a researcher wanted a sample of 200 students with these proportions of students accurately represented, stratifying could easily accomplish it. He or she would begin by developing a sampling frame with the students grouped according to class level. The researcher would then draw separate SRSs from each of the four class strata in numbers proportionate to their presence in the population: 70 freshmen, 50 sophomores, 40 juniors, and 40 seniors.

In actual practice, it is normal to stratify on more than one variable. In the case of a student popula-

Table 6.1 Hypothetical Proportionate Stratified Sample of University Students

Proportion in University		Stratified Sample of 200	
Seniors	20%	Seniors	40
Juniors	20%	Juniors	40
Sophomores	25%	Sophomores	50
Freshmen	35%	Freshmen	70
	100%		200

tion, the researcher might want to stratify on sex as well as class level. That would double the number of separate subsamples from four to eight: senior men, senior women, junior men, and so on. Even though stratifying on appropriate variables always improves a sample, researchers should use stratification judiciously. Stratifying on a few variables provides nearly as much benefit as stratifying on many. Because the number of subsamples increases geometrically as the number of stratified variables and their number of categories increase, attempting to stratify on too many variables can excessively complicate sampling without offering substantially increased benefits in terms of reduction in sampling error.

Disproportionate Sampling. In addition to reducing error, we use stratified samples to enable comparisons among various subgroups in the population when one or more of the subgroups is relatively uncommon. For example, suppose we were interested in comparing two-parent families receiving welfare with other welfare families. If two-parent families comprise only about 2 percent of families on the welfare rolls, a large SRS of 500 welfare families would be expected to contain only 10 such families. This number is far too small to make meaningful statistical comparisons. Stratifying in this case allows us to draw a larger sample of two-parent families to provide enough cases for reliable comparisons to be made. This is called *disproportionate* stratified sampling because we do not sample the strata proportionately to their presence in the popu-

lation. This type of sample is different from most probability samples where we achieve representativeness by giving every element in the population an equal chance of appearing in the sample. With a disproportionate stratified sample, each element of a stratum has an equal chance of appearing in the sample of that stratum, but the elements in some strata have a better chance of appearing in the overall sample than do the elements of other strata.

Selection of variables on which to stratify depends on the reason for stratifying. If we were stratifying to ensure sufficient numbers of cases for analysis in all groups of interest, as in the example of two-parent welfare families, then we would stratify on the variable that has a category with a small proportion of cases in it. This is often an independent variable and involves disproportionate stratified sampling. On the other hand, if the goal of stratifying is to reduce sampling error, as is the case in proportionate stratified sampling, then we might use variables other than the independent variable. Stratifying has an effect in reducing sampling error only when the stratification variables relate to the dependent variables under study. So we should select variables that we know or suspect of having an impact on the dependent variables. For example, a study of the impact of religiosity on delinquency might stratify on socioeconomic status because studies have shown that this variable is related to delinquency involvement. Stratifying on a frivolous variable, such as eye color, would gain us nothing, for it is unlikely to relate to delinquency involvement. It is worth noting, however, that stratifying never hurts a sample. The worst that can happen is that the stratified sample will have about the same sampling error as an equivalent-size SRS, and stratifying efforts will have gone for naught. Research in Practice 6.1 illustrates a fairly complex use of a stratified sample.

Area Sampling

Area sampling (also called **cluster sampling** or **multistage sampling**) is a procedure in which we obtain the final units to include in the sample by first sampling among larger units, called *clusters,* which contain the smaller sampling units. A series

RESEARCH IN PRACTICE 6.1

PROGRAM EVALUATION:

Sampling for Direct Observation of Seat Belt Use

During the 1960s, seat belts were mandated as standard equipment in all passenger cars. Millions of drivers, however, remained unimpressed by the belts and merely sat on them. There was talk of passive restraints and other mechanisms to ensure that people used their seat belts. Eventually, a compromise emerged between the automakers and the federal regulators in the form of an agreement that if a majority of the states passed mandatory seat belt use laws and if the compliance rate was high enough, then the regulators would not require passive restraints in new cars. This created the impetus for states to pass legislation requiring the use of seat belts by drivers and passengers. Do the laws work? Do people wear their seat belts in states that require them? Answering this question through observation required the development of some creative sampling procedures.

One approach might have been to take a random sample of driver's license holders and conduct a survey of seat belt use. Unfortunately, this is precisely the type of question that is likely to evoke a socially desirable response rather than an accurate one. Everyone knows they *should* wear their seat belts, so a survey is likely to produce results indicating substantially higher levels of belt use than is

actually the case. Faced with the undesirability of a survey, researchers at the University of Michigan Transportation Research Institute turned to direct observation of drivers and passengers to accurately determine levels of seat belt use (Wagenaar and Wiviott 1986). But direct observation had its own problems. Early on, researchers determined that to reliably code the desired information about each vehicle, the vehicle had to be stopped at least briefly. This requirement greatly affected both the sampling and observation procedures.

Because the main purpose of the study was to estimate seat belt use rates for the state of Michigan, a representative sample was crucial. Given the requirements for observation, the researchers needed a representative sample of places where vehicles temporarily stopped. They solved their unique sampling problem by selecting a sample of intersections with automatic traffic signals. The signals held the traffic long enough for accurate observations and in places with sufficient traffic to keep the observers efficiently busy. Specifically, using a multi-staged stratified probability sampling procedure, the researchers selected 240 intersections. First, they identified all counties in Michigan with at least three intersections controlled by electronic signals.

of sampling stages are involved, working down from larger clusters to smaller ones.

For example, imagine that we wanted to conduct a needs assessment survey that would determine the extent and distribution of preschool children with educational deficiencies in a large urban area. Simple random and systematic samples are out of the question because no sampling frame listing all such children exists. We could turn to area sampling, a technique that enables us to draw a probability sample without having a complete list of all elements in the population. The ultimate unit of analysis in this needs assessment would be households because children live in households and we can create a sampling

frame of households. We get there in the following way (see Figure 6.1). First, we take a simple random sample from among all census tracts in the urban area. (The Census Bureau divides urban areas into a number of census tracts, which are areas of approximately 4,000 people.) At the second stage, we list all the city blocks in each census tract in our sample and then select a simple random sample from among those city blocks. In the final stage, we list the households on each city block in our sample and select a simple random sample of households on that list. With this procedure, we have an "area probability sample" of households in that urban area. (Public opinion polling agencies, such as Roper, typically

They discovered that 20 of Michigan's 83 counties did not meet this criterion, so those were grouped with adjacent counties to form 63 counties or county groups.

The 63 areas were then grouped into seven regions, which became strata for a stratified sample, with a separate sample drawn from each region. Given the great differences in population density, from high in the southeastern part of the state to very low in the north and northwest, the researchers drew a disproportionate sample to ensure some inclusion of the low population-density areas. This was important, as they hypothesized that population density could relate to seat belt use rates. The counties and county groups in the seven regions constituted the primary sampling units (PSUs). They selected 60 PSUs, resulting in inclusion of 32 of the county and county groups in the sample.

For the next stage, the researchers selected a complete list of all intersections equipped with electronic signals in the selected counties and county groups to serve as a sampling frame. From this sampling frame, they randomly selected the final sample of intersections, for a total of 240 observation sites.

Sampling considerations did not end with the final sample of intersections. Because the goal was to estimate seat belt use at *all times* on Michigan roads, time sampling (discussed in more detail in Chapter 9) also was important. Unfortunately, the researchers could not meet this ambitious goal because they could not make accurate observations during the night. So the researchers restricted observations and conclusions to daylight hours. During the daytime, however, they distributed observations throughout the daylight hours and across all days of the week, expecting the resulting observations of the sample of intersections, days of the week, and times of day to reasonably approximate seat belt use rates for the population of Michigan motorists.

Care to know what the researchers found out? Actually, three observational studies were conducted, one prior to passage of a mandatory seat belt use law, one shortly after such a law was passed, and a third approximately two years after the law went into effect. (This is called a time-series design; we will discuss this type of study in more detail in Chapter 10). Results of the first survey revealed a relatively low level of seat belt use, 19.8 percent. After the law went into effect, use rose to 58.4 percent, clearly indicating that mandatory seat belt laws are effective in encouraging belt use. The last survey showed that the effectiveness of belt laws does wear off to some extent after the publicity dies down, and some people do revert to their old habits. Two years after the law was passed, seat belt use rate was down to 46.6 percent, still more than double the rate prior to the legal mandate.

use area sampling or a variant of it.) Finally, we interview each household in the sample regarding educational deficiencies among children in the household. If we were sampling an entire state or the whole country, we would include even more stages of sampling, starting with even larger areas, but eventually working down to the household or individual level, whichever is our unit of analysis.

A number of factors can complicate area sampling. For example, selected blocks within an area often contain vastly different numbers of people—from high-density inner-city areas to the lower-density suburbs. We must adjust the number of blocks and the number of households per block selected into the sample to take into account the differing population densities. Another complication involves the estimation of sampling error. Fairly straightforward formulas for estimating sampling error exist for the simpler sampling techniques. With area sampling, however, the many stages of sampling involved make error estimation exceedingly complex. It can be done, however, and those interested in the procedures are advised to see Kish (1965) or Scheaffer, Mendenhall, and Ott (1996).

Error estimation is quite important for area samples. They are subject to greater error than other probability samples because some error is introduced at each stage of sampling: the more stages involved,

Figure 6.1 Drawing an Area Probability Sample

Step 1:
Take a random sample of census tracts in an urban area (the shaded tracts are those sampled).

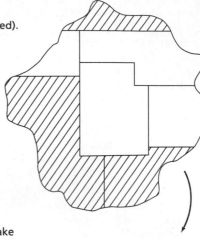

Step 2:
Identify city blocks in each census tract, and take a random sample from a list of those city blocks (the shaded blocks are those sampled).

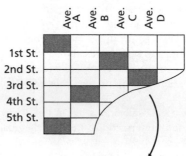

Step 3:
Using a table of random numbers, select a sample of five households from each city block sampled in each census tract sampled (addresses with an asterisk are those sampled).

1. 100 2nd St.*
2. 110 2nd St.
3. 120 2nd St.
4. 130 2nd St.*
5. 140 2nd St.*
6. 401 Ave. D
7. 415 Ave. D
8. 425 Ave. D
9. 435 Ave. D*
10. 201 3rd St.
11. 205 3rd St.
12. 209 3rd St.
13. 213 3rd St.*
14. 217 3rd St.
15. 400 Ave. C
16. 410 Ave. C
17. 420 Ave. C
18. 430 Ave. C

the more the sampling error accumulates. Other factors affecting sampling error are the size of the areas initially selected and their degree of homogeneity. The larger the initial areas and the greater their homogeneity, the greater the sampling error. This may seem odd because, with stratified sampling, greater homogeneity leads to less error. Remember, however, that with stratified sampling, we select a sample from *each stratum*. With area sampling, we draw samples only from *a few areas*. If the few areas in a sample are homogeneous in comparison with the others, they are less representative. Small, more numerous, heterogeneous clusters lead to more representative area samples. Despite the complexity, area sampling allows us to draw highly accurate probability samples from populations that, because of their size or geographical spread, we could not otherwise sample.

Estimating Sample Size

As we have seen, a key issue in selecting a sample is that it *represent* the population from which it was drawn. People sometimes assume that a larger sample is more representative than a smaller one, and thus one should go for the largest sample possible. Actually, deciding on an appropriate sample size is far more complicated than this. Five factors influence the sample size: research hypotheses, level of precision, homogeneity of the population, sampling fraction, and sampling technique.

Research Hypotheses. One concern in establishing desired sample size is that we have a sufficient number of cases to examine our research hypotheses. Consider a hypothetical study in which we have three variables containing three values each. For an adequate test of the hypotheses, we need a cross-tabulation of these three variables, and this would require a $3 \times 3 \times 3$ table, or 27 cells. If our sample were small, many cells would have few or no cases in them, and we could not test the hypotheses. Johann Galtung (1967, p. 60) has suggested that 10 to 20 cases in each cell provides an adequate test of hypotheses. We might use disproportionate stratified sampling here to ensure an adequate number of cases

in each cell. When that is not possible, Galtung suggests the following formula to determine sample size:

$$r^n \times 20 = \text{sample size}$$

where *r* refers to the number of values on each variable and *n* refers to the number of variables. Thus, for our hypothetical study:

$$r^n \times 20 = 3^3 \times 20 = 27 \times 20 = 540$$

So we would need a sample of 540 to feel reasonably assured that we had a sufficient number of cases in each cell. The formula works only if, as in our example, all variables have the same number of values. Furthermore, this technique does not guarantee an adequate number of cases in each cell. If some combination of variables is rare in the population, we may still find few cases in our sample.

Researchers often use statistical procedures in testing hypotheses, and most such procedures require some minimum number of cases to provide accurate results. What is the smallest legitimate sample size? This depends, of course, on the number of variables and the values they can take, but generally 30 cases is considered the bare minimum; some researchers conservatively set 100 as the smallest legitimate sample size (Bailey 1987; Champion 1981). Anything smaller begins to raise questions about whether researchers can properly apply statistical procedures.

Precision. Another factor influencing sample size is the level of precision, or the amount of sampling error, a researcher is willing to accept. Recall that sampling error refers to the difference between a sample value of some variable and the population value of the same variable. Suppose the average age of all teenagers in a city is 15.4 years. If we draw a sample of 200 teenagers and calculate an average age of 15.1 years, then our sample statistic is close to the population value, but there is an error of 0.3 years. Remember, however, that the ultimate reason for collecting data from samples is to draw conclusions regarding the population from which we drew those samples. We have data from a sample, such as the average age of a group of teenagers, but *we do not have those same data for the population as a whole*. If we did, we would not need to study the sample because we already would know what we want to know about the population. If we do not know what the population value is, how can we assess the difference between our sample value and the population value? We do it in terms of the likelihood or probability that our sample value differs by a certain amount from the population value. (Probability theory is discussed in more detail in Chapter 15.) So we establish a confidence interval, or a range in which we are fairly certain the population value lies. If we draw a sample with a mean age of 15.1 years and establish a confidence interval of $\pm$ (plus or minus) 1.2 years, we are fairly certain that the mean age in the population is between 13.9 and 16.3 years of age. Probability theory also enables us to be precise about how certain we are. For example, we might be 95 percent certain, which is called the confidence level. (The computation of confidence levels is beyond the intent of this book.) Technically, this means that if we draw a large number of random samples from our population and compute a mean age for each of those samples, 95 percent of those means would have confidence intervals that include the population mean and 5 percent would not. What is the actual population mean? We don't know because we have not collected data from the whole population. We have data from only one sample, but we can conclude that we are 95 percent sure that the population mean lies within the confidence interval of that sample.

Precision is directly related to sample size: Larger samples are more precise than smaller ones. Thus, probability theory enables us to calculate the sample size required to achieve a given level of precision. Table 6.2 does this for simple random samples taken from populations of various sizes. As an example of how to read the table, a sample size of 1,023 would give you a 95 percent chance to obtain a sampling error of 3 percent or less with a population of 25,000 elements and a relatively heterogeneous population (a 50/50 split identifies a heterogeneous population and an 80/20 split is a homogeneous population). In other words, a 95 percent chance exists that the population value is within 3 percent of (above or below) the sample estimate. Again, to be technical, it means

that if we draw many random samples and determine a confidence interval of 3 percent for each, 95 percent of those confidence intervals will include the population value. The table shows that sample size must increase when, other things being equal, the researcher wants less sampling error (that is, more precision) or the population size is larger or the population is more heterogeneous.

In actuality, of course, we draw only one sample; probability theory tells us the chance we run of a single sample's having a given level of error. There is a chance—5 times out of 100—that the sample will have an error level greater than 3 percent. In fact, there is a chance, albeit a minuscule one, that the sample will have a large error level. This is a part of the nature of sampling: Because we are selecting a segment of a population, there is always a chance that the sample will be unrepresentative of the population. The goal of good sampling techniques is to reduce the likelihood of that error. (Furthermore, one goal of replication in science, as discussed in Chapter 2, is to protect against the possibility that a researcher has unknowingly based the findings of a single study on a sample that contains a large error.)

If the 95 percent confidence level is not satisfactory for our purposes, we can raise the odds to the 99 percent level by increasing the sample size (this is not shown in Table 6.2). In this case, only 1 out of 100 samples is likely to have an error level greater than 3 percent. However, a sample size large enough for this confidence level might be expensive and time-consuming. For this reason, professional pollsters are normally satisfied with a sample size that enables them to achieve an error level in the 2 to 4 percent range. Likewise, most scientific researchers are forced to accept higher levels of error—often as much as 5 to 6 percent with a 95 percent confidence level. At the other end of the spectrum, exploratory studies can provide useful data even though they incorporate considerably more imprecision and sampling error. So the issue of sample size and error is influenced in part by the goals of the research project.

Population Homogeneity. The third factor impacting on sample size is the variability of the sampled population. As we have noted, a large sam-

Table 6.2 Calculating Sample Size Based on Confidence Level, Sampling Error, Population Heterogeneity, and Population Size

| | Sample Size for 95% Confidence Level | | | | | |
| | ±3% Sampling Error | | ±5% Sampling Error | | ±10% Sampling Error | |
Population Size	50/50 Split	80/20 Split	50/50 Split	80/20 Split	50/50 Split	80/20 Split
100	92	87	80	71	49	38
250	203	183	152	124	70	49
500	341	289	217	165	81	55
750	441	358	254	185	85	57
1,000	516	406	278	198	88	58
2,500	748	537	333	224	93	60
5,000	880	601	357	234	94	61
10,000	964	638	370	240	95	61
25,000	1,023	665	378	234	96	61
50,000	1,045	674	381	245	96	61
100,000	1,056	678	383	245	96	61
1,000,000	1,066	682	384	246	96	61
100,000,000	1,067	683	384	246	96	61

How to read this table: For a population with 250 members whom we expect to be about evenly split on the characteristics in which we are interested, we need a sample of 152 to make estimates with a sampling error of no more than ±5%, at the 95% confidence level. A "50/50 split" means the population is relatively varied. An "80/20 split" means it is less varied; most people have a certain characteristic, a few do not. Unless we know the split ahead of time, it is best to be conservative and use 50/50.

Numbers in the table refer to completed, usable questionnaires needed for various levels of sampling error. Starting sample size should allow for ineligibles and nonrespondents. Note that when the population is small, little is gained by sampling, especially if the need for precision is great.

Source From *How to Conduct Your Own Survey* by Priscilla Salant and Don A. Dillman, p. 55. Copyright © 1994 by John Wiley & Sons, Inc. This material is used by permission of John Wiley & Sons, Inc.

ple is more essential for a heterogeneous population than for a homogeneous one. Unfortunately, researchers may know little about the homogeneity of their target population and can make accurate estimates of population variability only *after* they draw the sample and collect and at least partially analyze the data. On the surface, this would appear to preclude estimating sample size in advance. In fact, however, probability theory still allows sample size to be estimated by simply assuming maximum variability in the population. In Table 6.2, the assumption of "50/50 split" means that we assume maximum variability. Such estimates are, of course, conservative: This means that the sample size esti-

mates are larger than needed for a given level of precision if the actual variability in the population is less than assumed.

Sampling Fraction. A fourth factor influencing sample size is the *sampling fraction,* or the number of elements in the sample relative to the number of elements in the population (or n/N, where n = estimated sample size ignoring sampling fraction and N = population size). With large populations, we can ignore the sampling fraction because the sample constitutes only a tiny fraction of the population. In Table 6.2, for example, a population of 10,000 calls for a sample size of only 370 (5 percent sampling error and 50/50 split), which is less than 4 percent of the population. For such samples, the research hypotheses, sampling error, and population homogeneity are sufficient to determine sample size. With smaller populations, however, a sample that meets these criteria may constitute a relatively large fraction of the whole population and, in fact, may be larger than it needs to be (Moser and Kalton 1972). This is so because a sample that constitutes a large fraction of the population contains less sampling error than if the sample were a small fraction. In such cases, the sample size can be adjusted by the following formula:

$$n' = n/[1 + (n/N)]$$

where:

n' = adjusted sample size
n = estimated sample size ignoring the sampling fraction
N = population size

As a rule of thumb, this correction formula should be used if the sampling fraction is more than 5 percent. For example, suppose that a community action agency is conducting a needs assessment survey for a Native American tribal organization with 3,000 tribal members. On the basis of the research hypothesis, sampling error, and population variance on key variables, it is estimated that a sample of 600 is needed. The sampling fraction, then, is $n/N = 600/3,000 = 0.2$, or 20 percent. As this is well over 5 percent, we apply the correction:

$$n' = 600/[1 + (600/3,000)]$$
$$n' = 600/1.20$$
$$n' = 500$$

Thus, instead of a sample of 600, we need only 500 to achieve the same level of precision. At costs that often exceed $50 per interview, the savings of this adjustment often are significant.

Sampling Technique. The final factor influencing sample size is the sampling technique employed. The estimates discussed thus far are for simple random samples. More complex sampling procedures change the estimates of sample size. Area sampling,

for example, tends to increase sampling error in comparison with SRS. We can obtain a rough estimate of sample sizes for area samples by simply increasing the suggested sizes in Table 6.2 by one half (Backstrom and Hursh-Cesar 1981). That estimate is crude and probably conservative, but it is simple to obtain. Stratified sampling, on the other hand, tends to reduce sampling error and decrease required sample size. Estimating sample sizes for stratified samples is relatively complex. Readers interested in this are advised to consult Kish (1965) or Scheaffer, Mendenhall, and Ott (1996).

In an assessment of the implications of scientific work for clinical application, the issue of precision in sampling comes to the fore. Practitioners need to exercise judgment regarding how scientifically sound the research is and whether it is sufficiently valid to introduce into practice. As we have emphasized, practitioners should view single studies with caution, irrespective of how low the sampling error is. As numerous studies begin to accumulate, we must then assess them in terms of how much error we can expect, given the sample size and the sampling technique. If the sampling errors appear to be quite low, then a few replications might confirm that the findings from these samples reflect the state of the actual population. With large sampling errors, however, the probability increases that the samples do not represent the population. In such cases, confidence in the outcomes results only if a number of studies arrive at the same conclusions. More studies mean the drawing of more samples, which in turn reduces the likelihood that *all* the samples contain large sampling errors.

Nonprobability Samples

Probability samples are not required or even appropriate for all studies. Some research situations call for **nonprobability samples,** in which the investigator does not know the probability of each population element's inclusion in the sample. Nonprobability samples have some important uses (O'Connell 2000). First, they are especially useful when the goal of research is to see whether there is a relationship between independent and dependent variables, with no intent to generalize the results beyond the sample to a larger population. This is sometimes the case, for instance, in experimental research where future research in other settings will establish generalizability (see Chapter 10). A second situation where non-probability samples are useful is in some qualitative research where the goal is to understand the social process and meaning structure of a particular setting or group (Maxwell 1996). Often in such qualitative research, the research goal is only to develop an understanding of one particular setting or group of people; issues of generalizing to other settings are either irrelevant or an issue for future research projects. As we will see in Chapters 9 and 16, some qualitative researchers see probability samples as inappropriate for, or at best irrelevant to, theoretically sound qualitative research.

A third situation in which nonprobability samples are useful is when it is impossible to develop a sampling frame of a population. With no complete list of all elements in a population, researchers cannot ensure that every element has a chance to appear in the sample. These populations are sometimes called "hidden populations" because at least some of their elements are hidden and difficult or impossible to locate. In fact, the members of hidden populations sometimes try to hide themselves from detection by researchers and others because they engage in illegal or stigmatized behavior, such as drug use or criminal activity. Rather than giving up on the study of such populations, researchers use nonprobability samples.

Although nonprobability samples can be useful, they do have some important limitations. First, without the use of probability in the selection of elements for the sample, we can make no real claim of representativeness. There is simply no way of knowing precisely what population, if any, a nonprobability sample represents. This question of representativeness greatly limits the ability to generalize findings beyond the level of the sample cases.

A second limitation is that the degree of sampling error remains unknown and unknowable. With no clear population represented by the sample, we have nothing with which to compare it. The lack of

probability in the selection of cases means that the techniques employed for estimating sampling error with probability samples are not appropriate. It also means that the techniques for estimating sample size are not applicable to nonprobability samples. Of the five criteria used in considering sample size among probability samples, the only one that comes into play for nonprobability samples is the first, namely, that researchers select sufficient cases to allow the planned types of data analysis. Even population homogeneity and the sampling fraction do not come into play because the researcher does not know exactly what either the size or the composition of the population is.

A final limitation of nonprobability samples involves statistical tests of significance. These commonly used statistics, which we will discuss in Chapter 15, indicate to the researcher whether relationships found in sample data are sufficiently strong to generalize to the whole population. Some of these statistical tests, however, are based on various laws of probability and assume a random process for selecting sample elements. Because nonprobability samples violate some basic assumptions of these tests, researchers should use them with caution on data derived from such samples.

Availability Sampling

Availability sampling (also called **convenience sampling** or **accidental sampling**) involves the researcher's taking whichever elements are readily available. These samples are especially popular and appropriate for research in which it is difficult or impossible to develop a complete sampling frame. Sometimes it is too costly to do so; in other cases it is impossible to identify all the elements of a population. Helen Mendes (1976), for example, used an availability sample in her study of single fathers. Because it was practically impossible to develop a sampling frame of all single fathers, she turned to teachers, physicians, social workers, and self-help groups for assistance. She asked these people to refer single fathers to her. The limitation on generalizability, however, seriously reduces the utility of findings based on availability samples. It is impossible for

Mendes to argue, for example, that the single fathers she studied were representative of all single fathers. It may well be that only fathers with certain characteristics were likely to become a part of her sample.

Availability samples are often used in experimental or quasi-experimental research. This is because it is often difficult to get a representative sample of people to participate in an experiment—especially one that is lengthy and time-consuming. For example, Ronald Feldman and Timothy Caplinger (1977) were interested in factors that bring about behavioral changes in young boys who exhibit highly visible antisocial behavior. Their research design was a field experiment calling for the children participating in the study to meet periodically in groups over an eight-month period. Groups met an average of 22.2 times for two to three hours each. Most youngsters could be expected to refuse such a commitment of time and energy. Had the investigators attempted to draw a probability sample from the community, they probably would have had such a high refusal rate as to make the representativeness of their sample questionable. They would have expended considerable resources and still had, in effect, a nonprobability sample. So they resorted to an availability sample. To locate boys who had exhibited antisocial behavior, they sought referrals from numerous sources: mental health centers, juvenile courts, and the like. For a comparison group of boys who were not identified as antisocial, they sought volunteers from a large community center association. Given the purpose of experimentation, representative samples were less important. Experiments serve to determine *if* we can find cause-and-effect relationships. The issue of how generalizable those relationships are becomes important only after the relationships have been established.

Availability sampling is probably one of the more common forms of sampling used in human service research, both because it is less expensive than many other methods and because it is often impossible to develop an exhaustive sampling frame. For example, in the 20 issues of the journal *Social Work Research* published from 1994 through 1999, at least 52 of the 88 research articles could be classified as reporting some form of availability sample. You can readily

grasp the problems of trying to develop a sampling frame in the following studies:

- Turning points in the lives of young inner-city men previously involved in violence, illegal drug marketing, and other crimes and now contributing to their community's well-being: The sample consisted of 20 young men, most of whom were referred by intervention programs, pastors, and community leaders.
- A study on methods for preventing HIV/AIDS transmission in drug-abusing incarcerated women: The sample consisted of inmates at Rikers Island who were recruited with posted notices and staff referrals.
- A study on effectiveness of a program to reduce stress, perceived stigma, anxiety, and depression for family members of people with AIDS: Participants were recruited from an AIDS service program.
- Depression and resilience in elderly people with hip fractures: The sample consisted of 272 patients over age 65 who were hospitalized following hip fractures.

An exhaustive sampling frame that would make possible the selection of a probability sample in each of these studies might be, respectively, as follows:

- All reformed/rehabilitated young adult offenders
- All drug-abusing, incarcerated women
- All family members of people infected with AIDS
- All elderly people with hip fractures

Clearly, such probability sampling is beyond the realm of most investigators. Availability samples, though less desirable, make it possible for scientific investigation to move forward in those cases where probability sampling is impossible or prohibitively costly.

Snowball Sampling

When a snowball is rolled along in wet, sticky snow, it picks up more snow and gets larger. This is analogous to what happens with **snowball sampling:** We start with a few cases of the type we want to study and let them lead us to more cases, which in turn lead us to still more cases, and so on. Like the rolling snowball, the snowball sample builds up as we continue to add cases. Because snowball sampling depends on the sampled cases being knowledgeable of other relevant cases, the technique is especially useful for sampling subcultures where the members routinely interact with one another. Snowball sampling also is useful in the investigation of sensitive topics, such as child abuse or drug use, where the perpetrators or the victims might hesitate to identify themselves if approached by a stranger, such as a researcher, but might be open to an approach by someone who they know shares their experience or deviant status (Gelles 1978).

Snowball sampling allows researcher to accomplish what Norman Denzin (1989) calls *interactive* sampling—that is, sampling people who interact with one another. Probability samples are all noninteractive because knowing someone selected for the sample does not change the probability of selection. Interactive sampling is often theoretically relevant because many social science theories stress the impact of associates on behavior. To study these associational influences, researchers often combine snowball sampling with a probability sample. For example, Albert Reiss and Lewis Rhodes (1967), in a study of associational influences on delinquency, drew a probability sample of 378 boys between the ages of 12 and 16. They then asked each of the members of this sample to indicate his two best friends. By correlating various characteristics of the juveniles and their friends, the researchers were able to study how friendship patterns affect delinquency.

This interactive element, however, also points to one of the drawbacks of snowball sampling: Although it taps people involved in social networks, it misses people isolated from such networks. Thus, a snowball sample of drug users is limited to those users who are a part of some social network but ignores those who use drugs in an individual and isolated fashion. It is possible that drug users involved in a social network differ from isolated users in significant ways. Care must be taken in making generalizations from snowball samples to ensure that we generalize only to those people who are like those in our sample.

Quota Sampling

Quota sampling involves dividing a population into various categories and setting quotas on the number of elements to select from each category. Once we reach the quota for each category, we put no more elements from that category in the sample. Quota sampling is like stratified sampling in that both divide a population into categories and then take samples from the categories, but quota sampling is a nonprobability technique that often depends on availability to determine precisely which elements will be in the sample. Quota sampling was at one time the method of choice among many professional pollsters. But problems deriving from efforts to predict the very close 1948 presidential election between Harry S. Truman and Thomas E. Dewey caused pollsters to turn away from quota sampling and embrace the newly developed probability sampling techniques. With its fall from grace among pollsters, quota sampling also declined in popularity among researchers. Presently, use of quota sampling is best restricted to those situations in which its advantages clearly outweigh its considerable disadvantages. For example, researchers might use quota sampling to study crowd behavior, for which they cannot establish a sampling frame given the unstable nature of the phenomenon. A researcher who is studying reaction to disasters, such as a flood or tornado, might use quota sampling where the need for immediate reaction is critical and takes precedence over sample representativeness.

Researchers normally establish quotas for several variables, including such common demographic characteristics as age, sex, race, socioeconomic status, and education. In addition, they commonly include one or more quotas directly related to the research topic. For example, a study of political behavior would probably include a quota on political party affiliation to ensure that the sample mirrored the population on the central variable in the study.

In quota sampling, interviewers do the actual selection of respondents. Armed with the preestablished quotas, interviewers begin interviewing people until they have their quotas on each variable filled. The fact that quota sampling utilizes interviewers to do the actual selection of cases is one of its major shortcomings. Despite the quotas, considerable bias can enter quota sampling owing to interviewer behavior. Some people simply look more approachable than others, and interviewers naturally gravitate toward them. Interviewers are also not stupid. They realize that certain areas of major cities are less-than-safe places to go around asking questions of strangers. Protecting their personal safety by avoiding these areas can introduce obvious bias into the resulting sample.

While there is a risk of bias with quota samples, the technique does have some major positive attributes; namely, it is cheaper and faster than probability sampling. At times, these advantages can be sufficient to make quota sampling a logical choice. For example, if we wanted a rapid assessment of people's reactions to some event that had just occurred, quota sampling would probably be the best approach.

Purposive Sampling

In the sampling procedures discussed thus far, one major concern has been to select a sample that is representative of and will enable generalizations to a larger population. However, generalizability is only one goal, albeit an important one, of scientific research. In some studies, the issue of *control* may take on considerable importance and dictate a slightly different sampling procedure. In some investigations, control takes the form of choosing a sample that specifically *excludes* certain types of people because their presence might confuse the research findings. For example, if a researcher were conducting an exploratory study of a psychotherapeutic model of treatment, he or she might wish to choose people for the sample from among "ideal candidates" for psychotherapy. Because psychotherapy is based on talking about oneself and gaining insight into feelings, ideal candidates for psychotherapy are people with good verbal skills and the ability to explore and express inner feelings. Because well-educated, middle-class people are more likely to have these characteristics, a researcher might choose them for the sample.

This is called **purposive sampling** or **judgmental sampling:** The investigators use their judgment and prior knowledge to choose people for the sample who best serve the purposes of the study. But this is not "stacking the deck" in the researcher's favor. Consider the illustration given earlier: The basic research question is whether this type of psychotherapy can work at all. If we select a random sample, we get a variation based on age, sex, education, socioeconomic status, and a host of other variables that are not of direct interest in this study but that might influence receptiveness to psychotherapy. Certainly, in a truly random sample, the effects of this variation would wash out. The sample, however, would have to be so large that we could not do psychotherapy on that many people. So rather than use some other sampling technique, we choose a group that is homogeneous in terms of the factors that are likely to influence receptiveness to psychotherapy. This enables us to see whether psychotherapy works better than some other form of therapy. If it does not work with this ideal group, then we can probably forget the idea. If it does work, then we can generalize *only to this group,* with further research still required among other groups to see how extensively we can generalize the results.

In a study of social supports among elderly women, Gertrude Goldberg and her colleagues (1986) used a purposive sample. Their basic interest was to investigate the sources of support among women who face old age with neither a spouse nor a child to provide them with support. For this exploratory study, they selected a sample of women who were single or widowed, childless, and not working full-time. Because the sources of support for women who are married or have children have been studied extensively, there was no need to repeat this. This enabled the researchers to look directly at such questions as whether kin and friends provide different kinds of support for these childless, spouseless women and whether widowed or divorced women have social supports that are different from those of women who never married.

Research in Practice 6.2 illustrates some of the kinds of research problems we can approach with nonprobability samples and how a sampling strategy might actually involve a creative combination of some of the sampling types discussed here.

BEHAVIOR AND SOCIAL ENVIRONMENTS:

Using Nonprobability Samples to Study Hidden Populations

One of the major advantages of nonprobability samples is that they enable us to gain access to hidden populations: people who are difficult to locate or who, for one reason or another, prefer to hide their identity or behavior from the prying eyes of authorities, social science researchers, and others (O'Connell 2000). Typically, we cannot construct sampling frames for such groups. Area or cluster sampling is not feasible either, so probability samples are out of the question. Thus, studies of illicit drug users typically use nonprobability samples, with sampling strategies involving variants on or combinations of such strategies as snowball, quota, and purposive sampling. Douglas Heckathorn (1997), for example, used a variant on snowball sampling, which he called **respondent-driven sampling,** in a study of intravenous drug users and AIDS. He began with a small group of drug users he called "seeds" who were known to the researchers; each seed was asked to contact three other drug users he or she knew. The seeds received a payment for their interviews and an additional payment when each of the people they contacted came in for an interview. Each recruit interviewed then became a seed and was sent out to contact others. The procedure, especially the incentives, proved successful in recruiting other drug users and protected the privacy of the users because researchers didn't learn anyone's name until he or she voluntarily came in for the interview.

One drawback of snowball samples is that they can produce "masking" when a respondent protects the privacy of others by *not* referring them to the researchers. Researchers must take care in making generalizations from snowball samples to ensure that we generalize only to those people who are like those in our sample. Actually, Heckathorn presents evidence to show that his respondent-driven sampling procedure substantially reduces the masking bias.

With all the incentives available in Heckathorn's study, consider that a subject might try to take ad-

vantage of the situation. Given the overlapping networks among drug users, it is highly likely that more than one recruiter might contact a single user, creating the possibility that one user could get interviewed twice by assuming a false identity at the second interview (and thus get two rewards). Heckathorn reduced the likelihood of this happening by recording visible identifying characteristics of each person interviewed: gender, age, height, ethnicity, scars, tattoos, and other characteristics that, in combination, identify a particular person. The concern here is less about money than about validity: If one person contributes multiple interviews, then the overall results become biased in the direction of that person.

Targeted sampling is a sampling strategy with similarities to both quota and purposive sampling; it involves strategies to ensure that people or groups with specified characteristics have an enhanced chance of appearing in the sample. In other words, researchers target specified groups for special efforts to bring them into the sample. We might identify the targeted groups for theoretical reasons because they would be especially useful for gathering certain kinds of information; or we might identify them during the data-collection process if we find that some groups are not showing up in the sample. So targeted sampling is interactive, with the results of data collection possibly changing the method of sampling.

An example of targeted sampling is a study of injecting drug users conducted by John Watters and Patrick Biernacki (1989). They began by constructing an "ethnographic map" of the city in which they were conducting their research. This told them where drug users and drug activity tended to occur, in what amounts, and what the characteristics of the users in different locations were. This information provided the basis for deciding where to start recruiting people for participation in their study. This ethnographic map also

continued on next page

told them that snowball sampling alone probably wouldn't work because the drug scene they found consisted of many nonoverlapping social networks. This meant that any network in which they could not find an initial informant probably would not show up in their sample.

Watters and Biernacki targeted neighborhoods in the city for sampling based partly on racial composition. They wanted to ensure adequate numbers of black and Latino drug users in their sample. To enhance Latino participation, for example, they sent two Latino males familiar with the drug scene into the community to inform people of the research, to encourage their participation, and eventually to drive people to the center where the data was collected. As data collection proceeded, Watters and Biernacki recognized that an insufficient number of female injecting drug users were showing up in the sample, so they revised the sampling techniques to enhance participation by women. One reason for the low participation by women, they learned, was that some of the female users were prostitutes, and going to the center to participate in the research meant they lost time working the streets to earn money. To help alleviate this, the researchers established a "ladies first" policy at the data collection sites: If there was a wait, women received precedence over men. This and other strategies were an effort to target women and get adequate numbers in the sample.

Heckathorn (1997), in his respondent-driven sampling, also used a form of targeted sampling to reduce bias problems that might arise because some groups of drug abusers are isolated from contact with other users. He used "steering incentives" in the form of bonus payments for contacting drug users with special characteristics. For example, female users were somewhat rare in his sample also, so anyone who contacted a female injector who then showed up for an interview received an extra $5.

So even though nonprobability sampling techniques such as those presented here are not suitable for population studies where the goal is to obtain precise estimates of population parameters, nonprobability approaches are extremely valuable for accessing hidden populations and increasing understanding of these groups. Researchers may not be able to compute sampling error as we could with random sampling, but we still can improve the representative quality of the sample with such techniques as targeted sampling and thus enhance the value of the study results. Given the goals of the study and the reality of accessing the population, a researcher's best option often is a nonprobability sampling strategy.

Dimensional Sampling

It is often expeditious, if not essential, to use small samples. Small samples can be very useful, but we must exercise considerable care in drawing the sample. (The smallest sample size, of course, is the single case, which we will discuss in Chapter 11.) **Dimensional sampling** is a sampling technique for selecting small samples in a way that enhances their representativeness (Arnold 1970). The two basic steps to dimensional sampling are these: First, specify all the important dimensions or variables, and second, choose a sample that includes at least one case that represents each possible combination of dimensions. We can illustrate this with a study of the effectiveness of various institutional approaches in the control of juvenile delinquency (Street, Vinter, and Perrow 1966). The population consisted of all institutions for delinquents. To draw a random sample of all those institutions, however, would have made a sample size that would tax the resources of most investigators. As an alternative, the researchers used a dimensional sample. The first step was to spell out the important conceptual dimensions. In terms of juvenile institutions, this investigation considered three dimensions, each containing two values as illustrated in Table 6.3: organizational goals (custodial or rehabilitative), organizational control (public or private), and organizational size (large or small). In the second step, the researchers selected at least one case to represent each of the eight possibilities that resulted.

Dimensional sampling has a number of advantages that make it an attractive alternative in some sit-

Table 6.3 An Illustration of Institutional Dimensions for a Dimensional Sample

	Custodial Goals		Rehabilitative Goals	
	Public	**Private**	**Public**	**Private**
Large Size				
Small Size				

uations. First, it is faster and less expensive than studying large samples. Second, it is valuable in exploratory studies with little theoretical development to support a large-scale study. Third, dimensional sampling provides more detailed knowledge of each case than we would likely gain from a large sample. With a large sample, data collection necessarily is more cursory and focused (which is justified if previous research has narrowed the focus of what variables are important).

Despite their limitations, nonprobability samples can be valuable tools in the conduct of human service research. However, we want to reiterate two points. First, some research uses both probability and nonprobability samples in a single research project, and we have given some illustrations of this. The point is that the two types of samples should not be considered competitors for attention. Second, we should view findings based on nonprobability samples as suggestive rather than conclusive, and we should seek opportunities to retest their hypotheses using probability samples.

Sampling with Minority Populations

The key to selecting scientifically valid samples is to ensure their representativeness so we can make valid generalizations. Accomplishing this is an especially difficult challenge when we are conducting research on racial or ethnic minorities. One problem is that some minorities have "rare event" status—that is, they constitute a relatively small percentage of some populations. African Americans and Hispanic Americans, for example, each constitute approximately 12 percent of the United States population, while Native Americans are about 3 percent (U.S. Census Bureau 2002). This means that a representative sample of

1,500 Americans would, if it included the proper proportions of minorities, contain 180 African Americans, 180 Hispanics, and 45 Native Americans. These numbers are too small for many data analysis purposes. The Native Americans especially are so few that any analysis that breaks the sample down into subgroups would result in meaninglessly small numbers in each subgroup. Furthermore, these small numbers mean that the error rate becomes much higher for minority groups than for nonminority groups because small samples are less reliable and have more error (A.W. Smith 1987). These small sample sizes make it difficult to assess differences of opinion or behavior within a minority group; thus, it is easy to conclude, falsely, that the group is homogeneous. As a consequence, we know little about gender, social class, regional, or religious differences among members of particular minorities. The outcome, according to Smith, is "little more than a form of stereotyping, an *underestimation* of the variability of opinions among blacks. This leads to an *overestimation* of the contribution of race, per se, to black–white differences" in attitude and behavior (1987, p. 445). The Committee on the Status of Women in Sociology (1986) makes the same recommendations regarding gender: "Research should include sufficiently large subsamples of male and female subjects to allow meaningful analysis of subgroups."

Some minorities have rare event status in another way that can cause problems in sampling. Because of substantial residential segregation of minorities in the United States, minorities who live in largely white areas are relatively small in number and researchers can easily miss them by chance even in a well-chosen, representative sample. The result is a biased sample that includes minorities living in largely minority communities but not minorities living elsewhere. Because minorities living in nonminority communities probably vary in terms of attitudes and behavior, such a biased sample gives a deceptively homogeneous picture of the minority.

So efforts must be made in sampling to ensure that those rare events have a chance at selection for the sample. In some cases, we can employ disproportionate sampling, in which some individuals or households have a greater probability of appearing in the sample than do other individuals or households. Another way to avoid some of these problems is to use both probability and nonprobability sampling techniques when studying minorities. Some researchers combine purposive, dimensional, and snowball sampling with some type of probability sample to ensure effective coverage of a minority population (Becerra and Zambrana 1985). A dimensional sample of Hispanics, for example, might specify an entire series of dimensions to cover in the sample. Thus, a researcher might specify certain age cohorts of Hispanic women (20–30 years of age, 31–40, and 41 and older) to include in the sample or some minimum number of single-parent and two-parent Hispanic families. This would ensure sufficient people with certain characteristics in the sample for valid data analysis. A study of mental health among Asian immigrants in the Seattle area used the snowball technique to ensure a complete sampling frame (Kuo and Tsai 1986). The researchers used local telephone directories and gathered names from ethnic and community organizations to develop part of the sampling frame. Then, given the dispersion of Asian Americans in the area, researchers added the snowball technique.

A Note on Sampling in Practice

Human service practitioners do not routinely engage in sampling procedures like those used for research purposes. Yet parallels exist between what occurs in practice and in research, and we can apply some of the sampling principles in this chapter to providing client services. The needs and characteristics of a particular client typically guide the assessments and actions of practitioners. But to what extent are judgments about one client based on experiences with other clients? The issue here, of course, is that

of *generalizability*. As human beings, we constantly dip into our own funds of experience to help us cope with situations that we confront. Practitioners use their past experience with clients—sometimes very effectively—to grapple with the problems of subsequent clients. The critical judgment to make in this regard is whether it is legitimate to generalize past outcomes to current situations.

Practice settings rarely involve dealing with probability samples. Irrespective of whether the clients are welfare recipients, elderly people receiving nursing home care, child abusers, or individuals with problem pregnancies, practitioners have no way of knowing whether *all* people with such characteristics had a chance to be in the "sample" (that is, to be one of their clients) or how great that chance was. For all practical purposes, then, practitioners deal with nonprobability samples and all the limitations that they entail. In most cases, practitioners have an availability sample of people who happen to come to their attention because they are clients. This means that practitioners need to show caution in making generalizations from their observations but is no reason for despair. Remember that many scientific investigations are based on availability samples. We simply need to recognize their limitations and use care in generalizing.

If the main concern is to generalize to other clients with similar problems, then a reasonable assumption is that the clients are representative of others with similar problems who seek the aid of a practitioner. Whatever propels people to see a particular practitioner is probably operative for many if not all of that practitioner's other clients. However, if the practitioner's research interest concerns all people experiencing a certain type of problem, then agency clients are not an appropriate sample. Agencies intentionally and unintentionally screen their prospective clients; thus, many people who could use services are not included in a sample of agency clients. The well-known study by Robert Scott (1975) on agencies that serve the blind is a classic example. Scott found that these agencies concentrated their efforts on young, trainable clientele, even though most blind people are elderly or have multiple handicaps. If workers in such an agency assumed that the agency clientele represented all blind people, they would have a distorted perspective on the actual blind population.

Ways of checking on such distortions exist, of course. For example, practitioners can compare notes with each other. Do they find the same kinds of problems among their clients? If so, that is support for an assumption that one set of clients is representative of all people with similar problems. Practitioners might also consider utilizing (at least informally) other sampling techniques, for example, adopting a snowball technique by asking clients to recommend someone they know who has a similar problem but is not receiving any services. Especially with people whose problems may be of a sensitive nature, this snowball approach is a mode of entry with a considerable likelihood of success. Another possibly effective sampling technique is purposive sampling. For example, in an agency dealing with unplanned pregnancies among teenagers, suppose that all clients are members of ethnic minorities. It might appear that the clients' behavior, such as hostility toward practitioners, is due either to the crisis of the pregnancy or to the animosity of a minority member toward the welfare bureaucracy. The problem is a sample that is homogeneous with respect to two variables that may be important: They all have problem pregnancies and they are all members of an ethnic minority. To get around this problem, the researcher might begin to choose a purposive sample in which the problem pregnancies occur among nonminority teenagers and thus be in a better position to determine the source of the hostility.

In some ways, dimensional sampling is the most feasible form for practitioners. In our previous illustration, for example, there are two variables—race and pregnancy status—with two values each: white versus nonwhite and pregnant versus not pregnant. Thus, the analysis contains four possible cells. If for some reason, such as past experience, the researcher believes that these two variables interrelate in important ways in determining such factors as clients' hostility or adjustment, he or she could make sure that at least one client was in each of those four cells in order to make some preliminary judgments regarding the importance of these two factors.

In summary, every client a practitioner encounters is part of a sample, and they are all a part of the larger population of clients that are of interest to practitioners. In Chapter 11, we discuss single-subject designs and the ways in which we can gain considerable scientific knowledge from studying changes in behavior of a single person or system. For now, however, it is important to have an awareness of how scientific sampling procedures can aid in assessing the validity of what we learn from a client. Once again, we can see that the gap between scientific research and human service practice is not nearly as large as many assume. Rather, research and practice are linked in a common endeavor—to gain useful knowledge of human behavior.

Main Points

- A population consists of all possible cases of whatever a researcher is interested in studying.
- A sample is composed of one or more elements selected from a population.
- A sampling frame is a list of the population elements used to draw some types of probability samples.
- The representativeness of a sample is its most important characteristic, referring to the degree to which the sample reflects the population from which it was drawn.
- Sampling error is the difference between sample values and true population values.
- Probability sampling techniques are the best for obtaining representative samples.
- The key characteristic of probability sampling is that every element in the population has a known chance of selection into the sample.
- Simple random, systematic, stratified, and area samples are all types of probability samples.
- Nonprobability samples do not assure each population element a known chance of selection into the sample and therefore lack the degree of representativeness of probability samples.
- Availability, snowball, quota, purposive, and dimensional samples are all types of nonprobability samples.
- Data based on properly drawn probability samples are reliable and generalizable within known limits of error to the sampled populations.

COMPUTERS IN RESEARCH

Software for Sampling

One question that confronts any researcher embarking on a research project is this: How big a sample do I need? Unfortunately, the only concise answer is this frustrating reply: It depends. It depends on many things, as we have seen in this chapter. Although understanding these factors conceptually helps clarify what influences sample size, the researcher needs a number, not a general explanation. Several software options are available to assist researchers with sampling decisions.

SamplePower is one such software program, available from SPSS (www.spss.com/spssbi/samplepower); another, Ex-Sample, is a part of a larger program called Methodologist's Toolchest (www.ideaworks.com/MToolchest.shmtl). These programs use information the researcher supplies, such as anticipated data analysis procedures, design power, effect size, confidence level, time, money, projected response rate, and so on, to help determine sample size. Besides generating a recommended sample size, these programs lead the researcher through a structured decision-making system that reduces the possibility of leaving some important considerations out of the sampling decision. The Ex-Sample program, for example, operates through a series of menus that guide the researcher through the choices in the program. He or she need only select the menu option for sample size and complete a limited number of information entries requested by the program, and the software will designate the sample size needed without requiring complex formulas or large amounts of data.

In addition to their use in estimating sample size, computers can also select the sample itself.

One sampling frame that computerization has rejuvenated is the telephone directory. In addition to the limitations covered in the discussion on sampling frames, telephone directories are physically cumbersome to work with. Furthermore, for anything other than a local survey, research requires amassing a large number of directories, certainly an impractical approach to selecting a national sample. However, personal computers are overcoming these problems with new high storage capacity and particularly with the development of CDs with the capacity to store vast amounts of data, such as encyclopedias, abstracts, and guides to professional literature, as well as millions of names from telephone directories. The ability to rapidly search the database and apply various selection criteria makes this kind of product a valuable sampling tool for many kinds of survey research. In addition to the U.S. database, similar products are available for Canada and European countries, along with regular updates sometimes as frequently as monthly, to ensure that the sampling frame is current.

Because of the proliferation and frequent modification of computer products for social research purposes, several professional publications regularly report on new developments. The journal *Social Science Computer Review* alerts readers to new developments in the field of computers and publishes feature articles on computer applications. Popular publications, such as *Byte, PC Week, PC World,* and *PC Connection,* often provide articles evaluating software, including survey, sampling, and statistical software products.

■ In studies of racial and other minorities, researchers must take care to ensure that sampling procedures do not result in unrepresentative samples, especially given the "rare event" status of many minorities.

■ Computer software is available to assist in such sampling tasks as selecting a sample size and selecting the sample itself through random digit dialing.

Important Terms for Review

accidental sampling
area sampling
availability sampling
cluster sampling
convenience sampling

dimensional sampling
judgmental sampling
multistage sampling
nonprobability samples
population
probability samples
purposive sampling
quota sampling
representative sample
respondent-driven sampling
sample
sampling error
sampling frame
simple random sampling
snowball sampling
stratified sampling
systematic sampling
targeted sampling

Exploring InfoTrac® College Edition and the Internet

InfoTrac® College Edition search terms:

probability sampl*
nonprobability sampl*
snowball sampl*
quota sampl*
stratified sampl*

InfoTrac® College Edition articles:

A Brief Telephone Interview to Identify Lesbian and Bisexual Women in Random Digit Dialing Sampling. (Statistical Data Included) Ilan H. Meyer, Lindsay Rossano, James M. Ellis, Judith Bradford. *The Journal of Sex Research* May 2002 v39 i2 p139(6) (4,648 words)

Drawing a Probability Sample of Female Street Prostitutes in Los Angeles County. David E. Kanouse, Sandra H. Berry, Naihua Duan, Janet Lever, Sally Carson, Judith F. Perlman, Barbara Levitan. *The Journal of Sex Research* Feb 1999 v36 i1 p45(1) (6,095 words)

Updating Howard Becker's Theory of Using Marijuana for Pleasure. Michael Hallstone. *Contemporary Drug Problems* Winter 2002 v29 i4 p821(26) (7,711 words)

In this chapter, we discussed many of the technical aspects of sampling. To expand your knowledge about sampling and how researchers use sampling in research, we recommend that you explore Internet sites affiliated with some of the major survey research endeavors that produce social science research data. Following are several sites that include information about the sampling processes in their surveys. Once you have accessed the main site, look for highlighted text about sampling procedures.

The General Social Survey (GSS) site (www.icpsr.umich.edu/GSS/) has its own search capacity, which makes locating material of interest fairly easy. Entering the term "sampling" in the search engine will lead to a variety of pages dealing with sampling. From this site, you can learn how the GSS sample is actually selected, how the procedure has changed over time, and what controversies have arisen over the sampling system modifications. Also, search for the term "primary sampling unit" and describe what it is and what role it plays in sampling procedures (see Research in Practice 6.1.)

The Crime Victimization Survey is another major survey conducted in the United States. You can learn about the sampling for this survey by going to the Bureau of Justice Statistics home page (www.ojp.usdoj.gov/bjs/welcome.html). Explore this site to find the actual results of the most recent crime victimization survey and to learn about the sampling procedures used in the study.

The Bureau of Labor Statistics and the Census Bureau cooperate in providing the Current Population Survey (CPS). To learn more about how sampling is done for this key survey, visit the CPS Web site (www.bls.census.gov/cps/cpsmain.htm). More specific data on the Basic Monthly Survey can be accessed from the main CPS site or by going directly to www.bls.census.gov/cps/bsampdes.htm.

For Further Reading

Henry, Gary T. *Practical Sampling*. Newbury Park, Calif.: Sage, 1990. This concise book is a handy guide to basic issues related to sampling. It also includes some interesting examples of research projects and the sampling procedures they used.

Hess, Irene. *Sampling for Social Research Surveys, 1947–1980.* Ann Arbor: University of Michigan Institute for Social Research, 1985. Sometimes a good example can enhance the understanding of complex subjects, and that is what Hess provides in her historical review of survey sampling. In addition, she provides further discussion of many sampling issues.

Kish, Leslie. *Survey Sampling.* New York: Wiley-Interscience, 1995. Considered the mainstay regarding sampling issues in social research, this book assumes that the reader has an elementary understanding of statistics.

Maisel, Richard, and Caroline Hodges Persell. *How Sampling Works.* Thousand Oaks, Calif.: Pine Forge Press, 1996. This book provides an excellent and detailed overview of scientific sampling, as well as software to assist students in learning through working problems.

Scheaffer, Richard L., William Mendenhall, and Lyman Ott. *Elementary Survey Sampling,* 5th ed. Belmont, Calif.: Wadsworth, 1996. As the name implies, this book is meant as an introductory text on the design and analysis of sample surveys. Limited to coverage of probability sampling techniques, it provides the information necessary to successfully complete a sample survey.

Stuart, Alan. *The Ideas of Sampling,* 3rd ed. New York: Oxford University Press, 1987. This book is another good review of sampling strategies that can be used in many human service settings.

Sudman, Seymour. *Applied Sampling.* New York: Academic Press, 1976. This book, along with the Kish work, will tell you almost all you need to know about sampling.

Wainer, Howard. *Drawing Inferences from Self-Selected Surveys.* New York: Springer-Verlag, 1986. This book focuses on the issue of self-selection into samples and the problems this can create in terms of making inferences from samples to populations.

Exercises for Class Discussion

A student is doing an internship with the Metropolis Senior Citizens Service Center (MSCSC), where she has been asked to help do a needs assessment. MSCSC is a publicly funded agency that is supposed to serve all residents of Metropolis who are 60 years of age or older. Spouses of such individuals are also eligible to receive services if they are at least 50 years old. As a part of the internship, the director wants the student to conduct interviews with all senior citizens in this city of 25,000 inhabitants. The student, having taken a research methods course, knows that this would be time-consuming and inefficient as well as unnecessary. She suggests that selecting a probability sample and conducting careful interviews with those selected will yield better information with less interviewing time. The director tells her to develop a plan to convince the agency board how she might accomplish this.

6.1 What is the population for this project? Define the population as specifically as possible.

6.2 Three sampling frames the intern might use are (a) the city directory, (b) the local telephone book, and (c) a Social Security Administration listing of recipients of benefits for the county. What might be the advantages and disadvantages of each? Can you think of any other sampling frames useful for this project?

6.3 Could you use a random digit dialing method to sample this population? Indicate reasons for and against using such a technique.

6.4 A staff member at the agency suggests dispensing with the sampling and just running a series of public service announcements on the local radio station and in the newspaper that ask senior citizens to call the agency to express their concerns. The researcher could interview those people who call in, and these interviews would constitute the needs assessment. What kind of sampling process is suggested? What are its advantages and disadvantages?

6.5 The elderly who reside in nursing homes make up a group of special interest to the center, although they represent only 1.5 percent of the eligible residents. Describe how sampling procedures could address the problem of including a representative group of nursing home elderly in the sample.

6.6 Use your local city directory to compile a simple random sample of 25 households, using the street address portion of the directory.

6.7 In the previous exercises, options included random digit dialing, the city directory, the telephone book, Social Security recipients, and respondents to radio announcements. Evaluate each of these options in terms of potential for underrepresenting minorities in the sample. Which method would be best?

Chapter 7

Survey Research

The term **survey** designates both a specific way of collecting data and identifies a broad research strategy. Survey data collection involves gathering information from individuals, called *respondents,* by having them respond to questions. We use surveys to gather data as a part of many of the research methods discussed in other chapters, such as qualitative studies, quantitative studies, experiments, field research, and program evaluations. In fact, the survey is probably the most widely used means of gathering data in social science research. A literature search in the online database *Sociological Abstracts* (SocAbs) for the five-year period 1998–2002, using the key-word search terms "social work" and "survey," identified more than 600 English language journal articles. Surveys have been used to study all five of the human service focal areas discussed in Chapter 1. This illustrates a major attraction of surveys—flexibility.

As a broad research strategy, the term **survey research** refers to asking questions of a sample of people, in a fairly short period of time, and testing hypotheses or describing a situation based on their answers. As a general approach to knowledge building, the strength of surveys is their potential for generalizability. Surveys typically involve collecting data from large samples of people; therefore, they are ideal for obtaining data that is representative of populations too large to deal with by other methods. Consequently, many of the issues addressed in this chapter center around how researchers obtain quality data that are in fact representative.

All surveys involve presenting respondents with a series of questions to answer. These questions may tap matters of fact, attitudes, opinions, or future expectations. The questions may be simple single-item measures or complex multiple-item scales. In whatever form, however, survey data are basically what people say to the investigator in response to a question. We collect data in survey research in two basic ways: with *questionnaires* or with *interviews.* A **questionnaire** contains recorded questions that people respond to directly on the questionnaire form itself, without the aid of an interviewer. A questionnaire can be handed directly to a respondent, it can be mailed or sent online to the members of a sample

who then fill it out on their own and send it back to the researcher, or it can be presented via a computer, with the respondent recording answers with mouse and keypad. An **interview** involves an interviewer reading questions to a respondent and recording his or her answers. Researchers can conduct interviews either in person or over the telephone.

Some survey research uses both questionnaire and interview techniques, with respondents filling in some answers themselves and being asked other questions by interviewers. Because both questionnaires and interviews involve asking people to respond to questions, a problem central to both is what type of question we should use. In this chapter we discuss this issue first and then analyze the elements of questionnaires and interviews separately. An important point to emphasize about surveys is that they only measure what people say about their thoughts, feelings, and behaviors. Surveys do not directly measure those thoughts, feelings, and behaviors. For example, if people tell us in a survey that they do not take drugs, we have not measured actual drug-taking behavior, only people's reports about that behavior. This is very important in terms of the conclusions that can be drawn: We can conclude that people report not taking drugs, but we cannot conclude that people do not take drugs. This latter is an inference we might draw from what people say. So surveys always involve data on what people say about what they do, not what they actually do.

Designing Questions
Closed-Ended versus Open-Ended Questions

Two basic types of questions are used in questionnaires and interviews: closed-ended or open-ended. **Closed-ended questions** provide respondents with a fixed set of alternatives from which to choose. The response formats of multiple-item scales, for example, are all closed-ended, as are multiple-choice test questions. **Open-ended questions** require the respondents write their own responses, much as for an essay-type examination question.

The proper use of open- and closed-ended questions is important for the quality of data generated as well as for ease of handling the data. Theoretical considerations play an important part in the decision about which type of question to use. In general, we use closed-ended questions when we can determine all the possible, theoretically relevant responses to a question in advance and the number of possible responses is limited. For example, The General Social Survey question for marital status reads, "Are you currently—married, widowed, divorced, separated, or have you never been married?" A known and limited number of answers is possible. (In research today, researchers commonly offer people an alternative answer to this question, namely, "living together" or cohabitating. Although cohabitation is not legally a marital status, it helps reflect accurately the living arrangements currently in use.) Another obvious closed-ended question is about gender. To leave such questions open-ended runs the risk that some respondent will either purposefully or inadvertently answer in a way that provides meaningless data. Putting "sex" with a blank after it, for example, is an open invitation for some character to write "yes" rather than the information wanted.

Open-ended questions, on the other hand, are appropriate in an exploratory study in which the lack of theoretical development suggests that we should place few restrictions on people's answers. In addition, when researchers cannot predict all the possible answers to a question in advance, or when too many possible answers exist to list them all practically, then closed-ended questions are not appropriate. Suppose we wanted to know the reasons people moved to their current residence. So many possible reasons exist that such a question has to be treated as open-ended. If we are interested in the county and state in which our respondents reside, we can generate a complete list of all the possibilities and thus create a closed-ended question. But the list would consume so much space on the questionnaire that it would be excessively cumbersome, especially considering that respondents should be able to answer this question correctly in its open-ended form.

Some topics lend themselves to a combination of both formats. Religious affiliation is a question usually handled in this way. Although a great many religions exist, there are some to which only a few respondents will belong. Thus, we can list religions with large memberships in closed-ended fashion and add the category "other" where a person can write the name of a religion not on the list (see Question 4, Table 7.1). We can efficiently handle any question with a similar pattern of responses—numerous possibilities, but a few popular ones—in this way. The combined format maintains the convenience of closed-ended questions for most of the respondents but also allows those with less common responses to express them.

When we use the option of "other" in a closed-ended question, it is a good idea to request respondents to write in their response by indicating, "Please specify." We can then code these answers into whatever response categories seem appropriate for data analysis. However, researchers should offer the opportunity to specify an alternative even if, for purposes of data analysis, we will not use the written responses. This is done because respondents who hold uncommon views or memberships may be proud of them and desirous of expressing them on the questionnaire. In addition, well-educated professionals tend to react against completely closed-ended questions as too simple, especially when the questions deal with complicated professional matters (Sudman 1985). The opportunity to provide a written response to a question is more satisfying to such respondents, and they are more likely to complete the questionnaire.

Another factor in choosing between open- and closed-ended questions is the ease with which we can handle each at the data analysis stage. Open-ended questions are sometimes quite difficult to work with. One difficulty is that poor handwriting or the failure of respondents to provide clear answers can result in data that we cannot analyze (Rea and Parker 1992). Commonly, some responses to open-ended questions just do not make sense, so we end up dropping them from analysis. In addition, open-ended questions are more complicated to analyze by computer because we

Table 7.1   Formatting Questions for a Questionnaire

Please indicate your response to the following questions by placing an X in the appropriate box.

1. Which of the following best describes where you live?

   [x] In a large city (100,000 population or more)

   [ ] In a suburb near a large city

   [ ] In a middle-sized city or small town (under 100,000 population) but not a suburb
       of a large city

   [ ] Open country (but not on a farm)

   [ ] On a farm

2. Have you ever shoplifted an item with a value of $10 or more?

   [ ] Yes

   [ ] No

   Filter Questions

If Yes: How many times have you taken such items?
[ ] Once
[ ] 2 to 5 times
[ ] 6 to 10 times
[ ] More than 10 times

   Contingency Question

3. Have you purchased a new automobile between 1995 and the present?

   [ ] Yes

   [ ] No (*If No*, please skip to Section C, question 1.)

4. Please indicate the religion to which you belong:

   [ ] Protestant

   [ ] Catholic

   [ ] Jewish

   [ ] Other. Please specify. _____

---

must first code a respondent's answers into a limited set of categories; this coding is time-consuming and can introduce error (see Chapter 14).

Another related difficulty with open-ended questions is that some respondents may give more than one answer to a question. For example, in a study of substance abuse, researchers might ask people why they use or do not use alcoholic beverages. As a response to this question, a researcher might receive the following answer: "I quit drink-ing because booze was too expensive and my wife was getting angry at me for getting drunk." How should this response be categorized? Should the person be counted as quitting because of the expense or because of marital problems created by drinking? It may be, of course, that both factors were important in the decision to quit. Researchers usually handle data analysis problems like this in one of two ways. First, the researchers may accept all the individual's responses as data. This, however, creates difficulties in data analysis; some people give more reasons than others because they are talkative rather than because they actually have more reasons for their behavior. A second way of handling multiple responses is to assume that each respondent's *first* answer is the most important one and to consider it to be the only response. This assumption, of course, is not always valid, but it does solve the dilemma systematically.

The decision about whether to use open- or closed-ended questions is complex, often requiring considerable experience with survey methods to assess. An important issue, it can have substantial effects on the type and quality of the data collected, as illustrated in a survey of attitudes about social problems confronting the United States. The Institute for Social Research at the University of Michigan asked a sample of people open- and closed-ended versions of essentially the same questions (Schuman and Presser 1979). The two versions elicited quite different responses. For example, with the closed-ended version, 35 percent of the respondents indicated that crime and violence were important social problems, compared with only 15.7 percent in the open-ended version. With a number of other issues, people responding to the closed-ended questions were more likely to indicate that particular issues were problems. One reason that the type of question has such an effect on the data is that the list of alternatives in the closed-ended questions tends to serve as a "reminder" to the respondent of issues that might be problems. Without the stimulus of the list, some respondents might not even think of some of those issues. A second reason is that people tend to choose from the list provided in closed-ended questions rather than writing in their own answers, even when provided with an "other" category.

In some cases, researchers can gain the benefits of both open- and closed-ended questions by using an open-ended format in a pretest or pilot study and then, based on the results, designing closed-ended questions for the actual survey. See Sudman and Bradburn (1982) for further discussion of open- versus closed-ended questions in surveys.

Wording of Questions

Because the questions that make up a survey are the basic data-gathering devices, researchers need to word them with great care. Especially with questionnaires that allow the respondent no opportunity to clarify questions, ambiguity can cause substantial trouble. We will review some of the major issues in developing good survey questions (Sudman and Bradburn 1982). (In Chapter 13, we will discuss some problems of question construction having to do specifically with questions that are part of multiple-item scales.)

Researchers should subject the wording of questions, whenever possible, to empirical assessment to determine whether particular wording might lead to unnoticed bias. Words, after all, have connotative meanings (that is, emotional or evaluative associations) that the researcher may not be aware of but that may influence respondents' answers to questions. In a study of attitudes about social welfare policy in the United States, for example, researchers asked survey respondents whether they believed the government should spend more money on welfare or less (T. W. Smith 1987). However, they were asked the question in three slightly different ways. Smith asked one group about whether we were spending too much or too little on "welfare," a second group about spending too much or too little on "assistance for the poor," and a third about money for "caring for the poor." At first glance, all three questions seem to have much the same meaning. Yet people's responses to them suggested something quite different. Basically, people responded much more negatively to the question with the word "welfare" in it, indicating much less willingness to spend more money on "welfare" than they were to "assist the poor." For example, 64.7 percent of the respondents indicated that too little was being spent on "assistance to the poor," but only 19.3 percent said we were spending too little on "welfare." This is a very dramatic difference in opinion, due to what might seem at first glance a minor difference in wording. Although the study did not investigate why these differing responses occurred, it seems plausible that the word "welfare" had connotative meanings for many people that involve images of laziness, waste, fraud, bureaucracy, or the poor as disreputable. "Assisting the poor," on the other hand, is more likely associated with giving and Judeo-Christian charity. These connotations lead to quite different responses. In many cases, the only way to assess such differences is to compare people's responses with different versions of the same question during a pretest.

In general, researchers should state questions in the present tense. Specialized questions that focus on past experiences or future expectations are an exception. In these situations, we use the appropriate past or future tense. Of major importance is that tenses are not carelessly mixed. Failure to maintain consistent tense of questions can lead to an understandable confusion on the part of respondents and, therefore, to more measurement error.

Researchers should keep questions simple and direct, expressing only one idea, and avoiding complex statements that express more than one idea. Consider the following double-negative question that appeared in a Roper Organization poll conducted in 1992 about the Holocaust: "Does it seem possible or does it seem impossible to you that the Nazi extermination of the Jews never happened?" (Smith 1995, p. 269). The results showed that 22 percent said "possible," 65 percent "impossible," and 12 percent "don't know." Could it be that over a fifth of Americans had doubts about the Holocaust and over a third questioned it or were uncertain that it occurred? Considerable controversy erupted over the survey results. In a subsequent Gallup Poll, researchers asked respondents the same double negative question with this follow-up question: "Just to clarify, in your opinion, did the Holocaust definitely happen, probably happen, probably *not* happen, or definitely *not* happen?" (Smith 1995, p. 277) Of those who had said it was possible that the Holocaust never happened in response to the first question, 97 percent changed their position to saying that it did happen with the second question.

Statements that seem crystal clear to a researcher may prove unclear to many respondents. One common error is to overestimate the reading ability of the average respondent. For example, a national study of adult literacy found that more than 20 per-

cent of adults in the United States demonstrate skills in the lowest level of prose, document, and quantitative literacy proficiencies. At this level, many people cannot total an entry on a deposit slip, identify a piece of specific information in a brief news article, or respond to many of the questions on a survey form (Kirsh et al. 1993). Such limited literacy skills are common among some clients of the human services, especially when English is a second language. Accordingly, the researcher should avoid the use of technical terms on questionnaires. For example, it would not be advisable to include such a statement as, "The current stratification system in the United States is too rigid." "Stratification" is a technical term in the social sciences that many people outside the field do not understand in the same sense that social scientists do.

Another practice to avoid is making reference to things that we cannot clearly define or that depend on the respondent's interpretation. For example, "Children who get into trouble typically have had a bad home life" is an undesirable statement because it includes two sources of vagueness. The word "trouble" is unclear. What kind of trouble? Trouble with the law, trouble at school, trouble with parents, or what? The other problem is the phrase "bad home life." What constitutes a "bad home life" depends on the respondent's interpretation.

Finally, for the majority of questions designed for the general public, researchers should never use slang terminology. Slang tends to arise in the context of particular groups and subcultures. Slang terms may have a precise meaning within those groups but confuse people outside those groups. Occasionally, however, the target population for a survey is more specialized than the general population, and the use of their "in-group" jargon may be appropriate. It would demonstrate to the respondents that the researcher cared enough to "learn their language" and could increase rapport, resulting in better responses. Having decided to use slang, however, the burden is on the researcher to be certain he or she uses it correctly.

Once a survey instrument is developed, it must be pretested to see if questions are clearly and prop-

Table 7.2 Common Errors in Writing Questions and Statements

Original Question	Problem	Solution
The city needs more housing for the elderly and property taxes should be raised to finance it.	**Two questions in one:** Some respondents might agree with the first part but disagree with the second.	Questions should be broken up into two separate statements, each expressing a single idea.
In order to build more stealth bombers, the government should raise taxes.	**False premise:** What if a person doesn't want more bombers built? How do they answer?	First ask their opinion on whether the bomber should be built; then, for those who respond "Yes," ask the question about taxes.
Are you generally satisfied with your job, or are there some things about it that you don't like?	**Overlapping alternatives:** A person might want to answer "Yes" to the first part (i.e., they are generally satisfied) but "No" to the second part (i.e., there are also some things they don't like).	Divide this into two questions: one measures their level of satisfaction while the other assesses whether there are things they don't like.
How satisfied are you with the number and fairness of the tests in this course?	**Double-barreled question:** It asks about both the "number" and the "fairness," and a person might feel differently about each.	Divide this into two questions.
What is your income?	**Vague and ambiguous words:** Does "income" refer to before-tax or after-tax income? To hourly, weekly, monthly, or yearly income?	Clarify: What was your total annual income, before taxes, for the year 2000?
Children who get into trouble typically have had a bad home life.	**Vague and ambiguous words:** The words *trouble* and *bad home life* are unclear. Is it trouble with the law, trouble at school, trouble with parents, or what? What constitutes a *bad home life* depends on the respondent's interpretation.	Clarify: Specify what you mean by the words: *trouble* means "having been arrested" and *bad home life* means "an alcoholic parent."

erly understood and are unbiased. We can handle pretesting by having people respond to the questionnaire or interview and then reviewing it with them to find any problems. The way a group responds to the questions themselves can also point to trouble. For example, if many respondents leave a particular answer blank, then there may be a problem with the question. Once the instrument is pretested and modifications made where called for, the survey should be pretested again. Any change in the questionnaire requires more pretesting. Once it is pretested with no changes called for, it is ready to use in research.

We present these and other problems that can arise in writing good survey questions in Table 7.2. One of the critical decisions in survey research—and it is a complex decision—is whether to collect data through questionnaires or through interviews. We discuss both types of surveys with an eye on the criteria to use in assessing which is more appropriate for a particular research project.

Questionnaires

Questionnaires are designed so that they can be answered without assistance. Of course, if a researcher hands a questionnaire to the respondent, as we sometimes do, the respondent then has the opportunity to ask the researcher to clarify anything that is ambiguous. A good questionnaire, however, should not require such assistance. In fact, researchers often mail questionnaires to respondents, who thus have no opportunity to ask questions. In other cases, researchers administer questionnaires to many people simultaneously in a classroom, auditorium, or agency setting. Such modes of administration make questionnaires quicker and less expensive than most interviews. But they place the burden on researchers to design questionnaires that respondents can properly complete without assistance.

Structure and Design

Directions.   One of the simplest, but also most important, tasks of questionnaire construction is the inclusion of precise directions for respondents. Good directions go a long way toward improving the quality of data that questionnaires generate. If we want respondents to put an X in a box corresponding to their answer, we tell them precisely to do so. Questionnaires often contain questions requiring different kinds of answers. At each place in the questionnaire where the format changes, we include additional directions.

Order of Questions.   An element of questionnaire construction that takes careful consideration is the proper ordering of questions. Careless ordering can lead to undesirable consequences, such as a reduced response rate or biased responses to questions. Generally, questions asked early in the questionnaire

should not bias answers to those questions that come later. For example, if we asked several factual questions regarding poverty and the conditions of the poor and later asked a question concerning which social problems people consider to be serious, more respondents will likely include poverty than would otherwise have done so. We can sometimes avoid these potentially biasing effects by placing opinion questions first when a questionnaire contains both factual and opinion questions.

Ordering of questions can also increase a respondent's interest in answering a questionnaire—this is especially helpful for boosting response rates on mailed questionnaires. Researchers should ask questions dealing with particularly intriguing issues first. The idea is to interest the recipients enough to get them to start answering. Once they start, they are more likely to complete the entire questionnaire. If the questionnaire does not deal with any topics that are obviously more interesting than others, then opinion questions should be placed first. People like to express their opinions, and, for the reasons mentioned earlier, we should put opinion questions first anyway. A pitfall we definitely want to avoid is beginning a questionnaire with the standard demographic questions about age, sex, income, and the like. People are so accustomed to those questions that they may not want to answer them again and may promptly file the questionnaire in the nearest wastebasket.

Question Formats.   All efforts at careful wording and ordering of the questions will be for naught unless we present the questions in a manner that facilitates responding to them. The goal is to make responding to the questions as straightforward and convenient as possible and to reduce the amount of data lost because of responses that we cannot interpret.

When presenting response alternatives for closed-ended questions, we obtain the best results by having respondents indicate their selection by placing an X in a box (❑) corresponding to that alternative, as illustrated in Question 1 of Table 7.1. This format is preferable to open blanks and check marks (✓), because it is easy for respondents to get sloppy and place check marks *between* alternatives, rendering their responses unclear and therefore useless as data. Boxes force respondents to give unambiguous responses. Though this may seem a minor point, we can attest from our own experience in administering questionnaires that it makes an important difference.

Some questions on a questionnaire may apply to only some respondents and not others. These questions are normally handled by what are called *filter questions* and *contingency questions*. A **filter question** is a question whose answer determines which question the respondent goes to next. In Table 7.1, Questions 2 and 3 are both filter questions. In Question 2, the part of the question asking about "how many items they have taken" is called a **contingency question** because whether a person answers it depends on (is contingent on) his or her answer to the filter question. Notice the two ways the filter question is designed. With Question 2, the person answering "Yes" is directed to the next question by the arrow and the question is clearly set off by a box; also in the box, the phrase "If Yes" is included to make sure the person realizes that this question is only for those who answered "Yes" to the previous question. With Question 3, the answer "No" is followed by a statement telling the person which question he or she should answer next. Either format is acceptable; the point is to provide clear directions for the respondent. By sectioning the questionnaire on the basis of filter and contingency questions, we can guide the respondent through even the most complex questionnaire. The resulting path that an actual respondent follows through the questionnaire is referred to as the *skip pattern*. As is true of many aspects of questionnaire design, it is important to evaluate the skip pattern by pretesting the questionnaire to ensure that respondents complete all appropriate sections with a minimum of frustration.

In some cases, a number of questions or statements may all have identical response alternatives. An efficient way of organizing such questions is in the form of a **matrix question,** which lists the response alternatives only once; a box to check or a number or letter to circle follows each question or statement. Table 13.1 on page 345 is an example of a matrix question. Multiple-item indexes and scales

often use this compact way of presenting a number of items.

However, researchers should use matrix questions cautiously because they contain a number of weaknesses. One is that, with a long list of items in a matrix question, it is easy for the respondent to lose track of which line is the response for which statement and thus indicate an answer on the line above or below where the answer should go. The researcher can alleviate this by following every third or fourth item with a blank line so that it is easier visually to keep track of the proper line on which to mark an answer. A second weakness of matrix questions is that they may produce response set. (We will discuss the problem of response set and techniques for alleviating it at length in Chapter 13.) A third weakness of matrix questions is that they may tempt the researcher, in order to gain the efficiencies of the format, to force the response alternatives of some questions into that format when another format would be more valid. Researchers should determine the response format of any question or statement by theoretical and conceptual considerations of what is the most valid way to measure a variable.

Response Rate

A major problem in many research endeavors is gaining people's cooperation so that they will provide whatever data are needed. In surveys, we measure cooperation by the **response rate,** or the proportion of a sample that completes and returns a questionnaire or agrees to an interview. With interviews, response rates are often very high—in the area of 90 percent—largely because people are reluctant to refuse a face-to-face request for cooperation. In fact, with interviews, the largest nonresponse factor is the inability of the interviewers to locate respondents. With mailed questionnaires, however, this personal pressure is absent, and people feel freer to refuse (Bridge 1974). This can result in many *nonreturns*, or people who refuse to complete and return a questionnaire. Response rates for questionnaires (especially mailed ones) vary considerably, from an unacceptably low 20 percent to levels that rival those of interviews.

Table 7.3 Items to Include in the Cover Letter of a Questionnaire or the Introduction to an Interview

Item	Cover Letter	Interview Introduction
1. Sponsor of the research	yes	yes
2. Address/phone number of the researcher	yes	if required
3. How the respondent was selected	yes	yes
4. Who else was selected	yes	yes
5. The purpose of the research	yes	yes
6. Who will utilize or benefit from the research	yes	yes
7. An appeal for the person's cooperation	yes	yes
8. How long it will take the respondent to complete the survey	yes	yes
9. Payment	if given	if given
10. Anonymity/confidentiality	if given	if given
11. Deadline for return	yes	not applicable

Why is a low response rate of such concern? The issue is the representativeness of a sample, as we discussed in Chapter 6. If we selected a representative sample and obtained a perfect 100 percent response, we would have confidence in the representativeness of the sample data. However, as the response rate drops below 100 percent, the sample may become less representative. Those who refuse to cooperate may differ in some systematic ways that affect the results of the research from those who do return the questionnaire. In other words, any response rate less than 100 percent may result in a biased sample. Of course, we rarely achieve a perfect response rate, but the closer the response rate is to that level, the more likely that the data are representative. Researchers can take a number of steps to improve response rates. Most apply only to questionnaires, but we can also use a few to increase response rates in interviews.

A Cover Letter. A properly constructed cover letter can help increase the response rate. A **cover letter** accompanies a questionnaire and serves to introduce and explain it to the recipient. With mailed questionnaires, the cover letter is the researcher's only medium for communicating with the recipient,

so he or she must carefully draft the letter to include information recipients will want to know and to encourage them to complete the questionnaire (see Table 7.3).

Researchers should feature the name of the sponsor of the research project prominently in the cover letter. Recipients want to know who is seeking the information they are asked to provide, and research clearly indicates that knowledge of the sponsoring organization influences the response rate (Goyder 1985; Rea and Parker 1992). Questionnaires sponsored by government agencies receive the highest response rates. University-sponsored research generates somewhat lower response rates, and commercially sponsored research produces the lowest rates of all. Apparently, if the research is at all associated with a government agency, stressing that in the cover letter may have a beneficial effect on the response rate. Researchers can increase the response rates of particular groups if their research is sponsored or endorsed by an organization that people in the group believe has legitimacy. For example, we can increase response rates of professionals if the research is linked to relevant professional organizations, such as the National Association of Social

Workers, the American Nurses Association, or the National Education Association (Sudman 1985).

The address and telephone number of the researcher should appear prominently on the cover letter. In fact, using letterhead stationery for the cover letter is a good idea. Especially if the sponsor of the research is not well known, some recipients may desire further information before they decide to participate. Although relatively few respondents will ask for more information, including the address and telephone number gives the cover letter a completely open and above-board appearance that may further the general cooperation of recipients.

The cover letter should also inform the respondent how people were selected to receive the questionnaire. It is not necessary to go into great detail on this matter, but people receiving an unanticipated questionnaire are naturally curious about how they were chosen to be a part of a study. A brief statement that they were randomly selected or selected by computer (if this is the case) should suffice.

Recipients also want to know the purpose of the research. Again, without going into great detail, the cover letter should explain why the research is being conducted, why and by whom it is considered important, and the potential benefits anticipated from the study. Investigations have clearly shown that we can significantly increase the response rate if we emphasize the importance of the research to the respondent. We must word this part of the cover letter carefully, however, so that it does not sensitize respondents in such a way that affects their answers to our questions. We can minimize sensitizing effects by keeping the description of the purpose general—certainly, do not suggest any of the research hypotheses. Regarding the importance of the data and anticipated benefits, the researcher should resist the temptation of hyperbole and instead make honest, straightforward statements. Respondents will see claims about "solving a significant social problem" or "alleviating the problems of the poor" as precisely what they are—exaggerated.

The preceding information provides a foundation for the single most important component of the cover letter: a direct appeal for the recipient's cooperation. General statements about the importance of the research are no substitute for a personal appeal to the recipient as to why he or she should take time to complete the questionnaire. Respondents must believe that their responses are important to the outcome (as, of course, they are). A statement to the effect that "your views are important to us" is a good approach that stresses the importance of each individual respondent and emphasizes that the questionnaire will allow the expression of opinions, which people like.

The cover letter should also indicate that the respondent will remain anonymous or that the data will be treated as confidential, whichever is the case. "Anonymous" means that *no one, including the researcher,* can link a particular respondent's name to his or her questionnaire. "Confidential" means that even though the researcher can match respondents to their questionnaires, he or she will treat the information collectively and will not link any individuals publicly to their responses.

With mailed questionnaires, two techniques assure anonymity (Sudman 1985). The best is to keep the questionnaire itself completely anonymous, with no identifying numbers or symbols; instead, the respondent gets a separate postcard, including his or her name, to mail at the same time he or she mails the completed questionnaire. This way, the researcher knows who has responded and need not send reminders, yet no one can link a particular respondent's name with a particular questionnaire. A second way to ensure anonymity is to attach a cover sheet to the questionnaire with an identifying number and assure the respondents that the researcher will remove and destroy the cover sheet once he or she has recorded the receipt of the questionnaire. This second procedure provides less assurance to the respondent because an unethical researcher might retain the link between questionnaires and their identification numbers. The first procedure, however, is more expensive because of the additional postcard mailing, so a researcher may prefer the second procedure for questionnaires that do not deal with highly sensitive issues that sometimes make respondents overly concerned about anonymity. If the material is not highly sensitive, assurances of confidentiality are adequate to ensure a good return rate.

No evidence indicates that assuring anonymity rather than confidentiality increases the response rate in nonsensitive surveys (Moser and Kalton 1972).

Finally, the cover letter should include a deadline for returning the questionnaire—a deadline calculated to take into account mailing time and a few days to complete the questionnaire. The rationale for a fairly tight deadline is that it encourages the recipients to complete the questionnaire soon after they receive it and not set it aside where they can forget or misplace it.

Payment. Research consistently shows that we can also increase response rates by offering a payment or other incentives as a part of the appeal for cooperation and that the incentives need not be large to have a positive effect. Studies find that, depending on the respondents, an incentive of between $2 and $20 can add 10 percent to a response rate (Warriner et al. 1996; Woodruff, Conway, and Edwards 2000). For the greatest effect, researchers should include such payments with the initial mailing instead of promising payment on return of the questionnaire. One study found that including the payment with the questionnaire boosted the return rate by 12 percent over promising payment on the questionnaire's return (Berry and Kanouse 1987). Researchers have used other types of incentives, such as entering each respondent in a lottery or donating to charity for each questionnaire returned, but these have shown mixed results as far as increasing response rates.

Mailing procedures also affect response rates. It almost goes without saying that researchers should supply a stamped, self-addressed envelope for returning the questionnaire to make return as convenient as possible for the respondent. The type of postage utilized also affects the response rate, with stamps bringing about 4 percent higher return than bulk-printed postage (Yammarino, Skinner, and Childers 1991). Presumably the stamp makes the questionnaire appear more personal and less like unimportant junk mail. A regular stamped envelope also substantially increases the response rate in comparison with a business reply envelope (Armstrong and Luck 1987).

Follow-Ups. The most important procedural matter affecting response rates is the use of follow-up letters. A substantial percentage of nonrespondents to the initial mailing will respond to follow-up letters. With two follow-ups, researchers can achieve 15 to 20 percent increases over the initial return (James and Bolstein 1990; Woodruff, Conway, and Edwards 2000). Such follow-ups are clearly essential; researchers can do them by telephone, if budget permits and speed is important. With aggressive follow-ups, the difference in response rates between mailed questionnaires and interviews declines substantially (Goyder 1985).

In general, researchers utilize two-step follow-ups. Some send follow-up letters encouraging return of the questionnaire to nonrespondents when response to the initial mailing drops off. This letter should include a restatement of the points in the cover letter, with an additional appeal for cooperation. When response to the first follow-up declines, the researcher then sends a second follow-up to the remaining nonrespondents and includes another copy of the questionnaire in case people have misplaced the original. After two follow-ups, we consider the remaining nonrespondents a pretty intransigent lot, as additional follow-ups generate relatively few further responses.

Length and Appearance. Two other factors that affect the rate of response to a mailed questionnaire are the length of the questionnaire and its appearance. As length increases, the response rate declines. However, no hard-and-fast rule governs the length of mailed questionnaires. Much depends on the intelligence and literacy of the respondents, the degree of interest in the topic of the questionnaire, and other such matters. However, it is probably a good idea to keep the questionnaire to less than five pages long, requiring no more than 30 minutes to fill out. Researchers must take great care to remove any extraneous questions or any questions not essential to the hypotheses under investigation (Epstein and Tripodi 1977). Although keeping the questionnaire less than five pages is a general guide, researchers should not strive to achieve this by cramming so much material onto each page that the respondent has difficulty using the instrument—because the appearance of the questionnaire is also important in generating a high response rate. As discussed earlier, the use of boxed response choices and smooth transitions through contingency questions help make completing the questionnaire easier and more enjoyable for the respondent, which in turn increases the probability that he or she will return it.

Other Influences on Response Rate.

Many other factors can work to change response rates. In telephone surveys, for example, the voice and manner of the interviewer can have an important effect (Oksenberg, Coleman, and Cannell 1986). Interviewers with higher-pitched, louder voices and clear, distinct pronunciation have lower refusal rates. The same is true for interviewers who sound competent and upbeat. Reminders of confidentiality can negatively affect the response rate (Frey 1986): If an interviewer reminds a respondent of the confidentiality of the information partway through the interview, the respondent is more likely to refuse to respond to some of the remaining questions than is someone who does not receive such a reminder. The reminder may work to undo whatever rapport the interviewer has already built up with the respondent.

A survey following all the suggested procedures should yield an acceptably high response rate. Specialized populations may, of course, produce either higher or lower rates. Because so many variables are involved, we offer only rough guidelines for evaluating response rates with mailed questionnaires. The desired response rate is 100 percent, of course. Anything less than 50 percent is highly suspect as far as its representativeness is concerned. Unless some evidence of the representativeness can be presented, we should use great caution when generalizing from such a sample. In fact, it might be best to treat the resulting sample as a nonprobability sample from which we cannot make confident generalizations. In terms of what a researcher can expect, response rates in the 60 percent range are good; anything more than 70 percent is very good. However, even with these response rates, we should use caution about generalizing and make attempts to check for bias due to nonresponse. The bottom line, whether the response rate is high or low, is to report it honestly so that those reading the research can judge for themselves about its generalizability.

Checking for Bias Due to Nonresponse

Even if researchers obtain a relatively high rate of response, they should investigate possible bias due to nonresponse by determining the extent to which respondents differ from nonrespondents (Groves 1989; Miller and Salkind 2002; Rea and Parker 1992). One common method is to compare the characteristics of the respondents with the characteristics of the population from which they were selected. If a database on the population exists, we can simplify this job. For example, if researchers are studying a representative sample of welfare recipients in a community, the Department of Social Services is likely to have data on age, sex, marital status, level of education, and other characteristics for all welfare recipients in the community. The researchers can compare the respondents with this database on the characteristics for which data have already been collected. A second approach to assessing bias resulting from nonresponse is to locate a subsample of nonrespondents and interview them. In this way, we can compare the responses to the questionnaire by a representative sample of nonrespondents with those of the respondents. This is the preferred method because we can measure directly the direction and the extent of bias that are due to nonresponse. It is, however, the most costly and time-consuming approach.

Any check for bias due to nonresponse, of course, informs us only about those characteristics on which we make comparisons. It does not prove that the respondents are representative of the whole sample on any other variables—including those that might be of considerable importance to the study. In short, although we can gather some information regarding such bias, in most cases we cannot *prove* that bias due to nonresponse does not exist.

The proper design of survey instruments is important to collecting valid data. Research in Practice 7.1 describes some of the key elements designed into a questionnaire used in an applied research project on the human services.

RESEARCH IN PRACTICE 7.1

NEEDS ASSESSMENT:

The Pregnancy Risk Assessment Monitoring System

During the 1980s, policymakers in the United States became increasingly aware of distressing pregnancy risk statistics. For example, while infant mortality rates were declining, they were still distressingly high, and the prevalence of low-birth-weight infants showed little change. At the same time, such maternal behaviors as smoking, drug use, and limited use of prenatal and pediatric care services were recognized as contributors to this lack of improvement. As a result of these concerns, the Centers for Disease Control and Prevention (CDC) developed the Pregnancy Risk Assessment Monitoring System, or PRAMS (Colley Gilbert et al. 1999). According to the CDC, the PRAMS survey (actually a questionnaire) is a "surveillance system" that focuses on maternal behaviors and experiences before and during a woman's pregnancy and during her child's early infancy. PRAMS supplements data from vital records for planning and assessing perinatal health programs within states. As of 1999, almost half of all states had grants to participate in the program, which currently covers more than 40 percent of all U.S. births. PRAMS is an excellent example of how researchers can put the advantages of questionnaires to use in applied research and social policy development.

The survey provides each state with data representative of all new mothers in the state. For a sampling frame, PRAMS relies on eligible birth certifi-

cates. Every month, researchers select a stratified sample of 100 to 250 new mothers in each participating state. Once the sample has been selected, the project is persistent in its efforts to reach the potential respondents. The sequence for PRAMS contact includes:

1. **Pre-letter.** This letter introduces PRAMS to the sampled mother and informs her that a questionnaire will soon arrive.
2. **Initial Mail Questionnaire Packet.** This packet goes to all sampled mothers 3–7 days after the pre-letter. The packet contains a letter explaining how and why the mother was chosen and eliciting her cooperation. The letter provides instructions for completing the questionnaire, explains any incentive or reward provided, and includes a telephone number the respondent may call for additional information. The questionnaire booklet itself is 14 pages long, with an attractive cover and an extra page for the mother's comments. A question-and-answer brochure contains additional information to help convince the mother to complete the questionnaire and a calendar to serve as a memory aid when answering the survey questions. Finally, the packet contains a participation incentive, such as coupons for birth certificates,

An Assessment of Questionnaires

Advantages.   As a technique of survey research, questionnaires have a number of desirable features. First, they gather data far more inexpensively and quickly than interviews. Mailed questionnaires require only four to six weeks, whereas obtaining the same data by personal interviews would likely take a minimum of several months. Mailed questionnaires also save the expense of hiring interviewers, interviewer travel, and other such costs.

Second, mailed questionnaires enable the researcher to collect data from a geographically dispersed sample. It costs no more to mail a questionnaire across the country than across a city. Costs of interviewer travel rise enormously as distance increases, making interviewing over wide geographic areas expensive.

Third, with questions of a personal or sensitive nature, mailed questionnaires may provide more accurate answers than interviews. People may be more likely to respond honestly to such questions when they are not face to face with a person they perceive as possibly making judgments about them. In practice, researchers may use a combination of questionnaire and interview to address this prob-a raffle for a cash award, postage stamps, bibs, or other inexpensive items.

3. **Tickler.** The tickler serves as a thank-you/reminder note, and is sent 7–10 days after the initial mail packet.

4. **Second Mail Questionnaire Packet.** This packet is sent 7–14 days after the tickler was sent to all sampled mothers who did not respond.

5. **Third Mail Questionnaire Packet (Optional).** This third packet goes to all remaining nonrespondents 7–14 days after the second questionnaire.

6. **Telephone Follow-Up.** Researchers initiate telephone follow-up for all nonrespondents 7–14 days after the mailing of the last questionnaire.

For 1997, PRAMS reported survey response rates that ranged from a low of 69 percent for West Virginia to a high of 80 percent for Maine.

Because PRAMS data are based on good samples drawn from the whole population, we can generalize findings from its data analyses to an entire state's population of women having live births. The questionnaire consists of a core component and a state-specific component that can ask questions that address the particular data needs of a state.

According to the CDC, findings from analysis of PRAMS data have enhanced states' understanding of maternal behaviors and experiences and their relationship with adverse pregnancy outcomes. Thus, these data are used to develop and assess programs and policies designed to reduce those outcomes. Some states have participated since 1987, so continuous data collection also permits states to monitor trends in key indicators over time. For example, one specific topic about which participants are queried is infant sleep position because infants who sleep on their backs are less susceptible to Sudden Infant Death Syndrome. Analyzing the data from 1996 to 1997 indicated that 6 of the 10 participating states reported a significant decrease in the prevalence of the stomach (prone) sleeping position.

In addition to illustrating the principles of sound survey design in action, the PRAMS project demonstrates the value of survey research as a tool in applied research. Although the data PRAMS generates may certainly be of use in expanding knowledge of human behavior, its primary role is as a tool for informing social policy, identifying needs requiring intervention, and assessing progress toward meeting policy objectives. Readers who would like to learn more about this project, including examining the core questionnaire itself, will find many useful resources at the CDC's Reproductive Health Web site at www.cdc.gov/nccd-php/drh/srv_prams.htm

lem. Written questions or computer-assisted self-interviewing have proven to generate more accurate information (Newman et al. 2002). A self-administered questionnaire increased reporting of male-to-male sexual activity over standard interview procedures in the General Social Survey (Anderson and Stall 2002).

Finally, mailed questionnaires eliminate the problem of interviewer bias, which occurs when an interviewer influences a person's response to a question by what he or she says, his or her tone of voice, or demeanor. Because no interviewer is present when the respondent fills out the question-naire, an interviewer cannot bias the answers to a questionnaire in any particular direction (Cannell and Kahn 1968).

Disadvantages. Despite their many advantages, mailed questionnaires have important limitations that may make them less desirable for some research efforts (Moser and Kalton 1972).

First, mailed questionnaires require a minimal degree of literacy and facility in English that some respondents may not possess. Substantial nonresponse is, of course, likely with such people. But nonresponse due to illiteracy does not seriously bias the results of most general-population surveys. Self-administered questionnaires are more successful among people who are better educated, motivated to respond, and involved in issues and organizations. However, some groups of interest to human service practitioners often do not possess these characteristics. If the survey is aimed at a special population in which the researcher suspects lower-than-average literacy, personal interviews are a better choice.

Second, the questions must all be sufficiently simple to comprehend on the basis of printed instructions. Third, there is no opportunity to probe for more information or evaluate the nonverbal behavior of the respondents. The answers they mark on the questionnaire form are final. Fourth, the researcher has no assurance that the person who should answer the questionnaire is the one who actually does so. Fifth, the researcher cannot consider responses independent, for the respondent can read through the entire questionnaire before completing it. Finally, all mailed questionnaires face the problem of nonresponse bias.

Interviews

In an interview, the investigator or an assistant reads the questions directly to the respondents and records their answers. Interviews offer the investigator a degree of flexibility not available with questionnaires. One area of increased flexibility relates to the degree of structure built into an interview.

The Structure of Interviews

The element of structure in interviews refers to the degree of freedom that the interviewer has in conducting the interview and that respondents have in answering questions. We classify interviews in terms of three levels of structure: (1) *unstandardized,* (2) *nonschedule-standardized,* and (3) *schedule-standardized.*

The *unstandardized interview* has the least structure. All the interviewer typically has for guidance is a general topic area, as illustrated in Figure 7.1. By developing his or her own questions and probes as the interview progresses, the interviewer explores the topic with the respondent. The approach is

called "unstandardized" because each interviewer asks different questions and obtains different information from each respondent. There is a heavy reliance on the skills of the interviewer to ask good questions and to keep the interview going; this can only be done if experienced interviewers are available. This unstructured approach makes unstandardized interviewing especially appropriate for exploratory research. In Figure 7.1, for example, only the general topic of parent–child conflicts guides the interviewer. The example also illustrates the suitability of this style of interviewing for exploratory research, as the interviewer is directed to search for as many areas of conflict as can be found.

Nonschedule-standardized interviews add more structure, with the topic narrower and specific questions asked of all respondents. However, the interview remains fairly conversational; the interviewer is free to probe, rephrase questions, or take the questions in whatever order best fits that particular interview. Note in Figure 7.1 that specific questions are of the open-ended type, allowing the respondent full freedom of expression. As in the case of the unstandardized form, success with this type of interview requires an experienced interviewer.

The *schedule-standardized interview* is the most structured type. An **interview schedule** contains specific instructions for the interviewer, specific questions in a fixed order, and transition phrases for the interviewer to use. Sometimes the schedule also contains acceptable rephrasings for questions and a selection of stock probes. Schedule-standardized interviews are fairly rigid, with neither interviewer nor respondent allowed to depart from the structure of the schedule. Although some questions may be open-ended, most are closed-ended. In fact, some schedule-standardized interviews are quite similar to a questionnaire except that the interviewer asks the questions rather than having the respondent read them. In Figure 7.1, note the use of cards with response alternatives handed to the respondent. This is a popular way of supplying respondents with a complex set of closed-ended alternatives. Note also the precise directions for the interviewer as well as verbatim phrases to read to the respondent. Relatively untrained, part-time interviewers

Figure 7.1 Examples of Various Interview Structures

The Unstandardized Interview
Instructions to the interviewer: Discover the kinds of conflicts that the child has had with the parents. Conflicts should include disagreements, tensions due to past, present, or potential disagreements, outright arguments and physical conflicts. Be alert for as many categories and examples of conflicts and tensions as possible.

The Nonschedule-Standardized Interview
Instructions to the interviewer: Your task is to discover as many specific kinds of conflicts and tensions between child and parent as possible. The more *concrete* and detailed the account of each type of conflict the better. Although there are 12 areas of possible conflict which we want to explore (listed in question 3 below), you should not mention any area until after you have asked the first two questions in the order indicated. The first question takes an indirect approach, giving you time to build up a rapport with the respondent and to demonstrate a nonjudgmental attitude toward teenagers who have conflicts with their parents.
  1. What sorts of problems do teenagers you know have in getting along with their parents?
     (Possible probes: Do they always agree with their parents? Do any of your friends have "problem parents"? What other kinds of disagreements do they have?)
  2. What sorts of disagreements do you have with your parents?
     (Possible probes: Do they cause you any problems? In what ways do they try to restrict you? Do you always agree with them on everything? Do they like the same things you do? Do they try to get you to do some things you don't like? Do they ever bore you? Make you mad? Do they understand you? etc.)
  3. Have you ever had any disagreements with either of your parents over:
     a. Using the family car
     b. Friends of the same sex
     c. Dating
     d. School (homework, grades, activities)
     e. Religion (church, beliefs, etc.)
     f. Political views
     g. Working for pay outside the home
     h. Allowances
     i. Smoking
     j. Drinking
     k. Eating habits
     l. Household chores

The Schedule-Standardized Interview
Interviewer's explanation to the teenage respondent: We are interested in the kinds of problems teenagers have with their parents. We need to know how many teenagers have which kinds of conflicts with their parents and whether they are just mild disagreements or serious fights. We have a checklist here of some of the kinds of things that happen. Would you think about your own situation and put a check to show which conflicts you, personally, have had and about how often they have happened. Be sure to put a check in every row. If you have never had a conflict then put the check in the first column where it says "never."
     (*Hand him the first card dealing with conflicts over the use of the automobile, saying,* "If you don't understand any of those things listed or have some other things you would like to mention about how you disagree with your parents over the automobile let me know and we'll talk about it.") (*When the respondent finishes checking all rows, hand him card number 2, saying,* "Here is a list of types of conflicts teenagers have with their parents over their friends of the same sex. Do the same with this as you did the last list.")

Automobile	*Never*	*Only Once*	*More Than Once*	*Many Times*
1. Wanting to learn to drive				
2. Getting a driver's license				
3. Wanting to use the family car				
4. What you use the car for				
5. The way you drive it				
6. Using it too much				
7. Keeping the car clean				
8. Putting gas or oil in the car				
9. Repairing the car				
10. Driving someone else's car				
11. Wanting to own a car				
12. The way you drive your own car				
13. What you use your car for				
14. Other				

Source From Raymond L. Gorden, *Interviewing: Strategy, Techniques, and Tactics,* 4th ed. Copyright © 1987 by the Dorsey Press. Reprinted by permission of the estate of Raymond Gorden.

can conduct schedule-standardized interviews be-cause the schedule contains nearly everything they need to say. This makes schedule-standardized interviews the preferred choice for studies with large sample sizes and many interviewers. The structure of these interviews also ensures that all respondents receive the same questions in the same order. This heightens reliability and makes schedule-standardized interviews popular for rigorous hypothesis testing. Research in Practice 7.2 explores some further advantages of having more or less structure in an interview.

RESEARCH IN PRACTICE 7.2

NEEDS ASSESSMENT:

Merging Quantitative and Qualitative Measures

That survey research is necessarily quantitative in nature is probably a common misconception. Certainly, survey results presented in the popular media support such a view. Virtually every edition of the evening news presents the results from one or more surveys indicating that a certain percentage of respondents hold a given opinion or plan to vote for a particular candidate or offers other information that is basically quantitative or reduced to numbers. Especially in the case of face-to-face interviewing, however, survey research is not necessarily limited to quantitative analysis. In fact, as we noted in the discussion of Figure 7.1, interviews run the gamut from totally quantitative in the highly structured type to fully qualitative in the least structured variety, as well as any combination in between. This flexibility has led some researchers to combine both quantitative and qualitative measures in individual studies to obtain the benefits of each approach.

Two studies of homeless families headed by females illustrate such a merging of interview styles. Shirley Thrasher and Carol Mowbray (1995) interviewed 15 homeless families from three shelters, focusing primarily on the experiences of the mothers and their efforts to take care of their children. Elizabeth Timberlake (1994) conducted another study, basing hers on interviews with 200 families not in shelters and focusing predominantly on the experiences of the homeless children. In both studies, the researchers used structured interview questions to provide quantitative demographic information about the homeless families and to get an idea about who makes up their ranks. For example, Timberlake found the ethnic composition of her sample to be 40 percent African American, 35 percent Caucasian, and 21 percent Hispanic, with 4 percent unclassified. She also found that the average length of time of homelessness, at the time of the interviews, was 7.7 months, with a range of 1.2 to 19.8 months. The other study noted that at the time of their interviews, all the women were unemployed.

As interesting as these numbers were, the researchers in both studies wanted to get at the more personal meaning of and feelings about being homeless. For this they turned to the unstructured parts of the interviews (sometimes called *ethnographic interviews*) designed to get the subjects to tell their stories in their own words. The goal of both studies was to assess the needs of the homeless families in order to develop new programs to assist them or to modify existing programs to better fit their needs. The researchers felt that the best way to accomplish this goal was to get the story of being homeless, in as pure a form as possible, from the people who lived it, without any distortion by the researchers' preconceived notions. The open-ended questions that Timberlake asked the homeless children illustrate this unstructured approach: "Tell me about not having a place to live." "What is it like?" "What do you do?" "How do you feel?" "How do you handle being homeless?" "Are there things that you do or say?" The questions Thrasher and Mowbray asked the homeless mothers were remarkably similar. Both studies used probes as needed to elicit greater response and clarify vague responses.

An example from Thrasher and Mowbray illustrates how responses to open-ended questions provide insight into what the respondent is experiencing. The researchers found that a common experience of the women in the shelters was that, before coming to the shelter, they had bounced around among friends and relatives, experiencing a series of short-term and unstable living arrangements. The researchers present the following quote from 19-year-old "Nancy":

I went from friend to friend before going back to my mother and her boyfriend. And all my friends they live with their parents, and so you know, I could only stay like a night, maybe two nights before I had to leave. So, the only thing I could do was to come here to the shelter and so that's what I did. After all, there is only so many friends. I went to live once with my grandmother for a week who lives in a senior citizens' high riser. But they don't allow anyone to stay there longer than a week as a visitor. So, I had to move on. I finally went to my social worker and told her I don't have any place to stay. She put me in a motel first because there was no opening in the shelter. Then I came here.

As this example illustrates, there is no substitute for hearing the plight of these people in their own words to help those who are not homeless gain some understanding of what it is like not to have a stable place to call home.

In part because of her much larger sample, Timberlake did not tape-record her interviews and so made no verbatim transcripts. Instead, she took field notes that summarized the responses of the homeless children. This resulted in a different approach to analysis because she did not have the long narratives that Thrasher and Mowbray had. Instead, she had a large number of summarized statements from her notes. She ended up doing a more quantitative analysis by categorizing and analyzing the respondents' statements. Timberlake found that the responses clustered around three themes: separation/loss, caretaking/nurturance, and security/protection. Within each theme were statements along two dimensions of the theme, which Timberlake refers to as "deprivation" and "restoration," respectively—the negative statements about what is bad about being homeless and the positive statements about what the children still have and how they cope. As we can see from Table 7.4, Timberlake tabulated the number of each kind of statement. It seems rather indicative of the devastation of homelessness on the children that Timberlake found approximately three times as many deprivation statements as restoration statements. It is important to note that these categories and themes were not used by the respondents themselves but were created by Timberlake in an effort to extract theoretical meaning from the narratives. Another researcher analyzing the same data, but with a different theoretical focus, might create different categories. Some critics of this sort of quantifying of narrative data suggest a danger of the researcher imposing too much of himself or herself into the analysis.

Neither of these studies used an interview format that would be suitable for interviewing a large, randomly selected sample of homeless people with the purpose of estimating the demographic characteristics of the entire homeless population. Imagine trying to organize and summarize data from several thousand interviews like those conducted by Thrasher and Mowbray! To reasonably accomplish such a population estimate, a schedule-standardized interview format, producing quantitative data, is far more appropriate. However, if the goal of the research project is to gain an understanding of the personal experiences and reactions to being homeless, as in the two studies just discussed, then presenting results in the respondents' own words is more effective.

Timberlake's study developed the concepts of deprivation and restoration, which she essentially discovered in her data. Although more abstract and removed from the respondents than direct quotations, the statements in Table 7.4 nevertheless communicate a sense of the personal meaning of homelessness while providing quantitative

continued on next page

summary data. If researchers were to design a schedule-standardized survey project to do a population description of the homeless, studies such as the two discussed here would be invaluable for determining what concepts to measure and for developing the quantitative indicators that such a study would demand.

These two studies illustrate that both qualitative and quantitative approaches are essential to social research. Which approach is most appropriate depends on the particular goals of the research; in some cases, a blend of both quantitative and qualitative approaches used in the same project obtains the desired results.

Table 7.4 Meaning of Homelessness

	Complaints About Deprivation (n = 2,835, 71.8% of total items)	Statements About Restoration (n = 1,111, 27.2% of total items)
Separation/Loss (n = 1,669, 42.3% of total items)	(n = 1,215, 72.8% of deprivation complaints) They take away your home. They make you move all the time. My friends are all gone. My dog is gone. I got no room. I can't do nothing. I got no privacy. I'm scared I'll get left. We got no privacy. We have to move a lot.	(n = 455, 27.2% of restoration statements) Mama stays with us. We got our car. We got our place to sleep. I got my doll/ball/favorite toy. I still got my clothes. I still got my school.
Caretaking/Nurturance (n = 1,400, 35.5% of total items)	(n = 945, 67.5% of deprivation complaints) We got no food. We got nothing left. We got no place to sleep. We got no clothes. We have nothing. Mama lost her job. Daddy left us. Mama's boyfriend left us.	(n = 455, 32.5% of restoration statements) We sleep in the car. We get food at the kitchen. Mama works. Mama stands in line to get money. I look after Mama 'cause she cries. I help out a lot. Mama gets us food. I get us money and food sometimes.
Security/Protection (n = 876, 22.2% of total items)	(n = 675, 77.1% of deprivation complaints) No place is safe. Weird things happen. It's too noisy and crowded. People get cut/shot/killed. People steal your stuff. Too many people tell you what to do.	(n = 201, 22.9% of restoration statements) We're safe in the car. Daddy protects us. John/Bill/Tom protects us. We get away from druggies/drunks.

Source Adapted from Elizabeth M. Timberlake, "Children with No Place to Call Home: Survival in the Cars and on the Streets," *Child and Adolescent Social Work Journal,* Vol. 4 (1994), p. 268. Used with permission of Kluwer Academic/Plenum Publishers.

Contacting Respondents

As with researchers who mail questionnaires, those who rely on interviewers face the problem of contacting respondents and eliciting their cooperation. Many interviews are conducted in the homes of the respondents; locating and traveling to respondents' homes are two of the more troublesome and costly aspects of interviewing. It has been estimated that as much as 40 percent of a typical interviewer's time is spent traveling (Sudman 1965). Because so much time and cost are involved and because researchers desire high response rates, they direct substantial efforts at minimizing the rate of refusal. The first contact of prospective respondents has substantial impact on the refusal rate.

Two approaches to contacting respondents that might appear logical to the neophyte researcher have, in fact, an effect opposite of that desired. It might seem that *telephoning* to set up an appointment for the interview is a good idea. In reality, it greatly increases the rate of refusal. In one experiment, for example, the part of the sample that was telephoned had nearly *triple* the rate of refusal of those contacted in person (Brunner and Carroll 1967). Apparently, it is much easier to refuse over the relatively impersonal medium of the telephone than in a face-to-face encounter with an interviewer. *Sending people a letter* asking them to participate in an interview has much the same effect (Cartwright and Tucker 1967). The letter seems to give people sufficient time before the interviewer arrives to develop reasons why they do not want to cooperate. Those first contacted in person, on the other hand, have only those excuses they can muster on the spur of the moment. Clearly, then, interviewers obtain the lowest refusal rates by contacting interviewees in person.

Additional factors can affect the refusal rate (Gorden 1987). For example, information regarding the research project should blanket the total survey population through the news media to demonstrate general community acceptance of the project. Information provided to the media should contain essentially the same information as in a cover letter for a mailed questionnaire, with a few differences (see Table 7.3). Pictures of the interviewers and mention of any props they carry (such as clipboards or zipper cases) should be included. This information assists people in identifying interviewers and reduces possible confusion with salespeople or solicitors. In fact, it is a good idea to equip the interviewers with identification badges or something easily recognizable so they are not mistaken for others who go door to door. When the interviewers go into the field, they should take along copies of the news coverage. If they encounter a respondent who has not seen the media coverage, they can show the clippings during the initial contact.

The timing of the initial contact also affects the refusal rate. It is preferable to contact interviewees at a time convenient for them to complete the interview without the need for a second call. Depending on the nature of the sample, predicting availability may be fairly easy or virtually impossible. For example, if interviewers can obtain the information required from any household member, almost any reasonable time of day will do. On the other hand, if the interviewer must contact specific individuals, timing becomes more critical. If we must interview the breadwinner in a household, for example, then we should probably make the contacts at night or on weekends, unless knowledge of the person's occupation suggests a different time of greater availability. Whatever time the interviewer makes the initial contact, it still may not be convenient for the respondent, especially if the interview is lengthy. If the respondent is pressed for time, it is better to use the initial contact to establish rapport and set another time for the interview, even though callbacks are costly. This is certainly preferable to the rushed interview that results in inferior data.

When the interviewer and potential respondent first meet, the interviewer should include certain points of information in the introduction. One suggestion is the following (Smith 1981):

> Good day. I am from the Public Opinion Survey Unit of the University of Missouri (shows official identification). We are doing a survey at this time on how people feel about police-community relationships. This study is being done throughout the state, and the results will be used by local and state governments. The

addresses at which we interview are chosen entirely by chance, and the interview only takes 45 minutes. All information is entirely confidential, of course.

Respondents will be looking for much the same basic information as with mailed questionnaires. As the preceding example illustrates, interviewers should also inform respondents of the approximate length of the interview. After the introduction, the interviewer should be prepared to elaborate on any points the interviewee questions. To avoid biasing responses, however, the interviewer must exercise care when discussing the purpose of the survey.

Conducting an Interview

A large-scale survey with an adequate budget often turns to private research agencies to train interviewers and conduct interviews. Smaller research projects, however, often cannot afford this and have to train and coordinate their own team of interviewers, possibly with the researchers themselves doing some of the interviewing. It is important, therefore, to know how to conduct an interview properly.

The Interview as a Social Relationship.   The interview is a social relationship designed to exchange information between respondent and interviewer. The quantity and quality of information exchanged depend on how astute and creative the interviewer is at understanding and managing that relationship (Fowler and Mangione 1990; Holstein and Gubrium 2003). Human service workers are generally knowledgeable regarding the properties and processes of social interaction; in fact, much human service practice is founded on the establishment of social relationships with clients. However, a few elements of the research interview are worth emphasizing because they have direct implications for conducting interviews.

A research interview is a secondary relationship in which the interviewer has a practical, utilitarian goal. It is easy, especially for an inexperienced interviewer, to be drawn into a more casual or personal interchange with the respondent. Especially with a friendly, outgoing respondent, the conversation might drift off to topics like sports, politics, or children. That, however, is not the purpose of the interview. The goal is not to make friends or give the respondent a sympathetic ear but to collect complete and unbiased data following the interview schedule.

We all recognize the powerful impact that first impressions have on perceptions. This is especially true in interview situations in which the interviewer and respondent are likely to be total strangers. The first impressions that impact a respondent are the physical and social characteristics of the interviewer. So we need to take considerable care to ensure that the first contact enhances the likelihood of the respondent's cooperation (Warwick and Lininger 1975). Most research suggests that interviewers are more successful if they have social characteristics similar to those of their respondents. Thus, such characteristics as socioeconomic status, age, sex, race, and ethnicity might influence the success of the interview—especially if the subject matter of the interview relates to one of these topics. In addition, the personal demeanor of the interviewer plays an important role; interviewers should be neat, clean, and businesslike but friendly.

After exchanging initial pleasantries, the interviewer should begin the interview. The respondent may be a bit apprehensive during the initial stages of an interview. In recognition of this, the interview should begin with fairly simple, nonthreatening questions. A schedule, if used, should begin with these kinds of questions. The demographic questions (reserved until the later stages of a mailed questionnaire) are good to begin an interview. Respondents' familiarity with this information makes the questions nonthreatening and a good means of reducing tension in the respondent.

Probes.   If an interview schedule is used, the interview progresses in accordance with it. As needed, the interviewer uses **probes,** or follow-up questions, intended to elicit clearer and more complete responses. In some cases, the interview schedule contains suggestions for probes. In less structured interviews, however, interviewers must develop and use their own probes. Probes can take the form of a pause in conversation that encourages the respondent to elaborate or an explicit request to clarify or elaborate on something. A major concern with any probe is that it not bias the respondent's answer by suggesting the answer (Fowler and Mangione 1990).

Recording Responses.   A central task of interviewers, of course, is to record the responses of respondents. The four most common ways are classifying responses into predetermined categories, summarizing key points, taking verbatim notes, and recording the interview with a tape recorder or videotape machine.

Recording responses is generally easiest when we use an interview schedule. Because closed-ended questions are typical of such schedules, we can simply classify responses into the predetermined alternatives. This simplicity of recording is another factor making schedule-standardized interviews suitable for use with relatively untrained interviewers because no special recording skills are required.

With nonschedule interviewing, the questions are likely to be open-ended and the responses longer. Often, all we need to record are the key points the respondent makes. The interviewer condenses and summarizes what the respondent says. This requires an experienced interviewer familiar with the research questions who can accurately identify what to record and do so without injecting his or her own interpretation, which would bias the summary.

Sometimes we may want to record everything the respondent says verbatim to avoid the possible biasing effect of summarizing responses. If the anticipated responses are reasonably short, competent interviewers can take verbatim notes. Special skills, such as shorthand, may be necessary. If the responses are lengthy, verbatim note taking can cause difficulties, such as leading the interviewer to fail to monitor the respondent or to be unprepared to probe when necessary. It can also damage rapport by making it appear that the interviewer is ignoring the respondent. Recording interviews can eliminate problems like this but increase the costs substantially. Though individual cassettes and recorders are not expensive, the number needed for a large-scale survey would certainly drive costs up considerably. The really big cost comes, however, in transcribing the tapes, which requires vast amounts of secretarial time (Gorden 1987).

The fear some researchers have that tape recorders increase the refusal rate appears unwarranted (Gorden 1987). If the recorder is explained as a routine procedure that aids in capturing complete and accurate responses, few respondents object.

Controlling Interviewers.   Once interviewers go into the field, the quality of the resulting data depends heavily on them. It is a naive researcher indeed who assumes that, without supervision, they will all do their job properly, especially when part-time interviewers who have little commitment to the research project are used. Proper supervision begins during interviewer training, stressing the importance of contacting the right respondents and meticulously following established procedures.

Although sloppy, careless work is one concern, a more serious issue is **interviewer falsification,** or the intentional departure from the designed interviewer instructions, unreported by the interviewer, which can result in the contamination of data (AAPOR Standards Committee 2003). A dramatic illustration of this was discovered in a National Institutes of Health survey of AIDS and other sexually transmitted diseases (Marshall 2000). Eleven months into the study, a data-collection manager was troubled by the apparent overproductivity of one interviewer. A closer look revealed that, while the worker was submitting completed interviews, some were clearly falsified. For example, the address of one interview site turned out to be an abandoned house. The worker was dismissed, and others came under suspicion. It took months to root out what was referred to as an "epidemic of falsification" on this research project. A cessation of random quality checks was identified as a major contributing factor to the problem.

Falsified data is believed to be rare, but survey organizations take this problem seriously and follow established procedures to address it. Factors that contribute to falsification include pressure on interviewers to obtain very high response rates and the use of long, complicated questionnaires that may frustrate both interviewer and respondent. The problem can be prevented by careful recruitment, screening, and training of interviewers; by recognizing incentives for falsification created by work quotas and pay structures; and by monitoring and verifying interviewer work (Bushery, Reichert, Albright, and Rossiter 1999).

Minorities and the Interview Relationship

Many respondents in surveys have different characteristics than those of the interviewers. Does it make a difference in terms of the quantity or quality of data collected in surveys when interviewer and interviewee have different characteristics? It appears that it does. In survey research, three elements interact to affect the quality of the data collected: minority status of the interviewer, minority status of the respondent, and minority content of the survey instrument. Researchers should carefully consider the interrelationships among these elements to ensure that the least amount of bias enters the data-collection process.

As we have emphasized, an interview is a social relationship in which interviewer and respondent have cultural and subcultural expectations for appropriate behavior. One set of expectations that comes into play is the social desirability of respondents' answers to questions. Substantial research documents a tendency for people to choose more desirable or socially acceptable answers to questions in surveys (DeMaio 1984; Holstein and Gubrium 2003), in part from the desire to appear sensible, reasonable, and pleasant to the interviewer. In all interpersonal contacts, including an interview relationship, people typically prefer to please someone rather than offend or alienate. In cases in which interviewer and respondent are from different racial, ethnic, or sexual groups, respondents tend to give answers they perceive to be more desirable (or at least less offensive) to the interviewer; this is especially true when the content of the questions is related to racial, ethnic, or sexual issues. A second set of expectations that comes into play and affects responses in interviews is the social distance between interviewer and respon-

dent, or how much they differ from each other on important social dimensions, such as age or minority status. Generally, the less social distance between people, the more freely, openly, and honestly they will talk. Racial, sexual, and ethnic differences often indicate a degree of social distance.

The impact of cross-race interviewing has been studied extensively with African American and white respondents (Anderson, Silver, and Abramson 1988; Bachman and O'Malley 1984; Bradburn and Sudman 1979; Dailey and Claus 2001). African American respondents, for example, express more warmth and closeness for whites when interviewed by a white person and are less likely to express dissatisfaction or resentment over discrimination or inequities against African Americans. White respondents tend to express more pro-black attitudes when the interviewer is African American. This race-of-interviewer effect can be quite large and occurs fairly consistently. Some research concludes that it plays a part mostly when questions involve race or other sensitive topics, but recent research suggests that its effect is more pervasive, affecting people's responses to many questions on a survey, not just the racial or sensitive questions (Davis 1997).

Fewer researchers have studied the impact of ethnicity on interviews, probably because the ethnicity of both interviewer and respondent is not as readily apparent in most cases as is race, which is visibly signified by skin color. In one study, both Jewish and non-Jewish interviewers asked questions about the extent of Jewish influence in the United States (Hyman 1954). Respondents were much more willing to say that Jews had too much influence when interviewed by a non-Jew.

Gender also has an effect on interviews. Women are much more likely to report honestly about topics such as rape, battering, sexual behavior, and male–female relationships in general when women interview them instead of men (Eichler 1988; Reinharz 1992). In a study of sexual behaviors with Latino couples, when women interviewed them, men reported fewer sexual partners and were less likely to report sex with strangers than when men interviewed them; male respondents were more likely to report sex with prostitutes or other men to older than to younger interviewers. Women were less likely to report oral sex to older interviewers (Wilson, Brown, Mejia, and Lavori 2002).

Some researchers recommend routinely matching interviewer and respondent for race, ethnicity, or gender in interviews on racial or sensitive topics, and this is generally sound advice. Sometimes, however, a little more thought is called for. The problem is that we are not always sure in which direction bias might occur. If white respondents give different answers to white as opposed to black interviewers, which of their answers most accurately reflect their attitudes? For the most part, we aren't sure. We generally assume that same-race interviewers gather more accurate data (Fowler and Mangione 1990). A more conservative assumption is that the truth falls somewhere between the data that the two interviewers collect.

When minorities speak a language different from that of the dominant group, conducting the interview in the dominant group's language can affect the quality of data collected (Marin and Marin 1991). For example, a study of Native American children in Canada found that these children expressed a strong white bias in racial preferences when the study was conducted in English; the bias declined significantly when interviewers used the children's native Ojibwa language (Annis and Corenblum 1986). This impact of language should not be surprising, considering that language is not just a mechanism for communication but also reflects cultural values, norms, and a way of life. So when interviewing groups where a language other than English is widely used, it is appropriate to consider conducting interviews in that other language.

An Assessment of Interviews

Advantages.   First, interviews can help *motivate* respondents to give more accurate and complete information. Respondents have little motivation to be accurate or complete when responding to a mailed questionnaire. They can hurry through it if they want to. The control an interviewer affords encour-

ages better responses, which is especially important as the information sought becomes more complex.

Second, interviewing offers an opportunity to *explain* questions that respondents may not otherwise understand. Again, if the information sought is complex, this can be of great importance, and interviews virtually eliminate the literacy problem that may accompany mailed questionnaires. Even lack of facility in English can be handled with multilingual interviewers. (When we conducted a needs assessment survey in some rural parts of Michigan's Upper Peninsula some years ago, we employed one interviewer who was fluent in Finnish because a number of people in the area spoke Finnish but little or no English.)

Third, the presence of an interviewer allows *control* over factors uncontrollable with mailed questionnaires. For example, the interviewer can ensure that the proper person responds to the questions and does so in sequence. Furthermore, the interviewer can arrange to conduct the interview so that the respondent does not consult with or is not influenced by other people before responding.

Fourth, interviewing is a more *flexible* form of data collection than questionnaires. The style of interviewing can be tailored to the needs of the study. A free, conversational style, with much probing, can be adopted in an exploratory study. In a more developed study, a highly structured approach can be utilized. This flexibility makes interviewing suitable for a far broader range of research situations than mailed questionnaires.

Finally, the interviewer can add *observational information* to the responses. What was the respondent's attitude toward the interview? Cooperative? Indifferent? Hostile? Did the respondent appear to fabricate answers? Did he or she react emotionally to some questions? This additional information helps to better evaluate the responses, especially when the subject matter is highly personal or controversial (Gorden 1987).

Disadvantages.   Some disadvantages associated with personal interviews may lead the researcher to choose another data-collection technique.

The first disadvantage is cost. Researchers must hire, train, and equip interviewers and pay for their travel. All of these expenses are costly.

The second limitation is time. Traveling to respondents' homes requires a lot of time and limits each interviewer to only a few interviews each day. To contact particular individuals, an interviewer may require several time-consuming callbacks. Project start-up operations, such as developing questions, designing schedules, and training interviewers, also require considerable time.

A third limitation of interviews is the problem of interviewer bias. Especially in unstructured interviews, interviewers may misinterpret or misrecord something because of their personal feelings about the topic. Furthermore, just as the interviewer's characteristics affect the respondent, so the characteristics of the respondent similarly affect the interviewer. Sex, age, race, social class, and a host of other factors may subtly shape the way in which the interviewer asks questions and interprets the respondent's answers.

A fourth limitation of interviews, especially with less structured interviews, is the possibility of significant but unnoticed variation in wording from one interview to the next or among interviewers. We know that variations in wording can produce variations in response, and the more freedom interviewers have in this regard, the more of a problem it is. Wording variation can affect both reliability and validity (see Chapter 5).

Telephone Surveys

Face-to-face interviews tend to be a considerably more expensive means of gathering data than either mailed questionnaires or telephone surveys (Rea and Parker 1992). As Table 7.5 shows, face-to-face interviews can be more than twice as expensive as phone or mail surveys. The table shows that face-to-face interviews incur substantially higher costs for locating residences, contacting respondents, conducting interviews, traveling, and training interviewers. Mail or telephone surveys require no travel time, fewer

interviewers, and fewer supervisory personnel. Although telephone charges are higher in telephone surveys, they are far outweighed by other savings. The cost advantages of the less expensive types of surveys make feasible much research that otherwise would be prohibitively expensive.

The speed with which a telephone survey can be completed also makes it preferable at times. If we want people's reactions to a particular event, for example, or repeated measures of public opinion, which can change rapidly, the speed of telephone surveys makes them preferable in these circumstances.

Certain areas of the country and many major cities contain substantial numbers of non-English-speaking people. These people are difficult to accommodate with mailed questionnaires and personal interviews unless we know ahead of time what language a respondent speaks. We can handle non-English-speaking people fairly easily with telephone surveys, however. All we need are a few multilingual interviewers. (Spanish speakers account for the vast majority of non-English-speaking people in the United States.) If an interviewer contacts a non-English-speaking respondent, he or she can simply transfer that respondent to an interviewer conversant in the respondent's language. Though multilingual interviewers can be and are used in personal interviews, this process is far less efficient, probably involving at least one callback to arrange for an interviewer with the needed language facility. A final advantage of telephone interviews is that supervision is much easier. The problem of interviewer falsification is eliminated because supervisors can monitor the interviews at any time. This makes it easy to ensure that specified procedures are followed and that any problems that might arise are quickly discovered and corrected.

Despite these considerable advantages, telephone surveys have several limitations that may make the method unsuitable for many research purposes. First, telephone surveys must be quite short in duration. Normally, the maximum length is about 20 minutes; most are even shorter. This is in sharp contrast to personal interviews, which can extend to an hour or longer. The time limitation obviously restricts the vol-

Table 7.5 Cost Comparison of Telephone, Mail, and Face-to-Face Surveys, with a Sample Size of 520

A. Mail Survey	Total Cost (dollars)		Total Cost (dollars)
Prepare for survey		Postage for return envelopes, 960 @	
Purchase sample list in machine-readable		$.55 each	528
form	375	Sign letters, stamp envelopes	100
Load database of names and addresses	17	Prepare mail-out packets	118
Graphic design for questionnaire cover		Third mail-out (960)	
(hire out)	100	Pre-stamped postcards, 4 bunches of 250 @	
Print questionnaires: 4 sheets, legal-size,		$.20 each	200
folded, 1,350 @ $.15 each (includes paper)		Address postcards	25
(hire out)	203	Print message and sign postcards	50
Telephone	100	Process, precode, edit 390 returned	
Supplies		questionnaires, 10 min each	545
Mail-out envelopes, 2,310 @ $.05 each,		Fourth mail-out (475)	
with return address	116	Print cover letter	25
Return envelopes, 1,350 @ $.05 each,		Address envelopes	25
pre-addressed but no return address	68	Sign letters, stamp envelopes	25
Letterhead for cover letters, 2,310 @		Prepare mail-out packets	168
$.05 each	116	Postage for mail-out, 475 @ $.55 each	261
Miscellaneous	200	Postage for return envelopes, 475 @ $.55 each	261
First mail-out (960)		Process, precode, edit 185 returned	
Print advance-notice letter	25	questionnaires, 10 min each	250
Address envelopes	25	**Total, excluding professional time**	**5,025**
Sign letters, stamp envelopes	50	Professional time (120 hrs @ $35,000 annual	
Postage for mail-out, 960 @ $.34 each	326	salary plus 20% fringe benefits)	2,423
Prepare mail-out packets	134	**Total, including professional time**	**7,418**
Second mail-out (960)			
Print cover letter	25		
Address envelopes	25		
Postage for mail-out, 960 @ $.55 each	528		

(continued on next page)

ume of information that interviewers can obtain and the depth to which they can explore issues. Telephone surveys work best when the information desired is fairly simple and the questions are uncomplicated.

A second limitation stems from the fact that telephone communication is only voice to voice. Lack of visual contact eliminates several desirable characteristics of personal interviews. The interviewer cannot supplement responses with observational information, and it is harder to probe effectively without seeing the respondent. Furthermore, a phone interview precludes the use of cards with response alternatives or other visual stimuli. The in-

ability to present complex sets of response alternatives in this format can make it difficult to ask some questions that are important.

Finally, as we noted in Chapter 6, surveys based on samples drawn from telephone directories may have considerable noncoverage because some people do not have telephones at all and others have unlisted numbers. Although modern telephone sampling techniques, such as random digit dialing, eliminate the problem of unlisted numbers, the approximately 6 percent of households without telephones remain unreachable and are concentrated among the poor and transient segments of

Table 7.5 *Continued*

B. Telephone Survey	Total Cost (dollars)	C. Face-to-Face Survey	Total Cost (dollars)
Prepare for survey		Prepare for survey	
Use add-a-digit calling based on systematic, random sampling from directory	84	Purchase map for area frame	200
Print interviewer manuals	37	Print interviewer manuals	29
Print questionnaires (940)	84	Print questionnaires (690)	379
Train interviewers (12-hour training session)	700	Train interviewers (20-hour training session)	1,134
Miscellaneous supplies	25	Miscellaneous supplies	25
		Conduct the survey	
Conduct the survey		Locate residences; contact respondents; conduct interviews; field-edit questionnaires; 3.5 completed interviews per 8-hour day	9,555
Contact and interview respondents; edit questionnaires; 50 minutes per completed questionnaire	2,786	Travel cost ($8.50 per completed interview; interviewers use own car)	4,420
Telephone charges	3,203	Office edit and general clerical (6 completed questionnaires per hour)	728
Total, excluding professional time	**6,919**	**Total, excluding professional time**	**16,570**
Professional time (120 hrs @$35,000 annual salary plus 20% fringe benefits)	2,423	Professional time (160 hrs @ $35,000 annual salary plus 20% fringe benefits)	3,231
Total, including professional time	**9,342**	**Total, including professional time**	**19,801**

Source Adapted from Priscilla Salant and Don A. Dillman, *How to Conduct Your Own Survey,* pp. 46–49. Copyright © 1994 by John Wiley & Sons, Inc. This material is used with permission of John Wiley & Sons, Inc.

the population. So some sampling bias remains even if we use random digit dialing. Because some human service clients are heavily concentrated in the population groups with lower rates of telephone service, we should exercise special caution before deciding on a telephone survey.

Online Surveys

The growth of the Internet has led to the possibility of conducting surveys using that medium rather than in person or through the mail or by telephone (Nesbary 2000). The term "Internet survey" or "Web survey" includes a diversity of methods with different purposes, populations, and target audiences. Some such surveys are sent as e-mail or an attachment to an e-mail; other surveys are available at a Web site. At one extreme, Web surveys serve an entertainment function, collecting data on every topic imaginable without pretext of being scientific or representative of any

population. For example, news, sports, and entertainment networks invite viewers to log on and give their opinion. Other Web surveys use probability-based sampling methods. One strategy is to restrict the population of interest to parties with Web access. A second strategy uses alternative methods such as random digit dialing to initially reach respondents and then uses the Web to collect data. One of the most ambitious efforts to reach a representative sample of the full population is InterSurvey (www.intersurvey.com). This organization recruits panel study members with random–digit-dialing and then provides them with Web TV units and free Internet access in exchange for participation (Couper 2000).

Online surveys have many advantages, but the field is so new that how well Web surveys will work out remains to be seen (Fricker and Schonlau 2002). Advantages include speed, low cost, and the ability to reach audiences anywhere in the world. One study, for example, found that a survey sent to 100 people cost $72 to distribute and collect by e-mail versus $503 by postal mail—quite a difference (Mavis and Brocato 1998). The same survey took an average of one day to return by e-mail versus 13 days by postal mail. However, a survey project that involves supplying participants with Web access and equipment is obviously not inexpensive.

Cost-saving is only one possible advantage. Administering questionnaires by computer rather than by mail or in person can also reduce error in data collection. Researchers may even find computer surveys a more ethical approach in terms of minimizing the harm associated with revealing sensitive data, such as child maltreatment (Black and Ponirakis 2000). The anonymity and impersonal nature of interacting with a machine rather than a human interviewer may reduce respondents' concerns about how their responses appear to others. It also makes it a good way to contact groups that are difficult to access in other ways, possibly because of their involvement in deviant interests or activities that they wish to hide from others (Wysocki 1999).

The versatility of the Internet means that we can supplement questionnaire text with a variety of visual and auditory elements such as color, graphics, animation, and even sound. Interactive features can aid with error checking and automate skip patterns so that respondents can move easily through the interview. At this point, little research has accumulated on the actual value or problems with such features.

Online surveys have their disadvantages, too. Sampling and representativeness are especially problematic (Kaye and Johnson 1999). The population of people who use the Internet tends to be skewed toward those who are affluent, well educated, young, and male. So unless the research has a clearly defined population, all of whose members have access to and actually use the Internet, questions of the representativeness of online respondents are difficult to resolve. Even with a clearly defined population and sampling frame, nonresponse can significantly distort results. For example, an online survey of the faculty members at a university would probably involve a population where all members have Internet access. However, it may be the younger faculty or those from particular academic disciplines who are most likely to respond. Thus, researchers need to

scrutinize the issues of response rate and representativeness, as they do with other types of surveys. Data available at this point suggest that postal surveys achieve a considerably higher response rate than do Web-based surveys (Mavis and Brocato 1998). However, for needs assessment surveys and some kinds of qualitative research where probability samples are not critical, researchers may find online surveys quite useful.

Another difficulty with online surveys is formatting: Different computer systems can change formatting in unpredictable ways. A survey that looks fine on the designer's computer screen may become partially (or totally) unintelligible when e-mailed to a respondent's computer. In addition, all Internet browsers and servers may not support the design features in some Web page design software. We mentioned earlier in this chapter the importance of survey appearance in terms of achieving high response rates and gathering complete and valid responses. If respondents with various computers receive differently formatted surveys, this may influence their willingness to participate or their responses and introduce error into measurement. This is a serious concern, although technological improvements will undoubtedly reduce the seriousness of this problem in the future.

Focus Groups

Research situations sometimes arise in which the standardization found in most surveys and interviews is not appropriate, and researchers need more flexibility in the way they elicit responses to questions. One area in which this is likely to be true is exploratory research. Here, researchers cannot formulate questions into precise hypotheses, and the knowledge of some phenomena is too sketchy to allow precise measurement of variables. This is also true in research on personal and subjective experiences that are unlikely to be adequately tapped by asking the same structured questions of everyone.

In such research situations, the **focus group,** or **group depth interview,** is a flexible strategy for gathering data (Krueger and Casey 2000; Morgan

1994). As the name implies, this is an interview with a whole group of people at the same time. Focus groups were originally used as a preliminary step in the research process to generate quantitative hypotheses and develop questionnaire items, and they are still used this way. Survey researchers, for example, sometimes use focus groups as tools for developing questionnaires and interview schedules. However, researchers now also use focus groups in applied research as a strategy for collecting data in their own right, especially when the researchers are seeking people's subjective reactions and the many levels of meaning important to human behavior. Today, tens of millions of dollars are spent each year on focus groups in applied research, marketing research, and political campaigns. One example of this is a study of the barriers that women confront in obtaining medical care to detect and treat cervical cancer, a potentially fatal disease readily detected and treated if women obtain Pap smears on a regular basis and return for follow-up care when necessary. The researchers decided that a focus group "would allow free expression of thoughts and feelings about cancer and related issues" and would provide the most effective mechanism to probe women's motivations for not seeking appropriate medical care (Dignan et al. 1990, p. 370).

A focus group usually consists of at least one moderator and up to 10 respondents and lasts for up to three hours. The moderator follows an interview guide that outlines the main topics of inquiry and the order in which they will be covered and may have a variety of props, such as audiovisual cues, to prompt discussion and elicit reactions. Researchers select focus group members on the basis of their usefulness in providing the data called for in the research. Researchers chose the women for the study on cervical cancer, for example, because, among other things, all had had some previous experience with cancer. Focus group membership is not normally based on probability samples, which Chapter 6 points out as the most likely to be representative samples. This can therefore throw the generalizability of focus group results into question. However, in exploratory research, such generalizability is not as critically important as in other research. In addition, most focus group research enhances its representativeness and generalizability by collecting data from more than one focus group. The cervical cancer study involved four separate focus groups of 10 to 12 women each; some research projects use 20 or more focus groups.

The moderator's job in a focus group is to initiate discussion and facilitate the flow of responses. Following an outline of topics to cover, he or she asks questions, probes unclear areas, and pursues lines of inquiry that seem fruitful. However, a focus group is not just 10 in-depth interviews. Rather, the moderator uses knowledge of group dynamics to elicit data an interviewer might not have obtained in an in-depth interview. For example, a status structure emerges in all groups, including focus groups; some people become leaders and others followers. The moderator uses this group dynamic by encouraging the emergence of leaders and then using them to elicit responses, reactions, or information from other group members. Group members often respond to other group members differently than they respond to the researcher/moderator. People in a focus group make side comments to one another—obviously not possible in a one-person interview—and the moderator makes note of these comments, possibly encouraging group members to elaborate. In fact, in a well-run focus group, the members may interact among themselves as much as they do with the group moderator. In a standard interview, the stimulus for response is the interviewer's questions; in contrast, focus group interviews provide a second stimulus for people's responses—the group experience itself.

The moderator also directs the group discussion, usually from more general topics in the beginning to more specific issues toward the end (Krueger and Casey 2000). For example, in the focus group study of cervical cancer, the moderators began with questions about general life concerns and the perceived value of health and ended with specific questions about cancer, cancer screening, and Pap smears. The general questions provided a foundation and a context without which the women might not have been as willing or able to provide useful answers to the more specific questions. Group moderators take great care in developing these sequences of questions. The moderator also observes the characteristics of the participants in the group to ensure effective participation by all members. For example, the moderator constrains a "rambler" who talks a lot but doesn't say much and encourages "shy ones" who tend to say little to express themselves. In short, moderating a focus group is a complex job that calls for both an understanding of group dynamics and skills in understanding and working with people.

During a focus group session, too much happens too fast to engage in any useful data analysis on the spot. The focus group produces the data, which is preserved on videotape or a tape recording for later analysis. During the analysis, the researcher makes field notes from the recordings and then prepares a report summarizing the findings and presenting conclusions and implications. Data from a focus group are usually presented in one of three forms (Krueger and Casey 2000). In the *raw data format,* the researcher presents all the comments group participants made about particular issues, thus providing the complete range of opinions the group expressed. The researcher offers little interpretation, unless to clarify some nonverbal interaction or nuance of meaning that could only be grasped in context. The second format for presentation is the *descriptive approach,* in which the researchers summarize in narrative form the kinds of opinions expressed in the group, with some quotes from group members as illustrations. This calls for more summary on the part of the researcher but also enables him or her to cast the results in a way that best conveys the meaning communicated in the group session. The third format is the *interpretive model,* which expands on the descriptive approach by providing more interpretation. The researcher can provide his or her own interpretations of the group's mood, feelings, and reactions to the questions. This may include the moderator's impression of the group members' motivations and unexpressed desires. The raw data model is the quickest manner of reporting results, but the interpretive model provides the greatest depth of information from the group sessions. Of course, the interpretive approach, because it does involve interpretation, is more likely to exhibit some bias or error.

Focus groups have major advantages over more structured, single-person interviews: The focus groups are more flexible, cost less, and can provide quick results. In addition, focus groups use the interaction between people to stimulate ideas and encourage group members to participate. In fact, when run properly, focus groups have high levels of participation and thus elicit reactions that interviewers might not have obtained in a one-on-one interview setting. Unfortunately, focus groups also have disadvantages: The results are less generalizable to a larger population and the data more difficult and subjective to analyze. Focus groups are also less likely than interviews to produce quantitative data; in fact, focus group data may more closely resemble the field notes produced in field research, which we will discuss in Chapter 9.

Practice and Research Interviews Compared

The interview is undoubtedly the most commonly employed technique in human service practice. Therefore, it is natural for students in the human services to wonder how research interviewing compares with practice interviewing. The fundamental difference is the *purpose* of the interview. Practitioners conduct interviews to help a particular client, whereas researchers conduct interviews to gain knowledge about a particular problem or population. The practitioner seeks to understand the client as an individual and often uses the interview to effect change; the researcher uses the data collected on individuals to describe the characteristics of and variations in a population. To the practitioner, the individual client system is central. To the researcher, the respondent is merely the unit of analysis; the characteristics and variability of the population are of primary concern.

The difference in purpose is the basis for differences between practice and research interviewing. Whereas we select *respondents* to represent a population, we accept *clients* because they have individual needs that the agency serves. Research interviews are typically brief (often single encounters); practice relationships are often intensive, long-term relationships. Clients (or clients' needs) often determine the topic and focus of a practice interview, whereas the nature of the research project predetermines the research interview's content. The ideal research interview presents each respondent with exactly the same stimulus in order to obtain validly comparable responses. The ideal practice interview provides the client with a unique situation that maximizes the potential to help that individual.

An emphasis on differences between the two forms of interviewing, however, should not obscure their similarities. Both require that the interviewer make clear the general purpose of the interview. Both require keen observational skills and disciplined use of self according to the purpose of the interview. This last point is crucial to answering another question about interviewing: Do practitioners make good research interviewers? The answer depends on the nature of the particular interview task and the interviewer's capacity to perform that task. Interviewers who display warmth, patience, compas-

sion, tolerance, and sincerity best serve some situations; other situations require reserved and controlled interviewers who bring an atmosphere of objective, detached sensitivity to the interview (Kadushin and Kadushin 1997). Some researchers have found that verbal reinforcement—both positive comments to complete responses and negative feedback to inadequate responses—results in obtaining more complete information from respondents (Vinokur, Oksenberg, and Cannell 1979). Although successful in terms of amount of information gained, such techniques might be foreign to the style of interviewing that a practitioner uses. Thus, for the structured, highly controlled interview, a practitioner who is used to improvising questions and demonstrating willingness to help may be a poor choice as interviewer. In situations requiring in-depth, unstructured exploratory interviews, that same practitioner's skills might be ideal. Again, the purpose of the interview and the nature of the task determine the compatibility of human service skills with the research interview.

COMPUTERS IN RESEARCH

Survey Design and Data Collection

Probably the most intensive application of computer technology to survey research is in the realm of **computer-assisted interviewing (CAI),** or using computer technology to assist in designing and conducting questionnaires and interviews. Originally, this took the form of **computer-assisted telephone interviewing (CATI),** where the interview is conducted over the telephone: The interviewer reads questions from a computer monitor instead of a clipboard and records responses directly into the computer via the keyboard instead of a paper form (Buetow et al. 1996; Groves et al. 1988). Superficially, CATI replaces the paper-and-pencil format of interviewing with a monitor-and-keyboard arrangement, but the differences are much more significant. Some of the special techniques possible with CATI include personalizing the wording of questions based on

answers to previous questions and automatic branching for contingency questions. These features speed up the interview and improve accuracy because the interviewer can concentrate fully on the questions at hand instead of searching through pages of items that do not apply. The CATI program may also include enforced probing when respondents give incomplete answers, editing of responses, and automatic call scheduling.

CAI involves two steps. The first is designing the interview schedule on specialized software that can produce either printed or online versions of the interview. The second step is conducting the interviews. The online survey forms are interactive, and the software enters the data from respondents directly into a data file for analysis. With the printed version, the filled-out survey forms are scanned into the data file.

In addition to customizing questions and utilizing branching routines, CATI programs help prevent errors from entering the data during the collection phase. For example, with a question that requires numeric data, such as "How old are you?," the program can require that only numeric characters be entered. Range checks also catch errors. Assuming one is interviewing adults, the age range might be set to 18-99 years. Any response outside that range would result in an error message or a request to recheck the entry.

Prerecording responses to which most people give the same answer simplifies data entry. For example, when asking about health status, very few respondents have probably had heart attacks. A "No" response can be prerecorded for this item so that data need be changed only for those few individuals who respond "Yes." The interview schedule can also warn of logical inconsistencies. If a respondent lists three family members as employed during the year, an error message would result if the interviewer attempted to enter zero annual income for one of those persons at a later point in the survey.

In some situations, the order in which questions are asked can affect the responses in a survey. Because of this, it is common to administer scale items in a random order in a questionnaire. Some software now includes a special feature to randomly order the items separately for each respondent.

Although telephone interviewing was the first application of computerized interviewing, we now also use what is called **computer-assisted personal interviewing** (CAPI), where face-to-face interviewers use computers in much the same way that the telephone interviewers did. Laptop and notebook computers prove especially versatile in this regard, as interviewers can take online, interactive questionnaires into the field. CAPI has all the advantages of CATI and is more versatile because it can be used in many field settings. An extension of this is called **computer-assisted self-interviewing** (CASI), where the respondents read questions on the computer screen and enter their responses at the keyboard themselves. Psychologists and social workers first used CASI for clinical tasks, and then researchers took it up for use in large-scale surveys. In some cases, computers are left in the homes of respondents for periodic responses to survey questions on a pre-arranged schedule. In other cases, CASI is used in combination with CAPI, with sensitive questions answered through CASI, which gives people a greater sense that their privacy is being protected. One disadvantage of CASI is its effect on response rates: Older and less educated respondents, as well as those with less computer experience, are less likely to give answers to CASI portions of interviews (Couper and Rowe 1996; Tourangeau and Smith 1996).

Research suggests that CAI clearly has some advantages over traditional methods but is not without its own problems. One advantage is that CATI, and especially CASI, yields substantially higher levels of reporting of sensitive behavior (Gribble et al. 1999). In studies of sexual behavior, for example, respondents reported that CASI was more comfortable; they were more likely to report stigmatized behaviors and less likely to report normative behaviors. A field experiment on using audio-CASI for the National Household Survey on Drug Abuse showed that audio-CASI generates an increased reporting of drug use among youth. Other research reports that audio-CASI resulted in estimates of the prevalence of male–male sex, injection drug use, and sexual contact with intravenous drug users that were higher by factors of 3 or more compared with other methods of interviewing (Turner et al. 1998). A second major advantage of CAI is its ability to reduce the error rate (deLeeuw and Nicholls 1996). Another advantage of CASI is that it enables respondents to correct inconsistencies in responses that the automated system detects and helps poor readers and less well educated respondents complete the survey (Lessler et al. 2000).

The advantages of CAI come at a cost, including spending more on specialized equipment and taking considerably more time to design and test the data collection system. In general, investment in CATI pays off only in large-scale or regularly repeated surveys (Weeks 1992). Another cost is that CAI can produce a lower overall response rate because some interviews take longer. A third cost results from computer downtime. If the computer system is inoperable for a period of time, which happens, then interviewing is delayed and some interviews may be lost entirely (Catlin and Ingram 1988).

Main Points

- Surveys are of two general types: (1) question-naires completed directly by respondents and (2) interviews with the questions read and responses recorded by an interviewer.

- Closed-ended questions provide a fixed set of response alternatives from which respondents choose.

- Open-ended questions provide no response alternatives, leaving respondents complete freedom of expression.

- Once developed, survey instruments should be pretested for clearly understood and unbiased questions; after changes are made in the instrument, it should be pretested again.

- Questionnaires must provide clear directions to indicate what respondents should do and to guide them through the questionnaire.

- Researchers should order questions so that early questions maximize the response rate but do not affect responses to later questions.

- Obtaining a high response rate (the percentage of surveys actually completed) is very important for representativeness in survey research.

- The cover letter, use of payments and follow-up letters, and length and appearance of the questionnaire are all central to efforts to maximize the response rate with the mailed questionnaire.

- Interviews are classified by their degree of structure as unstandardized, nonschedule-standardized, or schedule-standardized.

- Probes elicit clearer and more complete responses during interviews.

- Telephone surveys offer significant time and cost savings compared with interviews or mailed questionnaires and are a suitable alternative in many cases.

- Online surveys permit flexible formatting and design, but we have not yet developed standard practices in this new field.

- Focus groups rely on group dynamics to generate data that would not be discovered with a standard questionnaire or interview format.

- Computer software now enables interviewers to input responses directly into a computer file as well as check for errors or inconsistencies in the data.

Important Terms for Review

closed-ended questions
computer-assisted interviewing
computer-assisted personal interviewing
computer-assisted self-interviewing
computer-assisted telephone interviewing
contingency question
cover letter
filter question
focus group
group depth interview
interview
interview schedule
interviewer falsification
matrix question
open-ended questions
probes
questionnaire
response rate
survey
survey research

Exploring InfoTrac® College Edition and the Internet

InfoTrac® College Edition search terms:

focus group
questionnaire design
social survey research
survey interview*

InfoTrac® College Edition articles:

In Search of a Few Hundred Good Kids: Three Months in the Life of a Community-Based Survey Research Study. (Statistical data included.) John M. Bolland. *Families in Society: The Journal of Contemporary Human Services* Jan 2001 v82 i1 p79 (14,201 words)

Mode Effects for Collecting Alcohol and Other Drug Use Data: Web and U.S. Mail. Sean Esteban McCabe, Carol J. Boyd, Mick P. Couper, Scott Crawford, Hannah D'Arcy. *Journal of Studies on Alcohol* Nov 2002 v63 i6 p755 (7) (5,791 words)

Using Focus Groups to Determine What Constitutes Quality of Life in Clients Receiving Medical Nutrition Therapy: First Steps in the Development of a Nutrition Quality-of-Life Survey (research). Judith Barr, Gerald Schumacher. *Journal of the American Dietetic Association* July 2003 v103 i7 p844(8) (5,930 words)

A rich variety of resources awaits anyone who seeks information about survey research on the Internet. Most major survey research centers maintain Web sites, and some of them are extremely useful. At many sites, you can find a basic overview of survey research, a discussion of ethics in surveys, and information on how to plan a survey. Some of these sites contain minicourses on all aspects of conducting surveys. Some even provide the opportunity to examine questions used in actual surveys. It is also possible to download and read entire questionnaires and survey instruments. By reviewing these surveys, you can explore how the researchers structured the instrument and ordered the questions; you will see skip patterns and other features that enhance the research instrument's quality. Not only will you become more familiar with major survey projects around the world, but you can also learn a great deal about how to design good survey questions.

Many survey Web sites have search engines that enable you to locate questions on almost any topic imaginable. Try one of the search engines by entering a topic of interest to you, such as domestic violence, health care, or poverty. Are the questions open-ended or closed-ended? How are they worded? How might you improve them or adapt them to a project of interest to you? Depending on the source, you may be able to use or adapt questions from these surveys for use in your own survey instrument.

Here is a list of some worthwhile sites:

- The Odum Institute for Research in Social Science (IRSS): www2.irss.unc.edu/irss/home.asp.
- The General Social Survey: www.icpsr.umich.edu:8080/GSS/homepage.htm
- The Centre for Applied Social Surveys in England: www.socstats.soton.ac.uk/cass/
- The Survey Research Center: members.bellatlantic.net/~abelson/. (This site has some of the best links to organizations involved in survey research throughout the world that we have seen.)

- American Association for Public Opinion Research: www.aapor.org/ The "Best Practices" link is especially informative on planning and conducting surveys.
- Survey Research methods Section of the American Statistical Association: amstat.org/sections/srms/

Use the search engine on the Web browser available to you to look for other survey research centers like these:

- UK Data Archive-Major studies: www.data-archive.ac.uk/findingData/majorStudies.asp
- Statistics Canada: www.statcan.ca/
- National Center for Health Statistics: www.cdc.gov/nchs/express.htm

For Further Reading

Dillman, Don A. *Mail and Internet Surveys: The Tailored Design Method,* 2nd ed. New York: Wiley, 2000. This is an excellent introduction to survey research in general, and it also provides the most up-to-date overview of how to conduct surveys through the mail and on the Internet.

Gorden, Raymond. *Basic Interviewing Skills.* Itasca, Ill.: Peacock, 1992. This useful how-to book on interviewing covers everything from how to develop questions to how to motivate good responses to how to evaluate respondents' nonverbal behavior.

Gubrium, Jaber F., and James A. Holstein. *Handbook of Interview Research: Context and Method.* Thousand Oaks, Calif.: Sage, 2001. This complete handbook covers many forms of interviewing, including survey, qualitative, in-depth, and therapy. The book addresses technical issues, distinctive respondents, and analytic strategies.

Kadushin, Alfred, and Goldie Kadushin. *The Social Work Interview: A Guide for Human Service Professionals,* 4th ed. New York: Columbia University Press, 1997. This is the standard text for social work interviewing. It covers all aspects of the helping interview and presents a solid comparison for the survey interview.

Krueger, Richard A., and Mary Anne Casey. *Focus Groups: A Practical Guide for Applied Research,* 3rd ed. Thousand Oaks, Calif.: Sage, 2000. This book is the standard for learning how to conduct a focus group. This edition compares market research, academic, nonprofit, and participatory approaches to focus group research; it describes how to plan focus group studies and do the analysis, including step-by-step procedures.

Salant, Priscilla, and Don Dillman. *Conducting Surveys: A Step-by-Step Guide to Getting the Information You Need.* New York: Wiley, 1994. As the title states, this is a very useful guide to all the steps in conducting sound survey research.

Schuman, Howard, and Stanley Presser. *Questions and Answers in Attitude Surveys: Experiments on Question Form, Wording, and Content.* Thousand Oaks, Calif.: Sage, 1996. This is a comprehensive handbook on the rules, problems, and pitfalls of designing survey questions. It goes far beyond what this chapter is able to cover on this important topic.

Schwarz, N., and S. Sudman, eds. *Answering Questions: Methodology for Determining Cognitive and Communicative Processes in Survey Research.* San Francisco: Jossey-Bass, 1996. This collection discusses the methods involved in observation and/or taping and the subsequent coding and analysis of interviews. It also explores how to obtain, code, and analyze verbal protocols from respondents and examines other survey techniques, including sorting tasks and response latency measures.

Sudman, S., N. Bradburn, and N. Schwarz. *Thinking about Answers: The Application of Cognitive Processes to Survey Methodology.* San Francisco: Jossey-Bass, 1996. An exploration of what answers mean in relation to how people understand the world around them and communicate with one another. The authors present the survey as a social conversation and investigate and document the meanings of the answers respondents give.

Exercises for Class Discussion

Your state's Health and Human Services Department has recently released a controversial study that concludes that the state can provide better-quality foster care for less cost than private agencies can provide under a purchase-of-services contract. The private agencies are outraged and point out some serious flaws in the study. For example, the state study was made by people who might lose their jobs if the state contracts out for services. Furthermore, the study compared a state program in an urban area to a rural, private agency program. To resolve these concerns, the independent research firm where you are employed has been asked to conduct a survey that will generate results representative of the entire state.

The following exercises explore some of the tasks and decisions you face in undertaking such a survey.

7.1 Would you use mailed questionnaires, telephone surveys, or personal interviews with: (a) foster parents, (b) adolescents in care, (c) line workers? Defend your choices. What additional information would help you make these decisions?

7.2 If your organization decides to send a mailed questionnaire to foster parents, what could you suggest to improve the response rate?

7.3 One of the topics to cover with foster parents is their satisfaction with the services the foster care worker provides. Write a closed-ended question and an open-ended question to deal with this topic. Which type of question would, in your opinion, be best?

7.4 For interviewing the foster children, would you use a nonstandardized, a nonscheduled-standardized, or a schedule-standardized format? Why?

7.5 You have the task of selecting the interviewers to conduct face-to-face interviews with the adolescents, and you have the following options: Department of Health and Human Services workers; interviewers from a political polling organization, mostly middle-aged women; or teenagers between the ages of 16 and 19 eligible for a state-sponsored summer jobs program. Which group would you pick and why? What would be the advantages and disadvantages associated with each of these groups?

7.6 Approximately 30 percent of the young people in foster care are African Americans, and another 15 percent are Hispanic. What differences will racial composition of the population make in terms of the way you suggest doing the study?

7.7 To experience the importance of ordering questions in survey research, role-play a simulated interview on conflict tactics. Conduct one simulation using the CT scale discussed on pages 361–362. Conduct a second simulated interview using the scale in *reverse* order. Discuss how the participants felt about responding to the items about violent behavior.

Chapter 8

Analysis of Available Data

Normally, researchers prefer to organize and direct the collection of the data themselves. This enables them to tailor the nature and form of the data collected to their research hypotheses and the state of knowledge in the field (see Chapter 4). In some cases, however, this is far too costly and time-consuming. In other cases, it is impractical or unnecessary. Consider, for example, a study by Deborah Wingard (1987) of the characteristics of adopted children and their parents in California. Wingard could have gotten a list of the children and their parents from agencies and then conducted mailed questionnaires or interviews. As we saw in Chapter 7, however, questionnaires suffer from nonresponse problems, and interviews are expensive. Furthermore, as a routine part of service delivery, adoption agencies gather information about the characteristics of children and both their birth and adoptive parents. So in this case, Wingard did not need to collect data herself because the data to test the hypotheses already existed in a computerized agency information file.

Data of this type are called **available data:** observations collected by someone other than the investigator for purposes that differ from the investigator's but that nonetheless are available. A vast array of this type of data exists for scientific analysis. In some cases, such data take the form of *statistical data,* or quantified observations of some element of human behavior. For example, various branches of government collect large amounts of statistical data and provide quantified information about crime, health, birth rates, death rates, and so on. *Documents* are another form of available data and refer, in their broadest sense, to any form of nonquantitative communication. Documents include such items as books, magazines, letters, memoranda, diaries, Web pages, and other media of communication, such as radio, television, movies, and plays. Documents can also make up a part of records maintained by various institutions, such as military records, police records, court records, and social agency records. Some such records, of course, include both statistical and nonstatistical data.

Available data are a rich source for human service research and are sometimes used in conjunction with data collected from other sources, such as surveys. Furthermore, researchers can often treat available data as if they were data the researchers had collected themselves. Wingard, for example, could work with the agency data much as with the survey data she collected. Available data, however, does present researchers with some new problems, and these problems are the topic of this chapter.

Statistical Data

Human service professionals often complain about the mountains of paperwork associated with the procedures of trying to help people. But the facts and figures these procedures generate can be a rich source of data for research. Unfortunately, researchers often overlook the statistical data available to human service agencies or find it deficient in some critical respects. An important contribution that research-knowledgeable human service professionals can make to both practice and research is to help develop data-collection procedures that generate useful statistical data. This is a major theme of Research in Practice 1.2, which describes the social agency as a "research machine." To make such a contribution, human service professionals must have an understanding of how researchers use available statistical data and what qualities enhance the usefulness of available data for research.

Sources of Statistical Data

Statistical data are collected for many reasons, and much of these data are available to human service researchers. First, some statistical data are collected as part of many research projects. Many research organizations, such as the Institute for Social Research at the University of Michigan or the Institute for Research on Poverty at the University of Wisconsin, collect large amounts of useful data that others may reanalyze with different research questions in mind. In this way, data collected for one project may be reanalyzed by a number of different people in the years that follow. Table 8.1 lists just a few of these data sets and describes the kinds of data they contain. This re-

Table 8.1 Illustrations of Available Statistical Data Sets

Sample Data Set	Location	Types of Data Available
Boston Police Department Domestic Violence Research Project, 1993–1994	The National Archive of Criminal Justice Data (NACJD); www.icpsr.umich.edu/NACJD/home.html	Criminal justice data collections for research and instruction are available. NACJD provides access to over 550 criminal justice data collections free of charge.
KIDS COUNT	The Annie E. Casey Foundation, Baltimore MD; www.aecf.org/ kc1998/toc.html	This data set focuses on variables relating to the status of children and youth in society: infant mortality, infant and child health, teen pregnancy rates, suicide, school dropouts, and so on.
National Study of Protective, Preventive and Reunification Services Delivered to Children and Their Families, 1994	National Data Archive on Child Abuse and Neglect; www.ndacan.cornell.edu/holdingstable.html	The primary activity of the archive is the acquisition, preservation, and dissemination of high-quality data sets relevant to the study of child abuse and neglect.
Current Population Survey (CPS) and Public Use Microdata Samples (PUMS)	U.S. Census Bureau; www.census.gov www.icpsr.umich.edu	The CPS is a national sample of households with data on labor force participation, employment status, income, education, and other variables. The PUMS are a variety of data sets based on a sampling of households that were included in the decennial census.
Longitudinal Study of Generations and Mental Health by Bengston	The Murray Research Center; www.radcliffe.edu/murray/data/index.htm	A special emphasis is longitudinal studies of mental health. Special areas include the Video Archive and the Diversity Archive.

analysis of data collected for some other research project is called **secondary analysis** (Riedel 2000; Sieber 1991). In fact, some research organizations, such as universities or government agencies, have organized a national system of **data archives,** which are essentially libraries that lend or sell data sets much as libraries or bookstores lend or sell books. Among the better known are the Interuniversity Consortium of Political and Social Research (ICPSR) at the University of Michigan, the Roper Center at the University of Connecticut, the Na-

tional Institute of Child Health and Human Development, and the National Institute of Justice.

Also, some private organizations have created data archives in specialized areas. The Sociometrics Corporation, for example, offers numerous data sets from studies focusing on adolescent pregnancy issues. Many individual researchers also make data sets available to those with legitimate secondary uses of the data. Some funders of research, such as the National Science Foundation, now require, as a stipulation for receiving research funds, that the data eventually be delivered to a public data archive. Fienberg, Martin, and Straf (1985) list more than 50 major data archives in the social sciences. Data collected for research purposes and available for secondary analysis tend to be of fairly high quality because professional researchers collected them. Nonetheless, such data still suffer from some of the problems to be discussed shortly.

A second source of statistical data is the federal, state, and local human service agencies that collect data for either administrative or client service purposes. Community mental health centers, Head Start programs, departments of social services, and health and educational institutions are repositories of vast amounts of available data. Figure 8.1 illustrates some of the client data that human service agencies routinely collect. For instance, for each suspected case of child abuse or neglect referred to the Department of Social Services (DSS) in Michigan (now called the Family Independence Agency), practitioners complete this form. The upper part provides space for various specific bits of case information, and the lower half provides a convenient coding scheme to ease the entry of information. Some of these data are quantitative (such as age of the client, number of prior referrals, and number of days the client is in foster care), and these variables are amenable to statistical manipulation. Agencies collect such data for many reasons that may have nothing to do with their eventual research purposes. Sometimes agencies are simply required by law to collect such information, which is then stored in data banks and may be available to researchers. The authors combined the data on these forms with data from other organizational records in a study to assess the impact of a school social work program on the referral of cases of child abuse and neglect. Unfortunately, data from human service agencies are often not efficiently cataloged and indexed and therefore are often difficult for investigators to locate and use. Such data, nonetheless, have grown to voluminous proportions over recent decades. Research in Practice 8.1 gives further illustrations of agency records serving as a source of research data.

A third source of statistical data is the organizations and government agencies that collect data as a public service or to serve as a basis for social policy decisions. The Federal Bureau of Investigation (FBI) and the National Center for Health Statistics, for example, collect vast amounts of data, as do state and local governments. The U.S. Census Bureau also collects enormous amounts of data to use for establishing and changing the boundaries of political districts and allocating government funds that are based on population size. Often researchers can use data from these sources in conjunction with other types of data—from questionnaires, for example, or from agency records—to test hypotheses. One study of caseworker accuracy hypothesized that the political and economic characteristics of the local community might influence caseworker errors (Piliavin, Masters, and Corbett 1977). Data were based on interviews, questionnaires, and other sources. In addition, data from the Census Bureau measured the political and economic characteristics of each community regarding the percentage of poor people in the county, how the county voted in the most recent gubernatorial election, and the percentage of poor families headed by women. Thus, researchers can combine data from multiple sources to measure variables and test hypotheses in a single study.

Data collected by private organizations are distributed less widely than government statistics and for that reason may be more difficult to locate. Professional associations, such as the American Medical Association, the American Bar Association, and the National Association of Social Workers (NASW), produce statistics relating to their membership and issues of concern to their members. Additionally, research institutes and commercial polling firms also produce statistical data.

Using Statistical Data

When we use available statistical data, remember that most such data were not collected for research purposes—or at least not for the specific research questions for which we now intend to use them. They were compiled to meet the needs of whatever agency, organization, or researcher originally collected them, and the form in which the data were

Figure 8.1 An Example of a Client Information Form Used in a Human Service Agency

1. Primary Recipient Name	Date Received
	MANAGEMENT INFORMATION REPORT
2. Case Number	3. Referral Date
	Department of Social Services
	Reason issued
4. County / District / Unit / Worker	5. Referral Number
	CHILDRENS PROTECTIVE SERVICES
	Transaction Number
6. Action	7. Referral Source	8. No. Prefer Ref.	9. Hours to First Contact	10. Date Invest. Comp.	11. Living Arr.- Invest	12. ADC Status

ADDRESS OF PRIMARY RECIPIENT

13. In Care Of — Comments — 18. Document Number
14. Number and Street
15. City — 16. State — 17. Zip Code

19. Recipient Update Action	20. NAME (Last, First, Middle Initial)	21. PLANS CLIENT IDENTIFIER	22. BIRTH DATE	23. Sex	24. Race	25. Role	26. Abuse	27. Neglect	28. Living Arrangement at Closing

CLOSING DATA (Also Complete Item 28)

29. Close Date	30. Closing Code	If Item 30-6, Complete Item 31	31. Court Involvement/ Disposition	If Item 31-1, Complete Item 32	32. Non-Court Disposition	33. Greatest No. Days In Temp. Foster Care	34. Reason in Foster Care Over 21 Days	35. Reason Case Open Over 6 Months

Signature of Worker — Date

CENTRAL OFFICE

6. ACTION
1 • Investigation
2 • Close
3 • Invest/Close
4 • Change/Update

7. REFERRAL SOURCE
Mandated
01 • Pvt. Physician
02 • Hosp./Clinic Phys.
03 • Coroner/Med. Examiner
04 • Dentist
05 • Audiologist
06 • Nurse (Not school)
11 • School Nurse
12 • Teacher
13 • School Administrator
14 • School Counselor
21 • Law Enforcement
31 • Child Care Provider
41 • Hosp./Clinic Soc. Wkr.
42 • DSS Facil. Soc. Wkr.
43 • DMH Facil.Soc. Wkr.
44 • Other Pub. Soc. Wkr.
45 • Pvt. Agy. Soc. Wkr.
46 • Court Soc. Wkr.
47 • Other Soc. Wkr.

Non-Mandated
51 • Hosp./Clinic Personnel
52 • DSS Facil. Personnel
53 • DMH Facil. Personnel
54 • Other Pub. Soc. Agy. Pers.
55 • Pvt. Soc. Agy. Personnel
56 • Court Personnel
57 • Other School Personnel
61 • Victim
62 • Relative
63 • Sibling
64 • Parent/Sub In Home
65 • Parent/Sub Out of Home
66 • Anonymous
67 • Friend/Neighbor
68 • Other

11. LIVING ARR. AT INVESTIGATION
01 • Own Home
02 • Foster, Shelter, Group Home
03 • Shelter Facility
04 • DSS Facility
05 • DMH Facility
06 • Court Facility
07 • Pvt. Facility
08 • Resid. Ed. Facility
09 • Other Child Care Inst.
10 • Other Out of Home
11 • Mult. Plcmts.

12. ADC STATUS
01 • ADC
02 • GA
03 • ADC & GA
04 • None

19. RECIPIENT UPDATE
01 • Update Existing Recipient
02 • Add New Recipient
03 • Delete Recipient

23. SEX
M • Male
F • Female

24. RACE
Migrant
A • Caucasian
B • Negro
C • Indian
D • Other
E • Unknown
F • Sp. Surname

Non-Migrant
1. • Caucasian
2. • Negro
3. • Indian
4. • Other
5. • Unknown
6. • Sp. Surname

25. ROLE
11 • Victim
21 • Perp-Parent in Home
22 • Perp.-Sibling
23 • Perp.-Other Relat.
24 • Perp.-Other Household Memb.
25 • Perp.-Day Care
26 • Perp.-Fost. Parent
27 • Perp.-Inst. Staff
28 • Perp.-Parent Out of Home
29 • Perp.-Other
31 • Uninvolv.-Parent
32 • Uninvolv.-Sibling
33 • Uninvolv.-Other

26. ABUSE (Victim only)
1 • Physical Injury
2 • Congen. Drug Addict
3 • Rape
4 • Incest
5 • Molestation
6 • Exploitation
7 • Unnatural Acts

27. NEGLECT (Victim only)
1 • Physical
2 • Social
3 • Abandonment
4 • Inapp. Use of Funds
5 • Unlicensed Home/Improp. Guardianship

28. LIVING ARR. AT CLOSE (Victim and uninvolved siblings only)
1 • In Home
2 • Out of Home

30. Closing Code
1 • Unable to Locate
2 • No Evidence
3 • Not Sufficient
4 • Other Agency Contact
5 • Invest. Only
6 • Services Provided

31. COURT INVOLVEMENT/DISPOSITION
1 • No Court
2 • Accept PS Recom – Adjudication and Disposition
3 • Accept PS Recom – Adjudication Only
4 • Not Accept PS Recommendation
5 • Court - Other

32. NON-COURT DISPOSITION
1 • Satisfact. – No Referral
2 • Satisfact. – Refer to DSS
3 • Satisfact. – Refer Comm. Agency
4 • Unsatisf. Family Rsp. – Court Not Feasible
5 • Unsatisf. – Comm. Agency Not Avail. PS Not App.
6 • Unsatisf. – Refer to DSS
/ • Other

34. REASON FOSTER CARE OVER 21 DAYS
1 • Pending Court
2 • Other

35. REASON OPEN OVER 6 MO.
1 • Await Court Action
2 • Protective Payment
3 • Court Ward in Home
4 • Still Danger
5 • New Danger
6 • Other

RESEARCH IN PRACTICE 8.1

PROGRAM EVALUATION:

Evaluating Family Preservation Services through Agency Record Data

When child abuse or neglect occurs, the child is often removed from the parental home and placed in foster care. But such placements are expensive, temporary, and do not solve the problem of family dysfunction that produced the abuse. One promising alternative is intensive family preservation, in which the child's home becomes the primary site of service delivery instead of an agency or institution, and the entire family, rather than only a parent or the child, becomes the client. The premise of such programs is that treating the family within its own environment permits dealing with the family-interaction problems that may precipitate abuse and neglect. Such programs may include around-the-clock availability of family service workers using a wide range of skills and resources, such as teaching positive child-rearing skills, finding housing, advocating with a landlord to fix the heat, and showing parents how to repair a broken window.

With any such departure from traditional service delivery, evaluation is crucial to ensure that the programs do what they claim (Wells and Biegel 1991). A common feature of evaluation studies concerning family preservation services is that they rely extensively on available data gathered from human service agency records. The studies may also use interviews with service providers and questionnaires sent to clients, but the extensive data required

to trace delivery of services and to evaluate outcomes necessitates using data generated by the program itself. For example, Marianne Berry (1992) evaluated one such program by examining the characteristics of families and services that contributed to family preservation, including the match of services to the needs of the clients. She measured program success by skill gains among families as well as by avoiding the placement of a child outside the home. She studied a sample of about 400 families in the program. In addition to interviews with caseworkers, the project relied heavily on Department of Social Services (DSS) shelter and foster care logs as well as standard follow-up forms. These records provided demographic data on client families as well as information on amounts and kinds of services provided, location of contacts, and other agencies participating in the contacts.

The evaluation studies done so far do suggest that the programs are beneficial. In Berry's evaluation, 88 percent of the families receiving such services avoided having a child removed from the home for the year after receiving the services. Supporting one of the innovative features of intensive family preservation, researchers found that the location where services are delivered makes a difference: No families experienced a child placed outside the

collected limits the analysis. This leads to some special problems that call for caution.

Missing Data.   For a variety of reasons, a data set may not include complete data for every person studied or may fail to collect data from the entire population or sample of interest. For example, a person may refuse to answer certain questions, which results in a gap in his or her data set. Or researchers may not have collected data in a particular neighborhood considered too dangerous for interviewers to enter. Such gaps in a data set are referred to as

missing data and appear to some degree in practically all studies. The problem when using available data files is that we have no control over this failure to collect a complete set of data. Missing data result in incomplete coverage, which, if extensive, throws into question the representativeness of the data. Furthermore, because statistical procedures are based on the assumption of complete data, missing data can result in misleading statistical conclusions. As we dig back into data from the past, it is not uncommon to find data for whole periods missing. This can occur for many reasons, such as data destroyed by fires, lost home when more than half of the service time was spent in the home. Conversely, in those families where more than half of service time was in the agency, 28 percent later had a child placed outside the home. Furthermore, the service log provided a clue as to which services made a difference in treatment success. Families that remained intact had received more supplemental parenting, teaching of family care, and medical help.

Although the available DSS data provided a rich source of information for the project, those data were not without problems. For example, the author described the most commonly reported service provided—case planning—as a catchall category without much meaning. However, the vagueness of the category was considered an administrative problem, too, and DSS has since changed it to reflect more specific services.

Another study examined five home-based programs across several states (Nelson 1991). The focus of this study was the criticism that the only families kept together by family preservation programs were those families with few problems to begin with. Data were obtained for this study by having trained case readers (mostly graduate and undergraduate social work students) extract the data from case records. One portion of the data-collection task consisted of applying the Child Well-Being Scales to the case record data (Magura and Moses 1986). These scales are designed to rate problem levels based on assessments by the actual human service practitioner. Because of the lack of detail in the case records, case readers could only assess whether a particular problem was found in a case, rather than specifying the extent of the problem, as can be done when practitioners themselves complete the scales. So, although it was possible to use the scales, the researchers had to settle for less precision in measurement due to the necessity of using available data. Missing data is another problem common to studies based on available data. The researchers in this study reported that the proportion of missing data was comparable on most subscales to that found by Magura and Moses relying on direct data collection from workers. The study concluded that the family-based service sample had a consistent pattern of more problems than the comparison child welfare–based sample. Thus, the study does not support the criticism that family-based service success is an artifact of selecting families with fewer problems.

These two program evaluations illustrate some of the advantages and challenges of using available data from the records of social service agencies. Existing agency records eliminated the need for extensive interviewing and duplication of efforts. The agency logs proved to be a good supplemental data source in the first study, and the second study was able to rely entirely on existing data files. The potential for conducting sound evaluation studies underscores the need for human service agencies to provide good documentation of services, not only for administrative purposes but also with an eye toward applied research on program effectiveness.

data, changes in policy, and the like. Finding data that cover only a portion of our target population is also quite common. For example, researchers in a study of marriage rates among older Americans in the United States were forced to do without data from three states—Arizona, New Mexico, and Oklahoma—because those states did not maintain central marriage files (Treas and VanHilst 1976). Given the high concentration of retirees in Arizona, however, it is possible that the exclusion of data from that state might have affected their results. When working with data that suffer from noncoverage, we should assess the implications that noncoverage has for the results of the research.

Inductive versus Deductive Analysis.

In research investigations that collect data firsthand, we commonly use a deductive approach. That is, hypotheses are deduced from a theory, variables in the hypotheses are operationally defined, and data are collected based on these operational definitions. In short, research moves from the abstract to the concrete: The theory and hypotheses we are testing determine the kind of data we collect (see Chapter 2).

Figure 8.2 The Measurement Process with Available Statistical Data

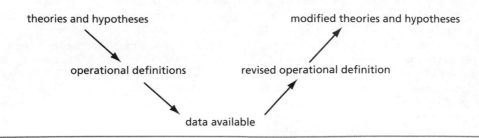

In the analysis of available data, however, such a deductive approach is often impossible because the data necessary to measure the variables derived from a theory may not have been included when the original data were collected. For example, a theory regarding caseworker effectiveness with clients might include the variable of the intensity of the casework relationship. Although intensity of relationship is a crucial concept in interpersonal helping, it is unfortunately not the type of variable that is included in routine agency data-collection procedures. In circumstances like this, it is not possible to operationalize the variable in the way most appropriate to the theory. If this difficulty is encountered, a compromise is often made. As we showed in Chapter 5, the measurement process often calls for modifying nominal and operational definitions (refer back to Figure 5.1). So we revise operational definitions and in some cases hypotheses so that we can test them with the data available (see Figure 8.2). In the example of caseworker effectiveness, we might measure intensity of relationship by looking at the amount of time a worker spent with a given client over the course of treatment, frequency of contacts, or duration of contacts. Although none of these variables may be the best measure of "intensity of relationship," we can readily derive them from the worker time sheets mandatory in many agencies. We may use total contact time, frequency of contact, duration of contact, or some combination of these, even though they are not thoroughly accurate measures of the variable of interest.

In other words, we modify our research to fit the data. When this occurs, research takes on a somewhat inductive character. In inductive research, we move

from the concrete to the abstract: Starting with the data collected, we develop hypotheses and theories to explain what we find. The situation we have described is actually somewhere in between induction and deduction. We have begun with theories and hypotheses, but we have also had to let the available data influence how we test the hypotheses. This is a frequent problem in the analysis of available statistical data.

Validity. Recall from Chapter 5 that *validity* refers to whether a measurement instrument actually measures what it is intended to measure. Many data in existing statistical files are valid indicators of certain characteristics that they directly describe, such as age, sex, and racial profiles of clients, along with the amounts of different kinds of services provided. However, validity problems frequently arise in three areas.

First, many elements of agency operation—such as achievement of goals, success of programs, or satisfaction of clients—may not be measured directly by any data normally collected by an agency. To study these, we would have to search for indirect measures among the agency data that might enable us to infer such things as goal achievement, success, or satisfaction. These situations create the same kinds of validity problems that confront researchers using other methods, except that when we use available data, we cannot consider and resolve validity problems *before* we collect the data. Because someone else has already collected the data, the problems are entrenched.

A second area in which validity problems frequently arise is data analysis that becomes inductive—that is, when we change operational definitions so we can measure variables with the available data. The more the definitions are changed, the more the validity of the measures is called into question. The operational definitions may be changed so drastically that they no longer measure the theoretical concepts they were first intended to measure.

Finally, validity questions arise when procedures an agency or organization uses in gathering data change over the years. Changing modes of collecting data, such as dropping some questions or developing new definitions of something, are quite common in any agency or organization. These procedural changes, however, can affect the comparability of data collected at various times and the validity of using the same operational definitions. Crime statistics are a good example. Researchers commonly use data from the Uniform Crime Reports (UCR) compiled by the FBI as a measure of the volume of crimes in the United States. Research in Practice 8.2 explores some of the problems that can arise when using this particular set of data.

RESEARCH IN PRACTICE 8.2

NEEDS ASSESSMENT:

Hazards in Estimating the Crime Problem from Available Data

Combating crime is a key objective for many human service programs, whether it is running a neighborhood watch to increase safety for the elderly, providing late-night basketball for inner-city youths, offering treatment groups for offenders, providing rape crisis counseling for victims, or monitoring ex-felons on parole. Whenever an organization embarks on an effort to design and implement a program like one of these, the planning process commonly requires that program planners demonstrate the need for the program by documenting the seriousness of the crime problem in a community. It is unlikely that most human service organizations have either the resources or the capacity to gather crime data themselves, so available data is an appealing alternative. As we noted in this chapter, one of the advantages to conducting research with available data is that somebody else paid to collect the data. It is, however, important to make serious inquiries about exactly how the data were collected and the numbers produced.

The human service agency that uses available crime data faces several possible pitfalls. The FBI produces one of the most widely used sources of crime data. The Uniform Crime Reports (UCR) is published annually and is available in practically every library. Some parts of it are now also available on the Web (www.fbi.gov or www.crime.org). On the surface, it might seem that data produced by an agency of the federal government, with all its authority and resources, would be reliable, and within limitations they are. But those limitations can cause problems if not understood. One of the most basic questions people have about crime is this: How much crime exists? UCR data cannot well answer even this apparently simple question. For an event to be recorded as a crime in the UCR, it must come to the attention of some police official. In a minority of cases, police chance across a crime taking place, and so it gets officially recorded. Most often, however, police must rely on citizens who are victimized by crime to report it to them—herein lies one of the problems with UCR data. A large percentage of even serious crimes never gets reported to the police. A recent estimate by the Bureau of Justice Statistics suggests that only about half of all violent crimes and only 40 percent of all property crimes are reported to the police and make their way into the UCR data (Rennison and Rand 2003). Clearly, this reporting gap causes the UCR data to significantly understate the true impact of criminal activity in the United States.

You may be wondering how such an estimate of unreported crime can be made. Another measure of criminal activity is the National Crime Survey (NCS), conducted every year on a representative sample of more than 100,000 citizens, inquiring if they have been victims of crimes. The disparity between the NCS data and the UCR data

continued on next page

provides an indicator of the amount of crime that goes unreported by the UCR and thus gives a clearer picture of actual criminal activity. Another possible pitfall awaiting users of UCR data is the fact that reporting to the FBI is voluntary on the part of local law enforcement agencies. This fact leads to a number of possible misinterpretations of the data. For example, researchers could not compare different regions or localities and conclude with any certainty which area had the higher or lower crime rate. Any differences noted might be real or merely differences in the willingness of officials to report to the FBI.

A related problem confronts anyone interested in longitudinal analysis. Over the long history of the UCR, the percentage of police agencies that report their numbers has steadily increased. This, of course, means that any comparison over time has a built-in problem. Even if crime has not increased, it will appear to have increased over time due to the higher rate of reporting in more recent years.

Yet another problem stems from the fact that during the first several decades of the UCR, crime rates were computed not from updated population estimates but from the most recent census count. The census is conducted only once every 10 years, and this for years meant that the basis for computing the crime rates stayed the same for a decade until the numbers from a new census became available. But, of course, a population does not remain stagnant and then suddenly appear to explode every 10 years. The population steadily increases from year to year, meaning that there are more people to commit crimes and to become crime victims. Using the same census number to compute crime rates meant that apparent increases in crime from year to year were inevitable. Then, when a new census number was used, there would appear to be a substantial drop in crime. Obviously this "drop" was not due to a real decline in criminal activity but to the census number used to compute the crime rate catching up with the population increase. This

is no longer a problem with UCR data because it now uses yearly population estimates, which are quite accurate, in computing the crime rates; however, it typifies the kind of traps that may await the unsuspecting researcher using other people's data.

Finally, when working with data collected over a long period of time, such as the UCR's, an important question is this: Have definitions or categorizations changed over time that would hamper making meaningful comparisons? Again, the UCR is illustrative. According to Barlow (1996), during the history of the UCR, the FBI's classification system for counting crime has changed several times. In fact, in 1979 the FBI added an additional crime, arson, to the crimes that make up the "crime index"—crimes that are tracked and used to compute the general crime rate. In addition to arson, the index crimes are homicide, aggravated assault, sexual assault, robbery, burglary, larceny, and auto theft. Naturally, when the crime of arson was added to the index, it appeared that crime had suddenly and dramatically increased when, of course, the change in measurement primarily caused the change in the numbers.

As illustrated by the UCR data, a researcher who uses available data must be careful not to fall into possible traps hidden in the data. Such risks do not mean that we should avoid available data but rather that we should use such data with caution. For example, the UCR data are not without value, as they reflect changes in people's willingness to report crime to the police. In recent years UCR data have shown a marked increase in the number of reported rapes, whereas the NCS data show no such increase (Perkins and Klaus 1996). This difference is evidence of increased willingness of victims to report the crime to the police. Women's changed roles in society, together with greater sensitivity on the part of authorities in handling rape cases, are probably responsible for the higher reporting rate. So we see that despite its limitations and potential for misinterpretation, the UCR data do have their uses.

Content Analysis

Whenever activity is recorded in some document—whether a book, diary, case record, film, or tape recording—it is amenable to scientific analysis. Although the data discussed in the previous section were already quantified when made available for research, the documents we now discuss have basically *qualitative* data that researchers must quantify. Consider the following research studies by various social scientists:

- A study of the lyrics in modern rap music shows that rap is a cultural form with messages of resistance and empowerment for minorities in the United States and serves as subcultural social criticism that expresses distrust and anger at what minorities perceive as a racist and discriminatory dominant white culture (Martinez 1997).
- A study of prime-time television programs explores what messages about alcohol use appear in this medium, especially as alcohol use affects adolescents (Mathios et al. 1998).
- A study of magazine advertisements determines whether the behavior displayed in advertisements is different for men and women and assesses whether stereotypical portrayals of men and women have changed over the past two decades (Kang 1997).
- A study of how emotions are expressed and interpreted in different settings reviews audiotapes of emergency 911 calls (Whalen and Zimmerman 1998).

Content analysis refers to a method of transforming the symbolic content of a document, such as words or other images, from a qualitative, unsystematic form into a quantitative, systematic form (Neuendorf 2002; Smith 2000; Weber 1990). In the above examples, the "documents" consist of music lyrics, television programs, magazine advertisements, and 911 audiotapes. Content analysis is a form of coding, a practice we discuss in Chapters 7 and 9 as a way of transforming data in some surveys and observational research. **Coding** refers to categorizing behaviors or elements into a limited number of categories. In surveys and observational research, we perform coding on data the investigator collects firsthand for particular research purposes. In content analysis, coding is performed on documents produced for purposes other than research and then made available for research purposes. In both survey data coding and content analysis, we develop categories and coding schemes to quantify verbal or symbolic content.

Coding Schemes

A major step in content analysis is to develop a coding scheme for analyzing the documents at hand. Coding schemes in content analysis, like those in coding observed behavior, are quite variable, and their exact form depends on the documents being studied and the hypotheses being tested in the research project.

Existing Coding Schemes. In some cases, researchers can find existing coding schemes for content analysis. For example, the coding categories Bales (1950) developed for the analysis of interaction in small groups are widely used in research and applicable to documents if they suit the purpose of the study (see Chapter 9). Another example of a general scheme is one commonly used for categorizing themes in fiction and drama. The basic themes are these: (1) love, (2) morality, (3) idealism, (4) power, (5) outcast, (6) career, and (7) no agreement (McGranahan and Wayne 1948). There are also categories for classifying endings, temporal settings, spatial settings, and patterns of love in the love theme. In the human services, researchers have developed coding schemes to analyze the content of a clinician's responses to patients in interviews. In a study of the impact of a clinicians' responses on whether clients continued with treatment, researchers developed a coding system utilizing three categories:

1. Substantive congruent responses: clinician responses that referred to the client's immediately preceding response or contained some elements of that response.

2. Nonsubstantive congruent responses: clinician responses, such as "I see" or "Yes," that indicate that the clinician is aware of and paying attention to the client's verbalizations.
3. Incongruent responses: clinician responses that appear unrelated to what the client has said.

Others interested in similar aspects of the practitioner–client interview might utilize the same coding scheme.

In conducting content analysis, then, we find it beneficial to search for an existing coding scheme that applies to the research problem at hand. The use of an existing coding scheme results in considerable savings for the researcher in terms of time, energy, and money; it also serves to make the research project comparable with other studies that use the same coding system.

We can find coding schemes in the many journals that report research relevant to the human services or in books, such as those by Holsti (1969) or Krippendorff (2003), that are devoted to the study of content analysis. Smith (2000) describes a number of coding schemes that have been developed to measure life span development, identity, problem-solving skills, and many other phenomena.

Characteristics.   Like categories in any measurement process, those used in content analysis should be exhaustive and mutually exclusive. Categories are *exhaustive* when a category is available for every relevant element in the documents. If there are only a few possibilities and they can be clearly defined, an exhaustive set of categories is not difficult to develop. If what we are trying to measure is rather open-ended with many possibilities, however, developing an exhaustive set of categories is difficult. For example, researchers have analyzed presidential speeches in terms of the values expressed. But so many values exist that developing an exhaustive list is unlikely. One such list contained 14 value categories, which undoubtedly cover the most important or commonly mentioned values (Prothro 1956). It is doubtful whether even that many categories are really exhaustive, however. If it is impossible to be exhaustive, then we use the most common or most

important categories and make available a residual category ("other") for those items that do not fit any of the categories.

Coding categories should also be *mutually exclusive,* which means that each coded item can fall into one—and only one—category. This requirement forces researchers to provide precise definitions for each category, so that no ambiguity exists concerning which items it includes and which it does not. Failure to meet this requirement can totally befuddle the measurement process because coders confused with overlapping categories will place items every which way. Lack of mutual exclusiveness will likely show up in low levels of reliability as the coders disagree on the placement of items into categories.

Units of Analysis

With the categories established, the next research decision concerns precisely what aspects of the documents to record. Generally, there are four units of analysis: a word, a theme, a major character, or a sentence or paragraph. (We have discussed the units of analysis commonly found in research other than content analysis in Chapter 4.) An often-convenient unit of analysis is a *single word* because we can code the presence of certain words in documents easily and with a high degree of reliability. If a single word qualifies as a valid indicator of what we wish to measure, it is a good choice for the unit of analysis. For example, as a part of their study of colonial families, Herman Lantz and his colleagues (1968) counted the frequency with which the word "power" was associated with men or women in colonial magazines. In this context, the single word was used as a measure of the perceived distribution of power between men and women during colonial times. When using single words as the unit of analysis, it is often helpful to make use of a context unit, which is the context in which the single word is found. The words surrounding the word used as the unit of analysis modify it and further explain its meaning. We then take this contextual information into account when coding the unit of analysis. For example, in the study just mentioned, the investigators needed to know whether the word "power" referred to men or to women. The context surrounding the word supplied this crucial information. The amount of context needed to explain the use of a given word adequately is, of course, variable.

The *theme* as a unit of analysis refers to the major subject matter of a document or part of a document. An entire document can be characterized as having a primary theme. Novels, for example, can be described as mysteries, science fiction, historical, and so on. In a study of the images of women during World War II and their treatment by government propaganda agencies, one researcher analyzed themes relating to the role of women in the workforce found in fiction pieces in two magazines popular during the war, *Saturday Evening Post* and *True Story* (Honey 1984). Themes can, however, be difficult to delineate. The overall theme may or may not be clear, or there may be multiple themes. Coder reliability is likely to be lower than when easily identifiable words are the unit of analysis.

A third unit of analysis in documents is the *main character*. The use of this unit of analysis is, of course, limited to documents that have a cast of characters, such as plays, novels, movies, or television programs. A study of children's television programs, for example, used the major dramatic character as the unit of analysis. The study, funded by the Ford and Carnegie Foundations, found that only 16 percent of the major characters were women, and "females were portrayed as married, less active, and with lower self-esteem" (Corry 1982).

The fourth unit of analysis is a *sentence* or *paragraph*. The study described earlier regarding congruency in clinician–client interaction used a similar unit of analysis: Each clinician's response, preceded and followed by a client comment, was considered the unit to code as congruent or incongruent. A paragraph or even a single sentence, however, often contains more than one idea, and this may make these larger units more difficult to classify while maintaining mutually exclusive categories and intercoder reliability. Indeed, reliability often is lower than with the word or main character units. Yet the larger units often are more theoretically relevant in the human services. In clinician–client interaction,

for example, it makes little conceptual sense to characterize an interchange as congruent on the basis of one word. Meaning in social interaction normally arises from a whole block of words or sentences. So, as we emphasized when discussing units of analysis in Chapter 4, the primary consideration in selecting a unit of analysis is theoretical: which unit seems to be preferable given theoretical and conceptual considerations.

Manifest versus Latent Coding

In content analysis, researchers distinguish between *manifest* and *latent* coding. The term **manifest coding** refers to coding the more objective or surface content of a document or medium (Holsti 1969). One example of manifest coding notes each time a particular word appears in a document. Another example of manifest coding occurs in a study of the portrayal of African Americans in children's picture books. This study observed whether blacks, whites, or people of other racial groups appeared in the pictures in a book (Pescosolido, Grauerholz, and Milkie 1997). In some cases it may be difficult to judge the race of a particular character—certainly more difficult than deciding whether a particular word appears in a document. However, this is still manifest coding because there is a fairly direct link between the image in the document and the coding category.

Latent coding, on the other hand, inherently involves some inference in which the coder has to decide whether the representation in the document is an instance of some broader category of phenomena. Coders assess the representations in the document for what they say about a more abstract or implicit level of meaning. The study just mentioned also used latent coding to judge the nature of the black representations in the picture books and of the black–white interactions portrayed. So the coders made judgments about how central the black characters were in the pictures and how intimate or egalitarian the black–white interactions were. "Centrality," "intimacy," and "egalitarianism" are qualities that a coder must infer on the basis of a judgment or assessment of the materials.

Another example that used both manifest and latent coding was the study of how alcohol use is portrayed in prime-time television shows (Mathios et al. 1998). The manifest coding involved recording incidents where alcohol use was a part of such shows, noting the type of alcohol used and the gender of the people involved, all of which was easily observed, with little need to make judgments or inferences. The latent coding involved judging the personality characteristics of those portrayed consuming alcohol. For example, the coders had to rate each such character on a four-point scale from "very powerful" to "very powerless" and from "very admirable" to "very despicable." To do this latent coding, the observers had to make some fairly sophisticated and subjective judgments about personality from the behaviors and overall portrayal of the characters on the television shows. As these two examples illustrate, manifest coding is generally more reliable than latent coding, but latent coding is often a more valid way to get at some fairly complex and theoretically important social processes and characteristics.

Issues in Content Analysis

When developing coding categories for content analysis, researchers confront several issues. Remember that content analysis is a form of measurement—measurement of aspects of a document's contents. As such, we encounter the familiar concerns regarding validity and reliability, along with problems of choosing a level of measurement and a sample (see Chapters 5 and 6).

Validity

In content analysis, validity refers to whether the categories we develop and the aspects of the content coded are meaningful indicators of what we intend to measure. Developing coding schemes that are valid indicators can be challenging. For example, Anne Fortune (1979) reported on an effort to study communication patterns between social workers and their clients in which recordings of interviews were content analyzed. The goal of the research was to discover which interview techniques bring about

cognitive and affective changes in clients. Fortune particularly wanted to know how techniques varied when the clients were adults rather than children. First, she developed a typology of communication techniques based on William Reid's work on task-centered casework. Because there are many ways to execute a particular verbal technique in a therapeutic setting, it was impossible to base the content analysis on a single word or phrase. Instead, Fortune provided coders with a description of each technique and examples of the verbal forms that each technique might take. For example, the communication technique of "exploration" was described as "communication intended to elicit information, including questions and restatements or 'echoes' of client's communications." Examples of this technique provided to the coders included such phrases as "What class was that?" and "You said your son misbehaved . . ." The communication technique of "direction" was exemplified by "I think the first step would be to talk this over with your daughter" (Fortune 1979, p. 391). By providing specific examples of how to code comments, she hoped the resulting coding would have greater validity than if coders were left on their own.

Depending on the nature of the research and the documents to analyze, researchers might apply any of the methods of assessing validity discussed in Chapter 5. The logical approaches of content validity and jury opinion are the most generally used assessments of validity in content analysis, although researchers sometimes use criterion validity. For example, in a content analysis of suicide notes, one study attempted to identify aspects of the content of real suicide notes that would differentiate them from simulated ones written by people who had not actually attempted suicide (Ogilvie, Stone, and Shneidman 1966). The researchers compared half of the genuine notes with half of the simulated ones and found that genuine notes made more references to concrete things and greater use of the word "love." The simulated notes, on the other hand, contained more references to the thought processes that went into the decision to commit suicide. Using these observations to predict which of the remaining notes were genuine, the researchers were able to make such predictions at a 94 percent level of accuracy, which suggests that the content aspects of the notes were valid indicators of genuine suicide notes.

Researchers must be able to argue convincingly that indicators are valid to attain acceptance of their scientific outcomes. Though most content analyses do not go beyond content validity or jury opinion, it is important to remember that these are the weakest demonstrations of validity. Whenever possible, more rigorous tests should be attempted.

Reliability

Reliability refers to the ability of a measure to yield consistent results each time we use it. In content analysis, reliability relates to the ability of coders to apply consistently the coding scheme. The question is this: Can several workers code the documents according to the coding scheme and obtain consistent results? Reliability in content analysis depends on many factors, including skill of the coders, nature of the categories, rules guiding the use of the categories, and degree of clarity or ambiguity in the documents (Holsti 1969; Scott 1990; Weber 1990). The clarity of the documents in any given study is largely fixed, so our discussion of control over reliability is limited to coders and categories utilized.

First, researchers can enhance reliability by thoroughly training the coders and by having them practice applying the coding scheme. Coders who continually deviate from the others in their coding during this practice period should not be relied on as coders. We must be cautious, however, about eliminating coders without assessing whether their deviation indicates poor performance or an ambiguous coding scheme.

Second, the nature of the categories to be applied to the document is also important for reliability. The simpler and more objective the categories, the higher the reliability. Vaguely defined categories or those requiring substantial interpretation decrease reliability because they create greater opportunity for disagreement among the coders.

Measuring reliability in content analysis is much the same as measuring reliability when coding observed behavior (see Chapter 9). One simple method is to calculate the percent of judgments on which coders agree out of the total number of judgments they must make:

$$\text{percent of agreement} = \frac{2 \times \text{number of agreements}}{\substack{\text{total number of observations} \\ \text{recorded by both observers}}}$$

This measure of intercoder reliability, however, does not take into account the extent to which intercoder agreement can occur by chance. Paula Allen-Meares (1984) presents other ways of measuring intercoder reliability. Accepted levels of reliability are 75 percent or better agreement between coders. Well-trained coders using well-constructed coding schemes should achieve better than an 85 percent agreement.

A certain tension exists between validity and reliability in content analysis. The simplest coding schemes—such as those employing word frequency counts—produce the highest reliability because they are very easy to apply in a consistent manner. As noted, however, word frequency counts may not validly measure what we want to measure. We may have to sacrifice some degree of reliability for the sake of validity. Researchers often end up performing a balancing act between the dual requirements of validity and reliability.

Level of Measurement

Like other methods of collecting data, content analysis involves a decision about the level of measurement to use (see Chapter 5). The level of measurement achieved depends on the variable measured and the process used to measure it. The variable measured puts an upper limit on the level of measurement that we can reach. For example, if we rate main characters in a book according to marital status, the highest level of measurement would be nominal because marital status is a nominal variable. No amount of measurement finesse can change this once we have selected the key variables. However, researchers have some control over the level of measurement, depending on the process used to measure the variables. The important factor is how we quantify the unit of analysis in the coding process. Coding systems in content analysis generally fall into one of four categories: (1) presence or absence of an element, (2) frequency of occurrence of an element, (3) amount of space devoted to an element, or (4) intensity of expression.

The simplest rating system is to indicate merely *the presence or absence of an element* in a document. For example, we might rate interviews as to whether the clinician mentions certain subjects, such as sexual behavior or parent–child relationships. This simple system yields nominal data and conveys a minimum of content information. Several important questions remain unanswered. We do not know whether the clinician addressed the subject in a positive or negative light, nor how the client reacted. Also unknown is how much time was devoted to that subject or how frequently it was repeated. Consideration of these factors would make the study more informative.

Frequency counts are common methods of rating. We simply count how often an element appears. For example, Jack Levin and James Spates (1970) sought to compare the dominant values expressed in middle-class publications with those in the so-called underground press. The investigators rated the frequency with which statements of various values appeared in the two types of publications. On the basis of the frequency counts, the study concluded that the underground press emphasized values related to self-expression, whereas the middle-class publications stressed values related to various types of personal achievement. Frequency counts reveal more information about the document than does the simple present-or-absent approach and open the way for more sophisticated statistical analysis because they can, with the appropriate theoretical concepts, achieve an interval or ratio level of measurement.

Coding systems based on *amount of space devoted to an element* have proved useful for analyzing the mass media. In newspapers or magazines, the normal approach is to measure column inches. The equivalent for films or television is time. For example, in a study of the contribution of social work writers to the development of professional knowledge, Merlin Taber and Iris Shapiro (1965) counted the number of column inches that selected social work journals

devoted to a discussion of different types of knowledge, such as theoretical versus empirical knowledge. We could measure over a period of years the amount of space devoted to a topic, such as family violence or the problems of lesbian mothers, to assess the impact of popular trends or political events on professional concern about various issues. The major attraction of space/time measures is their ease of use. We can measure the amount of space devoted to a given topic far more rapidly than we can measure word frequency counts or even whether key words are present or absent. As each document takes only a short time to analyze, space/time measures allow a larger sample size and possibly lead to greater representativeness. Space/time measures can also yield interval- or ratio-level measurement with theoretical concepts that are amenable to such a level of measurement.

Unfortunately, space/time measures are still somewhat crude. Other than the volume of space devoted to the particular topic in question, they reveal nothing further about the content. For example, time measures applied to the network news could tell us which types of news are allotted the most coverage but nothing about more subtle issues, such as whether the news coverage was biased. As Ole Holsti (1969, p. 121) notes, "A one-to-one relationship between the amount of space devoted to a subject and the manner in which it is treated cannot be assumed."

The most complex rating systems involve a *measure of intensity*—the forcefulness of expression in the documents. However, developing intensity measures is difficult. Intensity of expression is often quite subtle and dependent on many aspects of word usage, which makes it extremely difficult to specify clearly the conditions for coding content elements. Coders have to make many judgments before deciding how to categorize the content, and this leads to disagreements and low reliability.

Developing intensity measures that produce reliable results is quite similar to constructing measurement scales, as we will discuss in Chapter 13. We could, for example, have coders rate documents along a scale (as in the semantic differential or the Likert scales). Newspaper editorials dealing with public assistance programs might be rated as (1) very unfavorable, (2) unfavorable, (3) neutral, (4) favorable, or (5) very favorable. The study mentioned earlier on portrayals of alcohol use on television used an intensity measure: Coders had to rate characters on a four-point scale from "very powerful" to "very powerless" and from "very admirable" to "very despicable" (Mathios et al. 1998). The options for intensity scales are nearly endless given the vast variety of intensity questions that can arise concerning the contents of documents. Despite their complexity, intensity measures are the most revealing concerning a document's contents.

Sampling

In document analysis, the number of documents is often too vast for all to be analyzed; we have to take a sample from a group of documents. For example, we might want to study the extent to which concern for child abuse has changed among human service providers between the 1950s and the 1990s. We could do this by studying the extent of coverage of the topic in human service journals during those years. Considering the number of journals and thousands of pages involved, sampling is clearly necessary to make such a project feasible.

As with other types of sampling, representativeness is a critical issue. To generalize the findings of our document analysis, the sampling procedure must be likely to yield a representative sample, which is often difficult to achieve with documents. One problem is that the elements of the population of documents may not be equal. In studying child abuse, for example, some journals are more likely to publish articles on that topic than others—*Child Welfare* or the *Journal of Interpersonal Violence,* for example. A more general journal, like *Social Service Review,* would include a much smaller proportion of child abuse articles. Likewise, a journal specializing in a different area, such as the *Journal of Gerontology,* probably would not publish any articles on child abuse at all. A random sample of all human service journals, then, might include only a few journals most likely to publish articles on this topic. The random sample would be dominated by journals having a small like-lihood of publishing family violence articles, making it more difficult to measure changes in practitioner concern for family violence. We can solve this problem by choosing our sample from among those journals specializing in areas related to family violence. Or we can stratify the journals by type and then select a stratified random sample, taking disproportionately more journals that are likely to publish articles on family violence (see Chapter 6).

A second issue in sampling documents is the difficulty in defining the population of documents. For example, for a study of the changing image of the social work profession, James Billups and Maria Julia (1987) conducted a content analysis of advertisements for job vacancies in social work positions. Because such ads are published in many different places—in local, state, and national publications—defining that population of documents was difficult. To get around this problem, they limited themselves to advertisements in national publications on the grounds that these would most likely reflect national trends in the changing image of social work. At a national level, the most ads were placed in *Social Casework* in 1960 and 1970 and in the *NASW News* in 1980. To assess trends over time, Billups and Julia did not need to sample documents from each year. Instead, they took a random sample of 10 percent of the ads appearing in these journals in 1960, 1970, and 1980, which covered the period in which they were interested. The changing trends in practice the researchers found in their content analysis research reflected what other research had discovered: The distinction between casework and group practice had become less important over time, and social workers, especially those with graduate degrees, were more likely to find supervisory or administrative positions.

Assuming that we can adequately define the population to sample, we can apply to documents the normal procedures of sampling discussed in Chapter 6. Of those, simple random sampling is probably most common and most generally applicable (Scott, 1990). As we have seen, however, researchers may require stratified sampling to avoid bias when sampling from a population of unequal elements. We should approach systematic sampling cautiously because it is easy to be trapped by periodicity in documents. *Periodicity* is the problem in which elements with certain characteristics occur at patterned intervals throughout the sampling frame. For example, the size and content of newspapers vary substantially with the days of the week. If the sampling interval were seven or a multiple of seven, a systematic sample would include only papers published on the same day of the week and could be very biased, depending on the aspects of content under study.

Sampling documents often involves multistage sampling. As in all multistage sampling, we start with large units and work down through a series of sampling stages to smaller and smaller units. Levin and Spates's (1970) sample of the underground press illustrates multistage sampling. In the first stage, the researchers selected a sample of publications from the membership of the Underground Press Syndicate by choosing the top five publications in terms of circulation. In the second stage, they randomly selected a single issue of each publication for every other month from September 1967 through August 1968. This produced six sample issues of each of the five publications, a total of 30 issues. In the final stage, Levin and Spates selected for analysis every other nonfiction article appearing in the sample issues. The resulting sample contained 316 articles to represent the underground press.

Assessment of Available Data Analysis

Like other research techniques, the use of available data has both advantages and disadvantages. A consideration of these helps to determine when such analysis is the most appropriate and helps to point out some potential problems as well.

Advantages

Lower Costs.   Document analysis is one of the least costly forms of research, and using available statistical data can help reduce the costs of a research project. The producers of the documents and statistics bear the major expense of data gathering rather than the researcher. The sheer volume of data the U.S. Census Bureau, the NASW, or the many local and state social agencies collects is so massive that only the best-endowed research projects could possibly duplicate their data-collection efforts. Document analysis becomes expensive if the documents of interest are widely scattered and difficult to obtain or if very large samples are employed. Also, the more complex the coding process, the more expensive the study. Overall, however, available data offer an opportunity to conduct valuable research at reasonable cost.

Nonreactivity.   Like hidden observation and unobtrusive measures, available data are nonreactive (see Chapters 4 and 9). Unlike surveys or experiments, in which the participants are aware that they are being studied, producers of documents do not normally anticipate a researcher coming along at a later date to analyze those documents. The contents of the documents are, therefore, unaffected by the researcher's activities. This does not mean, of course, that those who produced the documents did not react to some elements that might have biased the documents. For example, police officers might be more likely to record an instance of physical or verbal assault in an arrest report when the suspect is nonwhite than when the suspect is white, thus generating data that make nonwhites appear more abusive and introducing bias into arrest records. In addition, people who compile documents may be reacting to how people other than researchers, such as a supervisor or politician, may respond to their document. Likewise, the preparer's hope for a "place in history" can shape the preparation of a document. Despite all this, researchers are not a source of reactivity with available data.

Inaccessible Subjects.   Properly cared for, documents can survive far longer than the people who produce them. Document analysis allows us to study the ways of society long ago and the behaviors of people long dead. The Lantz and colleagues (1968) study of the colonial family and the study of suicide notes by Ogilvie, Stone, and Shneidman (1966) dealt with the behavior of people quite inaccessible by research techniques other than document analysis.

Longitudinal Analysis. Many statistical data and documents are collected routinely over a period of years, even centuries. This contrasts sharply with the typical one-shot, cross-sectional survey data. With such longitudinal data, we can accomplish trend analysis—looking for changing patterns over time. For example, Reynolds Farley (1984) used a longitudinal analysis of available data in an evaluation of the progress of African Americans in the United States since the 1950s. Using census data from the 1950s, 1960s, and 1970s, Farley compared the position of African Americans relative to whites over three decades. He found mixed results. The census data revealed that African Americans as a whole had made substantial gains in the quality of employment, family earnings, and educational attainment. Other indicators were less encouraging, however, showing little or no improvement. In the areas of residential integration, unemployment rate, and school integration, African Americans' position relative to whites had not improved over 30 years. In general, Farley's analysis reveals that although African Americans have experienced significant gains in some areas, substantial gaps remain and appear quite persistent. This type of research is obviously valuable in putting today's conditions into a historical perspective; just as obviously, researchers can conduct this type of longitudinal analysis of *past* trends only through the analysis of available data. (Existing statistical data often lend themselves to the kind of time-series analysis we will describe in Chapter 10. In fact, the illustration of the multiple time-series analysis by Kohfeld and Leip [1991] in that chapter utilized existing data on alcohol-related traffic accidents in California.)

Sample Size. Many types of documents are abundant. As mentioned when discussing sampling, a researcher is likely to confront far more documents than he or she can analyze rather than too few. This means that a researcher can employ large samples to increase confidence in the results. The low cost associated with document analysis also contributes to the researcher's ability to use substantial sample sizes without encountering prohibitive costs.

Disadvantages

Variable Quality. Because documents are produced for purposes other than research, their quality for research purposes is quite variable. Unless researchers know the limitations of the documents, as with crime statistics, they may have little idea of the conditions under which the data were collected or the amount of attention to quality that went into them. Researchers should, of course, investigate the issue of quality when possible to discover any deficiencies in the data. When we cannot do this, we simply have to draw conclusions cautiously.

Incompleteness. Documents, especially those of a historical nature, are frequently incomplete. Gaps of weeks, months, or even years are not uncommon. In addition, data may be missing in available statistics. The effect of these gaps on a study is often impossible to know except that such gaps reduce confidence in the findings. Incompleteness is simply a common characteristic plaguing available data that researchers have to work around if they can.

Lack of Comparability over Time. Even though documents are commonly used in longitudinal analysis, this can be problematic because change over time may create statistical artifacts in the data and render comparisons useless. With crime statistics, changes in how the FBI collects data make it misleading to compare crime statistics over long periods of time. Researchers need to be careful of similar kinds of changes in other data.

Bias. Because documents are produced for purposes other than research, there is no assurance that they are objective. Data from private sources, for example, may be intentionally slanted to present a particular viewpoint. A researcher who blindly accepts such data can walk into a trap. Nonstatistical documents may suffer from biased presentation as well. A good example is the corporate annual report to stockholders, filled with glowing praise for management, impressive color photographs, and bright prospects for the future, presenting anything negative in the most favorable light or camouflaged in legalese.

Sampling Bias. Bias may creep into otherwise objective data during the sampling process. As we noted, sampling documents is often difficult due to unequal population elements and hard-to-define populations. We also commented that document sampling is frequently complex, requiring several stages. Errors or bad decisions made in the sampling process can result in a highly biased sample that will produce misleading results.

Using Available Data in Research on Minorities

When studying emotionally charged topics, such as racism or sexism, reactivity can be a very serious problem because people are inclined to disguise true feelings or motives that might result in disapproval. People may deny feelings of prejudice toward minorities or women when a survey researcher asks about such feelings, even though they may feel prejudice that influences their behavior. However, one of the major benefits of available data is that they are often less reactive than other data used to study behavior. Therefore, available data may be the preferred research method or a valued adjunct to other research methods when studying such emotion-laden topics.

Consider, for example, some of the uses to which researchers have put available data in the study of racism and sexism. If we ask people whether they are racists or sexists or whether they treat women or minorities unfairly, most people deny it, especially in the contemporary environment that frowns upon such attitudes and practices. Yet the records of agencies and organizations might contain evidence of sexism or racism despite the denial of those who run the organizations. Are whites or males found disproportionately in the more prestigious or better-paying

positions in an organization? Do whites or males earn substantially higher salaries than women or minorities in the organization? Such organizational practices suggest sexism or racism in the organization. It is often less reactive and more valid to measure the consequences of organizational decisions than to ask people about such things directly.

Another way to detect the persistence of prejudices and stereotypes is to study the portrayal of people in various cultural products, such as books, magazines, or movies. Two or more decades ago, the images of males and females presented in school textbooks, for example, typically reinforced traditional stereotypes: Males were pictured far more often than females; males were pictured in many occupations and women in few; and female pronouns such as *her* were uncommon. But haven't we seen change in the past 20 years? Not as much as one might think. Things have improved, especially when efforts are made to produce materials that are nonsexist in their presentation.

However, stereotyping persists. More recent studies of children's picture books, for example, find that more women are portrayed than in the past but still fewer than men (only one third of the illustrations are of women); women are still shown in fewer occupations than men; women are still likely to be portrayed in traditional gender roles associated with household work; and women are portrayed as less brave and adventurous and more helpless (Crabb and Bielawski 1994; Peterson and Lach 1990; Purcell and Stewart 1990). A study of newspaper photographs found that men appear in these photos far more frequently than women and that men typically appear in professional roles while women are in domestic roles (Luebke 1989). Even college textbooks are not immune to these influences. Studies of the pictorial content of texts for college-level psychology and sociology courses found that women appear less often than men and more passively and negatively than men (Ferree and Hall 1990; Peterson and Kroner 1992). For example, the psychology texts portray women as the victims of mental disorders and the clients in therapy while picturing men as the therapists. Thus, cultural products, like books or newspapers, can serve as available data to detect gender stereotyping undetectable by other research methods.

Some differences in the portrayal of men and women in cultural products are quite subtle. In a creative series of studies involving an intriguing application of available data, Dane Archer and colleagues (1983) measured the amount of space in photographs devoted to people's faces. They divided the distance from the top of the head to the bottom of the chin by the distance from the top of the head to the lowest point of the body visible in the depiction. The result is a proportion with an upper limit of 1.00 (face fills entire picture) that indicates the degree to which the face is prominent in the picture. The first application of this measure was on 1,750 photographs drawn from *Time, Newsweek,* and *Ms.* magazines and from the *San Francisco Chronicle* and the *Santa Cruz Sentinel*. Before even measuring the photos, the researchers discovered an interesting finding: More than 60 percent of the photos were of men! When they applied their facial prominence indicator, they found another difference between the sexes: The average "face-ism" value was .67 for men and .45 for women, indicating that the pictures of

males tended to feature the face more prominently, whereas pictures of women featured more of the body; and more recent studies show that this tendency persisted into the 1980s (Nigro et al. 1988). A subsequent study by Archer and colleagues found that this pattern held across pictures in publications from 11 other countries. Applying the indicator to paintings going back as far as 600 years showed that the pattern had a long history and the difference seemed to be increasing.

What is the significance of this face-ism? It may represent another mechanism for perpetuating stereotypes about the sexes. Another part of their research showed that people depicted with more prominent faces are rated more intelligent, more ambitious, and as having a better physical appearance. The authors conclude that this face-ism could help to reinforce the stereotyping of women as less intelligent and capable and contribute to discrimination against women. The analysis of available data offers a way to detect these subtle, and possibly even unconscious, cultural tendencies that many people would simply deny if asked directly about them.

COMPUTERS IN RESEARCH

Access to Statistical Available Data

Modern computer technology, especially the Internet, has made research based on available statistical data much more extensive and efficient than was ever possible in the past. Basically, researchers can share data sets. But what is so revolutionary about this? Researchers have done that for decades. What is new is the ease of doing this; the Internet makes such sharing much quicker to do and much more accessible to researchers with limited budgets. It also means that data sets can be much more thoroughly analyzed than in the past because many more researchers can use each set of data.

To understand the process, go to a Web site called Data on the Net, which is maintained at the University of California, San Diego (odwin.ucsd.edu/idata/). This site is basically a portal to other sites that list locations of data sets. It has a search function that allows you to search for data sets on particular topics. You can browse through lists (sometimes long) of data sets that might be of interest to you or data archives that might contain data sets of interest. This Web site also lists many other online gateways to social science data sets and

continued on next page

data archives. So, the first step in searching for available statistical data is to explore, via the Internet, what might be available. Many of these sites provide you with the actual questions or measurement instruments used to collect the data. These measurement instruments, remember, are the operational definitions of the variables in the data set.

When searching for statistical data sets that you might use, determine whether you can have access to the complete raw data set, to only parts of the data set, or to only reports that have been prepared based on the analysis of the data. For most research purposes, access to the complete raw data set is most desirable, if not essential. With such access, you can conduct whatever kind of statistical analysis your research questions require, using as many of the variables in the data set as necessary. If you can gain access to only parts of the data, then you may not be able to test some hypotheses or conduct some statistical tests. Some data archives, for example, only give access to frequency distributions on separate variables. If this is the case, then you cannot conduct any statistical analysis involving the correlation or comparing of two or more variables. Such a limitation makes the data set useless for most social science and human service research, which almost always involves looking at two or more variables at the same time. If the only access a data archive permits is to reports summarizing the analysis of the raw data, then it may be useful in the literature review part of a research project but would not be of use in additional hypothesis testing and data analysis.

When searching for statistical available data, you also need to determine whether the data is free or involves some cost. The data, after all, come from many different kinds of data archives: government bureaus, private foundations, university research organizations, as well as private, commercial research firms. Commercial research firms, in particular, may charge a fee for the purchase of a data set they own, but some of the other data archives may also charge for use, if only a nominal fee to cover their costs. Even if a cost is attached, it is often quite small, and certainly is far less than it would cost a researcher to gather the data anew.

A final determination in using these statistical data sets is what stipulations and limitations you must agree to before you can download the data. Most suppliers of data will require that you cite the source of the data in any reports that are prepared using them. Many will also require that the data be made public only as aggregate data, not as individual cases, to prevent the identity of any research participants from being made public. Some data archives will also require that you make no effort to determine the identities of the people who were the subjects of the research. If such a stipulation is required, then you could not, for example, seek out the subjects for purposes of gathering additional data from them. Other stipulations may also be required before you can use the data, depending on the particular nature of the data. But the point is that you will be required to agree to these stipulations before you will be allowed to download the data. Once you agree, then you are morally bound to follow them; to violate the stipulations would be considered an unethical research practice

Main Points

- Available data include both statistical data collected by others and documents, which include any form of communication.
- Content analysis quantifies and organizes the qualitative and unsystematic information contained in documents.

- Content analysis is essentially a form of measurement making the issues of validity and reliability paramount. Available data must also be carefully analyzed in terms of level of measurement, which is determined by the nature of the variable being measured as well as the process used in measuring it from the available data used.

- Document analysis normally includes some form of sampling procedure, which must be performed carefully for the sake of representativeness.
- Document analysis offers the advantages of low cost, nonreactivity, ability to study otherwise inaccessible subjects, easy longitudinal analysis, and often large samples.
- Problems in using available data include the variable quality of the data, incomplete data, changes in data over time, possible bias in data, and possible sampling bias.
- The analysis of available data is often less reactive than other research methods, which can make it useful in the study of emotionally charged topics, such as racism and sexism, where people may be inclined to hide their true feelings and emotions.

Important Terms for Review

available data
coding
content analysis
data archives
latent coding
manifest coding
missing data
secondary analysis

Exploring InfoTrac® College Edition and the Internet

InfoTrac® College Edition search terms:

content analysis
current population survey
secondary data analysis

InfoTrac® College Edition articles:

Popular Video Games: Quantifying the Presentation of Violence and Its Context. (Industry Overview) Stacy L. Smith, Ken Lachlan, Ron Tamborini. *Journal of Broadcasting & Electronic Media* March 2003 v47 i1 p58(19) (9,295 words)

Social Work Advocacy in the Post-TANF Environment: Lessons from Early TANF Research Studies. (Temporary Assistance for Needy Families) Steven G. Anderson, Brian M. Gryzlak. *Social Work* July 2002 v47 i3 p301(14) (9,166 words)

We identified three major sources of statistical data in this chapter: research organizations; federal, state, and local human service organizations; and organizations that collect data as a public service or as a basis for policy decisions. You can find each of these three general types of data sources on the Internet. First, explore the site of the Interuniversity Consortium of Political and Social Research at www.icpsr. umich.edu/. Click on "Data Access and Analysis" and you will find a page to help you discover what this data archive contains. Use ICPSR's Thematic Categories and Subject Thesaurus and report to the class about the kinds of data that can be found there.

Another site to explore is the Web site of the National Archive of Computerized Data on Aging (NACDA), funded by the National Institute on Aging: www.icpsr.umich.edu/NACDA/index.html. NACDA's mission is to advance research on aging by helping researchers profit from the underexploited potential of a broad range of data sets. By preserving and making available the United States' largest library of electronic data on aging, NACDA offers opportunities for secondary analysis on major issues of scientific and policy relevance.

Julian Faraway of the University of Michigan maintains an extensive list of data sources at www.stat.lsa.umich.edu/~faraway/data.html. Exploring just a few of the many sites listed here will give you a sense of the wide array of data sites. Some of the better sites are the Roper Center, the Gallup Organization, the U.S. Census Bureau, and Statistics Canada. Another excellent site is called "Data On the Net" and is maintained at the University of California at San Diego (odwin.ucsd.edu/idata/).

A recently established Web site useful for those interested in issues related to content-analysis research is called "Content Analysis: For Qualitative Analyses of Texts, Transcripts, and Images" (www. gsu.edu/~wwwcom/content.html). It includes links that lead to summaries of recent publications on content analysis, analyses of software used for content analysis, and links to related Web sites. You might explore this Web site by identifying materials found at the site that we have discussed in this chapter.

For Further Reading

Davies, James A., Tom W. Smith, and Peter V. Marsden. *General Social Surveys, 1972–2000: Cumulative Codebook.* Chicago: National Opinion Research Center; Storrs, Conn.: The Roper Center for Public Opinion Research, University of Connecticut, 2001. This book describes a body of available statistical data based on surveys conducted since the 1970s. It includes data on a wide range of topics of interest to people in the social sciences and human services.

Jacob, H. *Using Published Data: Errors and Remedies.* Beverly Hills, Calif.: Sage, 1984. An excellent guide to the problems and pitfalls of using existing data sets. The book focuses primarily on issues of validity and reliability.

Lee, Raymond M. *Unobtrusive Methods in Social Research.* Philadelphia: Open University Press, 2000. This book provides an excellent overview of the different types of unobtrusive or nonreactive measures as well as the advantages and problems in using them.

Price, J. *Handbook of Organizational Measurement.* Marshfield, Mass.: Pitman, 1986. This volume describes a diversity of ways of measuring organizational variables, many of which are based on available data.

Riedel, Marc. *Research Strategies for Secondary Data: A Perspective for Criminology and Criminal Justice.* Thousand Oaks, Calif.: Sage, 2000. Although it focuses on the field of criminology, this useful guide to the many sources of data available for secondary analysis also reviews some of the methodological issues important to consider in doing such data analysis.

Rutman, L., ed. *Evaluation Research Methods,* 2nd ed. Beverly Hills, Calif.: Sage, 1984. Although devoted to evaluation in general, it also contains an excellent discussion of how to make agency information systems of maximum utility for research purposes.

West, M. D. *Applications of Computer Content Analysis.* Westport, Conn.: Ablex, 2001. This is a basic introduction to the procedures used in conducting content analysis research, with special emphasis on the role of computers.

Exercises for Class Discussion

8.1 Agency records are a valuable source of available data. If you are in a field placement, an internship, or doing volunteer work in a human service agency, ask the agency to provide sample copies of required and routine data collected on clients. Of course, you should be certain to obtain the forms and reports in a way that will not infringe on client or service-user confidentiality.

a. Compare the types of information gathered in the agency with which you are affiliated to that gathered by other students in other agencies. Can you think of some specific research questions you could explore with these data? Can you suggest some changes in agency data-gathering procedures that might produce more data for research at little additional effort?

b. What steps are required to obtain existing data on clients so as to meet ethical safeguards for confidentiality?

8.2 A researcher is interested in studying the impact of changing economic conditions on the retention of minority students in college. The researcher's hypothesis is that an economic recession will have a greater negative effect on the retention and graduation of minorities than on nonminority students. Using your own institution as the site for the project, what sources of data, already available in some data bank in your institution, might you use in such a study? What problems do you envision with these data in terms of sampling, unit of analysis, and levels of measurement?

8.3 The negative portrayal of public welfare service users in the media is a concern of human service professionals. Is the image of welfare recipients really negative? Has there been a trend toward improvement? Does the image portrayed improve or deteriorate in conjunction with changes in the national economy? These are questions that you might approach through a content analysis of the news media. Suppose you were to conduct such a content analysis research in your community:

a. Suggest what elements you think the population being studied contains.

b. Identify some sampling issues the research would confront.

c. What different problems are involved in answering the second and third questions in the above paragraph, in contrast to the first question about negative image?

d. Assume the research is confined to daily newspapers. Suggest some possibilities for the unit of analysis.

e. How could operational definitions of "negative image" and "welfare recipient" be developed?

Chapter 9

Field Research and Qualitative Methods

Observational techniques refer to the collection of data through direct visual or auditory experience of behavior. With observational techniques, which include video or audio recordings of behavior, the researcher actually sees or hears the behavior or words that are the data for the research. Observational techniques can be either quantitative or qualitative in nature. As we discussed in Chapter 1, qualitative research basically involves research in which the data come in the form of words, pictures, narratives, and descriptions rather than in numerical form. A second way that observational techniques differ from one another is in whether the observations are done in a naturalistic setting or in a laboratory or contrived setting. A naturalistic setting is a "real-life" situation in which people behave as they routinely would if they weren't the subjects of scientific observation. In fact, in some cases, people in naturalistic settings may not even know that they are under observation. Contrived settings are created by the researcher and would not have occurred were it not for the research project. This chapter focuses on observation done in naturalistic, or field settings. (We will discuss observation in contrived settings, such as laboratory experiments, in Chapter 10.)

Field research involves observations made of people in their natural settings as they go about their everyday life. Surveys involve people's reports to the researcher about what they said, did, or felt. With surveys and available data, the researcher does not directly observe what will be the focus of the research. With field research, on the other hand, the researcher actually sees or hears the behaviors that are the data for the research. Field research is most closely associated, in many people's minds, with the work of anthropologists who live among indigenous peoples for extended periods and write ethnographic reports that summarize people's way of life. Yet researchers in other social sciences and the human services also find field research a useful way to gather data. This chapter focuses mostly on qualitative field research but also explores methods of collecting quantitative data in the field and some other types of qualitative methods. It is helpful to begin with a quick overview of some of the characteristics that set qualitative research methods apart from quantitative methods.

Characteristics of Qualitative Methods
Contextual Approach

Chapters 2 and 4 introduced the distinctions between positivist and nonpositivist approaches to science and between qualitative and quantitative research. Although qualitative research methods might at times be conducted by people who take a positivist approach and might sometimes involve collecting some quantitative data, qualitative research has been closely associated over the years with nonpositivist or interpretive paradigms. Proponents of such paradigms argue that qualitative and contextual approaches offer access to a valuable type of data: a deeper and richer understanding of people's lives and behavior, including some knowledge of their subjective experiences (Benton 1977; Guba and Lincoln 1994; Gubrium and Holstein 1997). Because these subjective experiences are so central to the debate between positivists and nonpositivists and so important to qualitative research methods, let's explore what each approach has to say about these subjective experiences and their role in understanding human behavior.

Positivism argues that the world exists independently of people's perceptions of it and that scientists can use objective techniques to discover what exists in the world (Durkheim 1938; Halfpenny 1982). Astronomers, for example, use telescopes to discover stars and galaxies, which exist regardless of whether we are aware of them. So, too, researchers can study human beings in terms of behaviors that can be observed and recorded using some kind of objective technique. Recording people's gender, age, height, weight, or socioeconomic position are legitimate and objective measurement techniques—the equivalent of the physicist measuring the temperature, volume, or velocity of some liquid or solid. For the positivist, quantifying these measurements—assessing the average age of a group or looking at the percentage of a group that is male—is simply a precise way of describing and summarizing an objective reality. Such measurement provides a solid and objective foundation for understanding human social behavior. Limiting study to observable behaviors and using objective techniques, positivists argue, is most likely to produce systematic and repeatable research results that are open to refutation by other scientists.

Subjectivism (also called the interpretive or *verstehen* approach) provides a more nonpositivist perspective on these issues. It argues that these "objective" measures miss an important part of the human experience: the subjective and personal meanings that people attach to themselves, what they do, and the world around them (Wilson 1970). Max Weber, an early proponent of this view, argued that we need to look not only at what people do but also at what they think and feel about what is happening to them (Weber 1957, orig. pub. 1925). Researchers cannot adequately capture this "meaning" or "feeling" or "interpretive" dimension through objective, quantitative measurement techniques. They need to gain what Weber called **verstehen,** or a subjective understanding. They need to view and experience the situation from the perspective of the people themselves. To use a colloquialism, the researchers need "to walk a mile in the shoes" of the people being studied. They need to talk to these people at length and to immerse themselves in their subjects' lives so they can experience the highs and lows, the joys and sorrows, the triumphs and the tragedies from the perspective of the people they are studying. Researchers need to see how the individuals experience and give meaning to what is happening to them. Qualitative research methods are an attempt to gain access to that personal, subjective experience. These qualitative approaches stress the idea that knowledge, especially of the subjective dimension, best emerges when researchers understand the full context in which people behave. For interpretivists, quantitative research, by its very nature, misses this important dimension of social reality. Positivists, for their part, do not necessarily deny the existence or importance of subjective experiences, but they question whether qualitative methods, with their emphasis on the subjective interpretations of the *verstehen* method, have any scientific validity.

Grounded Theory Methodology

Many qualitative methods are closely grounded in the data, in that they let meaning, concepts, and theories emerge from the raw data rather than being imposed by the researcher. In many research methodologies in the social sciences, the role of theories parallels the positivist approach and the deductive model we discussed in Chapter 2. Theories are abstract explanations containing a variety of concepts and propositions. From these theories, the researcher derives testable hypotheses and operational definitions of concepts. Then he or she makes observations to determine whether the hypotheses are true. This deductive approach, however, is not always appropriate or even useful: Some research projects are exploratory in nature, meaning that there is little existing theory, concepts, or propositions from which to shape hypotheses or develop operational definitions. Another reason such a deductive approach is not useful for some research projects is that it involves the scientists, through theory and measurement, imposing structure, categorization, and meaning onto reality rather than letting the structure and meaning emerge from reality.

So, proponents of more inductive approaches to theory development argue that deducing hypotheses from existing theories is sometimes limiting, especially in the early stages of theory development, when the theory may not include some relevant variables (Strauss and Corbin 1994). If the variables are not in the theory, they cannot be part of hypotheses and thus may be ignored. In other words, strict adherence to deductive hypothesis construction might blind researchers to some key phenomena. One of the more widely used approaches to these issues is called *grounded theory*. **Grounded theory** is a research methodology for developing theory by letting the theory emerge from the data or be "grounded" in the data. With this method, there is a continual interplay between data collection, data analysis, and theory development. In the positivist model, these three elements are sequenced: first data collection, followed by data analysis, followed in turn by theory development. Using a grounded theory method, these three elements can occur simultaneously as one goes constantly back and forth among them. Thus, theory development occurs in the midst of data collection rather than following it.

In the absence of theory, researchers begin by making observations; those who use grounded theory often do qualitative research by making direct observations or conducting interviews in field settings. Without the restrictions of a preexisting theory, they describe what happens, identify relevant variables, and search for explanations of what they observe. Beginning with these concrete observations, researchers develop more abstract concepts, propositions, and theoretical explanations that would be plausible given those observations. Inductive research of this sort can serve as a foundation for building a theory, and the theory that emerges can later serve as a guide for additional research, possibly even as a source of testable hypotheses through deductive reasoning.

Proponents of qualitative methods argue that concepts and theories produced by such grounded approaches provide a more valid representation of some phenomena because they emerge directly from the phenomena being studied. In fact, in positivist science, we can engage in theory development without engaging in any data collection or data analysis at all. This is impossible in grounded theory because the theory emerges from the data or observations. However, theory produced in this manner could also be subject to further verification by deducing and testing hypotheses. In fact, a common misconception of grounded theory is that it is entirely inductive in nature. To the contrary, grounded theory does at times use existing theory to understand and explain data, and it does include procedures for verifying theories. Thus, some of the considerations of more positivist approaches are relevant to grounded theory: Grounded theory uses evidence to verify theories, it rigorously follows precise procedures, it makes efforts at replication, and as one of its goals it generalizes about social processes across a variety of social settings.

We will discuss grounded theory in more detail in Chapter 16 in the context of analyzing qualitative data. However, it is helpful to review these ideas about the contextual and grounded nature of quali-

tative research in order to recognize the commonalities among the different types of qualitative methods that we will explore.

Field Research

Field research is one of the more common types of qualitative methods in the social sciences and human services. A number of different approaches to conducting field research exist. Although there is some overlap among them, each introduces some special techniques of data collection.

Participant Observation

One technique for doing field research is **participant observation,** a method in which the researcher observes people in their natural environment (the "field"); the researcher is a part of and participates in the activities of the people, group, or situation that is being studied (DeWalt and DeWalt 2001; Lofland and Lofland 1995). Participant observation research is naturalistic and involves some participation by the investigator, although, as we will see, the degree of such participation varies. In some cases, the investigator may have belonged to the group prior to the start of the research and can use this position as a group member to collect data. For example, a social worker might be interested in staff adaptation to antidiscriminatory hiring legislation. If he or she is on the agency personnel committee, such a position might serve as the context for participant observation. As the agency hires new staff members, the social worker can observe the reactions of the other staff in dealing with the new regulations. In other cases, a researcher must first gain access to a group in order to be a participant observer. Anthropologist Sue Estroff (1981) did this to learn more about the daily lives and problems of former mental patients. For two years she joined in the lives of a group of deinstitutionalized mental patients, experiencing the drudgery and degradation of their daily routine. She worked at low-paying jobs (such as slipping rings onto drapery rods) that were the lot of these ex-patients. She took the powerful antipsychotic drugs that were routinely administered to them and that had distinctive side effects, such as hand tremors and jiggling legs. She also experienced the extreme depression and despair that result when patients suddenly stop taking these potent drugs. From her position as participant in their subculture, she could observe the con games that characterized the relationships between patients and mental health professionals.

Through this type of participant observation, practitioners have access to a view of client groups that they cannot gain in an interview or therapy session. It is a unique view because the researcher sees from the perspective of the client, a perspective especially valuable to anyone who works with groups that are stigmatized or commonly misunderstood by both practitioners and laypeople. Though many practitioners may not have the opportunity to engage in such observations personally, such research efforts by behavioral scientists can be utilized to develop a better understanding of client groups. Human service professionals should seek opportunities to conduct this kind of research themselves to understand particular groups or subcultures. In fact, practitioners might consider periodically engaging in participant observation of their clients, if possible, to detect ways in which the practitioner perspective may limit understanding of client groups.

Proponents of participant observation argue that it is the only method that enables the researcher to approximate *verstehen,* an empathic understanding of the subjective experiences of people. Of course, actual access to such experience is impossible; thoughts and feelings, by their very nature, are private. Even when someone talks about how he or she feels, the person has objectified that subjective experience into words and thus changed it. Participant observers, however, can gain some insight into those subjective experiences by immersing themselves in the lives and daily experiences of the people they study. By experiencing the same culture, the same values, the same hopes and fears, researchers are in a better position to take on the point of view of these people. However, despite its focus on subjective experiences, participant observation is still empirical in the sense that it is grounded in observation, and issues of reliability and validity also concern those who use this method. Researchers who use participant observation consider it no less systematic or scientific than the more positivistic research techniques.

So one reason researchers select participant observation and qualitative methods is because they have determined that an interpretive approach best advances knowledge in a particular area. A second reason for choosing these research methods is because the research is exploratory in nature, and theoretical development does not enable researchers to spell out relevant concepts or develop precise hypotheses. Participant observation permits the researcher to view human behavior as it occurs in the natural environment without the restrictions of preconceived notions or explanations. Through observation, the researcher can begin to formulate concepts, variables, and hypotheses that seem relevant to the topic and grounded in the actual behavior of people.

It is important to recognize that, in participant observation, knowledge is gained from two distinct but linked kinds of observations. One kind of observation is based on *participation,* where the researcher learns about the social world of those he or she observes by personally experiencing that world. This is the *verstehen* method Weber proposed, and it provides understanding through empathic experience. This empathic experience is an important source of knowledge that offers an intersubjective understanding of other people's lives. The second kind of observation is produced by *observation,* noting and recording how others behave and what occurs at a social setting. Observation provides understanding through a deep appreciation of the full context within which people live their lives. It enables social scientists to make rich descriptions of everyday social life.

Examples of Participant Observation.   Some examples of participant observation can flesh out this discussion. In the mid-1980s, anthropologist Philippe Bourgois (1995), recently married at the time and looking for an apartment he could afford, moved into "El Barrio," an East Harlem neighborhood in New York. Although fieldwork was not his intent in moving there, he eventually used his residence there as a springboard for doing research on the underground economy, social marginalization, and how the poor families in that community managed to survive. He lived there for three and a half years and got to know many of the community members. He visited their homes often and attended parties and celebrations with them. He observed how people managed to get by when they could get no jobs at all or only poorly paying ones. Most of El Barrio's residents were law-abiding, but a small, publicly visible portion of them were involved in the drug trade. Bourgois became friends with two dozen street dealers and their families. He spent many nights on the streets and in the crack houses with both dealers and addicts. He saw how the residents who had nothing to do with drugs coped with the vibrant and sometimes violent drug world that pervaded their community.

As another example, a sociology research team used participant observation as one tool to explore what happens when two major policy shifts—one in welfare and the other in education—collide in the lives of the poor (Newman and Chin 2003). One current policy trend is the insistence on work over welfare; the other is an end to social promotion in school. The researchers point out that these seemingly unrelated changes are backed by wholly different research findings and implemented by totally different bureaucracies. Crunching numbers for millions of participants on dollars earned, hours worked, math scores achieved, and reading levels attained would be in danger of missing the behind-the-scenes breakdowns and crises as families cope with the pressure to both move into the low-end labor market in response to welfare initiatives and simultaneously to assist their children with their education. The researchers sought to put a face on this struggle by focusing on 12 families—four African American, four Puerto Rican, and four Dominican. They used participant observation in the neighborhoods where these people lived, the schools their children attended, the churches they frequented, and the social service providers they encountered. This research strategy enabled the researchers to unveil the stark reality of a single mother trying to work as she struggled to find day care for her young children and worried about her older children in a school where gangs were recruiting new members.

With participant observation, then, researchers can observe processes and grasp levels of meaning that other, more objective methods—such as surveys or available statistical data—cannot uncover and identify differences between what people say they do and their actual behavior.

Observer Roles.   In many types of research, the relationship between the researcher and those participating in the research is fairly clear-cut. In surveys, for example, participants know who the researchers are and that they as respondents are providing data to the researchers. In observational research, and especially with participant observation, the researcher–participant relationship becomes more problematic in that it can take a number of different forms. Two critical issues arise: the extent to which the observer will change the setting under observation and the extent to which people should be informed that they are being used for research purposes. The way in which a researcher resolves these issues determines the nature of the observer–participant relationship for a given research project.

A participant observer is a part of the activities being studied and is therefore in a position to influence the direction of those activities. For example, Sue Estroff might have wanted to organize the deinstitutionalized mental patients she studied into a lobbying group demanding better living conditions and improved treatment from mental health professionals. But if she had done this early in her participant observation, would it have interfered with her research goals? Would she have learned all the sources of despair and degradation that these people experienced? Would she have learned how such groups, without benefit of an intervening anthropologist, adapt to their plight? The resolution of this issue of the extent of intervention, of course, rests partly on the research question. If Estroff were interested in how such groups adapt without outside aid, then she should limit her influence on the group, even though humanitarian values might push her toward involvement. On the other hand, if she wanted to assess effective strategies for improving the lot of these groups, then intervention on her part would be called for by the research question. Human service providers, in particular, need to be sensitive to this issue because an important part of their role as practitioners is intervention. Providers need to recognize that intervention may at times be counterproductive to research goals.

This problem of the degree of intervention is often a question of whether the researcher is, first and foremost, a participant or an observer (Gold 1958). Which of these two aspects should he or she emphasize? Let us look at each side of the issue. Those who emphasize the importance of the participation of the observer argue that the investigator plays two roles—that of scientist and that of group member. To fully comprehend the activities of the group and the dynamics of the situation, the researcher must become fully involved in the group. Otherwise, group members may not confide in the researcher. In addition, the researcher who does not participate is hampered in achieving *verstehen,* that is, an empathic understanding of the deep meanings and experiences important to the group. To become fully involved, the researcher must act like any other group member—and this means intervening in those situations in which other group members might do so.

On the other side of the issue, those who emphasize observation over participation argue that the more fully one becomes a group member, the less objective one becomes. The real danger is that researchers will "go native": become so immersed in the group that they take on completely the perspective of the group and can no longer view the situation from a less interested perspective (Shupe and Bromley 1980). Most participant observers attempt to strike a balance between total immersion and loss of objectivity on the one hand and total separation with its consequent loss of information on the other.

The second critical issue in the researcher–participant relationship is both practical and ethical: To what extent should the people studied be informed of the investigator's research purposes (Piquemal 2001)? This is an especially troubling problem in participant observation because in some cases fully informing people undermines the researcher's ability to gather accurate data. For example, a study of staff treatment of patients in a mental hospital was conducted by having researchers admitted to the hospital as patients without informing the staff of their research purposes (Rosenhan 1973). Undoubtedly, hospital staff would have behaved quite differently had they known they were under surveillance. Therefore, some researchers take the position that concealment is sometimes necessary to conduct scientific work and that researchers must judge whether the scientific gain justifies the deception and any potential injury—social or psychological—that might result. Others, however, hold adamantly to the position that any research on human beings must include "informed consent": fully inform the people involved about the purposes of the research, any possible dangers or consequences, and the credentials of the researcher. Anything less, they argue, is both unethical and immoral because it tricks people into cooperation and may lead to undesirable consequences of which they are not aware. (We dealt with this complex ethical dilemma at greater length in Chapter 3.)

In a classic piece on observational research, Raymond Gold (1958) identified three distinct observer roles that can emerge depending on how the issues of observer influence and informed consent resolve: complete participant, participant-as-observer, and observer-as-participant. The distinguishing feature of the *complete participant role* is that the observer's status as observer is not revealed to those who are being studied. The observer enters a group under the guise of being just another member and essentially plays that role while conducting the study. The researcher must be able to sustain this pretense for long periods because studies using the complete participant role are usually characterized by lengthy involvement with the group studied. The complete participant role has proved valuable in studying groups, such as drug users or dealers, that otherwise might be closed to research if the observer's true identity were known. Research in Practice 9.1 provides an interesting illustration of the complete participant role used to better understand life in prison.

RESEARCH IN PRACTICE 9.1

BEHAVIOR AND SOCIAL ENVIRONMENT:

The Complete Participant Role in a Prison

Field research can be difficult and complicated to conduct, and it can put the researcher in situations where it is difficult to know what proper action is. In fact, sociologist Richard Leo put it this way: "Fieldwork is a morally ambiguous enterprise that is fraught with moral hazards, contingencies and uncertainties" (1996, p. 125). A participant observation research study by James Marquart (2001) conducted in prisons well illustrates some of these issues. Marquart's research also illustrates many of the steps in conducting field research discussed in this chapter.

Marquart first came into contact with the world of prisons while working on a project to evaluate the training of prison guards. He met a prison warden who invited him to visit his prison, which he did a number of times over a period a year or two. During these visits, Marquart came to know many guards and inmates, who encouraged him to learn what prison life was "really" like by working as a full-time prison guard. Marquart's specific research goal was to evaluate the effectiveness of a practice in the prison called the "building tender system," in which the prison used particularly dominant and aggressive inmates to control other inmates by meting out punishments, which included beatings. He recognized that becoming a prison guard and taking the complete participant role would give him a perspective on this system that he could gain in no other way. So with the support of the warden, he began work as a full-time prison guard, a job he kept for about a year and a half.

One major issue a field researcher confronts is what to tell the people he is observing in the field. Marquart's research was not truly disguised observation because the warden and some of the guards knew that he was a sociologist making field observations of prison life. To those who knew of his research role, he never lied or misrepresented himself. Yet he wasn't completely honest with them either. Although one of his major interests was in evaluating the building tender system, he didn't tell the prison officials this because he feared they would become defensive about a practice they had implemented and refuse him access. Instead, he stated his interests to be something more general involving the study of guards and guard work. This is what Richard Leo calls an "act of omission" (withholding information) rather than an "act of commission" (intentionally giving false information). Leo and some other field researchers argue that acts of omission are morally acceptable in field research because they are often necessary to get the research done (see Chapter 3). Marquart's belief was that, if he had not withheld certain information, he could not have done his research. Yet he clearly recognized that intentional falsification was morally unacceptable.

Prison life is filled with fear, danger, paranoia, suspicion, and factionalism—for both inmates and guards. It is a challenging environment in which to attempt to gain the rapport so essential to good fieldwork. Both guards and inmates came up with all kinds of theories as to who Marquart was and why he was working in the prison: He was a government agent, a spy, or a close relative of the warden. Marquart did a number of things over a period of time to build rapport. He worked hard and took on difficult and dangerous assignments, such as breaking up inmate fights. He lifted weights, boxed, and jogged with inmates to gain their respect. He also got into some serious and dangerous physical altercations with inmates. All of this enabled him gradually to become "invisible," perceived by both guards and inmates as just another prison guard.

One of the more difficult and morally ambiguous aspects of field research involves the researcher's responsibilities to those he or she observes in the field. In Marquart's case, the prison guards and even the prisoners let him into their world and their lives. What obligations did he have to them for doing this? When they accepted him in the role of prison guard, they expected him to perform that role well,

continued on next page

and one part of that role was to provide support for other guards. This meant assisting the guards in their various tasks, coming to the aide of a guard attacked by a prisoner, and even possibly not informing on a guard who beats a prisoner. As Marquart put it, "The ability to 'keep one's mouth shut' was a highly prized asset and I quickly internalized this important value" (2001, p. 40). A good guard was expected to keep his mouth shut. Leo, Marquart, and some other field researchers argue that Marquart took on an implicit moral obligation when he moved into the role of prison guard. Implicit in the guards' and prisoners' acceptance of him is that he be a good guard and carry out all aspects of that role.

Prison is a violent place. Marquart observed prisoners brutalizing other prisoners. He watched guards beat inmates senseless with clubs as the inmates pleaded for mercy. He was so disturbed by some incidents he observed that he almost quit. Yet he remained and developed a coping strategy of indifference. He also kept his mouth shut, not telling authorities outside the prison of any illegal or brutal actions he had observed. He respected the moral obligation he had incurred by going into the field. But it is surely a complex and ambiguous moral obligation. Other researchers might dispute the acceptability of his choices. Surely there must be a line that can be crossed that nullifies the moral obligation. What if a guard killed an inmate? Some would argue that some of the actions Marquart observed crossed that line.

The prison context in which Marquart conducted his field research is a difficult and extreme one in comparison to many field settings. Yet his position as complete observer provided him with a perspective on the practice of using building tenders that could not be obtained with any other research technique.

The *participant-as-observer role* differs from the complete participant role in that the researcher reveals his or her status as observer to those who are being studied. In this role, the observer enters a group and participates in their routines but is known to be doing so for research purposes. As in the case of the complete participant role, the participant-as-observer spends a considerable amount of time observing in the group being studied. Community research often uses the participant-as-observer role, probably due to the large size of these groups and the need for direct access to information that the complete participant might find difficult or too time-consuming to obtain while maintaining a disguise. Whyte's (1955) classic study, "Street Corner Society," is a fine example of the use of the participant-as-observer role.

The *observer-as-participant role* is similar to the participant-as-observer role in that the observer's true status is known to those being studied but differs with regard to the length of time the observer spends with the group. The participant-as-observer role assumes a lengthy period of observation. The observer-as-participant role involves brief contact with the group being studied, possibly for as little as one day. This brief contact tends to preclude the deep, insightful results that characterize studies utilizing the two previous roles. The observer-as-participant role is likely to generate more shallow, superficial results. In fact, the brief contact that characterizes this role may lead the observer to misunderstand aspects of the group being studied. Because of these problems, the observer-as-participant role has been less popular for conducting serious social research.

Unobtrusive Observation

Some research questions call for or require the investigator to refrain from participation in the group being investigated. This is the case when the intrusive impact of an outsider might change the behavior of group members in ways detrimental to the research question. In such cases, the relationship adopted by the investigator is what Gold (1958) labeled the *complete observer role*—the observer has no direct contact with or no substantial influence on those being observed. One way of doing such nonparticipant observation is an observational technique called **unobtrusive** or **nonreactive observation:** Those under study are not aware that they are being studied, and the investigator does not change their behavior by his or her presence (Lee 2000; Webb et al. 1981). Unobtrusive observation can be done in naturalistic or contrived settings and involves both quantitative and qualitative observations. Two forms that unobtrusive observation can take are hidden observation and disguised observation.

Hidden Observation. In some research projects, we can observe behavior from a vantage point that is obscured from the view of those under observation—through a one-way mirror, perhaps, or by videotaping with a hidden camera. For example, some studies of aggressive behavior among children utilize observations in naturalistic settings by videotaping children at play in school yards with the camera in a hidden location (Pepler and Craig 1995). The camera can be set up in a classroom window, out of sight of the children; zoom lenses make possible clear observation of children's behavior from long distances. As long as the children are not aware of the cameras and of the fact that they are being observed, the research is truly nonreactive in nature. This naturalistic, hidden observation is important in the study of aggression among children because children behave more normally under these conditions; in a contrived setting or an interview, it is probably impossible to make the same honest, natural observations. In fact, one group of researchers of such behavior noted that "the use of knives on our school playground tapes was so covert that it often took several passes through the audiovisual tapes to discern their presence" (Pepler and Craig 1995, p. 550). Because the children clearly attempt to hide the knives from others, they are extremely unlikely to display such aggressive behavior to researchers in surveys or in a contrived setting. Naturalistic and hidden observations are key to making such discoveries.

A major problem with hidden observations is ensuring that the observations are, in fact, hidden and truly unobtrusive. The unobtrusive nature of the study of children's aggression just mentioned was compromised in two ways. First, the school principal,

teachers, and other adults supervising the children at play knew about the observations. All people have a tendency to react differently when they are being observed—they put their best foot forward or behave in a fashion they think is acceptable to the observer. The adults supervising these children may well have done the same thing—watching the children more closely or reacting more quickly to behaviors that hint of aggression. If these adults behaved differently with the children than they would have if the children were not being observed, this would compromise the unobtrusive nature of the observations. A second compromise occurred because the researchers also wanted an audiotape of the children's conversations to fully understand the nature of their aggressive behavior. So the children had wireless microphones clipped to their clothing while they played in the school yard, thus making them aware that they were being observed. The researchers decided that both of these compromises were essential and that they had only minor effects on the validity of the observations made. The adults, for example, did not know exactly which children on the playground were being observed at a given time; the children seemed, after a short period of being aware of the microphone, to ignore it and play naturally. Other research supports this idea that people often tend to forget they are being observed and to behave normally, especially if the observation occurs over a long period. This research on aggression among children does illustrate, however, the ways in which what appears at first to be hidden observation is not actually completely unobtrusive.

Disguised Observation. With some types of behavior, we can conduct what we call *disguised observation:* Researchers observe people in a naturalistic setting, but without participating and without revealing that they are observing them. This is an example of the complete participant role. Any setting in which one can be present and not participate without calling attention to oneself is a potential scene for disguised observation. The observer enters a group under the guise of being just another member and plays that role while conducting the observations.

One setting, for example, that might lend itself to such disguised observation is a public establishment, like a bar or a tavern. A group of investigators interested in alcohol-related aggressive behavior (Graham et al. 1980) conducted exactly this kind of disguised observation. They decided that they could best gather information through unobtrusive observation of the behavior of people as they consumed alcohol in various bars in Vancouver, British Columbia. Teams of observers spent from 40 to 56 hours per week making observations in drinking establishments. Each team consisted of a male–female pair who would enter an establishment, locate a table with a good view of the saloon, and order a drink. They made every effort not to influence the people in the bar in any way. We consider such research nonparticipant rather than participant because the investigators made efforts to have no contact with or influence on the behavior of the patrons. At times, this was impossible—a patron would wander over to their table and engage them in a conversation. In those cases, they quickly terminated the observations and left the bar. In other ways, we might question the unobtrusive character of their observation: The female observer was often the only Anglo female in the bar, the observers were sometimes the only people in the bar who were not at least slightly inebriated, and there were often social class differences between the dress and behavior of the observers and the observed. Nonetheless, their impact on the behavior of the clientele was probably minimal, so we can consider this disguised, nonparticipant observation.

Steps in Field Research

The exact steps taken in conducting field research vary depending on whether it is participant observation, unobtrusive observation, or some variant. We will describe the steps taken in participant observation, recognizing that some parts of what follows may be unnecessary in other types of field research.

Problem Formulation

The first step in field research is to engage in problem formulation, including a literature review and conceptual development. From this assessment, the researcher establishes the specific goals of the research and decides whether field research is the most appropriate research strategy. A part of problem formulation also includes learning as much as we can about the people, groups, and settings that will be the focus of observation by reviewing previous research on the groups as well as any historical and literary materials that might enlighten us about the group and its culture. The more we learn before going into the field, the more effective we will be at making observations in the field.

Selecting a Field Setting

The second step is to decide which specific group to study. Whether we are studying deinstitutionalized mental patients, cocaine dealers, or motorcycle gangs, we have to decide exactly which group we will join and observe. One way to decide this is by finding a group that is accessible. Sometimes a field setting presents itself as a by-product of some research or other activities. Barrie Thorne's (1993) participant observation in elementary schools arose because she was asked to assess issues of gender equity in the schools. She designed her field observations to achieve that goal, but she also obtained permission to make additional observations for her own research purposes. Clifford Stott was interested in how violence escalates among fans of British soccer teams, so this focus determined the necessity of making field observations of fans before, during, and after soccer matches (Stott and Reicher 1998). A soccer fan himself, Stott joined other fans of the team he supported at international soccer matches, and these matches and fans became the focus of his participant observation. Anthropologist Nancy Scheper-Hughes (1992) selected a particular shantytown in Brazil as her field setting because she had lived there years earlier, before becoming an anthropologist, as a Peace Corps volunteer. Her earlier exposure had resulted in continuing ties with some people who lived there and made this shantytown a relatively accessible field setting for her.

Entering the Field

The third step is challenging: gaining entry into the group to be studied. In the complete participant role, this step is less of a problem because the people do not know they are being studied. However, we must be sufficiently like those studied to gain access. In the other participant roles, however, where they know that we are outsiders and researchers, we must find some way to convince the people to accept our involvement as researchers. Several methods increase the likelihood that people will cooperate (Feldman, Bell, and Berger 2003; Jorgensen 1989). One way to gain their cooperation is to win the support of those with more status or influence in the group and use our relationship with them to gain access to others. It would be best, for example, to approach the directors of a mental health center and enlist their aid before contacting caseworkers and ward staff.

Another way to increase cooperation is to present our reasons for conducting the research in a way that seems plausible and makes sense in the subjects' frame of reference. Esoteric or abstract scientific goals are unlikely to appeal to an agency director or to a struggling single parent on welfare. Instead, we should emphasize that our major concern is understanding their thoughts and behaviors as legitimate, acceptable, and appropriate. Nothing closes doors faster than the hint that we intend to evaluate the group. The door of a welfare recipient may open if we say we are studying the difficulties confronting parents on welfare; it will surely be slammed if we say we want to separate the good welfare recipients from the bad.

Cooperation is also enhanced if we have some means of legitimizing ourselves as researchers—perhaps through an affiliation with a university that supports the study or an agency with an interest in the research. In a study of a sexually transmitted disease clinic, for example, Joseph Sheley (1976) gained entrance because he was involved with a larger community study of sexually transmitted diseases (STDs). Such legitimation can backfire, of course, if the group we hope to study is suspicious of or hostile toward the organization with which we are affiliated. Sheley, for example, although allowed into the clinic, found himself with a degree of "outsider" status because of his association with the community STD study.

Finally, we may need to use informants to gain entry into some groups. An *informant* is an insider who can introduce us to others in the group, ease our acceptance into the group, and help us interpret how the group views the world. Especially with informal subcultures, the informant technique is a valuable approach.

Sometimes it takes a bit of creativity or even courage to gain entry into some field settings. Sociologist Ruth Horowitz (1987) wanted to study Latino gangs in a particular city. But as a Jewish woman, she did not have easy entry into these groups. So she sat on a bench in a park frequented by gang members until they approached her. Eventually, one of the leaders of the gang asked who she was—an obvious outsider on their turf. She told him that she wanted to write a book about Latino youth and then convinced him to introduce her to other members of the gang.

In some cases, the researcher may know members of the group being observed, and these personal contacts can ease entry into the group. For example, in a study of violence among British soccer fans, the anthropologist doing the study selected a particular group of fans to join and observe because he had grown up and gone to school with some of them (Armstrong 1993). These personal contacts made it easier to gain their cooperation.

Developing Rapport in the Field

The fourth step in participant observation is to develop rapport and trust with the people being studied so that they will serve as useful and accurate sources of information. This can be time-consuming, trying, and traumatic. It is a problem with which the human service professional can readily identify. The community organizer attempting to gain the trust of migrant workers, the substance-abuse worker dealing with a narcotics addict, and the child welfare worker running a group home for girls can all attest to the importance of establishing rapport. Although in many cases the human service worker can express a sincere desire to help as a means of establishing rapport, the researcher cannot always employ this approach because the research goals may not include providing such help. In the initial stages of the research, people are likely to be distant if not outright distrustful. We are likely to make errors and social gaffes that offend the people we have joined. More than one participant observation effort has had to be curtailed because the investigator inadvertently alienated the people being studied.

Many elements are involved in developing rapport or trust with our informants (Feldman, Bell, and Berger 2003; Jorgensen 1989). Rapport can emerge if the informants and group members view the investigator as a basically nice person who will do them no harm. It matters little if the informants know of or agree with the research goals—only that they develop a positive attitude toward the investigator. Trust and rapport can also emerge if the investigator shows through behavior that he or she agrees with or has some sympathy for the group's perspective. If we join our field contacts in some of their routine activities, such as drinking beer or playing cards, they are likely to view us as someone who accepts them and someone they can trust. Of course, the researcher must balance the need for acceptance against personal and professional standards of behavior. Another way to enhance trust and rapport is to reduce the social distance between the researcher and those being observed. In field studies of schoolchildren, this can often be achieved by avoiding positions of authority or by avoiding intervening with the children in ways that other adults, teachers, or school officials do. For example, field researchers observing children avoid intervening in fights or other behavioral problems unless some serious accident or injury might occur (Mandell 1988; Thorne 1993). Finally, researchers can enhance rapport if the relationship between investigator and group members is reciprocal; that is, both the observer and the group members have something the other needs and wants. We might, for example, gain scientific data from our informants, whereas they hope to gain some publicity and attendant public concern from the publication of our results.

Becoming Invisible

In field research, being "invisible" means that those present perceive the observer as a natural part of the setting, not an outsider or in any way unusual. Even in the participant-as-observer role, when the people know we are researchers, we can become invisible if the others begin to see us as "just one of them." This has something to do with rapport: As rapport develops, the observer comes to be seen as a natural part of the setting by the people being observed. Becoming invisible is also partly a matter of time: The longer a person is in the scene, the less he or she is noticed as unusual or as an outsider. Initially, the presence of the observer may change behavior, but this effect often dissipates as time passes. People also become invisible when they join in the routine activities in the setting, whether working side by side at some task, drinking beer or smoking marijuana with the others at the scene, or joining in on some illegal behavior. By doing these things, the group comes to see the observer as a routine part of their setting. Another way to become invisible is to develop friendships with those being observed. When this happens, the friendship role becomes more important in the eyes of those being observed than does the researcher role. As the friendship role becomes more salient, people become more open and honest and less guarded in their interactions with the observer.

Attitude of the Researcher

In positivist research, the researcher's attitude is presumed to be one of objectivity and detachment. In field research, however, researcher–subject relationships are more extensive, complex, and personal. As Philippe Bourgois put it, "in order to collect 'accurate data,' ethnographers violate the canons of positivist research; we become intimately involved with the people we study" (1995, p. 13). Another anthropologist put it this way: "The ethnographer must be intellectually poised between familiarity and strangeness, while socially, he or she is poised between 'stranger' and 'friend'" (Powdermaker 1966, p. 20). So, the researcher's role may be that of friend or stranger or somewhere in between. This complexity and ambiguity means that each field observer needs to address the issue of what his or her attitude should be toward those being observed.

In most field settings, the researcher's attitude should probably be one of *openness* to a wide range of types of behavior and *respect* for the dignity of the research subjects. As the examples in this chapter show, field researchers sometimes find themselves observing behavior that they find morally offensive or politically unpalatable. However, the researcher's goal is not to judge but to observe, record, and learn. Moral or political reactions can interfere with these goals and may threaten the rapport necessary to achieving good field research. In addition, ethical principles (see Chapter 3) dictate that the people who let us into their lives should not be harmed by that, and taking moral or political offense can be a form of attack. Researchers who cannot achieve this attitude of openness and respect toward particular groups might be best served by not doing field research on those groups.

The researcher's attitude also needs to be *reciprocal,* recognizing that the subjects make as significant a contribution to the production and interpretation of knowledge as the researcher does. A dangerous attitude is one that Barrie Thorne calls "studying down," where the researcher assumes that it is the researchers who produce or "discover" knowledge, while the subjects are less informed and less able to contribute to the production of knowledge (1993, p. 12). Thorne ran across this attitude on research on children, where many researchers seemed to dismiss the possibility that the children being observed could teach the researchers something and that the children could help produce knowledge and understanding. Thorne approached her field observations "with an assumption that kids are competent social actors who take an active role in shaping their daily experiences. I wanted to sustain an attitude of respectful discovery, to uncover and document kids' points of view and meanings" (1993, p. 12).

Finally, the researcher needs to *balance* his or her attitude in terms of identifying both the positive and negative aspects of the settings or cultures being observed. Philippe Bourgois, in his field research on inner-city street culture, points out that:

> . . . the methodological logistics of participant observation require researchers to be physically present and personally involved. This encourages them to overlook negative dynamics because they need to be empathetically engaged with the people they study and must also have their permission to live with them. (1995, p. 14)

This can produce an unwitting self-censorship when the researcher fails to notice or report on some of the negative aspects of the behavior or lifestyle of the subjects. Bourgois found aspects of the street culture he studied to be violent, dangerous, and abhorrent. Yet a balanced attitude requires that the researcher's overall picture is neither unrealistically negative nor unrealistically positive.

Observing and Recording in the Field

The center of attention in field research, of course, is observing and recording what occurs. However, this cannot truly begin until we have accomplished the other steps just described. Although field researchers keep track of what they observe while entering the field and gaining rapport, the best observations depend on those things having been achieved. What observations to record and how to record them are discussed later in this chapter.

Going Native

Because of the deep immersion in the group that can occur in field research, along with the strong relationships with people that can develop, one danger that can arise is what some ethnographers call *going native:* becoming so involved in and identified with the group as to take on its perspective and find it difficult to see the group from more objective (or at least different) perspectives. Any semblance of a scientific perspective or judgment is lost. For example, one British social scientist who was a strong soccer fan admitted to strong feelings of partisanship toward a particular team and its fans, who were also the subjects of his field observations (Hughson 1998). On at least one occasion this went so far that he joined (albeit reluctantly) in physical confrontations when "his" fans came into physical conflict with fans supporting opposing teams. Going native is something to be concerned with, but it is a delicate balance. After all, going native can assist in developing the empathic understanding that is one of the goals of field research. As we have said, the field researcher must be somewhere between a stranger and a friend; it requires some judgment to detect the point beyond which friendliness has more negative than positive consequences for the research.

Exiting the Field

In most field research, the period of observations in the field ends because the researcher has collected sufficient data (or run out of grant money). When this time comes, the researcher must leave the field in a way that brings no negative consequences to the people being observed. Because field research involves the researcher living in some degree of intimacy with those being studied, it is not uncommon for some level of personal relationship to develop. Acquaintances, friendships, and maybe even more intense relationships can emerge. The researcher needs to sever these relationships in such a way that people don't experience significant social or emotional loss. This may mean that, throughout the period of being in the field, the researcher remains somewhat socially or emotionally distant so that complicating personal relationships don't develop to the point where difficulty in exiting the field occurs. This is one way to avoid expectations of excessive intimacy or permanency in a relationship. Of course, there is a balance here because some level of friendly involvement may be essential to developing rapport. However, from the very beginning, the researcher has an eye on the exit in terms of developing relationships with respondents.

Recording Observations in Field Research

Field research is most closely associated with qualitative research, but observations made in the field can involve either qualitative or quantitative data or both. Accordingly, the manner in which field researchers record observations depends on whether the observations are primarily quantitative or qualitative in nature. Qualitative observation typically calls for less structured *field notes,* whereas quantitative observation typically uses more structured recording of data on *coding sheets.*

Qualitative Observation: Field Notes

Detailed, descriptive accounts of the observations made during a given period are called **field notes.** The precise nature of field notes varies greatly from one study to another, but all field notes should include six elements (Bogdan and Taylor 1975; Lofland and Lofland 1995).

1. A *running description* makes up the bulk of the field notes and is self-explanatory—simply a record of the day's observations with a primary concern of recording accurately the concrete events that were observed. The researcher should avoid analyzing persons or events while in the field because there is not the time and it interferes with observation of the ongoing scene. Instead, he or she should concentrate on faithfully recording what occurs.

2. Field notes also include *accounts of previous episodes that were forgotten or went unnoticed* but that the investigator remembered while still in the field. When preparing the field notes from any observation session, it is likely that the researcher may forget or leave out certain events. Subsequent observations may bring the forgotten episodes back to mind. The researcher should record these events when remembered, with the proper notation concerning when they originally occurred.

3. *Analytical ideas and inferences* refer to spur-of-the-moment ideas concerning such things as data analysis, important variables, speculation regarding causal sequences, and the like. Researchers should record these "flashes of insight" regarding any aspect of the study when they occur. Reviewing these ideas after the completion of observations can greatly benefit the final data analysis and writing of the report. Although most data analysis is reserved until after the observation period, no researcher wants to forget whatever analytical ideas occurred in the field.

4. *Personal impressions and feelings* should be noted because the possibility that bias might color our observations is always present. Recording personal impressions and feelings helps minimize this bias by giving a sense of the perspective

from which the observer is viewing various persons, places, or events. Does the observer simply dislike a certain person in the setting? If so, the observer should honestly record such a feeling when it first occurs. This can prove beneficial when reviewing accounts relating to this person to see if the researcher's personal feelings influenced the description.

5. *Notes for further information* are notes observers write to and for themselves: plans for future observations, specific things or persons to look for, and the like. It is risky to rely on memory for anything important relating to the study.

6. *Methodological notes* refer to any ideas that relate to techniques for conducting field research in this setting. As researchers, we should note any difficulties we have in collecting data, any biases that might be introduced by the data-collection techniques, or any changes in how we make and record observations. The purpose of this is to better prepare us to assess validity (to be discussed shortly) and to provide insight for future researchers who might make observations in similar settings.

How to Record. Field notes can take a number of different forms (Bernard 2001; Lofland and Lofland 1995). For example, parts of field notes might consist of brief jottings where researchers make note of something that is happening or something that occurs to them. Many field researchers carry a notepad at all times, even when not in the field, to make note of things as they occur or as they think of them. Other parts of field notes might contain a more detailed and complete written recording of what is happening in some setting. In some cases, instead of writing field notes, researchers use laptop or notebook computers or audiotapes to make their recordings. In other cases, conversations or interviews conducted in the field might be tape-recorded or videotaped for later analysis. Which of these formats to use depends on which most accurately preserves the record without interfering with rapport.

Recording field notes is particularly problematic for participant observers whose status as observer is disguised. Because such observers must constantly guard against having their true identity revealed, they must take notes surreptitiously. In some settings, a bit of ingenuity on the part of the researcher can handle the problem quite nicely. For example, in her study of people's behavior in bars, Sheri Cavan (1966) solved the note-taking problem by making frequent trips to the restroom and recording her observations there. Given the well-recognized effect of alcoholic beverages on the human body, her trips probably raised little suspicion among the other bar patrons. The study mentioned earlier, conducted by researchers who were admitted as patients to mental hospitals, found another wrinkle on note taking in participant observation: Researchers could take notes openly because the staff defined note taking as the meaningless activities of people who were "crazy" (Rosenhan 1973).

In many participant observation settings, no amount of innovation will allow the researcher to record observations on the scene. In these situations, there is no alternative but to wait and record observations after leaving the observational setting. Relying on memory in this fashion is less than desirable because memory is fallible. The observer should record observations as soon as possible to minimize the likelihood of forgetting important episodes.

What to Record. For someone who has never conducted participant observation research, collecting data through field notes can be particularly frustrating and confusing. What to watch for? What to include in the field notes? These are difficult questions even for veteran observers. In addition, because participant observation research may be exploratory, researchers are often only partially aware of what might be relevant. It is possible, nevertheless, to organize our thoughts around some general categories of things to observe and record (Bogdan and Biklen 1992; Lofland and Lofland 1995; Runcie 1980).

1. *The setting:* Field notes should contain some description of the general physical and social setting being observed. Is it a bar, a restaurant, or a ward of a mental institution? Are there any physical objects or barriers that might play a role

in the social interaction in the setting? Bogdan and Taylor (1975) suggest beginning each day's field notes with a drawing of the physical layout being observed. Such things as time of day, weather, or the presence of others who are not the focus of your observations are useful information in some field research. In short, the field notes serve to remind us—when we review them weeks, months, or years later—of the characteristics of the setting in which we observed behavior.

2. *The people:* Field notes should include a physical and social description of the main characters who are the focus of our observations. How many people? How are they dressed? What are their ages, genders, and socioeconomic characteristics (as well as we can observe from physical appearance)? Again, field notes should tell us, for each separate day of observation, who was present, who entered and left the setting during observation, and how the cast changed from one day to the next.

3. *Individual actions and activities:* The central observations in most studies are the behaviors of the people in the settings. How do they relate to one another? Who talks to whom, and in what fashion? What sequences of behavior occur? In addition, we may want to record the duration and the frequency of these interactions. Do repetitive cycles of behavior occur? Is there a particular sequencing of behavior?

4. *Group behavior:* In some cases, the behavior of groups is an important bit of information. How long does a group of people remain on the scene? How does one group relate to another? It might be useful, for example, to know what cliques have formed in a setting. What we record here describes the social structure of the setting: the statuses and roles that various people occupy and the relationships between them.

5. *Meanings and perspectives:* Field researchers are sensitive to the subjective meanings that people give to themselves and their behavior (which is one of the reasons for doing qualitative field research). So field notes should contain observations about these meanings and what words or behaviors are evidence of those meanings. *Perspectives* refers to general ways of thinking that people exhibit, evidence of which should appear in the field notes.

Quantitative Observation: Coding Sheets

When it is possible to do quantitative observation in field research, this often involves a process of **coding,** or categorizing behaviors into a limited number of preordained categories. To do this, researchers specify as clearly as possible the behaviors to be observed or counted during data collection. When possible, use of coding sheets is desirable. A *coding sheet* is simply a form designed to facilitate categorizing and counting of behaviors. For example, a typical coding sheet lists various behaviors with blanks following them for checking off the behaviors as they occur. If duration of a behavior is also important, additional blanks record the timing.

The coding sheet for a particular research project is likely to be a unique, highly specific document that reflects the special concerns of that project. Nevertheless, a number of coding schemes have sufficient generality to use in a number of different settings. For example, one coding scheme that has been applied to a diversity of research projects was developed by sociologist Robert F. Bales (1952) to study the elements of social interaction in small, face-to-face groups. Bales's categories are specific and behavioral (see Figure 9.1): They refer to behaviors that the coder is to look for, such as "jokes," "laughs," "concurs," "withholds help," and so on. Bales's coding categories emerged from his operationalization of social processes and interactional strategies common to all groups. Bales argued that all behavior in groups can be classified as relating to either task issues (instrumental or goal-oriented behavior) or social-emotional issues (behavior relating to the expression of feelings or the integration of motivations). Furthermore, he maintained that all groups must contend with six separate problem areas in accomplishing these task and social-emotional goals. With this coding scheme, researchers can develop a profile of any group in relation to these issues and processes.

Figure 9.1 Categories for the Observation of Social Interaction

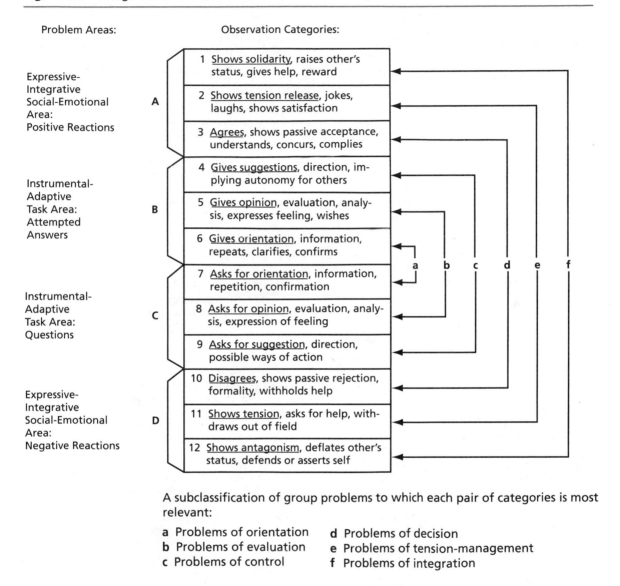

Problem Areas:

Observation Categories:

Expressive-Integrative Social-Emotional Area: Positive Reactions — **A**

1 Shows solidarity, raises other's status, gives help, reward

2 Shows tension release, jokes, laughs, shows satisfaction

3 Agrees, shows passive acceptance, understands, concurs, complies

Instrumental-Adaptive Task Area: Attempted Answers — **B**

4 Gives suggestions, direction, implying autonomy for others

5 Gives opinion, evaluation, analysis, expresses feeling, wishes

6 Gives orientation, information, repeats, clarifies, confirms

Instrumental-Adaptive Task Area: Questions — **C**

7 Asks for orientation, information, repetition, confirmation

8 Asks for opinion, evaluation, analysis, expression of feeling

9 Asks for suggestion, direction, possible ways of action

Expressive-Integrative Social-Emotional Area: Negative Reactions — **D**

10 Disagrees, shows passive rejection, formality, withholds help

11 Shows tension, asks for help, withdraws out of field

12 Shows antagonism, deflates other's status, defends or asserts self

a   b   c   d   e   f

A subclassification of group problems to which each pair of categories is most relevant:

a Problems of orientation   **d** Problems of decision
b Problems of evaluation   **e** Problems of tension-management
c Problems of control   **f** Problems of integration

Source From *Readings in Social Psychology,* 3rd edition by Hartley. Copyright © 1958. Reprinted with permission of Wadsworth, a division of Thomson Learning; www.thomsonrights.com.

Table 9.1 presents a coding scheme with similarities to that of Bales, used in a study of group work among institutionalized elderly. The goal of the research was to devise and evaluate intervention strategies that would increase people's participation in group activity. At each group meeting, two observers sat adjacent to the group where they could observe interaction without interfering with the group (a modified form of nonparticipant observation). Each observer had a stopwatch and a coding sheet (see Figure 9.2)

Table 9.1 Behavioral Definitions and Symbols Used to Record Data

Behavior	Recording Symbols*	Definitions
—Social Group Worker Behaviors—		
Questions	G, I	Verbal behavior that demands or suggests a response from one or more group members, indicated by words that suggest a question (i.e., why, how) or a direct request or demand for a response.
Statements	G, I	Verbal behavior that gives information does not call for a response from group members, and is not a direct consequence of a previous behavior of individual or group of residents. Includes reading to residents.
Positive Comments	G, I	Verbal behavior that followed the behavior of one or more group members and relates to this behavior to encourage similar responses. Suggests recognition, approval, or praise.
Negative Comments	G, I	Verbal behavior that followed the behavior of one or more group members and relates to this behavior to discourage similar responses. Suggests disapproval or displeasure.
Listening	√	Silence on the part of the worker, either while a group member verbalizes or while waiting for resident response in the absence of other worker behavior.
Demonstration/ Participation	√	Demonstrating equipment or activity or participating in activity.
Attending to External Events	√	Watching, listening to, or talking to a stimulus outside of the activity.
—Group Member Behaviors—		
Appropriate Verbal Behavior	○	Verbal behavior related to current group task (subject under discussion, activity, or relating to activity stimuli, e.g., phonograph recording).
Verbal Behavior Related to Environment	○	Verbal behavior related to another person present at activity or related to the room or other aspects of the environment, but not related to the current group task.
Inappropriate Verbal Behavior	⊘	Verbal behavior that does not relate to group task or other residents or staff present or the environment. Verbalizations not audible to the entire group or observers.
Appropriate Attention	△	Visual or apparent listening attention, indicated by head orientation or other observable response, that is directed toward social worker, a resident who is making or has just made an appropriate verbal response, or activity stimulus.
Appropriate Activity	□	Manipulating equipment related to activity as worker has demonstrated or similar appropriate use, helping another resident to do so, nodding or head-shaking appropriately, raising hand for recognition.
Inappropriate Activity	/	Repetitive actions, aggressive actions, manipulating materials not related to group task or activity stimuli, leaving activity, sleeping, talking to oneself, any attention directed away from worker, group task, activity stimuli, or a resident making a verbal response.

*Questions, statements, and comments were judged as to whether directed to an individual (I) or to the group (G).

Source Adapted from N. Linsk, M. W. Howe, and E. M. Pinkston, "Behavioral Group Work in a Home for the Aged." *Social Work*, Vol. 20, No. 6 (November 1975), pp. 457–458. Copyright © 1975, National Association of Social Workers, Inc., Social Work. Reprinted with permission.

Figure 9.2   Sample Observation Form (Used to Record Data during Three-Minute Observation Periods at Group Meetings)

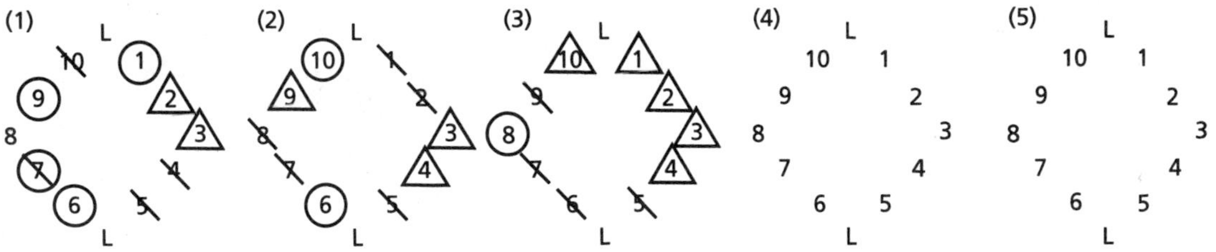

Source   Adapted from N. Linsk, M. W. Howe, and E. M. Pinkston, "Behavioral Group Work in a Home for the Aged," *Social Work*, Vol. 20, No. 6 (November 1975), pp. 457–458. Copyright © 1975, National Association of Social Workers, Inc., Social Work. Reprinted with permission.

and recorded behaviors on the coding sheet at one-minute intervals for the group members and at half-minute intervals for the group worker who led each group. In this fashion, the researchers developed a running account of the verbal and nonverbal interaction between group members and group workers. The effect of the group worker's various strategies, such as directing questions at individuals or using tangible rewards for specific behaviors, could then be measured in terms of changes in interaction patterns. The parallels between Bales's and Linsk's categories should be clear: Linsk's categories of "questions," "statements," "positive comments," and "negative comments" are virtually identical to Bales's categories of "asks for orientation," "gives orientation," "shows solidarity," and "shows antagonism," respectively. This illustrates the utility of examining existing general coding schemes to determine whether we can use them directly or modify them to serve our own purposes.

The development of an efficacious coding scheme requires considerable care. The coding categories should derive from the hypotheses being tested in the research. In Linsk's study, the researchers' concern was with the nature and quality of verbal and nonverbal interaction in a group, and the categories chosen reflect that focus. In addition, coding categories should be highly specific and behavioral. The degree to which we can achieve this is obviously limited because overspecificity soon becomes cumbersome and meaningless. For example, in Linsk's study, a category of "speaks" would be too general because it does not inform us of the type of verbal contribution. At the other extreme, a category such as "raises eyebrows" is so specific that we cannot determine the meaning of the behavior. Thus, we walk a fine line between too specific and too general in providing a coding scheme that enables us to answer our research questions. It is important to recognize that, although coding behavior with such schemes may appear quantifiable and objective, a considerable degree of subjective interpretation is involved. The coder must decide, for example, whether a given response is positive or negative and shows solidarity or antagonism; these judgments are necessarily subjective.

The use of coding schemes is not limited to situations in which a group is small, well organized, or engaging in highly structured behavior. If it is possible to specify concepts and hypotheses precisely—in other words, if the research is clearly hypothesis testing rather than exploratory—then it may be possible to develop a precise coding scheme for data collection. In their disguised observation study of alcohol-related aggression, Kathryn Graham and colleagues (1980) were able to do this. Their basic hypothesis was that aggressive behavior among men when they drink is due to situational factors as much as to psychological predispositions toward violence. They hypothesized that aversive stimuli in bars (their independent variable) serve as cues that allow or encourage aggressive behavior (the dependent variable). They coded the dependent variable using a dichotomous coding scheme: nonphysical aggression (swearing or other forms of abusive language) and physical aggression. Within the physical category, behavior was coded as physical threats or challenges to fight but no actual contact, aggressive but noninjurious physical contact (for example, grabbing and pushing), and actual physical violence (punching and kicking).

The independent variable—situational factors eliciting aggression—was, needless to say, more complex to code. First, the researchers spent some weeks in the field observing and developing precise definitions and coding schemes for the situational variables. Here are a few of the coding categories they developed:

location:	1 = downtown bar
	2 = suburban bar
time of day:	1 = 9 A.M. to noon
	2 = noon to 3 P.M.
	3 = 3 P.M. to 6 P.M.
	and so on
noise level:	1 = very quiet
	2 = medium quiet
	3 = medium loud
	4 = loud
sexual bodily contact:	1 = none, very casual
	2 = discreet necking
	3 = heavy necking, touching
	4 = flagrant fondling

friendliness to strangers: 1 = open, lots of
conversation with
strangers
2 = closed, people talk
only to members of
their own group

Each two-person observation team spent two to two-and-a-half hours in an establishment. Most recording of observations was done after leaving the establishment so that note taking would not attract attention.

This unobtrusive observation illustrates the manner in which field observers can use a precise, quantifiable coding scheme if the hypotheses to be tested are sufficiently developed. The investigators also found, however, that coding, although the major form of data collection, was not sufficient by itself. They also needed to collect qualitative data because, while they were in the field, more variables of importance began to emerge. They wanted to record descriptive accounts of aggressive incidents to ensure a complete record. This provides an illustration of a grounded theory approach where data collection changes while still in process because evaluation suggests that some new theoretical concepts, not originally planned for, are important.

Coding schemes can become highly complex, involving many categories of behavior, timing of the behaviors, measures of intensity, and the like. However, we can only use more complex coding schemes in situations where we can record accurately all that is necessary. Linsk's study of a single, small, task-oriented group enabled the use of a complicated coding scheme. In Graham's study, this would have been considerably more difficult because the group (the clientele of a bar) was large and shifting in composition, much was going on, and actual recording had to wait until after the observation concluded. This research setting necessitated a simpler coding scheme. Furthermore, investigations using complex coding schemes that require intense concentration on the part of the observer often require a number of observers, each of whom records for a short period and then is relieved by another observer. This reduces error due to observer fatigue or fluctuations in concentration. In some investigations, group behavior is recorded on videotape to reduce error and allow researchers to view the group as often as needed to code behavior properly. In developing a coding scheme, in short, researchers must make sure that the scheme does not become so complex as to become unusable, given the resources at hand.

Coding schemes are not appropriate forms of recording observations in all field research. In some cases, as with exploratory research, we cannot develop hypotheses with sufficient precision to operationalize concepts through coding schemes because the research is intended to explore and discover rather than to explain and predict. In other cases, a nonpositivist approach suggests that the nature of some phenomena does not lend itself to quantification; in fact, proponents of the nonpositivist approaches argue, quantification can lead to distortion and misunderstanding of what is going on. In these cases, the hypotheses involve variables and relationships that require considerable interpretive effort on the part of the observer in the field and cannot easily be condensed to a few coding categories. In still other cases, the complexity and lack of structure in the group being observed render coding schemes useless. In all these situations, the investigator is likely to turn to field notes as a means of recording observations.

Clearly, researchers can gather an enormous amount of information in any setting. In addition, the more exploratory the research, the more information researchers must record because it is more difficult to be sure what is relevant. With experience in the field and the development of more narrowly focused hypotheses, it is often possible to reduce the amount of information collected.

Other Qualitative Methods

In addition to field research, the social sciences and human services use a number of other important qualitative research methods—sometimes on their own, other times as a part of a field research study.

In-Depth Interviewing

Chapter 7 discussed the use of interviews in survey research, but those interviews are generally more structured and focused than the in-depth interviewing often used in qualitative research. **In-depth interviews,** sometimes called **ethnographic interviews,** are informal and unstructured interviews that explore a wide range of topics and may last for a long time, even days or weeks. Often, they are more like a rambling conversation, with the interviewer relatively nondirective and the person being interviewed fairly unconstrained in what they talk about (Fontana and Frey 1994; Patton 2002). Actually, there is some overlap between participant observation and in-depth interviewing because participant observation often gathers some data through informal interviews with people in the field.

These interview data are a third source of data collected in participant observation, in addition to gathering data through participation and observation. Yet the two methods are distinct because true participant observation research also gathers data through participation and observation. In addition, interviews can be a mechanism for collecting qualitative data apart from field research. For example, Sean Gilmore and Alicia Crissman (1997) studied the link between gender and violence among teens who play video games. Their main data-gathering tools were unstructured interviews, which enabled the researchers to explore issues of gender identity in great breadth and depth. This topic had been the focus of little previous research, so the researchers had no existing knowledge base from which to derive meaningful concepts or develop hypotheses. Instead, they wanted the concepts and hypotheses to emerge from the freewheeling and friendly conversations that were their unstructured interviews. These interviews were supplemented with some direct observation of the teens' conversations and behavior as they played the video games. As another example of in-depth interviews, Betty Dobratz and Stephanie Shanks-Miele (1997) conducted a study of the white separatist movement in the United States by conducting in-depth interviews with leaders and members of the movement. However, they also supplemented the interview data with field observations, such as attending white separatist rallies, dinners, congresses, and cross burnings. Although their data primarily came from the interviews, the field observations provided additional important information and insights that the interviews could not provide.

The researcher approaches an in-depth interview with some general topics of interest and asks questions that probe into those areas. However, the whole process is much more interactive and collaborative and much less directive than in survey interviews (Holstein and Gubrium 1995). It is more like a conversation. The researcher talks, rather than just asking questions, to keep the conversation going. The researcher may talk about him- or herself and life and even respond to questions the respondent asks—something not normally done in a survey interview. The researcher also permits the interview to take unexpected directions if they appear rewarding in terms of the research question or essential to maintaining the rapport and interest of the respondent. In fact, the relationship between interviewer and respondent often becomes one of equals conversing than of an expert gathering data from a subject. Yet the general topics the researcher needs to cover impose a structure of sorts on the interview. This is especially apparent when more than one person is interviewed because the researcher must make sure that he or she covers the same general topics with each person interviewed.

The goal of the in-depth interview is similar to participant observation: to explore how the world appears to the respondent without imposing inappropriate structure on the views they express by using preestablished categories or overly restrictive direction on what subjects explore and how they express it. The respondent's perspective should unfold and be framed in ways that make sense to him or her, not limited or constrained by the researcher's preconceived category systems or structures of meaning.

Case Studies, Life Histories, and Narratives

Another qualitative research technique is variously called *narrative inquiry, life histories,* or *case studies*

(Clandinin and Connelly 2000; Yin 2002). Although there are some differences among these approaches, they all involve a detailed descriptive account of part or all of a particular individual's life or, in some case studies, of an organization or an event. The goal is to gain understanding through depth and richness of detail. The description in case studies and life histories is a detailed and what is sometimes called "thick" description: a complete and literal accounting of the person or setting under study. Some quantitative data might be included, but the emphasis is on telling a story in prose or narrative. Researchers base case studies and life histories on direct observation, interviews, document analysis, organizational records, or some combination thereof—basically, any data that contributes to a description of the case under study.

Case studies and life histories share with participant observation a desire to understand how the social world looks from the perspective of the person being studied. Anthropologist Bourgois (1995), for example, used a life-history approach in his participant observation research in El Barrio: He tape-recorded long conversations with his informants to see how their current circumstances and behavior were part of the flow of their lives. One of the strengths of case studies and life histories is that they permit the people being studied to play a big part in framing and providing meaning for their lives, rather than having meaning and interpretation imposed by the observer. However, case studies take a much longer time perspective because they typically explore a good part (if not the whole) of a person's life. Case studies and life histories have proven to be useful methodologies in feminist research and in interpretivist and critical approaches (Lawless 1991).

The primary goal of most case studies and life histories is an idiographic explanation that focuses on an in-depth understanding of a particular case. Such an understanding might enhance our comprehension of other cases and situations, but the primary focus is description, not generalization. Their advantage is the rich and detailed descriptions they provide of people's lives, experiences, and circumstances. In addition, the ability of these methods to allow people to speak in their own voices makes them valuable sources of data. However, because they are based on one person's life, case studies and life histories are criticized on the grounds that the results are not generalizable beyond that one case. The data from such studies also contain a considerable element of subjectivity in it because of its dependence on the accounts of one individual. These methods also suffer from the normal errors of people's memories as well as from selective recall on the part of the individual. In fact, the data produced in narratives are sometimes the result of a collaboration between researcher and subject where the final story is one that they both find acceptable. To overcome some of these problems, people producing case histories sometimes check for errors or misinterpretations with others knowledgeable of people or events in the case history. Of course, errors in memory or selective recall may be valuable data in themselves in that we may learn as much about people from how they remember or reconstruct their past as from their actual past. In fact, proponents of case studies and life histories argue that a person's own story is important to understand, irrespective of the objective facts.

Focus Groups

We discussed focus groups as a form of survey research in Chapter 7 because they involve interviewing people, but focus groups also deserve mention here as a qualitative research method. Focus groups are also called *group depth interviews* because they are like an in-depth interview with a number of people at the same time. The advantage of focus groups is that they are flexible forms of data collection that leave the participants free to frame their answers and construct meaning as they wish. Although some quantitative data are collected as a part of focus groups, people are free to talk as much as they wish, and their complete responses serve as data for the research.

Research in Practice 9.2 offers an illustration of how we can use qualitative research techniques, such as in-depth interviewing and focus groups, to enhance our understanding of groups that are difficult to study with other research methods.

RESEARCH IN PRACTICE 9.2

BEHAVIOR AND SOCIAL ENVIRONMENT:

Listening to the Disabled through Qualitative Methods

One of the arguments in favor of using qualitative methods is that they offer access to a valuable type of data: a deeper and richer understanding of people's lives, including knowledge of their subjective experiences. But how does one access these data when the research participants themselves are afflicted with intellectual disabilities that severely hamper their capacity to communicate? This challenge faced a team of researchers engaged with the Lifespan and Disability Project, a two-year qualitative study designed to enhance understanding of social integration by including the perspectives of individuals with intellectual disabilities (Mactavish, Mahon, and Lutfiyya 2000). By discussing ways of including individuals with intellectual disabilities in the research process and of enhancing credibility of researcher's interpretations of their perspectives, the authors identified three guiding principles: presume credibility and inherent value of all perspectives, collect data in multiple and intensive ways over prolonged periods of time, and use concrete processes to elicit and confirm data.

The authors point out that qualitative and feminist researchers have emphasized that documenting the perspectives of individuals or groups who are typically excluded from the research process should be a goal of qualitative research. Individuals with intellectual disabilities are clearly one population whose perspective is easily ignored. In this project, the participants were 32 individuals, ranging in age from 17 to 82 years, including 18 women and 14 men. Of these, 14 had a mild level of disability, 10 had a moderate level, and 8 were severely to profoundly disabled. With the exception of the four oldest individuals, all of the participants were involved in daytime activities that took them out of their homes.

The Lifespan and Disability Project included several data-collection strategies. First, the researchers conducted 32 qualitative interviews to collect background information, build rapport, and explain the research and procedures. In addition to serving a data-collection function, the research team found that the interviews served to increase their sensitivity to potential barriers to participation, such as transportation. Next, they conducted eight focus groups to explore multiple perspectives on social integration. Finally, the researchers held two verification meetings with participants to verify the accuracy of their interpretation of the focus group data.

Issues in Observational and Field Research

Sampling

In most field research it is difficult, if not impossible, to use probability samples because we can establish no adequate sampling frame. In addition, the research questions that field research sometimes addresses do not call for probability samples. So, nonprobability samples are widely used in field research. Especially common are snowball sampling, targeted sampling, and purposive sampling. (In fact, in Chapter 6, we describe a number of field studies that used one of these sampling strategies or some combination of them.) These samples make possible sampling procedures in situations where sampling frames do not exist, and they also encourage the researcher, especially with targeted and purposive sampling, to avoid samples that are biased because some group was inadvertently missed by a particular sampling procedure.

In addition to the more common sampling issue of selecting participants for a project, observational and field researchers face another challenge—it is often impossible to conduct around-the-clock observation over the full length of the study, which may

Then they held eight focus groups, each involving four participants of roughly equal ages. Upon arriving for a group session, participants were greeted by the researcher who had conducted his or her initial interview. During the formal part of the group, the moderator reminded the participants about the purpose of the group meeting and then systematically explored questions related to social integration. Each session was audiotaped and later transcribed verbatim. One of the moderators recorded detailed field notes, including notes of nonverbal behavioral responses. Immediately following the session, the moderators discussed and noted any additional observations.

In keeping with the principle of using concrete ways of confirming interpretations by the researchers of participant communication, the researchers used what they called a "member checking" process. One technique employed in the verifying sessions was to use a prompting hierarchy of questions specific to social integration. For example:

1. What does social integration mean to you?
2. This question can be asked another way— what does a sense of belonging mean to you?
3. These are big words that mean different things to different people. For some people "social integration" and "a sense of belonging" mean "having friends that you can call to go out and do things with." What does "social integration" mean to you?

Another technique of verifying participant meaning was to use posters that visually depicted each of the theme areas that had emerged from the focus groups. The posters included brightly colored photographs, clipped from magazines, depicting the themes the researchers had identified from the focus groups. The posters were presented one at a time, and participants elaborated on the description the moderator provided.

Previous research had identified interaction with people with disabilities as a defining characteristic of social integration among the disabled. With the richer descriptions made possible by more qualitative data-gathering approaches, the researchers were able to determine that these participants viewed social integration as emanating from the sharing of time, activities, and experiences with family and friends independent of whether or not these individuals had a disability. Although the participants' capacity to verbally articulate their feelings and understanding may have been limited by their disabilities, the rich description, not only of their words but also of their behavior, enabled the researchers to step inside the participants' world and provide a forum where the disabled could say, "I can speak for myself."

involve a considerable period of time. Participant observers record things as they happen, and more quantitative observers mark coding schemes for as long as an interchange or social setting persists. However, in some situations continuous data collection is costly and unnecessary. In addition, as we discussed with other forms of sampling in Chapter 6, it is often not necessary to collect data from *all* elements of a population. In studies of child development, for example, we may not need to record all that occurs during an hour, a day, or a week. Instead, we can gather valid data through **time sampling,** or making observations only during certain selected

time periods (Irwin and Bushnell 1980). For example, for an observational study of adolescents in a group home, the prime hours for observation are those when the residents are most likely to be at the home, such as weekdays from 3 P.M. until lights out at 11 P.M. (40 hours per week) and Saturdays and Sundays from 7 A.M. until 11 P.M. (32 hours per week). The researcher can construct a sampling frame comprised of a weekly list of these 72 one-hour time segments and then select a random sample of these elements. To be sure to include both weekdays and weekends, the researcher might specify eight hours during the week and four hours from the weekend. The resulting sample of 12 one-hour time segments would provide sufficient time coverage for observation while reducing biases that might occur if, say, the researcher made all observations on weekdays after 8 P.M., when many youths are tired at the end of the day.

Keep some guidelines in mind when conducting time sampling (Suen and Ary 1986). The length of each time-sampling interval and the distance between intervals depend on the nature of the behaviors being observed: They should occur with sufficient frequency as to appear during the sampled time periods. Very infrequent behaviors might call for continual observations. The more frequently a behavior occurs, the smaller the number of intervals we have to sample. Furthermore, the time interval should be long enough for the behavior to occur and for the observer to make whatever recordings are called for.

Many of the considerations in time sampling are the same as the issues in sampling subjects or respondents that we discussed in Chapter 6. If our primary concern is to be assured of observing *some* occurrences of the behavior under study, it is advisable to use the equivalent of a purposive sample. For example, in studying domestic violence, we want to observe instances of family quarreling. Observing at mealtime is one way to increase the probability of witnessing the desired events. On the other hand, if we want to accurately estimate the frequency of occurrence of a particular event or to study the pattern of responses over a time period, we should use the equivalent of a probability sample. For example, to observe nursing home residents for frequency of contacts with nonresidents, we could divide the week into hourly segments and then use a random selection of hours as the basis for the observations.

Particularly when the observation process is highly complex and difficult to sustain for long periods of time, some form of time sampling can help to improve the quality of the data collected.

Validity and Reliability

We assess observational techniques, like other forms of data collection, in terms of how valid and reliable

they are (Kirk and Miller 1986). Observation rests on human sense organs and human perceptions—both of which are notoriously fallible. This is an especially difficult and insidious problem because we are often totally unaware of the ways in which our senses and our perspective lead us to misperceive situations. Especially with observational methods, people say resolutely, "I was there. I saw it. I comprehend what was going on." Yet as any trial lawyer will readily attest, eyewitnesses are often highly unreliable spectators to events; and considerable experimental evidence indicates that firsthand accounts of events are often partially inaccurate (Wells and Olson 2003). Given these problems, we need to consider the validity and reliability of observations carefully.

Little question exists that observational techniques have greater face validity as measures of behavior and events than do techniques that rely on secondhand accounts. Surveys depend on someone else's perception and recollection, which many factors beyond the control of the researcher can shape and cloud. Observational techniques, on the other hand, provide firsthand accounts of occurrences under conditions that the investigator at least partially controls. Misperception may still occur, of course, but the researcher is in a position to recognize its impact and possibly control its magnitude. For these reasons, observation has greater face validity than many other data-collection techniques.

As we showed in Chapter 5, we can sometimes measure the validity of an instrument by correlating the results of the instrument with the results achieved by some other instrument known to be a valid measure of the variable. Often, however, such direct measures of validity are not possible in qualitative field research; nevertheless, we can employ certain procedures in field research to enhance the validity of the observations:

1. *Be as thorough as possible in describing and interpreting situations.* This increases the likelihood that we will make important observations and produce a valid assessment of a situation. Observations that seem unimportant while in the field we may later recognize as important. Ob-

servations not recorded, of course, are lost forever as data. Obviously, observers cannot record everything that happens in a situation, but it is preferable to err on the side of being too complete rather than too skimpy.

2. *Carefully assess our own desires, values, and expectations to see if these might bias our observations.* People's expectations or lack of them drastically shape their perceptions. If we expect something to occur, we are much more likely to observe it—whether it actually occurs or not. If we expect welfare recipients to be lazy, then we will be acutely aware of all those behaviors among welfare recipients that might be interpreted as laziness. Thus, validity of observations is reduced to the extent that our expectations—recognized or not—mold our perceptions. We should assiduously look for the *opposite* of what we expect to happen, and we should be careful and critical if what we expect to find seems to be happening. On the other side of the coin, a lack of expectations may lead us to miss something of importance in a setting.

3. *Have other observers visit the same group or setting to see if they come to the same conclusions.* If they do, this provides validation that our conclusions are a response to the actual setting rather than to our expectations or biases—especially if the other observers had different expectations or biases.

4. *Compare the conclusions reached through field observations with conclusions reached by other research methodologies,* whether it is observational research in other settings or surveys, available data, or experimental research (Weinstein 1982). This is a variation on criterion validity discussed in Chapter 5. If the various methodologies yield the same conclusions, then we have greater confidence that the field observations have validity. Field research whose conclusions are at wide variance with the results of other research requires careful review, especially if none of these other checks on validity are available.

5. *Consider how the condition of the observer might influence observations and conclusions.* Hunger, fatigue, stress, or personal problems can lead to distorted perceptions and interpretations. Likewise, physical characteristics, such as the lighting in an establishment, may lead to invalid observations. (This is another good reason for keeping complete field notes—we can assess field conditions affecting validity later.) If a number of these conditions exist, we may decide to terminate observation and resume when conditions are more favorable.

6. *Look for behavior that is illegal, stigmatizing, or potentially embarrassing or that risks punishment.* If people engage in these kinds of behaviors, especially when they know they are being observed, then they are probably acting naturally and not putting on a performance for the benefit of the observer. In his study of a sexually transmitted disease clinic, Joseph Sheley (1976, p. 116) argued that the validity of his data was quite strong because "staff members dropped their professional masks and displayed quite unprofessional behavior and ideas in the company of the researcher." Under such conditions, we can assume that people are reacting to environmental stimuli that normally guide their behavior, rather than shaping a performance for the benefit of the investigator. If the people being observed do not have *anonymity,* their behavior may not be a true reflection of how they behave normally. Especially when controversial, sensitive, or potentially embarrassing issues are investigated, validity declines substantially if anonymity has not been ensured. For this reason, hidden or disguised observation and observation in which the researcher takes the complete participant role are more valid than other types of observation.

7. *If possible, make a video or audio recording of the scene.* Although such recordings have their weaknesses as records of what occurred, they do provide another way to check and validate our observations and conclusions. Others can also review such recordings, offering yet further checks on possible bias or misinterpretation.

Thus, researchers should follow as many of these guidelines as possible in designing field research; the more we incorporate, the more confidence we have in the validity of the results. Although many of the conditions influencing validity are beyond our control as investigators, it is important to honestly assess their impact on the research so that we can make accurate appraisal of the results.

As for reliability of observational research, an individual researcher who is studying a single group or setting through participant observation has no practical way to assess reliability (Kirk and Miller 1986). With more structured observations, such as when using a coding scheme, we can readily assess reliability with tests of *intercoder reliability,* or the ability of observers to code behaviors consistently into the same categories of the coding scheme: Two or more observers code the same behavior, with the resulting codes correlated to determine the degree of agreement between them. For example, in their study of barroom aggression, Graham and her colleagues (1980) correlated the coding results from the two observers who visited each bar. They achieved reliabilities ranging from $r = .57$ to $r = .99$. Many experts suggest that structured observation should achieve an intercoder reliability of $r = .75$ or better (Bailey 1987).

Reactivity

Reactivity, or the degree to which the presence of the researcher influences what is being observed, is a major concern in any research (Lee 2000). To take an extreme example, suppose a researcher enters a group for the purpose of studying it through participant observation. Suppose, in addition, that the researcher takes an active role in the group's proceedings by talking a great deal, offering suggestions, and so on. It should be clear that an observer behaving in this fashion will exert considerable influence on what occurs in the group, making the observer's presence highly reactive. This affects the validity of the observations because we do not know whether we have measured the group's *natural* activities or their *reactions* to the observer. We are never sure if events different from those observed might have taken place if the researcher had conducted the observation in a less reactive manner. Reactivity also

relates to the generalizability of findings. If the observer's presence is reactive, it is difficult to generalize findings to similar groups that have not had an observer in attendance.

Researchers generally agree that participant observation generates the best results when reactivity is kept to a minimum. This is a major argument in favor of the complete participant role, where the observer's true status is concealed. It is logical to assume that observation affects a group less if they are unaware of the observer's role as observer than if they are aware of it. Using the complete participant role does not, however, guarantee a lack of reactivity. Observers must play the role properly: as passively as possible without raising suspicion. Even when a researcher accomplishes the beginning of an observational study without undue reactivity, he or she must be careful that reactivity does not increase during the course of the project. Such a situation occurred in a study of a group that had predicted the end of the world (Festinger, Riecken, and Schachter 1956). On numerous occasions, situations arose that forced the observers to become active participants to the point where subsequent group activity was influenced by their actions.

Observational and Field Research on Minority Populations

We have discussed issues of validity and reliability in field observations; these issues take on added importance when the observations involve diverse groups with varying social and cultural patterns. In most cultures, for example, gender is an important determinant of behavior, which often means that men and women have distinctively different ways of interacting. In general, men tend to be louder, more aggressive, and more domineering in their interactions. This often produces a problem in field research that one anthropologist labeled the "big man bias": the tendency for the more powerful, more assertive, and louder individuals (who are also more likely to be males) to gain the attention of ethnographers and to have their behavior and lives recorded in ethnographies (Ortner 1984). But a field researcher cannot observe and record everything that occurs in the field. Selectivity is inevitable and can lead to bias when some important things are ignored. A field researcher overwhelmed with stimuli has a natural inclination to find ways to choose among them. In the remote village of some indigenous tribe, the ethnographer may choose to pay more attention to the village leaders, who are also likely to be elder males. Thus, the perspectives of younger tribal members and women are less represented in the ethnographic understanding of the village. To the extent that age and gender produce significant variations in perspectives in this village, the ethnographer's choices can produce a biased outcome.

Historians have noted for some time the danger that history can become more an account of the lives of societal elites than of nonelites. The elites, after all, leave more of the historical record that historians use as data in writing histories: They write books and memoirs, pass legislation, make speeches, and in other ways come to the attention of historians. To the extent that they are also mostly male, histories written primarily from these sources reflect the activities, interests, concerns, and perspectives of male elites.

Sociologist Barrie Thorne even detected a big man bias in field studies of preschool and elementary-school children:

> Large, bonded groups of boys who are physically assertive, engage in "tough talk," and actively devalue girls anchor descriptions of "the boys' world" and themes of masculinity. Other kinds of boys may be mentioned, but not as the core of the gender story. (1993, p. 98)

In other words, it was not just a bias in favor of males but of a limited range of males. The voices of females and the less visible or less dominant males are silenced or marginalized. Visibility could come from being a part of the large group of boys, or from their loud and aggressive behavior, or from popularity or athletic prowess. Thorne also argues that ethnographers are biased toward noticing things that are consistent with the ethnographers' own stereotypes or hypotheses. Like everyone else, ethnographers carry with them cultural assumptions and stereotypes about masculinity (that males are tough, are competitive, and tend to form dominance hierarchies).

Boys who conform to this stereotype in the classroom or school yard get noticed, whereas quiet boys who hang out with only a few other friends, and possibly even some girls, are less visible.

Thorne summarizes the problem by stating that "socially constructed contours of visibility skew ethnographic reports" (1993, p. 97). In her own and other field research, Thorne found a much richer and more complex social field among children's play groups than gender stereotypes suggest, for both boys and girls. She found boys who were quiet, shy, and cooperative and girls who were aggressive and hostile. Furthermore, given the diversity actually found, it is not clear whether the stereotype even portrays the experiences of the majority of boys and girls. When the ethnographer begins with the stereotype that the play worlds of boys and girls are different, then he or she tends to notice the differences in the field. It takes a special effort to notice instances that do not conform to the stereotype.

Assessment of Field Techniques and Qualitative Methods

As this chapter has shown, observational techniques differ from one another in terms of how qualitative and naturalistic they are. Not surprisingly, the advantages and disadvantages of observational techniques also differ depending on whether they are qualitative versus quantitative and contrived versus naturalistic. The first two advantages described next would apply to all forms of observational research. The remainder of the advantages and disadvantages apply particularly to the more qualitative, naturalistic, or unstructured types of observational research.

Advantages

1. Unlike surveys, which are limited to dealing with verbal statements, observational research can focus on both verbal and nonverbal behavior. This is an advantage because we can study *actual behavior* in addition to people's *statements* about how they behave. By dealing with behavior, observational research avoids a potential

source of error: the gap between what people say they do and what they actually do. The ability of observational techniques to consider both verbal and nonverbal behavior puts the researcher in a better position to link the verbal statements with behavior.

2. Much observational research is longitudinal in nature and thus enables researchers to make statements concerning changes that occur over the time of the research. In addition, by following activities over time, observers have less trouble establishing the correct causal sequence than they do with surveys. (As noted in Chapter 2, establishing the causal order with survey data can sometimes be difficult.)

3. The advantage most often claimed for observational research is that it provides deeper and more insightful data than most other methods generate. Especially with participant observation, researchers immerse themselves in the daily activities of those studied to a greater degree than with other techniques. This places them in a position to gain information they would likely miss with techniques such as a questionnaire or an interview. This is especially true for the complete participant or those who have become "invisible": as accepted members of the group, they see people behaving freely and naturally, unaware that they are being studied. Even such techniques as in-depth interviews and case studies can produce a deep, rich understanding of people's lives. The survey interviewer, on the other hand, may generate more socially acceptable responses and a carefully orchestrated presentation of self. But the participant observer and the in-depth interviewer can go beyond these public fronts and penetrate the behind-the-scenes regions of human behavior.

4. Observational research can study groups and behavior that is closed to other forms of research. Many studies cited in this chapter involve groups that, for various reasons, are not open to research by other methods. These people may have something to hide, or they may view a stranger's intrusion as threatening to their cohesion and values. The ability of the complete participant to conceal his or her identity and conduct research where we cannot otherwise go is a major advantage of this observational technique. Even participant observers and in-depth interviewers, whose status as researcher is known, may, over time, gain access to groups through the development of trust and rapport; these same groups might reject the more brief and superficial entreaties of an interviewer.

5. A frequently overlooked but nevertheless significant advantage of observational research is that the most qualified person is often directly involved in collecting data because the senior researcher is often one of the observers (Denzin 1989). This is very different from surveys, for example, in which the project director rarely conducts interviews, leaving this task to part-time interviewers hired for the job. This places the most knowledgeable person the farthest from the data-collection effort.

Disadvantages

Most of the disadvantages of observational research relate to the more qualitative, naturalistic, and unstructured types. With less structure, the quality of the results of an observational study depends heavily on the individual skills of the researcher, and this leads to several criticisms.

1. A nagging concern with participant observation research is the possible effect of observer bias on the results. Such research does not have the same structured tools of other methods to help reduce such bias. If researchers are not careful, personal attitudes and values can distort research findings, rendering them virtually useless for scientific purposes.

2. Closely related to the issue of observer bias is the problem of the observer going native or overidentifying with those who are studied. As the observer frequently becomes a part of a group for a substantial period of time, this possibility is quite real.

3. The lack of structure also makes exact replication—an important part of scientific research—

difficult if not impossible. Observational studies are often such individualized projects that the possibility for replication is slight. Any observer in a natural setting will be forced to record what occurs selectively owing to sheer volume. There is little chance that a replication attempt would select precisely the same aspects of a given setting on which to focus.

4. The nature of the data gathered in some observational research makes them very difficult to quantify. Some participant observers generate field notes that are basically rambling descriptions, which makes data in this form difficult to code or categorize in summary form and thus makes traditional hypothesis testing more difficult. As a result, many observational studies fail to get beyond a description of the setting. Of course, some nonpositivist researchers consider this an advantage of qualitative research.

5. Although unrelated to its lack of structure, some critics have called the ethics of participant observation into question, with the complete participant role generating the most controversy. Some social scientists see it as unethical to conceal one's identity for the purpose of conducting research because it deprives people of the opportunity to give informed consent. Whether disguised observation is ethical is still an open controversy in the social sciences. (As noted in Chapter 3, disguised observation is considered a questionable practice that requires approval by an institutional review board.) As long as the research is not trivial and the identities of participants are not revealed, disguised observation would probably be allowed.

6. As mentioned earlier, participant observation affords the researcher little control over the variables in the setting. A great deal may be happening that the researcher is not in a position to control or moderate. This often leads to situations in which the researcher is at a loss to select the important causal factors in a situation.

7. Because of the physical limitations on any researcher's observing capabilities, a participant-observation study will almost certainly study a limited sample of people. Although we could, with a sufficient number of observers, study a large sample, we rarely do. Observation is more commonly limited to a small group (such as a family or gang) or one setting (such as a bar or restaurant). The explanatory power that comes from a large sample size is, therefore, not available.

Observation in Human Service Practice

Observation is the foundation of human service practice, and our analysis of scientific observation in this chapter has some important implications for observation in practice settings. Even though the goals of practice and research are somewhat different, we can carry over some of the observational techniques researchers have developed into practice. Here are a few of the lessons to be learned:

1. The type of observation we engage in affects the kind of information we can gather. Structured observation in a therapeutic setting offers practitioners considerable control over what occurs and comparability of information from one setting to the next. Yet it is a somewhat artificial setting (from the client's perspective) and may not capture the dynamics of real-life situations the client experiences. For this, participant observation is more valuable.

2. Reactivity is a serious concern in any observation, whether done by a researcher or a practitioner. Human service workers must be sensitive to the extent to which their presence affects—possibly profoundly—the behavior of others. Clients may put their best foot (or their worst foot!) forward when a caseworker is present. The effect may be subtle; even the client may not be aware of the change. A concern about reactivity may dictate the use of observational techniques that reduce the extent of the problem. We may choose unobtrusive observation or the disguised observer role to reduce the extent of reactivity.

3. Good observational techniques rest on sound methods of recording information. This means that the practitioner should spell out as clearly

as possible beforehand the kinds of behaviors that will be observed. The more specificity, the better: "Aggression" is too general; one should plan to look for "hitting, kicking, or verbal insults." Thus, a precise and specific coding scheme is an important tool in both research and practice observation. This leaves fewer decisions to make during observation, when the observer is likely to be rushed and concerned about other matters.

4. Observation in research and practice has different purposes: In research, observation focuses on hypothesis testing and knowledge accumulation, whereas in practice, observation is a tool for change or amelioration of undesirable con-

COMPUTERS IN RESEARCH

Handheld Computers in Observational Research

An interesting example of computer application to observational research comes from a group designing programs to reduce drinking-related problems. The researchers wanted to measure the propensity of servers to illegally serve alcohol to underaged or intoxicated patrons at community events such as art fairs or music and food festivals (Fletcher, Erickson, Toomey and Wagenaar 2003). The research involved disguised observation; a team of three staff attended various community events with one research team member posing as an underaged buyer, another posing as an intoxicated buyer, and the third as an observer. Some of the data collected were quantitative in nature, such as whether particular events occurred or not; some data were more qualitative, involving written comments by the observers. Both the actor posing as a buyer and the observer collected descriptive details of alcohol purchase attempts. The study is of special interest because it also compared the effectiveness of data collection via a Personal Digital Assistant (PDA), which is a handheld computer, to the more traditional paper-and-pencil data collection forms.

The PDA is a small, handheld computer that commonly uses a pen or stylus to enter data. Other researchers had argued that handheld computers can be effective in ethnography to write down field data, search it, and cross-reference and analyze it onsite (Greene 2001). For this project, the data collection staff recorded all data twice, once using paper forms and once using a PDA. They alternated the order on a weekly basis. Forms very similar in content to the paper forms were designed for the PDAs. In addition, the PDAs were automated to follow the skip or branching pattern so that as questions were answered, the PDA displayed the next logical item on the data form.

The researchers report that they collected more than 6,000 data points at 47 community events, and the overall agreement between PDA and paper forms was an impressive 95.5 percent. One advantage of the PDA approach was a big savings in time and resources compared to the paper-and-pencil method for data entry and data cleaning to prepare the data for analysis. While the PDA's data was ready almost immediately for analysis, it took up to three months to get the paper-and-pencil data ready. On the other hand, it took longer to program the PDAs to collect the data than it did to prepare the paper-and-pencil forms. A second advantage of PDA data is a management feature: PDA data can automatically be stamped with time and date to confirm that it was collected and entered on the appropriate schedule. A common concern in observation research is the erosion of data quality due to memory/recall deficits. The time- and date-stamp information aids researchers with quality control and scheduling of observations. Compared to paper-and-pencil forms, the researchers found that use of the PDA required more training of observers, particularly for entering longer, narrative information. Overall, however, the handheld computers are a promising additional tool for the observational field researcher.

ditions. However, as stressed in Chapter 1, practice observations, if done properly, can add to our body of scientific knowledge.

5. Both research and practice observations should be done systematically, with certain explicit and publicly agreed-on rules followed so that others know precisely how the observations were made and could repeat them if desired. At times, departure from a previously established, systematic plan of observation may be called for in practice. As a practitioner–client relationship develops or circumstances change, the intuition of the practitioner calls for such departures to maintain progress toward the goals of practice. However, such departures are rarely justified in research and are practically always detrimental to the research process because observations made using different procedures are not comparable.

Main Points

- Observational techniques involve data collection through direct visual or auditory experience of behavior. In qualitative research, the data come in the form of words, pictures, narratives, and descriptions rather than in numerical form. Field research is one type of qualitative research. Two important characteristics of qualitative research are that it is contextual in nature and uses a grounded theory approach.

- One type of field research is participant observation, which is similar to the anthropologist's ethnographic research. Many field researchers base their work on the nonpositivist approach and often use the method of *verstehen*. Knowledge in participant observation is gained through both participation (empathic understanding) and observation (deep appreciation of context).

- A major decision for the participant observer is whether to reveal his or her status as observer to those studied and the extent to which the researcher's role will stress participation or observation.

- Unobtrusive observation, including both hidden observation and disguised observation, is designed to minimize reactivity.

- Steps involved in conducting field research include problem formulation, selecting a field setting, entering the field, developing rapport with people in the field, becoming invisible, observing and recording, and exiting the field.

- When variables cannot be easily quantified or when using the *verstehen* strategy, observers collect data in field research in the form of field notes, which are detailed, descriptive accounts of the observations made during a given period. When researchers can measure variables quantitatively in field research, they use coding schemes to measure and record observations. Coding sheets contain the categories of the coding scheme and facilitate the recording process.

- Another form of qualitative research is in-depth interviewing, an informal and unstructured interview that can explore a wide range of topics and may last for a long time, even days or weeks. It is quite different from the interviews done in survey research. Qualitative research also takes the form of narratives, life stories, or case studies, which all involve a detailed descriptive account of part or all of a particular individual's life or, with some case studies, of an organization or an event. The goal is to gain understanding through the depth and richness of detail achieved with this method in comparison to quantitative methods. Focus groups are also a form of qualitative research.

- Time sampling in observational research reduces the volume of observations researchers have to make. Validity and reliability in observational research mean that the observations correctly and accurately reflect reality.

- Some observational techniques, especially unobtrusive observation, minimize reactivity and are thus good for studying sensitive topics, such as racism and sexism.

- Observational techniques are relevant to both research and practice settings.

Important Terms for Review

coding
ethnographic interviews
field notes
field research
grounded theory
in-depth interviews
nonreactive observation
observational techniques
participant observation
reactivity
time sampling
unobtrusive observation
verstehen

Exploring InfoTrac® College Edition and the Internet

InfoTrac® College Edition search terms:

grounded theory
observation AND field research
participant observation
qualitative methods

InfoTrac® College Edition articles:

Experiences of Illicit Drug Overdose: An Ethnographic Study of Emergency Hospital Attendances. Joanne Neale. *Contemporary Drug Problems* Fall 1999 v26 i3 p505 (7,325 words)

The Organizational Career of Gang Statistics: The Politics of Policing Gangs. Albert J. Meehan. *The Sociological Quarterly* Summer 2000 v41 i3 p337 (19,024 words)

As you look online, pay attention to the number of different fields in the social sciences and human services that show an interest in qualitative research. A good way to begin is by searching under such terms as "qualitative methods," "participant observation," or "field research," although the last will produce many sites relating to the natural sciences because they also conduct something called "field" research. However, this offers an important learning exercise: Can you identify the ways that the research or science discussed at the natural science Web sites is similar to or different from what we as social scientists do? For example, do the natural scientists appear concerned with the positivist versus nonpositivist debate?

One of the better launching points for an Internet exploration of observational methods is a site maintained by the School of Social and Systemic Studies at Nova Southeastern University (www. nova.edu/ssss/QR/web.html). One resource available through this site is *The Qualitative Report,* an online journal devoted to qualitative and critical inquiry. This site includes an extensive collection of links to qualitative research sites and materials available through the World Wide Web. Papers, dissertations, and syllabi are just some of the useful materials in the Resources section.

Another qualitative research site on the Internet is QUALIDATA at the University of Essex in England (www.qualidata.essex.ac.uk/). This site provides information relating to qualitative data analysis, along with a number of useful links to other social science research resources that include observational methods. Yet another good Web site is *Forum: Qualitative Social Research (FQS),* an online journal devoted to qualitative research (www.qualitative-research.net/fqs/fqs-eng.htm).

For assistance with analysis of qualitative data obtained through observation, Computer Assisted Qualitative Data Systems (CAQDAS) is a worthwhile site to explore (caqdas.soc.surrey.ac.uk/). In addition to information on computer programs for analyzing data, the site includes an extensive bibliography on qualitative data analysis and links to other sites. Another Web site with an emphasis on qualitative observational research is maintained by the Centre for Applied Research in Education (CARE), a community of researchers that specialize in action research, naturalistic inquiry, evaluation, and the development of new methodologies to study sensitive issues. CARE is based in the School of Education and Professional Development, University of East Anglia, in Norwich, United Kingdom, and may be accessed at www.uea.ac.uk/care/. The Web site includes descriptions of projects with which

CARE is involved. You can review the descriptions for examples of how qualitative methods are used in applied research projects in such fields as education and health care. Another comprehensive site is Resources for Qualitative Research (www.qualitative research.uga.edu/QualPage/) at the University of Georgia.

For Further Reading

Anderson, Elijah. *Streetwise: Race, Class, and Change in an Urban Community.* Chicago: University of Chicago Press, 1990. This is an excellent example of participant-observation research in a community setting. In this case, changes in community life are described as the racial and social class composition of a neighborhood changes.

Berg, Bruce L. *Qualitative Research Methods for the Social Sciences,* 4th ed. Boston: Allyn & Bacon, 2001. Berg provides more detail on the qualitative research methods discussed in this chapter, as well as some others that we have not included.

Denzin, Norman K., and Yvonna S. Lincoln, eds. *Handbook of Qualitative Research,* 2nd ed. Thousand Oaks, Calif.: Sage, 2000. This book of readings provides a comprehensive overview of all aspects of qualitative research, including the historical development of the field. It is one of the most complete and authoritative statements about this form of research.

Ferrell, Jeff, and Mark S. Hamm, eds. *Ethnography at the Edge: Crime, Deviance, and Field Research.* Boston: Northeastern University Press, 1998. This remarkable book takes the pioneering and not necessarily popular stance that *verstehen* in field research requires that researchers gain experiential immersion in the criminal and deviant activities of those being studied. It is a realistic view of what happens in field research and raises many key methodological and ethical issues.

Liebow, Elliot. *Tell Them Who I Am.* New York: Free Press, 1993. This book is an observational research account in the genre of *Talley's Corner.* The author carefully documents the patterns and routines of homeless women, showing how they meet their needs and struggle to keep hope and humanity alive.

Marshall, Catherine, and Gretchen B. Rossman. *Designing Qualitative Research,* 3rd ed. Newbury Park, Calif.: Altamira Press, 1999. The authors of this book provide a good introduction to qualitative research methods in applied research and policy analysis. Although it emphasizes educational research, the book includes vignettes from other social science and human service areas.

Silverman, David. *Interpreting Qualitative Data,* 2nd ed. Newbury Park, Calif.: Sage, 2001. This book discusses the theoretical issues involved in collecting and analyzing data from qualitative research and describes some of the particular data-collection techniques.

Strauss, Anselm, and Juliet Corbin. *Basics of Qualitative Research: Grounded Theory Procedures and Techniques.* Newbury Park, Calif.: Sage, 1990. This is a good overview of how to do qualitative research.

Whyte, William Foote. *Learning from the Field: A Guide from Experience.* Beverly Hills, Calif.: Sage, 1984. A delightful book by one of the premier field researchers in the social sciences. Whyte used his 50 years of experience in the field to produce a practical and accessible volume on the gamut of issues related to field research.

Williams, Constance C. *Black Teenage Mothers: Pregnancy and Child Rearing from Their Perspective.* New York: Lexington Books, 1991. This book is a fine example of applying the ethnographic approach to the study of a human problem that is of great interest to human service practitioners. It is enlightening for its coverage of a social issue as well as being an example of a research approach.

Exercises for Class Discussion

9.1 A teacher asks a school counselor to assist her in controlling the behavior of four boys in her fifth-grade class. The teacher complains that the boys "horse around" a great deal. They don't work on their assignments, throw paper wads, disrupt other children, get out of their seats, and make "smart remarks" instead of answering questions. The counselor suggests setting up a behavioral intervention but first wants to observe the class.

a. What problems will the counselor face in doing an observation?

b. One idea is to observe at random intervals throughout the week. Another is to observe for one full morning. What do you think would be the advantages and disadvantages of each approach? Can you think of a better method of time sampling for this situation?

c. Develop a coding sheet that the counselor could use to record the frequency of the problems mentioned by the teacher.

d. Besides the occurrence of these specific behaviors, what else should the counselor attempt to observe?

e. What ethical issues need to be addressed in conducting and reporting on this type of observation? For example, is it necessary to have the students' permission? What about the parents'? What steps should the counselor take to ensure confidentiality of the data collected as a result of the observation?

9.2 Select one of the following locations for an observational study and spend approximately one hour there in actual observation: a veterinarian's waiting room, a beauty shop, a shoeshine stand, an adult bookstore, a fast-food restaurant, a bus stop, a hospital emergency room, or a garage sale. Answer each of the following questions:

a. For the location selected, what general categories of data will you look for?

b. How will you gain entry to the setting? Whose permission will you need, and how will you obtain it?

c. Are any particular time periods preferable for making observations at the setting you have selected?

d. Which observational approach will you use—nonparticipant or one of the participant forms?

e. Conduct the observations and report your experiences to the class.

f. For the observational setting you selected, is it more appropriate to collect data in the form of field notes or to develop a coding scheme? Why?

9.3 For the observational settings discussed in Exercise 9.2, consider the issue of when a participant observer should intervene and bring about some changes in the setting. What would have to occur to warrant such intervention even though intervening would be detrimental to research goals? Given the examples the class has developed, can you deduce any principles that might help others make a decision about when intervention is justified?

Chapter 10

Experimental Research

When people think of "science" and "research," experiments are often the first words that come to mind. These terms conjure up images of laboratories and white coats and electronic gear. This points to a considerable misunderstanding of the nature of experimentation. In fact, we all engage in casual experimenting in the course of our everyday lives. For example, when a mechanical device malfunctions, we probe and test its various components in an effort to discover the elements responsible for the malfunction. In essence, we are experimenting to find the component (or variable) that caused the malfunction.

Human service practitioners also often engage in casual experimentation. For example, when working with clients with particular problems, human service workers often try new intervention strategies to see if they will prove beneficial to particular clients. For instance, if behavior modification or role rehearsal does not bring about the desired effect, then the worker might try a cognitive learning strategy. Though these are illustrations of casual rather than systematic experiments, they point to the essence of an **experiment:** It is a controlled method of observation in which the value of one or more independent variables is changed to assess its causal effect on one or more dependent variables.

The term "experimentation" as used in research, then, concerns a logic of analysis rather than a particular location, such as a laboratory, in which observations are made. In fact, experiments can be conducted in many settings. **Laboratory experiments** are conducted in artificial settings constructed in such a way that selected elements of the natural environment are simulated and features of the investigation controlled. **Field experiments,** on the other hand, are conducted in natural settings as people go about their everyday affairs.

The logic of scientific experiments can be illustrated by a more careful look at two elements of the impromptu or casual experimenting that occurs in everyday human service practice. First, many casual experiments fail. That is, manipulating the variables involved may not produce the desired result. No matter which approach to a client is used, for example, improvement in functioning may not be forthcoming. In part, failures in casual experiments stem from the fact that they are *casual* and thus not carefully planned. For example, the wrong variables may have been selected for manipulation, so that no matter how they were changed, the desired result could not be obtained. In scientific experimentation, on the other hand, criteria exist to increase the likelihood of success by ensuring that the experiment is soundly planned and that crucial procedures are carried out. It is not that following formalized procedures guarantees success—it does not. Failure in the sense of not achieving desired results is an unpleasant but fully expected outcome of experimenting. Actually, it may be best not to conceive of failure to achieve predicted results as failure per se. Not achieving predicted results—assuming the results are not due to poor research techniques—serves to rule out one possible explanation.

The second feature of casual experimenting is a tendency to jump to conclusions that later prove incorrect. An effort to improve the performance of a client, for example, may produce temporary changes that later disappear. What went wrong? Maybe the practitioner's change in intervention strategy was not the real source of the change in the client's behavior. Something else may have actually caused the temporary changes. For example, perhaps the client found a job or his or her mother-in-law recovered from surgery, and these led to temporary improvements in performance. Or it may be that *any change* from one intervention strategy to another will result in short-term improvements that quickly dissipate. The point is that many things influence people's behavior, and casual experimentation is not organized to sort out these influences. Scientific experimentation is designed to do this and thus reduce the likelihood of reaching false conclusions.

The focus of this chapter is experimental research, but the techniques discussed here can be applied to practice settings. The impromptu experimenting attributed to human service practice certainly has its place. But the approach of evidence-based practice stresses the idea that knowledge based on experimentally designed research and practice is the most desirable foundation for practice decisions. A thorough grasp of the principles of experimentation can enhance the practitioner's knowledge-building and decision-making efforts.

The Logic of Experimentation
Causation and Control

The strength of experiments as a research technique is that they are designed to enable us to make inferences about causality. The element that makes this possible is *control:* In experiments, the investigator has considerable control over determining who participates in a study, what happens to them, and under what conditions it happens. To appreciate the importance of this, let us look at some of the key terms in experimental research.

At the core of experimental research is the fact that the investigator exposes the people in an experiment, commonly referred to as *experimental subjects,* to some condition or variable, called the *experimental stimulus.* The **experimental stimulus,** or **experimental treatment,** is an independent variable directly manipulated by the experimenter to assess its effect on behavior. (Recall from Chapter 2 that independent variables are those variables in a study that are hypothesized to produce change in another variable. The variable affected by the independent variable is the dependent variable—so called because its value is dependent on the value of the independent variable.) An **experimental group** is a group of subjects exposed to the experimental stimulus. **Experimental condition** describes the group of people who receive the experimental stimulus.

We can illustrate the logic underlying experimentation by means of a series of symbols. The following symbols are commonly used to describe experimental designs:

O = Observation or measurement of the
    dependent variable
X = Exposure of people to the experimental
    stimulus or independent variable
R = Random assignment to conditions

In addition, the symbols constituting a particular experimental design are presented in time sequence, with those to the left occurring earlier in the sequence than those farther to the right. With this in mind, we can describe a very elementary experiment in the following way:

$$O \quad X \quad O$$

In this experiment, the researcher first measures the dependent variable (the pretest), then exposes the subjects to the independent variable, and then remeasures the dependent variable (the posttest) to see if there has been a change. One major yardstick for assessing whether the independent variable in an experiment has had an effect is a comparison of the pretest scores or measures with those of the posttest. (Note that this is a slightly different use of the term "pretest" from its use in Chapters 1 and 7. In those contexts, the purpose of the pretest was to assess the adequacy of a data-collection instrument before actual data collection. In this context, the pretest involves actual data collection, but before the introduction of the experimental stimulus.)

Suppose, for example, that we were interested in the ability of developmentally disabled children to remain attentive and perform well in classroom settings. We might hypothesize that behavior modification techniques, in the form of reinforcement with praise, would improve the children's performance. To test this hypothesis, we first measure the children's performance so as to have a baseline against which to assess change. Then we expose the children to rewards for performance, the independent variable. For a specified period, we give the children praise each time they show certain specified improvements in performance. Finally, we again measure their performance—the dependent variable—to see if it has changed since the first measurement.

This illustration shows one of the major ways that experiments offer researchers control over what happens: The researcher manipulates the experimental stimulus. In this illustration, the researcher uses praise as reinforcement. The experimenter specifies how and under what conditions the reinforcement is delivered, including how much is delivered for a given response. The researcher might use one standard level of reinforcement or use multiple levels of reinforcement to assess the impact of such variation. The key point here is that the researcher controls the "when" and "how much" of the experimental stimulus.

The purpose of an experiment, again, is to determine what effects independent variables produce on dependent variables. Variation in the dependent variable produced by the independent variable is known as **experimental variability** and is the focus of interest in experiments. However, variation in the dependent variable can occur for many reasons other than the impact of the independent variable. For example, measurement error may affect the dependent variable (see Chapter 5), or the people in the experiment may have peculiar characteristics that influence the dependent variable separately from any effect of the experimental stimulus.

It is also possible that chance factors can affect the dependent variable. Variation in the dependent variable from any source other than the experimental stimulus is **extraneous variability;** it makes inferences about change in the dependent variable difficult. Every experiment contains some extraneous variability because chance factors other than the experimental stimulus always exist that influence the dependent variable. Researchers need some way of discovering how much variation is experimental and how much extraneous; experiments can be designed to provide this information through the use of *control variables* and *control groups.*

Control variables are variables whose value is held constant in all conditions of the experiment. By not allowing these variables to change from one condition to another, any effects they may produce on the dependent variable should be eliminated. In the study of developmentally disabled children, for example, we might have some reason to believe that, in addition to the presumed impact of the experimental stimulus, the environment in which learning occurs—factors such as the lighting and heating—could affect how well the children perform. To control this, we would conduct all the observations in the same setting with no changes in lighting or heating. With such controls, we have greater confidence that changes in the dependent variable are caused by changes in the independent variable and not by the variables that are controlled.

A **control group** is a group of research subjects who are provided the same experiences as those in the experimental condition with a single exception: The control group receives no exposure to the experimental stimulus. **Control condition** refers to the state of being in a group that receives no experimental stimuli. When we include the control group in the elementary experimental design just described, we end up with the following design:

Experimental group: O   X   O
Control group: O   O

The control group is important in experiments because it provides the baseline from which to measure the effects of the independent variable. For example, in the study of developmentally disabled children, the experimental condition involves receiving reinforcement in terms of praise. However, it might be possible that the children's performance would increase even in the absence of praise, possibly because of the attention received just by being a part of an experiment. To test for this, it would be desirable to have a control group that receives the same attention as the children in the experimental group but is not rewarded with praise. Because both experimental and control groups experience the same conditions with the exception of the independent variable, we can more safely conclude that any differences in the posttest value of the dependent variable between the experimental and control groups is due to the effect of the independent variable. So another yardstick for assessing whether an independent variable has an effect—in addition to the pretest/posttest comparison—is the posttest/posttest comparison between experimental and control groups.

It is important that the ideas of a control variable and a control group be kept distinct because they serve quite different functions. Researchers use a control variable is an attempt to minimize the impact of a single, known source of extraneous variability on the dependent variable. They use a control group, on the other hand, to assess the impact of extraneous variability from any source—including variables that are not known to the researcher—on the dependent variable.

Matching and Randomization

When making comparisons between the experimental and control groups to determine the effect of the independent variable, it is of crucial importance that the two groups be composed of people who are as much alike as possible. If they are not, any comparison could be meaningless as far as the effects of the independent variable are concerned. For example, imagine that a teacher decides to experiment with a new teaching technique. As luck would have it, she has two classes on the same subject, one meeting in the morning and the other in the afternoon. She uses the new teaching technique in the afternoon—the experimental group—and her conventional teaching methods in the morning section—the control group. At the end of the term, she notes that the afternoon class did substantially better on tests than the morning class. Can she conclude that the new technique is more effective than her old methods? Not with any great certainty. The students in the two classes may have differed from one another in systematic ways, and it may have been these differences between students, rather than variation in teaching technique, that caused differences in performance. It may be, for example, that students involved in extracurricular activities took morning classes so that their afternoons were free for those activities. Furthermore, the students active in extracurricular affairs may have had less time to study or were less academically inclined. Thus, given the kind of students who tended to take morning classes, we would expect the afternoon class to perform better even if there had been no variation in teaching technique.

Two methods avoid the problem this teacher encountered and ensure that the experimental and control groups are equivalent: *matching* and *random assignment*. The first has a certain intuitive appeal, but on closer inspection, it proves to be the less desirable of the two. As the name implies, **matching** involves matching individuals in the experimental group with similar subjects for a control group. People are matched on the basis of variables that we presume might have an effect on the dependent variable separate from the effect of the independent variable. By

matching, we make the experimental and control groups equivalent on these variables so that these variables could not account for any differences between the two groups on the dependent variable. For example, the teacher described earlier might use an IQ test as a matching tool. A high-IQ student in the morning class would be matched with a high-IQ student in the afternoon class. Any students without equivalent matches on IQ in the other class would simply not be used in the data analysis. But other variables in addition to IQ could affect the outcome. Race, sex, socioeconomic status, study habits, reading ability, and math proficiency—the list goes on and on. Though matching on IQ would not be too great a problem, the difficulty of matching would increase geometrically with the addition of more variables. For example, the teacher might need to find a match for an African American female of middle-class background with good study habits and a ninth-grade reading ability who is also in the 95th percentile in math proficiency.

This illustrates one of the problems with matching: So many variables might be needed for matching that it becomes impractical to consider more than a few at a time. A second problem is that the researcher needs to know in advance which factors might affect the dependent variable so that these can be included in the matching process; but often such information is not available. On the positive side, matching is better than no attempt at all to control and may sometimes be the only type of control available. In our illustration, the teacher may have no control over which students get assigned to which class. Consequently, the best she can do is select subgroup members in one class who have counterparts in the other class on a few key variables.

The second approach to ensuring equivalent groups is random assignment. As the name implies, **random assignment** uses chance to reduce the variation between experimental and control groups. This can be done in a number of ways. For example, each person in the experiment can be given a random number, then the numbers arranged in order and every other person on the list placed in the experimental condition. Or the names of all the

Table 10.1   Randomization and Blocking Illustration

Subject	Sex	Height	True Dependent Variable Score
A	Male	Short	2
B	Male	Tall	4
C	Male	Tall	6
D	Male	Short	8
E	Female	Tall	12
F	Female	Short	14
G	Female	Short	16
H	Female	Tall	18
Total N = 8			Mean = 10

	Possible Groupings			
	Group 1	Group 1 mean	Group 2	Group 2 mean
Ideal groups	BCFG	10	ADEH	10
Worst random	ABCD	5	EFGH	15
Worst block on sex	ABEF	8	CDGH	12
Worst block on height	ABCD	5	EFGH	15

people in the experiment can be listed alphabetically and given a number, then a computer randomly assigns each number to either the experimental or the control group. (See Appendix B on generating and using random numbers.) The point is to make sure that each person has an equal chance of being placed into either the experimental group or the control group. In the long run, this technique offers the greatest probability that experimental and control groups will have no systematic differences between them, so that differences on the outcome measures can be confidently attributed to the effect of the independent variable. Chance rather than *a priori* knowledge of other variables is the foundation of random assignment.

The problem with relying on chance is that, even though in the long run and over many applications randomization generates equivalent groups, this approach can still yield nonequivalent groups on occasion, especially when the study sample is small. Table

10.1 illustrates the extreme difference between groups that can occur by chance when using randomization. In this hypothetical data, eight subjects have been identified by sex and height. The subjects are ranked according to their true position on the dependent variable prior to the experiment, with scores ranging from 2 to 18. The mean score for the entire group is 10. Thus, when divided into an experimental and a control group, the ideal situation (the row labeled "Ideal groups") is for each group to have the same mean score of 10, or at least very close to it, on the dependent variable. Probability theory tells us that, with random assignment, it is most likely that experimental and control group means will be close to the overall mean, but it is possible to obtain groups with very different means because, by chance, any combination of subjects in the two groups is possible. Table 10.1 shows one possible arrangement of subjects into one group with a mean score of 5 and another with a mean score of 15 (labeled "Worst random").

To reduce the likelihood of such occurrences, researchers often use a combination of matching and randomization known as **blocking.** In blocking, the subjects are first matched on one or more key variables to form blocks. Members of each block are then randomly assigned to the experimental and control conditions. Blocking works by reducing the extreme range of groups that are possible. For blocking to be effective, the variable on which cases are blocked must be associated with the dependent variable. Notice in Table 10.1 that males have low scores and females have high scores; the variable of sex and the dependent variable are clearly associated. But no such association exists between height and the dependent variable. When blocking on the basis of sex, two males are randomly assigned to each group and two females to each group. The most extreme difference between groups that is possible in our hypothetical illustration with sex as the blocking variable is group means of 8 and 12 (labeled "Worst block on sex").

This is a considerable improvement over the extremes of 5 and 15 that are possible with randomization alone. Notice, however, that when the groups are blocked on the basis of height (labeled "Worst block on height"), there is no improvement; the worst possible group difference is still 5 and 15, as it was under randomization. This demonstrates that blocking on an appropriate variable can help reduce differences between groups. Choosing a variable for blocking that is unrelated to the dependent variable does not make matters any worse than random assignment, but neither does it improve the chances of achieving equivalent groups. Whether or not blocking is worthwhile basically comes down to the anticipated improvement in group equivalency versus the cost and complexity of carrying out the blocking procedure. Research in Practice 10.1 describes a field experiment that combined randomization and blocking with other procedures to ensure equivalence between experimental and control groups.

RESEARCH IN PRACTICE 10.1

PROGRAM EVALUATION:

Meeting the Challenges to Experimentation in a Drug Prevention Program

The proliferation of school-based substance abuse prevention programs has produced a need to evaluate their effectiveness. These evaluations suffer from a number of weaknesses that reduce their capacity to provide direction for program development. One weakness has been samples that include too few schools to make reasonable generalizations; other common weaknesses are studies that do not include enough students or adequately address ethnic and racial diversity. Lack of random assignment, faulty implementation of intervention, questions about accuracy of reported drug use, and inadequate statistical controls are other flaws.

One research team attempted to overcome some of these weaknesses in their evaluation of a program called Project ALERT (Ellickson and Bell 1992). Their study not only illustrates that true experimental designs are feasible in drug prevention research but also shows the clear benefits that can be derived from a well-planned and executed design.

What really makes this project noteworthy are its mechanisms for ensuring equivalence between experimental and control groups and the care taken to make sure that the treatment was implemented correctly—two elements of field experiments that often detract from the validity of the experimental design.

The program was based on a social influence model of prevention. According to this model, the key factors that keep young people from using drugs are influence by family, friends, and others, plus the young person's own beliefs about drugs. The program also focused on teaching skills to aid in resisting internal and external pressures to use drugs. This was accomplished through skill demonstrations by instructors, role-playing of solutions by students, and reinforcement of successful performance. In addition to learning if the program content was effective or not, the researchers were interested

continued on next page

in whether the program could be delivered more effectively by adults or by other teenagers. Consequently, the study used three groups: a control group with no treatment, a treatment group with instruction delivered by an adult educator, and a treatment group using an educator assisted by teenage peers from neighboring schools.

One concern in designing the study was to ensure that the program would be tested in different environments. Many previous studies had focused on white, middle-class, suburban communities. To avoid this, the researchers began by listing all California and Oregon school districts and then distinguishing them by several dimensions, such as geographic location, racial/ethnic composition, socioeconomic level, and school size. As some districts joined in, the researchers concentrated on obtaining other districts that would complement them in terms of demographic features. The process netted eight school districts, including 19 in California and 11 in Oregon.

Although the process generated a sample of schools that met the researchers' requirements in terms of diversity, the next challenge was to assign the schools to treatment and control conditions. It was not feasible to assign individual students randomly to study conditions because the nature of the intervention required that it be delivered to a whole school at one time. Consequently, whole schools were assigned to treatment and control groups; thus, the study sample consisted of all 30 schools. For reasons covered in our discussion of randomization and blocking, simple random assignment could produce nonequivalent experimental and control groups, especially with a sample as small as 30 cases. To reduce the likelihood of this, the researchers buttressed randomized assignment with blocking, but with a special twist that they labeled "restricted assignment."

School district was used as the blocking factor. The researchers reasoned that schools within the same district could be expected to have similar underlying substance-abuse rates. Socioeconomic status, norms about drug use, and school policy about substance use were also likely to be similar, if not the same, across schools in the same district. With such a small sample, then, it is possible by chance that most or all of the schools in one district would end up, even with random assignment, in the same experimental condition. To prevent this, schools from each district were randomly spread over the experimental conditions. If a district contained three schools, one was randomly assigned to each study condition. In the case of four schools, each condition was assigned one school, and the remaining school was randomly assigned to one of the study conditions. For districts with five schools, one condition received one school, and the other conditions got two schools each. Blocking in this fashion helped ensure that schools from the same district were spread more evenly among the three experimental conditions.

Although blocking could be expected to be of some help, the researchers also knew from their demographic analysis that substantial differences did exist within some districts. Because there were only 30 schools from eight districts to be distributed over three experimental conditions, the researchers were concerned that randomization, even with blocking, might result in nonequivalent groups. Their solution to this problem was to make use of publicly available data on each school and the results of an 11-item questionnaire that eighth-graders had previously completed at potential Project ALERT schools. These sources provided valuable information not only about demographic variables, such as parental education and mobility between schools, but also about cigarette and marijuana use as well.

Under the design of the research, pairs of school districts entered the project at about the same time. So, instead of assigning schools from each district to experimental conditions independently, the researchers created blocking units by pairing schools from one district with schools from another district and then randomly assigning these pairs of schools to treatments. The secret to this procedure was to create the best possible pairings. Figure 10.1 identifies school districts by letters and individual schools by numbers. (Schools A1 and A2, for example, are different schools, but both are in district A.) As the figure illustrates, there are six possible ways that three schools from one district (A1, A2, and A3) could be paired with three from a second (B1, B2, and B3).

The researchers evaluated each of the six sets of pairs to see which set had the best balance on the available variables, such as race, socioeconomic status, and reported drug use. The best set was the one in which the three pairs were most equivalent on

continued on next page

these variables. This set was then used as the basis for blocking. One pair of schools in the set was randomly assigned to the adult educator condition, the second to the peer instructor condition, and the third to the control group. The researchers called this restricted assignment: Randomization and blocking were used, but the outcomes of that process were restricted by eliminating those possible combinations of schools that were most likely to differ on important variables.

Collection of preliminary data and assignment to conditions by blocking with restricted assignment was a painstaking process but resulted in three groups of schools that were well balanced on almost all variables thought to possibly produce differences in the outcome variable. This increased the researchers' confidence that outcomes would be produced by experimental variability rather than by nonequivalent groups. The results of the experiment showed that the program effectively pre-

vented or reduced both cigarette and marijuana use during the junior high years and had modest effects on adolescent drinking.

In reflecting on the research experience, the researchers identified several lessons they learned:

- Communities and organizations will abide by experimental conditions, including randomization, if they understand the importance and feel that the inconvenience of doing so has been dealt with.
- Field experiments using large and limited units of assignment, such as school districts, need to go beyond simple random assignment to ensure balanced groups.
- When large organizations, such as schools, must be used as the unit of assignment, a large-scale study may be needed to meet the research objectives. No alternative may exist to a large-scale study when such issues as diversity and generalizability are at stake.

Figure 10.1 Randomization Process Employing Blocking with Restricted Assignment

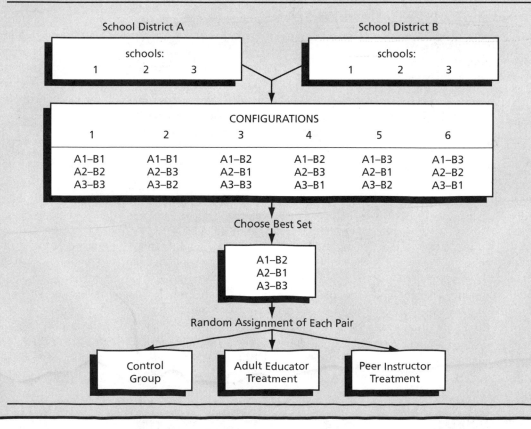

Internal Validity

The central issue in experimentation is that it allows us to make statements about causal relationships between phenomena. This is the reason for control variables, control groups, randomization, and matching. In what has come to be considered the definitive work on experiments and experimental designs, Donald Campbell and Julian Stanley (1963) discussed the importance of *internal validity* in experiments (see also Shadish, Cook, and Campbell 2002). Recall from Chapter 5 that the *validity* of a measure refers to whether it accurately measures what it is intended to measure. Likewise, **internal validity** in experiments refers to whether the independent variable actually produces the effect it appears to have had on the dependent variable; it is concerned with ruling out extraneous sources of variability to the point where we have confidence that changes in the dependent variable were caused by the independent variable.

In the preceding discussion, we presented the basic logic involved in designing experiments that have internal validity. However, the problem is much more complex because internal validity can be threatened in many ways. We now turn to the seven most serious threats to internal validity, as identified by Campbell and Stanley.

History. The threat of history concerns events other than the experimental stimulus that occur during the course of an experiment, events that could affect the dependent variable. History is more of a problem for field experiments than for those conducted in the confines of a laboratory because field experiments typically last longer, allowing more time for events that affect the outcome to occur. For example, the homicide rate in the United States declined dramatically between 1980 and 2000—by almost one half—and many commentators attributed this decline to policy changes in the criminal justice system, such as more police officers, better policing, and longer prison sentences for convicted felons. Yet during the same time period, dramatic improvements occurred in emergency care, including the spread of 911 emergency systems, the development of rapid re-

sponse emergency teams, and more effective trauma units at hospitals. These developments may well have produced some of the declines in homicide: By 2000, people had a better chance of surviving a knife or gun assault that, before 1980 with less effective emergency interventions, would have resulted in death (Harris, Thomas, Fisher, and Hirsch 2002). The effects of these historical events make it difficult to ascertain what effect the changes in criminal justice policies actually had on homicide rates.

Maturation. Maturation refers to changes occurring within experimental subjects due to the passage of time. Such things as growing older, hungrier, wiser, more experienced, or more tired are examples of maturation changes. If any of these changes are related to the dependent variable, their effects can confuse the effect of the independent variable. For example, many believe that people pass through a natural series of stages when grieving over the loss of a loved one: shock, then intense grief and sense of loss, followed by recovery (Kamerman 1988). In other words, time brings its own changes, or maturation, to the grieving individual. If we want to assess the effectiveness of some therapeutic intervention in helping people cope with the death of a loved one, any improvements people show over time might be due to maturation or the natural progression of the grief process rather than to the therapeutic intervention.

Testing. The threat of testing may occur any time subjects are exposed to a measurement device more than once. Because many experiments use paper-and-pencil measures and "before" and "after" measurements, testing effects are often of concern. For example, people taking achievement or intelligence tests for a second time tend to score better than they did the first time (Frankfort-Nachmias and Nachmias 2000) even when researchers use alternative forms of the same test. Similar changes occur on personality tests. These built-in shifts in paper-and-pencil measures can lead to changes in the dependent variable that are due to testing rather than to the impact of the independent variable.

Instrumentation. The threat of instrumentation refers to the fact that the way in which variables are measured may change in systematic ways during the course of an experiment, so that observations are measured differently at the end than they were in the beginning. In observing and recording verbal behavior, for example, observers may become more adept at recording and do so more quickly. This means that they could record more behaviors at the end of an experiment than at the beginning. If the observers do learn and become more skillful, then changes in the dependent variable may be due to instrumentation effects rather than to the impact of the independent variable.

Statistical Regression. The threat of statistical regression arises any time subjects are placed in experimental or control groups on the basis of extremely high or low scores on a measure in comparison to the average score for the whole group. When remeasured, those extreme groups will tend, on the whole, to score less extremely. In other words, they will *regress toward the overall group average.* For example, suppose the bottom 10 percent of scorers on a standard achievement test are singled out to participate in a special remedial course. On completing the course, they are measured with the achievement test again and show improvement. Could we conclude that the remedial course was responsible for the higher scores? We would certainly be hesitant to make this inference because of the effects of testing and maturation. In addition, however, there would also be a regression effect. Some of those people scoring in the bottom 10 percent undoubtedly did so for reasons other than their actual level of ability—because they didn't get enough sleep the night before, were ill, or were upset over a quarrel. (How many times do students score lower on an exam than they normally do because of factors like these?) When these people take the exam a second time, the conditions mentioned will have changed, and they will likely perform better—even without the special remedial course. Recognize that many (possibly most) people at the lowest 10 percent *are* performing at their normal level. However, in any such group based on a single test administration, a certain number of people will probably score lower than their normal level. If the whole group repeats the exam—even without any intervening experimental manipulation—they can be expected to perform better, and thus the average score of the group will improve.

Selection. Selection is a threat to internal validity when the kinds of people selected for one experimental condition differ from the people selected for other conditions. The threat of selection derives from improperly constituted experimental and control groups. Recall the importance of random assignment or matching to equalize these groups. As noted, improper composition of these groups can make findings based on comparisons between them meaningless.

Experimental Attrition. The attrition threat occurs when there is a differential dropout of subjects from the experimental and control groups. Especially in experiments that extend over long time periods, some people fail to complete the experiment. People die, move away, become incapacitated, or simply quit. If there is a notable difference in attrition rates between the experimental and control groups, the groups may not be equivalent at the end of the experiment, even though they were at the beginning. An example of the attrition threat can be found in a study of the effects of sex composition on the patterns of interaction in consciousness-raising counseling groups (Carlock and Martin 1977). One group was all women, and the other was both men and women. The women were randomly assigned to one or the other of the groups. Originally the all-female group contained nine members; the male-female group had 16 members. Before the experiment was completed, however, two female members of the male–female group dropped out. When the interactional patterns in the groups were compared, substantial differences were found. The authors concluded that these differences were due to the differing sex compositions of the groups, but, as they noted, their findings were weakened because of the dropouts from the male–female group. With such small groups to begin with, the loss of two members from one group can substantially affect results.

With this lengthy list of threats to the internal validity of experiments, can we ever be confident that changes in the dependent variable are due to the impact of the independent variable and not to some extraneous variability? In fact, such confidence can be established—and threats to internal validity controlled—through the use of a good experimental design.

Experimental Designs

There are three categories of experimental designs. **Preexperimental designs** lack both the random assignment to conditions and the control groups that are such a central part of good experimental designs. Although they are still sometimes useful, they illustrate some inherent weaknesses in terms of establishing internal validity. The better designs are called *true experimental designs* and *quasi-experimental designs*. **True experimental designs** are more complex and use randomization and other techniques to control the threats to internal validity. **Quasi-experimental designs** are special designs used to approximate experimental control in nonexperimental settings.

Preexperimental Designs

On the surface, Design P1 in Table 10.2 might appear adequate. The subjects are pretested, exposed to the experimental condition, and then tested again. Any differences between the pretest measures and posttest measures should be due to the experimental stimulus. However, this design as it stands has serious weaknesses. With the exceptions of selection and attrition, which are irrelevant owing to the lack of a control group, Design P1 is subject to the other five threats to internal validity. If a historical event related to the dependent variable intervenes between the pretest and the posttest, its effects could be confused with those of the independent variable. Maturation changes in the subjects could also produce differ-

Table 10.2   Preexperimental Designs

P1 The One-Group Pretest–Posttest Design:

	pretest	treatment	posttest
Experimental Group:	O	X	O

P2 The Static Group Comparison:

	pretest	treatment	posttest
Experimental Group:		X	O
Control Group:			O

ences between pretest and posttest scores. If paper-and-pencil measures are used, a shift of scores from pretest to posttest could occur due to testing effects. Regardless of the measurement process, instrumentation changes could produce variation in the pretest and posttest scores. Finally, if the subjects were selected because they possessed some extreme characteristic, differences between pretest and posttest scores could be due to regression toward the mean. In all these cases, variation on the dependent variable produced by one or more of the validity threats could easily be mistaken for variation due to the independent variable.

The other preexperimental design—the Static Group Comparison, or P2 in Table 10.2—involves comparing one group that experiences the experimental stimulus with another group that does not. In considering this design, it is important to recognize that the comparison group that appears to be a control group is not a control group in the true sense. The major validity threat to this design is selection. Note that no random assignment is indicated that would make the comparison groups comparable. In Design P2, the group compared with the experimental group is normally an intact group picked up only for the purpose of comparison. There is no assurance of comparability between it and the experimental group. For example, we might wish to test the impact of a local assistance program by comparing a city that has the program to one that does not. Any conclusions we might reach about the effects of the program could be inaccurate because of other differences between the two cities.

Despite their weaknesses, preexperimental designs are used when resources do not permit the development of true experimental designs. Human service practitioners especially are likely to be faced with this dilemma. However, conclusions based on such designs should be regarded with the utmost caution and the results viewed as suggestive at best. These designs should be avoided if at all possible. If they are used, efforts should be made to test the validity of the findings further with one of the true experimental designs.

True Experimental Designs

The Classic Experimental Design.   Diagrams of true experimental designs are presented in Table 10.3. Probably the most common true experimental design is the Pretest–Posttest Control Group Design with random assignment, which is identical to the design on page 258 except for randomization. This design is used so often that it is frequently referred to by its popular name: the *classic* experimental design. In all true experimental designs, the proper test of hypotheses is the comparison of posttests between experimental and control groups. This design utilizes a true control group, including random assignment to equalize the comparison groups, which eliminates all the threats to internal validity except certain patterns of attrition. Because of this, we can have considerable confidence that any differences between experimental and control groups on the dependent variable are due to the effect of the independent variable.

Let us take a closer look at how the classic design avoids the various threats to validity. History is removed as a rival explanation of differences between the groups on the posttest because both groups experience the same events except for the experimental stimulus. Because the same amount of time passes for both groups, maturation effects should be equal and therefore do not account for posttest differences. Similarly, as both groups are pretested, any testing influences on the posttest should be the same for the two groups. Instrumentation effects are also readily controlled with this design because any unreliability

Table 10.3   True Experimental Designs

T1 The Pretest-Posttest Control Group Design with Randomization—the "classic" experimental design

		pretest	treatment	posttest
Experimental Group:	R	O	X	O
Control Group:	R	O		O

T2 The Solomon Four-Group Design:

		pretest	treatment	posttest
Experimental Group 1:	R	O	X	O
Control Group 1:	R	O		O
Experimental Group 2:	R		X	O
Control Group 2:	R			O

T3 The Posttest-Only Control Group Design:

		pretest	treatment	posttest
Experimental Group:	R		X	O
Control Group:	R			O

T4 The Multiple Experimental Group with One Control Group Design:

		pretest	treatment	posttest
Experimental Group 1:	R	O	X_1	O
Experimental Group 2:	R	O	X_2	O
Experimental Group 3:	R	O	X_3	O
Control Group:	R	O		O

T5 The Factorial Design:

		pretest	treatment	posttest
Experimental Group 1:	R	O	X_1Y_1	O
Experimental Group 2:	R	O	X_1Y_2	O
Experimental Group 3:	R	O	X_2Y_1	O
Control Group:	R	O	X_2Y_2	O

in the measurement process that could cause a shift in scores from pretest to posttest should be the same for both comparison groups.

In situations where regression can occur, the classic experimental design controls it through random assignment of subjects with extreme characteristics. Thus, whatever regression does take place should be the same for both groups. Regression toward the mean, therefore, should not account for any differences between the groups on the posttest. Randomization also controls the validity threat of selection by assuring that the comparison groups are equivalent. Furthermore, the pretest results can be used as a check on precisely how similar the two groups actually are. Because the two groups are similar, attrition rates should be about the same for each group. In a lengthy experiment with a large sample, we would fully expect about the same number of subjects in each group to move away, die, or become incapacitated during the experiment. These can be assumed to be more or less random events. Attrition due to these reasons, therefore, is unlikely to create a validity problem. Attrition due to voluntary quitting is another matter. The experimental stimulus may affect the rate of attrition. That is, subjects might find something about the experimental condition either more or less likable than the subjects find the control condition, so the dropout rate could differ. If this occurs, it raises the possibility that the groups are no longer equivalent at the time of the posttest. Unfortunately, there is no really effective way of dealing with this problem. About all researchers can do is to watch for its occurrence and interpret the results cautiously if attrition bias appears to be a problem.

The Solomon Design. A second true experimental design—the Solomon Four-Group Design—is more sophisticated than Design T1 in that it uses four different comparison groups. In comparing Designs T1 and T2 in Table 10.3, we see that the first two groups of the Solomon design constitute Design T1, indicating that it is capable of controlling the same threats to internal validity as did that design. The major advantage of the Solomon design is that it can tell us whether changes in the dependent variable are due to some *interaction effect* between the pretest and the exposure to the experimental stimulus. Experimental Group 2 is exposed to the experimental stimulus without being pretested. If the posttest of Experimental Group 1 differs from the posttest of Experimental Group 2, it may be due to an interaction effect of receiving both the pretest and

the experimental stimulus—something we would not find out with the classic design.

Suppose, for example, that we wanted to assess the effect on prejudice toward racial minorities (the dependent variable) of receiving positive information about a racial group (the independent variable). We pretest groups by asking them questions regarding their prejudice toward particular groups. Then we expose them to the experimental stimulus: newspaper articles reporting on civic deeds and rescue efforts of members of those racial groups. Lower levels of prejudice in Experimental Group 1 than in Control Group 1 might be due to the independent variable. But it could also be that filling out a pretest questionnaire on prejudice sensitized people in the first group to these issues and they reacted more strongly to the experimental stimulus than they would have without such pretesting. If this is the case, then Experimental Group 2 should show less change than Experimental Group 1. If the independent variable has an effect separate from its interaction with the pretest, then Experimental Group 2 should show more change than Control Group 1. If Control Group 1 and Experimental Group 2 show no change but Experimental Group 1 does show a change, then change is produced only by the interaction of pretesting and treatment.

Thus, the Solomon design enables us to make a more complex assessment of the causes of changes in the dependent variable. In addition, the combined effects of maturation and history can be controlled (as with Design T1) and measured. By comparing the posttest of Control Group 2 with the pretests of Experimental Group 1 and Control Group 1, these effects can be assessed. However, our concern with history and maturation effects is usually only in controlling their effects, not measuring them.

Despite the superiority of the Solomon design, it is often passed over for Design T1 because the Solomon design requires twice as many groups, thus effectively doubling the time and cost of conducting the experiment. Not surprisingly, many researchers decide that the advantages are not worth the added cost and complexity. If a researcher desires the strongest design, however, Design T2 is the one to choose.

The Posttest-Only Control Group Design.

Sometimes, pretesting is either impractical or undesirable. For example, pretesting might sensitize subjects to the independent variable. In these cases, we can still use a true experimental design, the Posttest-Only Control Group Design (see Table 10.3). Despite the absence of pretests, Design T3 is an adequate true experimental design that controls validity threats as well as do the designs with pretests. The Posttest-Only Control Group uses random assignment to conditions, which distinguishes it from the preexperimental Design P2. The only potential validity question raised in conjunction with this design is selection. The absence of pretests means that random assignment is the only assurance that the comparison groups are equivalent. Campbell and Stanley (1963), however, argued convincingly that pretests are not essential and that randomization reliably produces equivalent groups. Furthermore, they argued that the lack of popularity of Design T3 stems more from the tradition of pretesting in experimentation than from any major contribution to validity produced by its use.

The Multiple Experimental Group Design.

The preceding experimental designs are adequate for testing hypotheses when the independent variable is either present (experimental group) or absent (control group). Yet many hypotheses involve independent variables that vary in terms of the *degree* or *amount* of something that is present. For example, *how much* treatment of a client (intensity level) is needed to produce some desired behavioral change? In a study of abusive parents, the independent variable was exposure to positive parenting sessions (Burch and Mohr 1980). Rather than just assess the effect of the presence or absence of such sessions, the researchers exposed some groups to *more* sessions than others. In cases such as this, Design T4 can be used—an extension of Design T1 with multiple experimental groups and one control group. The symbols X_1, X_2, and X_3 refer to differing amounts or intensities of a single independent variable or treatment. Comparing the posttests of the experimental groups enables us to determine the impact of the differing amounts of the independent variable.

The Factorial Design.

The experimental designs considered thus far can assess the impact of only a single independent variable at a time on the dependent variable. We know, however, that variables can *interact* with one another, and the combined effects of two or more variables may be quite different from the effects of each variable operating separately. For example, one experimental study investigated the impact of both social class and race on stereotypes of women (Landrine 1985). People in the study were asked to describe society's stereotype of four different women: a middle-class black, a middle-class white, a lower-class black, and a lower-class white. They found that social class and gender did affect stereotyping: Lower-class people received more negative stereotyping than middle-class people, and blacks were viewed less favorably than whites. Landrine did not find an interaction effect, however. In other words, various class/race combinations did not produce more changes in stereotyping than the effects of class and race separately.

The experimental design used in this study is called a Factorial Design (see Table 10.3). Design T5 illustrates the simplest factorial design in which two independent variables (X and Y, or race and social class) each have only two values (X_1 or X_2 and Y_1 or Y_2). In factorial designs, each possible combination of the two independent variables constitutes one of the experimental conditions. Technically, there may not be a control group, as in the example above, when there can be no "absence" of the factors involved. One cannot be without race or without social class. However, if variables involve the presence or absence of something, then a condition that looks like a control group appears in the factorial design. Factorial designs involve enough groups so that all possible combinations of the independent variables can be investigated. Assessment of interaction is accomplished by the comparison of Experimental Group 1, which is exposed to both independent variables, with Experimental Groups 2 and 3. We can see whether the combined effects of the independent variables differ from their separate effects.

Factorial designs can be expanded beyond this simple example. More than two variables can be investigated, and each variable can have more than two values. However, as the complexity increases, the number of groups required increases rapidly and can become unmanageable. For example, with three independent variables, each with three values, we would need a 3 × 3 × 3 factorial design, or 27 different groups. However, field experiments designed to assess the impact of social programs sometimes involve such complex designs.

We have covered the major types of true experimental designs in this section. However, circumstances often require researchers to use a variant of one of these designs. Research in Practice 10.2 illustrates such a variation that, nonetheless, retains randomization. The designs presented here also form the basis for many other more complex designs capable of handling such problems in experimenting as multiple independent variables and order effects.

RESEARCH IN PRACTICE 10.2

PROGRAM EVALUATION:

Field Experiments on the Police Handling of Domestic Violence Cases

The police telephone operator answered the call from a weeping woman: "Police."

Voice: I want a . . . a battered woman.
Operator: What, ma'am?
Voice: I am a battered woman.
Operator: Do you want the police to come, ma'am?
Voice: (sob) Yes.
Operator: Is he in the house now?
Voice: Yes—he's in the house now and I'm scared.
[Sherman 1992, p. 80]

This interchange between a victim of wife battering and the police was recorded in the course of a landmark experiment on law enforcement intervention in domestic violence conducted in Minneapolis. At first glance, the dialogue appears to stand as eloquent testimony to ethical and logistical barriers that prohibit using true experiments in the real world of human service. No matter how valuable the potential research findings, it is unthinkable to tell a victim, "Sorry, you're in the control group. We can't help you." And how could the researcher get the police officer on the scene to administer treatment A and not treatment B or C on a truly random basis?

On the other hand, the urgency of human need demands that researchers find the best ways of responding to such critical social problems. The most powerful rationale for using experiments in this way is that they deliver a more convincing case for causal relationships between variables than other research methods indicate due to the control that

researchers have over the variables—independent, dependent, and extraneous—in experimental research. If an intervention does prevent future assaults, a randomized experiment is the best way to find that out. Lawrence Sherman (1992) presents a fascinating account of the Minneapolis study and five replications in Omaha; Charlotte, N.C.; Milwaukee; Metro-Dade, Miami; and Colorado Springs. His presentation documents how researchers can overcome the barriers to experimentation in field settings and the lessons learned from the experience. We will highlight three of these studies on responding to domestic assault and focus on how they dealt with three potential barriers to experimentation—the ethics of withholding treatment, randomization, and ensuring that treatments are actually delivered as assigned.

The first of these studies was an investigation by criminologist Lawrence Sherman and sociologist Richard Berk (1984). The researchers randomly assigned 314 misdemeanor domestic assault cases to three types of police intervention: advising the couple (including informal mediation), separating the couple by ordering the offender to leave the house for eight hours, and arresting the offender so that he or she stayed in jail overnight. The independent variable was the mode of police intervention, and the dependent variable was whether or not the perpetrator was involved in another domestic violence incident in the six months following police intervention.

For ethical and practical reasons, the study was restricted to misdemeanor assaults, milder cases lacking severe injury or a life-threatening situation. With such misdemeanor offenses, police *could* make an arrest, or they could advise or separate, but no one of these responses was *required*. Under normal conditions, police would use their own judgment as to which intervention is called for. When participating in the Sherman–Berk study, police officers responding to a call first determined if the case fit the study criteria and then applied one of the three intervention techniques if it did. The ethical concerns raised by withholding treatment and random assignment to treatments were thus addressed by responding to all calls, by providing one of three standard treatments to each case, and by restricting the study to only misdemeanor cases.

Random assignment to experimental conditions was achieved by requiring each police officer to use a pad consisting of color-coded forms corresponding to the three different treatments: arrest, separation, and mediation. The forms were randomly ordered in the pad, and the officers were instructed to select their intervention according to whatever color form came up when they intervened in a case that met the study guidelines. In this study, the officers doing the intervening were responsible for making sure that the randomization was done properly. For the study to work as planned, officers had to follow the instructions faithfully. In addition, the forms were sequentially numbered so that the researchers could monitor how well the officers followed the assigned interventions. The researchers tried riding patrol with some of the officers to check, but this proved impractical because of the sporadic occurrence of assault complaints. Another approach was to have officers complete a brief form after each call describing what happened. In spite of these efforts, the study was criticized on the grounds that the treatments might not have been delivered as assigned.

Sherman and Berk concluded that arrest was the most effective of the three options for dealing with a spouse abuser: Those arrested were significantly less likely to be involved in a repeat episode of domestic violence in the following six months. Encouraged by these findings, many communities developed more aggressive arrest policies toward domestic assault. However, researchers and policymakers cautioned against placing too much faith in the results of a single study. One criticism was that the study had a small sample size. In addition, a few officers had submitted a disproportionately large number of cases. This may be because these officers patrolled a more violent section of town and, because of experience, were particularly effective at making an arrest an effective deterrent. The officers who did not arrest many offenders may have been more effective at mediation or separation. If so, then the study was really about variations in the skills of police officers rather than variations in the effectiveness of different treatments. This points to the importance of assessing *internal validity:* Is it variation in the independent variable that produces changes in the dependent variable, or is something else producing these changes?

Yet another criticism of Sherman and Berk's study was inadequate control over which treatments were actually delivered and the possibility that surveillance effects from the multiple follow-up interviews distorted the impact of the treatment. Finally, if the sample was biased for any of the foregoing reasons, the results would not be generalizable to other settings (Hirschel, Hutchison, and Dean 1992).

A follow-up study in Omaha differed from the Minneapolis project in several key respects (Dunford, Huizinga, and Elliott 1989). First, in addition to evaluating the three treatments—arrest, mediation, or separation—the research included a unique facet. If the assailant was not present when officers arrived but the case otherwise met study criteria, the suspect was randomly assigned to either receive or not receive a warrant for his or her arrest.

To improve generalizability, the researchers wanted to be sure the project covered all areas of the community, including sections populated by minorities. A competing goal was to maintain control by using those officers most likely to encounter assault cases rather than by training and monitoring the entire police force. A review of the 911 dispatch log revealed that about 60 percent of domestic assault calls occurred on the "C" shift (4 P.M. to midnight).

continued on next page

Focusing the project only on this shift kept the project more manageable. As in Minneapolis, the Omaha study was restricted to cases of probable cause of misdemeanor-level assault.

A criticism of the Minneapolis study had been the reliance on police officers to carry out randomization. The Omaha project addressed this criticism by having random assignment to treatment performed by the Information Unit of the Omaha police force. Upon establishing control at the scene, responding officers determined if the case met project eligibility requirements, such as being a misdemeanor offense. After information such as time, date, and victim and suspect characteristics had been reported to the Information Unit, the operator assigned an intervention treatment based on a computer-generated randomization procedure. In this way, randomization was centralized and data about the case and the assigned treatment immediately stored in the computer file.

For results to be valid, it was crucial that officers actually deliver the assigned treatment. This problem was controlled by three forms of monitoring. First, officers reported dispositions on a Domestic Violence Report form and forwarded it to the project. Second, victims were asked to describe what treatment was delivered. Finally, official records of police, prosecuting attorneys, and courts were compared with the other forms of monitoring data. Analysis of these various case-monitoring systems indicated that 92 percent of the treatments were delivered as assigned.

Another replication of the original Minneapolis study, this time in Charlotte, N.C., also had unique features (Hirschel, Hutchison, and Dean 1992): It included only cases involving female victims and male offenders in which both parties were at least 18 years old. The study covered the entire patrol division in around-the-clock, citywide sampling. The interventions also differed somewhat from the other studies. In addition to arrest, the police could issue citations requiring a court appearance by both victim and offender, or they could advise and separate (a combination of the mediation and separation treatments of the other studies). An additional explicit criterion addressed the concern of victim and officer safety: Cases were excluded if the victim insisted on arrest, if the assailant threatened or assaulted the police, or if officers believed that the offender posed an imminent danger to the victim. After restoring order at the scene, all victims were provided information on community resources, including the Victim Assistance Program and the battered women's shelter.

Choosing the best way to operationalize key variables is an important lesson from these studies. A related issue was whether to rely on official arrest records or interview reports of victims (Maxwell, Garner, and Fagan 2001). If repeat incidents of domestic assault are measured by re-arrest of the perpetrator, then repeat incidents appear to be rather small in number. However, if the occurrence of repeat events is measured by victims' reports to interviewers, then repeat incidents appear common—another example of the issue of validity discussed in Chapter 5: How accurately does a measurement tool measure some theoretical concept?

The original Minneapolis study, based on 314 cases, concluded that arrest significantly reduced future assaults, and the policy implication appeared clear-cut: Implement an aggressive pro-arrest policy to reduce spousal assault. Based on a total sample of thousands in six cities in the various replications, the general conclusions now are less clear-cut and more cautious and complicated (Maxwell, Garner, and Fagan 2001; Sherman 1992):

- Arrest does, in general, reduce future episodes of domestic violence, but the effect is modest.
- Arrest increases domestic violence among people who have nothing to lose, especially the unemployed.
- A small but chronic portion of all violent couples produces the majority of domestic violence incidents.

The research underscores the point that social problems and societal responses are complex and unlikely to yield singular solutions.

Quasi-Experimental Designs

Many times it is impossible for practical or other reasons to meet the conditions necessary to develop true experimental designs. The most common problems include an inability to assign people randomly to conditions and the difficulty of creating a true control group with which to compare the experimental groups. Although these can be problematic in experiments in any context, they are especially acute in field experiments and practice settings. Rather than rule out experimentation in such settings, however, the researcher may be able to use a *quasi-experimental design* that approaches the level of control of true experimental designs in situations where the requirements of the latter cannot be met. Quasi-experimental designs afford considerable control, but they fall short of the true experimental designs and should therefore be used only when conditions do not allow the use of a true experimental design (Achen 1986). As we will see in Chapter 11, quasi-experimental designs also form the basis of single-system designs used in clinical practice.

The Time-Series Design. One of the simplest and most useful of the quasi-experimental designs is the Time-Series Design (see Table 10.4), which involves a series of repeated measures, followed by the introduction of the experimental condition, and then another series of measures. The number of pretest and posttest measurements can vary, but it is unwise to use fewer than three of each. Time-series designs can be analyzed by graphing the repeated measures and inspecting the pattern produced. We can conclude whether the independent variable produced an effect by observing when, over the whole series of observations, changes in the dependent variable occur.

Figure 10.2 illustrates some possible outcomes of a time-series experiment. Of major interest is what occurs between O_4 and O_5 because these are the measures that immediately precede and follow the experimental stimulus. The other measures are important, however, because they provide a basis for assessing the change that occurs between O_4 and O_5.

Table 10.4 Quasi-Experimental Designs

Q1 The Time-Series Designs:

	pretests	treatment	posttests
Experimental Group:	$O_1 O_2 O_3 O_4$	X	$O_5 O_6 O_7 O_8$

Q2 The Different Group Time-Series Design:

	pretests	treatment	posttests
R	O_1		
R	O_2		
R		O_3	
R		O_4	
R		X	
R			O_5
R			O_6
R			O_7
R			O_8

Q3 The Multiple Time-Series Design:

	pretests	treatment	posttests
Experimental Group:	$O_1 O_2 O_3 O_4$	X	$O_5 O_6 O_7 O_8$
Control Group:	$O_1 O_2 O_3 O_4$		$O_5 O_6 O_7 O_8$

As Figure 10.2 shows, some outcomes suggest that the stimulus has had an effect, whereas others do not. In cases A, B, and C, stimulus X appears to produce an effect. In each case, the differences between measures O_4 and O_5 are greater than the differences between any other adjacent measures. Cases E and F illustrate outcomes where we can infer that changes result from something other than the stimulus because the differences between measures O_4 and O_5 are not substantially different from those between some other adjacent measures. The results of a time series design are not always clear-cut, as illustrated by case D. The sharp change between measures O_5 and O_6 could be a delayed effect of X, or it could be due to something else. More careful analysis would be required to come to a firm conclusion in that case.

In field studies involving a time-series analysis, the experimental stimulus is often not something the researcher manipulates; rather, it is something that

Figure 10.2 Possible Outcomes in a Time-Series Quasi-Experimental Design

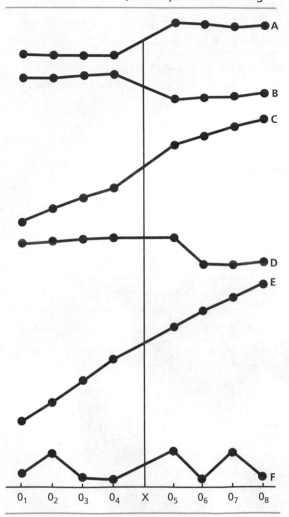

the daily homicide rates after championship prize-fights. The researchers found a sharp increase in homicides after such fights, peaking on the third day after each fight. Apparently, in some Americans, viewing heavyweight prizefights stimulates aggressive behavior that turns fatal in a few cases.

The time-series design fares quite well when evaluated on its ability to control threats to internal validity. With the exception of history, the other threats are controlled by the presence of the series of premeasures. Maturation, testing, instrumentation, regression, and attrition produce gradual changes that operate between all measures. As such, they cannot account for any sharp change occurring between O_4 and O_5. Because this design does not use a control group, selection is not a factor. Thus, history is the only potential threat to internal validity. It is always possible that some extraneous event could intervene between measures O_4 and O_5 and produce a change that could be confused with an effect of X. In many cases, there may not be an event that plausibly could produce the noted effect, and we could be quite sure it was due to X. Nevertheless, the inability of the time-series design to control the threat of history is considered a weakness.

The Different Groups Time-Series Design.

The time-series design requires that we be able to measure the same group repeatedly over an extended period. Because this requires considerable cooperation from the subjects, there may be times when the time-series design cannot be used. A design that avoids this problem and yet maintains the other characteristics of the time series is the Different Group Time-Series Design (see Table 10.4). Rather than make repeated measures on one group, this design substitutes several randomly selected groups, each of which is measured only once but at different times. Design Q2 produces the same type of data as the regular time series and can be analyzed using the same graphing procedure. In terms of internal validity, Design Q2 controls the same threats as the time series. Random sampling is relied on to equate the several comparison groups. Design Q2 also has the same weakness as the time-series design: Historical events can intervene between O_4 and O_5, possibly confusing the results.

occurs independently of the research. Thus, any natural event presumed to cause changes in people's behavior can serve as an experimental stimulus. In a study of the mass media and violence, for example, the experimental stimulus was the heavyweight championship prizefights that occurred between 1973 and 1978 (Phillips 1983). The dependent variable was the daily counts of all homicides in the United States provided by the National Center for Health Statistics, so an assessment could be made of

Because of the many random samples this design requires, it is limited to situations in which the cost of those samples is low. For example, if it is possible to draw the samples and collect data by telephone, the design is ideal. This is essentially the approach commercial pollsters use to measure public opinion by conducting weekly or monthly telephone surveys of different random samples. Although the pollsters do not conduct experiments, their repeated measures allow the assessment of the impact of events on public opinion. The event in question becomes the X in the design, and levels of opinion are compared before and after it occurred. For example, the terrorist attacks on New York and Washington in 2001 and the Iraq War in 2003 each caused the popularity of President George W. Bush to climb considerably. His popularity ratings dropped again a short time after each event, but because of the many before-and-after measurements, we have considerable confidence that it was the terrorist attacks and the war that temporarily increased the president's popularity.

The Multiple Time-Series Design. As noted, both of the preceding designs suffer from the validity threat of history. The addition of a control group to that time-series design controls this last remaining threat. Design Q3, known as the Multiple Time-Series Design, illustrates this (see Table 10.4). Design Q3 controls all the threats to internal validity, including history. Events other than X should affect both groups equally, so history is not a rival explanation for differences between the groups after the experimental group has been exposed to X. A design that uses a control group without random assignment might be thought suspect on the threat of selection, but this is less of a problem than with preexperimental designs because the series of before measures affords ample opportunity to see how similar the comparison groups are.

Data from Design Q3 are plotted and analyzed the same way as for the two preceding designs. This time, however, two lines on the graph represent the experimental group and the control group. The patterns of the two groups are compared to see what effect X produced. As a demonstration of the utility of quasi-experimental designs, Carol Kohfeld and

Leslie Leip (1991) looked at the impact of a California policy restricting the sale of beer and wine in stores that also sell gasoline. The idea was that people would be less likely to drink and drive if they could not purchase gasoline and alcohol at the same place. They measured the effectiveness of the policy in terms of the percentage of all alcohol-related automobile accidents. They collected data on 77 cities from 1981 to 1987; 37 of the cities had instituted a ban on concurrent sales of alcohol and gasoline by 1986. As Figure 10.3 illustrates, the percentage of alcohol-related accidents did decline over the period, especially between 1983 and 1986, from a high of about 24 percent to a low of about 18 percent. This would suggest that the ban had an effect. But was the decline due to the ban? Comparing cities with the ban to a control group of cities without such a ban over the same period, it appears that the ban had little effect because the "no ban" cities had a comparable decline. The best that could be said is that the cities with the ban experienced the decline slightly sooner than the "no ban" cities.

Quasi-experimental designs have considerable potential for human service research, much of which involves repeated contact with the same clients. Records of clients' situations and progress are routinely kept, so the repeated measures that time-series designs require may be easy to obtain. Various treatments or programs used with clients constitute the experimental condition. Plotting the data as suggested for time-series analysis would reveal whatever impacts those procedures produced. (We will discuss some of these topics and the intricacies of such designs in more detail in Chapter 11.)

Modes of Data Collection in Experiments

A good grasp of experiments in research makes this clear: Experiments are defined by a logical and orderly way of collecting data rather than by the form those data take. The research methods discussed in Chapters 7 to 9 are defined by the type of data collected: Surveys collect data in the form of verbal reports, available data uses archival records, and field research uses direct observation. Experiments, on

Figure 10.3 Example of Multiple Time-Series Data: Percent of Alcohol-Related Accidents for "Ban" and "No Ban" Cities (California, 1981–1987)

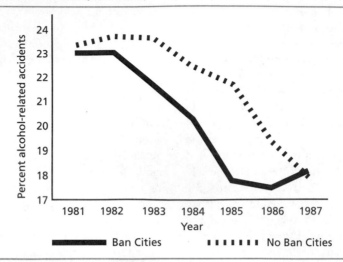

Source Carol W. Kohfeld and Leslie A. Leip, "Bans on Concurrent Sale of Beer and Gas: A California Case Study," In *Sociological Practice Review,* Vol. 2 (April 1991), p. 109. Reprinted with permission of the American Sociological Association and the authors.

the other hand, can collect data through all three of those sources—surveys, available data, and direct observation. Whatever kind of data is collected, what makes a research design an experiment is the presence of an experimental group, a control group, random assignment to conditions, and the other factors described in this chapter.

Some experiments, then, measure variables by getting people's responses to survey questions. The study discussed earlier on the impact of social class and race on gender stereotypes was of this sort: People were asked to state what society's stereotypes of different types of people were (Landrine 1985). The Minneapolis study of domestic violence and its replications described in Research in Practice 10.2 relied partially on interviews with victims to measure variables and also used available data in the form of arrest data (Sherman 1992). Archival records for the study of alcohol-related accidents illustrate a multiple time-series design: The study used government records on automobile accidents over a period of years (Kohfeld and Leip 1991).

Direct observation is also a way of collecting data in experiments, as illustrated by a quasi-experimental

field study assessing child care program quality (Ridley, McWilliam, and Oates 2000). In this case, the researchers compared the quality of care delivered by two different licensing levels of child care centers in North Carolina. A key outcome variable was "engagement," defined as the amount of time children spent interacting with the environment in a developmentally and contextually appropriate manner. Observers used a systematic process to code group engagement. They simply counted the number of children visible in one pass and then made a second pass, counting the number of children nonengaged (e.g., wandering aimlessly, crying, fighting). The percentage of engaged children was then computed and used as the dependent variable.

Technological advances in recording devices such as video recorders and computers have enhanced researchers' capacity to collect data by observation. The Computers in Research section of this chapter explores some of the tools available to aid researchers in gathering high-quality observational data for use in experiments.

In designing an experiment, then, a researcher also has to consider the issues involved in the particular kind of data collection used. If data will be collected for an experiment through a survey, for example, all the issues of question design, nonresponse, and others of Chapter 7 must be addressed. This chapter focuses on the logic behind experiments and leaves the issues related to the various forms of data collection to their respective chapters.

External Validity

In experiments, researchers make something happen that would not have occurred naturally. In laboratory experiments, for example, they construct a social setting that they believe simulates what occurs in the everyday world. In addition to its artificiality, the setting is typically simpler than what occurs naturally because researchers try to limit the number of social or psychological forces operating so they can observe more clearly the influence of the independent variables on the dependent variable. Even field experiments, which are considerably more natural than those in the laboratory, involve a manipulation of an independent variable by the researcher—a change in the scene that would not have occurred without the researcher's intervention.

This "unnaturalness" raises a validity problem different from internal validity discussed earlier in the chapter. **External validity** concerns the extent to which causal inferences made in an experiment can be generalized to other times, settings, or groups of people (Shadish, Cook, and Campbell 2002). The basic issue is whether an experiment is so simple, so contrived, or in some other way so different from the everyday world that what we learn from the experiment does not apply to the natural world. This problem is a part of the problem of generalizing findings from samples to populations (discussed in Chapter 6). With experiments, however, some special problems arise that are not found with sampling in other types of research methods. Indeed, resolving the problem of external validity can be difficult and is less straightforward than is the case with internal validity. Campbell and Stanley (1963, p. 17) succinctly state the problem:

> Whereas the problems of internal validity are solvable within the limits of the logic of prob-

ability statistics, the problems of external validity are not logically solvable in any neat, conclusive way. Generalization always turns out to involve extrapolation into a realm not represented in one's sample.

We will review four major threats to external validity and ways that these threats can be reduced.

Reactive Effects of Testing

In any design using pretesting, the possibility exists that experiencing the pretest can alter subjects' reactions to the independent variable. For example, items on a paper-and-pencil pretest measure might make subjects more or less responsive to the independent variable than they would have been without exposure to those items. The problem this raises for generalizability is not difficult to understand: The populations to which we wish to generalize findings are composed of people who have not been pretested. Therefore, if the subjects are affected by the pretest, findings may not accurately generalize to the unpretested population.

Whether reactive effects of testing are a threat to generalizability depends on the variables involved in the experiment and the nature of the measurement process used. Paper-and-pencil measures may be quite reactive; unobtrusive observation is likely not to be reactive. When a researcher plans an experiment, it is therefore important to consider whether the reactive effects of testing are likely to be a problem. If so, then it is desirable to choose a research design that does not call for pretesting, such as Design T3, or one that includes groups that are not pretested, such as the Solomon design. With the latter, it is possible to measure the extent of any pretesting effects.

Unrepresentative Samples

As emphasized in Chapter 6, the representativeness of the people studied in any form of research is crucial to the issue of generalizability. Unfortunately, it is often difficult to experiment on truly representative samples of any known population. Often, experimental subjects are volunteers, people who are enticed in some way to participate, or people who happen to be available to the researcher. The implications of this for generalizing experimental findings are quite serious. For example, repeated studies over the decades have demonstrated that people who volunteer to participate in experiments often differ in systematic ways from the people in the population from which they are drawn. The exact nature of the differences varies from one study to another: In some cases, volunteers are better educated, from a higher social class, or female (or in other cases, male) have a greater need for social approval or a higher achievement motivation (Boynton 2003; Rosnow 1993; Zelenski, Rusting, and Larsen 2003). Some studies show no such differences. Clearly, if these differences exist in a particular study, they could be related to any number of the variables likely to be used in human service research. Generalizing findings from such volunteer subjects could be quite hazardous. The best-designed experiments make an effort to measure such differences by comparing the characteristics of the volunteers with those of the population from which they were taken, if such comparative data exists.

Although the use of coerced subjects may reduce the differences between experimental subjects and the general population from which they are drawn, this has problems of its own as far as generalization is concerned. Coerced subjects are likely to have little interest in the experiment and may be resentful about the coercion used (Cox and Sipprelle 1971). This effect has been found even where the nature of the coercion was quite mild, such as gaining extra credit in a college class for agreeing to participate in an experiment. One can reasonably assume that these effects are amplified where the level of coercion is greater, such as court-ordered participation in a treatment program under threat of incarceration. In fact, a study of a drug treatment program involving court-ordered clients found this anticipated pattern (Peyrot 1985): The coerced clients were resentful, uncooperative, and unwilling to commit to the therapeutic objectives of the program.

The threat to external validity created by unrepresentative samples is of great importance to human service workers because we conduct most efforts to evaluate the effectiveness of treatment approaches on volunteers or coerced subjects. Volunteers may make programs look good because they are interested in the treatment and motivated to change in the direction promoted by the treatment. Not surprisingly, apparently effective treatment approaches on volunteers often fail when applied to nonvolunteer groups. Alternatively, because of their lack of interest and resentment, coerced subjects tend to make treatments appear ineffective when they might be effective on persons who are not coerced.

Reactive Settings

In addition to reactivity produced by testing, the experimental setting itself may lead people to behave in ways that are different from their behavior in the everyday world. One reason for this is that experimental settings contain **demand characteristics:** subtle, unprogrammed cues that communicate to subjects something about how they should behave. For example, people in experiments tend to be highly cooperative and responsive to the experimenter. In fact, the psychologist Martin Orne (1962) deliberately tried to create boring and repetitive tasks for subjects so that they would rebel and refuse to do them. One task was to perform a series of additions of random numbers. Each page required 200 additions, and each person was given 2,000 pages. After giving instructions, the experimenter told them to continue working until he returned; hours later the subjects were still working—it was Orne who gave up and ended the experiment! On the basis of this and other research, it has become evident that experimental settings can exercise a powerful enough influence on subjects to damage the generalizability of experimental findings. This has been labeled as the problem of the *good subject*—that is, the subject in an experiment who will do whatever the investigator asks, even to the point of confirming the experimenter's hypotheses if they are communicated to the subject (Aronson, Brewer, and Carlsmith 1985).

Subjects' reactions are not the only way that experimental settings can be reactive. Experimenters themselves can introduce distortion into the results that reduce generalizability. Experimenters, of course, usually have expectations concerning the results of the experiment, wanting it to come out one way or another. These **experimenter's expectations** can be communicated to subjects in such a subtle fashion that neither experimenter nor subjects are aware the communication has taken place (Rosenthal 1967). A classic illustration of how subtle this can be is recounted by Graham (1977) and involves a horse, not humans. The horse was called Clever Hans because of his seeming ability to solve fairly complex arithmetic problems. Hans and his trainer toured Europe in the early 1900s, amazing audiences and becoming quite famous. Hans would stand on stage pounding out the answers to problems with his hoofs. Amazingly, Hans was hardly ever wrong. Hans would perform his feats as well even when his trainer was not present. Could the horse really do arithmetic? After very careful observation, it was discovered that Hans was picking up the subtle cues given off by those who asked him questions. As Hans approached the correct number of hoofbeats, questioners would move or shift just enough to cue the horse that it was time to stop.

The same phenomenon has been thoroughly investigated in the physician–patient relationship (Kline 1988). When giving a patient a treatment known to be effective, a physician exudes confidence, and the patient picks up on this and expects to get better. The patient's hopeful mood then increases the likelihood that he or she will actually improve. However, when a physician is giving a patient a placebo—an inert substance the physician doesn't expect to work—his or her manner communicates doubt; the patient senses, without being aware of it, what the physician's expectations are and then helps create that reality. People in experiments often do the same thing. Subjects react to subtle cues unconsciously given off by an experimenter that tell them to behave in a way the researcher would like them to.

Reactive experimental settings can threaten external validity because changes in the dependent variable might be due to demand characteristics or experimenter expectancies rather than to the independent variable. One procedure for reducing reactivity in experimental settings is to conduct the experiment in such a way that subjects are *blind*—that is, unaware of the experimental hypotheses—so that this knowledge will not influence their behavior. In fact, subjects are commonly given a false rationale for what they are to do in order to reduce the reactions of subjects that might interfere with the generalizability of the findings. As an ethical matter, subjects should be informed of the experiment's true purpose during the postexperimental debriefing session.

The surest way of controlling reactivity due to the experimenter is to run what is called a *double-blind* experiment. In a **double-blind experiment,** neither the subjects nor the experimenter knows which people are in the experimental and which are in the control condition. This makes it impossible for the experimenter to communicate to subjects how they ought to behave because, for any given subject, the experimenter does not know which responses confirm the experimental hypotheses. Though simple in theory, maintaining a double-blind procedure in practice can be difficult. Another layer of personnel must be added to accomplish the assignment of subjects, issue sealed instructions to the experimenter, and keep track of the results. Furthermore, all information relating to these activities must be kept from those actually running the experimental groups. It is easy for this structure to break down so that the double-blind feature is lost. However, for true protection against such reactivity, double-blind experiments need to be used. Unfortunately, sometimes the nature of the treatment interferes with the use of the double-blind approach. Because of the different activities involved, it may be obvious which condition is experimental and which is control, thus clearly preventing the use of a double-blind experiment.

Multiple-Treatment Interference

In an experiment with more than one independent variable, the particular combination and ordering of experimental treatments may produce change in the dependent variable. If this same combination and this same ordering do not occur outside the experimental setting, the findings from the experiment cannot be generalized. Suppose, for example, that an experiment calls for subjects to experience four independent variables in succession. Furthermore, suppose that the last variable in the series appears to produce an interesting effect. Could the effect of that fourth variable be safely generalized on the basis of the experimental findings? The answer is no. The subjects in the experiment have experienced the three other independent variables first, which might in itself have affected the way they reacted to the last variable. If people outside of the experimental setting do not experience all the variables in sequence, generalization concerning the fourth variable is risky. The problem of multiple-treatment interference is similar to reactive effects of testing in that the subjects in the experiment experience something that the people in the population at large do not.

The threat of multiple-treatment interference can be effectively eliminated through the use of complex designs in which the different experimental groups experience the independent variables in every possible sequence. If a given variable produces a consistent effect regardless of the ordering of the variables, then multiple-treatment interference is not a threat to the generalizability of the findings. An alternative is to isolate the variable of interest in a multiple-treatment experiment and conduct a follow-up experiment with that variable as the only treatment. If it produces an effect similar to that found when it was a part of a series of treatments, multiple-treatment interference can be ruled out.

In designing experiments, especially those to be conducted in laboratory settings, problems of external validity need to be considered. Properly designed experiments can offer researchers substantial confidence in generalizing from an experimental sample to other settings or groups. However, efforts to enhance external validity may affect our ability to achieve internal validity, which brings us to the importance of replication for external validity.

Enhancing the External Validity of Experiments

Although both internal and external validity are important to experimental research, a tension ex-

ists between the two. On the one hand, internal validity is enhanced through greater control. Consequently, the researcher seeking internal validity is attracted to the laboratory experiment and to precise testing. Yet we have just seen that the reactive effect of testing is a threat to external validity. Seeking control, the researcher may use a homogeneous sample to avoid the confounding effects of other variables. In the effort to achieve internal validity, the researcher might, for example, use a sample of 18-year-old white males. Although the effects of race, sex, and age are now controlled, the external validity threat of unrepresentative samples increases. We have suggested the use of complex designs to reduce the threat to external validity of multiple-treatment interference. However, complex designs are more difficult to implement in a way that retains the integrity of the research design. Thus, there appears to be a dilemma between seeking internal validity on the one hand and external validity on the other.

Another way to approach the problem of external validity is, when possible, to conduct field experiments rather than laboratory experiments. Although issues of external validity do arise in field experiments, field experiments on the whole have greater external validity because they are conducted in the real world. This means that the results are more clearly generalizable to some settings in the real world, at least to settings similar to the setting in which the field study was conducted.

However, the basic solution to this dilemma is not to seek an answer to both internal validity and external validity in a single study. Ultimately, external validity is established through replication (Shadish, Cook, and Campbell 2002). Confidence in generalizing from experimental findings increases as other researchers test and support the same hypotheses in a variety of settings with a variety of designs. Often this takes the form of initial testing in the laboratory under ideal conditions to see if the hypothesis is supported at all. Then the same hypothesis can be tested under the less-than-ideal conditions of the field. Through replication, the dual objectives of internal and external validity can be achieved.

Lack of Minority Participation and Analysis

Depending on the setting in which an experiment is conducted, women and minorities may find themselves underrepresented in laboratory or field experiments—a problem that can affect both external and internal validity. Researchers often choose as subjects for experiments people who are easily accessible to them. In basic research in psychology and sociology, for example, students in introductory psychology or sociology classes are often selected as research subjects. The sex ratio of college students is fairly even: 46 percent male and 54 percent female. African Americans constitute about 11 percent of all college students but account for 13 percent of the total U.S. population (U.S. Census Bureau 2002). Thus, experiments using a representative sample of college students will tend to underrepresent African Americans, Hispanics, and some other minorities. And this underrepresentation is more severe at some colleges than at others: Some major research universities even today have only 1 percent or 2 percent black enrollment. So whenever experimental subjects are selected from a setting, care must be taken to ensure representation of minorities in a sample if the minorities are to be included in the generalizations made from the data. Otherwise, mention should be made that no special procedures were used in the sampling to enhance minority involvement.

A related problem is what one sociologist calls *gender insensitivity:* "ignoring gender as an important social variable" (Eichler 1988, p. 66). In experiments, this can happen when no mention is made of the sex ratio of the subjects in the experiment or data are not analyzed separately for each gender. Eichler reports one issue of a psychology journal in which the only article to mention the sex of the subjects was one that used rhesus monkeys; none of those using human subjects did so, despite the fact that practically all those articles focused on variables (such as perception, verbal ability, and learning) on which people's gender might well have an influence.

A final problem relating to minority participation in experiments is failure to consider the gender or minority status of all participants in the experiment. In addition to the researcher and the subject, this might include interviewers, confederates of the experimenter, and any others who interact with the subjects during data collection. We know, for example, that people of the same gender interact differently from people of the opposite gender. Thus, a male interviewer responds differently when asking questions of a female subject than when interviewing a male subject. In the former case, he might be friendlier, more attentive, or more engaging without even realizing it, and this can influence the subject's response to questions.

These threats to external validity can be reduced by reporting the sex or minority status of the various people involved in experiments and by analyzing the data with sex or minority status as an experimental or control variable. There are, of course, reasons for a homogeneous sample in an experiment: to reduce extraneous variation when trying to establish a causal relationship between independent and dependent variables. However, if the results are to be generalized to all racial and ethnic groups and both sexes, then experiments need to be replicated using subjects from these groups.

Assessment of Experiments
Advantages

Inference of Causality.   The major advantage of experimental research is that it places us in the most advantageous position from which to infer causal relationships between variables. (Recall from Chapter 2 that causality can never be directly observed. Rather, we infer that one thing caused another by observing changes in the two things under the appropriate conditions.) A well-designed and well-controlled experiment puts us in the strongest position to make that causal inference because it enables us to control the effect of other variables, which raises our confidence that the independent variable is indeed bringing about changes in the dependent variable. Experiments also permit us to establish the time sequence necessary for inferring causality. We can measure the dependent variable to see if it has changed *since* the experimental manipulation. With other research methods, such as the survey, it is often not possible to directly observe whether the changes in one variable preceded or followed changes in another variable.

Control. Experimenters are not limited by the variables and events that happen to occur naturally in a particular situation. Rather, they can decide what variables to study, what values those variables will take, and what combination of variables to include. In other words, researchers can create precisely what their hypotheses suggest are important. This is in sharp contrast to other research methods, such as the use of available data (see Chapter 8) or observational techniques (see Chapter 9), in which hypotheses need to be reshaped to fit the existing data or observations.

The Study of Change. Many experimental designs are longitudinal, which means that they are conducted over a period of time with measurements taken at more than one time. This makes it possible to study changes over time. Many other research methods, such as surveys, tend to be cross-sectional—they are like snapshots taken at a given point in time. In cross-sectional studies, we can ask people how things have changed over time, but we cannot *directly observe* that change.

Costs. In some cases, experiments—especially those conducted in laboratory settings—can be considerably cheaper than other research methods. Because of the element of control, the sample size can be smaller, and this saves money. Costly travel expenses and interviewer salaries found in some surveys are eliminated. Some field experiments, however, can be expensive because they may require interviewing—possibly more than once—to assess changes in dependent variables.

Disadvantages

Inflexibility. Experimental designs generally require that the treatment, or independent variable, be well developed and that the same treatment be applied to all cases in the experimental group. If the nature of the independent variable changes as the experiment progresses, this is extraneous variation, which makes it difficult to say what changed the dependent variable. Because of this inflexibility, experimental designs are not suitable in the early stages of research when treatments may not be well developed. This requirement for consistently measuring the independent variable is especially true of large-scale, longitudinal experiments, which are best suited for clearly designed treatments (Rossi, Freeman, and Lipsey 1999).

Randomization Requirement. Human service organizations may be unwilling to accept random assignment to treatment and control conditions, in spite of the value of this technique for controlling extraneous effects. This is especially so when the design calls for a control group to receive no treatment at all. Organizations may have ethical concerns about randomization, or they may want to be sure that they "get something" for participating in a study and so be reluctant to serve as the control condition. In addition, with field experiments, it is sometimes impossible to find or create a control group that is truly comparable to the experimental groups, and thus the true experimental designs are ruled out. In spite of the fact that randomization was achieved, both Research in Practice illustrations in this chapter emphasize the considerable difficulty in carrying out randomization.

Artificiality. The laboratory setting in which some experiments are conducted is an artificial environment created by the investigator, which raises questions of external validity. We often do not know what the relationship is between this artificial setting and the real world in which people live. We cannot be sure that people behave in the same fashion on the street or in the classroom as they do in the laboratory. Even field experiments of human service interventions are vulnerable to this criticism to an extent, especially when they create conditions that never exist naturally. For example, the recipients of social services who are the subjects of research may be treated better by the research team than they would be in their everyday contacts with human service agencies. Under the watchful eye of a research team, much greater care may be taken in the form of monitoring and supervision to ensure that the treatment delivered is true to the theoretical model than might be taken when the same intervention is delivered as a routine part of an agency's service.

Experimenter Effects.   Thus, artificiality of experimental settings in comparison to the real world exists. And there is another side to this coin: The experimental setting itself is a real world—a social occasion in which social norms, roles, and values exist and shape people's behavior. Social processes arising within the experimental setting—and not a part of the experimental variables—may shape the research outcome. Thus, changes in the dependent variable may be due to the demand characteristics of experiments (such as repeated measurement) or to the impact of experimenter expectations, factors that obviously do not influence people in the everyday world.

Generalizability.   The logistics involved in managing an experiment often necessitate that experimenters use small samples. Furthermore, the goal of holding measurement error to a minimum often compels researchers to make these samples as homogeneous as possible. Despite the advantages of random sampling, experimenters must frequently settle for availability samples to obtain subjects who will participate in the study. The net result is that experiments are often conducted on small, homogeneous availability samples, and it may be difficult to know to whom such results can be generalized. It is often assumed that representative sampling is not as essential in experiments as in other types of research because of the randomization and control procedures used. Although these help, we still must be cautious regarding the population to which we make such generalizations.

Timeliness of Results.   Although experiments may produce the strongest evidence of causation, they are often time-consuming to conduct. The urgency of policy decisions may preclude using experimentation simply because it takes too long to generate funding for the project, design the research, and carry it out. If results do not come in quickly enough, they may not be considered in the debate over a rapidly developing policy (Rossi, Freeman, and Lipsey 1999).

COMPUTERS IN RESEARCH

Computer Applications in Experimental Research

In defining experiments, we stated that the essence of experimentation is a *controlled method of observation* in which the value of one or more independent variables is changed to assess its causal effect on one or more dependent variables. Researchers endeavor to eliminate variation due to any variables other than the independent variable. In this effort to reduce extraneous variation, computer technology can be helpful.

One strategy to reduce extraneous variation and produce higher-quality data is to have research participants record data on computers themselves.

Not only can this approach help obtain high-quality data, but the computer may also incorporate a signaling function that alerts participants when it is time to record data. Computerization can also include timing functions to assess when data were entered or how long the participant engaged in a target behavior (Fahrenberg 1996). For example, one researcher used pocket computers to assess urges to smoke and lapses during smoking cessation programs (Shiffman et al. 1996) by equipping participants with PSION Organizer II handheld

continued on next page

computers with software developed specifically for the project, referred to as an "Electronic Diary." A four-line, 20-character LCD screen presented questions, and a user interface recorded responses. To respond to a question, users simply scrolled through alternative responses and pressed *Enter* to record their choices. In addition to the user's response, the computer recorded the date and time of the response. Participants recorded smoking behavior up to a target quit date and then monitored temptations to smoke following the quit date. Throughout the monitoring period, the Electronic Diary also prompted the participants at random times for assessments approximately four to five times per day.

Collecting the data immediately—while the participant is feeling the urge to smoke—eliminated the distortion associated with recall of the event at a later time. Shiffman and his colleagues (1997) conducted a comparison of data secured using the computers to retrospective recall. They found that retrospective recall of smoking lapses was quite poor compared with the immediately collected computer data. They also concluded that in

recall, subjects overestimated their negative effect and the number of cigarettes they had smoked during the lapse.

The number of available tools for data collection is expanding rapidly as computers become smaller, more portable, and less expensive. A recent review of computerized data-collection systems included 15 different products (Khang and Iwata 1999). One example is the MOOSES Program (Multiple Option Observation System for Experimental Studies), which allows the researcher to capture frequency, duration, interval, and time-sampling data for 200 different responses. In addition, the program can calculate inter-observer agreement, and be adapted to record data from video sources. Another example—called !Observe—also uses handheld computers; users record behavioral observations by touching on-screen "buttons" to access code sets that come with the program or create new templates to fit the needs of the study. Up to 24 different responses can be recorded during a session. In addition to specific responses, the user can record a variety of other useful variables, such as duration and intervals associated with responses.

Main Points

- Experiments are a controlled method of observation in which the value of one or more independent variables is changed to assess the causal effect on one or more dependent variables.
- Owing to the control experiments afford, they are the surest method of discovering causal relationships among variables.
- Major elements of control in experiments include control variables, control groups, matching, and randomization.
- Internal validity refers to whether the independent variable does in fact produce the effect it appears to produce on the dependent variable.
- Numerous conditions may threaten the internal validity of experiments, but using true experimental designs can control all of them.

- Quasi-experimental designs are useful for bringing much of the control of an experiment to nonexperimental situations.
- External validity is the degree to which experimental results can be generalized beyond the experimental setting.
- Threats to external validity are generally not controllable through design but are more difficult and less straightforward to control.
- Double-blind experiments, in which neither the subjects nor the experimenters know which groups are in the experimental or control condition, are used to control both experimental demand characteristics and experimenter bias.
- To avoid race, ethnicity, or gender insensitivity, the minority composition of experimental groups should be reported, consideration should be given to analyzing the data by con-

trolling for minority impact, and the minority status of all experimental participants should be considered.

- An understanding of experimental procedures can contribute to practice effectiveness as well as research endeavors.

Important Terms for Review

blocking
control condition
control group
control variables
demand characteristics
double-blind experiment
experiment
experimental condition
experimental group
experimental stimulus
experimental treatment
experimental variability
experimenter's expectations
external validity
extraneous variability
field experiments
internal validity
laboratory experiments
matching
preexperimental designs
quasi-experimental designs
random assignment
true experimental designs

Exploring InfoTrac® College Edition and the Internet

InfoTrac® College Edition search terms:

clinical trial* AND mental health
field experiment AND _____ (insert human service field: mental health, aging, delinquency, etc.)
quasi-experiment* AND social

randomized AND _____ (insert human service field: mental health, aging, delinquency, etc.)

InfoTrac® College Edition articles:

Death and Divorce: The Long-Term Consequences of Parental Loss on Adolescents. (Statistical Data Included) Miles Corak. *Journal of Labor Economics* July 2001 v19 i3 p682 (13,934 words)

The Ethics of Randomization. (editorial) Eric Kodish, John D. Lantos, Mark Siegler. *Ca* May–June 1991 v41 n3 p180(7) (3,747 words)

School Violence: Prevalence and Intervention Strategies for At-Risk Adolescents. Kathleen J. Cirillo, B. E. Pruitt, Brian Colwell, Paul M. Kingery, Robert S. Hurley, Danny Ballard. *Adolescence.* Summer 1998 v33 n130 p319(12) (3,326 words)

If you've been taking advantage of Internet resources that apply to the previous chapters, then you've no doubt discovered the value of using key chapter terms with various Internet search engines. For example, putting such terms as "random assignment" or "randomized control group" into the AltaVista search engine locates a number of Web sites that relate to experimental design in social science. The National Institutes of Health's Web page serves as a portal to information about experimental research on human volunteers. Its Web page uses the term "clinical trials," but focuses mostly on experimental research. Use this Web page to find illustrations of the different experimental designs discussed in this chapter. You can begin by looking for research on depression. Click on "Browse by Condition," then "Alphabetically," and then look under "D" for Depression. Once you have explored depression, look for research on other conditions.

For Further Reading

Adair, J. *The Human Subject: The Social Psychology of the Psychological Experiment.* Boston: Little, Brown, 1973. A good analysis of the many kinds of reactivity and experimenter expectancies that can be found in experimental settings.

Campbell, Donald T., and M. Jean Russo. *Social Experimentation*. Thousand Oaks, Calif.: Sage, 1999. Donald Campbell was one of the giants in the field of social experimentation. This book presents his views on how social experiments can be used for the betterment of society.

Fairweather, George W., and William S. Davidson. *An Introduction to Community Experimentation: Theory, Methods, and Practice*. New York: McGraw-Hill, 1986. An interesting book ideally suited to those involved in community action programs. It outlines the reasons for experimentation and supplies the designs to evaluate the effectiveness of various intervention programs.

Field, Andy, and Graham J. Hole. *How to Design and Report Experiments*. Thousand Oaks, Calif.: Sage, 2003. This textbook provides a good overview to experimental design and statistical analysis.

Gabor, Peter A., and Richard M. Grinnell, Jr. *Evaluation and Quality Improvement in the Human Services*. Boston: Allyn & Bacon, 1994. Although this book covers many other research issues, it is especially good at showing the importance of experimental designs in program evaluations. It describes the use of many different kinds of designs used in human service settings.

Gottman, John M. *Time-Series Analysis: A Comprehensive Introduction for Social Scientists*. New York: Cambridge University Press, 1981. "Comprehensive" is certainly the operative word in describing this book as it details the mathematical analysis of time-series designs. The author also argues persuasively against the common "eyeballing" approach to time-series analysis.

Kirk, R. E. *Experimental Design: Procedures for the Behavioral Sciences*, 2nd ed. Belmont, Calif.: Brooks/Cole, 1982. This is a thorough overview of how to design experiments, both simple ones and complicated ones. It goes well beyond the review in this chapter.

Exercises for Class Discussion

A senior citizens' service organization is concerned about the large number of purse snatchings and other attacks on elderly people in the community and decides to apply for a Department of Justice grant intended to assist local communities in fighting crime. A requirement for receiving such a grant is that an evaluation be performed to assess the effectiveness of any program established.

The center staff's first idea is to hire local teenagers to work out of the center as escorts to those people who request the service. Second, they plan to use the teenagers as a crime watch in those areas where attacks have been fairly frequent. Initially, the center will not be able to serve everyone, and the crime watch staff will only be able to cover some of the neighborhoods.

The senior center staff believes this program will serve two objectives. First, it will reduce the threat of crime to the elderly. Second, putting young people into positions where they can work with and help the elderly will increase feelings of understanding between the generations.

You have been asked to help the center develop a research design with the purpose of assessing how well the program attains its objectives.

10.1 What would be the independent and dependent variables for such a project? Give some examples of possible indicators for these variables. Which two experimental designs would be most appropriate to the research question? Which would be the most feasible?

10.2 One decision is whether to use the presence or absence of the program as the independent variable or to test different combinations of the independent variables. List some possible combinations of intervention efforts that could be used in a factorial design.

10.3 A major issue in experimental research is how to assign participants to experimental and control conditions.

a. Consider just the escort service. How could participants be assigned to treatment and control conditions? Would random assignment be ethical? Indicate why or why not.

b. Now consider the crime watch component, which serves anyone who happens to be in the patrolled area. Assume the center serves about a 50-block area of the city. Suggest some ways of developing experimental and control conditions.

c. What control variables might be useful in this study? How would these control variables assist you in making causal inferences?

10.4 How would you collect data to evaluate the effectiveness of the program in meeting its goals of reducing crime and increasing intergenerational understanding? Consider the alternatives of personal interviews, mailed questionnaires, observations, and existing data.

Now there's trouble in River City. It seems a local, very influential politician has gotten wind of the project. His mother lives in the impact area, and under no circumstances will he support an evaluation where his mother may wind up as a control subject who will not be provided services. Without his support, there will be no grant.

10.5 How could you design a quasi-experimental study that would not involve designating certain people or areas as experimental and control? What deficiencies would this design have in comparison to a true experiment?

10.6 What are the major threats to internal and external validity in this research project? How have the designs considered in the preceding exercises helped to reduce these threats?

Chapter 11

Single-System Designs

The model of evidence-based practice begins with converting the need for information into answerable questions and then systematically seeking through print and electronic sources to track down the best evidence for guiding practice decisions. However, using the available scientific knowledge base as a guide is only one part of evidence-based practice. Human service professionals are also called upon to evaluate their own effectiveness and to seek ways to improve future practice efforts (Sackett, Straus, Richardson, Rosenberg, and Haynes 2000). Practitioners generally work with one client at a time. Even if the client system is a family or a group or a community, the practitioner does not have randomized control groups or placebo treatments or other features that make clinical trials such a highly valued form of evidence for advancing practice. So beyond providing some interesting anecdotal evidence, how can the practitioner–client encounter serve as part of research process? Seeking to answer this question has led many human service professionals to revise the conception of their roles as clinician–researchers.

The purpose of this chapter is to present a fundamental tool of this role and a central mechanism through which valid research can be conducted in clinical settings: the *single-system design*. **Single-system designs** are quasi-experimental research designs that involve assessing change in a dependent variable on a single research case or subject. In psychology, the term "single case" appears to be replacing "single subject" as the designation of choice (Levin 1992). We have adopted a term more common to social work, single system, to signify the fact that the unit of analysis for this research may just as well be a couple, family, group, organization, or other human aggregate and not necessarily just an individual person. Our own students have designed single-system projects where the unit of analysis was an individual child with poor study behavior, a pair of squabbling siblings, a nursing home group with poor interaction among participants, and a medication-dispensing program in a mental health setting. In the latter case, the program was the system, and the dependent variable was the proportion of clients who received their weekly dosage of medication on time.

So although the most common application is to focus on the behavior of an individual client, the design is flexible and lends itself to the study of a wide range of practice issues.

When performing a literature search, however, keep in mind that there is no universal agreement on terminology. Studies with the features of a single-system design may be found in the literature under a variety of labels, including single case, case study, same subject, repeated measures, intensive, clinical–experimental, applied behavior analysis, time series, idiographic, $N=1$, and single subject.

The distinguishing feature of the single-system design is that the dependent variable is repeatedly measured, most commonly during a baseline phase and again during one or more intervention phases, when the independent variable is manipulated. Experimental effects are inferred by comparisons of the subject's responses across baseline and intervention phases. We begin by discussing how and why a *clinical research model* has emerged in the human services. Then we analyze the clinical research process, showing how research can be merged with clinical practice. Building on the discussion of experimental designs in Chapter 10, we then present the various kinds of single-system designs available to clinician–researchers. Finally, we analyze the advantages and disadvantages of single-system designs.

The Clinical Research Model

A fundamental force behind the development of single-system designs is the human service practitioner's professional concern about knowing how a client is responding to intervention. This basic desire to know has been intensified by the pressure for more accountability in the human services. Funding sources, insurance providers, and regulatory organizations demand documentation that services are delivered according to standards, and they want to see evidence that clients do in fact improve. Unfortunately, traditional research designs have significant limitations for meeting these needs in the practice community (Barlow and Hersen 1984; Gingerich 1990; Russell 1990). A major source new knowledge for many practitioners has been group experiments. However, group experiments are often impractical or impossible to conduct in practice settings. It may be too time-consuming and costly to assemble clients with similar problems and randomly assign some to treatment and others to control groups. A second problem with group experiments in terms of practice implications is that the results are often an average of the whole group's response, obscuring individual reactions. It is, of course, precisely the effects on individuals that are of most interest to clinicians. For example, knowing that a given treatment was effective on 70 percent of an experimental group may be interesting, but it helps relatively little in predicting the reaction of a particular client in a practitioner's office.

Another problem in some traditional group experimentation is failure of the research design to capture the process by which change was induced. Thus, traditional research has sometimes been referred to as "black box" research because subjects receive some treatment and are then compared with other subjects who did not receive the treatment. With only a pretest and posttest measure, experimenters may not have information on the process of how the change occurred, only on whether or not it occurred at all. It is as if the subjects passed through a mysterious black box and came out either improved or not improved. A fourth complaint about traditional group experiments has been that reliance upon statistical procedures for data analysis often requires a high degree of statistical expertise plus access to data analysis technology; this situation may necessitate relinquishing control of the study by practitioners to outside methodologists. Such a reliance on direction from outside of practice may have contributed to the view that these studies are not relevant to practice.

Finally, the use of control groups from which treatment is withheld is a source of ethical concern to human service professionals. Thus, although group experiments are appropriate for some purposes, the deficiencies inherent in the method have led both practitioners and researchers to seek alternative approaches for evaluating individual change and refining intervention techniques. Single-system

designs, as we shall see, effectively avoid the unattractive features of group experiments.

A second source of clinical knowledge prior to single-system designs was case histories. A case history, of course, is a report from a clinician about a client who has undergone treatment. Although many of these reports are intriguing, they often do not provide a sound basis for the accumulation of knowledge. First, they exhibit to only a limited degree the characteristics that distinguish science from other sources of knowledge (see Chapter 2). For example, vague treatments are often reported to have produced vague improvements. Because of this, other practitioners would have grave difficulty replicating the procedures if they wished. The ability to replicate is, of course, a fundamental characteristic of the scientific method, especially when one is working with a single case at a time. In addition, case histories are often prepared only on successes; information about failures, which may be of equal importance, is not communicated to other practitioners. Another problem with case histories is failure to report valid and reliable data to support conclusions. Exaggerated claims of success become common in the absence of hard data (Barlow and Hersen 1984). Finally, with no controls, these studies fail to consider the possible impact of extraneous variables on the client.

So it was against this backdrop of unsatisfactory research techniques for clinical settings that the clinical research model emerged. The **clinical research** or **empirical practice model** became an effort to merge research and practice, and it includes much more than single-system designs. It involves a stance toward practice that is defined by the following characteristics (Siegel 1984):

1. Maximum use is made of research findings for understanding human service practice issues.
2. Data is collected systematically to monitor the intervention.
3. Interventions are evaluated empirically to determine their degree of effectiveness.
4. Problems, interventions, and outcomes are specified in terms that are concrete, observable, and measurable.

5. Research ways of thinking and research methods are employed in defining clients' problems, formulating questions for practice, collecting assessment data, evaluating effectiveness of interventions, and using evidence.
6. Research and practice are viewed as parts of the same problem-solving process.
7. Research is accepted as a tool to be used in practice.

The systematic evaluation of practice through the use of single-system designs is a core component of this model of practice. Through the mechanism of single-system designs, research and practice merge into one enterprise. It should be noted, however, that this approach does not reject traditional large-group research, which is still necessary for testing total programs and for confirming the generalizability of intervention effectiveness.

The Clinical Research Process

At the outset, we wish to make clear that the clinical research model is not a radically new approach to intervention. In fact, many parallels exist between this model and traditional practice, and many practitioners are likely to do much of what the model calls for anyway. The model does, however, inject greater specificity, objectivity, and empiricism into the clinical process. By following the model, the clinician–researcher is in a position to know precisely what treatment was applied and how much effect was produced, along with supporting data for proof. The model links research and practice by putting the practitioner in the enviable position of not only bringing about change but also having valid evidence as to why the change occurred. What follows in this section is an outline of the clinical research process divided into six stages, which are summarized in Figure 11.1.

Identify Problems

Like all practice approaches, the clinical research model begins with an assessment of the client's prob-

Figure 11.1 Steps in the Clinical Research Process

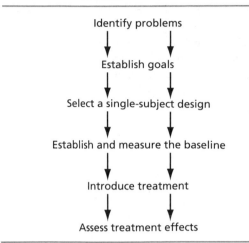

Identify problems

↓   ↓

Establish goals

↓   ↓

Select a single-subject design

↓   ↓

Establish and measure the baseline

↓   ↓

Introduce treatment

↓   ↓

Assess treatment effects

lem. Typically, the problem involves some aspect of the client's functioning: behaviors, perceptions, attitudes, or feelings. During the initial stage, the practitioner strives to obtain as clear and specific an understanding of the problem as possible through commonly used assessment strategies, such as interviewing or paper-and-pencil assessment tools.

Establish Goals

After the problem is identified, the next step is to determine treatment goals. At this point we encounter the first real difference between the clinical research model and traditional practice. The model requires, first, that goals be more specific and precisely defined than is often done in conventional practice and, second, that they be measurable in some way (Kazdin 1982). Although these requirements of specificity and measurability are more rigorous under the clinical research model than in traditional practice, they are best seen as an extension of normal practice procedures rather than as something strangely different. As to the requirement of measurability of outcomes, some practitioners argue that some beneficial outcomes of intervention are so subtle as to be unmeasurable. Countering this attitude in the field of social work is "The First Rule of EPM" (Empirical Practice

Model): "There is and can be no such thing as effectiveness until there is measurable positive change in the client's problem" (Nugent, Sieppert, and Hudson 2001, p. 3). The self-delusion is believing that a real but unmeasurable change has occurred when actually it has not. Effectiveness requires desired, positive change in the level of the client's problem.

One common difficulty in establishing goals is that goals are often long-term, making it impractical for the clinician–researcher to monitor progress all the way to achievement of the final goal. In these cases, it may be necessary to identify proximate, intermediate goals whose achievement is evidence of progress toward the final goal. For example, the final goal for an underachiever might be improved academic performance—a long-term goal. Proximate goals that would evidence progress might include improved note taking, longer study hours, and more regular class attendance. Achievement of these proximate goals would be expected to relate to achievement of the final goal. Which measurable, intermediate goals can serve as valid indicators of long-term goals depends, of course, on a theoretical understanding of the long-term changes sought through intervention.

Select a Single-System Design

Once a problem and a corresponding goal for intervention have been identified, the next phase of the clinical research process is to select an appropriate single-system design. Whereas the general principle of single-system research consists of comparing a series of pre- and postintervention measurements, many variations on this basic scheme exist. Later in the chapter we present several common designs and discuss their strengths and limitations. At this point, however, we simply want to note that we can choose from many design options; we also want to point out that early in the process, the practitioner should be thinking about the design choices that will best suit the goals and constraints of a particular clinical case. For example, if his or her primary objective is to provide treatment and simply monitor the client's progress, then a simple design is adequate. For a general behavior deficit where the proposed intervention involves working on increasing the desired behavior in different realms of the client's life, such as at home, in school, and when visiting with friends, more complicated designs take advantage of such an intervention strategy both to monitor client behavior and to maximize validity for research goals.

The point is that single-system designs are flexible and adaptive to many practice situations. Taking advantage of this flexibility requires the practitioner to have a clear notion of the problem to be addressed, an understanding of how the proposed intervention is supposed to effect changes, and an awareness of single-system design strengths and limitations. Once a particular design is chosen, the practitioner can address the next step in the clinical research process—establishing and measuring a baseline.

Establish and Measure the Baseline

Single-system designs are based on the quasi-experimental time-series designs discussed in Chapter 10 but are modified to make them more appropriate for use with a single subject. As such, single-system designs call for repeated measures of the client's condition so that trends and changes can be noted. Typically, the frequency, intensity, or duration of some behavior of the client is measured, such as how many cigarettes are smoked, the severity of pain, or how long a depression lasts.

Thus, the fourth step in the clinical research process is to establish a **baseline**, or a series of measurements of the client's condition prior to treatment and the basis from which to compare the client's condition after treatment is implemented. By comparing measurements after treatment with those of the baseline period, the clinician can trace the effect the treatment is having. Typically, three measurements are needed as an absolute minimum to establish a baseline (Barlow and Hersen 1973). More measurements are better, especially if the variable's condition is unstable. It is important to note that all single-system designs rule out the simple procedure of using only two measurements—one pretest and one posttest—because this results in a preexperimental design that is extremely weak on internal validity (see Design P1 in Chapter 10).

Figure 11.2   Hypothetical Baseline Followed by Successful Treatment

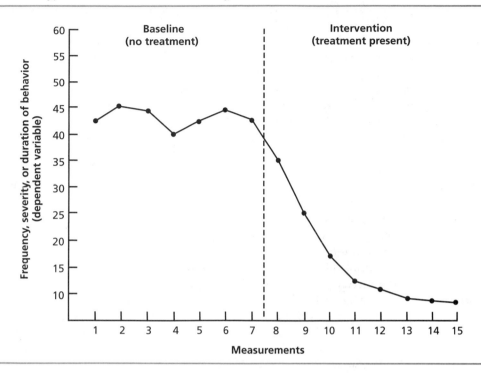

Figure 11.2 illustrates how baseline measurement can serve as a basis for assessing treatment effects. The hypothetical data show a high level of undesirable client behavior prior to treatment. After treatment is instigated, this level drops sharply. Results are not always as dramatic as these, so making interpretations can be more difficult. We deal with the issue of assessing treatment effects in more detail later.

Two major issues in establishing the baseline are (1) what to measure and (2) how to measure it. Typically, the clinical problem itself suggests the appropriate trait to measure. In general, what we seek to change through treatment is what we need to measure. For example, a child whose problem is disruptive behavior in school could be monitored as to the frequency of disruptions he or she causes each day. On the other hand, treatment philosophy might suggest monitoring frequency of *appropriate* behavior as a means of not only measuring behavior but also setting the stage for change. (As emphasized in Chapter 5, measurement and operational definitions

should be deduced from theoretical concepts, whether or not those concepts emerge from research or practice theories.)

Client problems without specific behavioral outcomes or manifestations are more difficult to measure (Bloom, Fischer, and Orme 1999). Depression, for example, can be displayed in many different behavioral forms, and in such cases it is preferable to use several measures. Also, where such an indirect link exists between a concept and behavioral manifestations, multiple indicators help reduce the effects of error in those measures. For depression, we might establish a separate baseline for a behavioral indicator (say, percentage of day spent alone), a paper-and-pencil measure of depression, and a self-report from the client for his or her subjective assessment. If the treatment produced positive gains on all measures, we would have greater evidence of the treatment's effectiveness than if we relied on only one indicator.

Having decided on what aspects of the client's condition to measure, we confront the issue of how to measure them. Basically, the clinician–researcher has four choices: observation, existing records, paper-and-pencil measures, and client self-reports. Of these, observation is of the most general utility and is the most valid and reliable (Jayaratne and Levy 1979; Weiss and Frohman 1985).

Unfortunately, many client problems are not directly observable, so there is a limit to the applicability of observation. When it is used, however, there are three important considerations. (These issues regarding observation were discussed in greater detail in Chapter 9.) First, the observations should be unobtrusive. If they are not, the client may behave differently due to the presence of the observers. This could result in faulty baseline data, which could obscure treatment effects. Second, multiple observers should be used where possible to assess the extent of observer reliability. In some cases, videotapes might be substituted for multiple observers, but in natural settings their use is likely to be difficult. Third, if possible, observers should not be aware of when treatment is begun. If they are, their expectations for improvement might affect their objectivity. For example, borderline behaviors that were counted as disruptive during the baseline phase might be ignored during the treatment phase, thus tending to overstate the apparent effectiveness of the treatment to reduce disruptive behavior.

A second measurement approach is existing records. Some client problems relate to matters on which people other than the clinician or client routinely gather data. For example, existing records, such as grades and school attendance, are often used in assessing a child's school performance. Where existing records are appropriate, they are often a good choice. They are unobtrusive because they are collected whether the client is under treatment or not. Furthermore, because persons other than the clinician–researcher collected them, time and cost factors are likely to be favorable. (We reviewed problems associated with using existing records for research purposes in Chapter 8.)

A third common measurement approach is paper-and-pencil measures, often useful when the client's problem does not lend itself to direct observation. If the decision is made to use a paper-and-pencil measure, it is advisable to use an existing one, if available, rather than to devise a new one. In addition to the practical benefits of avoiding the time and trouble of developing a new measure, existing measures usually have established levels of validity and reliability. Furthermore, their use contributes to the accumulation of knowledge because the standardized measuring devices make for greater comparability across studies. Fortunately, a large number of measures are available, covering a wide array of client problems. The following are only some of the compilations of such measures: Groth-Marnat 1984; Mitchell 1985; Magura and Moses 1986; Corcoran and Fischer 2000; Fredman and Sherman 1987; Miller and Salkind 2002; Plake, Impara, and Spies 2003; and Zalaquett and Wood 1997. Other sources are available on the Internet, including Health & Psychosocial Instruments (HaPI) from Ovid Technologies at www.ovid.com/site/products.

Paper-and-pencil measures have some characteristics that make them less than ideal for use in single-system designs, however. First, they are obtrusive because clients obviously know they are being measured, and this can create many problems. For example, completing a questionnaire concerning family relationships might make parents aware that they have been paying less attention to their children than they should, and this awareness could change their behavior. (Recall from Chapter 10 that this is the "testing" threat to internal validity in experiments. Although such change may be desirable, the problem from a research standpoint is that it is not possible to determine if the treatment or the measurement process caused the change.)

The second problem with paper-and-pencil measures is that of *demand characteristics* (also discussed in Chapter 10). Clients may deliberately change responses in the direction indicating improvement because of a desire to fulfill the expectations of the clinician for improvement. Furthermore, frequent exposure to the measure makes the client familiar with it and raises the specter of multiple-testing effects (see Chapter 10). The same issues appear to apply to computerized administration. A study comparing paper-and-pencil testing versus computerized testing found no difference in social desirability effects between the two modes of testing (Fox and Schwartz 2002). Finally, some paper-and-pencil measures are projective tests, such as the Rorschach Inkblot Test, the Thematic Apperception Test, sentence completion tests, and figure drawings. These tests all rely heavily on the examiner's interpretation of client responses. After reviewing the evidence, Barlow and Hersen (1984) strongly advised against the use of such measures because they do not have sufficient validity and reliability to provide a sound basis for single-system experiments.

The last measurement alternative is self-reports by clients who monitor their own behavior or feelings. Although clients' perceptions of their condition are important, many problems are associated with overreliance on self-reports.

First, evidence shows that self-reports do not correlate well with objective indicators. For example, studies of assertiveness among female college students have made use of subjects' own reports of how assertive they are and of trained observers' assessments of how assertively these people actually behave. Generally, researchers find that the self-reports do not correlate with the observers' assessments (Frisch and Higgins 1986).

Second, self-monitoring is reactive because it sensitizes the client to some aspect of his or her behavior (Barlow et al. 1992). Research has shown that the mere process of monitoring can change one's behavior. In one study, for example, objective baselines were gathered on how many cigarettes were consumed by a group of smokers (McFall 1970). Half the subjects were then asked to monitor and record the extent of their smoking. The other half was to keep track of the times when they didn't smoke. Both groups showed a change from their baseline levels but in the opposite direction. Those monitoring their smoking smoked more, and those monitoring their nonsmoking smoked less!

Similar self-monitoring effects have been noted concerning study habits among college students (Johnson and White 1971). This phenomenon has been put to use in a variety of treatment programs that include self-monitoring as the intervention that brings about behavior change. This effect, however, is hardly desirable when the goal is to assess the effects of treatments other than self-monitoring. Because of the multitude of problems associated with self-report data, such measurements should be used with caution, preferably as an adjunct to other measures that are less subject to false reports.

Thus, it is evident that some of the measurement options available to clinician–researchers are better than others, and so the most objective, valid, and reliable measure available in a given research context should be selected. As noted, direct observation is usually best if the client's problem lends itself to such observation. Otherwise, a more indirect measure is necessary, although these do have limitations. However, by using multiple measures, the weaknesses of the indirect measures can be reduced and the quality of the single-system experiment improved (Gottman 1985).

Introduce Treatment

Once the baseline is established, the next stage in the clinical research process is to begin treatment. It is important to the clinical research model that only a *single,* coherent treatment be applied (Barlow and Hersen 1984) because each application of the model is essentially an experiment, with the treatment the independent variable in that experiment. If more than one treatment is used and the client exhibits behavior change in comparison to the baseline, we do not know which treatment produced the change and cannot learn anything that might be valuable with similar clients in the future. To assess the effects of the independent variable, we must be able to specify precisely what the treatment consisted of and also to be consistent in its application during the treatment phase.

The demand for a single, specific treatment is one aspect of the clinical research model that has led to a cold reception in some human service circles, particularly among nonbehaviorists (Nelsen 1981). Nonbehavioral treatments often lack the specificity that allows practitioners to trace a particular treatment over the period of the treatment phase. In addition, nonbehavioral treatments can be very complex and may even mix a number of treatment modes, making it difficult to identify the precise factors that presumably resulted in change. However, this is less a criticism of the clinical research model than a challenge to those using nonbehavioral treatments:"[Nonbehaviorists] must work hard at choosing interventions that may be effective and at defining their interventions precisely, preferably by addressing both what they do and how they do it" (Nelsen 1981, p. 35).

Resistance to the discipline imposed by the clinical research model appears to be greatest among those who are least familiar with it. After some initial frustration with the specificity and single treatment required by the model, practitioners learning to apply the model generally come to accept it (Johnson 1981). They come to appreciate that the model increases rationality in the selection of treatments, forces explicit consideration of the assumptions on which treatment is based, and requires specific practice skills rather than reliance solely on intuition or ingenuity. The greatest satisfaction, however, comes from the fact that the model provides solid evidence regarding whether the client benefited from treatment. Although it is rewarding to feel that one has been of assistance, it is even more rewarding to have objective evidence to support those feelings.

During the treatment phase, the measurement of the client's condition, started during the baseline phase, continues to track what changes (if any) the treatment is producing in the client's condition. It is crucial that the conditions under which measurements are made during the treatment phase remain consistent with those under which the baseline measurements were obtained (Jayaratne and Levy 1979). Any change in such things as observers, settings, examiners, or instructions could confound apparent treatment effects. Remember that a single-system design is an experiment, and only one variable—the treatment—should be allowed to change from one phase to another.

Assess Treatment Effects

When is a treatment judged to be effective? This seemingly simple question, which is addressed in the last stage of the clinical research process, has a surprisingly complex answer. Assessing effectiveness de-

Figure 11.3 Types of Baseline Patterns

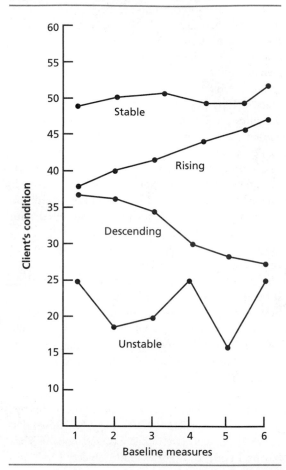

pends, first of all, on the pattern produced during the baseline measurements: The ease and clarity with which baseline measures can be compared with treatment measures depends in part on the *stability* of the baseline measures.

Figure 11.3 illustrates four possible baseline patterns: (1) a stable baseline, (2) a rising trend (client worsening), (3) a descending trend (client improving), and (4) an unstable baseline. In this discussion of baseline stability, we will assume that lower measurement scores represent improvement, as in the case of reducing the incidence of some problem behavior. If the goal of treatment is to increase some aspect of client functioning, as it often is, higher measurement scores indicate improvement. A stable baseline is the ideal because posttreatment comparisons then readily reveal treatment effects. If the treatment is helpful, we see a pronounced downward move in measurement levels. A treatment producing negative effects yields an upward move in measurement levels. And little change from baseline levels reveals ineffective treatment. The value of a stable baseline is that it allows all three possible treatment outcomes to be readily noted.

Unfortunately, client conditions are often not stable but worsen, improve, or vary considerably. Assessing treatment effects with baselines like these is more difficult and often puts limits on what we can infer. A baseline with a rising trend (client worsening) is not too problematic because an effective treatment will produce a reversal of the baseline trend. Such a change provides strong evidence that the treatment was effective. With ineffective or harmful treatments, however, it is difficult to tell if this is just a continuation of the baseline trend (ineffective treatment) or if the continued deterioration is due to some harmful treatment. A baseline with a decreasing trend, showing client improvement, has the opposite effect. If the treatment proves harmful, the trend reverses, and the negative effect becomes readily apparent. But if the client continues to improve during treatment, it is unclear whether the treatment produced that improvement (effective treatment) or whether it was just a continuation of the baseline trend (ineffective treatment).

The unstable baseline is the most troublesome. With the client's condition changing from one measurement to another, it becomes difficult to identify changes due to treatment. A couple of strategies do exist, however, for dealing with an unstable baseline (Barlow and Hersen 1984). One extends the period of baseline measurements with the hope that a stable pattern will emerge—with, of course, no guarantee of stabilization. In addition, we may find practical as well as ethical constraints on how long treatment can be postponed while awaiting baseline stability. A second strategy is the application of statistical techniques that can reveal trends and differences between pre- and posttreatment that are too subtle to be noted by visual inspection

(Achen 1986; Gottman 1981). These statistics have limited effectiveness, however, if the pattern is extremely unstable.

The use of statistics to assess treatment effects also raises a problem beyond that of baseline stability—namely, how much change is necessary before we can say a treatment is effective. From a research perspective, any change from pretest to posttest measures is evidence that the treatment was effective in the sense of bringing about change in the dependent variable. However, in clinical settings, change can take the form of improvement or deterioration in a client's status. Practitioners seek improvement, of course, so treatment effectiveness in single-system designs is normally defined as an improvement in performance after treatment. Yet assessing whether improvement has occurred is complex because effectiveness can be based on three different criteria: therapeutic, experimental, or statistical.

A treatment is *therapeutically effective* when it leads clients to fully achieve the goals set for them. The disruptive student is no longer disruptive, the underachiever is now achieving, or the teenage mother can care for her infant independently. When treatment produces these kinds of improvements, its effectiveness is obvious. Visual inspection of the measurements taken during the treatment phase clearly reveals the improvement when compared with the baseline measurements.

A treatment is *experimentally effective* when it produces a pronounced improvement in the client's condition even though the ultimate goals have not been reached. For example, a claustrophobic person may have come to the point where he or she can use an elevator alone but remains unable to use a crowded one. As with therapeutic effectiveness, the change in the client's condition from baseline to treatment phase is sufficiently dramatic that visual inspection is normally adequate to reveal it. Figure 11.4 displays two data plots from single-system designs conducted in a school classroom.

In the first case, the teacher monitored disruptive classroom behavior. The second case represents a child in kindergarten who had difficulty adjusting to school. The problem was monitored by counting the number of requests she made during school to

Figure 11.4 Establishing Experimental Effectiveness in Single-System Research

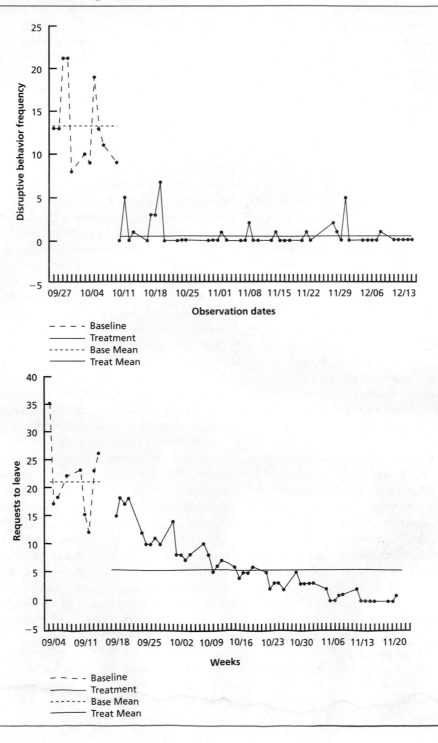

go home. These cases illustrate two criteria for establishing experimental effectiveness (Kazdin 1982). The first case has nonoverlapping data. All the measurements taken during the treatment phase are higher or lower (whichever direction represents improvement) than those taken during the baseline phase. Stated another way, performance during treatment does not overlap with that of the baseline period. This is a fairly severe guideline and one that, if met, is a strong demonstration of experimental effectiveness. The criterion achieved by the second case is somewhat less rigorous: All the measurements taken during the treatment phase are higher or lower than the *average* level of the baseline. This guideline is preferable if the baseline is not especially stable, but it is important to emphasize that these are only guidelines, not rigid rules. Quite possibly, a given single-system experiment could evidence clear experimental effectiveness and achieve neither of these guidelines. Following them, however, does make visual inspection more systematic and less a matter of judgment on the part of the clinician–researcher.

Statistical effectiveness is achieved when the treatment produces statistically significant improvement in the client's condition. In other words, the difference between baseline and treatment levels is sufficiently large that it is not likely to be due to chance variation. (We will discuss the concept of statistical significance in detail in Chapter 15.) In addition to the magnitude of the difference between baseline and intervention, the number of observations in each phase also determines statistical significance— more is better. So assuming a relatively large number of observations in each phase, say 20 or more, statistics may be sufficiently sensitive to detect smaller changes than visual inspection can. With many observations in each phase, statistical effectiveness sometimes requires the least improvement in the client to detect change.

This raises the issue of the difference between statistical significance and therapeutic or experimental significance. A treatment judged to be effective because it produced a statistically significant improvement in the client might be a near failure according to the other criteria. For example, reducing a juvenile fire-starter's behavior from seven episodes

a week to three might be a statistically significant reduction, but we would hardly call the treatment a rousing success. Because statistical significance may be only remotely related to treatment success, statistical analysis is most useful in cases with an unstable baseline, where visual analysis is difficult. Because single-system designs involve repeated measurement of the same subject, data generated by such designs may exhibit "serial dependency" or "autocorrelation." Autocorrelation may be thought of as pattern in the data whereby later observation values can be predicted from earlier ones. Without going into great detail, many statistical procedures assume that data are independent from one another. For example, if you flip a coin nine times and you get nine heads, the probability of getting a head on the tenth flip is still 50-50 because coin flips are independent. If we use a depression inventory to measure 20 clients who have been taking an antidepressant drug, we would not expect scores to decrease systematically from the first subject to the last. However, when we take 20 daily measurements on one subject, we might well see an association or pattern from earlier scores to later ones on this one subject. Such autocorrelation violates a key assumption of many statistical tests and may result in erroneously concluding that a statistically significant change has occurred. There is considerable debate among statisticians on the problem of autocorrelation and how to deal with it, which go beyond the scope of this text. (See Bloom, Fischer, and Orme 1999 for a complete discussion.) One recommendation is to rely on visual analysis. A second is to conduct statistical tests but interpret the results conservatively. Another alternative is to use statistical procedures that do not require the assumption of independence or that control for trend and cycles in the data. Several such procedures, specifically designed for analyzing single-system data, are available (see Achen 1986; Barlow and Hersen 1984; Gottman 1981; Jayaratne and Levy 1979; Kazdin 1982; and Marascuilo and Busk 1988).

So we see that the question of treatment effectiveness depends in part on the particular criterion of effectiveness applied. With the varying criteria, it is important to be aware of their differences and to

RESEARCH IN PRACTICE 11.1

PRACTICE EFFECTIVENESS:

Protecting Human Subjects and Single-System Designs

The linkages between practice and research emphasized throughout this text are especially strong in the case of single-system designs. However, as desirable as the fusion between practice and research may be, blurring boundaries between the two can cause confusion in the area of ethical responsibilities and raise questions concerning the protection of human subjects in practice. For example, how do such principles as informed consent (discussed in Chapter 3) apply to conducting single-system evaluations of practice? If systematic evaluation is an integral part of service delivery, does the practitioner need to obtain approval from an institutional review board (IRB) before implementing an *AB* design as a means of documenting client progress, or is such routine evaluation exempt from review? Every practitioner who seeks to employ systematic evaluation must address questions like these.

Although research and practice evaluation may involve many of the same procedures (such as measurement via direct observation or the use of standardized scales), several writers argue that it is important in terms of ethical conduct to distinguish between research and evaluation. Judith Nelsen (1994) makes a primary distinction between practice models in which objective monitoring of target problems is routine (such as behavioral and task-centered models) and other models in which clients do not expect to participate in objective measure-

ment (such as psychosocial or family treatment). She argues that where routine, systematic monitoring is part of the normal service delivery, the evaluation is an integral part of practice and is therefore part of practice rather than research. Research ethics issues arise in cases where practitioners or students want to do monitoring that their practice model does not ordinarily require. For example, which clients get selected for special monitoring? To what extent does the client have the right to refuse additional monitoring or observation? Do issues of gender or racial bias influence which cases get selected for special monitoring? Nelsen suggests that such concerns may require that informed consent be exercised in these cases and possibly even formal IRB review required.

Grigsby and Roof (1993) directly address the issue of IRB involvement. Like Nelsen, they distinguish between evaluation and research. They argue that the principle of generalizability is the distinction between evaluation (to determine whether the client's condition has improved over time and conducted for the benefit of client and practitioner) and research (to pursue knowledge for its own sake or to generalize knowledge). They argue that evaluation of practice using single-system designs is not research as technically defined in federal regulations. However, the matter is not entirely clear-cut. If evaluation data, originally collected as part of practice evaluation, are subsequently used to make

be precise when discussing what we mean by effectiveness. Furthermore, it is important to recognize that the effect of a treatment may be relatively permanent, or the effect may decrease after treatment is withdrawn. To test for this, the posttreatment measurements become, in effect, a new baseline. Deviation from this baseline as time passes suggests a limit to how long the treatment is effective.

Before turning to a discussion of the various types of single-system designs, Research in Practice

11.1 addresses some of the special ethical considerations that arise in this kind of research.

Types of Single-System Designs

Although numerous types of single-system designs exist, all involve repeated measurements during baseline and treatment phases and a comparison across phases as evidence of treatment effects. The generalizations and printed in any publications to report the generalizations, then IRB review would be required. Grigsby and Roof recommend that clinicians and researchers who use evaluation designs be encouraged to inform potential subjects from the outset that their records may be used for research purposes and that they be given the opportunity to consent or object to the use of their individual records. The basic principle that triggers the need for IRB involvement is the intent of the practitioner–researcher to contribute to generalizable knowledge beyond the particular case by publishing the results of the evaluation.

Bloom and Orme (1993) advocate for the routine use of systematic evaluation in practice. To enhance the ethical implementation of evaluation as part of practice, they offer a set of 10 principles to ethically implement single-system designs in practice. They also provide a model consent form as a way of operationalizing them:

1. Provide demonstrable help. The clinician-researcher should be able to document that actual improvement or help has been delivered.
2. Demonstrate that no harm is done.
3. Because evaluation is intrinsic to good practice, involve the client in the evaluation of his or her situation while coming to agreement on the overall practice relationship.
4. Involve the client in the identification of the specific problem and/or objective and in the data-collection process, as far as possible.
5. Evaluation should enhance practice, not impede it. Evaluation should intrude as little as possible on the intervention process while still collecting useful and usable information.
6. Stop evaluation whenever it is painful or harmful to the client, physically, psychologically or socially, without prejudice to the services offered.
7. Maintain confidentiality with regard to the data that result from evaluation of the client/situation.
8. Balance the benefits of evaluating practice against the costs of not evaluating practice.
9. A client bill of rights is an intrinsic part of a code of ethics for evaluating practice.
10. Evaluation should be part of any formal or informal theory of practice; it should also be recognized that any evaluation process reflects the values of the researcher.

Use of the model consent form that Bloom and Orme provide serves as one mechanism to safeguard clients from ethical risks; Nelsen also advocates for the use of such a procedure. She goes on to suggest that human subject review committees should be formed for immediate review within settings where single-case research or objective evaluation of practice will occur. Such review committees would help ensure that implementation of the principles identified by Bloom and Orme not rest solely in the hands of the practitioner conducting the evaluation. By distinguishing clearly between practice evaluation and research and by consistent application of ethical principles, the enterprises of both research and practice may be pursued while ensuring that the rights of service users are protected.

---

designs differ in the number of phases involved, the number of treatments applied, and the number of baselines employed. Perhaps the most important differences are in the internal validity of the designs. Some are more capable of providing evidence for the effect of a treatment when such an effect actually exists. Ideally, of course, clinician–researchers should select the most valid design that fits their particular case (see discussions of validity in Chapters 5 and 10).

Single-Treatment Designs

The Basic *AB* Design.   It has become customary to present single-system designs by using the first letters of the alphabet to symbolize various phases of the design. The letter *A* signifies a phase in which the client is not receiving treatment. This is the baseline period in all designs, but it can also refer to a period of treatment withdrawal in some of the more complex designs. The letter *B* indicates a treatment phase during which some specific intervention is in progress. Subsequent letters of the alphabet, *C, D,* and so on, symbolize the application of treatments different from *B.*

The *AB design* is the simplest of the single-system designs and forms the basis for the others. The *AB* design consists of one baseline phase followed by one treatment phase. Treatment effectiveness is determined by comparing the client's condition during treatment with that of the baseline. The basic *AB* design is less than ideal because its validity is threatened by history: Events other than the intervention could be responsible for the change in the client. Despite the limitations of the *AB* design, it provides better evidence of treatment effects than nonexperimental case histories. The *AB* design also has the advantage of applying to most clinical situations, especially to cases where more rigorous designs might be precluded.

Reversal and Withdrawal Designs.

The *AB* design can be strengthened substantially by moving to a *reversal* or *withdrawal design,* so called because, after one treatment phase, the treatment is interrupted for a period of time. Some sources distinguish between a withdrawal design (in which the treatment stops entirely after the first intervention phase) and a reversal design (in which the treatment is transferred to a different behavior). For example, a juvenile in a residential facility may participate in a token economy study on completing math homework. After a baseline period, he receives tokens each day for an intervention period based on the number of math problems he completes. In a withdrawal design, giving tokens is terminated (withdrawn) for another baseline. If a reversal design is used, tokens might be made contingent on a different behavior (reversed) such as pages of English read, while the number of math problems completed continues to be monitored for the study. We use the term "reversal design" to apply to both approaches in this discussion. There are basically two versions of the reversal design: *ABA* and *ABAB;* they differ only in that the *ABA* design ends in a no-treatment phase, whereas in the *ABAB* design the treatment is reintroduced a second time (see Figure 11.5).

The value of reversal designs stems from their ability to demonstrate more conclusively that the

treatment (not some extraneous factor) is producing change in the client's condition. If the client's condition deteriorates when the treatment is withdrawn, we have evidence that the treatment is the controlling factor. Even more evidence is provided with the *ABAB* design if the reintroduction of the treatment coincides with renewed improvement of the client. Although it is possible for a set of extraneous factors to produce the first client improvement, it is less likely that the same set of factors would recur at precisely the right time to produce improvement on reintroduction of the treatment. As Figure 11.5 illustrates, especially with the *ABAB* design, we have great confidence in the efficacy of a treatment that produces similar real-life results. In certain circumstances, the design can be expanded to include even more phases.

Despite their strengths on internal validity, practical considerations often restrict the use of reversal designs. First, treatments that produce permanent changes in clients—often the goal of intervention—are not reversible. For example, if the treatment involves clients' learning something, it is obvious that they cannot "unlearn" it at the command of the clinician–researcher. In such cases, reversal designs are simply not applicable. Second, it might be unwise or unethical to attempt to return clients to their pretreatment states. An obvious example would be a case where the suicidal tendencies of a client were alleviated. It is up to the clinician–researcher to decide on a case-by-case basis whether a reversal design is ethically justified.

Multiple-Baseline Designs.

The *multiple-baseline design* involves establishing baselines for more than one aspect of a client's condition. Multiple baselines can be established for multiple behaviors, for one behavior in different settings, or for multiple clients who suffer from the same problem. For example, a practitioner working with several alcoholics might establish separate baselines for each, thus applying the multiple-baseline design across individuals. Although it is recommended that a minimum of three baselines be utilized, clinician–researchers should not be deterred from using only two if conditions do not

Figure 11.5   Hypothetical Examples of Reversal Designs

The *ABA* Design

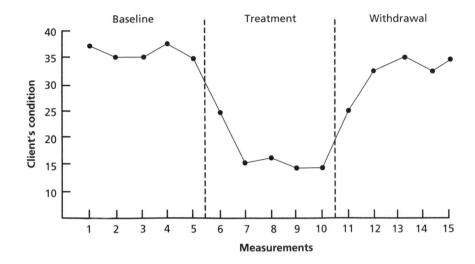

The *ABAB* Design

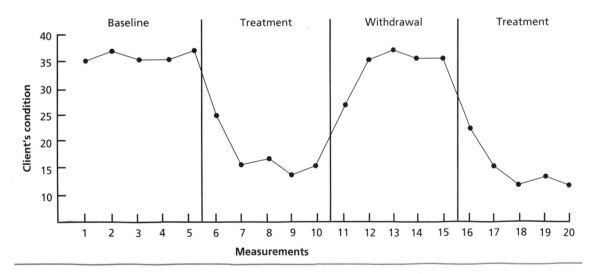

permit more. The more baselines, however, the stronger the design becomes in terms of internal validity (Barlow and Hersen 1984; Jayaratne and Levy 1979).

The multiple-baseline design is essentially a stacked set of *AB* designs, with the same treatment introduced sequentially into each of the baseline conditions:

First client: A_1B
Second client: A_1A_2B
Third client: $A_1A_2A_3B$

In the illustration, the initial baseline measurement (A_1) is made on each client, and then the treatment is introduced to the first client only. A second baseline measurement is taken from the remaining two clients, and then treatment is introduced to the second client.

A third baseline measurement is taken from the third client, who then receives treatment. Figure 11.6 illustrates the multiple-baseline design with a successful outcome. In each of the three conditions, the introduction of the treatment is followed by improvement.

Figure 11.6   Hypothetical Example of Multiple-Baseline Design

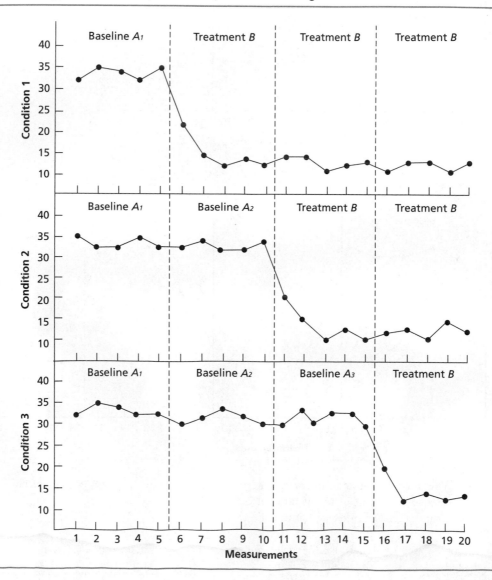

The multiple-baseline design is fairly strong on internal validity. The efficacy of the treatment is assessed across three or more behaviors, settings, or individuals. Furthermore, sequential introduction of treatments makes it highly unlikely that extraneous factors can account for apparent treatment effects across the several baseline conditions. The multiple-baseline design is thus generally superior to the *AB* design, but the *AB* design with replication also overcomes some of the threats to internal validity, such as history (Harris and Jenson 1985). The multiple-baseline design is not as strong on internal validity as reversal designs; but where reversal designs are inappropriate, the multiple-baseline design is a good alternative.

Multiple-baseline designs can provide strong evidence for the validity of single-system outcomes, as Research in Practice 11.2 illustrates. They do have weaknesses, however. The seepage of treatment effects from one setting to another is a major limitation of the multiple-baseline design. The behaviors, settings, or individuals traced by the several baselines must be relatively independent, or else the treatment effects in one condition can produce changes in other, as yet untreated conditions. For example, it would be unwise to attempt a multiple-baseline design with members of the same family. Because of their routine interaction, treatment applied to one family member could affect the others. If the baseline conditions are highly interrelated, the treatment will show effects after the initial introduction not only in the condition where it is applied but also in one or more of the other conditions as well. If interrelatedness is sufficiently severe, the power of the multiple-baseline design can be destroyed, rendering it little more than an *AB* design with multiple indicators.

The multiple-baseline design also can reveal *contra-variation:* positive changes in one area but negative changes in another (Jayaratne and Levy 1979). For example, a multiple-drug abuser might respond to treatment by reducing intake of one substance but increasing intake of another. If we traced only one drug, perhaps the most dangerous, the contra-variation would remain undetected. A multiple-baseline design covering all the abuser's drugs would readily reveal such an occurrence.

Specialized Designs

The designs we have just discussed comprise the simplest and most generally useful single-system designs and have in common the use of only a single treatment (although applied more than once in the *ABAB* design). However, some situations call for variations of these simpler designs to handle special

RESEARCH IN PRACTICE 11.2

PRACTICE EFFECTIVENESS:

A Multiple-Baseline Evaluation of Treating Panic Disorder

"It just happened . . . I was walking and all of a sudden my heart started to beat fast and I started to sweat . . . I didn't know what was going on . . . I just felt weird . . . that something bad was happening to me but I didn't know what."

(Quoted in Ollendick 1995, p. 217)

These are the words of a 14-year-old adolescent describing her first panic attack, a condition characterized by periods of intense fear or discomfort in which certain somatic and cognitive symptoms develop abruptly. Imagine the concern that such experiences raises for a person, wondering what caused it and when it might happen again, as well as suffering the embarrassment of behaving in such a bizarre manner.

One research project set out to evaluate the effectiveness of cognitive behavioral treatments on panic disorders in adolescents. The researcher chose the multiple-baseline design because it is

continued on next page

superior to the *AB* design in reducing the threat of history while still providing a detailed record of individual process through treatment (Ollendick 1995). The particular research design was a multiple-baseline across subjects. Four adolescents who were being seen at an outpatient clinic specializing in anxiety disorders of children and adolescents participated in the study. The subjects were evaluated on several screening instruments, and each met full criteria for panic disorder with agoraphobia. They reported that "they sometimes felt really scared, for no reason at all, that out of the blue they felt really scared and that they didn't know why," and that there were places that they didn't want to go because they were afraid they "would get scared all of a sudden and couldn't get help or get away." The researchers hypothesized that the cognitive behavioral treatments found effective among adults in treating such conditions would also prove effective with adolescents.

Multiple measures were used to assess the effectiveness of treatment. One indicator was the frequency of panic attacks. The adolescents were asked to monitor the date, time duration, location, circumstance, and symptoms experienced, using a Panic Attack Record (PAR) based on a recording format that the researcher located in the literature (Rapee, Craske, and Barlow 1990). This provided a weekly measure of the frequency of panic attacks. Another indicator was self-efficacy in coping with three potential agoraphobic situations included in one of the screening tests used during assessment. Subjects were asked to rate from 1 to 5 how sure they were that they could cope with situations (1 = not at all sure, 5 = definitely sure). The subjects considered three circumstances: simply being in the agoraphobic situation, first noticing some symptoms, and experiencing more intense symptoms. The adolescents were also asked to rate the extent to which they had actually avoided agoraphobic situations, such as going to school, being in an auditorium, or going to restaurants. The self-efficacy and avoidance measures were also modeled on measures in the existing literature (Clum 1990).

Baseline measures were obtained for one week for S1 (Subject 1), for two weeks for S2, three weeks for S3, and four weeks for S4 (see Figure 11.7). Following baseline, a treatment regimen began that included providing information on the nature of panic attacks and training in progressive muscle relaxation and proper breathing techniques. The adolescents learned to use positive self-statements and cognitive coping strategies. Later sessions involved *in vivo* exposure to the situations that had aroused panic symptoms. The actual length of treatment varied from one subject to another based on the termination criterion of two consecutive weeks with an absence of attacks. Brief maintenance sessions were held two weeks and one month following treatment, with a systematic follow-up six months posttreatment.

The data plots for frequency of attacks, agoraphobic avoidance, and self-efficacy provided positive evidence that the treatment was effective in eliminating panic attacks. In addition, standardized self-report measures at pretreatment, posttreatment, and follow-up also showed improvement. The project illustrates several points about single-system designs in support of practice:

- Ollendick relied on the empirical literature to identify promising intervention methods. The literature helped him devise measurement strategies consistent with previous research and likely to be reliable and valid.
- Flexibility of the single-system design permitted this researcher to avoid interference with treatment and permitted documentation of the progress of each case while demonstrating that the intervention was the most likely cause of change.
- By using standardized tests prior to treatment, after treatment, and at the six-month follow-up, the researcher obtained independent, supporting evidence that corroborated the multiple-baseline data. Alone, such a pretest/posttest data are weak but in combination with the multiple-baseline strategy strengthened the entire project.

Figure 11.7 Outcomes Assessment Using a Multiple-Baseline Design

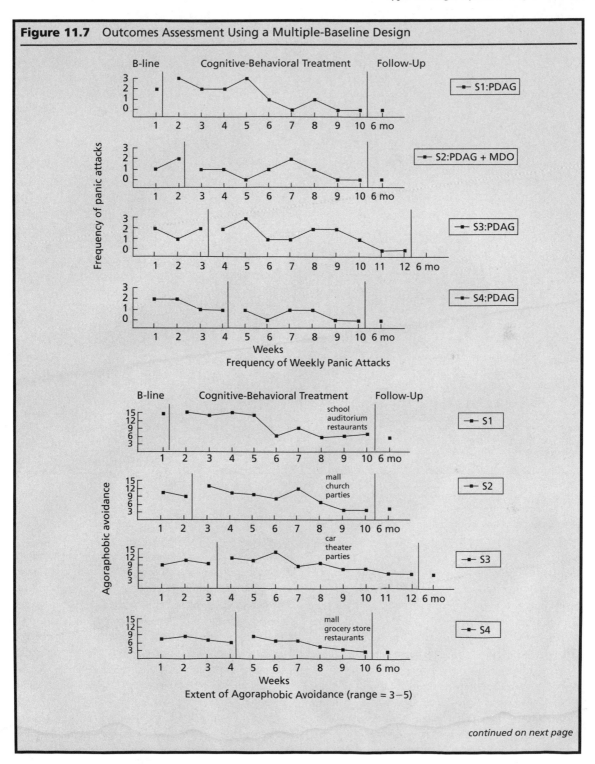

Frequency of Weekly Panic Attacks

Extent of Agoraphobic Avoidance (range = 3–5)

continued on next page

Figure 11.7 Outcomes Assessment Using a Multiple-Baseline Design—Continued

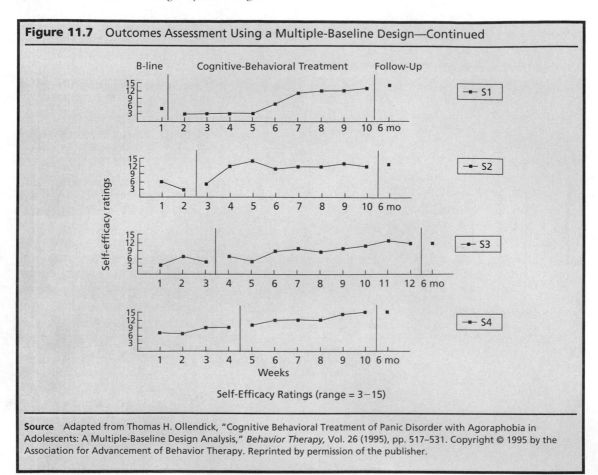

Self-Efficacy Ratings (range = 3–15)

Source Adapted from Thomas H. Ollendick, "Cognitive Behavioral Treatment of Panic Disorder with Agoraphobia in Adolescents: A Multiple-Baseline Design Analysis," *Behavior Therapy,* Vol. 26 (1995), pp. 517–531. Copyright © 1995 by the Association for Advancement of Behavior Therapy. Reprinted by permission of the publisher.

problems. So many complex and specialized designs exist that we can touch on only a few of them here.

Multiple-Treatment Designs. In some settings, the practitioner may need to apply several treatments before finding an effective one. By an extension of the reversal designs, *multiple treatments* can be accommodated. A fairly simple extension is the *ABA-C-A* design. It should be apparent that the *ABA* segment comprises a basic reversal design. To that is added a second treatment phase with treatment *C* instead of *B* and another return-to-baseline phase. This design can be extended to include as many treatments as a given case requires. One important limitation of this design is that it is not pos-

sible to determine which is most effective if both treatments show some effect (Barlow and Hersen 1984). The culprit is history, as extraneous variables occurring during the *B* phase cannot be assumed to be the same as those occurring during the *C* phase.

Special designs can also be used when treatments are not applied individually but in combination to assess the relative effects of the components of the treatment package. The *ABAB-BC-B-BC* design, a complex extension of the reversal designs, accomplishes this. The first part, *ABAB,* is one of the basic reversal designs and provides a strong demonstration of component *B*'s effects. The *BC-B-BC* segment indicates the effects of *C* beyond those of *B* alone. This design can, of course, be extended farther to

Figure 11.8 Hypothetical Example of the Changing-Criterion Design Applied to Phased Withdrawal of Smoking

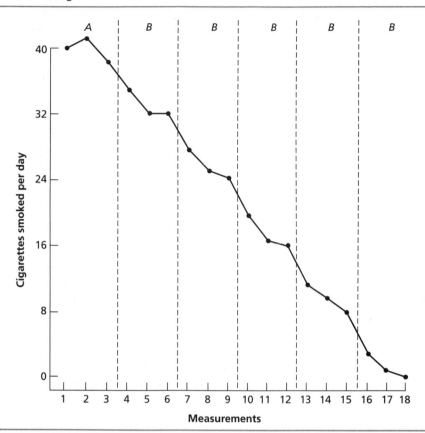

indicate additional treatments. Because both of these design extensions are based on reversal designs, they cannot be used with treatments that are irreversible or unethical to reverse.

Changing-Criterion Designs. Another specialized design with considerable utility is the *changing-criterion design* (Barlow and Hersen 1984). With this design, the goal or criterion of success changes over time as the client is led to attainment of the final treatment goal in stages by achieving a series of subgoals.

For example, a smoker can be brought to the final goal of abstinence through phased withdrawal. Figure 11.8 illustrates what a successful application of such treatment with a changing-criterion design might look like. Following the baseline measurement of cig-

arettes smoked per day, treatment begins. For example, assume the treatment consists of reinforcement. During the first treatment phase, the client is reinforced for achieving the first subgoal—say, a reduction of eight cigarettes per day. In the second treatment phase, reinforcement is received for achieving a reduction of an additional eight cigarettes—the second subgoal. The third treatment phase requires another reduction to receive the reinforcement. The process continues until the client progresses through the subgoals and achieves the final goal of no longer smoking.

The changing-criterion design is related to the multiple-baseline design. In the multiple-baseline design, intervention is independently implemented in relatively distinct areas of the subject's environment. In the changing-criterion design, each time a subgoal is achieved and a new, more stringent subgoal is established, the preceding level essentially becomes a new baseline from which further improvement is measured. Like the multiple-baseline design, the changing-criterion design provides greater evidence of treatment effectiveness than the simple *AB* design. Each time the treatment leads to the achievement of another subgoal, further evidence of its effectiveness is obtained. The only major limitation associated with the changing-criterion design is that it can only be applied to client problems that can be meaningfully broken up into subgoals.

Generalizability of Single-System Designs

To build a knowledge base for clinical practice, researchers must have findings that can be generalized to a wide variety of situations and cases. Of course, *one* successful single-system experiment has little generalizability beyond that particular case. Despite success and hard evidence to prove that the treatment produced change, there is no assurance that the same treatment would be effective on other clients, in different settings, or when used by another practitioner. This lack of generalizability, however, does not detract from the value of single-system experiments because generalizability can be achieved through replication. It requires many replications before we develop a knowledge base concerning which clients can be helped by which treatment, which settings it will work in, and what the clinician must do to apply it successfully. This is a process of slow accretion, as each replication provides a little more knowledge concerning the extent of generalizability of treatment effectiveness.

It is valuable in this context to make a distinction between *direct* and *systematic* replication. **Direct replication** involves the repeated application of the same treatment by the same clinician to clients suffering from the same basic problem. In direct replication, only the individual clients vary, with all other conditions remaining constant. Direct replication serves two important functions. First, it increases confidence in the reliability of the findings. For example, a clinician with a series of successes in treating claustrophobics will have far greater confidence in the effectiveness of

the treatment than he or she did after success with the first case. Second, direct replication builds generalizability across clients. As the treatment repeatedly proves effective with additional clients, we discover that the initial success was not a fluke. Direct replication is the beginning of establishing the generalizability of a treatment. It cannot, however, answer questions concerning generalizability across settings, practitioners, or other client problems.

Systematic replication is the attempt to extend a treatment to different settings, practitioners, or client disorders by varying one of these conditions or any combination of them. It is normally conducted after there is evidence from direct replication that the treatment may work. For example, the clinician mentioned earlier with the successful history of intervention with claustrophobics might begin systematic replication by applying the treatment to agoraphobics. If this is successful, it indicates that the treatment is generalizable to a different client disorder from that with which success was originally obtained. Additional replications that vary settings and clinicians would, of course, be required to establish generalizability across these conditions.

A study of using biofeedback to treat depression (Earnest 1999) provides an example of a successful systematic replication involving different clients. The investigator presented examples of earlier case studies that demonstrated the effectiveness of EEG biofeedback training in treating depression in adults. In this case the intervention method was successfully extended to an adolescent client. Systematic replication with different clients and different therapists was also illustrated by a study on verbal self-guidance (Martini and Polatajko 1998). The authors reported that this intervention had been useful in helping children with developmental coordination disorder. They successfully replicated the intervention using a different therapist with four different children, thus adding further evidence of the potential of this intervention for effective treatment. When the same treatment proves effective in a replication with so many differences from a previous situation, it suggests that the treatment may have broad generalizability. Many more successful replications, of course, are needed before the parameters of effectiveness for this or any other treatment can be firmly established.

When single-system experiments and their replications are conducted, two practices are crucial. First, substantial information about client characteristics and backgrounds should be collected to serve as *control variables* in assessing the complex effects that treatment can have on dependent variables. The necessity for this arises from the fact that replications often show that treatment is not consistently effective or ineffective. The background information may be useful in sorting out the reasons for these mixed results. A simple example would be a treatment that was effective with men but either ineffective or less effective with women.

A second essential practice is that treatments be kept uniform from case to case so that the results of replications are truly comparable. In addition, reports must be clear and include all information relevant for future replication efforts. At the outset, we noted that one source of dissatisfaction with traditional case histories is the tendency of reports to be too vague to allow for replication. The full potential of single-system experiments will not be realized if reports include inadequate information for sound replication.

Assessment of the Clinical Research Model

Advantages

Promotes Better Service for Clients. The requisites of the clinical research model—careful assessment of treatment goals, use of specific treatments, and continuous monitoring of client progress—promote more effective treatment for clients and encourage the use of scientifically tested intervention strategies. The model encourages the application of specific practice skills in a systematic and rational fashion rather than a reliance on personal idiosyncrasy, intuition, or vague and shifting treatment efforts. Furthermore, the model promotes a consideration of the assumptions underlying various treatment approaches, such as why a given treatment should produce positive results with a particular case. The net result is an increased likelihood that a successful intervention will be selected and that the client will be helped.

Promotes Research Activity. The merger of practice and research in the clinical research model allows practitioners to conduct research when they might otherwise not do so. For obvious and practical reasons, the opportunities for most human service practitioners to be involved in traditional group research are limited. The clinical research model makes each client a possible subject for a single-system experiment. In addition, single-system research is more practical for the typical clinician because it is research on a small scale, involving minimal cost and avoiding the complexities of group research. Furthermore, involvement in single-system research can enhance the status of the practitioner because publication of results is often possible. On a broader scale, increased research activity can promote the image of the human services as scientifically based professions.

Results Are of Both Immediate and Future Value. The clinical research model provides hard evidence of a client's progress, which is of immediate value to the practitioner. Tracking progress aids in the selection and application of effective treatments. After successful treatment, the data provide a clear demonstration that the client has been helped. In an age of increasing accountability, vague feelings of having helped clients or even client testimonials are no longer adequate. To document that intervention does work, critics increasingly demand scientifically based evidence, and single-system experiments hold the promise of providing that evidence (Russell 1990).

Disadvantages

Impracticality. Under current practice conditions, application of the clinical research model may often be impractical. Some of the most rigorous of the single-system designs, such as the reversal designs, are especially difficult to apply because irreversible treatments and ethical considerations may preclude their use. Furthermore, some designs contain many phase segments that may require too much time to complete. Beyond these problems is the fact that some client disorders call for immediate attention, precluding the baseline measurements so crucial to single-system designs.

COMPUTERS IN RESEARCH

Computer-Aided Single-System Data Analysis

In the discussion of data analysis for single-system designs, the point was made that visual analysis is often preferred. You can use common spreadsheet software such as Microsoft Excel to conduct a visual assessment. A convenient approach is to design an analysis template—a reusable form that contains no data. Once the template is created and saved, you need only enter new data for each case rather than re-create the entire spreadsheet. Here are the basic steps for setting up a template, but you can embellish and expand this model to meet your own research needs. Enter some hypothetical data during the design process, just to make sure that the spreadsheet works properly. Once you have tested the spreadsheet, clear these data before saving the final version.

For illustration purposes, assume that a practitioner has collected data on a child's temper tantrum behavior for a baseline of 12 days and a treatment period involving the use of "time out" for another 12 days. The practitioner wants to document whether or not tantrum activity has declined. The example has room for 28 total observations, more than enough for most practice situations. The **Observation** column is the numbers 1 through N (in this case, 1 to 28, representing 28 possible observations). Enter the dependent variable values for the baseline phase in the **Baseline** column and intervention phase data in the **Treatment** column. Use the **Comparison** column to enter one of three standards for comparing

baseline to intervention: the baseline mean, the baseline maximum, or the baseline minimum.

A common practice for visual analysis is to see if all intervention data points are better than some baseline standard, such as the baseline mean, maximum, or minimum. In this illustration, the purpose of intervention is to decrease the number of tantrums, so the research question is: Are all treatment observations below the baseline mean? This value is calculated in cell C35 of the illustration. A more stringent standard for visual analysis would be this: Are all the treatment observations better than the best of baseline? In this case "better" would be below the baseline minimum, which is calculated in cell C37. (If the goal were to increase the behavior, the value to use would be the maximum from cell C36.) By using the "Copy" and "Paste Special" functions, the selected value is entered into the comparison column. All the necessary data are now in place to generate a graph.

Three series of data points are printed on the graph:

- Baseline data
- Treatment data
- Comparison (either baseline mean, maximum, or minimum)

Once you have tested the template, you can reuse it with other clients by simply clearing the contents from the Baseline, Treatment, and Comparison columns and entering new data.

Limited Generalizability of Results. As noted, results from one single-system experiment have virtually no generalizability beyond that particular case, and they provide less powerful tests of therapeutic effects than do traditional group experiments. Generalizability is obtained only through successful replication across clients, settings, disorders, and practitioners. This is a slow process, and the potential of single-system research to increase the knowledge base of the profession will not be realized quickly.

Main Points

- Single-system designs are quasi-experimental designs used to trace changes induced by treatments to individual clients in a clinical setting.
- Interest in single-system designs developed out of dissatisfaction with group experiments and case histories as sources of knowledge useful in clinical settings.
- The clinical research model utilizing single-system designs is not a radical departure from tra-

Figure 11.9   Graphing Single-System Data with Spreadsheet Software

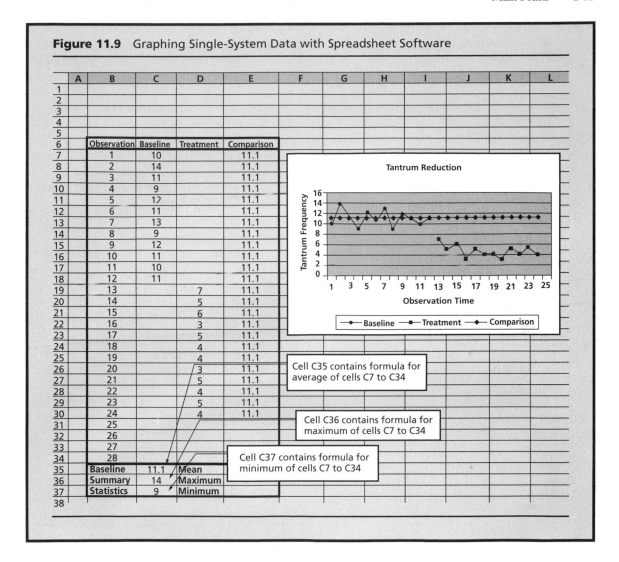

	Observation	Baseline	Treatment	Comparison
1	1	10		11.1
2	2	14		11.1
3	3	11		11.1
4	4	9		11.1
5	5	12		11.1
6	6	11		11.1
7	7	13		11.1
8	8	9		11.1
9	9	12		11.1
10	10	11		11.1
11	11	10		11.1
12	12	11		11.1
13	13		7	11.1
14	14		5	11.1
15	15		6	11.1
16	16		3	11.1
17	17		5	11.1
18	18		4	11.1
19	19		4	11.1
20	20		3	11.1
21	21		5	11.1
22	22		4	11.1
23	23		5	11.1
24	24		4	11.1
25	25			
26	26			
27	27			
28	28			

Baseline	11.1	Mean
Summary	14	Maximum
Statistics	9	Minimum

Cell C35 contains formula for average of cells C7 to C34

Cell C36 contains formula for maximum of cells C7 to C34

Cell C37 contains formula for minimum of cells C7 to C34

ditional clinical practice but rather an effort to increase the specificity and objectivity of practice and to enhance opportunities for replication and knowledge accumulation.

■ Although we have many specific single-system designs from which to choose, all involve a series of pretreatment measures (the baseline) and a series of posttreatment measures that are then compared with the baseline.

■ Measurements typically consist of observations, available records, paper-and-pencil measures, or self-reports; observations are usually the most desirable and self-reports the least desirable.

■ Effectiveness may be judged against three different standards—therapeutic, experimental, or statistical—with therapeutic effectiveness demanding the greatest client improvement and statistical effectiveness the least.

■ The simple *AB* design is highly flexible but not strong on internal validity.

■ Reversal designs, such as *ABA* or *ABAB,* are strong on internal validity but often impractical to apply.

■ Multiple-baseline designs are quite strong on internal validity and reasonably flexible, making them a good choice when a reversal design cannot be used.

■ In addition to these basic designs, many specialized designs can accommodate such things as changing treatments, combined treatments, or phased achievement of the treatment goal.

■ Positive results from one single-system experiment are not generalizable, but generalizability can be built up over time through replication.

■ Computer software can simplify and speed both the visual analysis and the statistical analysis of data from single-system research.

Important Terms for Review

baseline
clinical research model
direct replication
empirical practice model
single-system designs
systematic replication

Exploring InfoTrac® College Edition and the Internet

InfoTrac® College Edition search terms:

single subject design
multiple baseline

InfoTrac® College Edition articles:

Reducing Anxiety through a Structured Writing Intervention: A Single-System Evaluation. (journal writing) Michelle D. Barrett, Terry A. Wolfer. *Families in Society: The Journal of Contemporary Human Services* July 2001 v82 i4 p355 (5362 words)

Single-Subject Research Design for School Counselors: Becoming an Applied Researcher. Linda H. Foster, T. Steuart Watson, Caroline Meeks, J. Scott Young. *Professional School Counseling* Dec 2002 v6 i2 p146(9) (5,313 words)

Education & Treatment of Children, May 1999 v22 i2 p189 Level 1 Research: Where the Rubber Meets the Road in the Treatment of Serious Mental and Physical Health Problems. Kevin J. Moore.

Single-system design is a relatively narrow, specialized topic, so locating related resources on the Internet is more challenging than seeking material on more general subjects. Using such terms as "single case experiments" with standard search engines may locate some useful sites, but the search process can be frustrating. As an alternative, you can turn to some specialized tools for assistance. Single-system designs have long been used in the field of psychology, so a promising starting point is the American Psychological Association's home page (www.apa.org) and some of the databases that can be accessed there. One of the resources it offers is PsychCrawler (www.psychcrawler.com), a search engine that focuses on psychology-related topics.

An interesting way to explore how single-system designs have been applied to various human service practice evaluation studies is to use the search engine of the *Journal of Applied Behavior Analysis* (www.envmed.rochester.edu/wwwrap/behavior/jaba/jabahome.htm.), which provides a menu of suggested search terms and allows you to include your own as well. Searching on the term "multiple baseline" returns a list of previously published journal articles related to multiple-baseline designs. You can then select articles of interest to you and review an abstract of each. If you have a practice situation in mind for evaluation, these abstracts can provide guidance for planning and conducting a single-system design.

For Further Reading

Bloom, M., ed. *Single-System Designs in the Social Services: Issues and Options for the 1990s.* New York: Haworth, 1993. A compilation of thought-provoking articles by leading human service professionals on the application of single-system designs to practice.

Bloom, M., J. Fischer, and J. Orme. *Evaluating Practice: Guidelines for the Accountable Professional,* 4th ed. Boston: Allyn and Bacon, 2003. A thorough textbook on all aspects of single-system design for social work and other human services. Includes software for analysis.

Franklin, R. D., D. B. Allison, and B. S. Gorman. *Design and Analysis of Single-Case Research.* Mahwah, N.J.: Lawrence Erlbaum Associates, 1996. A complete source for in-depth information on single-case design, especially visual and statistical analysis issues.

Haynes, S. N., and W. H. O'Brien. *Principles and Practice of Behavioral Assessment.* New York: Kluwer Academic/Plenum Publishers, 1999. Psychological assessment is the primary focus of this book, which also includes substantial information related to using the single-case approach to assessment.

Kazdin, A. E. *Single-Case Research Designs.* New York: Oxford University Press, 1982. A concise overview of single-system research with illustrative applications in several areas of human service practice.

Kratochwill, T. R., and J. R. Levin. *Single-Case Research Design and Analysis: New Directions for Psychology and Education.* Hillsdale, N.J.: Lawrence Erlbaum Associates 1992. This source provides an overview of single-case research and includes detailed information on philosophical and statistical foundations of single-case designs, visual analysis, nonparametric tests, and meta-analysis for single-case research.

Richards, S. B., R. L. Taylor, R. Ramasamy, and R. Y. Richards. *Single Subject Research: Applications in Educational and Clinical Settings.* San Diego: Singular Publishing Group, 1999. For the reader seeking a basic, clear, concise coverage of single-system design, this is an excellent source. Very readable and well illustrated.

Exercises for Class Discussion

11.1 A foster parent complains to the foster care worker that the 14-year-old placed in her home chronically oversleeps in the morning and is late for school. She wakes him every morning about 7 A.M., leaving him two hours to get ready for school and be there on time.

a. Establish the problems that the foster care worker might tackle with this youngster and the goals to be accomplished. As you do this, keep in mind the importance of specificity and measurability.

b. Identify some alternative ways of measuring a baseline for assessing change in this case.

c. What would be the advantages and disadvantages of having the foster parent versus the foster son do the data collecting? Can you identify any outside sources of data?

11.2 Select a behavior from one of the following, devise a means of measuring it, and collect baseline data for a week, using yourself or someone else as the client. Report your results to the class.

a. Cigarette smoking

b. Speeding while driving

c. Snacking

d. Feeling depressed

e. Praising your child

f. Completing homework

11.3 A counselor in a spouse abuse shelter has been working with women in the shelter on assertiveness in dealing with men. She would like to do a single-system design with a woman client to evaluate the effectiveness of the assertiveness training. She intends to have the staff collect data on the client's level of assertiveness in a variety of situations, using a coded observation form.

What would be the advantages and disadvantages of the following designs for this research?

a. *AB*

b. *ABA*

c. *ABAB*

What steps would need to be taken to conduct this study in an ethical manner? Are there any special problems that are unique to each design type (*AB, ABA,* or *ABAB*)? Are there more complex designs that you might want to use in this situation?

11.4 An intensive foster care worker is responsible for six adolescent clients in separate foster homes. She has been receiving complaints from most of the foster parents that the kids do not pick up their clothes or do other chores around the house, such as washing dishes, mowing lawns, or cleaning walks. She decides to implement a reinforcement program by enabling the foster children to earn points toward special activities, such as a trip to a large amusement park. One such activity would be scheduled each week.

a. Describe how this worker might design a multiple-baseline study across clients.

b. Describe how the worker might design a multiple-baseline study across behaviors.

c. How might she devise a changing-criterion design?

Chapter 12

Evaluation Research

A major theme of this book is the benefits accorded to the human service field by linking human service practice with scientific research to form a single endeavor seeking common goals. (We labeled this "evidence-based practice" and "scientific practice" in Chapter 1 and the "clinical research model" in Chapter 11.) In this chapter, we encounter a new element of this linkage in the form of *evaluation research,* which points to a reason for conducting research rather than to a new research methodology. **Evaluation research** refers to the use of scientific research methods to plan intervention programs, monitor the implementation of new programs and the operation of existing ones, and determine how effectively programs or clinical practices achieve their goals.

Although evaluation research has been around for many years, it has risen to considerable prominence over the past two decades as the amount of public and private funds channeled into social programs has grown. As funding increased, those providing the funds sought valid and reliable evidence regarding whether programs achieved their goals, how efficiently they did so, and whether they produced any unintended consequences. Evaluation research is a mechanism for gathering evidence about these issues, and it has become an integral part of most modern social programs.

What Is Evaluation Research?

Evaluation research offers a means of supplying valid and reliable evidence about the operation of social programs or clinical practices—how they are planned, how well they operate, and how effectively they achieve their goals. For example, a medical care facility may need to know if a community need exists for a day care program for the elderly. Corrections officials may want to know the size at which a probation officer's caseload becomes too large to provide effective services. Or hospital administrators may need to assess the impact on patient care of a 15 percent reduction in the nursing staff. In these situations and others like them, evaluation research uses many of the research techniques discussed in other chapters to provide evidence about the workings of programs and practices in the human services. A typical evaluation effort might involve some combination of interviews, questionnaires, observation, available data, and an experimental design. (In fact, we have already discussed evaluation research in many places in this book without calling it by this name. In Chapter 11, for example, many of the single-subject design studies described can be considered evaluation research of the effectiveness of clinical interventions.)

Why Evaluate?

Evaluation research is conducted for three major reasons (Rossi, Freeman, and Lipsey 1999). First, it can be conducted for *administrative purposes,* such as to fulfill an evaluation requirement demanded by a funding source, improve service to clients, or increase efficiency of program delivery. Evaluations for administrative reasons tend to focus on assessing the daily operations of a program rather than on its overall impact, with the goal of finding the most efficient means to run a program or agency.

A second reason for conducting evaluation research is *impact assessment* to see what effects, if any, a program is producing. Typically, impact assessment identifies program goals and measures how well the program achieves those goals. The results are then used to make policy decisions regarding whether to expand, change, or curtail a program.

Third, evaluation research may be conducted to *test hypotheses* or *evaluate practice approaches.* These often amount to the same thing because practice strategies are often based on hypotheses derived from social and psychological theories. Such evaluation not only provides information about a particular practice intervention but also adds to the fund of social-scientific knowledge, which may be useful in the design of new intervention strategies.

Evaluation Research and Basic Research

Evaluation research is another form of applied research (see Chapter 1) that involves a special application of the general techniques of basic research.

Because of this, there are similarities between the two. But there are also some important differences (DeMartini 1982; Weiss 1998). First, the results of evaluation research have immediate practical use in assessing operating programs. Basic research, on the other hand, is oriented toward more general information gathering and hypothesis testing.

Second, in contrast to evaluation research, in which the needs of the decision makers sponsoring the study are paramount in shaping the form and content of the research, the basic researcher has more control over which issues to investigate (Rossi, Freeman, and Lipsey 1999). Some evaluations may allow some latitude to expand beyond the issues of direct interest to the decision makers. But control over the content of the research is shared with them. This can become a source of conflict between researchers and sponsors.

A third difference is that evaluation, by its very nature, has a judgmental quality that is often not a part of basic research. The evaluation may deem a program a success or failure based on how well it achieved its purposes; this judgmental quality also can be a source of tension between an evaluator and the sponsors of the evaluation. Understandably, the sponsors are concerned that a negative evaluation could have dire consequences for the existence of the program and for their own livelihoods and careers.

The fourth difference between basic and evaluation research relates to the issues given priority in the research process. In basic research, quite naturally, the requisites for producing a scientifically sound study are given strong weight. Evaluation research, on the other hand, takes place in the context of an ongoing, operating program, and the demands of that program may conflict with the demands for sound scientific practices. When this happens, the program administrators may give higher priority to the program than to the evaluation. The scientific demands of an evaluation, for example, might call for the random assignment of nurses from a home health care agency to each new client of the agency. But the agency administrator may prefer to assign nurses on the basis of his or her assessment of their competencies and fit with the client. The agency head likely will be able to override the evaluators'

requests and force them to modify their scientific procedures.

The differences in approach sometimes found between practitioners and researchers (Weiss 1972) can sometimes aggravate these conflicts. Practitioners tend to emphasize the importance of providing services to people and the role of empathy and concern in the intervention process. Researchers, on the other hand, may give more weight to the understanding provided by rigorous scientific analysis and objectivity. Although these differences should not be overdrawn—for researchers do have empathy and practitioners do recognize the value of scientific analysis—there can be a difference in emphasis between practitioners and researchers, and it can be another source of tension. In fact, one of the beneficial outcomes of developing linkages between practice and research is that the process encourages people to develop ways of combining the two approaches so that advantages accrue to both.

A final difference between basic and evaluation research relates to making the results of the research public. One of the canons of science is that research results be made public for others to see and criticize, in order to reduce the likelihood that errors or personal bias might have found their way into the research (see Chapter 2). In the past, wide dissemination of evaluation results was uncommon. A review of the journals *Social Work* and *Social Casework* between 1958 and 1972 found not even one article describing a carefully conducted evaluation. The few references to evaluation were more in the nature of "afterthoughts" (Segal 1972). Not until 1976 did a journal specifically devoted to evaluation reports, *Evaluation Quarterly,* come into existence. Today, numerous journals in every human service field cover this topic, and a number of professional organizations serve as outlets to disseminate the results of evaluation research. However, all too frequently, sponsors of an evaluation receive a few copies of the report, which they promptly file away and forget, thus thwarting the accumulation of information so necessary for progress. Even if evaluation results show no effect, those findings are valuable in preventing similar ineffective programs from proliferating.

Despite the differences between evaluation research and basic research, there are important similarities. First, both may choose from the entire array of data-gathering techniques those that best fit their needs. In fact, as noted, evaluation projects often involve a synthesis of data gathered in a variety of ways. Second, both forms of research can focus on determining cause-and-effect relationships. In basic research, researchers seek cause-and-effect relationships between variables of their own choosing, whereas in evaluation research investigation focuses on variables that are a part of the program being assessed.

The differences between evaluation and basic research are of a practical nature, deriving mainly from the context in which evaluation research is conducted. Although these differences are important—and the potential conflicts alluded to are quite real—the actual process of inquiry is much the same in both types of research. In fact, evaluation research illustrates the dynamic and flexible quality of basic social research methods in that the core methods and techniques can be expanded and changed to confront new problems and issues. Evaluation research is a novel and challenging application of methods that have been used in many other contexts. As such, the distinction between basic and evaluation research is one of degree rather than of kind.

The Politics of Evaluation Research

Decades ago, many evaluation researchers took a fairly straightforward, positivist view of their activities. By this we mean that they viewed the social programs they were evaluating as interventions that attacked clearly identifiable problems in the world. The researchers viewed these problems as obvious social ills that needed rectifying, they assumed that almost everyone agreed on what the betterment of those social ills would entail, and they saw their own methods as objective and scientific tools to assist in achieving that social betterment. But the arguments of nonpositivist paradigms (discussed in Chapter 2) have led many evaluation researchers to recognize that reality is not as simple as the straightforward positivist view would suggest (Greene 1994; Patton

1987; Rule 1978). In particular, these approaches have led to recognition that evaluation research and the programs they evaluate are inherently political in nature. Politics has to do with power—who has it, who exercises it, and who controls its resources. Social interventions have to do with controlling and distributing resources.

Let us illustrate these issues with an example: programs to reduce teenage pregnancies. The problem of teen pregnancy can be approached in a number of different ways, such as programs to encourage sexual abstinence, to make available safe and reliable contraceptives, or to provide abortion services to those who become pregnant. Which of these approaches a particular social program takes is determined by the values of those who fund and control the program and thus have the power to see that their values prevail. These people shape what the program is like, which services it provides, and how it provides them. In so doing, policymakers and program managers have great influence on shaping people's definitions of the problem of teenage pregnancy and acceptable solutions to that problem. Thus, social programs are the product of political decisions that involve the establishment of priorities and the allocation of resources.

In recent decades, evaluation researchers have come to recognize the importance of **stakeholders** in social programs—all the people who have an interest in whether a social program operates or how well it does so. Evaluation researchers also recognize that any program has a large variety of stakeholders, including its funders, administrators, personnel, and clients or beneficiaries. In most cases, these stakeholders have varied and competing interests. The teenagers receiving services from a pregnancy prevention program, for example, may benefit from different kinds of interventions than the bureaucrats who run the program or the policymakers who fund it.

However, evaluations are typically sponsored by only one or a few stakeholders, such as the government agency that funds the evaluation or the managers who run the program. These sponsors may want to see the evaluation come out a certain way and may pay for an evaluation that addresses some questions but not others. If the sponsors want to promote sexual abstinence, for instance, they may include in the evaluation measures that assess how well abstinence works. But they may not even ask the teens if they would use contraceptives or abortion referral services if these were available. Thus, it is possible that an evaluation can be directed toward some conclusions and away from others because only some stakeholders in the program are funding (and in part directing) the evaluation.

The new approach recognizes that social ills and their betterment are not objective conditions about which social consensus exists. Rather, social ills and social betterment are political issues based on differing social definitions of reality, about which people disagree and come into conflict. In designing and conducting evaluation research, then, researchers must recognize these competing viewpoints and interests and consider the possibility that some research methodologies may be biased in the direction of certain conclusions and the interests of certain stakeholders.

Types of Evaluation Research

The term "evaluation research" is somewhat misleading in that there is not a separate set of research techniques that are distinctly applied for this single purpose. Rather, the phrase applies to a diverse collection of strategies that can be used for a broad range of evaluative purposes. One way that evaluation research methods may be classified is in terms of the unit of analysis. (For example, the single-system designs covered in Chapter 11 may be considered evaluation methods where the unit of analysis is a single system or individual. Because of the unique features involved in doing such individual studies, we have chosen to devote a separate chapter to them.) This chapter considers evaluations that focus on programs or organizations as the unit of analysis.

Another useful way to conceptualize the diversity of evaluation research is in terms of the goals of the study. Evaluation research can achieve two basic goals. **Formative evaluation research** focuses on providing information to guide the planning, development, and implementation of a specific program. It is primarily concerned with ensuring a smooth-running, well-integrated program rather than with the ultimate worth or impact of the program. **Summative evaluation research** is concerned with the program's effects. Here the purpose centers on assessing the effectiveness and efficiency of programs and the extent to which the outcomes of the project are generalizable to other settings and populations. Formative evaluation research has received less attention in the evaluation literature than has summative evaluation. However, the two forms are closely linked and may be likened to a foundation and a building. The formative component of evaluation may not be especially glamorous or attract much attention, but unless it is carefully prepared and well done, the summative study is difficult to carry out for high-quality results.

Formative Evaluation Research

Formative research poses the questions that arise in the planning, implementation, and operation of social programs. To initiate a program, certain basic information is essential. First, it is necessary to gather data on the target population and their characteristics. The nature of their problems, the number of potential program users, their location in the community, and other demographic information are essential to planning a good program. Second, it is important to be aware of existing services that the program under development might duplicate or on which it may rely for referrals or auxiliary services. Third, program planners need to know about specific intervention strategies that might apply to the problems they uncover. Fourth, program operators must be able to specify the staff skills required to deliver the program. Fifth, planners must determine if the program as conceptualized is feasible to offer and monitor.

To answer these questions, formative research might take the form of a **needs assessment**: collecting data to determine how many people in a community need particular services and assessing what level of services or personnel already exists to fill a need (McKillip 1987). In needs assessments, researchers commonly utilize a sampling strategy and then survey members of the target population. Thus, survey research methods form the backbone of such needs assessments. We can also rely on direct observation or existing data to gain a profile of the population and identify its needs. Essentially, any techniques used for descriptive research may be employed to answer this question. We might learn about existing and related services through interviewing potential clients and representatives of existing agencies. Knowledge of possible intervention strategies and program components often results from a thorough literature search, a fundamental step in any research project. (Appendix A, on the use of the library, is directly applicable to such a task.)

Formative evaluations also sometimes utilize *focus groups* (the group interview technique discussed at length in Chapter 7). Focus groups are especially useful when the formative evaluation is exploratory in nature or when planners want to learn about people's personal and subjective meanings and experiences. Focus groups are a useful strategy for drawing out such information.

Formative evaluation research can also take the form of a *pretest* or *trial run,* which tests all the procedures to be used in a program before the full program is implemented. An example of this can be found in a program to provide financial aid to newly released offenders (Rossi, Berk, and Lenihan 1980). The researchers began with a very modest project involving six released inmates who received six weekly payments of $60 and 20 controls who received no payment. Relying on a review of the literature and existing statistics on the problems of released offenders, this modest project helped prepare for a large-scale program in several ways. It helped determine that it was logistically possible to make the payments and to interview and keep track of ex-inmates in the community. Had this pilot project shown that these operational elements could not be accomplished effectively, then it would have been foolish to continue with a larger project even though the researchers were convinced of the overall value of the program.

Because the questions formative research addresses are often modest in scope, the staff of the agency administering the program frequently conducts the research itself. However, such research may also be done on a national scale in conjunction with large programs. Programs such as Temporary Assistance to Needy Families (TANF), food stamps, and vocational rehabilitation involve large sums of money, and initiation of such programs involves estimating the number of potential recipients, which can vary considerably depending on what definition of poverty is applied. Before initiating such programs, formative research based on needs assessment is essential. Although formative evaluation cannot ensure success, it can help reduce instances of unnecessary intervention and increase the potential for success among those programs that are initiated.

Besides serving as a tool for planning an intervention program, formative research may also monitor the implementation of new programs and the ongoing operation of existing ones. Several basic issues in program monitoring are counterparts to program planning. First, is the target population in fact being served? It is not uncommon to discover that people do not use programs in spite of obvious need. Even major social welfare programs have been plagued by this problem, referred to as the "take-up rate."

Studies have found that less than 50 percent of eligible recipients participated in the food stamps program. Inadequate information about food stamps and personal attitudes toward food stamp use had the greatest impact on the decision to participate (Coe and Hill 1998). Another study (Kalra, Fieldhouse, and Alam 2001) reported on the reasons for nonparticipation and avoidance of the New Deal for Young People (NDYP), a public policy program that tries to reduce unemployment among the age 18–25 group. Negative experiences at previous youth training programs and the perception that NDYP could not offer desirable jobs were identified as major barriers to involvement. As a means to assess the extent of such problems, a census of program users can compare their characteristics with the characteristics of the population for whom services were intended. Any discrepancy suggests that some members of the target population are not receiving services intended for them. Unless such issues are addressed during the formative evaluation stage, a full-scale program may be destined for failure.

Next, are the services that are supposed to be delivered actually being delivered, and is the quality of the service adequate? Experience with program effectiveness evaluations has shown that a key issue is program fidelity during intervention—that is, operating the program exactly as it was designed to run. Without implementation data, an evaluator might conclude that a program model is ineffective when the real culprit is inadequate implementation that did not permit a valid test of the program (Lynch et al. 1998). Service delivery may be assessed in a variety of ways, including questionnaires and direct observation. As in single-system designs, time samples may be used to determine if behaviors associated with service delivery are occurring as planned. Quality control techniques not unlike those used in industry can monitor the delivery of services in many settings. State departments of social services routinely monitor major financial assistance services, such as TANF. Typically, the process involves selecting a random sample of recipients and examining the most recent action on their files to determine if the action resulted in a correct payment, an overpayment, or an underpayment. States are expected to keep their error rate within certain specific limits. Other settings use follow-up questionnaires to determine if expected services were delivered.

Finally, agencies commonly use a time-reporting system to make sure that staff members are spending the expected amount of time on specified aspects of the program. Figure 12.1 illustrates one type of time-reporting system. Such studies do not address the question of whether or not the program is actually doing any good but rather address the narrower issue of the extent to which the services actually being delivered are true to the intended plan.

Summative Evaluation Research

Summative evaluation research involves assessing the impact of a program, and good summative evaluations usually investigate other matters concerning the program's operation as well. The results of summative evaluations are intended for policymaking decisions—whether to continue, expand, or cancel a program and whether to generalize the findings of a particular project to other settings and populations. Summative evaluations are typically large-scale projects involving considerable time, personnel, and resources. For this reason, as well as to avoid the biasing effect of personal interest, outside consultants rather than agency staff often conduct these evaluations.

Although the steps in the research process are much the same for all types of research, including evaluation research, some special planning is called for to take into consideration the unique problems of evaluation research.

Evaluability Assessment

During the planning of evaluation research, an **evaluability assessment** is often conducted to enable investigators to decide whether a program has the necessary preconditions to be evaluated. An evaluability assessment involves four steps (Rutman 1984; Smith 1989). First, the purpose of the evaluation—from the standpoint of the eventual users of the results—is determined. This identifies which aspects of the program to assess for impact. To be evaluated, a program needs clearly specified goals because they are the major criteria of the program's success. Goals are the dependent variables that the input variables are supposed to affect. Unfortunately, the goals of many programs are either so vague or so global ("improve family functioning," for example) as to be unusable for evaluation purposes. It may be necessary for an evaluator to become actively involved with the staff in developing a set of clear goals before a program can be evaluated.

The second step in an evaluability assessment is to study and gather information about the program. What are the inputs, the expected results or goals, and the linkage between them? This linkage is essentially the theory on which the program is based. It involves answering the question, "Why, given these program inputs, should certain outcomes be expected?" This theoretical linkage may be explicitly recognized as the basis of the program, or it may be implicit but derivable from the program's operation. The purpose of identifying this rationale is that

Figure 12.1   Example of a Time-Reporting Form

Case Name _____

Case No. _____

Worker _____   Page _____

Date	Type	Time	

Code:

1—Telephone Contact
2—In-office Visit
3—School Visit
4—Foster Home Visit
5—Referring Worker Visit
6—Paperwork
7—Driving Time

8—Foster Parent Training
9—Court Visit
10—Visit to Family of Origin
11—Case Staffing and Supervision
12—Other Collateral
13—Client

Time Interval—
1–15 Min.

it is important in understanding the success or failure of the program. For example, some programs may identify certain outcomes as goals but not direct any effort toward realizing them. (Quite obviously, if evaluated against these goals, the program would probably turn out to be a failure.) If we do not specify the linkage, the reason for failure may be unclear and, in the case of a success, we would be at a loss to explain why. Knowledge of the linkage reveals the source of the problem as the failure to direct input resources toward those particular goals. During this step, it is important to monitor the program *as implemented* because gaps sometimes develop between the stated program and the program as operated.

Third, information gathered during the second stage is used to develop a flow model of the program. This model traces program inputs, clients, and interventions as they affect the expected results, specifying any assumed causal linkages along the way. Modeling of programs is extremely useful in evaluation research because it provides a clear picture of the structure and operation of the program. It can also help explain a program's successes or failures. For example, as a part of an evaluation of a group-counseling program in a correctional system, a careful model of the program was developed (Kassebaum, Ward, and Wilner 1971). When the results of the evaluation showed that inmates in the counseling program did not have lower recidivism rates than other inmates, the evaluators were not surprised, because their model revealed that counselors were poorly trained and unmotivated, counseling sessions tended to be unfocused bull sessions, inmate participation was motivated largely by a desire to impress the parole board, and the inmates did not view the sessions as helpful. Against this backdrop, the failure of counseling to reduce recidivism is understandable. The flow model of the program helped identify these elements.

The final stage of an evaluability assessment is to review the program model to identify those aspects that are sufficiently unambiguous in terms of inputs, goals, and linkages to make evaluation feasible. The result of the assessment may be that the whole program can be evaluated, none of the program can be evaluated, or, most commonly, only certain parts of the program are amenable to evaluation.

Specification of Variables

As in any research, an important part of evaluation research is the specification of variables and how they will be measured. In some evaluations, the variables of interest take the form of independent and dependent variables. The inputs to a social program, for example, might constitute the independent variables. In some cases, the independent variable takes the form of a dichotomous variable: participation or nonparticipation in a program. In other cases, the independent variable is the degree or duration of participation in a program, such as the frequency of contact with a counselor, the level of financial aid received, or the length of time a service is provided. Commonly, the dependent variables in evaluation

research are the goals of a program: precisely what it is supposed to accomplish. Some evaluation research, of course, especially the formative type, does not involve independent and dependent variables. But whatever form the variables take, a central issue in evaluation research is that the variables be clearly and properly specified, as numerous problems can arise along these lines. This is especially true when measuring the goals of a program.

A frequent problem is that the goals, as articulated by program administrators, do not easily lend themselves to evaluation. They may be vague, overly broad, or so long term that evaluation is not feasible. For example, a goal of Head Start preschool education is to develop capable and functioning adults who can rise out of poverty. Although the success of Head Start in achieving this goal may be its ultimate test, it would be necessary to wait 20 to 30 years before evaluating the program. Although this goal is a laudable and essential part of the program, funding agencies are understandably reluctant to expend funds for that length of time with no evaluation. Thus, such programs normally include what are called *proximate goals,* or goals that can be realized in the short run and are related to the achievement of the long-term goals (Weiss 1998). In the case of Head Start, academic achievement is a reasonable proximate goal because performance in school is associated with social and occupational success in adulthood.

For other programs, of course, it is possible and desirable to assess the long-term impact—for example, a 30-year follow-up of the Cambridge-Sommerville Youth Study, a five-year experiment in delinquency prevention begun in Boston in 1939 (McCord 1978). This field experiment focused on 506 boys, half of whom received counseling and other assistance, while the other half served as a control group. The experimental condition consisted of counseling sessions every two weeks, tutoring, medical and psychiatric assistance, summer camps, and organized youth activities. Thirty years later, researchers located 95 percent of the participants in the experiment. Many of the comparisons showed no differences between the two groups. But the differences that were found suggested that the experimental variables had the *opposite* effect from what was expected! The experimental group committed more crimes as adults, had higher rates of alcoholism, poorer mental and physical health, and less occupational success. The only positive result for the program appeared to be the participants' own subjective evaluations. Two-thirds of the experimental group thought the program had been helpful to them even though their objective situation was worse than that of those in the control group. The program may have produced harmful effects because it raised participants' expectations to an unrealistically high level. When those expectations were not realized, participants suffered frustration and added stress, which resulted in a greater tendency toward criminality and alcoholism and deleterious effects on their mental and physical health (McCord 1978). Despite the need for early program evaluations, long-term evaluation, accomplished so well in this study, is still essential in assessing many programs.

Vague or overly broad goals must be clarified or reduced in scope so that they are amenable to evaluation. In this regard, it is helpful if program administrators consult with evaluators to develop program goals. During discussions with program administrators, it is important that evaluators not simply accept as all-inclusive the goals the administrators articulate. In fact, one of the major reasons for finding that a program does not have the intended result is that program goals are too limited (Chen and Rossi 1980). Too often, administrators state program goals from the standpoint of what they desire, which results in goals that are unattainable given program inputs. When evaluated against these goals, the program naturally appears to be a failure. Evaluators should cast a wide net in seeking program effects, including not only those suggested by administrators but also others logically expected given the nature of the program. The model developed during the evaluability assessment and the theoretical basis of the program are productive places to look for possible program effects to include in the evaluation. This approach promises a better chance of finding nonzero program effects and supplying information on what the program does, as well as what it does not do.

Another problem in specifying the goals and variables for evaluation is that different stakeholders may have different conceptions of what the program should accomplish. All sides may be clear about what the goals should be, but disagree with one another on them. This points again to the political dimensions of evaluation research and the possibility that those who control the resources (usually the program funders or administrators) will impose their version of what the program goals should be. The evaluation researcher needs to ensure that other significant stakeholders have input into the process of defining and clarifying the goals.

Measuring Variables

The goals specified for an evaluation program tend to be abstract statements of desired outcomes. Before an actual evaluation can proceed, measurable criteria or operational definitions must specify exactly what observations will be made to determine goal achievement. Evaluators thus distinguish between *goals,* which are the desired end states for a program, and *objectives,* the measurable criteria for success. For example, a goal of a substance abuse prevention program might be to reduce experimentation with alcohol and cigarettes among junior high students. An objective of the program might be that 85 percent of program participants be able to correctly list at least five health hazards associated with alcohol use. Some goals can be readily measured because they have clearly quantifiable outcomes. For example, standard achievement tests readily measure the academic effects of compensatory education programs. But measuring such effects of Head Start as improved self-esteem, better adjustment to the classroom environment, or enhanced parent–child relationships requires more inventiveness on the part of the evaluator.

When measures for program effects are considered, alternative indicators of the same program effect may exist. For example, in measuring the effects of a family planning program, we might use as a measure (1) the proportion of participants adopting contraceptive practices, (2) average desired number of children, (3) average number of children born, or

(4) attitudes toward large families. All these indicators logically relate to the effects of a family planning program. Multiple indicators—though sometimes prohibited by budget—are more useful than single ones.

Multiple indicators are more sensitive and therefore more likely to show an effect if the program produced one (Weiss 1998). If multiple indicators are impractical, a decision must be made as to which of the alternatives is best. In the case of the four alternatives for the family planning program, the clearest indicator of program success is a low birthrate among participants. This indicator, however, might be impractical for some purposes because we have to wait many years before the evaluation can be completed. The two indicators dealing with attitudes are not the best choices because attitudes can change and sometimes only a weak relationship exists between attitudes and behavior. Indeed, attitudinal measures should be avoided whenever a behavioral alternative is available. Of the four possible measures, then, the proportion of participants who adopt contraception is probably the best single indicator of the effectiveness of the family planning program. It is not perfect as a measure, because contraceptives must be used conscientiously to be effective, but it is adequate for the short run.

As we have noted, it is preferable to use existing measures where possible. This avoids the work involved in creating new measures, pretesting them, and establishing their validity and reliability. Furthermore, existing measures contribute to the accumulation of knowledge because they make evaluations of different programs more comparable. But the preference for existing measures extends only to the point where good existing measures for the variables of interest can be found. If existing measures are only tangentially related to what we seek to measure, then it is far better to develop new measures. Good measurement is crucial to meaningful evaluation; shortcuts that compromise quality cannot be tolerated.

Assuming that some new measures must be created, it is important to keep in mind the dual criteria for assessing them: validity and reliability. Measures used in evaluation research must meet the same standards of validity and reliability as those used in basic research, and the methods for assessing those characteristics (considered in Chapter 5) apply here as well.

The Evaluation of Minorities in Evaluation Research

One area in which evaluation research has played an important role is in assessing the operation and impact of policies and programs affecting minorities. When the women's movement hit full stride in the 1970s, women began rapidly to enter what had generally been considered exclusively male occupations. Before long, studies were assessing the relative performances of men and women working the same jobs. As more of this research was amassed, serious questions were raised concerning the quality and fairness of the evaluations, particularly toward the women in traditionally male occupations.

Take the case of evaluating male and female police officers. Merry Morash and Jack Greene (1986) reviewed the nine major evaluations of women police officers that had been conducted up to that time. Not surprisingly, given the varying methodologies of the several studies, the results were inconsistent. With one exception, however, the studies concluded that female police officers were neither better nor worse than their male counterparts but that they were different. That is, women were better than the male officers at some policing activities, but they were not as good as the male officers at others. If these differences are real, such information can be quite valuable in allocating police personnel to maximize the strengths and minimize the weaknesses of both male and female officers. But what if the differences are merely artifacts of a faulty study design? Because assignments in police departments have implications for career advancement, we had better be sure that the findings of such evaluations are indeed valid before proceeding to use them as a basis for allocating personnel—or for any other reason.

Morash and Greene's review of the nine studies is not encouraging on the validity issue, but it does point out issues that future researchers should address. Among the problems they found in the research were a tendency to choose variables based on male stereotypes of what is important in police work (such as marksmanship or frequency of arrests), failure to evaluate performance on a representative sample of police tasks, overemphasis on the violent and dangerous aspects of police work, failure to consider the differences between men's and women's experiences in the workplace (greater camaraderie among male officers, for example), failure to evaluate variations in performance among male officers as well as variation between the sexes, and unclear or unspecified definitions of what constituted good police work. Quite a litany of criticisms!

The authors also found that performance evaluations may be subject to deliberate political manipulation. A study conducted in Philadelphia concluded that women performed at least as well as the men did. In a second study, certain behaviors that had been positively evaluated in the first study were now negatively evaluated. This time the results came out against the female officers.

Morash and Greene's analysis clearly indicated that conducting performance evaluations of men and women in job settings is difficult and fraught with possibilities for invalid conclusions. The fact that such evaluations continue and their results are acted upon means that those who conduct evaluations must be cognizant of the potential pitfalls and ready to guard against biased results through the use of sound study designs and firm resistance to any efforts at political manipulation.

Designs for Evaluation Research

Summative evaluation research is often concerned with cause-and-effect relationships. For example, the program being evaluated is presumed to bring about changes in such factors as client behavior. A research design developed for such an evaluation needs to be based on an awareness of this cause-and-effect dimension. (In Chapter 10, we noted that true experimental designs involving randomization are the better choice for establishing cause-and-effect relationships because they best control the validity threats that can lead to false causal inferences.) The ideal approach to determining the effects of a program, therefore, is the randomized experiment. Any

of the true experimental designs discussed in Chapter 10 is appropriate for evaluation purposes. However, quasi-experimental designs are quite common because these are often far more feasible and expedient than true experimental designs.

Randomized Experimental Designs.   As we have noted, the requirements of a true experiment are two randomized equivalent groups, one that experiences the experimental condition and a control group that does not. In summative evaluation research, the experimental condition requires some level of participation in the program under consideration. The crucial feature of the true experiment is that members of the comparison groups are randomly assigned. This is the surest and most reliable way of producing equivalent groups.

Virtually all randomized experiments in evaluation are field experiments, taking place in the setting where the actual program is administered. Because of this, evaluators may encounter a number of impediments to conducting a randomized experiment. The first centers around the control group and the randomization procedure used to obtain it. It is necessary, in order to create a control group, to deny some members of the target population access to the program under evaluation, and that denial must be made on a random basis. Evaluators may encounter substantial resistance to such denials. For example, the enabling legislation of some programs mandates that all persons who meet the eligibility requirements have a legal right to participate in the program. If such is the case, random denial of service is ruled out.

In other programs, resistance to random denial of services may spring from program administrators and staff. Practitioners are accustomed to providing services on the basis of need and may be disinclined to use a table of random numbers instead. It seems cold, insensitive, and even immoral to withhold available services from people who need them, especially if intuition leads the practitioner to believe that the provision of services would have beneficial effects. In advocating a randomized experiment, evaluators sometimes find themselves in a no-win situation. If they discover that the program produces harmful effects, they are blamed for subjecting the experimental group to the harmful program. If the program produces positive results, they are blamed for withholding this valuable service from the control group. Imagine the ethical implications of a randomized experiment for evaluating something like a suicide prevention program where life-and-death issues are at stake.

Along these lines, it is important to keep in mind that intuition regarding the impact of programs is often faulty. In fact, the literature on evaluation research strongly suggests that practitioners' assumptions of positive program effects are often wrong. Leonard Gibbs (1991) documented this point with a diverse list of well-intentioned intervention efforts from the annals of medicine and human service—efforts that appeared to be reasonable in their time but proved to be ineffective. Included were bloodletting, mercuric chloride as a drug, oxygen therapy for premature infants, neuroleptic medication for tardive dyskinesia, a juvenile awareness program known as "Scared Straight," encounter groups, and aggressive relocation of the aged. In the last illustration, a study on providing a full range of human services to the mentally impaired elderly reported that the death rate for clients receiving the intensive services was 25 percent in contrast to only 18 percent for the controls. Although not statistically significant, the results should make us pause before we assume that good intentions assure a positive outcome. Because services our intuition may suggest are effective often turn out not to be, the arguments against withholding services in a randomized experimental design are severely weakened, and, as demonstrated in Research in Practice 10.2, studies involving true control groups are clearly feasible.

A second impediment to conducting randomized experiments in evaluation research is that they may be more time-consuming and expensive than other designs. Experimental evaluations of programs are typically longitudinal: Sufficient time must pass for programs to have an effect. With many social programs, such as compensatory education or job training, the minimum length of the experiment might be at least one year. Furthermore, a listing of the target population, required for randomization, may be difficult or expensive to obtain. These practical considerations mean that randomized experiments are limited to those cases where the money and time are available for an elaborate, rigorous evaluation.

Before succumbing to the pressure to settle for a weaker design, however, consider the lesson of the Salk polio vaccine trials. Two experimental methods were used. One was a nonrandomized trial wherein one million volunteer second-graders were given the vaccine, and unvaccinated first- and third-graders served as the control group. The other study was an experiment involving 800,000 volunteers randomly assigned to receive either the vaccine or a placebo without doctors, parents, or children knowing which group they were in. Although the first study involved a larger sample and may have seemed easier to conduct without complicated randomization, its design proved inadequate for estimating the effect of the vaccine. It seems that polio was more prevalent in the middle classes because better hygiene prevented building up the natural immunity that lower-class children developed. Second-graders who volunteered tended to be middle class and thus different from second-graders who did not volunteer and also different from the first- and third-grade controls. In citing this case in his argument for randomized experiments, Lawrence Sherman (1992, p. 59) concluded, "Only the randomized, fully controlled Salk vaccine experiment provided the clear estimate of the vaccine's benefits which was needed to adopt a national policy of vaccination."

Randomized experiments are clearly the best designs from which to assess causality, and many statistical procedures are based on the assumption of equivalent experimental and control groups. Reports in such journals as *Evaluation Quarterly* document the widespread use of these designs. With some inventiveness on the part of evaluators, much of the resistance to randomized experiments can be overcome. Indeed, there is a growing consensus about the desirability of randomized experiments and an expanding literature documenting their use (Orr 1998), which should work to reduce the barriers to future randomized experiments in evaluation.

One common situation in particular contributes to the possibility of a randomized experiment.

When the target population is larger than the program's capacity to serve it—in short, when demand for services exceeds supply—services must be denied to some people. Because many programs are initially instituted on a small scale, excess demand often occurs. Because some members of the target population will not be served anyway, the determination of who will be served might as well be random unless there is some other clear-cut and defensible criterion, such as severity of need. In fact, a reasonable argument can be made that random allocation of services is the fairest method when resources are inadequate to serve all and no other criteria seem applicable.

If an evaluator is successful in obtaining approval for a randomized experiment, the random assignment process must be carefully monitored to ensure proper implementation. Lack of such monitoring can destroy the experimental design. For example, an employment and training program with which one of the authors of this book once consulted had agreed to a randomized study. However, when a large group of eager youths appeared at the agency on the first day, the staff was overwhelmed and simply threw the program open to all of them, thus totally destroying the randomization procedure. When such events go undiscovered, the comparison groups are not equalized and the eventual results are misleading. A two-step procedure is desirable in which client information is gathered by personnel different from those who do the random assignment. In this way, those handling the assignment do so without knowledge of client identities or characteristics. Insulating the assignment process in this way reduces the opportunity for deviations from randomness to creep in and eases the monitoring task (Cook, Cook, and Mark 1977).

The Alternatives to Randomized Experiments.

The barriers to randomized experiments may be sufficiently formidable as to require an alternative design. It is important to remember that anything other than a randomized experiment produces results in which confidence is reduced because such alternative designs are weaker on internal validity (see Chapter 10). Properly conducted, however, these designs allow evaluation with a reasonable degree of certitude.

One alternative to the randomized experiment is to use a *quasi-experimental design*. When a program is meant to affect behavior about which data are routinely collected, a time-series design may be appropriate. One research group, for example, used a time-series design to evaluate the impact of a Massachusetts gun control law that mandated a one-year minimum prison sentence for anyone convicted of carrying a firearm without a permit (Deutch and Alt 1977). The law went into effect in April 1975. The researchers traced the monthly occurrences of homicide, assault with a gun, and armed robbery in Boston from 1966 to 1975, which provided a baseline of gun-related offenses for about nine years prior to the introduction of the gun control law. Their analysis revealed that in the first seven months the law was in effect, statistically significant decreases occurred in both armed robbery and assaults with a gun. No change was registered for homicide, however. Despite their frequent utility for evaluation, it is important to remember that the chief weakness of time-series designs is the validity threat of history. Unless it is possible to use a control group, as in the multiple time-series design, it is always possible that some extraneous variable can intervene and confound the results.

A second alternative to randomized experiments is *matching*. If randomization is not feasible, it may be possible to match persons in the experimental group with persons having similar characteristics in a control group. However, matching can be unreliable because we can use relatively few variables, which leaves uncontrolled variables that might confound the results.

An example of an evaluation in which a form of matching was used was a study of the effects of a housing allowance program implemented by the Department of Housing and Urban Development (HUD) in 1970 (Jackson and Mohr 1986). Because of the nature of the program, people could not be assigned to experimental and control groups. Instead, for the experimental group, a random sample of clients enrolled in the program was used. For a control group, a sample was selected from the

Annual Housing Survey administered by HUD. The HUD survey contained data similar to that collected from the experimental group. The matching involved selecting clients from the Annual Housing Survey who were eligible for but not enrolled in the housing allowance program. This provided a comparison group to assess the impact of enrollment in the housing allowance program on such characteristics as changes in housing quality and the extent of the rent burden.

A third alternative to the randomized experiment, really another form of matching, is the use of *cohort groups.* Cohorts are groups of people who move through an organization or a treatment program at about the same time. For example, the following are cohorts: students in the same grade in a school, people receiving public assistance at the same time from a particular agency, and people in a drug rehabilitation program at the same time. Cohorts are valuable alternatives to randomized experiments because we may be able to assume that each cohort in an organization or program is similar to the cohort preceding it in terms of the characteristics that might affect a treatment outcome. In other words, each group should be alike in age, sex, socioeconomic status, and other characteristics that may be important. However, there can also be very significant differences, and cohorts should always be assessed to detect any possible systematic variation.

An elaborate cohort study evaluating curriculum revision and televised instruction was conducted in El Salvador from 1969 to 1973 (Mayo, Hornick, and McAnany 1976). Seventh-grade classes in 1969, 1970, and 1971 made up three separate cohorts of students. Within the cohorts, some classes received a new curriculum, some received the new curriculum with televised instruction, and some received the old curriculum. The cohorts from 1969 and 1970 were followed for three years, and the one from 1971 was followed for two years. Comparisons among the groups produced mixed results. The new curriculum was consistently superior to the old one, and televised instruction was superior during its first year. However, the superiority of televised instruction wore off as the students became accustomed to it.

The major weakness of cohorts is, again, the threat to validity from history. Because the measurements are taken at widely spaced times, extraneous variables may intercede and affect the results. The El Salvador example is instructive on this point. It would be unlikely that a similar cohort study could have been reliably conducted 10 years later, as the country became unstable owing to guerrilla warfare. Comparing a cohort from a period of peace with one from a period of near civil war has obvious problems.

A fourth alternative to the randomized experiment is the *regression discontinuity design:* People are selected to receive a treatment based on their score on a test, their eligibility for a program, or some other criterion. The study of recidivism in California discussed in Research in Practice 12.1 was a regression discontinuity design in which prison inmates were eligible for the experimental group if they had worked sufficient hours in prison to be eligible for unemployment benefits when released. Inmates who had worked fewer hours were put in the control group. This design is often implemented for evaluation research field experiments, and it can be useful. However, regression discontinuity designs suffer from some of the threats to internal validity, particularly selection and, in some cases, statistical regression. Incidentally, the summative evaluation described in Research in Practice 12.1 was an outgrowth of the formative evaluation project described earlier in this chapter about the provision of financial aid to newly released prisoners.

The last major alternative to randomized experiments is the use of *statistical controls,* procedures that allow the effects of one or more variables to be removed or held constant so that the effects of other variables can be observed. These procedures allow comparisons to be made between groups that differ from one another on some characteristics thought to be important. The effects of the variables on which the groups differ are removed through statistical manipulation so they cannot obscure the results. Statistical controls, however, even in their most elaborate application, can only approximate the level of control achievable in randomized experiments. As with matching, only variables the researcher knows to be

RESEARCH IN PRACTICE 12.1

PROGRAM EVALUATION:

The Effectiveness of Financial Assistance in Reducing Recidivism

Even the most reformed and well-intentioned former prisoner faces a host of obstacles in his or her efforts to begin a new life outside prison. Family members often are not supportive or too poor to help, or the ex-inmate has no relatives or friends outside prison on whom to rely. The newly released prisoner suddenly becomes responsible for innumerable decisions: where to live, buy clothes, obtain meals, and find work and how to make friends and keep out of trouble. These problems are frequently compounded by an uncertain financial status: no job prospects, a bus ticket to one's hometown, and $25 to $200 gate money.

Policymakers concerned about the welfare of former prisoners and hoping to reduce recidivism have considered programs that provide financial assistance to former prisoners to help them make a successful transition to civilian life. The thrust of such programs is typically to provide a payment, like unemployment insurance, to provide financial support while the ex-inmate gets settled and finds a job. Because many crimes are economically motivated, it seems reasonable to hypothesize that such financial assistance would reduce the likelihood that a newly released inmate would turn to such crimes.

To test this hypothesis, the Baltimore Living Insurance for Ex-prisoners (or Baltimore LIFE) Project was developed (Lenihan 1977; Rossi et al. 1980). This field experiment was an intermediary stage between a small pilot project involving only six people and a much larger program involving several thousand inmates in Texas and Georgia. In the Baltimore LIFE Project, high-risk inmates scheduled for release by the Maryland Department of Corrections were randomly divided into four groups: three experimental groups and one control. One experimental group received financial assistance of $60 per week for 13 weeks after release and was offered job placement services. The second group received financial assistance but no job placement services. The third experimental group received only job services, whereas the control group received neither financial assistance nor job ser-

vices. The intent of this phase of research was to determine if the two independent variables—financial assistance and job placement services—would have any positive effect on recidivism. For two years, the ex-prisoners were observed, and their experience in employment and criminal activity was noted. When the analysis was complete, a number of factors were considered, such as race, age at first arrest, number of prior arrests, education, marital status, parole status, and work experience.

The Baltimore LIFE Project illustrates several key features of careful program evaluation. First, the project was preceded by a much smaller exploratory study that enabled the project staff to test and refine some of their procedures. Second, the evaluation utilized a variety of research techniques. In addition to the basic experimental design, the research relied on structured interviews and case studies of several participants to provide insight into the problems, reactions, and frustrations of these men as they attempted to cope with life in the community. Third, a cost-benefit analysis was conducted to ascertain if the program was worthwhile. Finally, great care was taken in selecting participants, in explaining the program to the participants, and in dispensing financial aid and job counseling according to the design.

The results of the study indicated that the men who received financial aid had an 8 percent lower rate of arrest for charges of theft. Arrests for other types of crime were not significantly different. Also, those not receiving financial aid were arrested earlier, were more likely to be convicted, and were more likely to be returned to prison. Job placement services had no apparent impact on recidivism or occupational success.

Based on the modestly optimistic findings of this research, a much larger program, which involved dispensing financial aid through the existing Employment Security Offices in Texas and Georgia, was implemented. In that project, the overall findings were not positive. The researchers

continued on next page

concluded that the disappearance of positive outcomes may have resulted from the way the larger program was administered, thereby emphasizing the need for careful program implementation as well as research. Thus, evaluation research focuses not only on the outcome of programs but also on how they can be best implemented.

The Baltimore LIFE Project also served as a model for a legislatively mandated program in California (Berk et al. 1985). It was designed much like the Baltimore LIFE Project except the inmates actually applied for unemployment benefits once released from prison and were eligible if they had worked sufficient hours per week in prison. Because of this, however, the random assignment of inmates to experimental and control groups for evaluation purposes was not done, and thus the best research design for assessing program impacts—the randomized experiment—was not used.

Instead, investigators used a regression discontinuity design, in which the experimental group consisted of those inmates who had worked enough to be eligible for unemployment benefits and the control group contained those who had not. This did not affect the operation of the program, but it did make the evaluation of it more difficult and less certain. Nonetheless, a conservative evaluation of its effects concluded that the program saved California $2,000 for each inmate involved. In other words, the costs of the program were far outweighed by the money saved because some inmates in the program did not commit further crimes and the state saved the cost of incarcerating them. Despite this, the program was ended, partly because of ideological hostility to the idea of giving support to inmates and partly because California was facing a budget crisis.

potentially important can be statistically controlled, so there is always the possibility of leaving important extraneous variables uncontrolled. Furthermore, statistical controls tend to underadjust for differences between groups because of the error component in the measurement of the control variables (Berk and Rossi 1990). The error allows at least some of the effects of the control variables to remain even after the statistical controls have been applied. Because of these limitations, statistical control alone may not be appropriate. However, it is well suited as an adjunct to the physical control obtained through design. For example, in a matched design, we might find out after the fact that an important variable was left unmatched. Assuming the necessary data were collected, we could make up for this error by applying statistical control to that variable.

The use of both design control and statistical control is probably the best overall approach for evaluation because statistical control can even be useful in randomized experiments.

Nonpositivist Approaches to Evaluation

Nonpositivist approaches make quite different assumptions from positivist approaches about what is going on in a summative evaluation. First of all, nonpositivists assume that there are multiple stakeholders in—and thus multiple perspectives on—social interventions (Greene 1994). A given research methodology may assess the program in terms of the interests of some stakeholders but not others. In fact, some critics of positivist approaches to evaluation argue that because such evaluations are typically funded and supported by the sponsors and managers of the program, the evaluations tend to address issues of concern to those stakeholders—such as economic efficiency of the program, numbers of people served, or other issues that can be measured in quantitative (often monetary) ways. These approaches tend to focus on the importance of assessing program outcomes, efficiency, and accountability and in fact are the issues most readily addressed through the randomized experimental designs that positivists consider to be the ideal evaluation methodology. For evaluators who address different issues or the interests of other stakeholders, the randomized experimental design with control groups may be less important or possibly irrelevant as a research design (Cook 1985).

A second assumption of nonpositivist evaluators, especially those using an interpretive approach, is that interpretation and social meaning are at the core of social interventions (Denzin 1989; Smith 1989; Weiss 1998). In this view, social reality does not just exist "out there" but is created by people as they interact and exchange meanings. An interpretivist program evaluation focuses attention on how all the stakeholders experience a social intervention—the sponsors and managers as well as the recipients of services. From some perspectives, such as that of those receiving the services, economic efficiency and other quantitative matters may not be the key elements of the program at all. The point is that nonpositivist evaluators refuse to define issues and solutions solely from the perspective of the more powerful and dominant stakeholders. These concerns lead nonpositivist evaluators to research methodologies that are more useful for discovering the interpretations and perspectives of the various parties to the program: participant observation, in-depth interviewing, case studies, and other more qualitative approaches. In these approaches, control groups, random assignment, and random samples are less important than discovering meaning in the social contexts in which people live and allowing participants to frame their own issues and define problems using their own meaningful categories.

A third assumption of nonpositivist evaluators, especially those using a critical approach, is that social interventions typically reflect and reinforce inequitable distributions of power and resources in society. A central goal of the critical program evaluator is to reveal the mechanisms whereby inequities are reinforced and increased and to show how social programs promote the agenda of the powerful while doing relatively little for the less

powerful. Critical evaluators might use either quantitative or qualitative approaches, but their approach is more participatory in nature: Less powerful stakeholders participate in designing and carrying out the evaluation, thus increasing the likelihood that the research designed will discover facts and relationships beneficial to them. They are consulted about the research all along the way, and one of the research goals is the empowerment of these groups. A part of this empowerment involves the evaluation serving as a catalyst for social change.

Research in Practice 12.2 provides an illustration of a program evaluation that utilizes a nonpositivist approach. Of course, the distinction between positivist and nonpositivist research does not rigidly follow the separation between quantitative and qualitative research, although there is a relationship. This is also true in the field of evaluation research. Although positivists and nonpositivists do have the methodological inclinations we describe, the key distinctions between them have to do with assumptions rather than with particular research methodologies. Looking at both the positivist and nonpositivist perspectives achieves a much broader view of what evaluation research can accomplish and what issues and values can be attended to in such research.

Cost-Benefit Analysis

One particular type of evaluation research, *cost-benefit analysis,* involves some unique issues and premises and thus warrants special attention. In an era of increasing accountability for social programs, this approach often serves as a foundation for social policy decisions, and so it is important that it be used properly, with its strengths and limitations well understood (Hummel-Rossi and Ashdown 2002).

On the surface, **cost-benefit analysis** appears seductively simple: Add up the costs of a program, subtract them from the dollar value of the benefits, and get the result: either a net gain (benefits exceed costs) or a net loss (costs exceed benefits). Such an approach is appealing to many policymakers because it seems to clarify complex issues and programs through quantification. They would logically support

RESEARCH IN PRACTICE 12.2

A Nonpositivist Evaluation of a Juvenile Gang Intervention Program

PROGRAM EVALUATION:

Research in Practice 12.1 presented a program evaluation that was positivist in nature, using quantitative measures of variables and focusing a lot of attention on the economic efficiency of the program. Little consideration was given to treating the released inmates as stakeholders in the program; their views were not solicited. A more nonpositivist approach was used in an evaluation of a juvenile gang intervention program in a rural community (Stum and Chu 1999). The program evaluated in this study was a school partnership program that followed the philosophy of community policing. The basic idea was to build positive police–citizen partnerships based on trust and mutual respect, accomplished, in part, through daily visits to schools by the police to interact with and get to know the youths. Because there had been little prior research on such programs, especially as they operate in rural communities, the researchers decided that a more nonpositivist, exploratory, qualitative approach was appropriate.

The researchers decided that focus groups (see Chapter 7) and content analysis (see Chapter 8) would be the best methodologies. Earlier in this chapter, we discussed using focus groups as a part of formative evaluations, but this research provides an illustration of the use of focus groups in summative evaluations. The research focused on gang members and at-risk youth and explored their perceptions of themselves, their peers, their communities, and the gang prevention and intervention programs operating in their schools. (As discussed in Chapter 9, these qualitative approaches better enable us to understand the subjective experiences of the people being studied, and they better avoid the possibility that a researcher will impose his or her own meanings in a way that misses or distorts what is going on.)

Recall (from Chapter 7) that focus groups, also called group depth interviews, involve a moderator asking questions of a group and recording people's responses. The questions asked guide the discussion, but the moderator is free to ask additional questions and even to digress into new topics that seem fruitful based on the discussion. In addition, group interaction can stimulate responses that might not have occurred with other methodologies. Overall, focus groups are exploratory and encourage people to respond in their own words and by creating their own meanings. This is based on the assumptions made by nonpositivist program evaluators: The thoughts and perspectives of all stakeholders in a program should be assessed, and powerless or disadvantaged groups should have an opportunity to be heard.

In this study, data collection occurred in three separate focus groups in which each participant was involved. One addressed the school partnership policing program by asking youth about their contacts or relationships with the police. A second focus group addressed the youths' perceptions of themselves, their activities, and the crimes they committed as well as their perceptions of police, probation officers, judges, and others in positions of authority. This focus group also explored whether the youths felt they had changed because of their experience with the program. The third group had to do with how the youths felt about their peers and their communities.

All focus group discussions were tape-recorded, and a research assistant prepared notes based on his or her observation of the group discussion so the tapes and notes could be compared as a way of assessing reliability and validity. Then the tapes and notes were reviewed repeatedly to identify major themes in the data. If researchers disagreed about themes, they went back to the raw data (tapes and notes) to identify what led to the identification of a particular theme.

One of the conclusions the study came to was that, based on the opinions expressed by the youths in the focus groups, the school partnership program had serious weaknesses and might not be an effective intervention program for teens at risk. Most of the youth reported that they didn't know, or at best hardly knew, the police officers with whom they were supposed to be developing positive relationships. In addition, they expressed concerns that contact with police authorities might bring them difficulties—police could identify them as potential troublemakers because of their involvement in a program for at-risk teens. With no prior research in these programs, this exploratory, qualitative methodology is more likely to discover attitudes like these.

and perhaps expand programs showing a net gain and curtail those with a net loss. If only it were that simple. As we shall see, quantifying benefits and costs can be extremely difficult and often involves a number of unproved assumptions and estimates.

Cost-benefit analysis can be applied to a program during its planning stages, called *ex ante analysis,* or after the program has been in operation, or *ex post analysis* (Rossi, Freeman, and Lipsey 1999). The major difference is that an *ex ante* analysis requires more estimates and assumptions because no hard data exist on either costs or benefits. An *ex post* study has records of actual cost outlays and can determine benefits empirically through normal evaluation research procedures. The use of estimates in *ex ante* analyses means that results are far more tentative and accounts for why *ex ante* analyses conducted by different parties sometimes come to widely divergent conclusions: They use different estimates and assumptions. Sorting out whose estimates are most valid has produced some lively debates among policymakers. *Ex post* analyses require fewer estimates and are, therefore, more reliable.

Estimating Costs.   The easy part of cost-benefit analysis—although by no means simple—is determining the **direct costs** of a program. The program has either a record of actual expenditures (in *ex post* analysis) or a proposed budget for the program (in *ex ante* analysis). A budget proposal, however, is based on assumptions that may not be accurate. For example, the budget for a supplemental unemployment compensation program must assume a certain unemployment rate. If the actual rate changes, the cost of the program can skyrocket or fall dramatically.

Considerably more difficult to estimate than direct program costs are what economists call *opportunity costs.* **Opportunity costs** are the value of forgone opportunities. Suppose, for example, that you are fortunate enough to win a $1,000 prize in a contest. You can invest the money or spend it on anything you like—a stereo, for instance. The direct cost of the stereo is the $1,000 you spent on it, but there are opportunity costs. The opportunity costs are what you forgo by buying the stereo. You lose the return you could have earned by investing it or the value of

other items you might have purchased, such as new clothes or the down payment on an automobile.

So it is with the funding of social programs. Agencies have limited resources. If they decide to fund a certain program, the cost of the program includes the opportunity costs of not funding alternative programs. Normally, the estimated value of the benefits of competing programs is used as the basis for computing the opportunity costs of the program being analyzed. Computing the benefits lost by not initiating a program is complex, which makes it difficult to calculate the opportunity costs of the funded program. Such estimates need to be made, however, to provide an accurate picture of the total costs of a program.

Estimating and Monetizing Benefits.   The really difficult and often unreliable part of cost-benefit analysis comes in determining program benefits and *monetizing,* or attaching a dollar value to them. This process may be fairly straightforward or mystical, depending on the program. In general, if a program's benefits are related to some economic activity, they are easier to monetize—for example, the value of subsidized day care. The market price of private day care plus the added income of the parent who otherwise could not work constitute the major dollar benefits from the program. But what about program benefits less related to economic activity? How can we place a dollar value on such program benefits as improved mental health, improved self-esteem, reduced domestic violence, or other noneconomic outcomes? Cost-benefit analysis attempts through complex procedures to place a dollar value on practically anything. Doing so, however, requires many often-controversial assumptions and value judgments. Thus, cost-benefit analysis is of the greatest utility when the relationship between program benefits and a certain dollar value is fairly clear.

Another complicating factor in cost-benefit analysis is that benefits and costs do not accrue at the same time. Costs are incurred immediately upon the program's implementation, whereas benefits may not accrue until some later date, possibly far in the future. In some programs, such as education or job training, at least part of the benefits are long-term indeed. This temporal gap is a problem because the value of both costs and benefits change with time. A dollar today does not have the same purchasing power it did 10 years ago. To make meaningful comparisons over time, we must adjust costs and benefits so that comparisons are made in constant dollars. This involves the calculation of what is called the *discount rate*. The discount rate is the amount that future costs and benefits are reduced to make them comparable to the current value of money. Actual calculation of the discount rate involves some accounting procedures. There are also several competing approaches to its calculation (Rossi, Freeman, and Lipsey 1999). As many disheartened investors will attest, predicting the future value of money is a risky business. Furthermore, the discount rate used has a marked effect on the outcome of the analysis. For all these reasons, it is common to run several analyses with differing discount rates to see how the program fares under different sets of assumptions.

Whose Costs, Whose Benefits?   An important consideration in cost-benefit analysis is that costs and benefits are calculated from particular perspectives. Three different perspectives may be used: program participants, the funding source, or society as a whole. A comprehensive cost-benefit analysis would include all three.

Take the example of early childhood intervention programs, which are efforts by government or other agencies outside the family to support and improve the quality of life for youngsters from the prenatal period into the school years. These programs focus on providing health, education, and social service interventions. The theory behind such programs is that they will provide broad benefits to society because the children they support will generally be healthier, do better in school, and be less likely to create problems of crime or welfare dependence as adults. In Table 12.1, we have listed some of the po-

Table 12.1   Perspectives on the Costs and Benefits of an Early Childhood Intervention Program

Benefits and Costs	Society	Perspective Participants	Funding Source
Costs of home visits to children	−	+	−
Reduction in emergency room visits by child	+	+	0
Increase in taxes paid by mother because of her increased employment income	+	−	+
Decrease in cost of government welfare payments to mother	0	−	+
Decrease in mother's arrest and jail costs	+	+	0
Decrease in child's arrest costs as an adolescent	+	+	0
Decrease in child's arrest cost as an adult	+	+	0
Income from mother's increased employment	0	+	0
Decrease in welfare payments to mother	0	−	+
Decrease in losses to crime victims	+	0	0

Key: + = an expected benefit from a given perspective

− = an expected cost from a given perspective

0 = neither a cost nor a benefit

Source   Adapted from Lynn A. Karoly et al., *Investing in Our Children: What We Know and Don't Know about the Costs and Benefits of Early Childhood Interventions* (Santa Monica, CA: Rand, 1998).

tential costs and benefits of such early intervention programs, along with an indication of which perspective might see each as a cost or benefit.

Let us look at some elements in the table. For the mothers (participants) who can work at paying jobs because of the services provided by the programs, their costs are the loss of welfare payments they would receive if they did not work. Their benefits are the income received by working (together with less tangible benefits, such as enhanced social status, job satisfaction, and freedom from child care responsibilities). Participants also benefit from any reductions in criminal activity the mother or child experience because of participation in the program.

From the perspective of the funding sources—in this case the federal government—the costs and benefits are quite different. The costs are the direct costs of running the program (e.g., costs of home visits) together with the opportunity costs of not using the money for something else. The benefits are the reduced costs of other public assistance programs and an increase in tax revenues on the incomes of working mothers.

The societal perspective is the broadest and frequently the most difficult to calculate. (If the funding source is the government, we should not assume that the government's perspective coincides with the societal perspective. The government represents only those who control a particular government agency.) The costs to society of the early intervention program are the increased taxes or federal borrowing necessary to fund the program, plus the opportunity costs. Benefits are increased productivity of the mothers who are now freer to make economic, social, and cultural contributions to society (although we need to remember that performing as a parent or homemaker is also an essential contribution). Other less direct benefits might accrue if working and the additional income it provides have positive effects on family relationships, the children's well-being, future aspirations, and the like. Of course, society as a whole benefits when costs associated with crime are reduced.

Early intervention programs involve more elements—and more costs and benefits—than we listed in Table 12.1, but the table helps clarify the idea that program costs and benefits need to be assessed from a variety of perspectives. People might also disagree over whether a particular element in the table is a cost or a benefit from a particular perspective, which only reinforces the point that cost-benefit analysis is difficult, complicated, and often contentious. Incidentally, most cost-benefit analyses of these early childhood intervention programs conclude that, if run well, the programs do provide substantially more benefits than costs (Karoly et al. 1998).

Cost-Effective Analysis

Because it is difficult to monetize benefits, interest has developed in an alternative approach that does not require that benefits be ascribed a dollar value. **Cost-effective analysis** compares program costs measured in dollars with program effects measured in whatever units are appropriate, such as achievement test scores, skill performance level, coping abilities, or whatever effect the program is supposed to produce. Such analysis is most useful for choosing among competing programs rather than evaluating a single program. For example, cost-effective analysis is often used in evaluating HIV prevention programs (Holtgrave 1998). The challenge to comparing prevention programs is having a meaningful standard of comparison. One approach is to employ cost-benefit analysis by comparing programs based on the benefit of money saved in medical care by preventing an infection. However, such cost-benefit analysis is insufficient for policymakers because medical care dollars saved hardly represent the positive impact of a prevention program.

Evaluators have developed an alternative, non-monetary measure, the QALY, for cost-effective analysis. The term "QALY" refers to "quality-adjusted life years," or the number of years of additional life that result because infection did not occur, as well as the quality of that life (perfect health versus some diminished level of capacity). We will not get into the complexity of measuring QALYs except to make the point that a variety of prevention programs can be directly compared in terms of money spent for each additional QALY achieved. Based on experience with the standard of program costs per

QALY saved, policymakers consider a ratio of $40,000 per QALY to be cost-effective.

Such cost-effective analyses of many competing programs make it possible to select the most efficient approach. Interpreting a single cost-effective analysis, however, is less clear-cut than a cost-benefit analysis because the costs and benefits are not expressed in the same units. For this reason, cost-effective analysis is not an interchangeable substitute for cost-benefit analysis because they answer different questions.

Although cost-benefit analysis is a valuable tool in assessing programs, it is important that it be neither oversimplified nor overemphasized but carefully interpreted in light of the data. The complex components that go into a cost-benefit analysis need to be considered when interpreting the results. Like all forms of analysis, cost-benefit analysis is only as good as the data, the estimates, and the assumptions on which it is based. All these components should be explicitly discussed in the report and the users encouraged to evaluate their soundness. The real risk associated with cost-benefit analysis comes when bottom-line results are accepted blindly and become the overriding factor in decision making. At its current level of development, cost-benefit analysis is useful, but it must be cautiously interpreted as only one of many factors in the decision-making process concerning social programs.

Barriers to the Use of Evaluation Research

At the beginning of this chapter, we described the purposes of evaluation research as improving service to clients, aiding in the policymaking process, and testing social science theories and practice approaches. In all these areas, the assumption is made that the research results will be used to produce some change in the status quo. In actuality, this is often not the case because there are many barriers to the use of the results of evaluation research.

One barrier is the fault of evaluators. Owing to poor design or execution, the evaluation may not produce clear-cut results. It is difficult to overcome resistance to change unless the reasons for change are strong and the direction that change should take is clear. All too often, the basic conclusion of an evaluation is this: "The program as currently operated is not achieving its intended goals." What is one to do with such a conclusion? It offers no indication of why the program is failing or suggestions for improving it. To avoid results like this, evaluation should be broadly conceived so the findings indicate not only what the program does not do but also what it does do and why. Such detailed findings are of far greater utility for pointing the way for the future and for producing positive program changes (Bedell et al. 1985).

A second barrier to the use of evaluation research results is poor communication on the part of evaluators (Miller 1987). Researchers are used to communicating with other researchers who share a common technical language and background. When communicating with one another, they assume those commonalities and write their reports accordingly. If this is done in an evaluation report, the results may be quite unclear to the practitioners, program administrators, and policymakers who are to use those results. Evaluation reports should be written so they are clear and understandable to the audience who will use them, and evaluators should work through the report with sponsors, explaining it thoroughly and answering all questions. Those sponsoring an evaluation or using the results should demand such accountability from evaluation researchers.

A third barrier to the use of evaluation research is the failure of the researchers to press for the adoption of their research findings. Such an advocacy role is foreign to many researchers, who may feel that their job terminates once the data have been analyzed. However, implementation of modifications to a program is often complex, and program staff are faced with competing interests. Without active participation by the researcher, adoption of recommendations may not take place at all.

A fourth barrier is the ever-present resistance to change. People become accustomed to established procedures. Vested interests are difficult to overcome.

One of the most arrogant rejections of research was President Richard Nixon's reaction to the findings of the President's Commission on Pornography. Nixon appointed the commission to study the societal impact of pornography, fully expecting negative effects to be found, thus justifying a crackdown. When the commission reported no negative effects of viewing pornography and possibly even some salutary ones, Nixon simply dismissed the report as wrong.

Such blatant dismissals are rare, however. More common is what happened to a study of group counseling in a correctional system (Kassebaum et al. 1971). This well-conducted study not only found few positive effects of counseling but also provided many suggestions as to why these effects did not occur. The reaction to the report by the Department of Corrections was swift but not what was predicted given its contents. The counseling program was not dropped but was expanded to every prison in the system, and the expanded program was not modified to take into account the suggestions in the report (Ward and Kassebaum 1972). Discouraged, the evaluators speculated that the main effect of their report would be to limit future outside evaluations of prison programs.

One change suggested to improve research utilization is increased dissemination of results (Weiss 1998). Earlier we expressed concern over the fact that evaluation reports are not often widely circulated. Broader dissemination may bring a report to the attention of someone willing to use the results.

Evaluation research reports are published in a number of ways. Sometimes they are published in social science or human service research journals, such as *Evaluation Review, Journal of Applied Behavioral Science*, or *Journal of Applied Sociology*. Over the past few years, more outlets for the publication of evaluation research have developed. Evaluation research reports are also published in government documents and reports, especially when the study concerns a government program; these can be accessed like other government documents (see Appendix A).

Some evaluation reports are not published, however, and this can make them more difficult—but not impossible—to find. Unpublished results may be presented at meetings of applied research organizations, such as the Society for Applied Sociology, the NTL Institute for Applied Behavioral Science, and the National Association of Social Workers. In some cases, unpublished research reports can be obtained from the researchers themselves or from the organizations or agencies for which the research was done. Unpublished reports can be difficult to locate because they are often not included in the databases that can be accessed online or through libraries to search for published research reports (see Appendix A). Some may be found through an Internet search or by participating in networks of professionals doing research in the same area.

Another change that increases the use of the evaluation results is to involve the potential users in the evaluation research itself. Users can help design the research or serve as interviewers. This results in better communication between evaluators and users: The users perceive the evaluation as more relevant and credible, and they are more committed to the evaluation (Dawson and D'Amico 1985).

What is really needed to improve research utilization is for policymakers and program administrators to develop an increased willingness to put evaluation results to use. In fact, resistance to research utilization does appear to be declining, and there may be a growing awareness that common sense and conventional wisdom are inadequate bases for designing and operating effective social programs (Rossi, Freeman, and Lipsey 1999). Years of experience with ineffective programs have made this conclusion evident. Such changing perspectives are encouraging for the future of evaluation research and its increased utilization.

Main Points

- Evaluation research is the use of scientific research methods to plan intervention programs, to monitor the implementation of new programs and the operation of existing ones, and to determine how effectively programs or clinical practices achieve their goals.

■ Formative evaluation focuses on the planning, development, and implementation of intervention programs.

■ Summative evaluation assesses the effectiveness and efficiency of programs and the extent to which program effects may be generalized to other settings and populations.

■ Prior to beginning evaluation, an evaluability assessment is conducted to gain knowledge about the program as operated and to identify those aspects of it that can be evaluated.

■ Proximate goals are evaluable, short-run goals logically related to the achievement of long-term goals that are impractical to evaluate.

■ Despite frequent difficulties associated with their use, randomized experiments constitute the strongest, most desirable designs for assessing program impact.

■ Cost-benefit analysis, through the use of complex assumptions and estimates, compares the costs of a program with the dollar value of its benefits.

■ Cost-benefit analysis and cost-effective analysis are not interchangeable. Cost-benefit analysis is useful for evaluating a single program, whereas cost-effective analysis is useful for choosing the most efficient program from among competing approaches.

■ It is important that bottom-line results from either cost-benefit or cost-effective analyses not be accepted blindly, but that the data, estimates, and assumptions on which the results are based be carefully considered.

Important Terms for Review

cost-benefit analysis
cost-effective analysis
direct costs
evaluability assessment
evaluation research
formative evaluation research
needs assessment
opportunity costs
stakeholders
summative evaluation research

Exploring InfoTrac® College Edition and the Internet

InfoTrac® College Edition search terms:

program evaluation AND _____ (insert human service field: delinquency, aging, etc.)
cost benefit analysis AND social
needs assessment AND social
evidence based AND mental health

InfoTrac® College Edition articles:

Assessing the Effects of School-Based Drug Education: A Six-Year Multilevel Analysis of Project D.A.R.E. Dennis Rosenbaum. *Journal of Research in Crime and Delinquency* Nov 1998 v35 n4 p381(31) (12,199 words)

Cost-Effectiveness of a School-Based Tobacco-Use Prevention Program. Li Yan Wang, Linda S. Crossett, Richard Lowry, Steve Sussman, Clyde W. Dent. *Archives of Pediatrics & Adolescent Medicine* Sept 2001 v155 i9 p1043 (6,548 words)

The Cash and Counseling Demonstration: An Experiment in Consumer-Directed Personal Assistance Services. Pamela J. Doty. *American Rehabilitation* Summer 1998 v24 i3 p27(1) (3,039 words)

One way to broaden your understanding of evaluation research is to review examples of completed evaluation studies. The Internet is an excellent source for locating illustrative projects in any human service field. For instance, if the field of substance abuse interests you, then we suggest that you go to the National Clearinghouse for Alcohol and Drug Information (NCADI) prevention database (www.health.org). NCADI offers substance abuse information via searchable databases. Click on "Databases," then "Prevention Materials Database," and you can access each database by clicking on its button and using the search mode attached. You can research these databases for bibliographic abstracts pertaining to such subjects as alcohol, tobacco, marijuana, cocaine, and other drugs.

The National Criminal Justice Reference Service (www.ncjrs.org) provides access not only to bibliographic references but also to the full-text versions of a wide range of evaluation projects in criminal justice. By searching this site, you can review projects and learn about the actual methodology used to evaluate them. One of the pages associated with this site is devoted to evaluation grants (www.ncjrs.org/fedgrant.html). Here you can review grant application instructions.

We pointed out that evaluation research differs from basic research in the role of the decision makers in program evaluation. We suggest that you review the specifications for one of the program evaluation projects with an eye toward how the sponsoring organization's needs affect the design of the research project. The Bureau of Justice Assistance also maintains a Web site with many resources and Web links related to evaluating criminal justice programs (www.bja.evaluationwebsite.org).

An excellent source of program evaluation–related resources in the field of education is the ERIC Clearinghouse on Assessment and Evaluation (www.ericae.net). In addition to directing you to various evaluation studies, the site provides links to assessment tools and professional organizations involved in evaluation. One such site worth mentioning in its own right is the American Evaluation Association, or AEA (www.eval.org). This international professional association of evaluators is devoted to the application and exploration of program evaluation, personnel evaluation, technology, and many other forms of evaluation. The AEA maintains a current listing of Internet sites of interest to program evaluators, so whether you are interested in health, education, or any other human service area, this site will help you to locate additional resources.

For Further Reading

Blalock, Ann Bonar, ed. *Evaluating Social Programs at the State and Local Level: The JTPA Evaluation Design Project.* Kalamazoo, Mich.: W. E. Upjohn Institute, 1990. This book provides an excellent overview of how to conduct program evaluations by analyzing specific evaluations of employment and training programs. It is a useful case study approach.

Boruch, Robert. *Randomized Experiments for Planning and Evaluation.* Thousand Oaks, Calif.: Sage, 1996. This author stresses the point made in this chapter that good program evaluations should be based on randomized experimental designs. The book is packed with useful examples of how to do this, often in situations where it might seem impossible.

Campbell, Donald T., and M. Jean Russo. *Social Experimentation.* Thousand Oaks, Calif.: Sage, 1999. Donald Campbell was one of the giants in the fields of experimentation and evaluation research. This book presents his approaches to how social experiments should be designed and how they can improve society.

Fitzpatrick Jody L., James R. Sanders, and Blaine R. Worthen. *Program Evaluation: Alternative Approaches and Practical Guidelines,* 3rd ed. Boston: Addison-Wesley, 2004. This text provides an overview of a wide variety of approaches to evaluation and extensive practical guidelines for carrying out evaluation studies.

Ginsberg, Leon H. *Social Work Evaluation: Principles and Methods.* Boston: Allyn and Bacon, 2001. In addition to traditional methods of outcome evaluation, this source includes chapters on licensure, accreditation, internal program evaluation, and user satisfaction that make the book relevant to the human service practitioner.

Guba, Egon G., and Yvonna S. Lincoln. *Fourth Generation Evaluation.* Newbury Park, Calif.: Sage, 1989. This book focuses mostly on program evaluation in educational settings. It challenges conventional thinking in that it takes an interpretive approach, viewing all knowledge as a social construction. Even scientific knowledge is seen as socially constructed, as only one version of reality.

Gupta, Kavita. *A Practical Guide to Needs Assessment.* San Francisco: Jossey-Bass/Pfeiffer, 1999. This book provides both an overview of needs assessment and step-by-step details for several models of needs assessment, along with illustrations of various data-collection tools. It is especially useful for staff training program assessment.

Nas, Tevfik F. *Cost-Benefit Analysis: Theory and Application.* Thousand Oaks, Calif.: Sage, 1996. The author shows, in much more detail than could be included in this chapter, how to conduct good cost-benefit analyses. The book covers all the relevant issues.

Patton, Michael Quinn. *Qualitative Research and Evaluation Methods,* 3rd ed. Thousand Oaks, Calif.: Sage, 2002. This book considers both theoretical and practical issues in conducting program evaluations. It also emphasizes the use of qualitative research and stresses the perspective that good program evaluations must be designed to be useful to program managers and policymakers.

Shadish, William R., Jr., Thomas D. Cook, and Laura C. Leviton. *Foundations of Program Evaluation*. Newbury Park, Calif.: Sage, 1993. This volume looks at the origins of program evaluation and at the accumulated experiences of veteran program evaluators to provide an insightful discussion of the development of the field and of key issues that are relevant today.

Exercises for Class Discussion

It is commonly known that many elderly people have strong emotional attachments to their pets. However, the necessity of moving into a nursing home or medical care facility generally entails severing that relationship. Recently, experts in gerontology have "discovered" the important role that animals can play in making residents feel at home in residential facilities. Consequently, some facilities have begun experimenting with pet therapy, a program in which volunteers bring pets to the nursing home on a regular basis so that interested residents may pet and play with the animals.

Assume you are a human service worker with a nursing home, and you have been approached by some residents or staff about starting such a program. You are aware that some local foundation money may be available to support the project, and some local organizations—the Humane Society, an area kennel club, a cat fanciers' group—could probably be induced to provide both the animals and the volunteers to help with the project. You also know that to get the money for the program, you have to convince the administration that the program is worth the trouble and show the foundation that you have a well-designed program that is effective in meeting its goals.

12.1 To make a formal proposal for funding, you must first do some formative evaluation research to determine if the program is needed and, if so, feasible. What are some initial research questions to ask in this regard?

12.2 What kinds of data will you need, and how might you collect them?

12.3 State some specific goals that such a program might be expected to achieve. Assume you have done some formative evaluation work, and the facility administrator has given the go-ahead to apply for a grant for the project. However, the board was somewhat skeptical about the idea, so the compromise that resulted specifies the program be tried for six months, at the end of which time a thorough evaluation must be done to determine the effects of the program and the relative costs and benefits.

12.4 What are some possible effects that the program might have? Remember to look for both positive and negative impacts. How would you suggest measuring these potential effects?

12.5 For a cost-benefit analysis, make a list of both costs and benefits. For each list, make a column with headings for three different accounting perspectives—society, the nursing home residents, and the funding source. For each cost and each benefit you identify, place a plus (+) sign in the column if that party stands to benefit, a zero (0) if the impact is neutral, or a minus (−) if that party stands to have a net cost. (See Table 12.1 for an example.)

12.6 Given the kinds of benefits that might result from such a program, which ones lend themselves to cost accounting? Which ones are not readily translatable into dollars? All things considered, is a cost-benefit analysis appropriate for this project?

12.7 The program as planned will be available to any resident in the facility who wants to participate. Thus, it is not possible to assign residents randomly to receive or not receive the program. Given this condition, what are some alternate ways of providing experimental control for the project? What potential validity problems do your suggestions pose?

Chapter 13

Scaling

We discussed measurement in research at some length in Chapter 5 and explained that some measurement is fairly straight-forward and involves the use of only a single *item,* or indicator of a variable. We can, for example, measure a person's age with one question that asks how old the person is. Likewise, such variables as marital status or number of children in a family are normally measured with a single item. These variables refer to phenomena that are fairly unambiguous and for which a single indicator provides a valid and reliable measure.

Many other variables, however, are much more difficult and complex to measure. In some cases, we may have more than one indicator of a variable. In other cases, the variable may involve a number of dimensions and call for multiple indicators. In still other cases, we may be concerned with the *degree* to which a variable is present. In cases where a single-item measuring instrument is probably inadequate, we use a **scale:** a number of items that combine to form a composite score on a variable. To measure people's attitudes toward having children, for example, we could ask how much they agree with a series of questions; together, those questions make up the scale that would indicate their overall attitude toward having children.

Advantages of Scaling

Scales have four major advantages over single-item measures.

Improved Validity

When measuring abstract or complex variables, a multiple-item measure is generally more valid than a single-item measure. Consider the variable of self-esteem. The Rosenberg Self-Esteem Scale contains 10 statements (see Table 13.1) because no single question or statement could possibly measure something as complex, multifaceted, and constantly changing as a person's self-esteem. What single question could we ask that might encompass all the feelings that we have about ourselves? Clearly, self-esteem involves many aspects of a person's life situation—family, occupa-

tion, financial, and social status, to name only a few. Multiple-item scales provide more valid measures of such complex phenomena.

Improved Reliability

In general (as we showed in Chapter 5), the more items a measure contains, the more reliable it is because the statements making up a scale are actually just a sample of the entire universe of statements that could have been used. A single-item measure is a sample of one, and it is less likely to be *representative* of the universe of statements than more than one item is. Multiple-item scales are larger samples from this universe and are more likely to be representative and, therefore, more reliable than single-item measures.

Increased Level of Measurement

Single-item measures are likely to produce data that are nominal or at best *partially ordered data,* a term that refers to data with a few ordered categories but with many cases tied for each category. Although superior to nominal data, partially ordered data are less desirable than fully ordered data, in which nearly every case has its own rank (see Chapter 14). Multiple-item scales can produce fully ordered and possibly interval-level data. A higher level of measurement means better measurement in terms of precision and increased flexibility in data analysis.

Increased Efficiency in Data Handling

Because the items in a scale are all related (in that they all measure the same variable), we can summarize responses to these items into a single number or score for each respondent. This achieves the quantification goal of measurement and means that all the separate responses to each of the items do not have to be analyzed individually. Each score summarizes a great deal of information about each respondent and facilitates analysis of the data.

So when the concept to be measured is complex, multiple-item scales offer substantial advantages for the researcher—advantages that often outweigh the difficulty of the scale's construction.

Table 13.1   Rossenberg Self-Esteem Scale

	1 Strongly Agree	2 Agree	3 Disagree	4 Strongly Disagree
(1) On the whole, I am satisfied with myself.	SA[4]	A[3]	D[2]	SD[1]
(2) At times I think I am no good at all.	SA[1]	A[2]	D[3]	SD[4]
(3) I feel that I have a number of good qualities.	SA[4]	A[3]	D[2]	SD[1]
(4) I am able to do things as well as most other people.	SA[4]	A[3]	D[2]	SD[1]
(5) I feel I do not have much to be proud of.	SA[1]	A[2]	D[3]	SD[4]
(6) I certainly feel useless at times.	SA[1]	A[2]	D[3]	SD[4]
(7) I feel that I'm a person of worth, at least on an equal plane with others.	SA[4]	A[3]	D[2]	SD[1]
(8) I wish I could have more respect for myself.	SA[1]	A[2]	D[3]	SD[4]
(9) All in all, I am inclined to feel that I am a failure.	SA[1]	A[2]	D[3]	SD[4]
(10) I take a positive attitude toward myself.	SA[4]	A[3]	D[2]	SD[1]

Source   Morris Rosenberg, *Conceiving the Self,* rev. ed. (Malabar, Fla.: Krieger Publishing Company, 1986). Reprinted by permission of Morris Rosenberg.

Developing Scales

Once a researcher decides to use a scale as a measuring device, he or she needs to find or develop an appropriate scale. In most cases, scales consist of questions to which people respond or statements to which they indicate their level of agreement. (In Chapter 7, we presented guidelines for writing questions in questionnaires or interviews, and those same general rules apply to the development or selection of scale items. Readers should review those guidelines now, considering them in the context of scale construction.)

In many cases, it is possible to use a complete scale developed by someone else if it is a valid and reliable measure of the variables under investigation. A scale can also be made up of statements or even whole sections taken from previously developed scales. A major advantage of existing items or scales is that their validity and reliability usually have already been established. A few of the many compilations of measurement scales are listed in the For Further Reading section of this chapter. In addition, scales are reported and described in the many research journals dedicated to the behavioral sciences.

If no existing scale will do the job, then a new scale should be developed (DeVellis 2003). A certain logic is common to the development of scales, which generally involves the following steps:

1. Develop or locate many potential scale items, far more than will appear in the final scale.
2. Eliminate items that are redundant, ambiguous, or for some other reason inappropriate for the scale.
3. Pretest the remaining items for validity, reliability, or other measurement checks to be described shortly.
4. Eliminate items that do not pass the tests of Step 3.
5. Repeat Steps 3 and 4 as often as necessary to reduce the scale to the number of items required.

Sources of Scale Items

One of the most accessible sources of scale items is a researcher's own imagination. Once he or she has developed and refined a concept, the researcher has a pretty good idea of what is to be measured and can then generate a range of statements to satisfy the criteria to be discussed. At this early stage in scale construction, we need not be too concerned with honing and polishing the statements to perfection because much pretesting remains before an actual respondent ever sees any statement.

A second source of scale items is a group of people, sometimes called judges, who are considered to be especially knowledgeable in a particular area. If we are seeking items for a delinquency scale, for instance, it is reasonable to discuss the issue with juvenile probation officers and others who have daily contact with delinquents.

Two social psychologists used this approach to find items for a scale to measure people's tendency to manipulate others for their own personal gain (Christie and Geis 1970). They turned to the writings of Niccolò Machiavelli, a 16th-century advisor to the prince of Florence in Italy. In his classic book *The Prince,* Machiavelli propounded what is essentially a con artist's view of the world and politics: According to Machiavelli, people are to be manipulated for one's own benefit, in a cool and unemotional fashion. Lying, cheating, and underhandedness are justified to advance one's own personal position. In the writings of this Florentine four centuries ago, these social psychologists found such statements as "It is safer to be feared than to be loved" and "Humility not only is of no service but is actually harmful." They constructed a scale made up of Machiavelli's statements, somewhat revised, and asked people whether they agreed with each statement. Now known as the Machiavellianism Scale, it has been used widely in scientific research. One is tempted to wonder whether Signore Machiavelli, were he able to peer through the mists of time, would consider this scale a sufficiently cunning and beguiling use of his prose. In any event, this illustrates a particularly creative use of judges in the development of scales.

A third source of scale items is the people who are the focus of the research project. Claudia Coulton (1979), for example, was interested in person–environment fit among consumers of hospital social services. In developing her scale, she obtained a large number of verbatim statements from hospital patients and then began to form them into a scale. In a similar manner, if we were interested in attitudes among teenagers toward unwanted pregnancies, an excellent beginning would be to discuss the topic with teenagers themselves and gather from them as many statements as possible regarding the issue. When items are garnered from people in this fashion, only rarely are statements usable without editing. Many statements would ultimately be rejected, and most would have to be considerably rewritten. Still, such people are likely to provide a range of statements with meaning from the perspective of the group under investigation.

Characteristics of Scale Items

Once the researcher has amassed a large number of scale items, he or she must select the best ones for the final scale. Good scale items have the following characteristics.

Validity.   A primary concern in item selection is the validity of the statements (see Chapter 5). Each statement considered for inclusion should be assessed for content validity. For example, if we are creating a self-report delinquency scale, we assess each statement by how it relates to measuring delinquent activity. Statements concerning participation in delinquent acts are reasonable as valid measures of how delinquent that person is. On the other hand, an item relating to how well the respondent gets along with his or her siblings probably is not a valid indicator of delinquency.

Range of Variation.   Variables that are measured with multiple-item scales normally consist of a number of possible values or positions that a person can take. If we want to measure attitudes toward growing old, for example, people's positions on that variable could be extremely positive, extremely negative, or anywhere in between. In selecting items for measurement scales, we should ensure that the items cover the actual range of possible variation on the variable being measured. Failure to do so results in a poor scale. When selecting items on the basis of variability, the researcher needs to exercise care to avoid defining the range either too narrowly or too broadly. Failure to include a sufficiently wide range of items results in responses that pile up at one or both ends of the scale's range. If many respondents tie with either the lowest or highest possible score, the range in the scale is inadequate. This piling-up effect reduces the precision of the measurement because we are unable to differentiate among the respondents with tied scores.

Going to extremes with items to define the range is not desirable, either. If we include items that are too extreme, they apply to few, if any, respondents. In the case of a delinquency scale, for example, an item pertaining to engaging in cannibalism would be such an extreme item as to warrant exclusion. The act is so rare in our culture that it is unlikely that any juvenile has done it, and it thus contributes nothing of benefit to the scale. The goal is to select items with enough variation to cover the actual range of alternatives that people are likely to choose, without including items so extreme that they do not apply to anyone.

Unidimensionality. In the construction of a multiple-item scale, the goal is to measure one specific variable. We do not want the results confounded by items on the scale that actually measure a different (although possibly related) variable. The items of a **unidimensional scale** measure only one variable. If a scale actually measures more than one variable, then it is called multidimensional. In creating our delinquency scale, we might be tempted to include an item about school performance on the grounds that delinquents seem to perform poorly in school. Although an empirical relationship may exist between delinquency and school performance, these are separate variables and should be treated and measured as such.

In assessing the unidimensionality of scales, we distinguish between *different variables* and *different aspects of the same variable*. A single variable may have more than one aspect, and we need to be careful to recognize these so that they can be measured appropriately. Delinquency, for example, contains at least two aspects: severity and frequency. In terms of severity, it is reasonable to distinguish between an adolescent who commits petty theft and one who commits aggravated assault. In terms of frequency, an adolescent who regularly commits petty theft might be properly considered delinquent, or even more delinquent, than one with a single case of assault.

The different aspects of a variable need to be distinguished and analyzed carefully because one may correlate with an independent or dependent variable, whereas another may not. This again suggests the complexity of some variables. In a study of person–environment fit, for example, Claudia Coulton (1979) distinguished between the many aspects that might be parts of this variable. "Person–environment fit" refers to the extent to which an individual's needs can be satisfied and aspirations fulfilled in the context of the demands and opportunities available in a particular environment. Coulton distinguished between "fit" in relation to one's economic activities, "fit" in terms of the amount and relevance of available information, "fit" in terms of one's family relations, and the like. In this case, the "person–environment fit" scale is unidimensional in that it measures one underlying variable, but it also contains a number of distinct aspects that are a part of that variable.

To gain systematic evidence of the unidimensionality of a scale, the researcher can intercorrelate each item in the scale with every other scale item, usually during a pretest. If some items do not correlate with the others, it is possible that they do not measure the same variable or that they are separate aspects of the variable and vary independently of one another. If we suspect that these items measure a different variable, we should eliminate them from the scale. If we find a few items that have nearly perfect correlations, we only need to use one of them in the scale. Two items to which people respond identically are simply redundant; using both adds nothing to the measurement abilities of the scale. Occasionally, however, highly correlated items should be included to detect response inconsistency or random answering. That exception notwithstanding, the final scale should be composed of statements that correlate fairly highly, but not perfectly, with one another.

A knowledge of the characteristics and sources of scale items provides an important and necessary foundation for the development of scales. By themselves, however, these offer only a general guide to scale development. The more complex intricacies of developing scales are best grasped by looking at specific types of scales and illustrations of how they were developed. Moreover, some types of scales have unique requirements that are not adequately covered by our previous discussion. We turn, then, to a discussion of the most important types of scales used in human service research.

Scaling Formats

Scaling can utilize a number of formats, and each format calls for some unique design elements.

Likert Scales

Rensis Likert (1932) developed one of the most popular approaches to scaling. A **Likert scale** consists of a series of statements, each followed by four or five response alternatives. An illustration of a Likert scale is presented in Table 13.1. Five is the most common number of alternatives because it offers respondents a sufficient range of choices without requiring unnecessarily minute distinctions in attitudes. However, more or fewer than five alternatives are sometimes used. Notice in Table 13.1 the numbers ranging from 1 to 4 in brackets next to each response alternative. These numbers are included on the scale here for purposes of illustration only; they would not be printed on a scale for actual use because their presence might influence respondents' answers. The numbers are used when scoring the scale. The numbers associated with each response are totaled to provide the overall score for each respondent. In this case—a 10-item scale—individual scores can range from a low of 10 (if alternative 1 were chosen every time) to a high of 40 (if alternative 4 were chosen every time). The Likert scale is one example of a **summated rating scale,** in which a person's score is determined by summing the number of questions answered in a particular way. Summated rating scales can take a number of different forms, although the Likert format is the most common.

Note that (as discussed in Chapter 5) each item in a Likert scale is an ordinal measure, ranging from a low of "strongly disagree" to a high of "strongly agree." Because the total score of a Likert scale is the sum of individual, ordinal items, many researchers contend that a Likert scale is therefore ordinal in nature. Technically, one should refrain from using such statistics as the mean and standard deviation with ordinal-level data. However, especially with well-established Likert scales, it is common to see published studies in which scores are treated as if they were interval level. Whether this application of interval procedures is appropriate is a debated topic among researchers and cannot be resolved here.

Constructing a Likert scale, as with all scales, requires considerable time and effort. The researcher begins by developing a series of statements relating to the variable being measured. The general criteria for such statements, as outlined previously, should be carefully considered during this stage. No matter how diligent we are in following those guidelines, however, some of the statements turn out to be inadequate, for a variety of reasons. Because we anticipate having to drop some unacceptable items, we should initially write more substantial statements than desired in the final scale. A common rule of thumb is to start with three times the number of statements desired for the final scale.

A final criterion in deciding which items to use ultimately in a Likert scale is whether the scale items *discriminate* among people. That is, we want responses to an item to range over the four or five alternatives rather than bunch up on one or two choices. Imagine a scale with an item that reads, "People convicted of shoplifting should have their hands amputated." If such an item were submitted to a group of college students, it is likely that most would respond with "strongly disagree" and maybe a few "disagrees." It is highly unlikely that any would agree. Of what use is this item to us? We cannot *compare* people—assess who is more likely to agree or disagree—because they all disagree. We cannot correlate responses to this item with the social or psychological characteristics of the students because there is little or no variation in responses to the item.

We want, then, to eliminate nondiscriminating items from consideration for our scale. *Nondiscriminating items* are those that are responded to in a similar fashion by both people who score high and people who score low on the overall scale. Nondiscriminating items in a scale can be detected on the basis of results from a pretest in which people respond to all the preliminary items of the scale. One way to identify nondiscriminating items is to compute a **discriminatory power score** (or DP score) for each item. The DP score essentially tells us the degree to which each item differentiates between respondents with high scores and respondents with low scores on the overall scale. Although this approach is now used less in actual practice because of the availability of other, more complex procedures that depend on computer support, it is a straightforward technique that illustrates well the principles of item selection.

The first step in obtaining DP scores is to calculate the total scores of each respondent and rank the scores from highest to lowest. We then identify the upper and lower quartiles of the distribution of total scores. The *upper quartile* (Q_3) is the cutoff point in a distribution above which the highest 25 percent of the scores are located, and the *lower quartile* (Q_1) is the cutoff point below which the lowest 25 percent of the scores are located. With the quartiles based on total scores identified, we compare the pattern of responses to each scale item for respondents whose scores fall above the upper quartile with the pattern for respondents whose scores fall below the lower quartile. Table 13.2 illustrates the computation of DP scores for one item in a scale to which 40 peo-

ple responded. Ten respondents are above the upper quartile, and 10 are below the lower quartile. We see that the high scorers tended to agree with this item because most had scores of 4 or 5. Low scorers tended to disagree because they are totally concentrated in the 1 and 2 score range. The next step is to compute a weighted total on this item for the two groups, multiplying each score by the number of respondents with that score. For example, for those above the upper quartile, the weighted total is:

$$(1 \times 0) + (2 \times 1) + (3 \times 2) + (4 \times 4) \\ + (5 \times 3) = 0 + 2 + 6 + 16 + 15 = 39.$$

Next, we compute the weighted mean (average) by dividing the weighted total by the number of cases in the quartile. For the upper quartile, we have $39 \div 10 = 3.9$. We then obtain the DP score for this item by subtracting the mean of those below the lower quartile from the mean of those above the upper quartile. In this example, we have $3.9 - 1.8 = 2.1$ DP. This process is repeated for every item in the preliminary scale, so that each item has a calculated DP score. (Statistical and spreadsheet software can be readily programmed to accomplish this task.)

Once we have DP scores for all the preliminary items, final selection can begin. The best items are those with the *highest* DP scores because this shows that people in the upper and lower quartiles responded to the items very differently. As a rule of thumb, as many items as possible should have DP scores of 1.00 or higher, and few, if any, should drop below 0.50. Applying this rule to the item in Table 13.2, we would conclude that it is a very good item, and we would include it in the final scale.

Table 13.2 Calculation of Discriminatory Power Score for One Item in a Scale

Quartile	N	Response Value					Weighted Total	Weighted Mean	DP Score
		1	2	3	4	5			
Upper	10	0	1	2	4	3	39	3.90	
Lower	10	2	8	0	0	0	18	1.80	2.10
								2.10	

Occasionally researchers encounter DP scores with negative signs. Under no circumstances should an item with a negative DP score be included because this means that high scorers on the overall scale scored lower on this item than did low scorers. If the size of the negative DP score is small, it is probably an ambiguous statement that is being variously interpreted by respondents. If the negative DP score is large, however, it is possible that the item was accidentally mis-scored; that is, a negative item was scored as if it were positive or vice versa.

Many computer software packages have procedures for item analysis that rely on other principles but accomplish largely the same task. For example, the popular package SPSS includes the procedure Reliability Analysis, which performs an item analysis on the components of additive scales by computing commonly used coefficients of reliability. The procedure computes a correlation matrix that shows how each item correlates with every other item and with the overall scale. It also provides the reliability coefficient Cronbach's alpha (see Chapter 5) for the proposed scale, with each item deleted. Using the output of this procedure, the researcher can exclude from the scale those items that detract from or contribute little to the overall reliability of the instrument.

The Likert scale is one of the most popular multiple-item scales because of the many advantages it possesses. First, it offers respondents a range of choices rather than the limited yes–no alternatives of some other scales. This makes Likert scales valuable if the theoretical assessment of a variable is that it ranges along a continuum rather than being either present or absent. Second, data produced by Likert-type scales are considered to be ordinal level, which enables us to use more powerful statistical procedures than with nominal-level data. Third, Likert scales are fairly straightforward to construct.

Although its advantages make the Likert scale one of the most widely used attitude scales, it has the same disadvantages as many other scales. In particular, we must be careful in interpreting a single score based on a Likert scale because it is a summary of so much information (separate responses to a number of items). Whenever we summarize data, we lose some information. (A college course grade is a summary measure of a student's performance, and in calculating it the instructor loses information regarding high—or low—scores on individual exams.) The summary score might hide information about patterns of variation in responses or about possible multidimensionality of the scale.

Research in Practice 13.1 discusses the development of a Likert scale for research in human service practice settings.

RESEARCH IN PRACTICE 13.1

PROGRAM EVALUATION:

Developing a Scale to Measure Client Satisfaction

Managed care has become a major force shaping the way human services are delivered today. One of the signs of that impact is the rise of quality assurance and quality improvement (QA/QI) in human service settings (Nabors et al. 1999). In the quest to demonstrate that services are of high quality and do produce effective outcomes, we have seen a growing need for convenient, valid, and reliable tools to measure variables that serve as indicators of outcome, including client satisfaction. Researchers have responded by developing a variety of client satisfaction measures: the Service Satisfaction Scale-30 (Greenfield and Attkisson 1999), the Client Satisfaction Inventory (McMurtry and Hudson 2000), and instruments for special populations, such as nursing home residents (Ryden et al. 2000). An interesting illustration of the process of creating a useful instrument is presented by Reid and Gundlach (1983). Their scale construction strategy illustrates many of the points made in our discussion of scale construction.

The first step in the process involved collecting possible scale items to reflect social service consumer attitudes. The researchers relied on two main sources for scale items. First, one of the authors had extensive experience in practice and consultation with service users, so this personal expertise served as a source. Second, the authors consulted the provocative book *The Client Speaks,* which was based on interviews with family service agency users in London (Timms and Mayer 1971).

Items were developed to measure three attributes of a service:

1. Relevance—Did a service correspond to the client's perception of his or her problem and needs?
2. Impact—Did the service reduce the problem?
3. Gratification—Did the service enhance self-esteem and contribute to a sense of power and integrity?

The items were included in a study of social service use and involved 166 families served by a Head Start program. The authors described the sample as a high-service user group. During the three months prior to the study, 78 percent had received Aid for Families with Dependent Children (AFDC), 75 percent had received Medicaid, and 56 percent had received food stamps. The sample also had used a variety of other public services.

To analyze the scale items, the authors turned to the SPSS software and its procedures for item analysis. They used Cronbach's alpha to determine which items to eliminate. A full explanation of the process is beyond the scope of this book; however, it basically involves comparing the reliability coefficient of the scale when an item is included with the reliability coefficient obtained when an item is dropped from the scale. If the reliability is greater without a given item included, it is dropped. Items that contribute little to the overall reliability may also be dropped to make the scale as concise and convenient to complete as possible.

On completion of the scale construction process, the authors reported that the total scale had a reliability of .955. Reliability for the Relevance subscale was .848, Impact was .821, and Gratification was .857.

Additional analysis was conducted to determine relationships between the subscales and background characteristics of the service users, such as race, sex, and marital status. Comparisons were also made between respondents based on the particular service they viewed as most important. The authors concluded that a measurement tool for client satisfaction was feasible and recommended that the scale could be used by agencies seeking to assess the effect of differing services on client attitudes.

Thurstone Scales

L. L. Thurstone and E. J. Chave (1929) developed another approach to scaling. **Thurstone scales** are constructed so that they use *equal-appearing intervals*—that is, it is assumed that the distance between any two adjacent points on the scale is the same. This provides data of interval-level quality and enables us to use all the powerful statistical procedures that require interval-level data. (We have discussed levels of measurement in Chapter 5.)

Construction of a Thurstone scale begins in much the same way as for Likert scales—with the selection of many statements that relate to the variable being measured. Once a sufficient number of statements is at hand, the next step is to provide a value between 1 and 11 for each statement. Figure 13.1 illustrates the Thurstone scale pattern ranging from 1, the most favorable statement regarding an object, event, or issue, to 11, the most unfavorable. However, scale items may be arranged positively (high scores represent a favorable attitude) or negatively (high scores indicate an unfavorable attitude). Point 6 on the scale is called "neutral" and is used for statements that are neither favorable nor unfavorable. For example, the statement "teenage girls who get pregnant are immoral" would be considered very unfavorable toward teenage pregnancies.

Figure 13.1 Equal-Appearing Intervals as Used in Thurstone Scale Construction

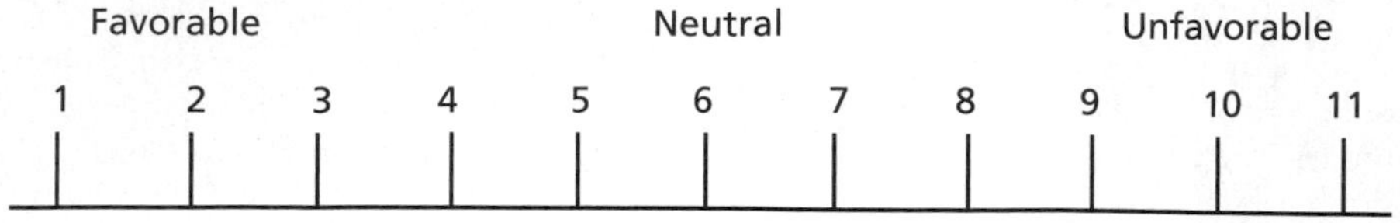

Table 13.3 Attitude toward Church Scale

Check (✓) every statement below that expresses your sentiment toward the church. Interpret the statements in accordance with your own experience with churches.

(8.3)*   1. I think the teaching of the church is altogether too superficial to have much social significance.

(1.7)   2. I feel the church services give me inspiration and help me to live up to my best during the following week.

(2.6)   3. I think the church keeps business and politics up to a higher standard than they would otherwise tend to maintain.

(2.3)   4. I find the services of the church both restful and inspiring.

(4.0)   5. When I go to church, I enjoy a fine ritual service with good music.

(4.5)   6. I believe in what the church teaches but with mental reservations.

(5.7)   7. I do not receive any benefit from attending church services, but I think it helps some people.

(5.4)   8. I believe in religion, but I seldom go to church.

(4.7)   9. I am careless about religion and church relationships, but I would not like to see my attitude become general.

(10.5)   10. I regard the church as a static, crystallized institution, and as such it is unwholesome and detrimental to society and the individual.

(1.5)   11. I believe church membership is almost essential to living life at its best.

(3.1)   12. I do not understand the dogmas or creeds of the church, but I find that the church helps me to be more honest and creditable.

(8.2)   13. The paternal and benevolent attitude of the church is quite distasteful to me.

*Scale value

Source   L. L. Thurstone and E. J. Chave, *The Measurement of Attitude* (Chicago: University of Chicago Press, 1929). Used with permission of the University of Chicago Press.

The task of rating each statement as to how favorable or unfavorable it is with regard to the measured variable is again assigned to judges. With each of the preliminary statements printed on a separate card, the judges rate the items by placing them in piles corresponding to points on the 11-point scale. The judges place in each pile statements they assess to be roughly equivalent in terms of their favorableness. All the judges will not agree on the exact rating of statements, so the scale value of a particular Thurstone item is determined by using the median of the judges' ratings. The scale values derived by this process are displayed in the first column of Table 13.3.

Once the scale values are computed for all the preliminary items, the next step is to determine which items are the least ambiguous and therefore best for inclusion in the final scale. If the judges differed widely in their ratings on an item, something is likely unclear about the statement itself, leading to varying interpretations. So the degree of agreement among judges about the rating of an item is one indicator of ambiguity.

Scales should include the items with the most agreement among judges, and there should be a roughly equal number of items for each of the 11 scale values, ranging from unfavorable to favorable, moving upward in half-point increments. This requires a minimum of 21 items, although some argue that if reliability of .90 or better is desired, as many as 50 statements may be needed (Seiler and Hough 1970). Regardless of the number actually used, the last step in Thurstone scale construction is to order the items randomly for presentation to respondents.

Table 13.3 presents the first 13 statements contained in the original 45-item scale developed by Thurstone and Chave, with the scale value of each item indicated in parentheses. This particular scale is designed so that items with high scale values are "unfavorable" toward the church, and items with low scale values are "favorable." The scale values would not, of course, be included on a working version of the scale and are presented here for purposes of illustration. Note that respondents are required only to check the statements with which they agree, which makes the Thurstone format particularly easy for respondents.

Scoring a Thurstone scale is different from the simple summation procedure used with Likert scales. Because respondents agree to differing numbers of statements with different values, the simple sum of the item values is worthless. Rather, a respondent's score is either the mean or median of the scale values of the items that the person agrees with. For example, if a person agreed with statements 2, 4, 8, and 12 in Table 13.3, that person's Thurstone scale score would be 3.13. Another person choosing 1, 7, 10, and 13 would have a score of 8.18. This scoring procedure distributes respondents along the original 11-point scale.

Thurstone and Likert scaling techniques are essentially interchangeable methods of measuring attitudes. A major advantage of the Thurstone technique is that it provides interval-level data. However, if the interval-data properties are not needed, the Likert technique is probably preferable, owing to its higher reliability with fewer items and its reputed greater ease of construction. A second advantage of Thurstone scales is that people can respond to the items more quickly than with a Likert scale because they need only indicate whether they agree with an item and need not ponder how much they agree or disagree. However, because reliability calls for Thurstone scales to be longer, this advantage may be minimal and can even become a disadvantage if the longer scale leads people to be overly quick or careless in responding to statements. Another major disadvantage of Thurstone scales is that they are costly and difficult to construct. However, modern data-processing techniques have substantially reduced this construction time (Seiler and Hough 1970).

Semantic Differential Scales

Another scaling format that has proved to be quite popular is the semantic differential (SD) developed by Osgood, Suci, and Tannenbaum (1957). The **semantic differential** format presents the respondent with a stimulus, such as a person or event, to be rated on a scale between a series of polar opposite adjectives. Normally the scale has seven points but can have more or fewer if theoretical or methodological considerations call for it.

Table 13.4 illustrates an SD designed to measure people's attitudes toward the elderly. In this study, college students were shown pictures of people of varying ages and then asked to describe the characteristics of each person by placing an X on the line between each adjective pair that best represented their assessment of the person. So, on the first line, placing an X over the 6 means that you view the person as quite active; placing an X over the 1 is an assessment of quite passive. In this example, all the positive adjectives are on the left and the negative adjectives on the right. Sometimes the positive responses to some adjectives are put on the right to discourage uninterested respondents from pl~ all their responses in the same column. If ~ respondents who had done so, we wou~

Table 13.4 Semantic Differential Scale Assessing Attitudes toward the Elderly

	Scale							
	7	6	5	4	3	2	1	
Active	—	—	—	—	—	—	—	Passive
Competent	—	—	—	—	—	—	—	Incompetent
High IQ	—	—	—	—	—	—	—	Low IQ
Powerful		—	—	—	—	—	—	Weak
Healthy	—	—	—	—	—	—	—	Sickly
Secure	—	—	—	—	—	—	—	Insecure
Creative	—	—	—	—	—	—	—	Uncreative
Fast	—	—	—	—	—	—	—	Slow
Attractive	—	—	—	—	—	—	—	Ugly
Pleasant	—	—	—	—	—	—	—	Unpleasant
Reliable	—	—	—	—	—	—	—	Unreliable
Energetic	—	—	—	—	—	—	—	Lazy
Calm	—	—	—	—	—	—	—	Irritable
Flexible	—	—	—	—	—	—	—	Rigid
Educated	—	—	—	—	—	—	—	Uneducated
Generous	—	—	—	—	—	—	—	Selfish
Wealthy	—	—	—	—	—	—	—	Poor
Good memory	—	—	—	—	—	—	—	Poor memory
Involved	—	—	—	—	—	—	—	Socially isolated

Source William C. Levin, "Age Stereotyping: College Student Evaluations," *Research on Aging,* Vol. 10 (March 1988), pp. 134–148, Copyright © 1988 by Sage Publications. Reprinted with permission of Sage Publications, Inc.

discard their data because they obviously had not marked the scale seriously. Incidentally, this study found considerable age stereotyping still persists among college students: The elderly were consistently evaluated more negatively than younger people on most of these adjectives.

Based on their research with the SD, Osgood and colleagues have suggested that, depending on the sets of adjectives used, three different dimensions of a concept can be measured: evaluation, potency, and activity. Semantic differentials can be designed to measure any one or all three of these dimensions. The measure illustrated in Table 13.4 contains adjectives relating to all those dimensions.

One major problem in constructing an SD is the selection of relevant adjectives for rating a given concept. For example, the adjective pair "alive–dead" is not relevant to an SD rating self-concept. If the researcher is uncertain about the relevance of a set of adjectives, it is possible to supply the adjectives to a group of subjects and have them rank-order them according to their relevance to the concept to be rated. The researcher would then use the pairs of adjectives ranked highest by the subjects (Mitsos 1961).

A second problem with SDs is determining which of the three dimensions a given pair of adjectives is measuring. Generally, intuition is not reliable for making this determination (Heise 1970). Accurate identification of the dimension measured by a given adjective pair can be accomplished through the use of a rather complex statistical procedure called *factor analysis,* which correlates each variable with every other variable. Its use in SD construction is to indicate which of the three dimensions correlates most highly with a given set of adjectives and hence which dimension is being tapped by those adjectives. Unfortunately, it is often impractical to do a factor analysis every time we want to construct an SD because of the large sample size needed for reliable results.

Many SDs are set up like the one in Table 13.4, with only the ends of the scale labeled with the adjectives. Some scales, however, employ such adverbs as "extremely," "quite," and "slightly" at appropriate points between the adjectives. One study found that the use of adverbs improved the quality of responses to SD scales (Wells and Smith 1960). In light of these findings, it appears advisable to include adverbs when constructing SDs.

Scoring an SD can be done in a variety of ways, depending on the researcher's needs. One way is to treat the response to each adjective pair separately. This procedure is not common, however, because usually we want a summary score for each respondent. To accomplish this, responses on the adjective pairs that constitute each dimension can be summed to provide an overall score on each of the dimensions measured—another variant of the summated ratings scale.

Semantic differentials have several advantages in comparison with both Likert and Thurstone formats. Unlike the other scaling techniques that require 20 or more items for adequate reliability, SDs require only four to eight adjective pairs for each dimension to reach reliabilities of .80 or better. Approximately 10 adjective pairs are often used to ensure adequate validity. This brevity means that many concepts can be rated by respondents in a reasonable amount of time. In addition, because an SD is fairly easy to respond to, people can be expected to make at least 25 judgments in 15 minutes (Heise 1970; Miller and Salkind 2002). Another advantage is that SDs are much easier and less time-consuming

to construct than either Likert or Thurstone scales. Adjective pairs are easier to develop than are unambiguous and unbiased statements about an issue. In addition, adjective pairs from prior studies are more readily adaptable to other studies because of the general and nonspecific nature of the adjectives. This is particularly important if a measuring scale is needed quickly. For example, if we wanted people's reactions to some unanticipated event, time would be of the essence. We would have to get their reactions while the event was still fresh in their minds. Only an SD type scale could be readied in time.

About the only disadvantage of an SD is that, like Likert scales, SDs generate ordinal data. If interval data are desired, a Thurstone scale is preferable.

Guttman Scales

Researchers make efforts to create scales that are unidimensional—that is, scales that measure a single variable or a single aspect of a variable. With a **Guttman scale,** the procedures used in the construction of the scale help ensure that the resulting scale will truly be unidimensional (Guttman 1944).

Researchers using Guttman scaling achieve unidimensionality by developing the items in such a way that a perfect Guttman scale has only one pattern of response that will yield any given score on the scale. For example, if an individual's score is 5, we expect that he or she agreed with the first five items on the scale. This contrasts with other scaling techniques that allow obtaining the same score by agreeing or disagreeing with any number of items and having completely different response patterns. Guttman scaling is able to do this because the items in the scale have an inherently progressive order, usually relating to the intensity of the variable being measured. The least intense items are referred to as "easy" because more people are likely to agree with them, and the most intense items are considered "hard" because fewer are expected to agree with them. If a person agrees with a certain item, we would expect him or her also to agree with all the less intense items; conversely, if a person disagrees with a particular item, we would also expect that person to disagree with all the more intense items.

Table 13.5 illustrates a Guttman scale designed to measure attitudes toward gun control. The items are arranged with the "easiest" first and the "hardest" last. Often, only two response categories, either "agree" and "disagree" or "yes" and "no," are provided. Some Guttman scales, however, make use of the Likert-type response categories, as does the scale in Table 13.5. Because these categories are collapsed to a dichotomy at a later point in working with the scale, little is gained by their inclusion other than allowing the respondents greater freedom of expression.

The fact that the items in a Guttman scale are progressive and cumulative leads to the basic means of assessing whether a set of items constitutes a Guttman scale. This criterion is called *reproducibility,* or the ability of the total score of all respondents to reproduce the pattern of the responses to the scale items of each individual. For example, all persons with scores of 2 will have agreed with the two "easiest" items and disagreed with the rest, persons with scores of 3 will have agreed with the three "easiest" items and disagreed with the rest, and so on. In a perfect Guttman scale, each respondent's score reproduces one of these patterns, as illustrated in Table 13.5. There is always one more perfect response pattern, zero agreements, in a Guttman scale than there are items in the scale; therefore, the nine-item scale in Table 13.5 would have 10 possible response patterns. In actual practice, perfect Guttman scales are virtually nonexistent. Usually, some respondents do deviate from the expected pattern. Nevertheless, Guttman scales with high levels of reproducibility have been developed.

Constructing a Guttman scale is difficult and risky (to a certain extent) because we do not know whether the scale we have devised has sufficient reproducibility to qualify as a Guttman scale until after we apply it to a sample of respondents. As with the other scaling techniques, to create and select items for inclusion in the scale is a basic first step. In Guttman scaling, this task is further complicated by the need for those items eventually selected to have the characteristic of progression.

The procedure for selecting items for a Guttman scale is known as the *scale discrimination technique* (Ed-wards and Kilpatrick 1948). As with both Likert and Thurstone scaling techniques, we begin by writing a large number of statements that relate to the variable to be measured. These statements are then rated by a group of judges along the 11-point Thurstone equal-appearing interval scale. Scale values and interquartile ranges (upper quartile minus lower quartile, or $Q_3 - Q_1$) of the judges' ratings are obtained for each item. The half of the items with the lowest interquartile ranges are kept and the remainder discarded. The items on which judges were in the greatest agreement are given a Likert-type response format and presented to a pretest group. The pretest results are used to calculate DP scores as described under Likert scaling. Items for inclusion in the final Guttman scale are selected so they cover the full Thurstone scale range and have the highest DP scores. Despite the effort involved in this approach, all it accomplishes is to increase the likelihood that the selected items will have sufficient reproducibility to constitute a Guttman scale; it does not guarantee reproducibility.

The only way to determine if we have succeeded in developing a true Guttman scale is to administer it to another pretest group and see if it has adequate reproducibility (Dotson and Summers 1970). Table 13.6 illustrates the most common way of assessing reproducibility of items. For the sake of simplicity, the illustrated scale contains only four items and data from only 20 subjects. As can be seen from the table, subjects are arrayed according to their total score for the four statements, from highest (4) to lowest (0). Subjects' responses to each statement are indicated by an X under either 1 or 0 corresponding to an "agree" or a "disagree" response, respectively. The statements are arranged from left to right from "hardest" (most disagreements) to "easiest" (most agreements). The lines drawn across each of the statement columns are called *cutting points* and indicate where the pattern of responses tends to shift from agree to disagree. The position of the cutting points must be determined carefully because these points form the basis from which error responses are counted. Any "1" (agree) responses below the cutting points and any "0" (disagree) responses above the cutting points constitute

Table 13.5 A Guttman Scale Measuring Attitudes toward Handgun Control

Do Not Favor or No Opinion	Strongly Favor or Somewhat Favor	Here are some proposals that have been made for controlling handgun violence. Would you please tell us how you feel about each of these proposals?
0	1	1. Institute a waiting period before a handgun can be purchased, to allow for a criminal record check.
0	1	2. Require all persons to obtain a police permit before being allowed to purchase a handgun.
0	1	3. Require a license for all persons carrying a handgun outside their homes or place of business (except for law enforcement agents).
0	1	4. Require a mandatory fine for all persons carrying a handgun outside their homes or places of business without a license.
0	1	5. Require a mandatory jail term for all persons carrying a handgun outside their homes or places of business without a license.
0	1	6. Ban the future manufacture and sale of non-sporting-type handguns.
0	1	7. Ban the future manufacture and sale of all handguns.
0	1	8. Use public funds to buy back and destroy existing handguns on a voluntary basis.
0	1	9. Use public funds to buy back and destroy existing handguns on a mandatory basis.

Note The response alternatives in this study were "strongly favor," "somewhat favor," "do not favor" "no opinion" and "no response." They were collapsed into two categories for Guttman analysis: 1 = strongly favor or somewhat favor; 0 = do not favor or no opinion.

Guttman Scale Pattern

% Favoring	Item	0	1	2	3	4	5	6	7	8	9
87%	1. Waiting period	no	yes	yes	yes	yes	yes	yes	yes	yes	yes
61	2. Permit to purchase	no	no	yes	yes	yes	yes	yes	yes	yes	yes
72	3. License to carry	no	no	no	yes	yes	yes	yes	yes	yes	yes
66	4. Mandatory fine for no license	no	no	no	no	yes	yes	yes	yes	yes	yes
52	5. Mandatory jail term for no license	no	no	no	no	no	yes	yes	yes	yes	yes
40	6. Ban non-sporting manufacture/sale	no	no	no	no	no	no	yes	yes	yes	yes
23	7. Ban all handgun manufacture/sale	no	no	no	no	no	no	no	yes	yes	yes
19	8. Voluntary buy-back	no	no	no	no	no	no	no	no	yes	yes
17	9. Mandatory buy-back	no	no	no	no	no	no	no	no	no	yes
N = 1442	Coefficient of Reproducibility: .915										

Source Reprinted from *Journal of Criminal Justice*, Vol. 13, Raymond H. C. Teske, Jr. and Michael H. Hazlett, "A Scale for the Measurement of Attitudes Toward Handgun Control," pp. 373–379, Copyright (1985), with permission from Elsevier.

Table 13.6 Example of Error Computation for a Guttman Scale

	Statements								
	1		2		3		4		
Subjects	1	0	1	0	1	0	1	0	Scores
1	x		x		x		x		4
2	x			x	x		x		3
3	x			x	x		x		3
4		x	x		x		x		3
5		x	x		x		x		3
6		x	x		x		x		3
7		x	x		x		x		3
8		x	x		x		x		3
9		x		x	x		x		2
10	x			x		x	x		2
11		x		x	x		x		2
12		x		x	x		x		2
13	x			x		x	x		2
14		x	x			x	x		2
15	x			x		x		x	1
16		x		x		x	x		1
17		x		x	x			x	1
18		x	x			x		x	1
19		x		x		x	x		1
20		x		x		x		x	0
Frequency	6	14	8	12	12	8	16	4	
Error	3	0	2	2	1	1	2	0	e = 11

error responses. Cutting points are drawn at positions that minimize the number of error responses. Inspection of the cutting points in Table 13.6 reveals that locating them in any other position does not reduce the number of error responses.

With the cutting points established, tabulation of error responses is straightforward. In the example under Statement 1 are three "1" responses below the cutting point with no "0" responses above it. Note that in the row marked "error," these responses are tabulated as 3 and 0, respectively. The same counting procedure was followed for the other statements. As Table 13.6 illustrates, the error responses for individual statements are summed to indicate the total number of error responses. Tabulating error responses for a longer scale by hand is exceedingly tedious, but computer software, such as the SAS package, can assess the reproducibility of even a long scale quite rapidly.

The total number of errors is used in the following simple formula to calculate the coefficient of reproducibility (R_c):

$$R_c = 1 - \frac{number\ of\ errors}{(number\ of\ items) \times (number\ of\ subjects)}$$

Inserting the values from Table 13.6, we have:

$$R_c = 1 - \frac{11}{(4)(20)} = 1 - .14 = .86$$

Guttman (1950) suggested that a coefficient of reproducibility of .90 is the minimum acceptable for a scale to qualify as a Guttman scale. According to this criterion, our example does not qualify. However, scales with reproducibility coefficients of somewhat less than .90 have given satisfactory results. In general, the more items in a Guttman scale, the more difficult it is to achieve a high level of reproducibility. For a very short scale, .90 would be the minimum acceptable; with a longer scale, the minimum reproducibility level can be adjusted downward slightly.

Suppose we develop a scale of 11 items, submit it to a pretest group, determine the reproducibility coefficient, and find it to be too low. The game is not over because of this initial failure. It is perfectly legitimate to rearrange the order of the items or drop items to achieve the necessary reproducibility. We might, for example, drop three or four of the items containing the most error responses, leaving a seven- or eight-item scale with adequate reproducibility to qualify as a Guttman scale. In addition, situations arise in which the coefficient of reproducibility can be misleading, and A. L. Edwards (1957) suggests additional analysis may be necessary to assess the reproducibility of a scale.

It is important to note that a given Guttman scale may be group specific. This means that if we achieve adequate reproducibility with a given set of items with one sample of respondents, nothing guarantees that the same items will scale when applied to another sample. Only after-the-fact analysis of each sample will reveal if the Guttman scale properties hold for subsequent applications of a scale.

The data generated by Guttman scaling is ordinal level. Given the relatively few items characteristic of these scales and the common "agree–disagree" format, there are few possible scores for respondents to achieve. This means that large numbers of respondents will have tied scores on the scale, so many statisticians believe it is better to consider these numbers as ranks (ordinal) rather than interval- or ratio-level data (Chapter 5). Guttman scales are unique, however, for the characteristics of unidimensionality and reproducibility. If these attributes are desired, they are apt to more than outweigh the presence of all the tied scores.

Given the extreme complexity of creating Guttman scales, most human service workers seldom have occasion to develop one. However, a substantial number of such scales already are in existence, making an understanding of their operating characteristics worthwhile. This is especially true because of the need to check the reproducibility level of a scale each time it is applied to a new sample.

Multidimensional Scales

All the scaling techniques presented so far were developed a number of years ago. More recent activity has centered on what is called the **multidimensional scale** for measuring variables composed of more than a single dimension. These scaling techniques are too complex for full presentation here, but we can discuss the basic logic that underlies them.

One purpose of the preceding scaling techniques is to locate respondents' scores along some sort of continuum to determine that various groups or people exhibit more or less of the variable measured. With these unidimensional techniques, the straight line of a single scale is sufficient to indicate the location of all people on a given variable. When we come to variables of more than one dimension, however, this single line is no longer adequate. We must think of locating responses somewhere in either two-, three-, or N-dimensional space. A common analogy exists between multidimensional scaling and cartography, or mapmaking: Just as the cartographer locates various places along the dimensions of latitude and longitude, multidimensional

Figure 13.2 Hypothetical Two-Dimensional Space of Client Motivation

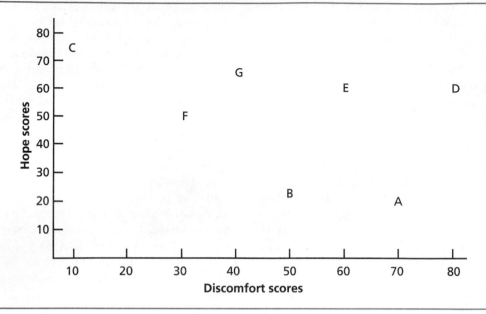

scaling locates people along the various dimensions of a variable. For example, if we conceive of people's motivation as composed of the two dimensions of "discomfort" and "hope," then Figure 13.2 illustrates how multidimensional scaling might serve to locate these people with regard to these dimensions (Kogan 1975). It might be possible to use multidimensional scaling of client motivation to predict chances of success with clients undergoing various forms of treatment.

Multidimensional scaling can, of course, deal with variables composed of many more than two dimensions. As more dimensions are added, however, presentation and interpretation become increasingly complex. (Those interested in a detailed presentation of multidimensional techniques should consult Schiffman, Reynolds, and Young 1981). Be forewarned that multidimensional scaling utilizes some fairly sophisticated statistical techniques that may require review before a thorough understanding is possible.

Scales are most commonly used in research problems in which the unit of analysis is the individual (see Chapter 4). However, scales can be used with other units of analysis, such as the characteristics of organizations.

Avoiding Response Bias

As we saw in Chapter 5, a key issue in measurement is whether people's answers to questions are accurate reflections of their actual feelings, beliefs, or behaviors. In other words, our measure of some phenomenon should be determined by the nature of the phenomenon itself and not by systematic or random errors (review the measurement formula on p. 121). One source of such error in responses to questions or statements is called **response bias:** the tendency for answers to questions to be influenced by something other than true feelings, beliefs, and behaviors. Response bias can result in a patterned overestimation or underestimation of variables (Bradburn 1983).

Sources of Response Bias

One source of response bias is called **response set:** Some people tend to be either yea-sayers or nay-sayers, tending either to agree or disagree with statements regardless of their content. This is sometimes called the *acquiescence response set* because it more often takes the form of people being predisposed to agree with statements. To illustrate this, look again at the self-esteem scale in Table 13.1. If the scale were constructed so that "strongly agree" always indicated high self-esteem, then people who tend to agree with statements would score higher on self-esteem than they actually should because they tend to agree with statements irrespective of content. This would throw into question the validity of the scale because it would produce the systematic error (discussed in Chapter 5).

Another source of response bias is **response pattern anxiety:** Some people become anxious if they have to repeat the same response all the time and change their responses to avoid doing so. If this occurs, then their reactions to statements do not reflect their actual attitudes but their reaction to certain response patterns, and the validity of the scale is reduced. (Students sometimes experience this when taking a multiple-choice exam. If several consecutive questions all have the same answer, they become concerned and may doubt answers they were fairly sure of just because the pattern of responses differs from the more random pattern they expect.)

Another source of response bias is the **social desirability effect:** people's tendency to give socially acceptable, popular answers to present themselves in a good light. For example, the Conflict Tactics Scale is an instrument for measuring modes of conflict resolution and violence between intimate partners (Straus et al. 1996). It does so by asking people (among other questions) whether they have ever used a gun or knife in resolving a dispute with an intimate partner. Because it is socially unacceptable for most people to admit using a knife or gun on a partner, this may affect how people respond to the Conflict Tactics Scale. People may deny using a knife or gun, even if they have done so, to avoid appearing socially unacceptable to an interviewer.

Reducing Response Bias

Researchers use a number of strategies in an attempt to reduce response bias. Response set and response pattern anxiety can be avoided by designing statements so that positive statements are not always an expression of the same attitude. Likert scales are routinely designed like this. In the items in Table 13.1, choosing "strongly agree" on items 1, 3, 4, 7, and 10 is an expression of high self-esteem; choosing "strongly agree" on items 2, 5, 6, 8, and 9, on the other hand, is an expression of low self-esteem. If "strongly agree" were an expression of high self-esteem for all items, then some respondents would have to choose the same alternative on every item in order to express their opinion. Mixing the response pattern of items is taken into account in scoring Likert scales. The alternatives that indicate an expression of the same opinion or feeling are given the same numerical score. In our example, for instance, all high-esteem alternatives (whether they are "strongly agree" or "strongly disagree") are given a score of 4. Then each person's responses to all items can be summed for a total scale score.

Another technique for avoiding response bias is to present sensitive issues in a neutral and nonjudgmental context. In the Conflict Tactics Scale, Murray Straus and his colleagues presented questions about violent acts in the context of disagreements and conflicts, which would presumably appear more socially acceptable to people than abuse and violence.

A third way to reduce response bias has to do with the ordering of questions: Questions can be asked in a hierarchical order, beginning with the less sensitive and gradually moving on to the more sensitive issues. The Conflict Tactics Scale begins with a few items that reflect positive ways of resolving conflict ("I explained my side of a disagreement to my partner") before moving into questions about psychological and physical abuse. Questions about the use of violence do not appear until well into the instrument. The rationale for this design was that people feel less reticent about divulging acts of violence if they have been given the chance to show that such acts were "the last straw" after attempting other means of conflict resolution.

A fourth strategy for reducing response bias is to use an interspersed pattern for the items, where socially acceptable items are interspersed with the less acceptable items. So, in the Conflict Tactics Scale, positive items, such as "I said I was sure we could work out a problem," are followed by such items as "My partner needed to see a doctor because of a fight with me." The reason for this pattern is that a straight hierarchical ordering may open the door to a form of "response set": A respondent may blindly answer "never" to every item once items began referring to violent acts. Interspersing sensitive items with positive ones encourages participants to think more carefully about each item. Thus, the Conflict Tactics Scale actually uses a combination of hierarchical and interspersed ordering of sensitive items. For any given scale, whether a hierarchical pattern or an interspersed ordering produces the least bias is an empirical question to be settled through research on the scale itself.

A fifth technique that helps to reduce response bias is called *funneling*. A researcher might ask respondents first about conflict in their city, then about conflict in their local community and among neighbors, and finally about conflict in their own family. As another example of this, Moser and Kalton (1972) suggested phrasing questions so that respondents can answer in the third person. For example, "Many men have hit their wives at one time or another. I wonder if you know under what circumstances it happens?" This can be followed with a direct question asking if the respondent has done it.

Scaling in the Human Services

Scaling is arguably the best example of a strong linkage between practice and research. Scales developed for research purposes may prove extremely useful in practice, and scales developed for human service practice may be equally useful for research. Practitioners use scales for several purposes. First, scales strengthen the general intake process by providing a systematic means of detecting areas for intervention. For example, the Multi-Problem Screening Inventory (MPSI) scale is a multidimensional self-report measure that helps practitioners assess the magnitude of client problems across a wide array of personal and social functioning areas (Hudson and McMurtry 1997). Second, human service practitioners use scales to assess specific problems for intervention. Research in Practice 13.2 describes several scales that are particularly useful for this purpose.

Third, the practitioner uses scales to document the progress of intervention. Although simply administering a scale before and after treatment makes for a weak research design, it still provides more rigorous evidence of improvement than the casual observation common in many practice situations. For the practitioner seeking to document case outcomes with stronger evidence, standardized scales may supplement repeated measures in a single-system design. This strategy was illustrated by a report on treatment of panic disorder. During baseline, treatment, and follow-up, social workers used the client's daily rating of anxiety level for the single-system *AB* design. In addition, the client also completed a standardized instrument, the Clinical Anxiety Scale, before and after treatment. Both the daily rating and the scale scores indicated client improvement (Alfonso and Dziegielewski 2001). Finally, human service organizations rely on scaling as part of their overall program quality and effectiveness monitoring process. One team of researchers described the use of a comprehensive set of scales to both assess individual clients and help guide program evaluation in the field of substance abuse treatment (Joe et al. 2002). Such use of scales to both inform the practitioner about individual client progress and provide data for program evaluation is a key element in the evidence-based practice approach that we introduced in Chapter 1. Because the documentation of practice effectiveness is measured using recognized valid and reliable scales, it can be used in evaluation research as a valuable source of evidence for guiding future practice decisions.

Properly employed, scales can be of immense benefit to practice. However, danger also exists that the uninformed use of scales or use of poorly constructed scales will provide false or misleading information. False data are in some ways worse than no data at all because people believe they have gained some understanding when in fact they have not. Social policy or practice techniques based on such erroneous data may actually exacerbate problems rather than alleviate them. For these reasons, we need to be exceedingly cautious about using scales developed without the

ASSESSMENT OF CLIENT FUNCTIONING:

Rapid Assessment Instruments

One of the most common applications of scaling in the human services is problem assessment. Protective service workers use scales to systematically assess the risk of child abuse (Children's Research Center 1999). At the other end of the age spectrum, gerontology practitioners use instruments such as the NEECHAN Confusion Scale for rapid and unobtrusive assessment of acute confusion in hospitalized older patients (Neelon et al. 1996) and the FEAR scale to assess generalized anxiety in elderly primary care patients (Krasucki et al. 1999).

Both the confusion scale and the anxiety measure are illustrations of an increasingly popular category of scale known as the *rapid assessment instrument,* or RAI. RAIs are distinguished from other measures by several main features. They are short, easy to administer, and easy to complete. RAIs are written in clear, easy-to-understand language with uncomplicated directions so disruption of the intervention process is minimized. Scoring normally takes only a few minutes, without the need for special equipment. RAIs have been developed to cover a wide array of settings and common targets of human service intervention. They have been applied in family service agencies (Toseland and Reid 1985) and in agencies serving children and youth (Edlesen 1985; Nelson-Gardell 1997). Ogles, Lambert, and Masters (1996) identified instruments for depression, anxiety, and phobias. A number of instruments have been developed in the area of substance abuse, such as the Hudson Index of Alcohol Involvement (Rapp et al. 1999). Probably the best current reference for practitioners seeking measurement instruments to aid in practice evaluation is Corcoran and Fischer (2000).

A good illustration of an RAI is the Michigan Alcoholism Screening Test (MAST), a 25-item questionnaire designed to provide a rapid and effective screening for lifetime alcohol-related problems and alcoholism. The MAST can be completed in less than 10 minutes and scored in less than five minutes; it can be used in either paper-and-pencil or interview format and has been productively used in a variety of settings with varied populations.

Practitioners may wonder whether it is worth the resources to go beyond a basic interview and utilize an RAI such as the MAST or to go a step farther and employ a more comprehensive scale. One agency undertook a systematic comparison of the relative benefits of each approach by comparing results obtained with the MAST to those from a screening interview and to information gathered via the Alcohol Use Inventory (AUI), a complex, 147-item, multiscale instrument (Skinner 1981). The researcher administered the three forms of measurement to a sample of 327 individuals with alcohol problems to assess the relative benefits and liabilities of each approach. In addition, several other instruments were used to assess further the validity of the three procedures, including the Lifetime Drinking History, a detailed, structured interview procedure that yields quantitative indexes of drinking patterns. Other measures included several scales to test for understanding of scale items and measures of the tendency to present oneself in a favorable light.

The study found that asking individuals a few simple questions during the intake process was effective in obtaining useful data about alcohol usage. However, although the intake interview permitted detection of a potential problem, the MAST procedure was superior because it produced reliable information on the severity and nature of the alcohol problem. Furthermore, this additional information was gained at only a slight increase in time and money required for the assessment process. In contrast, the AUI procedure required considerably more time to complete the 147-item, multiscale instrument and also required considerable time and skill to score and interpret the results. For the added cost, it did provide detailed information about styles of use, patterns of symptoms, and perceived benefits of use.

continued on next page

The researcher concluded that human service professionals who are in a position to detect alcohol related problems would definitely benefit from including a procedure such as the MAST in their client screening routine. The added reliability and validity over and above what can be obtained in a brief screening are obtained for very little additional cost. On the other hand, the added precision and fine distinctions that are possible through use of the AUI cannot be justified for referring agencies.

The AUI is better suited for specialized treatment facilities that can set up efficient procedures for scoring and analysis and that can make use of the added information in treatment planning for alcoholics. Therefore, the selection of measurement tools and the decision to incorporate scales into practice should be based on the demonstrated capacity of the measurement tools weighed against the added costs in terms of time, money, and skill required for their use.

extensive pretesting and analysis outlined in this chapter. Some people are under the mistaken impression that one can gather usable data from statements that have been constructed with no pretesting or analysis. It is tempting to believe that a couple of intelligent people can sit down and write unbiased, valid, and reliable statements to measure variables. It is also a dangerously erroneous belief. Great care is always called for in constructing scales. These concerns illustrate the profound responsibility of social researchers and practitioners to take all steps necessary to ensure that their findings are valid. Any investigator—including a human service practitioner—who casually develops scales without rigorous safeguards and distributes results based on those scales is, many would argue, engaging in unethical behavior.

The temptation to simply make up a scale rather than seek out a valid and reliable instrument may be especially strong in areas where understanding of the concepts seems obvious to the practitioner. Terms like "helpful," "supportive," and "sensitive" are commonplace in the human services, so it seems at first glance that a practitioner could quickly make up a good measurement scale by asking a few questions such as, "On a scale of 1 to 5, how helpful was the therapist?" But what concepts do these terms really represent, and how well do the items measure them? What it takes to answer these questions well can be glimpsed in the work of researchers who developed a multidimensional scale on social support (Goldsmith, McDermott, and Alexander 2000). Their work

involved three studies. The first study asked a sample of more than 100 participants to interpret the meaning of the terms "helpful," "supportive," and "sensitive." The second involved almost 400 participants rating 30 semantic differential items derived from the first study. A third was conducted to ascertain the scale reliability, validity, and conceptual distinctiveness of the terms. The work on this instrument is typical of the time, resources, and effort needed to design quality scales, and it underscores the value of carefully selecting valid, reliable instruments.

When human service providers select scales for use in practice or research, they need to assess whether research is methodologically sound. In scale construction, this requires considering how rigorous the investigator was in developing items, whether pretesting was conducted, and whether validity and reliability were tested. In some cases, after reviewing a piece of research, the practitioner may decide that, although the results are tantalizing, the study lacks the methodological rigor necessary to convince him or her to incorporate those results into practice.

Main Points

■ Multiple-item scales are particularly valuable for measuring complex variables because they enhance validity and reliability, increase the level of measurement, and improve the efficiency of data handling.

- The five basic steps common to most scaling techniques are these: develop many preliminary items, eliminate obviously bad items, pretest the remaining items, eliminate bad items on the basis of pretest results, and select items for the final scale.
- Likert scaling is a popular scale format that involves a series of statements with respondents selecting from five alternatives, ranging from strongly disagree to strongly agree.
- An important consideration in selecting items for inclusion in a Likert scale is discriminatory power—the ability of each item to differentiate between high and low scorers on the overall measurement scale.
- Thurstone scaling uses judges to assign a value from 1 to 11 to each item in the scale, which results in a scale capable of producing interval-level data.
- Items for inclusion in a Thurstone scale have scale scores that cover the full 1 to 11 range and were most agreed on by the judges.
- The semantic differential (SD) scaling format presents respondents with a concept to be rated and a series of opposite adjective pairs separated by a seven-point scale that is used to evaluate the concept.
- Semantic differentials are a convenient scaling format, as they are considerably easier to construct than the alternatives.
- Guttman scales have the unique characteristic of reproducibility, meaning that a given total score reflects one and only one pattern of responses to the items in the scale.
- Multidimensional scaling uses two or more dimensions or components of a complex variable to locate people with regard to the various components of the variable.
- The use of scales or the results of research based on measurement scales should be approached cautiously, with careful consideration given to whether adequate development has gone into the scale, particularly in terms of assessing its validity and reliability.

Important Terms for Review

discriminatory power score
Guttman scale
Likert scale
multidimensional scale
response bias
response pattern anxiety
response set
scale
semantic differential
social desirability effect
summated rating scale
Thurstone scales
unidimensional scale

Exploring InfoTrac® College Edition and the Internet

InfoTrac® College Edition search terms:

Likert scale
scale validity
semantic differential

InfoTrac® College Edition articles:

A Review of Factors Affecting Treatment Outcomes: Expected Treatment Outcome Scale. Farrokh Alemi, Richard C. Stephens, Shirley Llorens, Benjamin Orris. *American Journal of Drug and Alcohol Abuse* Nov 1995 v21 n4 p483(27) (9,033 words)

The Vicissitudes of Measurement: A Confirmatory Factor Analysis of the Emotional Autonomy Scale. Mark F. Schmitz, Judith C. Baer. *Child Development* Jan 2001 v72 i1 p207 (6,846 words)

Information about a potential scale for a research project, and sometimes copies of the scale itself, can be found at various Internet sites, for example, the scales Walter Hudson developed (www.walmyr. com/perscales.html). From this site, you can download samples of scales to view with an Acrobat file viewer program. Easy-to-follow instructions are provided for downloading both the sample scales and

Acrobat Reader, along with information about ordering scales and other products for professional and educational purposes.

Another way of using the Internet to learn more about scaling is to use such key terms as "Guttman" or "Likert" with a specialized search engine, such as the one provided in conjunction with the General Social Survey Internet site (www.icpsr.umich.edu:8080/GSShomepage.htm). The search engine returns bibliographic citations and full-text reports related to the General Social Survey. Many different scales have been used in the General Social Survey, making this site an excellent source of research articles about scaling issues.

Another excellent source for locating information on scales is the Buros Institute Test Reviews On-Line (buros.unl.edu/buros/jsp/search.jsp). The site includes a Test Locator. Not only can you search for scales, but you can also find review information on tests and scales. For scales related to children's services and program assessment, a useful source is the National Network for Family Resiliency (www.nnfr.org/eval), which provides information on scales related to children, adolescents, parenting, and violence prevention.

While exploring these sites or others related to scaling, pay attention to whether and in what ways the sites include information about the methods of assessing scales discussed in this chapter: validity, reliability, reproducibility, discriminatory power, and so on.

For Further Reading

Bech, Per. *Rating Scales for Psychopathology, Health Status, and Quality of Life: A Compendium on Documentation in Accordance with the DSM-III-R and WHO Systems.* New York: Springer-Verlag, 1992. Oriented particularly toward researchers and clinicians in the mental health field, the book provides details on a range of instruments suitable for measuring client problems and conditions and intervention outcomes.

De Vellis, Robert F. *Scale Development: Theory and Applications,* 2nd ed. Thousand Oaks, Calif.: Sage, 2003. This is an understandable guide to all the various stages in developing good scales. It includes discussions of how to generate items, how long scales should be, and other useful topics.

Fischer, Joel, and Kevin Corcoran. *Measures for Clinical Practice: A Sourcebook,* 3rd ed. New York: Free Press, 2000. A two-volume set that includes actual scales as well as reliability and validity data. Volume I covers instruments for couples, families, and children; volume II is devoted to instruments for adults.

Fredman, Norman, and Robert Sherman. *Handbook of Measurements for Marriage and Family Therapy.* New York: Brunner/Mazel, 1987. This volume is a compilation of scales useful in human service research.

McDowell, Ian, and Claire Newell. *Measuring Health: A Guide to Rating Scales and Questionnaires,* 2nd ed. New York: Oxford University Press, 1996. This volume discusses the theoretical and technical aspects of constructing and evaluating scales relating to such health issues as social health, psychological well-being, and depression. It presents and evaluates many actual scales.

Miller, Delbert C., and Neil J. Salkind. *Handbook of Research Design and Social Measurement,* 6th ed. Thousand Oaks, Calif.: Sage, 2002. The latest edition of a classic in the field of measurement. Miller's book provides an overview of the various types of scale construction along with many examples of proven scales.

Mueller, Daniel J. *Measuring Social Attitudes: A Handbook for Researchers and Practitioners.* New York: Teachers College Press, 1986. A step-by-step guide to developing any of the major scaling formats (Likert, Thurstone, semantic differential, etc.). It also contains many useful examples of existing scales.

Netemeyer, Richard G., William O. Bearden, and Subhash Sharma. *Scaling Procedures: Issues and Applications.* Thousand Oaks, Calif.: Sage, 2003. This current resource on scaling examines the issues involved in developing and validating multi-item self-report scales. The authors present a four-step approach for multi-indicator scale development. The book includes relevant empirical examples and a review of the concepts of dimensionality, reliability, and validity.

Robinson, J. P., P. R. Shaver, and L. S. Wrightsman, eds. *Measures of Personality and Social Psychological Attitudes.* San Diego: Academic Press, 1991. This volume is a compilation of scales useful in human service research.

Schutte, Nicola S., and John M. Malouff. *Sourcebook of Adult Assessment Strategies (Applied Clinical Psychology).* New York: Plenum, 1995. A text for practitioners, researchers, and instructors in the mental health field, this book presents more than 70 scales on a wide range of adult mental disorders, reviews of their psychometric properties, and user instructions. The scales include self-report, observer-based, and clinician-rating measures.

Streiner, David L., and Geoffrey R. Norman. *Health Measurement Scales: A Practical Guide to Their Development and Use,* 2nd ed. Oxford: Oxford University Press, 1995. A thorough discussion of issues related to locating and assessing scales for health-related research is the focus of this book.

Touliatos, John, Barry F. Perlmutter, Murray A. Strauss, and George W. Holden, eds. *Handbook of Family Measurement Techniques.* Thousand Oaks, Calif.: Sage, 2000. This three-volume set is intended for researchers, clinicians, and students in the family and related fields. It includes abstracts of family measurement instruments published from 1929 to 1996 as well as full versions and scoring instructions for many instruments.

Exercises for Class Discussion

One point we have made in this chapter on scaling is that the human service professional may not have occasion to construct new scales. In many situations you can use scales that have already been developed and reported in the literature.

13.1 For one of the following topics, find one or more scales that are included in the professional literature:

Depression
Life satisfaction
Alcoholism

Stress
Child abuse
Marital satisfaction or adjustment

We suggest using *Psychological Abstracts, Sociological Abstracts,* and *Social Work Research and Abstracts* as aids in your research. (See also Appendix A on information retrieval and the use of the library).

13.2 For each scale you locate, indicate what kind of scale it is—for example, Likert, Guttman, or semantic differential. Is reliability and validity information available on the scale? If you wanted to use a scale on this topic, what would be the problems with and advantages of using the one you found?

Among the Personal Adjustment Scales developed by Walter Hudson and colleagues, the WALMYR Assessment Scale Training Package, which contains the 10 most widely used scales, is especially useful. As a class project, have members complete and score the Generalized Contentment Scale. (Scales may be ordered from Walmyr Publishing: www.walmyr.com/shortform.html.)

13.3 What value does such a scale have over data gathered in interviews?

13.4 These scales are intended for repeated use with single-subject designs. How do you envision clients might respond to such a scale, especially with repeated applications?

Chapter 14

Data Analysis I: Data Preparation and Presentation

All research involves some form of **data analysis,** which refers to deriving some meaning from observations made during a research project. Data analysis can take many forms. In some cases, it is qualitative, such as a summary description of an investigator's field notes from a participant-observation study. The focus of this chapter, however, is with quantitative data analysis, in which observations are put into numerical form and manipulated in some way based on their arithmetic properties. The analysis of quantitative data typically involves the use of **statistics,** which are procedures for assembling, classifying, tabulating, and summarizing numerical data to obtain some meaning or information.

This chapter begins our coverage of common data analysis methods, which we will continue in Chapter 15. Primarily designed for those who have not taken a course in statistics, these chapters may also serve as a refresher for those who have. To learn to do statistical analysis requires at least a full course devoted solely to that topic, but our goals are more basic: to introduce the issues of preparing a data set for analysis, to guide selection of the most appropriate statistics to accomplish a particular task, and to provide guidance in the interpretation of statistical results. This knowledge prepares us to better understand various statistics when we encounter them in research reports and the popular media, and also to assess whether the statistics are being used properly. This chapter explores some of the fundamentals of preparing and managing data—an often-overlooked portion of the research process that falls between the generation of observations by the research design on the one hand and the production of statistical results on the other. Although it may not seem as challenging or intellectually demanding as developing the design or analyzing the data, it is still a critical step that can determine the success of the overall project.

Preparation for Data Analysis

In this chapter, we generally assume that the data have already been collected and that the task is now to enter the data into a computer file and begin the data analysis. Recall from Chapter 1 that data analysis is part of the overall research process and that many questions regarding data analysis should be resolved before any data are actually collected. As emphasized in Chapters 2, 4, and 5, theoretical and conceptual considerations are important in determining the nature of the data to be collected, and the nature of the data determines the kinds of statistics that can be applied. Furthermore, as we discussed in Chapter 7 in relation to survey data collection, procedures such as computer-assisted telephone interviewing (CATI) essentially merge the steps of data collection, data coding, and data set creation into one process because responses of participants are entered directly into a computer file data set. So even though the actual data analysis occurs toward the end of a research project, many of the issues discussed in this chapter will have been settled, or at least envisioned, *before* any data are actually collected.

Imagine that a researcher has completed a survey of sample size 400. The completed questionnaires are neatly stacked on the desk. Presumably, the questionnaires contain much information and the data for assessing the hypotheses he or she set out to test. But as long as the data are on the questionnaires—or in any other raw form, for that matter—they are useless. The raw data are in a highly inconvenient form from the standpoint of deriving usable meaning from them. Indeed, even if we tediously read through the 400 questionnaires, we would have little idea of the overall contents. The data were collected in an organized format that made sense in terms of the collection process but not for drawing conclusions. The collected data must be reorganized before we can go on and apply the necessary statistics for their analysis.

Coding Schemes

In the current context, *coding* refers to the process by which a researcher transforms raw data into a machine-readable format suitable for data analysis, which requires that each observation be translated into a numerical value or set of letters. The numbers or letters assigned to an observation of a variable are called a *code*. The raw data set may have resulted from an observational study, a survey, an experiment, or an analysis of existing data; and it can be in one of several forms, including completed written questionnaires, survey interview schedules, observation notes, or agency records. In the following discussion, we used survey data to illustrate the coding process, but the basic principles apply to other research methods as well.

Coding data requires adapting the data as collected to the constraints of the program used for statistical analysis. On the one hand, the researcher must consider the data source, such as a completed questionnaire, and determine how to translate the data into coded form. On the other hand, the researcher must also be cognizant of the capabilities and restrictions of the computer program that will analyze the data. Although we present these perspectives somewhat independently, in practice the researcher must give simultaneous attention to both. The plan by which the researcher organizes responses to a variable or item, together with how the variable is defined for computerization, constitutes the **coding scheme** for a variable. The initial purpose of the coding scheme is to provide the rules and directions for converting the observations into code. Referring to our example of the 400 completed questionnaires, the researcher's first task is to convert the responses into numbers and letters for computer entry.

As explained in Chapters 8 and 9, coding refers to categorizing a variable into a limited number of categories. Sometimes this coding is built into the way a question is asked and answered (see Chapter 7). This is the case with the following question format:

Which of the following best describes where you live? (Circle the number of your choice.)

1. Large city.
2. Suburb of a large city.
3. City of 50,000 or less.
4. Rural but nonfarm.
5. Rural farm.

In this case, the circled number is the code for how a particular respondent answered a question. This example also illustrates one reason why coding and

data analysis issues need to be considered before data collection is initiated. The number of options in the question predetermines the maximum number of response categories that can be used later to look at possible relationships between "residential area" and other variables. Because we did not provide an option for "City of 50,000 to 300,000," we could not use this as a category in our data analysis.

With some variables, the actual value of the response is a number and can be used to code the data. Family size, income, and number of arrests are variables of this type. However, when the data take the form of responses to open-ended survey questions, field notes, or other nonnumerical entities, the data must be translated into numbers for quantitative analysis. This process is essential for most data analysis because the substitution of numbers for observations greatly reduces the volume of data that must be stored and facilitates its analysis, especially by computer. (As we noted in Chapter 9, qualitative analysis often does not involve the substitution of numbers for the actual observations.) Many computer programs permit the use of words or letters to stand for categories, but these are generally more cumbersome and only infrequently used. (Recall from Chapter 5, however, that assigning a number to coding categories does not necessarily mean that we can perform the various mathematical functions, such as addition and subtraction, on them. Whether we can do this depends on the level of measurement.)

When establishing coding categories, the researcher should follow two general rules. First, the categories should be *mutually exclusive;* that is, a given observation is coded into one and only one category for each variable. The universal practice of categorizing people by sex as either male or female exemplifies mutually exclusive categories. Second, the coding categories should be *exhaustive,* which means that a coding category exists for every possible observation that was made. For example, it might be tempting not to bother to code the "no opinion" response with Likert-type questions, on the grounds that those responses will probably not be included in the data analysis. A researcher might well decide not to analyze those responses in the end, but the coding stage is not the time to make such decisions. If the researcher fails to code a response and later decides to include it in the analysis, it becomes necessary to develop a new coding scheme and reenter the data into the computer. A good rule of thumb when coding is to do it in such a way that *all* information is coded. Coding is usually a difficult task, and the coder can become careless and fatigued. But it is critical that the job be done well. Searching out errors after the fact is often time-consuming and expensive. Unless caught and rectified, coding errors can ruin the most carefully collected data set by causing distortions in relationships and resulting in meaningless or misleading results.

Today, virtually all quantitative (and much qualitative) data analysis is done with computers. This means not only that the coding scheme must specify logically meaningful categories but also that it must meet the specifications the computer program requires to use the data once it is entered into the computer. These specifications include attributes for each variable that permit the computer program to display the data on the monitor, to use the data in calculations, and to write the data to various files for storage and retrieval.

In its most basic form, a computerized data set can be conceptualized as a rectangular table of cells where the columns represent variables and the rows designate individual cases. Figure 14.1 illustrates a portion of a simulated data set showing how it would appear on a typical computer program data entry screen. The first column consists of respondent last names; the remaining columns designate first names, birthdates, prior arrests, date of offense, relationship to victim, and annual income. Notice that the top of each column displays the variable name (lname, fname, and so on). The variable names and other variable attributes, together with information about the position of the variable in the data set, are also vital elements of the coding scheme for computerized data. At a minimum, a computer-coding scheme identifies a variable name and a variable format.

For variable names, computer program data entry screens typically use a default designation, such

Figure 14.1 Data Entry Screen Commonly Used in Windows Versions of Statistical Software

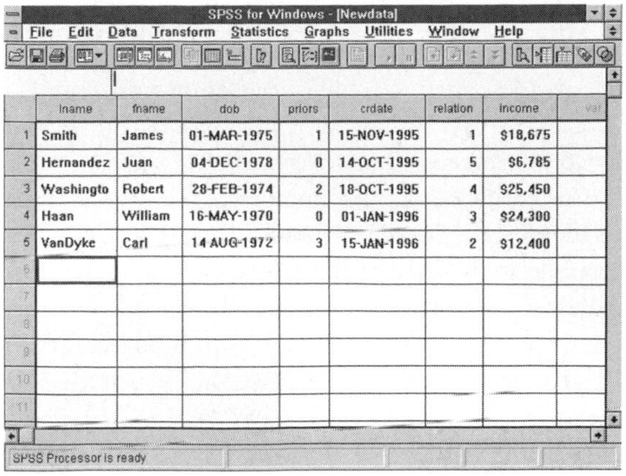

	lname	fname	dob	priors	crdate	relation	income
1	Smith	James	01-MAR-1975	1	15-NOV-1995	1	$18,675
2	Hernandez	Juan	04-DEC-1978	0	14-OCT-1995	5	$6,785
3	Washingto	Robert	28-FEB-1974	2	18-OCT-1995	4	$25,450
4	Haan	William	16-MAY-1970	0	01-JAN-1996	3	$24,300
5	VanDyke	Carl	14-AUG-1972	3	15-JAN-1996	2	$12,400

as C1, C2, C3 (in the case of Minitab) or var001, var002, var003 (in SPSS) to identify variables. Spreadsheet programs, such as Lotus, Excel, and Quattro, label them a, b, c, . . . aa, ab, and so on. Obviously, such designations convey little information about the meaning of a particular variable. With even a few variables, relying on such designations quickly becomes confusing, so the researcher needs to provide more recognizable variable names. Variable names should be short to minimize entering long lists of variable names when conducting statistical analysis. In addition, some statistical programs, such as SPSS, limit names to a maximum of eight characters. Although short, a variable name should be an indicator of the content of that variable. A common practice is to use a mnemonic device when naming variables. Thus, "lname" and "fname" clue the reader that the variable names stand for last name and first name, respectively.

Variable names may also be selected to help group variables together. For example, a data set on domestic violence may include similar variables on both the suspect and the victim, such as date of birth, age, and alcohol use. Beginning each variable related to victims with the letter "*v*" and each suspect-related variable with an "*s*" helps the researcher quickly distinguish to which party a given variable refers. Another benefit of this approach is that data analysis programs commonly display variable lists alphabetically. Beginning all victim-related variables with *v* causes them to be grouped together whenever the computer displays a variable list. This reduces the need to scroll through a long list of variables when selecting variables for inclusion in a data analysis procedure. When a variable is measured by combining responses to a number of separate items, it is often useful to use a number as part of the name to identify the variable's position in the set. Variables representing individual items of a 10-item self-esteem scale, for example, might be designated as se1, se2, se3, and so on through se10. Such a designation can reduce the amount of work in combining the items into a single score. Thus, a total score on self-esteem can be generated by a computer command like "Sum se1 to se10" instead of requiring a separate listing of all 10 individual items.

In addition to the variable name, a coding scheme specifies the *variable format,* which determines how many characters a coded entry may have, whether it is nonnumeric or some form of numeric variable, and where identifiers such as decimals, commas, or dollar signs should be placed. Figure 14.1 displays several types of variables; some consist of letters, others include letters and numbers, and some are only numbers.

Data analysis programs vary in terms of the kinds of variables they accept, but the two major types are numeric and alphanumeric. **Numeric variables** are sometimes called "values" because they have the property of a quantitative value. **Alphanumeric variables,** on the other hand, consist simply of type characters; they are sometimes also referred to as "string" variables or labels. An alphanumeric variable has no quantitative meaning and cannot be used in mathematical computations. Thus, the variable "lname" is clearly an alphanumeric variable because its field (column) consists of text, such as "Smith" and "Hernandez." However, what makes a variable alphanumeric is determined by how the variable is defined in the coding scheme and not simply by what characters are displayed on the computer monitor. For example, we could enter Social Security num-

bers in a data set and designate these as alphanumeric values. Even though the entire column consists of numerical characters, such as 375426174, a statistical program would not compute the mean, standard deviation, or other statistics on this variable because it is designated as an alphanumeric or string variable. Data analysis programs commonly accept almost any keyboard character in a variable designated alphanumeric. Although one can enter numeric characters in an alphanumeric variable, statistical packages such as SPSS and Minitab only accept numerical symbols in a variable designated numeric.

In addition to simply designating a variable as either string or numeric, many programs also permit the specification of subtypes of numeric variables. Typical options include integer, decimal, currency, and date or time. Although the format code is not visible on the screen, it is stored with the data file and tells the program how much space to reserve for a given variable in the data set and how to display it. These format codes are included in the variable information as "Print Format" and "Write Format" provided in the codebook, as shown in Table 14.1. In the case of the variable LNAME, these are specified as "A12." The "A" designates the variable as alphanumeric, and the "12" indicates the maximum number of characters that the computer will permit for printing the variable when it is displayed or when the program writes the variable to a file. Similarly, the date-of-birth variable is identified as DATE11, indicating that the variable is a date with 11 characters in it. The numeric variable PRIORS is designated as "F8," indicating that it is a numeric variable with no decimal places. If it were a decimal variable with two decimal places, it would be "F8.2." Currency variables are displayed with two decimal places, a dollar sign, and commas separating thousands. So, the variable INCOME has a format of DOLLAR8, indicating that it is a currency variable that can be as large as "99,999,999.99." In Table 14.1, the variables DOB and CRDATE are defined as date variables. If we want to determine how old each suspect was at the time of the offense, we can enter a computer command that will subtract DOB from CRDATE and display the result in years. Although different com-

Table 14.1 Domestic Violence Study Codebook

Item	Variable Name	Variable Label	Variable Formats	Position
1. List offender last name	LNAME	last name	Print Format: A12	1
			Write Format: A12	
2. List offender first name	FNAME	first name	Print Format: A10	2
			Write Format: A10	
3. Enter date of birth	DOB	date of birth	Print Format: DATE11	3
			Write Format: DATE11	
4. How many prior arrests for domestic violence?	PRIORS	number of prior arrests	Print Format: F8 Write Format: F8	4
			Missing values: −1,9	
5. What was the date of offense?	CRDATE	crime date	Print Format: DATE11 Write Format: DATE11	5
6. What was offender's relationship with victim?	RELATION	relation to victim	Print Format: F8 Write Format: F8	6
			Value Label	
			1 married	
			2 cohabitating	
			3 separated	
			4 divorced	
			5 dating	
			6 other	
7. What was offender's adjusted gross income reported to IRS for 1995?	INCOME	1995 income	Print Format: DOLLAR8 Write Format: DOLLAR8 Missing values: −1,99	7

puter programs use their own conventions of designating variable types, the important point is that how the variable is defined before data entry determines its type rather than being determined by how the variable looks on a computer monitor or printout. The researcher must plan how variables will need to be used in the analysis and define them accordingly.

Additional elements may be added to a coding scheme to enhance its usefulness. Besides a brief variable name, the researcher may specify a variable label, which is an extended description of a variable that the data analysis program will print in addition to the variable name whenever output is generated for that variable. Thus, in a table using the variable CRDATE, the designation "crime date" can be printed to make the table more understandable. Similarly, the coding scheme may include "value labels," which designate in words what a given value represents. For example, in Table 14.1, numbers are used to designate the following relationship possibilities between offender and victim: 1 = married, 2 = cohabitating, 3 = separated, 4 = divorced, 5 = dating, and 6 = other. Because this is a nominal variable and thus without an inherent quantitative meaning to the numbers, the value labels are printed on outputs to help make clear what quality each number represents.

Finally, the coding scheme should also show how to interpret special codes, such as *missing values.* Missing values arise when no response is recorded for a particular item. Depending on why the item is a nonresponse, the researcher may either leave the variable blank in the computer data set or enter a value that signifies why the item was missing. For example, an item might be coded "−1" if the respondent refused to answer the question or "99" if the item does not apply to a particular respondent. This could be an important distinction for some types of analysis, so the coding scheme must specify how these various entries should be handled in computations. For example, if "99" is a missing value code for a variable of respondent age, the computer program must treat this respondent's age as missing and not as 99 years old when computing statistics such as the mean or standard deviation on the variable.

Preparing and Using a Codebook

The coding scheme results in a specification of the variable name, variable format, the range of permissible response codes, location of the variable in the data set, and optional features, such as variable labels, value labels, and missing value codes. Researchers commonly develop a *codebook* for the data set, which is an inventory of all the individual items in the data collection instrument together with the coding schemes (see Table 14.1). We stated that the initial use of the coding scheme is to guide the process of converting responses into codes. But the need for a codebook does not end once the data are entered into a computer file. The codebook provides lasting documentation on how the data set is constructed. Anytime there is a question about how a variable is constructed or how it can be used in analysis, the researcher can turn to the codebook for help. Not only does the researcher who collected the data need the codebook, but without such documentation, it would be impossible to conduct a replication study on a previously collected data set or to explore new hypotheses with existing data. Finally, the codebook is invaluable for data file management. A data set may consist of hundreds of variables, so to make analysis more efficient, researchers commonly create subfiles containing only the variables needed for a particular analysis. The codebook plays an essential role in selecting the variables and creating new files.

The preliminary codebook is normally prepared before data are entered into the computer and then used as a guide for data entry. However, the codebook is not a static document. Researchers often recode original variables and compute new ones. It is critical that these manipulations of the original data also be documented in the codebook so that any researcher can determine how these new variables were derived, what they mean, and where they are located in the data set.

Data Entry

The goal of the data entry process is to produce a complete data set, free from errors, that the data analysis software program can access and process. Although sometimes seen as a laborious, repetitive task devoid of intellectual skill requirements, data entry is a critical part of the research process, and the researcher needs to take steps to ensure that it proceeds with accuracy and efficiency. Significant strides have been made in recent years to both minimize data entry error and increase the speed of transforming raw data into a data set that is ready for analysis.

Raw Data Entry

When the raw data must be extracted from existing documents, such as court records, or from printed questionnaires or survey schedules, the data must be manually entered into the computer. Several options exist for this process. Sometimes the questionnaire data are coded onto pages known as "transfer sheets," which consist of numbered rows and columns that look much like the computer screen in Figure 14.1. In other cases, questionnaires have space along the border for writing the code, referred to as "edge coding." Whether one uses a transfer sheet, edge coding, or simply the raw questionnaires themselves, a common way to enter a data set is to use the data entry facility of the statistical package that will eventually analyze the data.

Modern statistical packages for the personal computer, such as SPSS and Minitab, include full-featured data entry facilities as part of the package. Conventions and individual features vary from program to program, but the basic process is similar. The data entry screen is laid out in columns and rows (Figure 14.1). Each column represents one variable (field), and each row represents one case (record). Assuming that the variable names, labels, and other specifications have already been entered during the preparation of the codebook, the value for each variable is simply typed into the respective cell in the row corresponding to the individual case. Errors can be corrected by moving the cursor with mouse or arrow keys to the cell in question and reentering the correct code. If the coding scheme's data definition for the computer has not already been entered into the computer file, this step can be completed as data are entered into each variable.

Although data entry directly into a statistical package is relatively easy and convenient, additional options may be more attractive. On the one hand, a researcher may not have immediate access to the data analysis package itself. Another possibility is that the data are being collected for purposes other than this research project for use with a program such as a spreadsheet or a database that human service agencies commonly use to collect and store data for management purposes. Spreadsheet programs were originally developed for financial data but are now widely used for many other purposes, and human service agencies commonly use them to enter and store data. Such spreadsheets as Lotus, Excel, and Quattro have made popular the row-by-column cell display now used by statistical packages that we discussed earlier. Major statistical packages can read data files generated by popular spreadsheet programs. So even without the latest version of SPSS or Minitab, one can basically prepare a data set on the spreadsheet program, save it on disk, load it into the

statistical package, and begin analysis. In addition to the wide availability of spreadsheet programs, another reason for using them is their powerful capacity to compute complex variables through the use of formulas. It may be easier to compute a variable on the spreadsheet and import it into a statistical package than to rely on the statistical package's capacity to compute new variables.

Database programs, such as Microsoft Access and Corel Paradox, are also popular options for data entry. In fact, modern spreadsheets and database program features tend to overlap, although databases are designed primarily for storage, retrieval, and manipulation of data files, and a spreadsheet's strong suit is quantitative calculation. A major reason for turning to a database for data entry is the control such a program affords over the data entry process. An appealing database feature is the ability to specify a default value or an acceptable range of values for a variable. Thus, if males are coded "1" and females are coded "2" and the vast majority of respondents are males, the database can be set up to enter a default value of "1." The computer automatically enters that value for each case unless a "2" is manually inserted. Alternatively, an acceptable range, such as "1–5," may be defined for a variable. If the data entry person types a "6," the computer does not accept it, thus reducing the potential for error. Setting up a database program this way prevents entry of out-of-range values.

A second reason for choosing a database program for data entry is the form design feature that these programs offer. For example, the researcher can prepare a data entry form that looks very similar to the questionnaire. The form may also provide coding instructions to the data entry person for complex items. Instead of staring at an endless sea of rows and columns, the data entry person views a form with blanks in which data may be entered. The actual data are stored in a standard file structure, but the form helps guide the data entry process. The form can even be programmed to follow the skip pattern of the questionnaire (see Chapter 7), eliminating the need to make decisions about where to enter the next response.

In addition, data entry can be greatly simplified by the use of pull-down menus and buttons that are ideal for closed-ended questions. Pull-down menus display a small window and an arrow on the data entry form. The user simply clicks on the menu bar, and the program displays all the possible acceptable choices for that item. The user then selects the respondent's choice from the list with the mouse or arrow key, and the program enters that value in the database. For simple items, such as those with a yes–no response choice, the computer screen displays a button next to each response choice. The user simply clicks the mouse on the desired choice, and the response is coded into the data set. Such features greatly speed up the data entry process and reduce the possibility of error.

A final option worth considering for data entry is a specialized data entry program, such as QDATA, which we will discuss in the Exploring the Internet section of this chapter. QDATA is a modest program compared to a full-featured database or spreadsheet, but it is very effective for the specific task of data entry. It will define a data set, including specifying variable labels, value labels, and range of values. Once the data are entered, the file can be saved in a statistical package format or in ASCII, which is a generic format many programs accept.

Instead of making data entry a distinct step in the research process, it may be combined with data collection. One way of doing this is to use a data entry form prepared with a database as the actual questionnaire. Either the interviewer or the respondent views the items on the computer monitor and enters the responses. For studies consisting primarily of closed-ended question items, which readily lend themselves to employing buttons and pull-down menus, recording the responses directly into the computer data set can reduce error and increase the speed of data entry.

Another innovation in data entry is the use of optical scanning technology. A data-collection instrument is designed using a special program. Respondents either mark a circle corresponding to their choice or, in more sophisticated programs, write a response. The questionnaire is then read by a scanning machine or faxed into the computer, and the coded values are entered directly into the database for analysis. Whether one uses specialized data entry like this or relies on manual entry into the data analysis program depends on several factors. The specialized equipment is cost-effective for large projects where a staff of data entry personnel would otherwise be needed. But designing, setting up, and testing an automated data entry program is prohibitively expensive for a small data set. Researchers today have many options to choose from. The most important issue is to select the process that yields the most accurate, usable data set.

Data Cleaning

No matter how much care one takes during the data entry process, errors can be expected—skipping variables for certain cases, entering the wrong value, entering the value in the wrong column, or entering an alphanumeric character in a numeric variable column. If uncorrected, some errors can cause the analysis program to abort a statistical procedure or at least seriously distort the findings of the analysis. Thus, before analysis begins, the researcher should examine the data set carefully and make corrections. Although no system is foolproof, researchers have developed a variety of techniques for locating errors.

If the data set is small, he or she may be able to detect some errors simply by scanning the data with the data editor screen. Scrolling through the rows and columns of data on the screen can turn up obvious errors, such as blank cells, unusually large numbers, or stray alphanumeric characters. However, it is best to rely on a more systematic approach. One simple technique with a statistical package, spreadsheet, or database is to use a sort procedure. Sorting rearranges the order of all cases in the data set on the basis of the values of the variable selected as the sort key. Alphanumeric variables are sorted alphabetically, and numerical variables are sorted in numerical order. Scanning the sorted data on the monitor, the researcher can detect misspellings and missing or out-of-range values. For example, if the variable used in the sort procedure is a scale item where expected values are integers from 1 to 5, blank entries and entries of "0"would be at the top of the list, decimals such as 1.5 would show up between "1" and "2," and values of 6 or more would be at the end of the list. This can be a cumbersome process with large data sets, but for only 50 or so variables, sorting the data works well.

With a statistical package such as SPSS, another option is to generate a frequency distribution on all variables. This produces a list of every value that actually occurs in the data set for each variable in ascending order and the number of cases for each respective value. This helps detect variables with out-of-range values or values that should not be present. Of course, knowing that some cases exist somewhere with the wrong entries for a variable and finding those cases are very different things, especially when the data set may contain a thousand or more cases. Having identified a variable with one or more suspect cases, the researcher can use a conditional selection process. The exact command differs from program to program, but basically the researcher enters a command to select those cases for which the value for the variable in question meets a certain condition. For example, if no one in the data set should have an age greater than 18, execute a command to select all cases where AGE > 18, then include a second command to list the case numbers or the last and first names of all cases meeting that condition. Armed with this information, scroll through the data set to the identified cases and correct them. The researcher may edit the entry by replacing it with the correct value, enter a missing value code if the correct value is not available, or, in really serious cases, eliminate the whole case entirely.

These techniques help find data entries that are too large or too small, but sometimes the data are within the acceptable range but simply wrong for that case. Some of these errors can be detected by looking for logical inconsistencies. For example, if the value in a month variable is April, June, September, or November, then the value in a day variable associated with that month should not be greater than 30. If the variable entry for the number of adults in the household is 2, and the number of chil-

dren is 4, then the entry for total household size should be 6. Depending on the software program, it is possible to build queries that detect cases where such inconsistencies are present. QDATA has a built-in facility for doing such logical consistency checks. Large-scale professional surveys have the benefit of specialized software to help detect errors and employ supervisory personnel review data entry to detect problems, but most human service practitioners are unlikely to have access to such services. However, rigorous application of these procedures can locate many errors. Finally, error detection underscores the importance of numbering the questionnaires or other raw data sources and keeping the raw data in a safe, accessible location so that you can compare the original data to the computer file when needed.

Creating New Variables

The data have all been entered and checked for error, but one task remains before proceeding to data analysis: The variables as recorded may not be in the final form for the desired analysis procedures. If this is the case, the researcher needs to modify the variables or generate usable new ones. Such data manipulation may sound unusual, but it is a legitimate and necessary part of the research process.

Here is one example of how and why this is done. Recall from Chapter 13 that some scale items are stated in positive terms and other items stated in negative terms to avoid problems such as response set. With a 10-item Likert scale for depression, for instance, with choices ranging from 1 to 5, half of the items would be stated such that a positive response (such as "strongly agree" or "1") would indicate low depression. The other half of the items would be stated such that a negative response ("strongly disagree" or "5") would indicate low depression. To conduct statistical analysis, some items need to be reverse-scored so that a score of 1 on all items signifies a low value on the concept being measured and a 5 signifies a high value. This can be accomplished by use of a *recode* procedure in statistical programs. A recode statement specifies the existing values in a given variable and what the new values should be. In our example, for the five items in which a negative response (a "5") indicated low depression, we would change the values as follows:

Old Item Value	Revised Item Value
1 ⟶	5
2 ⟶	4
3 ⟶	3
4 ⟶	2
5 ⟶	1

Having recoded the negative items, we now have 10 consistent items where low values indicate low levels of depression and high values indicate high levels of depression. However, what we really need is a total scale score on depression. This can be obtained by using a *compute* procedure in the data analysis program. A compute procedure creates a new variable by performing mathematical computations using one or more existing variables. Depending on the conventions of the particular software, we enter a formula like this:

$$\text{DEPSCORE} = \text{sum (DEP1 to DEP10)}$$

A new variable called DEPSCORE is created. Its value is computed for each case by summing all 10 individual items that make up the depression scale (DEP1 through DEP10). The new variable, the total depression scale score, is added to the data file. As with the existing variables, the researcher can attach a variable label and value labels to such newly created variables. Whenever the researcher modifies the data set, whether by recoding or computing new variables, the steps used in the data manipulation must be recorded and added to the codebook. Fortunately, this is easy to do because statistical programs typically record all executed data transformations in a special file. In SPSS, it is called an output file; in Minitab it is a history file. Documenting these transformations ensures that any researcher using the data file will be able to confirm how new variables were generated. Recoding and computing new variables is an essential step in the process of unlocking the findings contained in the data set.

Data Distributions

Once the data have been stored as a computer file, systematically inspected for error, cleaned, and possibly revised through recoding and variable creation, we are ready to begin actual data analysis. Data analysis is the process of seeking out patterns within individual variables and, more important, seeking out patterns in relationships between variables. The term *univariate analysis* refers to the process of describing individual variables. Even though our ultimate goal in a research project is usually to determine how two or more variables are related, the process of describing the data by specifying the characteristics of individual variables is critical to a research project. Learning how individual variables are distributed can help determine which variables to use in studying relationships and which data analysis procedures we should use.

Types of Data Distributions

One of the first steps usually taken with a data set is to look at the range of values for each variable. To accomplish this, a *frequency distribution* is constructed. In Table 14.2, the variable is the grade for a college class, with the traditional five categories. The frequency column shows the number of class members who received each grade. Of particular interest is the *shape* of a frequency distribution. A

Table 14.2   Hypothetical Grade Distribution for a Social Science Research Class

Grade	Frequency
A	4
B	7
C	10
D	5
F	3
	$N = 29$

distribution's shape derives from the pattern the frequencies produce among the various categories of the variable. A number of labels are used to describe the shapes of distributions. First, distributions may be symmetrical or asymmetrical (see Figure 14.2). *Symmetrical distributions* are balanced, with one half of the distribution being a mirror image of the other half. In reality, most distributions only approach perfect symmetry. *Asymmetrical distributions* have cases bunched toward one end of the scale, with a long "tail" caused by a small number of extreme cases trailing off in the other direction. Asymmetrical distributions are said to be *skewed,* with positively skewed distributions having long tails extending in the direction of the higher values and negatively skewed distributions having tails going in the direction of lower values. (Note that the concepts of positive and negative skewness apply only to distributions of data of ordinal level or higher. Because the categories of nominal data have no inherent order, the shape of a distribution of nominal data is purely an arbitrary matter of how we choose to arrange the categories.) Determining the amount of skewness is an important preliminary step for later analysis. Certain inferential statistics, for example, are based on the assumption that the variables are normally distributed. One of the basic properties of a normal distribution is that of being symmetrical. Therefore, our analysis at this stage may be critical for helping decide later which inferential procedures are appropriate.

Figure 14.2 Symmetrical and Asymmetrical Distributions

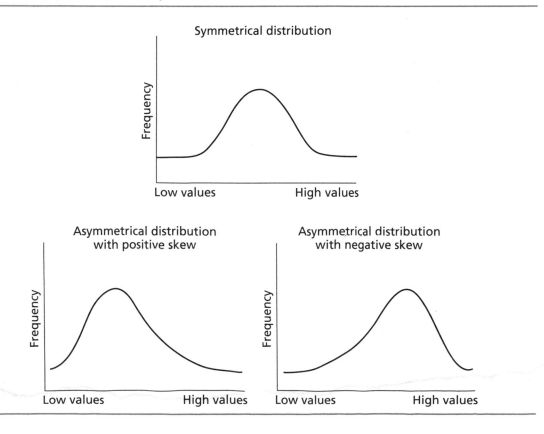

Constructing Frequency Distributions

Simple Frequency Distributions. When data are collected, they are in the form of a *raw data distribution,* which means that the distribution contains all the different values that were observed on a variable. Table 14.3 displays a raw data distribution of the ages of a sample of 71 residents in a veterans' facility. A first step in data analysis might be to construct a *simple frequency distribution,* in which each value of a variable is listed only once, along with the number of cases that have that value. Table 14.3 includes a simple frequency distribution of the ages of the people in the facility. The *X* column refers to the values or categories of the variable, while the *f* column indicates the frequency, or number of cases that have each value.

Simple frequency distributions can be constructed on variables at any level of measurement. In Table 14.3 it is much easier to gain some sense of the age distribution of the residents from the simple frequency distribution in comparison to the raw data distribution. However, sometimes simple frequency distributions are too cumbersome. Table 14.3 shows a lot of categories to look at, and many categories have no cases or only a few cases. In these situations, it is often preferable to collapse a distribution further by creating a grouped frequency distribution.

Grouped Frequency Distributions. At its core, data analysis is basically a search for patterns in data. However, sometimes searching for patterns in raw data is akin to the old adage of not being able to see the forest for the trees. Even if we order the observations with a simple frequency distribution, the large number of observations, the small variations between some observations, and large gaps between others combine to hide the pattern inherent in the data.

Grouping is the process of combining a large number of individual variable categories into a smaller number of larger categories. It permits us to step back from the data and see the big picture by ignoring minor variations between cases and focusing on larger patterns. One reason for grouping is to summarize the data into a manageable number of categories; a table or graph may be unreadable if it has too many categories. Another purpose is to eliminate categories with no or very few cases in them. In addition to making it easier to see patterns in the data, grouping is often necessary for certain data analysis procedures. For example, a statistical computation may require enough cases so that each cell in a table could theoretically have at least five cases in it. Grouping helps meet this requirement because reducing the number of categories increases the number of cases falling into the newer, larger categories.

The manner in which grouping is done depends in large part on the level of measurement of the data. Table 14.4 shows the hypothetical results of a small survey that includes the variable "religious affiliation." This frequency distribution clearly is in need of grouping: Some categories have no cases at all while others have few cases, and the coding scheme has a large number of categories. When grouping nominal data like these, we rely on logic and common sense to group categories together that fit in some way with each other. For example, it is logical to group all Protestant denominations into a new category called "Protestant" because they all share some core beliefs and practices. On the other hand, those categories with few or no frequencies could reasonably be grouped into a category called "other," simply because none of them contain a sufficient number of cases. The difference in reasoning behind each group is important to note because it may be significant for later analysis. For example, if we are evaluating how religious affiliation relates to attitudes toward volunteering for community service, "Catholic," "Jewish," and "Protestant" are meaningful categories, whereas "other" is a hodgepodge of cases that we really can't describe in terms of common theology. For analysis purposes, we may want to classify these latter cases as "missing" and exclude them from analysis.

Grouping ordinal data can be a very straightforward process of merging adjacent categories. For example, if we decide that the nine social-class

Table 14.3   Two Types of Data Distributions of Patients' Ages

A. Raw Distribution

98	82	78	70	68	60
96	81	76	70	68	60
95	80	76	70	68	59
92	80	75	70	68	59
91	79	74	70	68	59
89	79	73	70	67	58
87	79	72	70	66	56
85	79	72	70	66	54
85	79	71	70	66	52
84	79	71	69	64	51
82	79	71	69	63	50
82	79	71	69	63	

Total $N = 71$

B. Sample Frequency Distribution

X	f	X	f	X	f
98	1	76	2	59	3
96	1	75	1	58	1
95	1	74	1	56	1
92	1	73	1	54	1
91	1	72	2	52	1
89	1	71	4	51	1
87	1	70	9	50	1
85	2	69	3		
84	1	68	5		
82	3	67	1		
81	1	66	3		
80	2	64	1		
79	8	63	2		
78	1	60	2		

categories in Table 14.5 are too many, it is easy to collapse them down to the conventional three shown in the table. In this illustration, going from nine to three categories makes logical sense because the nine small categories are gradations of the three larger groupings.

However, this is not always the case. A survey may include an item that asks for years of education

Table 14.4   Illustration of Grouping a Nominal Variable

	Original Code Scheme RELIGION religious affiliation			Recoding Scheme RELIG2 religious affiliation groups		
Value	Label	Frequency		Value	Label	Frequency
1	Roman Catholic	10		1	Roman Catholic	10
2	Methodist	3		2	Protestant	20
3	Presbyterian	2		3	Jewish	10
4	Lutheran	5		4	Other	5
5	Baptist	4				
6	Unitarian	3				
7	Episcopalian	3				
8	Jewish	10				
9	Moslem	1				
10	Eastern Orthodox	0				
11	Hindu	1				
12	Buddhist	1				
13	Shintoist	0				
14	Atheist	2				
15	Other	0				

Total $N = 45$

Table 14.5   Grouping Ordinal Data

Social Class	f	Social Class	f
upper-upper	8		
middle-upper	14	upper	57
lower-upper	35		
upper-middle	56		
middle-middle	92	middle	212
lower-middle	64		
upper-lower	44		
middle-lower	32	lower	87
lower-lower	11		
Total (N) = 356		Total (N) = 356	

but not have a variable for highest degree attained. The desired variable could be approximated by grouping the existing variable. Although years of education could conceivably be construed of as a ratio-level variable, if it is applied as an indicator of preparation for employment, then it might better be treated as ordinal. In terms of getting a job, having a high school diploma, an associate degree, or a bachelor's degree may be the critical determinants. People who dropped out without completing the 12th grade are all dropouts, whether they completed 9, 10, or 11 years. People who have 13 to 15 years of education probably have some college but not a bachelor's degree. Rather than using equal multiples as in the social class example, a researcher might approximate employment preparation by grouping years of education into the following categories:

1 = < 9 years (no high school)

2 = 9–11 years (some high school)

3 = 12 years (high school graduate)

4 = 13–15 years (some college)

5 = 16+ years (college graduate)

The scheme would not be perfect because not everyone with 12 years of schooling graduated, but it would approximate the desired variable. As this example illustrates, the fact that the original categories are ordered is a starting point for grouping a variable, but the researcher must still rely on logic and knowledge of the application to which the grouped variable will be put to decide on the boundaries of the intervals.

Grouping interval-level data is a fairly direct process. Unlike ordinal data, the distance between units of interval-level data are by definition equal, so one general principle is to use equal-width intervals when grouping data. Nevertheless, common sense and knowledge of the use to which the grouped data will be put are essential to planning the group intervals. Intervals of $10 might make perfect sense if grouping data on weekly earnings of high school students but are completely inappropriate if the data concern annual income of single-parent households. All raw frequency distributions of interval data have units of 1, such as length of jail sentence in days, earnings in dollars, or live births per year. In grouping, we merely increase the number of units in each new interval from 1 to 3, 10, 1,000, or whatever amount makes logical sense given the data and provides the desired number of intervals for describing the data and doing data analysis. The size of the grouped intervals is called the *interval width*. Consider the distribution of ungrouped ages for the residents of the veterans' residential facility in Table 14.3. These scores are clearly in need of grouping, as they are so spread out that any pattern is difficult to see.

To illustrate grouping interval data, we will group the scores in Table 14.3 into 10 new intervals. We want enough intervals so that we do not obscure significant variation in the data, but we want to reduce the clutter of too many categories. Once the decision on the number of intervals is made, we must determine the number of measurement units that will go into each new interval—the interval width. In this example, with a range of 48

years in the age variable and the number of grouped intervals set at 10, it is quite obvious that the interval width should be 5. In other situations, however, the interval width may not be so easy to determine, so there is a formula that one can apply to find the interval width:

$$\text{Interval Width} = \frac{H_s - L_s}{N_i}$$

where:

H_s = Highest actual score in the distribution
L_s = Lowest actual score in the distribution
N_i = Number of desired intervals

If we applied this equation to the data in Table 14.3, we would have:

$$\text{Interval Width} = \frac{98 - 50}{10} = \frac{48}{10} = 4.8$$

In many cases, the result of this formula is a decimal of some sort that one merely adjusts up or down to the nearest convenient interval width. In our case, we would adjust upward for an interval width of 5. The resulting frequency distribution is displayed in Table 14.6.

When selecting interval widths, we suggest that the width be an odd number, such as 3, 5, or 7, because intervals with an odd-numbered width have a whole number for their *midpoints*. For example, an interval sized 5, 50–54 has a midpoint of 52, but an interval sized 4, 46–49 has a midpoint of 47.5. When working with grouped interval data, the midpoints have a number of uses (such as category labels in Table 14.6), and it is far more convenient to work with midpoints that do not have decimals. Compare the grouped data in Table 14.6 with the ungrouped and simple frequency distributions in Table 14.3. Do you notice anything in the grouped distribution that you did not see when you first looked at those distributions, especially the ungrouped distribution? The grouped distribution clearly shows the characteristic accumulation of people in the middle of a distribution with the frequencies tapering off toward both tails of the distribution. Such a distribution is commonly referred to as a "normal

Table 14.6   Patient Age Data Grouped by Intervals of 5 Years

Interval Width	Value	Frequency	Percent	Valid Percent	Cum Percent
50–54	52	4	5.6	5.6	5.6
55–59	57	5	7.0	7.0	12.7
60–64	62	5	7.0	7.0	19.7
65–69	67	12	16.9	16.9	36.6
70–74	72	17	23.9	23.9	60.6
75–79	77	12	16.9	16.9	77.5
80–84	82	7	9.9	9.9	87.3
85–89	87	4	5.6	5.6	93.0
90–94	92	2	2.8	2.8	95.8
95–99	97	3	4.2	4.2	100.0
	Total	71	100.0	100.0	

Valid cases   71   Missing cases   0

curve" and is an important characteristic of data distributions that is used in choosing some statistics in Chapter 15.

Graphical Display of Data Distributions

In addition to describing variables by means of a frequency distribution, another common procedure is to use a graph. The visual impact of a graph can help identify and summarize patterns in data that might not be detected as readily by perusing frequency distribution tables. Statistical software today can produce a diverse array of graphs that can be enhanced with color and editing capabilities. Used correctly, graphs are a powerful tool for communicating information about data; used incorrectly, they can confuse and even mislead viewers on the meaning of a distribution. One situation in which graphs are popular occurs when the results of a frequency distribution must be presented to an audience that is unfamiliar with reading such tables.

We present a few of the more common ways of graphing individual variables. Basically, these graphs are visual representations of a frequency distribution. Earlier, we discussed ways of grouping data for presentation in a frequency distribution table. Many of the same issues apply to graphing data. For example, a graph is more effective if there are a manageable number of categories. If several categories have a very low frequency, they will be hard to see on a graph. An effective graph, then, begins with organizing the data appropriately as one would for a frequency distribution table.

Bar Graphs

One of the most commonly used types of graphs is the **bar graph.** A distinguishing feature of the bar graph is the space between the bars. These spaces illustrate that the categories of the variable being represented are separate, or *discrete*. In Chapter 5 we pointed out that only certain categories are theoretically possible in a discrete variable such as race, religious affiliation, and household size. Nominal and ordinal variables are by definition

Figure 14.3   Example of a Bar Graph

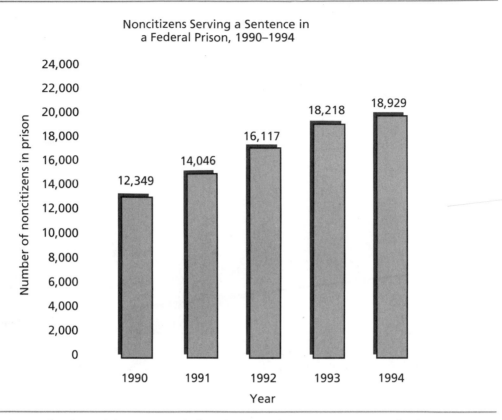

Noncitizens Serving a Sentence in
a Federal Prison, 1990–1994

Source   Based on Bureau of Justice Statistics, *Noncitizens in the Federal Criminal Justice System 1984–1994* (Washington, D.C.:
U.S. Department of Justice, 1996), p. 9.

discrete variables, so bar graphs are especially useful for these levels of data. Figure 14.3 illustrates a
typical bar graph, with the height of the bars representing the frequencies in each category of the
variable. As can be seen from the figure, a bar
graph makes it easy to note trends such as the upward one in Figure 14.3.

   When constructing a bar graph (and most other
types of graphs, for that matter), care should be
taken when establishing the dimensions of the
graph. The vertical axis, which represents the frequencies, and the horizontal axis, which represents
the categories of the variable, should be about
equal with reasonably equal spacing of the cate-

gories on both axes. Again, Figure 14.3 illustrates
this. This concern for roughly equal dimensions is
important because it is possible to accidentally or
purposely construct a graph that gives a false impression. For example, by expanding the dimensions of the vertical axis, a graph can be constructed
that makes small differences among categories appear large, at least to the casual observer. On the
other hand, expanding the horizontal dimension
has the opposite effect. A graph can be constructed
that appears to minimize differences among the
categories. Purposeful manipulation of graph dimensions in an attempt to deceive viewers is considered unethical. It should be noted, however, that

Figure 14.4   Histogram and Frequency Polygon of Hypothetical Exam Scores

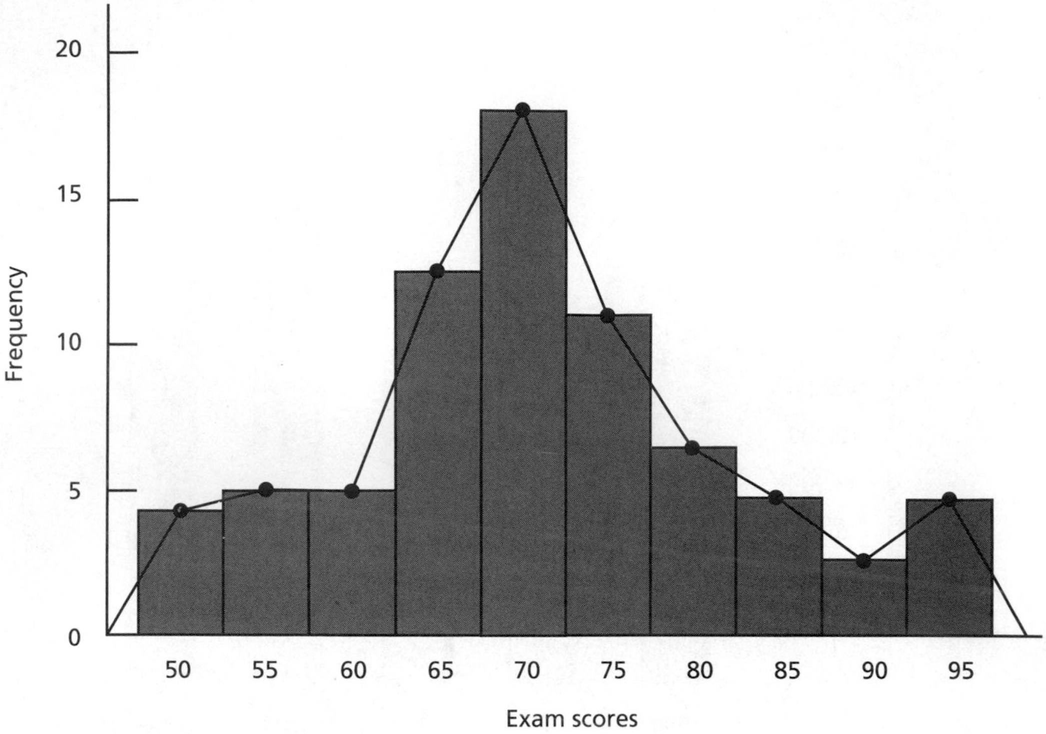

Histograms and Frequency Polygons

Although some variables, such as household size or a frequency count of a behavior, are discrete variables, at the interval or ratio level of measurement, variables are conceived of as *continuous,* meaning that, unlike the discrete variables, there are no gaps or spaces between the categories. Thus, age is a continuous variable. This continuous nature of interval and ratio data should be reflected in graphs used to present them. The researcher wishing to graph interval or ratio data has a choice of two popular methods. The **histogram** bears a considerable resemblance to the preceding bar graph.

misleading graphs are produced all the time, so anyone reading a research report should always carefully inspect any graph to be sure that viewers are not misled by its initial appearance.

Once again, as we see in Figure 14.4, bars of various lengths represent the magnitude of the frequencies from a frequency distribution. The only difference between a bar graph and a histogram is that the bars in a histogram touch, signifying the continuous nature of the data.

Figure 14.4 also illustrates the alternative technique of graphing interval or ratio data, the **frequency polygon,** which is simply a line graph that connects the midpoints of each category of the variable. The choice of either a histogram or a frequency polygon is purely a matter of personal preference as they are interchangeable.

Pie Charts

Pie charts are another type of commonly used graph that are particularly good for showing how some whole amount is divided. As such, pie charts are often

Figure 14.5 Example of a Pie Chart

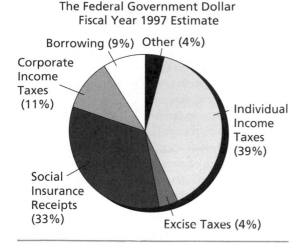

The Federal Government Dollar
Fiscal Year 1997 Estimate

- Borrowing (9%)
- Other (4%)
- Corporate Income Taxes (11%)
- Individual Income Taxes (39%)
- Social Insurance Receipts (33%)
- Excise Taxes (4%)

Source *Budget Supplement Fiscal Year 1997* (Washington, D.C.: U.S. Government Printing Office, 1996), p. 2.

used to illustrate how budgets are distributed for varying functions. Anyone who has occasion to prepare a grant proposal will most likely have to create one or more pie charts indicating how the money would be spent. Figure 14.5 is a pie chart based on projected revenue to the federal government for the 1997 fiscal year.

A pie chart gets its name from its resemblance to slices of a pie. The size of each slice gives a visual depiction of the percentage of the whole that each category represents. Preparing a pie chart via a computer program now involves simply choosing a variable and the pie chart option from the graphing menu. However, the process that the graphing program uses involves determining how many of the 360 degrees of an entire circle are to be allocated to each of the categories. For example, Figure 14.5 indicates that 11 percent of revenues are expected to come from corporate income taxes. To determine how large a slice to allocate to corporate income taxes, the data analysis software multiplies 360 by 11 percent, obtaining a value of 39.6 degrees. So, the slice devoted to corporate income taxes is drawn such that it occupies 39.6 degrees of the 360 degrees of the circle.

Research in Practice 14.1 provides an example of how the preparation and presentation of univari-

ate data described thus far in this chapter have utility in human service program planning.

Contingency Tables

Thus far, we have discussed ways of describing the distribution of cases on a single variable and ways of presenting single variable data in the form of frequency distributions and graphs. Now we turn our attention to ways of describing and exploring how two or more variables are distributed together. That is, given the values in a data set on one variable, how are values distributed on one or more other variables? Classifying or organizing the data on one variable according to values on a second variable is the basis for contingency table analysis.

Bivariate Relationships

The statistics we have considered so far describe the distribution of a single variable and are therefore called **univariate statistics.** Most data analysis in research involves dealing with two or more variables simultaneously. Statistical procedures that describe the relationship between two variables are called **bivariate statistics,** and **multivariate statistics** deal with three or more variables. When two or more variables are analyzed with descriptive statistics, the major feature of interest is the relationship between the variables, especially the extent to which they co-vary, or vary together. If two variables are related, a change in one of the variables is associated with a change in the other.

A convenient way of investigating bivariate relationships is to cross-tabulate the data in the form of a table. A *contingency table* contains raw frequencies, percentages, or both. We discuss the construction of such tables for only two variables. However, contingency table analysis can be applied to three or more variables.

Table 14.7 illustrates the general form of a contingency table. We use two conventions to standardize the construction of contingency tables. First, when we have an independent variable and a dependent variable, the vertical *columns* represent categories of the independent variable, and the horizontal *rows* represent categories of the dependent variable. In

Table 14.7 A Contingency Table with Frequencies and Percentages

dependent variable   independent variable

NUMBER OF HOURS OF
TELEVISION WATCHED

| | INCOME | | |
	Low	Medium	High
High	49 (19.2%)	19 (8.6%)	10 (6.7%)
Medium	164 (64.3%)	136 (61.5%)	86 (57.5%)
Low	42 (16.5%)	66 (29.9%)	53 (35.6%)
Totals	255 (100%)	221 (100%)	149 (100%)

cell frequency   cell percentage   column marginals

Source James A. Davis and Tom W. Smith. General Social Surveys (1972–1994). (Chicago: National Opinion Research Center; Storrs, CT: The Roper Center for Public Opinion Research, University of Connecticut)

RESEARCH IN PRACTICE 14.1

NEEDS ASSESSMENT:
Does Deer Hunting Really Prevent Domestic Violence?

One of the most significant ways that social science research methods and human service practice can be linked together is by using research data to make better-informed human service planning decisions. To illustrate this point, we have selected one of our own projects, the Marquette County (Mich.) Coordinated Response to Domestic Violence Program. Through a cooperative effort between community agencies, spearheaded by the Women's Center and the Marquette County Prosecuting Attorney, the project sought ways of responding more effectively to cases of domestic violence. A brief description of this project illustrates how the skills of data preparation and presentation are often used in human service settings.

A portion of this effort involved designing a data-collection system to identify domestic violence cases and track their progress through the various organizations involved in responding to the problem. Just setting up the data-collection system proved to be a complex undertaking. Several possible sources of data existed, including 911 calls to Central Dispatch; hotline calls to the Women's Center; legal system reports from police, the prosecutor, district court, and probation; and reports from hospitals and mental health and substance-abuse programs. These records include police report information as well as case disposition data. Using a database program, the researchers developed a data entry form, including coding directions, which permitted a student intern to enter data from all cases, beginning with 1995, the year before program initiation. These data were intended to serve as a baseline for program planning. Approximately 180 completed case files for offenses occurring in 1995 were entered into the initial data set.

Although the database was a good start, many of the variables were not in a form that lent itself to ready data analysis by a statistical package. For example, information on the severity of injury to the victim had been entered as descriptive labels, such as "Pushed and Shoved—No Lasting Pain" or "Weapon Involved—Wounded by Weapon." As a result, such variables were recoded into an ordinal scale, ranging from no physical contact through serious injury requiring medical attention. The database program is also being revised so that in the future, the data set will already contain a numerical code and not require recoding.

When data analysis is used to inform human service practice, an important part of the process is to identify variables that can be of practical use. In this case, one such variable turned out to be the victim's ZIP code. The simple frequency distribution in Table 14.8 shows the distribution of 1995 domestic violence cases in Marquette County, Mich., for ZIP codes of the larger communities. The county is the largest in the state in area, but in terms of population, communities are small. Marquette has only about 27,000 inhabitants. Under these circumstances, ZIP codes are convenient because they include surrounding suburban areas while still representing distinct communities for program planning. In this case, the data show that Ishpeming, about one half the size of Marquette, has a disproportionately large number of domestic violence cases. As the county seat, Marquette has many more human service resources, including a major hospital, a university, and the Women's Center. Analyzing cases by geographic distribution

Figure 14.6 Drinking Pattern in Cases of Male Abuse Suspects and Female Victims

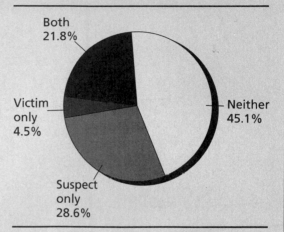

is hardly a groundbreaking data analysis procedure, but this simple analysis played a major role in deciding to allocate a new full-time staff member to Ishpeming, which, based on this data, was felt to be underserved.

Other basic descriptive data are also useful for program planning. An often-discussed issue in the field of domestic violence is the role of alcohol. The pie chart in Figure 14.6 shows the distribution of alcohol involvement by both perpetrator and victim. Such information can help agencies plan services based on actual data rather than on conjecture. The pie chart in Figure 14.7 depicts the distribution of severity of injury in the domestic violence cases that came to the attention of the police. Knowing not only how many cases were referred but also the severity of assaults can be useful in planning services. Such graphical presentations effectively share statistical data with audiences who have little knowledge of statistics.

Of course, not all data can be translated into program policy decisions. One variable we examined was the distribution of domestic violence cases by month. Figure 14.8 seems to suggest that domestic violence cases were comparatively low during November and relatively high during April.

continued on next page

Table 14.8 Program Evaluation Data Showing Domestic Violence Cases by ZIP Code

VZIP	victim ZIP code		
Value Label	Value	Frequency	Percent
Gwinn	49841	15	8.3
Ishpeming	49849	50	27.6
Marquette	49855	69	38.1
Neguanee	49866	24	13.3

Figure 14.7   Assault Severity for Domestic Violence Cases for 1995

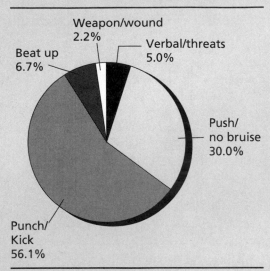

seems plausible. There are over 700,000 licensed deer hunters in Michigan. In the Upper Peninsula, deer season may be more important than Christmas. Schools close, fluorescent orange clothing appears everywhere, and men head off to deer camp in droves. If a large proportion of men are not around their partners, there's less opportunity for domestic violence. Tax time in April doesn't have quite the same impact, but the April rate is high.

However, before the National Rifle Association begins touting big-game hunting as domestic violence prevention or the Internal Revenue Service gets bad press for being the cause of domestic violence, we have some more likely—although less entertaining—explanations. Probably the most likely of these is simply random variation in the data. Furthermore, months are not equal intervals. Not only do some have more days than others, but some have more weekends, and one thing that is clear is that most violence happens between Friday evening and Sunday morning (see the bar chart in Figure 14.9). The pattern (or lack thereof) in the data is more apparent by graphing the data by week instead of month (see Figure 14.10). April 15 falls in week 15 and deer season opens on November 15 in week 46. The number of cases around tax time is

What could be the explanation? Several local people who looked at the graphs had an immediate explanation: It is deer season in November and tax time in April. On the face of it, this explanation

Figure 14.8   Domestic Violence Offenses per Month for 1995

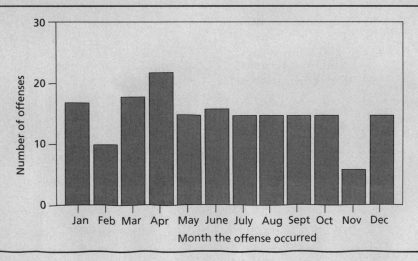

Figure 14.9 Domestic Violence Cases, Weekday of Offense (1995)

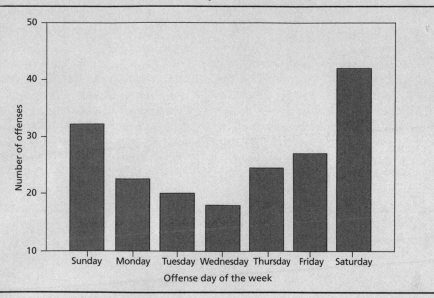

Figure 14.10 Domestic Violence Arrests by Week of the Year (1995)

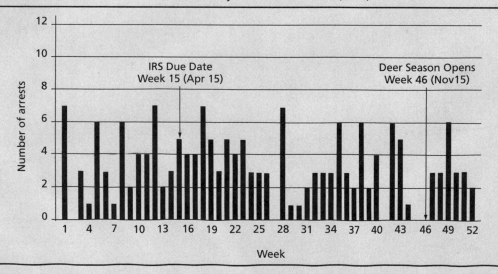

continued on next page

large, but many other weeks show the same or more numbers of cases. No cases of domestic violence were reported during the week of opening day, but there were three other weeks with no cases and several weeks with only one or two cases. So conclusions about the impact on domestic violence of both the tax deadline and deer season are less clear when we categorize data by week rather than month.

This situation illustrates some important points. First, there is more random variability to data than we often think. We must be cautious about reaching *ad hoc* conclusions just because they seem plausible or interesting. Second, how researchers organ-ize or group data in frequency distributions and graphs can reveal meaningful patterns but can also lead to confusion if the categories are flawed. Finally, the evaluator must keep in mind the purpose of the evaluation. In this instance, identifying in what communities domestic violence occurs is an important, useful contribution because it has direct implications for how services should be allocated. But finding a few more cases of domestic violence around tax time or a few less around deer season is not of much use for needs assessment or program planning. Such relationships might be of sociological interest, but the purpose of the study determines which variables are important.

Table 14.7, the variable *Income* is the independent variable and *Hours of Television Watched* is the dependent variable. Second, when ordinal-level or higher data are cross-tabulated, the categories should be ordered as illustrated in Table 14.7, with columns running from lowest on the left to highest on the right and rows from lowest at the bottom to highest at the top. These conventions are not universally applied; however, some tables are constructed differently. But following the conventions does contribute to consistency and ease of interpretation. Furthermore, the computational routines for some statistics assume that tables are constructed according to this convention and must be modified to produce correct results with differently structured tables.

Several labels refer to the various parts of tables. The squares of the table are called *cells,* with the frequencies within the cells labeled *cell frequencies.* Values in the "Totals" column or row are called *marginals* (only the column marginal is shown in Table 14.7). Tables are often identified according to the number of rows and columns they contain. A table with two rows and two columns becomes a 2 $\times$ 2 (read "2 by 2") table. A table such as Table 14.7 is a 3 $\times$ 3 table. In addition, because the number of rows is always designated first, a 2 $\times$ 3 table is not the same as a 3 $\times$ 2.

Contingency tables almost always include *cell percentages* because, by themselves, cell frequencies are difficult to interpret if the number of cases varies in each column and row. Converting frequencies to percentages makes interpretation much easier and can be done by dividing each cell frequency by the appropriate marginal total and multiplying the result by 100. We would use column marginals if we wanted to see how the dependent variable was distributed across categories of the independent variable. Percentages in the first column of Table 14.7 were obtained by dividing the cell frequencies 49, 164, and 42 by the column marginal 255, with the result multiplied by 100. Below each column, the percentages are totaled and indicated as equaling 100 percent. This informs the reader that the column marginals were used to compute the percentages. Sometimes the cells in a contingency table contain only percentages and no frequencies. In this case, the marginal frequencies should always be included because they supply valuable information regarding the number of cases on which the percentages are based and enable the reader to compute the cell frequencies if needed.

Reading percentage tables is a straightforward process similar to constructing them. Whereas we computed the percentages down the columns, we read percentage tables by comparing percentages along the rows. Of particular interest is the *percentage difference* (% d) between any two categories within a given row. For example, in Table 14.7, the difference between the low-income column and the high-income column in the top row is 12.5 percent, meaning that substantially more low-income people watch high levels of television. The % d suggests that high levels of television watching are less common among high-income groups. Note that with a 2 × 2 table, a single % d summarizes the complete table. As the number of rows and columns in a table increases, the number of % d's that can be calculated increases rapidly.

The magnitude of % d's is a crude indicator of the strength of the relationship between two variables: Small differences of 1 or 2 percent indicate weak and possibly meaningless relationships, while % d's of 15 percent or more usually indicate substantial relationships. Unfortunately, no hard-and-fast rules concerning evaluating the magnitude of % d's can be offered because of the complicating factor of sample size. For example, if we are dealing with employment data for the entire nation, a difference of 1 percent or less could represent a million more workers with or without jobs. With large samples, smaller % d's are more important. Alternatively, with small samples, % d's must be large before they indicate a substantial relationship. (We will discuss other statistics for assessing the strength of relationships in contingency tables in Chapter 15.)

Multivariate Analysis

As noted in Chapter 2, analyzing an independent and a dependent variable and finding a bivariate relationship between them does not prove that the independent variable actually *causes* variation in the dependent variable. To infer causality, the possible effects of extraneous variables must be investigated. Although research projects may focus primary attention on two variables, they typically consider others to assess the full complexity of social phenomena. A set of procedures for conducting this kind of multivariate analysis is called either **table elaboration** or **contingency control.** Contingency control in-

Figure 14.11 General Format for Partialing Tables:
X = categories of the independent variable
Y = categories of the dependent variable
Z = categories of the test variable

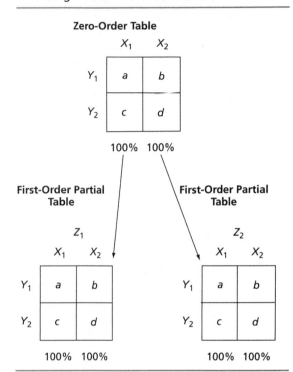

volves examining a relationship between an independent and a dependent variable while holding a third variable (also called a test factor) constant. Three variable tables are constructed such that the relationship between the independent and dependent variable can be examined within each category of that third variable. The general format of contingency control is illustrated in Figure 14.11.

The original table that the researcher begins the analysis with is called the *zero-order table,* and the relationship contained within it is known as a *zero-order relationship.* The zero in these labels indicates that no control or test variables are being used. As we introduce test variables, the tables produced are called *partial tables,* and the relationships within them are known as *partial relationships.* A partial relationship is a relationship between an independent and a dependent variable within one category of the test (or control) variable.

Partial tables are referred to by the number of test variables being controlled at one time. If we are controlling one test variable in our partial tables, they are referred to as *first-order partials,* indicating that the number of variables controlled is one. If more variables than one are simultaneously controlled, the tables are called second-order partials, third-order partials, and so on. Often, research does not go beyond the first order with contingency control. One reason is that as we add more test variables, the number of partial tables that are generated increases rapidly, and interpreting all of these tables becomes difficult. The other reason table elaboration is often not taken beyond the first order is that the sample gets divided quickly, to the point that individual cell frequencies may become too small and reduce our confidence in the results. We literally run out of cases. This effect can be seen in Figure 14.11, where

in the zero-order case the sample is divided among the four cells of the zero-order table; but when we move to the partials, the same number of cases is spread among eight cells, thus reducing the magnitude of the cell frequencies. For analyzing multivariate relationships beyond the first order, we normally use techniques other than table elaboration.

A number of outcomes can occur when a test variable is introduced and partial tables created. Describing some of these outcomes offers an idea of the basic logic behind multivariate analysis. First, the partial tables may show *no effect*. This is also called *replication* because the results in the partial tables replicate or repeat the results in the zero-order table: The relationship in the partial tables is approximately the same in terms of strength and direction as it was in the zero-order table. In this case, we have tested a variable that is unrelated to either the independent or the dependent variable; therefore, it could not affect the relationship between those variables. We have illustrated this in Figure 14.12, where the zero-

Figure 14.12 Table Elaboration Showing "No Effect" of the Test Variable (Replication)

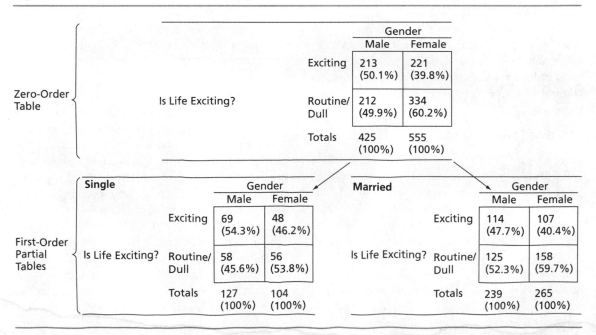

Source James A. Davis and Tom W. Smith. *General Social Surveys (1972–1994)* (Chicago: National Opinion Research Center; Storrs, CT: The Rope Center for Public Opinion Research, University of Connecticut).

order table shows the relationship between *gender* and *whether people believe life to be exciting, routine, or dull*. You can see in the zero-order table that about 10 percent more of the males believe that life is exciting. It is possible, however, that *marital status* might influence whether men and women perceive life to be exciting. So in the partial tables, we look at the relationship between the two variables separately for married and single people (we left the other possible marital statuses out to simplify the example). You can see that this third variable has almost no effect on the original relationship. In each of the categories of marital status, about 7 to 8 percent more men than women see life as exciting.

A second possibility when doing table elaboration is that the strength of the relationship found in the zero-order table may be substantially reduced or even disappear entirely in the partials. We described this kind of situation in the discussion of causality in Chapter 2 without calling it by these names. We have reproduced that data in Figure 14.13. The zero-order table shows how reading reports about the health consequences of smoking impacted on whether people quit smoking. The table shows that people who read such reports are substantially more likely to quit smoking (% d = 23%). However, when we control for education, the original relationship disappears. In each educational grouping, quitting smoking is as common among those who have not read the report as among those who have.

This result can be difficult to interpret because there are two possibilities and we need more information (which may or may not be available) to choose between the two. One possibility is that in terms of temporal order, the test variable intervenes between the independent and the dependent variable (see Figure 14.14). When such an intervening variable is controlled, it is called *interpretation;* the independent variable is changing the test variable, which in turn is changing the dependent variable. In other words, a causal sequencing is being specified. When there is such a causal chain, the relationship between the

Figure 14.13 Relationship between Reading Smoking Reports and Smoking Cessation, with Level of Education as a Control Variable

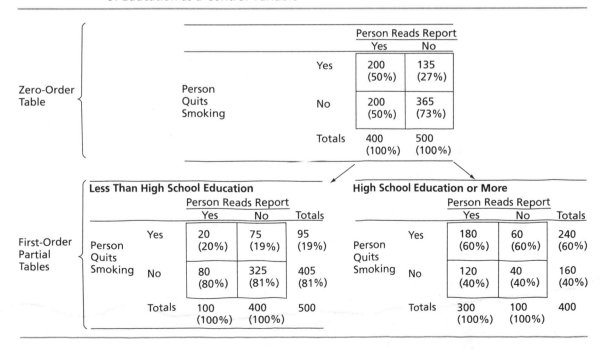

Figure 14.14   A Comparison of Intervening and Antecedent Variable Relationships

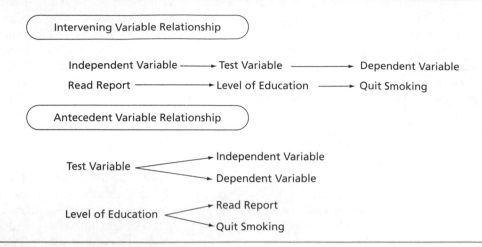

independent variable and the dependent variable is effectively blocked in the partial tables. In our example, an intervening variable relationship means that reading of the report is what produces their level of education, and level of education, in turn, causes them to quit smoking. However, this is probably not an appropriate assessment of these variables because there is no logical or theoretical reason to assume that reading a health report would change people's level of education. So interpretation is probably not what is going on in this table.

This brings us to the other possibility, namely, that the zero-order relationship is either all or partly *spurious*. In this case, which is called *explanation,* the test variable is temporally located before either the independent or the dependent variable and is related directly to both. This is called an *antecedent variable relationship.* When the effects of the test variable are controlled, the apparent relationship between the independent variable and the dependent variable is reduced or eliminated because the operation of the test variable was to inflate the actual relationship between the other two variables in the zero-order table. In other words, the relationship shown in the zero-order table was a false reading. In Figure 14.13, we know that people's educational levels are antecedent: Their educational levels were established

before they had a chance to read the report or quit smoking. In addition, theoretical reasons allow us to conclude that level of education can influence both whether people read the report and whether they quit smoking. This tells us that the relationship in the zero-order table is spurious.

So when a relationship disappears in a partial table, we need to establish the appropriate temporal location of the test variable or use some theoretical or logical considerations to determine whether interpretation or explanation is the proper assessment of what is going on. If that cannot be done, as might occur with survey data, we cannot be sure whether the partials are indicating the presence of an intervening variable or that of a spurious relationship. (As noted in Chapter 2, determining temporal order is crucial in sorting out causal relationships among variables.)

Yet another possibility can be discovered in table elaboration. *Specification* refers to a situation where the relationship between the independent and dependent variables is found in the zero-order table but the partial tables show different relationships from one table to another. One partial table may show no relationship or a weak relationship, while the other shows a strong relationship. In other words, the table elaboration specifies the categories

Figure 14.15 Table Elaboration Showing Specification: Relationship between Social Class and Self-Esteem, Controlling for Gender

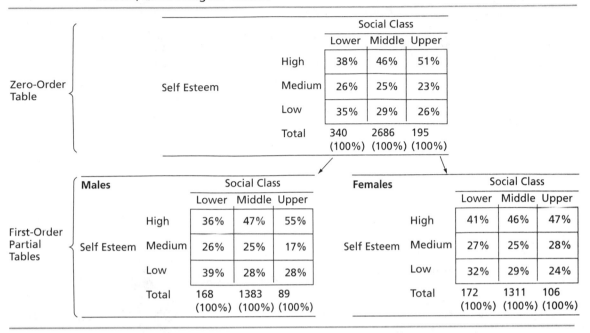

Source Morris Rosenberg, *Society and the Adolescent Self-Image* (Princeton, NJ: Princeton University Press, 1965), pp. 40–41.

of the test variable in which the relationship occurs or does not occur.

Figure 14.15 shows one example of what specification can look like. The figure shows the relationship found in one study between social class and self-esteem among adolescents. The zero-order table shows a fairly strong relationship, with adolescents in higher social classes being more likely to have high self-esteem (% d = 13% in the high self-esteem category). However, when gender is introduced as a test factor, the original relationship gets dramatically specified: Upper-class boys are substantially more likely to have high self-esteem than lower-class boys (% d = 19% in the high self-esteem category). However, the relationship is much weaker, although still in the same direction, among girls (% d = 6% in the high self-esteem category). So the introduction of the test factor enables us to specify that social class is a fairly powerful factor in shaping self-esteem among boys, but much less so among girls.

We want to mention one final possibility that can be found in table elaboration. The partial tables may show an even stronger relationship between the independent and dependent variables than was indicated by the zero-order table. This outcome occurs because the action of the uncontrolled test variable in the zero-order table is to suppress the relationship between the independent and the dependent variables. In fact, variables that produce this result are called *suppressor variables,* and the result itself is known as *suppression.* This occurs when the test variable and the independent variable are exerting forces on the dependent variable that are at least partly offsetting. That is, as values of the independent variable increase, they influence the dependent variable to increase, but as the test variable increases, it is influencing the dependent variable to decrease, thus masking part of the relationship between the independent and the dependent variables. When the influence of the test variable is controlled, this masking effect is removed, and the relationship between the independent variable and the dependent variable is revealed to be stronger than in the zero-order table.

A number of other possibilities can occur in table elaboration, but these examples illustrate the importance and difficulty of this kind of multivariate analysis. It is important because it enables us to discover the complexity of social reality where dependent variables are influenced by a number of factors at the same time. It is also a difficult kind of analysis because it requires time, patience, and creativity to tease out what can sometimes be hard-to-discover relationships.

Main Points

■ Data analysis refers to deriving some meaning from the observations that have been made as a part of a research project; quantitative data analysis involves putting observations into numerical form and manipulating them based on their arithmetical properties.

■ Most data analysis is currently performed by computer, with data entered into a computer file from a computer terminal.

■ Data analysis begins by developing a coding scheme and a codebook, which is a set of mutually exclusive and exhaustive numerical codes into which the raw data are categorized.

■ After data have been entered into a computer file, they must be carefully checked for coding or input errors.

■ New or revised variables may be created by recoding existing variables or by computing new variables based on existing variables.

■ Frequency distributions may be effectively communicated with bar graphs, histograms, frequency polygons, and pie charts.

■ Frequency distributions reveal the pattern the frequencies produce among the various categories of the variable and may be symmetrical or asymmetrical.

■ Contingency tables and percentage tables are particularly useful for analyzing bivariate and multi-variate relationships with categorical or partially ordered data.

Important Terms for Review

alphanumeric variables
bar graph
bivariate statistics
coding scheme
contingency control
data analysis
frequency polygon
histogram
multivariate statistics
numeric variables
pie charts
statistics
table elaboration
univariate statistics

Exploring InfoTrac® College Edition and the Internet

InfoTrac® College Edition search terms:

contingency tables
histogram

InfoTrac® College Edition articles:

Impression Management with Graphs: Effects on Choices. Vairam Arunachalam, Buck K.W. Pei, Paul John Steinbart. *Journal of Information Systems* Fall 2002 v16 i2 p183(20) (10,416 words)

HRS Data Set: Respondent Earnings and Social Security Benefits Files. (Health and Retirement Study)(Statistical Data Included). *Social Security Bulletin* Winter 2000 v63 i4 p72 (1,127 words)

Interactional Styles of Bullies and Victims Observed in a Competitive and a Cooperative Setting. (Statistical Data Included) ERSILIA MENESINI, ELENA MELAN, BARBARA PIGNATTI. *Journal of Genetic Psychology* Sept 2000 v161 i3 p261 (7,805 words)

The emphasis in most of the Exploring Info-Trac® College Edition and Internet sections in this text has been on locating information that will help expand your knowledge of research. But the Internet does more than just provide interesting illustrations of research methods; it can also provide you with tools for actually doing research. The step of data entry is an example of this. An important goal of the data entry step is to obtain a data set that is complete, free from errors, and ready for analysis. Although one can enter data directly into a statistical software program, such as SPSS, Minitab, or SAS, it is not always convenient to do so, nor are there always safeguards against entering incorrect values. A solution is a freeware program (so called because there is no charge for obtaining it) called QDATA (www.soc.qc.edu/QC_Software/qdata.html). QDATA is an easy-to-use program specifically for designing data sets, entering data, and cleaning data. You can begin by defining variables to be included in the data set, including variable names, extended labels, whether the variable is text or numeric, the range of acceptable values, and labels for the values. Once the variables are defined, you can enter your data set. After the data are entered, the program guides you through several data-cleaning steps. By downloading the program and its manual, you can either use the program with actual data that you collect or simply experiment by making up a hypothetical data set to gain a sense of the process involved.

Graphical aids to data analysis and presentation have exploded with the advent of the personal computer, and the Internet has an abundance of resources available to enrich your understanding of graphical data analysis and to provide tools to aid you in generating graphs of your data. One of the most inclusive sites on the Internet related to graphical use of data is Michael Friendly's site, Statistics and Statistical Graphics (www.math.yorku.ca/SCS/StatResource.html). This page provides a topic-based collection of available resources for statistics, statistical graphics, and computation related to research, data analysis, and teaching; it now contains more than 350 links. An interesting feature of this Internet site is a page devoted to illustrating some of the best and worst examples of graphs to depict data. Examining these graphical depictions of data will show

you the value of using graphs—and some of the pitfalls to avoid as well. Access "The Gallery of Data Visualization" at www.math.yorku.ca/SCS/Gallery.

For Further Reading

Craft, John L. *Statistics and Data Analysis for Social Workers,* 2nd ed. Itasca, Ill.: Peacock, 1990. This brief introduction to statistical analysis provides many good illustrations of the kinds of statistical analysis that involve human service workers.

Fox, William. *Social Statistics: A Text Using Microcase,* 4th ed. Belmont, Calif.: Wadsworth, 2003. Written in a light and accessible style, this book teaches statistics through the use of the increasingly popular and easy-to-use Microcase software, a copy of which is included with each book.

Gravetter, Frederick J., and Larry B. Wallnau. *Statistics for the Behavioral Sciences,* 6th ed. Belmont, Calif.: Wadsworth, 2004. This is a standard but well-written introductory textbook in statistics. It covers all the topics discussed in this and the next chapter, going into more detail and including additional topics.

Green, Samuel B., and Neil J. Salkind. *Using SPSS for Windows and Macintosh: Analyzing and Understanding Data,* 3rd ed. Upper Saddle River, N.J.: Prentice Hall, 2003. This book provides an introduction to the use of the most widely used statistical package today, SPSS. This handbook will show you how to do all of the things that are discussed in this and the next chapter.

Healey, Joseph F. *Statistics: A Tool for Social Research,* 6th ed. Belmont, Calif.: Wadsworth, 2002. This is another standard but well-written introductory textbook in statistics. Along with the Evans book, it can help you understand all the material in this and the next chapter.

Henry, Gary T. *Graphing Data: Techniques for Display and Analysis.* Newbury Park, Calif.: Sage, 1994. This book presents techniques for making data from the social sciences accessible to nontechnical audiences. Discusses insights from visual perception research relating to graphing data and explores graphs for data summarization, display of multiple units, tabular displays, alternatives to tables, two-variable scatterplots, and creating effective legends and titles on displays.

Jones, Gerald E. *How to Lie with Charts.* Alameda, Calif.: Sybex, 1995. An ideal guide for all who want to understand how presenters can use charts to deceive an audience. Readers will learn how to make their presentations more effective.

Journal of Technology in Human Services. New York: Haworth, quarterly. A journal that began publication in 1984, focusing on the potential of computer technology to help us deal with mental health, developmental disabilities, and other human problems. It provides a timely contribution to this area.

Wallgren, Anders, Britt Wallgren, Rolf Persson, and Ulf Jorner. *Graphing Statistics and Data: Creating Better Charts.* Walnut Creek, Calif.: Altamira Press, 1996. This book suggests how to create graphs and charts that make viewers aware of the qualities of data. Introduces the elements of charts, such as axes, scales, and patterns; describes steps to make charts clearer, using real data for examples; and walks through the entire process from data to finished chart.

Walsh, Anthony, and Jane C. Ollenburger. *Essential Statistics for the Social and Behavioral Sciences: A Conceptual Approach.* Upper Saddle River, N.J.: Prentice Hall, 2001. This text covers all of the standard procedures in statistics but does so in a briefer version than other texts and emphasizes the interpretation of results rather than the calculation of formulas.

Zeisel, Hans. *Say It with Figures,* 6th ed. New York: Harper & Row, 1984. A classic analysis of how to present data with statistics. It is very useful for policy makers who wish to improve their understanding of the statistics presented to them.

Exercises for Class Discussion

Assume that you have just completed the data collection on a needs assessment for a volunteer visitation program for the elderly in your community. You have a random sample of 500 questionnaires completed by people 55 years and older that must now be analyzed. The program will cost about $45,000 a year for the coordinator's salary and administrative and advertising costs. Variables included in the survey are sex, age, annual income, proximity to family members, a scale score on perception of neighbors' capacity to help, and a scale indicating desirability of a visitation program. Finally, the question was asked, "If this program were implemented, would you use it?" The question could be answered yes or no.

14.1 Describe the general process you would follow in analyzing the data by listing the main steps to be completed.

14.2 Develop a hypothetical coding scheme for the following variables: age, sex, income, and desirability scale score (assume the scale scores can range from 0 to 30).

14.3 In terms of bivariate relationships, using the final question as the dependent variable, indicate which indicators would be appropriate for each of the independent variables. What if the dependent variable is the scale score?

Chapter 15

Data Analysis II: Descriptive and Inferential Statistics

This chapter is a continuation of the introduction to data analysis that began in Chapter 14. You will recall that data analysis is the process of deriving some meaning from the observations made during the research process. Thus far, the focus has been on describing data using relatively simple procedures, such as frequency distributions, data plots, and contingency tables. Although these means of summarizing and displaying data are useful, researchers often rely on more sophisticated statistics to describe data precisely and to examine relationships between variables.

Statistics have become common to the lexicon of modern living. We often hear people casually referring to something being "above the norm," "below average," or "correlated" with something else. Tune in to the evening news and you might assume that death from cancer is imminent because research has shown a "statistically significant correlation" between your favorite food and the dreaded disease. Or you might hear a report stating that the relationship between underage drinking and traffic-related injuries to adolescents is "statistically significant." Because statistics are ubiquitous in our modern world, people often use statistical terms, such as "correlation" or "statistical significance," without fully comprehending what they mean. It is imperative to have a basic understanding of statistical concepts to be an informed consumer of both the popular media and the professional literature in the social sciences and human services.

Also, it is very likely that, as a human service professional, you will need to compile data, analyze it, and present the findings as part of a needs assessment, funding proposal, or documentation of program outcome. This requires knowing not only how to interpret a statistic but also which statistics to use and how to compute them. We believe that it is especially important to emphasize choosing the correct statistic. Computer technology has made statistical computation relatively easy, but the proper selection of statistical procedures and interpretation of statistical results cannot be done by the computer—it requires an intellect informed about statistical analysis.

This chapter is not intended as a thorough coverage of statistical procedures; to provide such coverage requires a book devoted solely to the subject. However, we do provide a basic introduction to the fundamentals of statistical analysis in order to draw conclusions from the data and to understand their broader implications.

Considerations in Choosing Statistics

Once the data are coded and in a computer file, the researcher is ready to begin the data analysis that will unlock the information that the data contain. One of the major errors that can occur in data analysis is selecting a statistic that is inappropriate for the kind of data gathered in a research project. Although many factors need to be taken into account in choosing statistics appropriately, five major considerations are especially important.

Level of Measurement

One consideration is the level of measurement of the data collected. Chapter 5 addresses the four levels of measurement: nominal, ordinal, interval, and ratio. Each level of measurement involves different rules of permissible mathematical operations that can be performed on the numbers produced while measuring variables at that level. The nominal level involves merely classifying observations into categories; the categories have no order, and the numbers associated with a category only serve as a label for the category—the numbers have no mathematical value and performing any arithmetic operations on them is inappropriate. On the other hand, a ratio level of measurement has a true zero point, making all mathematical operations permissible.

Each statistical procedure involves mathematical operations that are appropriate at one of the levels of measurement. For example, a nominal statistic assumes that the data have only mutually exclusive and exhaustive categories and none of the mathematical properties of the other levels of measurement. Like-

Table 15.1   Relationship between Statistics and Level of Measurement

Level of Measurement Statistic Is Designed For	Level of Measurement of the Data			
	Nominal	**Ordinal**	**Interval**	**Ratio**
Ratio	No	No	No	Yes
Interval	No	No	Yes	Yes
Ordinal	No	Yes	Yes	Yes
Nominal	Yes	Yes	Yes	Yes

No = Inappropriate to use the statistic with this data

Yes = Appropriate to use the statistic with this data

wise, a ratio statistic assumes that the data have a true zero point and requires mathematical operations appropriate to that.

The basic rule is that variables that are measured at a given level can be analyzed with a statistic designed for that level of measurement or with a statistic designed for a lower level of measurement. As Table 15.1 illustrates, nominal, ordinal, interval, or ratio data can be treated as nominal and used with a statistical procedure designed for nominal data. For example, a frequency distribution (as described in Chapter 14) can be used with a nominal-level variable, such as religious affiliation; however, a frequency distribution can also be used to classify data at higher levels of measurement, such as levels of agreement to Likert scale items (ordinal level) or annual income in dollars (ratio level). Because it can handle data at all levels of measurement, a frequency distribution is a good statistical procedure with which to begin data analysis.

However, even though data measured at higher levels can be analyzed with lower-level statistics, a trade-off results in terms of the kind of information and relationships that we can discover about the data based on the statistics. With annual income, for example, it is much more informative to be able to say that the people in the upper 10 percent of the income distribution range earn eight times more money than people in the bottom 50 percent than to simply report the number or percent of people who are in a particular income category. Therefore,

researchers generally prefer to use the highest level of statistic appropriate for a particular variable. In addition, it is definitely inappropriate to use a statistic designed for a higher level of measurement than the level of measurement of the data being analyzed.

Thus far, we have discussed the role of levels of measurement in selecting a statistic on the basis of individual variables. However, many research questions involve examining relationships between two or more variables simultaneously, and these may involve different levels of measurement. For example, we might study whether substance abusers abstain or use drugs (nominal) after attending one of several treatment programs (nominal) while also taking into account religious affiliation (nominal), age (interval), and severity of addiction (ordinal). One reason why so many different statistical procedures exist is that they address different possible combinations of levels of measurement among variables. For any data-analysis problem, then, the researcher must be able to classify each variable in terms of its level of measurement.

Goals of the Data Analysis

The second consideration in assessing the appropriateness of statistics is to determine what goals the statistic is to accomplish. Each statistical technique performs a particular function, revealing certain information about the data. A clear conception of the analytical goals of the data analysis is a prerequisite for selecting the best statistics for achieving those goals. Statistical techniques have one of two goals: *description* or *inference*. **Descriptive statistics** assist in organizing, summarizing, and interpreting data. The data might be from a sample, or they might be from a whole population (see Chapter 6); in either case, descriptive statistics organize and summarize the body of data. **Inferential statistics** allow us to make generalizations from sample data to the populations from which the samples were drawn. Recall from Chapter 6 that the ultimate reason for making observations on samples is to draw conclusions regarding the populations from which those samples were drawn. We make observations on a sample of clients in an agency because it is too expensive, time-consuming, or impractical to observe all the clients; yet we want to draw conclusions about all the clients. Inferential statistics are based on probability theory, and they basically tell us the probability of being wrong if we extend the results found in a sample to the population from which the sample was taken.

Statistics must be chosen that are appropriate to the goals of the data analysis. In some cases, we use both descriptive and inferential statistics because the analysis intends to accomplish both goals. However, if a population were small enough that the data could be collected from every element in the population, inferential statistics would not be necessary and would be inappropriate. In addition, inferential statistics should not be used if the goals of the analysis are descriptive, and descriptive statistics should not be used if the goal is inference.

Number of Variables

A third consideration in choosing an appropriate statistic is the number of variables to be analyzed. **Univariate statistics** are those that analyze only one variable; **bivariate statistics** analyze two variables; **multivariate statistics** analyze three or more variables. An example of a univariate statistical problem would be an investigation of the average income paid to correctional officers in a particular correctional facility. The only variable in the problem is "amount of income"; the correctional facility is not a variable but a constant—it has only one value or

category. This problem could be changed into a bivariate problem by introducing a second variable: How does gender affect the average income paid to the correctional officers in the facility? Now the problem has two variables: gender and amount of income. A multivariate problem could be hypothesized by adding additional variables: How do gender, race, and seniority influence levels of income in the facility?

Each statistic is designed to be used on either a univariate, bivariate, or multivariate problem. However, a point of clarification is warranted: Some univariate statistics are also calculated as a *part* of some bivariate or multivariate statistics. For example, among the statistics to be discussed in this chapter, the mean is a univariate statistic, but it is also calculated as a part of some bivariate statistics (such as Student's *t*) and some multivariate statistics (such as MANOVA). In these cases, however, the univariate statistic is only one step in the more complex and lengthy calculation of the bivariate and multivariate statistics.

Properties of the Data

To be properly used, some statistics require that the data to be analyzed have certain mathematical or other properties. We have already discussed an example of this as levels of measurement, which involves the mathematical properties required for particular statistical tests. This is discussed separately because it is of paramount importance and relates to every statistical procedure. However, other assumptions about the properties of the data also need to be considered.

One important assumption of many statistical procedures is that the observations on the dependent variable are independent of one another. For example, if we are evaluating the effectiveness of a counseling program for men who batter their partners, we might randomly assign 20 men to receive treatment and 20 to the control group. Upon completion of the program, each subject participates in a videotaped simulation exercise where an observer rates his use of controlling tactics with his partner. First, the 20 control tapes are graded, and then the 20 treatment tapes are graded. The grading process is a complex task, and the observer becomes more skilled in grading as he or she gains practice and counts more controlling behaviors as a consequence. In this situation, subjects scored later are likely to have higher scores than those rated first, so the scores are correlated with (are "dependent" on) rating order. This condition is referred to as *serial dependence* because the scores are dependent on their position in the series of measurements. Serial dependence is often hard to detect, but it can be a serious problem because one may reach erroneous conclusions when comparing the average rating for the treatment group with the average rating of the control group. (Statistical procedures exist to detect such a correlation with serial position and to estimate how much of the difference between groups is due to it.)

In other situations, it is more obvious that observations are not independent; in fact, some research problems call for designs that include related observations. This is particularly the case when we want to study change over time. For example, perhaps we classified homeless shelters by funding source in 1986 and again by funding source in 1996 to determine if there was a trend. A similar situation occurs when the same group of people is given a pretest and a posttest or possibly several tests over the course of an intervention. Single-system designs (discussed in Chapter 11) are another example of a research design that often fails to satisfy the assumption of independence. In these three examples, because the same organizations or individuals are being observed at different points in time, the observations are not independent, and we would consider this fact when selecting statistical procedures.

Another important assumption for some statistics concerns the shape of the distribution of observations on a variable. Some statistics require that this distribution be normal or symmetrical. If the distribution is not normal, the statistic calculated on the data may be misleading.

As a part of the process of selecting an appropriate statistic, researchers review these various assumptions about the nature of the data they are analyzing and assess the risk of using a statistic that requires assumptions not met (or not fully met) by the data.

The more the data violate these assumptions, the greater the risk of producing a misleading result.

Audience

If all the preceding considerations are weighed and more than one statistic can appropriately be used, we next consider the audience for whom the data analysis is intended. If that audience has limited statistical expertise, then a relatively simple, easily understood statistic is preferred over a more complex statistic that might confuse them. Among the simpler statistics are the visual forms of presenting data (discussed in Chapter 14) and univariate statistics. Some bivariate statistics, and especially the multivariate statistics, may be beyond the comprehension of most audiences without at least an elementary introduction to statistics.

With these considerations in mind, we now turn to the descriptive statistics that are most commonly used in the social sciences and human services.

Descriptive Statistics

Imagine that we are selected to spend a year studying abroad. We say good-bye to our friends and family and board a plane for Europe, Asia, or another far-off locale. In the course of our stay there, we will likely be asked by our hosts to describe what Americans are like. For example, we might be asked to describe American college students. We might talk about what is typical or common among American college students—American college students are middle-class kids who like to attend sporting events, such as football, basketball, and hockey. They head south during spring break to party; they eat junk food; they pay for school by relying on their parents and taking out loans. They love to use e-mail and the Internet to communicate, and they watch a lot of television.

That's not a complete description, however, and hardly a fair one. Many students don't attend athletic events at all, nor do they get to sport a tan after spring break. Some do not get any financial aid, and, although a majority of freshmen may be age 18, some are in their 50s! So in trying to describe what American college students are like, we really need to talk about the diversity among students, not just what is most common. Beyond describing similarities and differences, we might also discuss characteristics of particular groups. So we might say, for example, that women at our school are more likely to major in social work and men are more likely to major in criminal justice. As we engage in this process of describing what students are like, we would be using, albeit casually, the basic principles of descriptive statistics. Descriptive statistics provide quantitative indicators of what is common or typical about a variable, how much diversity or difference there is in the variable, and how values on one variable are associated with values on one or more other variables.

Measures of Central Tendency

Although valuable for revealing patterns within the data and the shape of the distribution, frequency distributions (discussed in Chapter 14) can be cumbersome. In fact, with variables that can take on many values, such as age or income, a frequency distribution can become so massive that it is difficult to detect patterns in it. **Measures of central tendency,** more commonly known as *averages,* summarize distributions by identifying the "typical" or "average" value and are one of the most commonly used statistics. The three most widely used measures of central tendency are the *mode, median,* and *mean,* each designed for use with a particular level of measurement and each having unique qualities.

The *mode* is the category in a frequency distribution that contains the largest number of cases. The mode for the grade distribution in Table 14.2 on page 378 is C because more people received that grade than any other. Although the mode can be determined for data of any level of measurement (such as the grade distribution, which is ordinal), mode is usually used with data of the nominal level for two reasons. First, the mode is the least stable of the three measures; that is, its value can be changed substantially by rather minor additions, deletions, or changes

in the values that make up the distribution. With the other measures of central tendency, adding more cases produces less dramatic shifts in their values. Second, if two or more categories are tied with the largest number of cases, we could have two, three, or more modes, none of which would necessarily be very typical of the distribution. The presence of several modes also undermines its utility as a summary statistic to describe the average case.

With ordinal data, the *median* is the appropriate measure of central tendency. The median is the point in a distribution below which 50 percent of the observations occur. For example, a distribution of six scores—10, 14, 15, 17, 18, 25—results in a median of 16. Note that when the distribution contains an even number of values, an observed score may not fall on the median. The median is then the value halfway between the two central scores. If we add another score greater than 16 to the preceding distribution so that it contains seven cases, the median is 17, an observed score. Because the median does not take into account the actual value of the scores, only the number of observations, whether the score we add is 17, 100, or 1,000 makes no difference—the median is still 17. This makes the median very stable because the presence of extremely high or low scores in a distribution has little effect on the value of the median.

The *mean,* the measure of central tendency most people think of when they hear the word "average," is calculated by summing all the values in a distribution and dividing by the number of cases. The mean, however, is only suitable for interval- or ratio-level data, where there is equal spacing along a scale and various mathematical functions can be performed (see Chapter 5). There is one exception to this: dichotomous nominal- or ordinal-level variables that have only two values. Many interval-level statistics, such as the mean, can be meaningfully computed on such variables. This is called dummy variable analysis and is beyond what we wish to introduce in this chapter.

Because the mean takes into account the actual value of all scores in a distribution, it is less stable than the median. The presence of a few extreme scores will pull the mean in that direction. Because of this, the median is often the preferred average when summarizing skewed distributions, even with interval-level data, as it more accurately reflects the central value. For example, although the mean could be used to summarize income data, the U.S. Census Bureau typically reports median income because the presence of the relatively few wealthy people tends to pull the mean to such a high level that it overstates typical family income. Because it is less affected by extreme scores, the median is also often preferred in clinical practice research, where treatment and control groups are usually small and violate the assumptions required for statistics based on the mean.

Selecting the most appropriate measure of central tendency for a given set of data is not difficult. Level of measurement and skewness are the primary considerations. With relatively symmetrical distributions, the only factor is level of measurement.

Measures of Dispersion

Like measures of central tendency, measures of dispersion describe and summarize distributions. Whereas central tendency indicators describe the middle or average of the distribution, **measures of dispersion** indicate how dispersed or spread out the values are in a distribution. Measures of dispersion add valuable information about distributions. On the basis of central tendency measures alone, we might assume that two distributions with similar averages are basically alike. Such an assumption would be erroneous, however, if the spread of the distributions were different. As illustrated in Figure 15.1, distribution *A* is more dispersed, with values deviating widely from the central value. The values in distribution *B* are more tightly clustered near the average. To avoid possible erroneous assumptions about the spread of distributions, researchers report a measure of dispersion along with a measure of central tendency.

Three commonly used measures of dispersion are the *range, semi-interquartile range,* and *standard deviation.* The *range* is the simplest of these, referring

Figure 15.1 Two Distributions with the Same Average but Different Dispersions

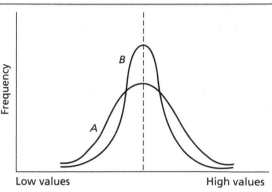

merely to the difference between the highest and lowest scores in the distribution. As such, the range indicates the total spread of a distribution. Knowing the end points of a distribution, however, tells us nothing about how the remainder of the values is dispersed within the distribution. Furthermore, because the range is based on only two values, it is unstable. Adding or deleting extreme scores causes the range to vary widely, whereas the bulk of the distribution may change little. Moreover, despite its simplicity, the range is suitable only for interval data. The operation of subtraction used to obtain the range assumes that the values of the scores in a distribution have meaning; that is true only for interval- and ratio-level data. Because of these limitations, the range is usually used as an adjunct to other measures of dispersion and not reported alone.

The *semi-interquartile range* (sometimes called the quartile deviation) is symbolized by the letter Q; it is closely related to the median and is the measure of dispersion usually reported with it. The semi-interquartile range is obtained by first dividing a frequency distribution into fourths, or *quartiles.* The first quartile (Q_1) is the score below which 25 percent of the scores occur, and the third quartile (Q_3) is the score below which 75 percent of the scores occur. (The median is actually the second quartile [Q_2] and is the point below which 50 percent of the scores occur.) The semi-interquartile range is equal to half the difference between the third quartile and the first quartile. The larger the value of the semi-interquartile range, the more dispersed the scores are from the median. Q is calculated as:

$$Q = \frac{Q_3 - Q_1}{2}$$

The *standard deviation,* symbolized by the letter *s,* indicates the average (or mean) spread of the scores from the mean and is therefore the measure of dispersion usually reported along with the mean. The larger the value of the standard deviation, the more dispersed the scores are from the mean. Actual calculation of the standard deviation is relatively complex and beyond the scope of this chapter. In addition to its use as a descriptive statistic, the standard deviation has important applications in inferential statistics.

One final note on measures of dispersion: Although their overall purpose is to assist in the description of distributions, a single dispersion value from a single distribution is not particularly revealing. The major utility of dispersion indicators is in comparing several distributions because they enable us to tell at a glance which has more or less spread.

Measures of Association

Measures of association describe the nature of relationships between variables, particularly the *strength* of the relationship or how closely variables are related. The strongest relationship is a *perfect* one in which a given change in one variable is always associated with a given change in the other variable. Perfect relationships are rarely found in human service research. A less-than-perfect relationship indicates only a tendency for the variables to vary together. With ordinal- or higher-level data, relationships between variables can also be positive, negative, or curvilinear. Recall that a positive relationship is one in which the change in value of the variables is in the same direction (i.e., both increase or both decrease), a negative relationship is one in which one variable increases while the other decreases, and a curvilinear relationship is one in which the direction of change in one variable is not consistent with changes in the other. For example, in a U-shaped curvilinear relationship, both low and high

Table 15.2 Nominal Data Suitable for Phi

Is Life Exciting?	Gender	
	Male	**Female**
Exciting	213 (50.1%)	221 (39.8%)
Routine/Dull	212 (49.9%)	334 (60.2%)
Totals	425 (100%)	555 (100%)
		Phi = 0.11

Source James A. Davis and Tom W. Smith. *General Social Survey (1972–1994)* (Chicago: National Opinion Research Center; Storrs, CT: The Roper Center for Public Opinion Research, University of Connecticut).

values of the independent variable may be associated with high values of the dependent variable. In this case, a negative relationship exists between the two variables for low values on the independent variable and a positive relationship with high values on the independent variable. Most measures of association indicate a perfect positive relationship by 1.00 and a perfect negative one by −1.00. The closer the value of the measure is to −1.00 or 1.00, the stronger the relationship. The closer the value is to 0, the weaker the relationship.

The overriding determinant in selecting a measure of association is the level of measurement of the data at hand, so we will consider measures of association according to the level of measurement for which each was designed.

Nominal Data. Some data are dichotomous in form. That is, the variables have only two values, such as yes–no or male–female. A useful measure of association for two dichotomous variables is the *phi* (pronounced *phee*) coefficient (ϕ). The data are cast into a 2 × 2 table as illustrated by Table 15.2. Phi indicates the strength of the relationship between variables by yielding a value between −1.00 and 1.00. Although phi may yield negative values, the negative sign is simply ignored because it has no meaning in the case of nominal data.

Phi is considered a good measure of association for three reasons. First, it is quite easy to compute. Sec-

Table 15.3 Nominal Data Suitable for Lambda and Goodman and Kruskal's Tau

		Region			
		Northeast	Midwest	South	West
Religious Preference	Protestant	54 (41.2%)	140 (64.5%)	206 (84.8%)	80 (53.3%)
	Catholic	55 (42.0%)	56 (25.8%)	28 (11.5%)	43 (28.7%)
	Jewish	10 (7.6%)	1 (0.5%)	1 (0.4%)	3 (2.0%)
	None	12 (9.2%)	20 (9.2%)	8 (3.3%)	24 (16.0%)
	Totals	131 (100%)	217 (100%)	243 (100%)	150 (100%)

Lambda = 0.07
Goodman and Kruskal's tau = 0.07

Source James A. Davis and Tom W. Smith. *General Social Survey (1972–1994)* (Chicago: National Opinion Research Center; Storrs, CT: The Roper Center for Public Opinion Research, University of Connecticut).

ond, it is mathematically related to measures of association suitable for other levels of measurement, which makes comparing the strength of different relationships possible. Measures of association that are not mathematically related have different operating characteristics and produce values that are not comparable, precluding meaningful comparisons. Third, phi is a member of a group of measures of association that can be given what is called a **proportional reduction in error (PRE)** interpretation. The PRE interpretation means that the measure shows how much the independent variable helps reduce error in predicting values of the dependent variable. To interpret phi in this way, it is first necessary to square it (ϕ^2). For example, $\phi = 0.11$ is squared to become $\phi^2 = 0.01$. This latter value is treated as a percentage and is interpreted to mean that the independent variable reduced the error in predicting values of the dependent variable by 1 percent. All PRE statistics are interpreted in this way.

Because phi is suitable only for two dichotomous variables, a different measure of association must be used for nominal data with more categories. The most generally useful measure for data of this type is *lambda* (λ). As with phi, the data are cast into tabular form, as illustrated in Table 15.3.

Lambda is a bit different from most measures of association in that its value can range only from 0 to 1.00. Lambda is never negative, but this is not a disadvantage because the negative sign is meaningless with nominal data anyway. Lambda is always positive because it is a direct-reading PRE statistic. That is, lambda indicates the proportional reduction in error as calculated and need not be squared as phi does. This is an important point to remember because the values lambda produces usually look rather small. The reason is not that lambda understates relationships but that the lambda values are "presquared," which makes them appear small.

Although phi and lambda are the most common nominal measures of association, several others are available. For two dichotomous variables, an alternative to phi is Yule's Q. However, Q cannot be given the PRE interpretation and tends to make relationships appear stronger than they actually are. For nominal data with more categories, Goodman and Kruskal's *tau* (τ) is often used. Tau is sometimes preferred to lambda because the former uses data from all cells in the table, while the latter only includes in its computation data from some of the cells. However, tau does not always vary from 0 to

1.00, especially when the dependent variable has more categories than the independent variable.

Ordinal Data. Many commonly used measures of association exist for ordinal data. A major consideration in selecting one has to do with whether or not the data are *fully ordered*. In situations where every or nearly every case has its own unique rank and there are no or few ties, the data are said to be fully ordered. Table 15.4 illustrates fully ordered data. The most popular measure of association for fully ordered data is Spearman's *rho* (r_s). Rho, like phi, is mathematically related to other measures and thus facilitates comparisons of relationships. It also has the desirable characteristic of varying between -1.00 and 1.00. Note that now, with ordinal data, the negative sign has meaning and indicates a negative relationship. Rho also may be squared (r_s^2) and given the PRE interpretation.

When we have only a few ordered categories and many cases are to be placed into them, the data will contain many ties, far too many for Spearman's rho to be usable. Data of this type are called *partially ordered* and are handled in tabular form, as illustrated in Table 15.5. Several alternative measures of association are available for data of this type. *Gamma* (γ), *Somer's D,* and *Kendall's tau* (τ) are all suitable and vary between -1.00 and 1.00. However, some subtle differences among them make one or another most appropriate in a given situation.

Gamma is the easiest of the three to compute, but unfortunately it does not take into account any of the tied scores and tends to overstate the strength of the relationship. Indeed, on the basis of a positive gamma alone, we cannot safely assume that as X increases, Y also increases, which is a normal assumption of a positive relationship. Because of its failure to consider ties, all a positive gamma allows us to conclude is that as X increases, Y does not decrease, which is a much weaker conclusion.

Somer's D is used when we are only interested in our ability to predict a dependent variable from an independent variable. When predicting Y from $X,$ Somer's D takes into account ties on the dependent variable. This has the effect of reducing the value of D in comparison with gamma when the two are

Table 15.4 Ordinal Data Suitable for Spearman's Rho

Independent Variable	Dependent Variable
Ranks	*Ranks*
10	9
8	10
1	1
3	5
2	2
9	6
4	7
6	3
5	4
7	8
	$r_s = 0.77$

computed on the same data. Somer's $D,$ however, gives a more accurate indication of how much the independent variable reduces error in predicting the dependent variable.

Finally, Kendall's tau takes into account all the tied scores. It indicates the degree to which the independent variable reduces error in predicting the dependent variable and also how much the latter reduces error in predicting the former. Because it considers the relationship both ways, tau is particularly appropriate when we do not have a clearly identifiable independent and dependent variable and merely wish to determine if two variables are related. By including all the ties, a positive tau allows us to conclude correctly that as X increases, Y also increases. This is the type of statement we expect to make on the basis of a positive result, so Kendall's tau is more generally useful than gamma.

Interval Data. The most used measure of association for interval data is the *correlation coefficient,* or *Pearson's r.* The correlation coefficient is mathematically related to both phi and Spearman's rho, making comparisons among them possible. As with the other two, Pearson's *r* varies between -1.00 and

Table 15.5 Ordinal Data Suitable for Gamma, Somer's *D,* or Kendall's Tau

		Income		
		Low	Medium	High
Number of Hours of Television Watched	High	49 (19.2%)	19 (8.6%)	10 (6.7%)
	Medium	164 (64.3%)	136 (61.5%)	86 (57.5%)
	Low	42 (16.5%)	66 (29.9%)	53 (35.6%)
	Totals	255 (100%)	221 (100%)	149 (100%)

Gamma = –0.33
Somer's *D* = –0.18
Kendall's tau = –0.20

Source James A. Davis and Tom W. Smith. *General Social Survey (1972–1994)* (Chicago: National Opinion Research Center; Storrs, CT: The Roper Center for Public Opinion Research, University of Connecticut).

1.00 and may be squared (r^2) and given the PRE interpretation. When squared, this value is called the *coefficient of determination.*

The correlation coefficient has a unique characteristic that is important to remember when applying or interpreting it. Pearson's *r* indicates the degree to which the relationship between two interval-level variables can be described by a straight line when plotted on a scattergram, as in Figure 15.2. The formula for *r* mathematically determines the best-fitting line and then considers the amount the scores deviate from perfect linearity. This feature of Pearson's *r* means that, if the relationship between the two variables is curvilinear, *r* will understate the actual strength of the relationship, producing a coefficient that is smaller than it should be. Therefore, it is advisable to plot a *scattergram,* a table with the scores of both variables plotted on it. The scattergram provides a visual indication of the relationship between the two variables and is useful for uncovering curvilinearity. Figure 15.2 illustrates three typical scattergrams. In those instances in which curvilinearity is discovered, a measure of association other than Pearson's *r* should be selected. Curvilinear measures of association do exist, but they are beyond the scope of this discussion.

Before we leave measures of association, one important matter requires emphasis: Association or cor-relation does not imply causality! Just because one variable is labeled independent and another dependent and a relationship is found between them does not prove that changes in one variable caused changes in the other. Correlation is only one step toward inferring causality. In addition, it is necessary to affirm the appropriate temporal sequence and rule out rival causal variables.

The Normal Distribution

Chapter 14 discussed frequency distributions as descriptive statistical procedures that transform a raw data distribution into a form that is more meaningful. There is another way to transform raw data to derive additional meaning from it, and this transformation will also serve as our transition from descriptive to inferential statistics. A transformation is a set of arithmetical operations that are executed on a variable to obtain a new variable. One common transformation is known as *standardizing.* Raw scores are transformed into *standard scores,* also known as *z-scores.* Symbolically, a standardized score, *z,* is given by:

$$z = \frac{x - \bar{x}}{s}$$

Figure 15.2   Three Typical Scattergrams

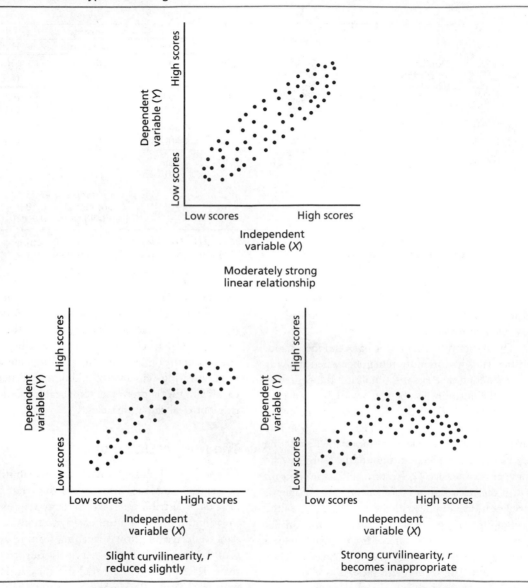

Moderately strong
linear relationship

Slight curvilinearity, *r*
reduced slightly

Strong curvilinearity, *r*
becomes inappropriate

Standard scores are obtained by following these two steps:

a. Subtract the mean, $\bar{x}$, from each raw score, x.

b. Divide the $x - \bar{x}$ difference by the standard deviation, s, of the distribution.

If all the raw scores in a distribution are transformed to z-scores, a new distribution is obtained

that will always have $\bar{x} = 0$ and $s = 1$. This is called a *standard normal distribution,* and, as it turns out, this distribution has some quite convenient properties.

One way to think about the z-transformation is that it expresses raw scores in a distribution in terms of standard deviation units rather than the original unit of measurement. A z-score of 1.5 indicates a score point that is 1.5 standard deviations greater than the mean, whereas a z-score of -1.5 indicates a score point 1.5 standard deviations below the mean. In other words, a standard score, z, is a number indicating the distance that a raw score deviates from the mean as measured in standard deviation units. Furthermore, the sign of a z-score indicates whether the score point is above ($+$) or below ($-$) the mean of the distribution.

On first encounter, it may seem strange to express raw scores in terms of standard deviation units, but doing so allows us to make comparisons between distributions that otherwise would be difficult to make because their original units of measurement differ. Standardizing equalizes the units so that a meaningful comparison can be made. For example, the comparison of a person's raw scores on two different IQ tests would not be legitimate unless the IQ tests have a common unit of measurement and operate on the same scale. Therefore, mental testers commonly employ the z-transformation as a way of making different IQ tests comparable.

Consider the data in Table 15.6. In both tests, someone received a score of 99, but are both scores really equal? In terms of raw scores they certainly appear to be, but in relative terms—that is, compared to the other scores in the distribution—the 99 on Test 2 is far more remarkable, and a z-score transformation will reveal this. On Test 1, with a relatively high mean and small standard deviation, the 99 transforms to a z-score of 1.46, which means it is 1.46 standard deviations above the mean of 94.6. The 99 on Test 2, with a low mean and high standard deviation, transforms to a z-score of 2.47, which means it is 2.47 standard deviations above the mean of 49.6. The comparison of z-scores shows that the two scores of 99 are, in fact, far from equal compared to the other scores in their respective distributions. Allowing for these types of comparisons to be made is one important use of z-scores.

Another important use of z-scores has to do with what is called the normal distribution. The normal distribution is a continuous, bell-shaped distribution, as shown in Figure 15.3. The **normal distribution** is a symmetrical, unimodal distribution in which the mode, median, and mean are iden-

Table 15.6 Two Sets of Hypothetical Test Scores

	Test 1	Test 2	
	99	99	
	98	45	
$\bar{x} = 94.6$	6	44	$\bar{x} = 49.6$
	95	44	
$s = 3$	95	4.	$s = 20$
	93	41	
	91	41	
	90	40	

tical. Actually, there is not a single normal distribution but many. Normal distributions may have different means and different standard deviations, for example. What makes them all normal is that they all are symmetrical and unimodal and have the three measures of central tendency at the same point. In addition, all normal distributions have the same proportion of cases between the same two ordinates. This statement means that between, say, $+1$ and -1 standard deviations from the mean for any normal distribution, the proportion of the total cases bounded by those points is the same for all those normal distributions.

In Figure 15.3, the shaded area is the proportion of the total area under the curve bounded by points that are 1 standard deviation on either side of the mean. For any normal distribution, no matter what the mean and standard deviation happen to be, the area bounded by $\bar{x} - s$ and $\bar{x} + s$ is always equal to 68.26 percent of the total area under the curve, whereas 95.46 percent of the total area is between $\bar{x} - 2s$ and $\bar{x} + 2s$. In place of $\bar{x} - s$ and $\bar{x} + s$, we may substitute any two points we wish and carve out a proportion of the total area that will be the same for all normal distributions. Figure 15.3 shows selected points and the proportions of the total area that fall between them for any and all normal distributions.

This indicates another use of z-transformations: to assess the relative position of a score in a distribution of scores. For example, suppose a

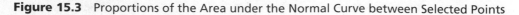

Figure 15.3   Proportions of the Area under the Normal Curve between Selected Points

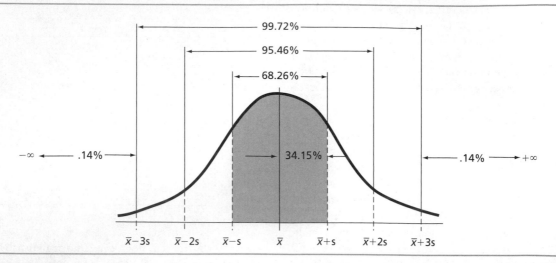

female student took a national merit exam and received a score of 580. How well did she do compared with the others who took it? If she knows that the scores on this exam are normally distributed, and she knows the mean score and standard deviation, then she can calculate her position relative to the others who took the exam. Suppose the mean was 490 and the standard deviation was 72. She could then use the z-formula to transform her exam score of 580 into a z-score as follows:

$$z = \frac{x - \bar{x}}{s} = \frac{580 - 490}{72} = +1.25$$

So her score is $+1.25$ standard deviations above the mean for all the students who took the test. By looking at Figure 15.3, she can determine that she scored better than at least 84 percent of the students who took the exam. She can figure this out because 50 percent of the students scored below the mean and another 34.15 percent scored between the mean and $+1.00s$ above the mean. To figure out what additional percentage is included between $+1.00s$ and $+1.25s$, she can refer to tables that tell what proportion of cases fall between any two points in a normal distribution. (These tables can be found in any introductory statistics text.) From those tables, she can determine that 89.44 percent of all cases in a normal

distribution fall below $+1.25$ standard deviations above the mean. So she did better than more than 89 percent of all the people who took that examination! Transforming her test score into a z-score enabled her to make a precise statement about her place in the distribution relative to others in the distribution.

The standard normal distribution is useful for comparing distributions with different means and standard deviations, and it helps us make precise statements about relative position in a distribution. A third important use of this distribution is that it serves as the foundation for inferential statistics.

Inferential Statistics

As noted in Chapter 6, most social research is conducted on relatively small samples drawn from much larger populations, and all the statistical procedures discussed so far are designed to assist in describing, summarizing, and interpreting data from samples. Findings from sample data, however, are of little scientific value if they cannot be generalized beyond the members of the sample to the larger population from which the samples were drawn. For example, it would do other practitioners little good to learn that a researcher had successfully raised the school performance of 50 underachievers unless they could reasonably expect the new approach to work on children who were not in the researcher's sample. In other words, for the new technique to be worthwhile, it must be generalizable to members of the population of underachievers.

Probability Theory

How do we know when research findings are generalizable? Generalization is always an uncertain business, but inferential statistics can reduce the uncertainty to the point where reasonably safe generalizations can be made and the probability of a given amount of error estimated. Inferential statistics are based on probability theory, the same probability theory that works to make probability samples representative. Because of this, inferential statistics can be meaningfully applied only to data based on probability samples or experiments in which random assignment has been implemented.

Probability theory allows the mathematical calculation of the likelihood or probability that random events or outcomes will occur. For example, if 10,000 raffle tickets are issued and the winning ticket is chosen in such a way that each ticket has an equal chance of being selected, then each person who purchases one ticket has 1 in 10,000 chances of winning. However, if you buy 10 tickets, then you have 10 in 10,000 or 1 in 1,000 chances of winning. You have increased the probability of your winning even though the mechanism for selecting the winner is unchanged. This does not mean, of course, that you *will* win. Less likely events do occur, although with less frequency than more likely ones, and a person who purchased only one ticket could certainly win the raffle. In other words, while probability theory tells us the *likelihood* of something occurring, it does not tell us what *will* occur. For this reason, inferential statistics can tell us whether the odds are on our side that a particular generalization is accurate, but they do not make it a sure bet.

As noted in Chapter 6, probability samples are supposed to represent the populations from which they were drawn, but we expect differences between a sample and its population owing to chance alone. Because these differences are due to the random process used in the selection of samples, their probability can be readily calculated. For example, suppose a researcher draws a probability sample of 50 delinquent boys and applies a special intervention designed to reduce future delinquency involvement. At the end of one year the success rate of the sample is 75 percent, whereas for the population of untreated delinquents the rate is 60 percent. Can we conclude that the experimental intervention was a success? At the level of the sample alone, it is clear that the treated boys had a better rate, but the differences could be due, all or in part, to sampling error. Even with random sampling, the researcher might have obtained a sample of boys who were better risks on average than those in the general population of delinquent boys. The question that inferential statistics answers is whether the difference between the sample results and the population results is too great to be likely on the basis of chance alone. In the example, running the appropriate inferential statistic would tell us what the chances are of obtaining, through random error, a 15 percent difference between a population and a probability sample drawn from that population. If such a difference were highly probable, we would conclude that the seeming effect of the experimental treatment was due to chance differences between sample and population. On the other hand, if the result indicated that there was only a small likelihood that a 15 percent differential was due to chance, we would reject chance variation as the explanation and conclude that there is a generalizable effect associated with the treatment group.

Sampling Distributions

Our ability to determine the likelihood that a sample difference is due to chance derives from the properties of the normal distribution, discussed earlier in this chapter, and what are called *sampling distributions*. To explain sampling distributions, let us return to the example of the 50 delinquents with the 75 percent success rate. If we had selected 10 samples of size 50 and computed a success rate on each sample, we would have found that the success rate differed somewhat from sample to sample because each sample consists of a different set of 50 boys. For the 10 samples, we might have found the following success rates: 72 percent, 71 percent, 73 percent, 69 percent, 66 percent, 70 percent, 73 percent, 69 percent, 71 percent, and 67 percent. The success rate for these 10 samples is distributed over the range of possible sample results. If we took many more samples of size 50, we would see a pattern emerge as the number of samples approached infinity. We would find the occasional extremely high or low value, but samples would most frequently lie in the middle of this range. A **sampling distribution** is a theoretical distribution of a statistic from all possible samples of a certain size drawn from a population; the distribution shows the probability of occurrence of each value of the statistic. If we actually knew the success rate among all delinquent boys in the population from which these samples were taken, this would be referred to as the *population parameter,* and it is this population parameter around which all the sample success rates are distributed in a statistically predictable pattern.

This sampling distribution has certain properties that are very important in inferential statistics. In particular, the **central limit theorem** from mathematics tells us that, when a large number of large random samples are selected from a population, the resulting distribution of sample statistics has two key properties: First, the sampling distribution approximates a normal distribution, and second, the population parameter is equal to the mean of the sampling distribution. In our example, the distribution of all sample success rates is normal, and the success rate in the population is equal to the average of all those sample success rates. This means that we can determine the probability that a sample result will fall between any two points in the sampling distribution, just as we did with z-scores and the normal distribution. It also means that we can determine the probability that a sample result will fall far away from the population parameter. Recall from the earlier discussion that approximately 68 percent of all cases in a normal distribution fall within 1 standard deviation above and below the mean of the distribution,

and approximately 95 percent of cases fall within 2 standard deviations. Likewise, in a distribution of samples, 95 percent of the sample results will fall within 2 standard deviations of the mean of the sampling distribution, which is also the population parameter. Only 5 percent of samples will fall more than 2 standard deviations away from the population parameter.

Going back to our example, we can choose one of two alternatives: (1) the treatment did not work, and we have selected a sample of boys that, by chance, is very different from the boys in the population (i.e., sampling error), or (2) the treatment worked, and this is what makes the treatment boys different from the nontreated boys in the population. However, if the success rate in the population is 60 percent and the sample success rate of 75 percent is more than 2 standard deviations away from 60 percent, then the z-transformation tells us that 75 percent is way out in one of the tails of the normal distribution and obtaining such a sample by chance would be highly unusual. Therefore, we are on safer grounds, just in terms of probabilities, to conclude that the 75 percent is probably not due to sampling error but rather is showing that the treatment had an effect on this group of boys.

Although many different kinds of inferential statistics are used, they all follow the basic logic involving sampling distributions and normal distributions. The formal process by which researchers decide whether the results of data analysis could be due to chance or are better explained by relationships between variables is called statistical hypothesis testing.

Statistical Hypothesis Testing

When we utilize inferential statistics, we are engaging in a special form of hypothesis testing in which we develop two hypotheses that are precisely opposite of each other. The outcome of a statistical test is then used to determine which hypothesis is most likely correct. The first hypothesis, called the **null hypothesis,** states that no relationship exists between two variables in the population or that there is no difference between a sample statistic and a population parameter. "There is *no* relationship between variable X and variable Y in the population" or "There is *no* difference between the success rate of the sample and the success rate of the population" are two examples of null hypotheses. Alternatives to null hypotheses are called **research hypotheses.** Suitable research hypotheses to go with the two preceding null hypotheses are, "There *is* a relationship between variable X and variable Y at the level of the population" and "There *is* a difference between the sample success rate and the population success rate." In each application of a statistical test, we assess the research hypothesis by determining whether the opposite null hypothesis is probable or improbable.

It is not uncommon, on first exposure to statistical hypothesis testing, to question the utility of null hypotheses. If we believe the research hypothesis is true, why not just test that hypothesis? The need for null hypotheses stems from the fact that it is not possible with inferential statistics to prove research hypotheses directly. However, by determining the likelihood that the null hypotheses are false, we indirectly provide evidence that their opposites, the research hypotheses, are probably true. To illustrate this point, we will use an example in which there is a clear criterion to use in testing a hypothesis.

Imagine attempting to determine whether a die is unbiased. If it is, each side should appear approximately an equal number of times—about one sixth of the times the die is thrown. If the die is biased, one or more outcomes will occur a disproportionate number of times—one or more numbers occurring substantially more than one sixth of the time. Suppose the die is tossed 12 times, with each outcome occurring twice, or one sixth of the time. Would this prove the die unbiased? The answer is no. The bias, if it exists, might be too slight to appear after only 12 trials. What if the die is tossed 144 times and still each outcome occurs one sixth of the time? Such a result would still not make it certain that the die is unbiased, for a slight bias might be revealed by even more trials. Indeed, no number of trials would provide absolute assurance that the die is unbiased. However, a large number of trials with no evidence of bias would make the hypothesis of a biased die so unlikely that it is reasonable to reject it. By finding no evidence of support for one hypothesis, we indirectly obtain support for its alternative. In all applications of statistical hypothesis testing, if the evidence fails to support the null hypothesis, then the opposing research hypothesis is accepted as probably true.

Although their computational routines vary, all inferential statistical tests use the properties of sampling distributions and normal curves to yield a result indicating the probability that the null hypothesis is true. In choosing between the competing hypotheses, we ask, "How unlikely must it be for the null hypothesis to be true before we are willing to reject it as false and accept the research hypothesis?" This is determined by the **alpha level,** or the probability at which the null hypothesis will be rejected (see Table 15.7). Researchers have some discretion in setting alpha levels but must guard against the two types of inferential errors that can be made. **Type I** or **alpha error** is the probability of rejecting a null hypothesis that is actually true. The alpha level selected determines the amount of alpha error we are willing to tolerate, so the researcher directly controls Type I error by setting alpha. Alpha levels are usually written as "$p < .20$" and read as "a probability of less than 20 percent." Alpha levels can be understood in the following way. Suppose the null hypothesis is that "no relationship exists between variable X and variable Y in the population." We draw a sample from that population to test the hypothesis and indeed find a relationship in the sample data. An alpha level of .20 means that we would find a relationship as large as we did in 20 percent of the samples we draw, even though the null hypothesis is actually true and there is no relationship between the variables in the population. We are now faced with a difficult dilemma: "Is the null hypothesis true and our sample an unusual one, or is the null hypothesis false?" Inferential statistics cannot answer that question for us. It can tell us that, in the long run and by testing many hypotheses, we would be correct 80 percent of the time by rejecting null hypotheses when differences of a given size have an alpha level of .20.

Setting an alpha level as low as .20 makes it easy to reject the null hypothesis, but we are also assured of frequently rejecting true null hypotheses. To avoid so much Type I error, we might establish a very stringent alpha, such as .001, meaning that we

Table 15.7   Illustration of Type I and Type II Errors

Decision	Condition in Population	
	Null Hypothesis Is True	Null Hypothesis Is False

Reject null hypothesis	Type I (alpha) error
	    prob. = alpha
		Correct decision
		    (power of test)
		    prob. = 1 − beta

Fail to reject null hypothesis	Correct decision
	    prob. = 1 − alpha
		Type II (beta) error
		    prob. = beta

would reject the null hypothesis only if its odds of being true were less than 1 in 1,000. If the null hypothesis can be rejected at such an alpha level, we would be quite confident that it was false and that we were not committing a Type I error.

But setting extremely rigorous alpha levels raises the probability of making the other possible inferential error. **Type II** or **beta error** is the probability of failing to reject null hypotheses that are actually false. Alpha levels such as .001 make it so difficult to reject null hypotheses that many false ones that should be rejected are not. Thus, in selecting suitable alpha levels, we face a dilemma. Guarding against one type of error increases the chances of making the other type.

Fortunately, conventions regarding appropriate alpha levels have developed. In general, social researchers operate with alpha levels of .05, .01, or .001. Although these levels are the most common ones in research reports, nothing is sacred about them. The researcher must consider the purpose of the research and the alternative risks in selecting a given level. For example, medical research into the safety and effectiveness of new drugs or treatments typically operates with very stringent alpha levels because life-and-death issues are at stake. If the null hypothesis in a research project is "Drug X is not safe," then we want to reject it only if we are very sure that it is false. If it is wrongly rejected, people will be exposed to an unsafe product. On the other hand, a practitioner with a null hypothesis of "Reminder phone calls do not reduce the number of no-shows for clinic appointments" might select an alpha level as low as .10. If the procedure shows any chance of working, the clinic may want to try it. In this case,

the consequences of rejecting a true null hypothesis are not severe. Some additional issues related to hypothesis testing and alpha and beta errors are discussed in Research in Practice 15.1.

A common way of expressing that the null hypothesis was rejected is to indicate that a given result is "statistically significant" at some specified alpha level. Unfortunately, the use of the word "significant" can cause some confusion. In popular usage, "significant" means important or notable. Its meaning in statistics, however, does not have the same connotation. Whether a set of research findings is important or notable depends far more on the topic, theory, sample, and quality of measurement than it does on statistically rejecting null hypotheses. Research on trivial matters or research that is procedurally flawed cannot produce important results no matter how many "statistically significant" findings it might contain. Be sure to remember that the meaning of "significant" in statistics is simply that a null hypothesis has been successfully rejected.

Statistical Procedures

Some of the basic considerations for selecting inferential statistical procedures are much like those for selecting descriptive statistics. One important consideration is the nature of the dependent variable. For nominal dependent variables, the commonly used procedures, such as chi-square, are discussed later. Many additional procedures, such as log-linear analysis, go beyond the scope of this book but are rapidly gaining prominence in research literature. With ordinal dependent variables, many procedures are, in addition to being applicable to

RESEARCH IN PRACTICE 15.1

PROGRAM EVALUATION:

Designed for Failure: Statistical Power in Human Service Research

Although much attention is given to the issue of statistical significance or alpha levels in evaluation research, a related and equally important issue, statistical power, is often overlooked. *Statistical power* refers to the probability of *correctly* rejecting a null hypothesis in a research study (see Table 15.7). Another way of looking at statistical power is to conceptualize a study designed with low power as being a study with a high probability of failure because it cannot detect an intervention that works. If the number of cases in the treatment and control groups is small and the variation within each group is large, there may be insufficient difference between the groups to generate a statistically significant result. In technical terms, the problem is that the study has insufficient effect size. The concept of effect size has been receiving increasing attention among researchers (Bloom, Fischer, and Orme 1999; Prentice and Miller 1998; Schmidt 1998). Although various ways exist for measuring effect size, for illustration purposes we will use a simplified version:

$$ES = \frac{\overline{X}_t - \overline{X}_c}{S}$$

where:

ES = Effect size
$\overline{X}_t$ = Treatment mean
$\overline{X}_c$ = Control mean
S = Standard deviation of both groups combined

The effect size coefficient is basically a standardized indicator of how big a difference exists between treatment and control groups. Compare this formula to the one for standardized scores, or z-scores, on page 411; they are almost identical—both are formulas to transform raw scores into standardized scores. Basically, the formula shows that the larger the standardized difference between groups, the larger the effect size. Other things being equal, a larger effect size is more likely to generate a significant statistic. For example, assume that we conduct a

test of a family intervention program using a treatment group of 15 families that receive the intervention and a control group of another 15 families that do not. Assume also that the intervention program does work, although the effect is modest. If we perform a statistical test on the difference between the two groups, the results may not be statistically significant, despite the fact that the intervention works.

This is a quite real problem, as evidenced by examinations of published human service research indicating that almost half of the studies reviewed could not detect even a medium-sized effect (Orme and Combs-Orme 1986; West, Biesanz, and Pitts 2000). A consequence of this shortcoming is that policy decisions may be made to curtail or not implement potentially useful innovations. Another important consideration is that a research effort is wasted if it is unable to detect a program effect when it is present.

In the typical human service program evaluation, the investigator formulates a null hypothesis, such as "There is no difference between the treatment group and the control group," expecting to reject it at the specified level of statistical significance or alpha level. The sample data are analyzed and the null hypothesis is then rejected if the difference between the experimental group and the control group is sufficiently large to be considered an improbable event at the preselected alpha level, such as .05, .01, or .001. An unfortunate error of interpretation is to assume that failure to reject the null hypothesis is equivalent to proving that the treatment had no effect. A more correct assessment is that the data generated from this study, *as designed,* failed to detect a difference between the treatment and the control conditions. Unless care is taken in the design of the study, it could well be that the study could not detect an effect even if it were present.

Statistical power is determined quantitatively as:

$$1 - \text{beta}$$

continued on next page

or

$$1 - \text{(the probability of a Type II error)}$$

The beta level is complex to calculate and beyond the scope of this book. For a particular research problem, beta can be looked up in a reference work, such as Cohen (1988), or calculated by appropriate computer software. Once this is done, the adequacy of beta can be assessed by the following rule of thumb: The minimum acceptable ratio of Type II errors to Type I errors should be about 4 to 1. Thus, if alpha is set at .05, beta should be 4 × .05, or .20. Because power equals 1 − beta, power equals 1 − .20, or .80. (This means we have an 80 percent chance to correctly reject the null hypothesis.) Similarly, if alpha is .01, power should be a minimum of .96, and if alpha is .001, power should be a minimum of .996. However, the 4-to-1 rule is only a general guideline. The power level acceptable in a particular research project should be determined by the nature of the research project and its implications.

Reviews of published research studies in the human services and other fields have consistently reported that the actual power of a large proportion of studies is well below these standards of .80, .96, and .996 (Orme and Tolman 1986). What can be done to improve the power of a research project? Although the concept of power is complex, it has three major determinants: sample size, alpha level, and effect size. By manipulating them, one can improve statistical power.

The larger the sample, the greater the statistical power of a research project. Using the rule of thumb described above with an alpha level of .05 and power equal to .80, it can be shown that 52 total participants (26 treatment and 26 control) are needed to detect a large effect, 126 participants to detect a moderate effect, and 786 to detect a small effect (West, Biesanz, and Pitts 2000). Therefore, a straightforward solution to increasing power may be to increase sample size. Going back to our illustration of the family intervention program, it would obviously make sense to increase the size of our groups from 15 each to 30 each. However, it is also apparent that going to about 800 participants to detect a small effect could greatly complicate a research project and make it prohibitively expensive. Another option is to consider reducing the alpha level. Because Type I and Type II errors are related, it may be an acceptable trade-off to make alpha .1 with beta at .40 according to the rule of thumb of 4 times alpha. Under this scenario power is equal to $1 - .40 = .60$. This would make it easier to detect an effect, but it does increase the risk of a Type I error.

Of course, neither of these solutions is without drawbacks. Fortunately a researcher may use additional steps in an effort to increase statistical power (Lipsey 1997). The best approach may be to increase the effect size of the independent variable in the sample (or increase the difference between X_t and X_c in the ES formula). Other things being equal, the larger the effect of the independent variable relative to other factors, the more likely the null hypothesis will be rejected. One way to increase effect size is to select samples that minimize measurement error and ensure that a high proportion of the difference between treatment and control groups is due to the independent variable (see Chapters 6 and 10). Another solution lies in taking steps to eliminate as much extraneous variation as possible. Thorough training of service providers, careful rehearsal of procedures, and attention to program detail can all serve to eliminate variation due to factors other than the program effect (or reduce the size of the denominator, or variation, in the ES formula).

We don't often think of social interventions in terms of dosage, but the evaluation researcher should make sure that the participants receive a sufficient dose of the independent variable to make a difference. If the program is financial aid, it might be better to give a small sample large amounts of aid instead of giving a little aid to many. If the program is counseling, the program should provide an intensive counseling experience. Using the most valid and reliable measurement tools can help detect a difference that exists between groups.

ordered data, compatible with small clinical samples. Furthermore, many procedures that are technically appropriate for interval-level data are also used with ordinal variables because they are "robust," or not readily affected by violation of their theoretical assumptions. Finally, many procedures have been developed to handle interval-level data, such as Student's *t,* ANOVA (analysis of variance), and regression.

Beyond the level of measurement in the dependent variable, another consideration is the character of the independent variable. Some procedures are designed for single independent variables with only two levels. Other procedures handle two or more independent variables simultaneously as well as estimating combined effects.

Finally, another issue concerns how the data were generated. Some procedures, such as ANOVA, are intended for data generated by an experiment in which one or more control groups are compared with one or more treatment groups. Other procedures, such as regression analysis, are well suited for analyzing large samples, such as surveys, in order to estimate effects. Still other procedures, such as MANOVA (multivariate analysis of variance and covariance), are suitable for both statistical control of nonexperimental variables and analysis of experiment-generated variables at the same time. Many of these procedures are highly complex and beyond the scope of this text. The point is that specific factors favor the use of some statistical procedures over others. It is important to select the appropriate procedures. Through other courses, you may learn to utilize and select the procedures yourself, or, as a human service professional, you may rely on outside consultants to assist you with this aspect of your research.

In experimentation, researchers often make comparisons between a control group and a treatment group. If these two groups are comparable in all respects except for the treatment received, a commonly used statistic is Student's *t.* This statistic compares the mean of one group against the mean of the other. Recall from the chapter on sampling that the groups may have different means by chance alone. Large differences, however, suggest a treat-

ment effect. But what is a large difference? The answer depends on the scale of the variable being measured and on the size of the samples. The *t* test results in a statistical value that is referred to a table for samples of different sizes. The table indicates the probability of obtaining a value that is as large or larger by chance. If the table value is less probable than the alpha level, one rejects the null hypothesis and concludes that the difference is significant. Tables indicating the value of *t* and other inferential statistics necessary for rejecting null hypotheses at various alpha levels may be found in any introductory statistics textbook. Computer packages, such as SPSS, provide the significance value.

In many experimental situations, the research involves more than only two groups. The researcher may also want to measure the difference between groups. For example, if four treatment groups each receive different amounts of tutorial help, the researcher might be interested in the effect each level of help has on the number of problems the members of the different groups can solve. For this situation, involving an experimental design and an interval-level dependent variable (number of problems solved), a commonly applied statistical procedure is *analysis of variance* (ANOVA). ANOVA compares the variability in the scores of members within each group (within-group variance) with variability between treatment groups. We do not expect all members of a treatment group to do equally well. In fact, even if one level of treatment works better than another, some members of a lower group might do better than some members receiving a better tutorial program. ANOVA permits the researcher to estimate how much of the variance in performance between groups is due to the treatment.

Another commonly used statistical procedure is *multiple regression analysis.* Multiple regression is used for a variety of purposes, but a typical application involves estimating the effect of multiple independent variables. For example, we might be interested in determining if a person's income is influenced by gender, race, and age—plus *how much* each of these variables affects income. As discussed earlier, correlation indicates whether two variables are associated,

Table 15.8 Nominal Data from Table 15.3 Suitable for Chi-Square, Showing Observed and Expected Values

		Region				
		Northeast	Midwest	South	West	Totals
Religious Preference	Protestant	54 (exp = 85)	140 (exp = 141)	206 (exp = 157)	80 (exp = 97)	480
	Catholic	55 (exp = 32)	56 (exp = 53)	28 (exp = 60)	43 (exp = 37)	182
	Jewish	10 (exp = 3)	1 (exp = 4)	1 (exp = 5)	3 (exp = 3)	15
	None	12 (exp = 11)	20 (exp = 19)	8 (exp = 21)	24 (exp = 13)	64
	Totals	131	217	243	150	$N = 741$

Chi-Square = 107, $p < 0.001$

Source James A. Davis and Tom W. Smith. *General Social Survey (1972–1994)* (Chicago: National Opinion Research Center; Storrs, CT: The Roper Center for Public Opinion Research, University of Connecticut).

but regression permits the researcher to estimate how much change in the dependent variable is produced by a given change in an independent variable. Multiple regression is especially useful in that it can handle a large number of independent variables simultaneously, permitting researchers to estimate the effects of one variable while controlling for others. We know, for example, that income is correlated with race, education, age, and occupation, among many other variables. If we collect these data from a number of respondents, regression permits us to estimate the contribution of each independent variable to income. Multiple regression produces coefficients that indicate the direction and amount of change in the dependent variable to be expected from a unit change in the independent variables. Thus, if the dependent variable is dollars of income, a regression coefficient of +580 for the variable "years of education" indicates that one more year of education is worth an additional $580 per year in income, assuming the other independent variables are held constant. In our illustration, regression would produce an equation as follows:

$$Y'(\text{income}) = a + b_1 (\text{race}) + b_2 (\text{education}) + b_3 (\text{age}) + b_4 (\text{gender})$$

where a = value of Y before other factors' effects are considered, b_1 is an estimate of the effect of race on income, b_2 is the estimated effect of education, b_3 is the estimated effect of age, and b_4 is the estimated effect of gender.

A widely used inferential statistic suitable for nominal data is chi-square (χ^2), which is applied to data in tabular form. The several versions of chi-square allow its application to data of different types. All these versions, however, operate by comparing the number of cases actually found in the cross-classification of two or more variables with what would be expected by chance. For example, Table 15.8 shows the relationship between region and religious preference in a sample of 741 people in the United States. The null hypothesis for this table would be that there is no relationship between the two variables. Chi-square compares the actual values in a table like this with what would be expected if the variables were unrelated. Table 15.8 also contains these expected values in parentheses in each cell. Expected values can be calculated from the marginals in the table. The expected proportion of cases in each cell is what would be found in the population if there were no relationship between the two variables. For example, because people in the Northeast

COMPUTERS IN RESEARCH

Statistical Software

Although computing statistics by hand or by calculator is possible, virtually all data analysis today is done on a computer. Personal computers are sufficiently powerful that they can run sophisticated statistical packages, such as SPSS, SAS, and MINITAB, which have placed state-of-the-art statistical capabilities at the disposal of virtually everyone, and at a relatively low price. At the same time, the bewildering array of software has made software selection a complicated choice.

Because researchers now use computers for so many different tasks, we can no longer evaluate statistical software solely on the basis of the number of statistical procedures it can run—we must also consider the other applications of the software. Fortunately, several excellent sources are available for assistance in selecting statistical software. Many popular periodicals about computers, such as *PC Magazine, PC World,* and *InfoWorld,* publish articles evaluating software. In addition, many professional journals publish articles on statistical software. One of the better sources for social research applications is *Social Science Computer Review.*

As for selecting the correct statistic to use for a set of data, computer software is available to help the researcher identify key issues and systematically put that knowledge to use. One example is the program Methodologist's Toolchest (Brent and Thompson 2000). This program does not analyze data; rather, it presents options for data analysis from more than 200 statistical procedures and a description of how well

each option fits the stated objectives and assumptions of the research. Methodologist's Toolchest is an example of a so-called expert system in that the program contains information for decision making. The software leads the user through an interview by presenting questions on the screen. The answer to one set of questions determines the next set of questions to appear. Through these questions, the researcher tells the program whether the data analysis is descriptive or inferential, how many variables are involved, and so on—basically the kind of information discussed in this chapter. It should be emphasized that the program does not select the statistic for the user; rather, it guides the user through the steps necessary to choosing a proper statistic. The program prepares a report that includes as many as four statistical procedures, rated by how well they match the assumptions and objectives of the researcher as well as the expectations of the intended audience. The report also includes a comprehensive description of each selected test, complete with references and a list of statistical software packages that include the test.

Using a computer program like this does not ensure that a researcher will always select the appropriate statistic. Nor can one expect it to replace a knowledge of research methods and data analysis. But the program systematizes the selection process, makes a large amount of technical information immediately accessible, and encourages the researcher to consider design options that might otherwise be overlooked.

make up 17.6 percent of the whole sample, we expect 17.6 percent of all Protestants in the sample, or 85 out of 480, to be from the Northeast if the variables of religious preference and region are unrelated. Due to random variation, we would expect that the actual values in the sample will not be exactly the same as the expected values in the population even when there is no relationship. However, the more the actual cell frequencies in a sample diverge from the expected frequencies, the more likely it is that the null hypothesis is false and that an association does exist between the two variables in the population.

Small values of chi-square indicate little or no association, whereas large values indicate that an association is likely. With chi-square, the value of the statistic is influenced by sample size and by the number of categories on each variable. Computer data analysis packages automatically take this into account in reporting significance level; however, when doing hand calculations, researchers must refer the statistical value to a special table that states the probability of obtaining a χ^2 of that magnitude by chance, given the sample size and number of variable categories. Chi-square does not indicate the strength of the association but whether one exists at the level of the population.

For the consumer of research, this introduction provides some basic guidelines for interpreting statistical analyses encountered in reading research. Those who will conduct research and engage in statistical analysis themselves need to go beyond the materials presented here to books such as those mentioned in the following For Further Reading section.

Main Points

- The major considerations in choosing statistics properly are level of measurement of the variables, goals of the research, number of variables involved, properties of the data, and audience.
- Descriptive statistics are procedures that assist in organizing, summarizing, and interpreting sample data.
- Measures of central tendency, or averages, summarize distributions by locating the central value of frequency distributions.
- Measures of dispersion indicate how dispersed or spread out the values are in a distribution, with most indicators revealing the average spread of the scores around the central value.
- Measures of association indicate the strength of relationships and, with ordinal- or higher-level data, also indicate the direction of relationships.
- Data are sometimes transformed into z-scores or standard normal distributions. These distributions enable us to compare distributions with one another, assess the relative position of cases in a distribution, and conduct inferential statistics. The properties of the normal distribution are important in this regard.
- Inferential statistics allow generalizations to be made from sample data to populations from which

the samples were drawn. Inferential statistics derive from the properties of the normal distribution, sampling distributions, and the central limit theorem.

- In inferential statistics, a research hypothesis is paired with an opposite null hypothesis, and the results of a statistical test are used to decide which is most likely correct.
- Particular inferential statistics are linked to level of measurement. Among the inferential statistics are Student's t, analysis of variance, regression, and chi-square.

Important Terms for Review

alpha error
alpha level
beta error
bivariate statistics
central limit theorem
descriptive statistics
inferential statistics
measures of association
measures of central tendency
measures of dispersion
multivariate statistics
normal distribution
null hypothesis
proportional reduction in error (PRE)
research hypothesis
sampling distribution
Type I and Type II errors
univariate statistics

Exploring InfoTrac® College Edition and the Internet

InfoTrac® College Edition search terms:

statistical hypothesis testing
statistical power
levels of measurement

InfoTrac® College Edition articles:

The Disappearing Bell Curve. Dawn M. Horton. *Journal of Secondary Gifted Education* Spring 2001 v12 i3 p185 (2,063 words)

Statistical Power in Stuttering Research: A Tutorial. (Statistical Data Included) Mark Jones, Val Gebski, Mark Onslow, Ann Packman. *Journal of Speech, Language, and Hearing Research* April 2002 v45 i2 p243(13) (9,230 words)

Some Web sites can help you actually carry out data analysis tasks. For example, we have discussed the issue of statistical power in Research in Practice 15.1. Some Internet sites permit you to enter parameters about your data set and receive statistical power calculations as output. One such site is Power Calculator (www.stat. ucla.edu/calculators/powercalc), which permits you to determine power statistics for several different kinds of data analysis problems.

Finally, we have mentioned several different data analysis software programs in the course of this chapter. You can learn more about data analysis software by contacting software firms at their Internet addresses. One way to locate these sites is simply to enter the name of the software, for example, "SPSS," in a search engine. Many social science research–related sites also include links to these sites. For example, at the Internet site for ERIC (www.ericae.net), click on "resources," "assessment and evaluation on the Internet," and "statistics" to find links to software sites.

For Further Reading

Aron, Arthur, and Elaine N. Aron. *Statistics for the Behavioral and Social Sciences,* 2nd ed. Upper Saddle River, N.J.: Prentice Hall, 2002. This very readable introduction to statistics explains the issues clearly and minimizes the use of formulas.

Cuzzort, R. P., and James S. Vrettos. *Elementary Forms of Statistical Reasoning.* New York: St. Martin's, 1996. This fairly brief textbook introduces statistical analysis to the student. It focuses more on the logic of statistics and how to reason through problems than on computational issues.

Frankfort-Nachmias, Chava, and Anna Leon-Guerrero. *Social Statistics for a Diverse Society,* 3rd ed. Thousand Oaks, Calif.: Pine Forge Press, 2002. This book provides a comprehensive overview of descriptive and inferential statistics and also stresses the applications of statistics by using them to elaborate on issues of race, class, and gender diversity—especially of interest to those in the human services.

Gravetter, Frederick J., and Larry B. Wallnau. *Statistics for the Behavioral Sciences,* 6th ed. Belmont, Calif.: Wadsworth, 2004. This text provides a fairly comprehensive introduction to both descriptive and inferential statistics. It can serve as an important resource and reference work for learning statistics.

Healey, Joseph F. *Statistics: A Tool for Social Research,* 6th ed. Belmont, Calif.: Wadsworth, 2002. This is another standard but well-written introductory textbook in statistics. Along with the Gravetter and Wallnau book, it can help you understand all the material in this and the preceding chapter.

Exercises for Class Discussion

A community mental health agency operates a program called Assertive Community Treatment for chronic mentally ill people. The goal of the program is to enable the mentally ill to live in their own community with as few restrictions as possible and to prevent rehospitalization, which is extremely expensive. In addition to providing and monitoring medications, the program provides a drop-in center, therapy groups, arts and crafts, a 24-hour emergency service, and regular contact with a case management team. The agency converted its record keeping to computer databases several years ago but has not used the data in any systematic way to evaluate program effectiveness. The agency asks your help in deciding which of several hundred variables they should use and what statistical procedures would be appropriate. The table on page 426 presents a selection of some of the variables available, together with coding information.

15.1 Classify each of the variables in this data set as nominal, ordinal, interval, or ratio. Compare your classification with other students and discuss any cases that are difficult to classify.

15.2 You run a frequency distribution procedure on all the variables. There are 120 total cases. You notice that *HOSPDAYS* range from 0 to

57. However, 117 of the cases had 15 days or less hospitalization, whereas the remaining four cases are 35, 48, and 57 days, respectively. Which measures of central tendency and dispersion would you use with this variable and why?

15.3 Which measure(s) of association would be appropriate for examining each of the following relationships?

HOSPDAYS—CMANHRAL
HYESNO1—MEDUSE
MEDUSE—GAS1

CRISIS1—HYESNO1
HYESNO1—CMANHR1
CRISIS1—GAS1
GAS1—GAS2

15.4 Similar programs are used throughout the state with approximately 15,000 patients. Assume that the same data are available from the other programs and that a random sample of 600 patients is selected. Identify three research questions that you could ask from this data. For each question, state the research and null hypotheses and indicate the alpha level to use for Type I error.

Variable Name	Description	Permissible Range of Values
HOSPDAYS	Number of days hospitalized during fiscal year	Integer values from 0 to 366
HYESNO1 to HYESNO12	Was patient hospitalized at all during a given month? (HYESNO1 = January, HYESNO2 = February)	0 = No, 1 = Yes
CMANHR1 to CMANHR12, CMANHRAL	Case manager hours devoted to the case each month (CMANHR1 = January, CMANHR2 = February, CMANHRAL = sum for year)	Any value from 0 to 200
GAS1 TO GAS12	Goal attainment rating score; completed by case manager on each client each month on client progress toward treatment goals	1 = low, 2 = medium, 3 = high
RESSTAT	Residential status; living alone, with roommate, in group home, or with family member	1 = alone, 2 = roommate, 3 = group home, 4 = family, 5 = other
MEDUSE1 to MEDUSE12	Case manager estimate about patient compliance with medication regime	1 = poor, 2 = good, 3 = excellent
CRISIS1 to CRISIS12	Did the patient have an emergency contact with center during month?	0 = No, 1 = Yes

Chapter 16

Analysis of Qualitative Data

The parallels and linkages between practice and research are most readily apparent in qualitative approaches to research. In fact, it has been argued that many traditional social work methods for evaluating and assessing practice are also traditional qualitative methods for collecting and analyzing data (Smith 1998). So as we present the ways by which qualitative researchers make sense of their data, it should help the student of the human services to see that the techniques used for drawing meaning from qualitative research data lend themselves equally well to making sense of practice information.

For example, process recording, a technique long used in social work for training students in clinical methods and for documenting case progress, is closely related to the case study method used by qualitative researchers. Social workers are commonly required to write case summaries, and these reports closely parallel a qualitative researcher's report that analyzes, interprets, and integrates data from a qualitative study. Human service students in internships or field placements are often required to maintain a log or journal of their experiences. Again, the student's task of synthesizing and summarizing the content of such a journal is similar to the qualitative researcher's task of analyzing field notes. Students who have covered the use of such techniques as genograms, sociograms, and timelines to graphically represent practice phenomena will find themselves on familiar ground as we present some of the same approaches here (although sometimes with different labels). What differentiates these research and practice approaches is the greater emphasis on systematic and rigorous application found in research as compared with practice.

The raw material for qualitative data analysis is often in the form of the field notes and in-depth interviews discussed in Chapter 9. However, qualitative data may also come in the form of diaries, narratives, video recordings, and other sorts of texts that are nonquantitative. In qualitative data analysis, the researcher attempts to transform this raw data and extract some meaning from it, mostly without quantifying the data. (We pointed out in Chapter 9 that field research can produce some quantitative data; when it does, this data is analyzed using the procedures discussed in Chapters 14 and 15.)

Goals of Qualitative Data Analysis

The goals of qualitative data analysis are both similar to and different from the goals of quantitative data analysis. Though the specific strategies used in qualitative data analysis are different from those used in quantitative data analysis, it is still, nonetheless, data analysis: extracting meaning from observations. The goals of a qualitative research project might be the same as those discussed in Chapter 1, especially description, explanation, and evaluation. In addition, qualitative research often strives for understanding by generalizing beyond the data to more abstract and general concepts or theories. The ultimate end may, in some cases, be to generalize the results to people, groups, or organizations beyond those observed. Thus, qualitative data analysis creates meaning in part by using raw data to learn something more abstract and general. In this respect, qualitative and quantitative data analyses are similar.

Beyond the similarities, however, qualitative and quantitative approaches have obvious differences. First, qualitative research recognizes that abstraction and generalization are matters of degree and that they may be of less importance in some studies. Second, qualitative research gives more emphasis to the effort to contextualize—to understand people, groups, and organizations within the full context or situation in which they act. In fact, some qualitative data analysis strategies devote more effort to contextualizing than to abstracting or generalizing. This is based on the position that scientific knowledge is not found only in abstracting and generalizing; such knowledge can also derive from a deep and full description of a context. In other words, some qualitative research focuses on idiographic explanations rather than nomothetic ones (see pages 34-37 in Chapter 2 on different types of explanations). Third, qualitative research tends to place more emphasis on inductive reasoning than on deductive reasoning. Qualitative researchers stress the value of letting

Figure 16.1   The Stages of Social Research as Conceptualized by Some Qualitative Researchers

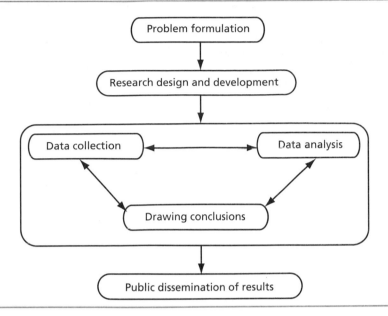

concepts and abstract ideas emerge from the data rather than using the data to provide evidence for preexisting concepts and theories.

As a part of the goal of stressing the contextual, qualitative research maintains a close, interactive link between data collection and data analysis. In Chapter 1, we presented the stages in the research process as a sequence in which one stage is mostly completed before the next one is begun. In particular, we suggested that the data collection stage is completed before the data analysis stage begins and that data analysis is largely finished before conclusions are drawn (see Figure 16.1). This is the way many quantitative and positivist researchers describe the process. One major reason for this sequencing is to ensure that the data-collection procedures used are the same over time; if the measurement procedures change from the beginning to the end of the data collection phase, then researchers may be measuring different variables (see Chapters 5 and 13). This is an important consideration in research where there are clearly stated and quantifiable variables and hypotheses and quantitative measurement procedures are used.

For many qualitative researchers, on the other hand, the process looks more like Figure 16.1: The stages of data collection, data analysis, and drawing conclusions are more simultaneous and interactive (Maxwell 1996; Seidman 1998). The researcher begins to analyze and draw conclusions almost as soon as data collection begins, and these analyses and the conclusions provide direction for whatever additional data collection needs to occur. Unlike the positivists, for whom comparability over time is essential, many qualitative researchers see that aspect of data collection as problematic in the sense that it is a decision to be weighed given the particulars of a research project. In many cases, the advantages gained by adjusting and refocusing the data-collection efforts as they proceed outweigh the disadvantages of changing the manner in which they collect the data. One of the advantages gained when data collection and analysis overlap is **theoretical sensitivity:** having data collection and analysis closely guided by emerging theoretical issues (Glaser 1978; Strauss 1987). Now, data collection and analysis are guided by theoretical issues in all research, but in a different way. In most research, theoretical issues are used to create measuring devices before collecting the data, and what occurs during the process of data collection does not lead to changes in the measuring devices. However, because many qualitative researchers do not see a rigid separation between data collection and data analysis, their stance opens the door for the possibility of theoretical issues arising *during* data collection to change what kind of data is collected or from whom it is collected. So theoretical sensitivity involves a constant interaction between theory and data collection. Data collected in one interview, for example, may raise some theoretical issues for the researcher, such that later interviews are modified to collect data addressing those issues.

Following Miles and Huberman (1994), we find it helpful to organize qualitative data analysis into three categories: data reduction and analysis, data displays, and drawing conclusions and verifying theories. Keep in mind that these are not sequential steps but overlapping activities that mutually support one another. As Miles and Huberman (1994, p. 12) state it, "The three types of analysis activity [data reduction, data displays, and conclusion drawing] and the activity of data collection itself form an interactive, cyclical process." All three activities occur, at least in part, during the process of data collection and may influence and change that process.

Data Reduction and Analysis

As we describe different kinds of qualitative data analysis, it may seem at times as if we are talking again about the process of data collection in the field (the topic of Chapter 9). That confusion can arise because in qualitative research, data collection and data analysis often occur simultaneously. In qualitative field research, for example, the data-collection phase involves collecting field notes and other materials. *Data analysis* refers to the application of coding schemes and other procedures to those field notes that are described in this section. So the analysis is sometimes occurring as the data are being collected.

The data analysis strategies discussed in this section tend to be of two types. **Categorizing strate-**gies attempt to generalize and abstract by generating concepts and even theories from the raw data. **Contextualizing strategies** attempt to treat the data as a coherent whole and retain as much of the raw data as possible in order to capture the whole context (Maxwell 1996). Actually, many specific qualitative data analyses can involve elements of both.

We will first review categorizing strategies in the form of coding, reflective remarks, and memos. Then the contextualizing strategies will be discussed.

Codes and Coding

We have talked about the process of *coding* at a number of points in this textbook—as a part of doing content analysis of available data in Chapter 8, as a part of making structured field observations in Chapter 9, and as a part of quantitative data analysis in Chapter 14. Coding is also a form of data analysis with qualitative data, and it has some similarities to coding done in other contexts.

Coding refers to the categorizing of observations into a limited number of categories. However, coding in most qualitative data analysis is distinct from the other forms of coding in at least three important ways. First, it is not an effort to quantify the data or create a set of numerical categories, as is often the case with other types of coding. Coding in qualitative analysis reduces and simplifies the data, but it does so by retaining words and their essential meanings. Second, in qualitative analysis, codes and coding schemes are created at least partly from the data themselves during the process of data collection; in other words, the data create the codes. Quantitative coding schemes are more typically derived from some preexisting theoretical stance, and then an effort is made to see if the data fit the coding scheme. Third, the purpose of coding in qualitative analysis is different. In quantitative research, coding is usually a part of the process of measurement: The coding categories constitute the operational definition of the underlying variable. Although this principle applies to an extent, in coding in qualitative research, qualitative coding goes beyond measurement: It is also an integral part of conceptual development and theory building. So the

Table 16.1   A Section of Transcribed In-Depth Interview, with Codes

Codes	Interview Statements
Self-perception *Awareness of difference* *Identifying self-through ill health* *Comparing health to others'*	*A 29-year-old man with renal failure was discussing his high school years, and events that occurred long before he was diagnosed.* *. . . I knew I was different. I caught colds very easily and my resistance was very low, and so I knew that generally speaking my health wasn't as good as everybody else's, but I tried to do all the things that everybody else was doing.*

Normalizing the context of illness
Self-esteem:
    feelings of failure
    failure of self
Reality contradicts idealized
  experience
	A 29-year-old woman with colitis was recounting her first episode of illness.
	. . . I was under a great deal of stress as a result of all this bouncing around and trying to get a job and trying not to have to go home to my parents and admit that I had failed. [I] failed at life. I had left college, and left there saying, "Gee, I can do it on my own," so I was trying this exciting existence I read about and there was something wrong; I had all this pain. I didn't know what to do about it.

Self in retrospect *Self-esteem* *Outcome of timed struggle* *Improving self-esteem as treatment goal*	*A 54-year-old woman who had had cancer and currently had a crippling collagen disease was explaining her view on why she had had a recurrence of cancer.* *. . . When I look back on my second bout of cancer, I was not feeling good about myself and the whole struggle of the last three years put met into X (a cancer institute) to try and get me to feel better about myself.*

Source   Reprinted by permission of Kathy Charmaz, from Kathy Charmaz, "The Grounded Theory Method: An Explication and Interpretation." In Robert M. Emerson, ed., *Contemporary Field Research: A Collection of Readings* (Prospect Heights, IL: Waveland Press, Inc., 1983 [reissued 1988]).

process of coding in qualitative research spans the realms of both measurement and the more abstract process of developing concepts and theories.

In qualitative research, then, the data is in the form of field notes, narratives produced by respondents, or possibly written documents or archival material. Coding is the process of categorizing sections of that data—a phrase, a sentence, a paragraph. Coding is a way to see which parts of the data are connected to one another in terms of some issue, concept, theme, or hypothesis. Some researchers use different terms, such as *thematic analysis,* for data analysis strategies that basically involve categorizing the data (Seidman 1998). Table 16.1 is an example of this, with a few sections of the transcript of an in-depth interview on the right-hand side and the codes that the researcher applied to each section on the left. These interviews were conducted as a part of a study of how people with chronic illnesses experience time and personal identity. Many of the

conceptual codes the researcher identified have to do with self-esteem and feelings about oneself—the concepts that this researcher identified as important in each part of what was said in the interview.

Approaches to Coding.   Three approaches exist to developing the coding schemes used by qualitative researchers. One is to create a fairly complete coding scheme prior to going out into the field to collect observations (Miles and Huberman 1994). This would be based on theoretical considerations regarding what will be observed in the field and what the important variables, social mechanisms, and causal processes are. This approach might rely on prior research or on preexisting coding schemes developed by others and used in research on similar topics. For example, a qualitative evaluation of a high school mental health program involved coding focus-group responses according to four topics: (1) positive aspects of the program, (2) suggestions for improving services, (3) how to reach youth in need of mental health services, and (4) ideas for measuring treatment outcomes (Nabors, Reynolds, and Weist 2000). Examples of coding categories included therapist behaviors and academic, personal, and neighborhood changes.

This coding scheme can be readily adapted to studies of similar programs. When using this approach, the list of coding categories should be fairly complete in terms of what the observer expects to see in the field and may be quite detailed and lengthy. However, one thing that distinguishes this approach to coding from what most quantitative researchers do is that the qualitative researcher still expects to change and adapt the coding scheme as observations are made in the field. With almost any coding scheme, some categories prove more useful and others less so. Some categories might not be used at all, whereas others get used too much—so many observations fall into the category that it needs to be divided into subcategories based on differences among the various observations. Thus, the coding scheme continues to develop as the data are collected.

The second approach to developing coding schemes is the reverse of the first: Observers enter the field with no preestablished coding scheme (Strauss 1987). Coding categories are developed as observations are made in the field context. One example of this is the grounded theory approach (described in Chapter 9), a very data-driven, contextualized approach to data analysis. Without the restrictions of a preexisting coding scheme, the observer describes what happens, tries to identify relevant variables, and searches for explanations of what is observed. Beginning with these concrete observations, the researcher then develops a coding scheme that points toward more abstract concepts, propositions, and theoretical explanations that would be plausible given those observations. In this way, preexisting theory does not limit the kind of data collection that occurs.

This general approach was used in a qualitative study of the role of the family in the achievement of African-American males (Maton, Hrabowski, and Greif 1998). The researchers interviewed sons and parents in 60 African-American families, generating more than 800 single-spaced pages of text data. Through reading the transcripts, the research team developed initial coding categories related to things that might influence achievement, such as discipline, high expectations, love, and community resources. The researchers then moved back from the coding categories to the original text and developed a final set of categories. Eventually, the process resulted in a formal coding system of the 20 most salient factors contributing to outstanding academic achievement.

However, even this open approach to coding is given some structure by some proponents of grounded theory, such as Anselm Strauss, who argue that coding should address four general categories of phenomena:

- conditions or causes
- interaction among people
- strategies and tactics
- consequences

A third approach to developing coding schemes falls in between the first two: A general coding scheme is developed that identifies domains of observation rather than referring to specific content within those domains. Then coding schemes are inductively developed within those domains (Bogdan and Biklen 1992; Lofland and Lofland 1995). These domains are more specific and detailed than the four general categories just mentioned that are used by some grounded theory researchers. A possible list of such domains might include the following:

- actions/events
- activities (actions of some duration)
- meaning (what people say and do to define a situation)
- perspectives (ways of thinking or orientations)
- relationships
- setting/context
- social structure (statuses, roles, and their relationships)

Most or all of these domains are likely to be relevant in a field setting, yet the categories are so general that context still plays a strong part in shaping the observations made and the specific coding scheme that emerges.

Table 16.2   Excerpts from Ethnographic Interviews of Gang Members, with Suggested Coding

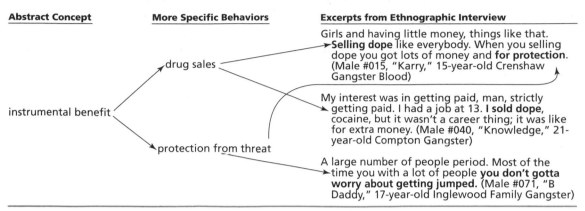

Abstract Concept	More Specific Behaviors	Excerpts from Ethnographic Interview
instrumental benefit	drug sales	Girls and having little money, things like that. **Selling dope** like everybody. When you selling dope you got lots of money and **for protection**. (Male #015, "Karry," 15-year-old Crenshaw Gangster Blood)
		My interest was in getting paid, man, strictly getting paid. I had a job at 13. **I sold dope**, cocaine, but it wasn't a career thing; it was like for extra money. (Male #040, "Knowledge," 21-year-old Compton Gangster)
	protection from threat	A large number of people period. Most of the time you with a lot of people **you don't gotta worry about getting jumped**. (Male #071, "B Daddy," 17-year-old Inglewood Family Gangster)

Source   Adapted from Scott H. Decker and Barrick Van Winkle, *Life in the Gang: Family, Friends, and Violence.* (Cambridge, UK: Cambridge University Press, 1996), pp. 63, 153. Reprinted with the permission of Cambridge University Press.

To begin to show more concretely how coding is done, we can use an example from a field study of gang life that relied on ethnographic interviews as a source of data (Decker and Van Winkle 1996). The study began with some theoretical ideas regarding what attracted young men to join gangs—especially certain instrumental benefits of joining a gang, such as the ability to get protection from others or to join in the sale of drugs. Then the researcher went through the transcribed interviews to find words or phrases that seem to represent these behaviors as reasons for joining gangs. Table 16.2 presents some excerpts from the interviews, with the key words highlighted that indicate a particular coding category. The young men in these interviews were responding to questions about why they got involved in gangs. The researchers then use these codes to assess the extent to which, throughout all of the coded interviews, support was found for their theoretical ideas about the role of instrumental benefits.

Notice a couple of characteristics in the coding in both Tables 16.1 and 16.2. First, the coding does not focus on counts of how often things happen but rather on descriptions of what is applicable to a particular person or context. The data analysis produces words, phrases, and descriptions as meaning rather than numbers to extract meaning. Second, there is a close link between the codes and the data: When a code is applied, it is linked to a particular section (word, phrase, sentence, or paragraph) of the raw data. This is important in terms of assessing validity.

Descriptive versus Abstract Coding.   Coding schemes vary in terms of how general or abstract the coding categories are. Different qualitative researchers have developed different descriptions of this. Miles and Huberman (1994), for example, suggest three different types of coding. *Descriptive codes* are coding categories that involve fairly directly observed behaviors or events; the coder need not do a great deal of interpretation to place a statement in field notes into these categories. So field notes that say "Jane left the room" or "Jim shook hands with the nurse" can be fairly directly coded as "departure" and "greeting," respectively. *Interpretive codes* are coding categories that require field researchers to use some of their deep understanding of the social context to place a section of field notes into a category; in other words, they must interpret the meaning of a particular entry in the field notes. Interpretive codes might involve assessing people's motivations or moods or the meanings that people attach to things. So, if the field notes say that "Jane left the room angrily" or "Jim gave the nurse a cool greeting," the words "angry" and "cool" are interpretive in nature—they involve a judgment or interpretation by the researcher. Thus, placing these parts of the field notes into categories of "angry" and "distant" is more interpretive and subjective than are the descriptive codes.

The third type of coding involves *pattern codes:* "explanatory or inferential codes, ones that identify an emergent theme, configuration, or explanation. They pull together a lot of material into more meaningful and parsimonious units of analysis" (Miles and Huberman 1994, p. 69). Pattern codes reduce the amount of data into more manageable amounts and help focus later data collection on data that assists in better understanding the patterns or themes. A section of field notes is identified as representing some abstract or theoretical theme or pattern in the events that are occurring. An explanatory code may refer to some abstract social process. So, "Jane left the room angrily" might be coded as exemplifying the social process of "rejection of deviant," whereas "Jim gave the nurse a cool greeting" might be coded as the social process of "role distance." Pattern codes usually focus on one of four general categories of phenomenon: themes, causes or explanations, relationships among people, and theoretical constructs. The danger with pattern coding is that the researcher might prematurely impose a certain meaning on the data and then try to fit everything else into that pattern. To prevent that, Miles and Huberman recommend that the researcher remain tentative and flexible:

> The trick here is to work with loosely held chunks of meaning, to be ready to unfreeze and reconfigure them as the data shape up otherwise, to subject the most compelling themes to merciless cross-checking, and to lay aside the more tenuous ones until other informants and observations give them better empirical grounding. (Miles and Huberman 1994, p. 70)

Keep in mind that a single section of a text or field notes can be given more than one type of code; in fact, it might be given a descriptive, an interpretive, and a pattern code.

Going back to Table 16.2, notice that it is fairly straightforward to give a descriptive code to some segments, such as "sells drugs"; however, it is more difficult—requires more interpretation and judgment—to give interpretive codes. For example, it requires some judgment to say that "you don't gotta worry about getting jumped" is an instance of the code "protection from threat." It is even more inferential to assign a pattern code, such as "selling drugs as instrumental benefit that motivates joining a gang." Such abstract coding might be based on things said in other parts of the interview or on the researchers' deep knowledge of the field setting in which the interviewees live and the interviews occurred. This is why Miles and Huberman caution against settling on pattern codes too quickly.

Open versus Focused Coding.   Another approach to coding is to begin by looking for any types of codes that might emerge from the data and then focus on a limited number of codes to see how well they fit various parts of the data (Charmaz 1983; Glaser 1978). The initial coding of field notes, interviews, or other documents is called *open coding* and involves unrestricted coding to produce concepts and dimensions that seem to fit the data fairly well. These codes can be linked to the various dimensions mentioned above (conditions or causes etc.), and the coding categories are provisional and tentative. The point of open coding is to open up the data—to open up possibilities—rather than to finalize anything. Anything that is wrong or unclear at this stage will be rectified and clarified at later stages of coding. As Strauss (1987, p. 29) puts it, at this stage of the coding, researchers "play the game of believing everything and believing nothing." Whereas in quantitative research the goal of coding is to produce counts (how many cases fall into each category), the point of open coding, according to Strauss (1987, p. 29), is to "fracture, break the data apart analytically": to create new categories and to split apart and rearrange existing categories. There is nothing fixed about the category system, at least at this stage; it is emerging out of the data and is therefore in flux. Especially early in the process, open coding is likely to be more of the descriptive variety, but it may also include some interpretive and pattern codes.

After open coding has proceeded for a while, the field researcher can turn to *focused coding,* or what Strauss calls *axial coding:* intense analysis around one or a few of the coding categories. (Each of the general coding categories is called an "axis," hence the name "axial coding.") Focused coding is more selective and conceptual; it involves applying a limited set of codes to a large amount of data. Focused coding enables the researcher to assess how extensively a set of codes applies and to discover the various forms in which the categories appear. This enables the researcher to explore one of these dimensions of social reality throughout the field notes and thus expose relationships that may not have been obvious with open coding. Focused coding cannot be done until open coding has already provided a plethora of potential concepts, but after a period of open coding, focused coding can be done periodically. In open coding, the center of attention is the raw data; in focused coding, the emerging coding categories are the focus of attention. Focused coding begins to expose the core concepts and categories and the relationships among them that emerge from the data. However, focused coding is still strongly linked to the data because the researcher must constantly go back to the original texts to validate decisions about what the core concepts are and what the relationships appear to be among them. Furthermore, focused coding may lead to revisions in the coding done during open coding as new concepts emerge from the data. What occurs at this stage is essentially conceptual development (discussed in Chapter 4), but here conceptual development grows out of the process of data analysis rather than before research design development.

Selective coding is a term used by Strauss to describe coding that focuses on the core concepts and categories that emerged during focused coding. It is, in a sense, a more intense focused coding. All elements of the text are coded in terms of how they relate or do not relate to the core concepts and theories that are emerging from the data. This is similar to Miles and Huberman's pattern coding. Selective coding builds on open and focused coding and can begin only after some of those forms of coding have been accomplished. As data analysis proceeds, selective coding comes to predominate in the process. In addition, as core concepts and theories emerge from selective coding, they can point to what additional data needs to be collected to provide further tests and comparisons for the theory.

Operational Definitions and Reliability.

However a coding scheme is developed, each category in it must have a good operational definition to ensure that all observers use the coding scheme properly and consistently. The *operational definition* is a verbal statement of the kind of observations that should be placed in a particular category. The definition might emerge from some existing theoretical framework, or it might emerge out of the observations, as in grounded theory. Nevertheless, it is critical that this be clearly specified and understood by all observers. Otherwise, observations that are placed in one category by one observer might be placed in another category by another observer or ignored altogether. One way to clarify these operational definitions is through *double coding:* Two observers code the same set of field notes, and then cases where they disagree on the coding can be evaluated. Discussion about their disagreements usually produces a sharper, clearer operational definition or a revision in the coding scheme to take the difficulty into account.

Reliability of coding schemes can be assessed in a number of different ways. As discussed in Chapter 8, one way is double coding, and then the degree of agreement between the two coders can be assessed. One simple way to do this is to calculate the percent of judgments on which coders agree out of the total number of judgments that they must make:

$$\text{percent of agreement} = \frac{2 \times (\text{number of agreements})}{\substack{\text{total number of observations} \\ \text{recorded by both observers}}}$$

Some disagreement exists about what level of agreement is acceptable, but many researchers argue that the final coding scheme, after revisions and adjustments, should achieve at least 85 to 90 percent agreement. Another way to check the reliability of a coding scheme is to have each observer code the same set of field notes twice, separated by a period of at least a few days. Again, the ultimate code–recode reliability should achieve at least 85 to 90 percent.

Reflective Remarks and Memos

In performing qualitative data analysis, researchers need some mechanisms for moving away the immediate, raw data and toward the general and abstract. Pattern coding and selective coding are ways to achieve this, but field researchers have also identified other methods. One is **reflective remarks** on field notes: reflections, interpretations, connections, or other thoughts that occur to the researcher while transcribing field notes or coding the data. This can take many different forms: questioning the original interpretation of some event in the field notes, a recollection of something about the relationship between two people that didn't get put into the field notes, an elaboration on something that was only sketchily described in the field notes, or a new hypothesis to explain something that happened in the field. All of these might be useful in understanding and coding the field notes and should be committed to writing.

If the field notes are being transcribed when the reflective thoughts occur, such thoughts can be incorporated directly into the field notes. However, it is a good idea to keep the data recorded in the field separate from reflective remarks because the latter could be influenced by selective recall or retrospective interpretation. One way to keep the field notes separate from the reflective remarks is to set the remarks apart from the notes with some device—a different font, double parentheses, brackets, or any other device not be used anywhere else in the field notes—that clearly identifies what it is. If the reflective thoughts occur during coding, they can be written into a margin of the field notes but not in the margin where codes are placed.

Another significant step away from the raw data are what are variously called memos, analytical memos, or theoretical memos. **Memos** refer to attempts at theorizing: The researcher writes down ideas about the meanings of the codes that are emerging from the data and the relationships between the various codes (Glaser 1978; Strauss 1987).

Memos do not just describe the data; they are more conceptual and abstract in nature, showing that a particular part of the data is an instance of a particular concept or social process. Or a memo might link various pieces of data together as sharing some abstract property in common. Whatever form they take, memos represent a move beyond the raw data toward more abstract theorizing. Memoing can be done as data collection and data analysis proceed. In fact, memoing can begin as soon as abstract ideas begin to occur to the researcher, which may be fairly early in the data-collection process. This is quite different from quantitative research, where data collection and analysis must be pretty much complete before the theoretical implications begin to emerge.

Memos can be short or long, a few sentences to a few pages. Most researchers identify on the memo exactly what parts of the field notes the memo refers to. This is theoretically important for such approaches as grounded theory because of their stance about the close link between raw data and abstract theory: All abstract ideas should be tied to specific parts of the data. In these approaches to qualitative data analysis, it is not adequate for researchers to report on general impressions from the data; this has low validity. Instead, memos should identify the lines in the field notes or other memos to which they relate so that there is a clear link between bits of data and abstract conclusions. The memos should also identify what codes or concepts they refer to and be dated, so that it is clear when the thoughts occurred in the research process. Some of the memos, or at least parts of them, may later be incorporated into the final research report.

Beyond saying that memos are abstract and general, it is difficult to specify their content because it is so highly variable. A memo might clarify an idea or an existing coding category, suggest some new coding categories or subcategories, or link data from different parts of the field notes or possibly even from other research projects. A memo might propose a hypothesis or a new pattern code, or it might identify something puzzling that does not fit in with the conceptual framework emerging in other memos. As the memoing process continues, what begins to emerge, either gradually or in some cases

Figure 16.2 The Data Analysis Process in Some Types of Qualitative Research

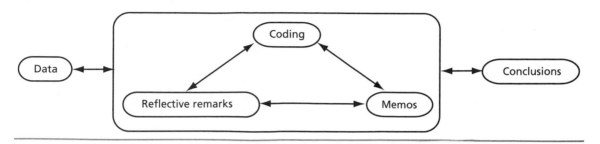

quickly, is a more formalized and coherent set of propositions or explanations of what is found in the data. (We discussed the development of propositions and theories at length in Chapter 2.) The propositions in qualitative data analysis emerge out of the data in an inductive process. In fact, some qualitative researchers eventually force themselves to state some tentative propositions that they can then review in light of all the memos, codes, and data to see if the propositions have any validity. In some cases, propositions may emerge early in the process of data analysis. Some propositions will eventually be discarded as they are shown to be inconsistent with much of the data. But eventually a set of propositions emerges that seems to be consistent with all or most of the observations. Propositions can take a number of different forms, such as these:

When *A* happens, *B* is also found.
A causes *B* to occur.
A is found when *B, C,* and *D* exist.
A is found when *B* and *C* but not *D* occur.

In whatever form they take, the propositions are abstract explanations of phenomena. In qualitative research, these explanations are viewed as tentative; another sweep through the data by the same or different researchers could produce different coding, memoing, and proposition development. In addition, field observations of different groups or different locations could produce different outcomes. Figure 16.2 diagrams these categorizing strategies; the double arrows illustrate once again how interactive this process is. As analysis proceeds, the researcher constantly goes back and forth among the

memos, reflective remarks, and coding; in addition, he or she goes back and forth between these three elements and the data and conclusions.

Contextualizing Strategies

Qualitative researchers in general stress the importance of context and of viewing and analyzing data with an appreciation of the complete context in which the data were produced. However, the categorizing strategies we have just discussed tend, to a greater or lesser degree, to move the researcher and the analysis away from the concrete data and toward more abstract categories and propositions. Some qualitative researchers argue that something is lost using this strategy (Maxwell 1996; Seidman 1998). They argue for *contextualizing strategies:* approaches to data analysis that treat the data as a coherent whole and retain as much of the raw data as possible in order to capture the whole context. Contextualizing strategies are less concerned with abstracting from one set of data in order to generalize to other people or circumstances and more interested in a deep, rich appreciation of the individuals or situations from whom the data were collected. In other words, these contextualizing strategies focus more on idiographic than nomothetic explanations (see Chapter 2).

One type of contextualizing strategy is the use of profiles, as promoted by Irving Seidman (1998). **Profiles** refer to vignettes of a person's experience, usually taken from in-depth interviews, that are stated largely in the person's own words, with relatively little interpretation or analysis by the researcher. Profiles are, fundamentally, a narrative that tells a story. Telling stories is a key way for people to make sense of themselves and their world, and hearing others' stories is a valuable way to learn about their lives. Profiles are constructed by transcribing in-depth interviews and then identifying parts of the interview that seem to the researcher to be especially important in telling the person's story. Then the parts of the interview are put together into a preliminary profile. This profile is then reviewed with a critical eye to see if any passages are redundant or irrelevant and whether the passages are sequenced properly to tell the most effective story. This review process continues until the researcher is satisfied with the profile. The final profile is mostly in the person's own words, although the researcher might include some comment to clarify or provide transitions. Any comments of the researcher should be clearly identified as such.

The researcher has to exercise considerable judgment about what to include in the story and how to sequence passages, and the possibility exists that some bias might enter into this selection process. Yet Seidman argues that the researcher is in the best position to make these judgments. It is, after all, the researcher who has "done the interviewing, studied the transcripts, and read the related literature . . . mentally lived with and wrestled with the data" (Seidman 1998, p. 110). Certainly the researcher might consult with those interviewed to see if they concur with the researcher's judgment, but ultimately the researcher needs to be confident that his or her intuitive and professional judgments about how to shape the best profile are the right ones. The final step in developing a profile is analogous to the conceptualizing or theorizing of other researchers: The researcher spells out what he or she has learned from the whole process of collecting data, reviewing data, and developing the profile. Undoubtedly, some abstracting and conceptualizing is part of this conclusion, but it is probably grandiose to call it theory building.

An approach similar to profiling is **narrative analysis,** in which interviews, autobiographies, life histories, letters, and other personal materials are used to form a descriptive narrative of a person's life or circumstances (Clandinin and Connelly 2000;

Merriam 1998). As with the profile, this narrative tells a story and relies heavily on the person's own words as taken from their letters, autobiography, or other sources. However, narrative analysis does not rely so heavily on interviews; it uses a broader range of data sources than do profiles.

A similar contextualizing strategy, but one that doesn't rely so heavily on the subject's own words, is the **case study:** a detailed, descriptive account of one individual, situation, organization, group, or other entity (Merriam 1998; Patton 2002). As with profiles, data analysis in case studies focuses on description and narrative rather than on categorizing strategies. Furthermore, the description in case studies is detailed and what is sometimes called "thick": a complete and literal accounting of the person or setting under study. Some quantitative data might be presented as a part of a case study, but the emphasis is on telling a story in prose or narrative, although not completely in the words of the people being studied, as in the profile or narrative. The idea, however, is the same: The researcher describes people's lives and experiences in great detail.

In addition to the researcher's description, the case study might use quotations from those being studied, along with photos, videos, artifacts, and any other materials that help provide an in-depth description of the subject of the case study. Social work students who have to complete a process recording as part of their practice methods training find the case study method familiar because the two methods have many features in common. By way of illustration, Katherine Tyson (1999) essentially used process recording from therapy with a three-year-old boy in presenting a qualitative study demonstrating the effectiveness of an empowering approach to crisis intervention. The presentation of the research intersperses quotations of interchanges between therapist and child with analysis and discussion of the principles of the therapeutic approach.

Case studies can be based on direct observation, interviews, document analysis, organizational records, or some combination of these—basically, any data that would contribute to a description of the case under study. Historical research often focuses on a case study and might use a wide variety of materials as data: historical accounts, published newspapers and magazines, biographies, letters, government statistics, official records, and so on.

The primary goal of the case study and the other contextualizing strategies is an idiographic explanation that focuses on an in-depth understanding of this particular case. Such an understanding might enhance one's comprehension of other cases and situations, but the primary focus is description, not generalization. The advantage of profiles, narratives, and case studies is the rich and detailed descriptions they provide of people's lives, experiences, and circumstances. A disadvantage of these contextualizing strategies is that they depend heavily on the subjective and intuitive judgments of the researchers closest to the data. Another researcher producing a case study or profile of the same person or situation might come up with quite a different story. Yet another disadvantage is limited ability to generalize beyond the individual case.

Displaying Data

A **data display** is an organized presentation of data that enables researchers and their audiences to draw some conclusions from the data and to move on to the next stage of the research (Miles and Huberman 1994; Strauss 1987). In any data analysis, the researcher must display the data so that a convincing argument can be made to support the conclusions reached in the research. In science, we don't take the researcher's word in regard to conclusions; we need to be convinced by a display of the data. In quantitative data analysis, an important part of the display of data is the numbers, in the form of contingency tables, charts, or descriptive and inferential statistics (see Chapters 14 and 15). Some narrative is required to explain how the numbers were arrived at and to clearly explain their interpretation, but the core of the argument is the display of the numbers. In qualitative data analysis, the core of the argument is not numbers. Although the qualitative researcher may have some numbers to show, he or she uses different kinds of data displays. Creating data displays is very much a part of data analysis; creating the displays as-

sists the researcher in identifying and clarifying the concepts and categories that are emerging from the coding and other strategies used on the data.

Narrative Text

One key type of data display in qualitative research is the description, narrative, or verbal argument made by the researcher. In the contextualizing strategies, the narrative provides as full a description as possible to give an in-depth picture of the field, interview, or person that is the center of attention. The narrative attempts to be true to the meaning of the original experience, as interpreted by the researcher. The anthropologist Philippe Bourgois (1995, p. 341), in his study of street drug dealers, points to "the impossibility of rendering into print the performance dimension of street speech. Without the complex, stylized punctuation provided by body language, facial expression, and intonation, many of the transcribed narratives of crack dealers appear flat, and sometimes even inarticulate." The challenge for Bourgois was to produce a narrative that conveyed the rich, detailed meanings that he perceived in the field setting, based on all the linguistic and nonlinguistic cues available to him.

In the categorizing strategies, the researcher's narrative describes the concepts and propositions that emerged from the research, along with excerpts from the field notes or other data sources that illustrate the concepts and propositions and corroborate the conclusions drawn (see Tables 16.1 and 16.2). In neither quantitative nor qualitative research do researchers report *all* the data, which would mean the raw data. A research report is always a summarization of the data, and it is ethically incumbent on the researcher to give an accurate summarization of the data. For the qualitative researcher, this means that the illustrations presented to corroborate the conclusions are representative illustrations and not selective or distorted.

Visual Displays

Qualitative researchers also use a variety of visual formats to display data, just as quantitative researchers use contingency tables, graphs, and charts in their data analysis (Miles and Huberman 1994; Patton 1981; Strauss 1987). These visual data displays are considered a part of data analysis because the process of their development serves as an assist in conceptualization and theory development. By summarizing what is found in the data, these displays help clarify conceptual categories and give further insight into relationships between categories. They also enable the researcher to see weaknesses in the analysis and thus suggest areas where additional data analysis is called for. Of course, visual data displays also are an effective adjunct to the narrative text in communicating results to a variety of audiences. Although these visual displays can take a variety of formats, there are generally two types. One is a figure that serves as a visual mapping of some physical or conceptual terrain. The second is a table, chart, or matrix into which some text, phrases, or other materials are placed. Although the specific form these visual displays can take is highly variable and dependent on the specific data and concepts, we can provide a few illustrations to offer a sense of their nature, function, and development.

One type of visual display is a **context map,** which describes in graphic form the physical or social setting that is the context of the observations. Qualitative researchers stress the centrality of the context in understanding people's behavior; they are fond of pointing out that everything must be contextualized or situated. Positivist, quantitative research often collects and analyzes data without regard to the context. A survey researcher, for example, will collect data on a questionnaire without regard to whether those attitudes might be important, different, or possibly irrelevant *depending on the context in which the person is behaving.* Many nonpositivists refer to this as "decontextualized" data collection and analysis and argue that those attitudes only take on a life (i.e., become important) in a particular context. Just as a percentage table informs the audience about some of the meaning in data, a context map provides meaning to the data by describing the context in which the behaviors occurred.

In some cases, the context map is a drawing of the physical or geographic setting in which observa-

tions are made. In fact, we suggested in Chapter 9 that each session of field observation might begin by drawing a map of the setting. The map might be a drawing of a room, building, street, or neighborhood; it might include physical objects, entrances and exits, the location of people or groups, and whatever else is relevant to understanding the social interaction described in the narrative. In other cases, the context map describes the social setting: the individuals, statuses, roles, groups, or organizations relevant to the observations; it would also show connections and relationships between these elements by the use of lines and arrows. Some forms of this are called **sociograms** or **network analysis.** Figure 16.3 gives an example of what this might look like, showing the friendship choices made among a group of people. Network analysis may be the primary analytical approach used in a study, as was the case in a research project on the role that social networks play in the daily survival of homeless Latino and African-American men (Molina 2000).

A common strategy for developing a sociogram is to conduct a sociometric interview with each member of a group. Each member is asked questions, such as these:

- Whom of your group would you like to always be beside you during classes (or work or other relevant activity)?
- Who do you think can get the group organized best of all?
- Whom of your group would you invite to a party at your home?
- Whom would you not invite?
- Whom do you work with if you have to but really don't like very much?

The visual representation that results helps us better see certain social phenomena, such as particular patterns of relationships. Figure 16.3 provides evidence for certain social phenomena, such as the clique (a group of people who all make mutual friendship choices) or the star (a person who is selected as a friend by a large number of people). Figure 16.3 is based on friendship or attraction choices, but it could map other aspects of relationships, such as deference, submission, dominance, or giving and re-

Figure 16.3   A Sociogram as an Example of a Context Map

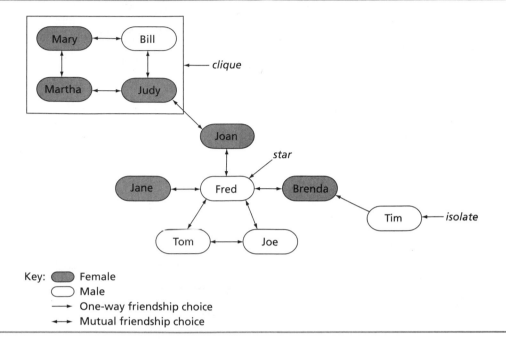

Key: ⬭ Female
      ◯ Male
      → One-way friendship choice
      ←→ Mutual friendship choice

ceiving help. As with other context maps, the specifics depend on the particular observational setting and the concepts that emerge from it.

Another type of visual display in qualitative research is called a **matrix display.** A matrix looks very much like a contingency table with rows and columns. The difference is that, whereas the cells of a contingency table contain numbers or percentages, the cells of a matrix contain text, quotations, phrases, or symbols from the field notes or other sources of qualitative data. The rows in the matrix may represent the categories of a variable (as in contingency tables), or they may represent different concepts that emerged from the field notes or different points in time. The columns may also represent such a range of possibilities. Table 16.3 is a matrix used to analyze data in a study of the implementation of a new reading program in a grade school. The rows represent different conditions that affected the acceptance and implementation of the reading program, whereas the columns represent different kinds of people (users of the reading program, such as teachers, versus educational adminis-

trators). Notice that the material in the cells is not an attempt to quantify how many people felt or acted a certain way but rather to give an overall assessment or judgment of each group's reaction to the innovation and then include some quotes from the field notes to support that judgment. In this study, for example, the researchers' analysis of the field notes suggested that users of the reading program were strongly committed to it, whereas the administrators were only weakly committed. Sometimes in matrix analysis, the rows might be each individual who was observed and the columns are different categories from the data.

Thus, matrix displays are a good way to summarize data from the field notes. It is possible to summarize as many as 20 pages of field notes into one matrix, which makes this a much easier and more effective way to communicate the results with an audience. Matrix displays are also used as an assist in the data analysis because the researcher can review the matrix in an effort to detect patterns, themes, or trends that may be difficult or impossible to detect by reading and rereading the field notes or other

Table 16.3 Example of a Matrix Display

	Presence of Supporting Conditions	
Condition	For Users	For Administrators
Commitment	*Strong*—"wanted to make it work."	*Weak* at building level. Prime movers in central office committed; others not.
Understanding	*"Basic"*—("felt I could do it, but I just wasn't sure how.") for teacher. *Absent* for aide ("didn't understand how we were going to get all this.")	*Absent* at building level and among staff. *Basic* for 2 prime movers ("got all the help we needed from developer.") *Absent* for other central office staff.
Materials	*Inadequate:* ordered late, puzzling ("different from anything I ever used"), discarded.	N.A.
Front-end training	*"Sketchy"* for teacher ("it all happened so quickly"); no demo class. *None* for aide: ("totally unprepared. I had to learn along with the children.")	Prime movers in central office had training at developer site; none for others.
Skills	*Weak-adequate* for teacher. *"None"* for aide.	One prime mover (Robeson) skilled in substance; others unskilled.

Source Matthew B. Miles and A. Michael Huberman, *Qualitative Data Analysis: An Expanded Sourcebook,* 2d ed., p. 95, copyright © 1994 Sage Publications, Inc. Reprinted by permission of Sage Publications, Inc.

texts. This is analogous to what a quantitative data analyst would do in looking at a contingency table rather than the raw numerical data.

Beyond what we have said here, there are few fixed rules about creating matrices. It is a creative process, and the exact nature of the matrix is very much driven by the data. However, if we begin qualitative data analysis thinking in terms of matrices, then it may be easier to discover in the data how possible matrices can be created.

Conclusions and Verification

Data analysis involves discovering meaning in the data. In qualitative research, this means identifying themes, patterns, and regularities and in some cases stating propositions, causal connections, and developing theories. In this regard, qualitative research is identical to quantitative research. However, the differences between the two are important to emphasize. One difference is that drawing conclusions in qualitative research occurs, at least in part, during

the process of data collection and analysis, whereas in quantitative research this stage usually occurs after the data have been collected and analyzed (compare Figure 1.1 on page 10 and Figure 16.1). Second, most qualitative researchers hold their conclusions more tentatively or "lightly," especially in early stages of the analysis, because they recognize that additional analysis could lead to reinterpretations or reconceptualizations of the data. However, as analysis proceeds, conclusions become more complete and certain. Third, the conclusions in qualitative research are more grounded in the data, which means that the conclusions are more clearly allowed to flow out of the data rather than be imposed on the data by measurement devices created before the data are collected. In a grounded approach, the data analysis and conclusions are allowed to adapt to what is discovered in the data. Finally, in qualitative research more than in quantitative research, the primary data-gathering instrument is the researcher herself or himself, and that raises concerns about the many ways in which the instrument/observer may bias the observations.

This is also a problem in quantitative research; we have discussed ways in which a researcher might build a bias into, for example, a question or a multiple-item scale used in survey research. However, when the observer is the data-gathering instrument, then his or her own personal values or biases can seriously compromise the collection of data and must be taken into account in assessing conclusions.

Qualitative researchers not only draw conclusions but also make efforts to verify those conclusions by finding evidence of their truth and validity. Are the conclusions reasonable and plausible? Without verification, one researcher's conclusions are simply his or her own account of what is going on. This verification is a part of the overall argument that a researcher makes to convince both him- or herself, along with any relevant audiences, that the conclusions are reasonable and justified. In Chapter 5, we discussed some of the procedures used to assess validity in quantitative research, such as criterion and construct validity. In Chapter 9, we discussed ways to assess the validity of observations made in qualitative research. Here, we are discussing the validity of the data analysis and conclusions, but some of the points made about observations also apply to conclusions. Some additional points can also be made:

1. *Assess whether the conclusions are based on a thorough description and interpretation of the situation, including competing interpretations and explanations.* As soon as something resembling a pattern, generalization, or conclusion seems to be emerging from the data, researchers need to ask what rival explanations or conclusions are possible. This serves as a check against bias, misinterpretation, or laziness and will likely require additional passes through the data to see what evidence supports the rival explanations. It can be helpful to enlist other researchers in this process because the researcher's own bias may prevent him or her from recognizing and clearly evaluating alternatives. If the conclusions are justifiable, then the rival explanations will find considerably less support in the data and thus more verification for the conclusions.

2. *Consider negative evidence and deviant cases.* Although much data analysis is a search for evidence to support a theme or conclusion, it is also important to search for evidence that does not support it. Especially in qualitative research, it can be easy to miss negative evidence because the researcher is so focused on developing evidence to support a conclusion. (As one example of how this can occur, recall the Big Man bias in the discussion of research on minorities in Chapter 9.) If possible, have other researchers go back to the raw data—the field notes—to see if they can find any negative evidence. If they don't, the researcher has fairly powerful support for the conclusions. A part of this is to search for *deviant cases* or *outliers,* cases that don't follow the themes or patterns that are being discovered in the data. Deviant cases may be difficult to find, but the search for them is important and can be assisted by some of the data displays discussed in this chapter. It is important not only to discover the deviant cases but also to explain them. Can their deviation be understood within the context of the overall themes and propositions of the research? Explaining deviant cases may call for modification in the concepts and propositions or, in extreme cases, a total revamp of the theoretical approach.

3. *Carefully assess the desires, values, and expectations of the person analyzing the data to see if these might bias the conclusions drawn.* People's perceptions are drastically shaped by their expectations or lack of them. If we expect something to occur, we are much more likely to observe it—whether it actually occurs or not. If we expect welfare recipients to be lazy, then we become acutely aware of all those entries in field notes that might be interpreted as laziness. Thus, the validity of conclusions is reduced to the extent that expectations—whether recognized or not—mold interpretations of data. On the other side of the coin, a lack of expectations may lead us to miss entirely something of importance in the data.

4. *Have other researchers analyze the data to see if they come to the same conclusion.* There are problems

with this because these other researchers were probably not involved collecting the data in the field, and that experience of being in the field provides all kinds of information and insights that may not appear in the raw data (the field notes). Nonetheless, if these other researchers do come to the same conclusions, they provide validation that the conclusions are valid.

5. *Compare the conclusions reached through field observations with conclusions reached by other research methodologies,* whether it is observational research in other settings or survey, available data, or experimental research. This is a variation on criterion validity (discussed in Chapter 5). It is also sometimes called *triangulation,* or approaching a problem from a number of different directions. If various methodologies yield the same conclusions, then we have greater confidence that the field observations have validity. Field research whose conclusions are at wide variance with the results of other research should be accepted with caution, especially if none of the other checks on validity are available.

6. *Consider how the condition of the observer might influence observations and conclusions.* Hunger, fatigue, stress, or personal problems can lead to distorted perceptions and interpretations. Likewise, physical characteristics, such as the lighting in an establishment, may lead to invalid observations. (This is another good reason for keeping complete field notes—field conditions affecting validity can be assessed at a later point.) If a number of these conditions exist, it may be judicious to terminate observation and resume when conditions are more favorable.

7. *Look for behavior that is illegal, stigmatizing, or potentially embarrassing or that risks punishment.* If people engage in these kinds of behaviors when they know they are being observed, then they are probably acting naturally and not putting on a performance for the benefit of the observer. For example, in his study of a sexually transmitted diseases clinic, Joseph Sheley (1976, p. 116) argued that the validity of his data was quite strong because "staff members dropped their professional masks and displayed quite unprofes-

sional behavior and ideas in the company of the researcher." Under such conditions, we can assume that people are reacting to environmental stimuli that normally guide their behavior rather than shaping a performance for the benefit of the investigator. When these kinds of behaviors constitute the evidence for conclusions, then we can have added confidence in the conclusions.

8. *If possible, make a video or audio recording of the scene.* Although such recordings have their weaknesses as records of what occurred, they do provide another way for observers to check and validate their observations and conclusions. These recordings can also be reviewed by others, which offers further checks on possible bias or misinterpretation.

9. *Assess the representativeness of the individuals, groups, informants, and observational sites.* Qualitative researchers do not typically use probability samples, but this does not absolve them from addressing the issue of how representative their observations are and how valid their generalizations are. (We already addressed this issue in Chapter 6 when talking about some types of nonprobability samples.) To generalize beyond the individuals, groups, or sites observed, we need to make a case that those individuals, groups, or sites are representative of other individuals, groups, or sites. We do this by showing that the characteristics of those observed are similar to the characteristics of other individuals, groups, or sites that were not observed. If we cannot make claims of representativeness, this does not completely invalidate the research, but it does throw into question any conclusions that claim to generalize. Of course, with some qualitative methodologies, especially the contextualizing strategies, generalization may be of secondary importance in the research.

10. *Evaluate whether the subjects of the research agree with or support the conclusions.* Who knows the field better than those whose field it is? This point is poignantly illustrated by Sarah, a developmentally disabled young woman participating in a qualitative study. At one point, posters that displayed the themes found in the data by the researchers were presented to the group.

Sarah walked to a poster that displayed the theme of "sense of belonging" at school and work. In response to a question, she smiled broadly and swung her arms out as far as she could reach to communicate just how much she agreed (Mactavish, Mahon, and Lutfiyya 2000).

Thus, an important clarifying and validating step in qualitative research is to assess the reactions of those being observed to the conclusions. Do they agree with the themes, patterns, and propositions that form the conclusions? Depending on who is being observed, they may or may not understand the more abstract and theoretical parts of the conclusions, but many of the patterns and themes will be comprehensible to them, possibly with a little explanation. If they generally agree with the conclusions, then this provides additional evidence of validity for them. If they disagree with some or all of the conclusions, then this can have two positive effects. One

effect is to stimulate the researcher to consider changing or clarifying the conclusions to take into account the objections. Of course, it is possible that the researcher will conclude that no change or clarification is necessary. This can lead to the second positive effect: explaining why the people disagree with the conclusions. In other words, their objections become further observations to be described and explained by the research. This may, in fact, provide more support for the conclusions.

As many of these guidelines as possible should be followed in verifying the conclusions drawn in qualitative data analysis. No one of them, of course, is the key to having confidence in the conclusions; the key is that the more that are incorporated, the more confidence we can have. Research in Practice 16.1 discusses a research project that illustrates a number of elements of qualitative data analysis, including the use of a number of mechanisms for enhancing validity.

RESEARCH IN PRACTICE 16.1

BEHAVIOR AND SOCIAL ENVIRONMENTS:

Pregnancy after Perinatal Loss

Getting through the first 12 weeks of just being scared [that was hard]. Every time I went to the bathroom you watched for blood and you sort of panic. After that you go week-by-week instead of day-by-day . . . I haven't gotten to the month-to-month thing yet. There's a lot of apprehension. . . . Once we reached 24 weeks [the age that our first was born prematurely and subsequently died] it was great, but it was nerve wracking. We also decided that we couldn't deal with it again after this; we could bury one more child but that would be the last one we buried. . . . You rely on faith a lot. (Cote-Arsenault and Marshall 2000, p. 473)

For an expectant mother, pregnancy is supposed to be a time of excitement and anticipation as she awaits the birth of a healthy infant. But how

does a woman who has seen these feelings dashed by the disappointment of premature birth and death deal with a new pregnancy? The powerful quotation above offers some insight into the world of couples whose dreams of having children have previously been broken by tragedy. The quotation also illustrates the potential of qualitative research for communicating the experience of the research participant.

Certainly for the health care professional, understanding the dynamics of coping with pregnancy after perinatal loss can be vital to working with patients, and this fact motivated the study described here by Denise Cote-Arsenault and Robin Marshall (2000). Specifically, the researchers sought answers to these questions: (a) What is the experience of pregnancy after loss like? (b) What is the significance of specific or particular milestones during

continued on next page

the pregnancy? (c) What are the woman's major concerns or worries? (d) What did health care providers do for these women that was helpful or not helpful?

To seek answers to these questions, the researchers employed a qualitative strategy. They conducted three focus groups and interviewed two additional participants whose restrictions prevented their participation in groups. The inclusion of interviews as well as focus groups permitted comparison of the methods in terms of depth and data content for each approach. Focus-group sessions were audiotaped and documented using field notes. In addition, the researchers held debriefing sessions to capture additional information.

The researchers based their data analysis on the work of Morse and Field (1995), who identify the principles of comprehending, synthesizing, theorizing, and recontextualizing. Comprehending entails coding and sorting the data and searching for underlying meanings and metaphors. Next, the researchers sought to identify commonalities and arrive at a representative case of the phenomenon through the process of synthesizing. The researchers identified theorizing as the stage in which they tried out various explanations for the data, seeking a simple model that fit the data well. The final principle, recontextualizing, involved integrating new findings into what was already known.

The transcribed tapes of focus groups and interviews were verified by at least two research team members, using field notes and the audiotapes to add information on such features as intonations, pauses, emotions, body language, and gestures to clarify meaning of transcribed words. The completed transcripts were then transferred into a software program to search the text and identify themes.

We have made the point that data collection and data analysis often occur simultaneously in qualitative methods, and that was the case in this study. Prior to the second focus group, the first focus group was transcribed and the data from this transcription used in the second group to look for topics and discussions that were not consistent with those of the first group. Data analysis also included

gaining feedback from participants. After the synthesis phase, a written report of tentative findings in the form of metaphors and themes was mailed to participants. The researchers report that seven of the 13 participants returned written feedback. In the terminology of Morse and Field (1995), this step involved the participants "trying on the data" to see if what the researchers had derived was a "true fit" to the experience of the participant. Notice also that this qualitative method engages the participant, not merely as a data source but also as an active contributor to the analysis process. Thus, the research becomes more of a collaborative process between researcher and participants than is the case in typical quantitative methods.

Under the general topic of conclusions and verification, the researchers in this study made several points in support of the trustworthiness of their findings, including the following:

1. Use of multiple data collection strategies (focus groups and interviews)
2. Inclusion of participants with diverse perinatal loss histories
3. Involvement of multiple research team members in the process, including independent review of transcripts
4. Use of "member checks" during focus groups, in which participants were asked for clarifications or expansions of other's accounts
5. Use of participant review of tentative findings
6. Use of independent research team review of transcripts and findings for agreement with metaphor and theme descriptions

Each of these points contributes to acceptance of the findings and conclusions as reasonable and plausible.

On the basis of their research, a metaphor that emerged from the data was "One Foot In—One Foot Out." On the one hand, women were engaged in the new pregnancy in hopes of a positive outcome; on the other hand, they were painfully aware that things could go wrong and were unable, in the words of one participant, to "jump into the pregnancy with both feet." In addition to this overall metaphor, the researchers extracted from the data some more specific contexts and themes. In presenting the contexts and themes, the researchers made ample use of the contextualizing strategy of profiling. For example, in presenting the theme of "setting the stage," the researchers include this segment from a participant's discussion:

> It was a very much wanted pregnancy. I always knew something was wrong or different, but when I started bleeding at 10 weeks my husband tried to convince me that it would be OK. It kind of started and stopped and I rode the roller coaster of maybe it is normal spotting, maybe it is not. But then it was like labor and I would pass a little tissue each day. I just wanted to be alone with the loss, nothing invasive.

Looking back, it was very hard. (Cote-Arsenault and Marshall 2000, p. 479)

The understanding of the special dynamics of pregnancy after perinatal loss that emerges from this study provides valuable insights for nurses, social workers, and other human service professionals who work with pregnant women and their families. Quantitative studies based on structured interviews and available health data enable us to estimate the demographics of perinatal loss, but qualitative research like this study sensitizes the human service professional to the world and emotions of the woman whose experience of pregnancy is tempered by the somber reality of past experience.

Using Computers in Qualitative Research

Most people are at least somewhat familiar with what computers do with quantitative data: They "crunch the numbers" by performing various statistical procedures on the numerical data. However, when the data take a more qualitative form, such as field notes or the text of a magazine article, the manner in which computers analyze the data is less widely understood. Yet as early as the 1960s, computer programs could perform content analysis on such texts. Since then, advances in computer hardware and software, artificial intelligence, and optical scanning technologies have expanded dramatically the kinds of tasks that computers can do in qualitative research (Fielding 2002; Flick 2002; Weitzman and Miles 1995). We won't discuss specific software programs here but rather the general capabilities of some or all versions of what is now called **computer-assisted qualitative data analysis** (CAQDA).

Computers haven't substantially changed qualitative data analysis; they simply assist the researcher in doing many of the tasks described in this chapter. CAQDA software definitely does not do the researcher's work. Qualitative data analysis is still difficult and time-consuming and calls for substantial

creativity on the analyst's part. It is analogous to writing: Even with word processors, writing is still a difficult job that requires a creative mind. But computers definitely make writing, as well as qualitative data analysis, easier and more effective than they would be without them.

To illustrate what computers can do these days, consider a qualitative study of eating disorders among people referred to an addiction treatment center. The data in this study might consist of open-ended interviews with the clients, client social histories and treatment plans, and chart logs taken from client records. There might also be videotapes of meetings where the staff discusses cases. Many of these documents would be in narrative form, and the first step would be either to type or to scan them into a computer as text files.

Coding and Retrieving Data

At a very elementary level, computer software can provide counts of how often particular words or phrases appear in a text or field notes and which words and phrases tend to appear together or near one another in the text. However, most qualitative data analysis goes far beyond this. A more important use for CAQDA software is to assist the researcher in creating and using a coding scheme and coding the qualitative data. To do this, the researcher displays the text on the screen and selects a portion of interest. In some software, this is done by blocking the section of text on the screen much the way you block a section of text in a word processor to copy it or cut it; other software automatically divides the text into sections based on lines, sentences, or paragraphs, and then the researcher places a marker at the beginning or end of the section to code. For example, a section of text describing the way a mother disapproved of her daughter's behavior could be selected and marked with a code for "Mother disapproval of daughter behavior." CAQDA software can then search through the text identifying and counting the number of times various codes appear in field notes. Advanced software can also analyze whether certain words, phrases, or codes tend to be used together, how far apart from one another they tend to be, whether words or codes in a text tend to be positively or negatively evaluated, and whether certain words or codes tend to be associated with certain other words or codes (Kelle 2004; Seale 2000; Weitzman and Miles 1995). Some software assists in the coding with search procedures and what are called "wild cards." If the researcher requests a search for "moth," the program will go through the field notes and identify all words that begin with "moth" and display them. Such a search might produce such words as "mother," "motherly," "motherhood," and "mothballs," and the researcher can then decide which code to assign to each .

To begin analyzing the data, the researcher uses the program's search function. In this hypothetical study, we begin by locating all cases that contain the codes "Mother pressured" or "Father pressured." This process is similar to conducting a computerized literature search by entering combinations of key words. By using these codes joined by the key term "OR," we can identify a subset of all cases where parental pressure was indicated and then save that group of files for further analysis. Having selected a subset of cases based on one or more codes, the program can produce a report with whatever information the researcher wishes: the individual's name, the name given to various codes, the frequency of use of various codes, and which source material the data were taken from.

Most CAQDA software programs store the codes for a given case in a special file, sometimes called an "index card." When done coding the material for one case, the index card file contains all the codes the researcher used for all the materials pertaining to that individual. Thus, the computer program follows a logical procedure much like the traditional practice of manually preparing note cards for cross-referencing cases. To help with coding, the program provides a code list containing all the codes used thus far for all cases in the study. Some programs can also "autocode," which means to give the same code to all identical words or phrases in a document. We can also store information about each case or individual in the study, such as age, gender, or whatever else is available in the data. In addition, the software allows us to give more than one code to a given segment of text. We can also revise the coding scheme in a variety of ways. For example, we can create different levels of codes. If a number of codes all share something in common, we can group them under a higher-level or more abstract code. The program retains all levels of coding, and the data can be retrieved using any level of code. Or we can go the opposite way: A single coding category can be elaborated into a series of more specific or concrete categories.

Data Analysis and Hypothesis Testing

Some content analysis software can test hypotheses by performing searches for all cases containing particular combinations of codes. Suppose our hypothesis is that "mothers who are critical of their daughter's body image have a negative effect on their daughter's self-image." The software could search for all cases that include the codes "Mother critical of daughter's body image," "Mother–daughter relationship strained," and "Daughter experiencing weight loss." To each of those cases, it then adds the code "Mother negative influence on daughter self-image," indicating that these cases confirm the hypothesis. Only cases meeting all three conditions have the new code added to their files. In a similar way, we can construct codes for other combinations of interest.

Some content analysis software can perform statistical analyses of the frequency of occurrence of various codes and display the data in graphical form, using some of the graphs and matrices discussed in this chapter. Some software can also import data from and export data to statistical programs and spreadsheets. In addition, beyond merely automating content-analysis procedures, some programs provide important advances in the validation, reliability, and generalizability of qualitative data analysis. For example, an independent researcher can code the same data with the codes already developed and stored and thus determine interrater reliability. To assess validity, an independent researcher might code the same material blindly, that is, without benefit of the existing coding scheme, to determine if the second coder develops the same or similar meanings as the first.

Conceptualization and Theory Building

Some CAQDA software is designed to assist in the tasks of conceptualization and theory building (Dohan and Sánchez-Jankowski 1998; Fielding 2002). Of course, the software doesn't actually create coding schemes or build theories, but it can provide the researcher with some assistance in these tasks by showing links in the data between concepts, coding categories, and observations that he or she might not have observed without such assistance. In fact, this CAQDA software has been used heavily by some proponents of grounded theory methodology because the software assists in going back and forth from data to concepts, a key feature of grounded theory.

One way the software supports theory building is by providing opportunities for the process of memoing discussed earlier in this chapter: Researchers can write their own comments, and the software will link those comments/memos to sections of identified text. The memos can be stored separately from the field notes or inserted as annotations directly into the field notes or other text. Annotations to field notes are identified as such by the

software, and the annotations themselves can be coded. As explained earlier in the chapter, these memos and annotations are expressions of conceptual and theoretical ideas, and the software assists in this process by enabling the researcher gradually to build a conceptual scheme and theory that provides a more abstract understanding of the data while still closely linked to the data. Also, by being able to code these memos, the researcher is helped to notice linkages that might have escaped attention otherwise. Some software also provides graphical maps that provide a visual representation of links between concepts and other concepts and between concepts and data. This visual picture can be a substantial assist in theory building: "Maps may help the analyst picture the project's theoretical shape, the concepts in use, the relationships between those concepts, and the ethnographic data that have been collected regarding each of those concepts and links. Theory-building software facilitates experiments with different concepts and links within the research process" (Dohan and Sánchez-Jankowski 1998, p. 490).

Main Points

- Qualitative data analysis focuses on extracting meaning from nonnumerical data without transforming the data into numbers. Though nonpositivist paradigms have been receptive to qualitative approaches, a one-to-one link does not exist between a particular paradigm and a tendency to use qualitative rather than quantitative research.

- In qualitative research, the stages of data collection, data analysis, and drawing conclusions tend to overlap. One of the advantages of this overlap is greater theoretical sensitivity. Qualitative research pursues goals of description, explanation, and evaluation, as well as attempts to abstract and generalize, and also seeks to contextualize the analysis.

- Qualitative data analysis can pursue a categorizing strategy or a contextualizing strategy. One approach to the former is to code the data. One approach to coding is to create a fairly complete and detailed coding scheme before gathering data; other approaches let the coding scheme emerge as the data is collected and analyzed.

- Specific types of coding can focus on the concrete versus the abstract or on the open versus the more focused coding. Coding schemes should have clear operational definitions and be tested for reliability.

- Reflective remarks and memos can assist in coding, conceptualization, and theory building. Contextualizing strategies include profiles, narrative analysis, and case studies. Their primary goal is idiographic: to understand a particular case rather than to generalize to other cases.

- Data displays are important in helping the researcher to develop coding schemes and conceptual categories as well as to communicate conclusions to audiences. Data displays come in the form of narrative texts and visual displays, such as context maps and matrix displays.

- Qualitative data analysis produces conclusions that must be verified. A variety of guidelines are applied, and confidence in the conclusions increases as more of the guidelines are satisfied.

- Qualitative data analysis is often accomplished with computers, which can assist in coding and retrieving data, analyzing data, testing hypotheses, and engaging in memoing and other strategies that help in conceptualization and theory building.

Important Terms for Review

case study
categorizing strategies
coding
computer-assisted qualitative data analysis
context map
contextualizing strategies
data display
matrix display
memos
narrative analysis
network analysis
profiles

reflective remarks
sociograms
theoretical sensitivity

Exploring InfoTrac® College Edition and the Internet

InfoTrac® College Edition search terms:

qualitative data analysis
qualitative AND coding
qualitative AND hypothesis testing

InfoTrac® College Edition articles:

Using Computer Software for the Analysis of Qualitative Market Research Data. Miriam Catterall, Pauline Maclaran. *Journal of the Market Research Society* July 1998 v40 n3 p207(16) (6,400 words)

Contagion of Deliberate Self-Harm among Adolescent Inpatients. Tero J. Taiminen, Kristiina Kallio-Soukainen, Hannele Nokso-Koivisto, Anne Kaljonen, Hans Helenius. *Journal of the American Academy of Child and Adolescent Psychiatry,* Feb 1998 v37 n2 p211(7)

The Internet is a useful resource for learning about qualitative data analysis. As you try various search strategies, pay attention to the number of different fields in the social sciences and human services that show an interest in this topic. A good way to begin (mentioned in Chapter 9) is to search under such terms as "qualitative methods," "participant observation," or "field research," although the last will produce many sites relating to the natural sciences because they also conduct field research. However, this can produce an important learning exercise: Can you identify the ways in which the research or science discussed at the natural science Web sites is similar to or different from that done by social scientists and discussed in this book? For example, do the natural scientists appear concerned with the positivist versus nonpositivist debate? Beyond these terms, you can search for various terms discussed in this chapter, such as computer-assisted qualitative data analysis, coding, narrative, case studies, and so on.

Look for Web sites that deal with qualitative data *analysis,* not how to conduct field research.

A number of Web sites contain useful information and/or links to other valuable sites. For example, at the School of Social and Systemic Studies at the Nova Southeastern University Web site, "The Qualitative Report" (www.nova.edu/ssss/QR) is an online journal dedicated to qualitative research. The same site has a comprehensive section on ethics in qualitative research (www.nova.edu/ssss/QR/nhmrc.html). Two other comprehensive sites are Resources for Qualitative Research (www.edu.oulu.fi/sos/kvaltutk.htm) and QualPage: Resources for Qualitative Researchers (www.qualitativeresearch.uga.edu/QualPage/). Another good Web site, for the CAQDAS Networking Project (www.soc.surrey.ac.uk/caqdas), includes an extensive bibliography as well as opportunities to review qualitative data analysis software.

For Further Reading

Coffey, Amanda, and Paul Atkinson. *Making Sense of Qualitative Data: Complementary Research Strategies.* Thousand Oaks, Calif.: Sage, 1996. This book focuses on the analysis stage and gives a good overview of the various analysis strategies used, including how computers are used in qualitative data analysis.

Fielding, Nigel G., and Raymond M. Lee. *Computer Analysis and Qualitative Research.* Thousand Oaks, Calif.: Sage, 1998. This book focuses on the ways that computers can be used in qualitative data collection and analysis, including discussions of available software and how qualitative research might change to adapt to computer capabilities.

Flick, Uwe. *An Introduction to Qualitative Research,* 2nd ed. Thousand Oaks, Calif.: Sage, 2002. This book covers all aspects of qualitative research, including how to analyze data and how to present the data visually.

Gahan, Celia, and Mike Hannibal. *Doing Qualitative Research Using QSR NUD.IST.* Thousand Oaks, Calif.: Sage, 1998. These authors describe in clear prose how to use QSR NUD.IST software for analyzing qualitative data. It both explains this software and shows clearly how qualitative analysis is done.

Merriam, Sharan B., ed. *Qualitative Research in Practice: Examples for Discussion and Analysis.* San Francisco: Jossey-Bass, 2002. Qualitative research has been popular in human service fields such as education for decades, and this book gives a good introduction to how to collect and analyze qualitative data in such practice settings.

Richards, Lyn. *Using NVivo in Qualitative Research.* Thousand Oaks, Calif.: Sage, 1999. This book provides a good overview of how CAQDA is done as well as focusing on how to use one fairly popular CAQDA software package.

Rossman, Gretchen B., and Sharon F. Rallis. *Learning in the Field: An Introduction to Qualitative Research,* 2nd ed. Thousand Oaks, Calif.: Sage, 2003. These authors describe the complexity of doing field research while still making the basic data-analysis tools accessible to the student.

Strauss, Anselm, and Juliet Corbin. *Basics of Qualitative Research: Techniques and Procedures for Developing Grounded Theory,* 2nd ed. Thousand Oaks, Calif.: Sage, 1998. This book offers a complete introduction to the data analysis techniques developed to support the grounded theory approach. It is both readable and practical.

Exercises for Class Discussion

16.1   One approach to coding is to enter the field with no preestablished coding scheme. The chapter suggests that four general categories of phenomena should be addressed when doing this kind of field observation: conditions or causes, interactions among people, strategies and tactics, and consequences. Have teams of students conduct observations of various settings for about an hour each. In recording observations, identify examples that would fit each of these four categories. Here are some suggested observation opportunities:

a. children, parents, officials and spectators at a youth sporting event, such as a soccer, junior hockey, or Little League game

b. supermarket checkout area

c. traffic court or misdemeanor court arraignment or sentencing

d. student campus organization meeting

e. local government commission meeting or public hearing on a controversial issue

16.2 Another approach to coding suggested in the chapter is to develop a coding scheme that identifies domains of observation. The text provides an illustration of a listing of possible domains. Using the observation experiences suggested in Exercise 16.1, develop examples that would fit each of the seven domains.

16.3 One of the ways that qualitative researchers visually display data is through sociograms. Construct a sociogram for yourself, based on a social network in which you function, such as fellow employees in a work group, students in your housing unit, or a voluntary organization to which you belong.

Chapter 17

Writing for Research: Grant Proposals and Report Writing

The Grant-Funding Process
Federal Government Funding Sources
State Government Grants
Private Funding Sources
Learning about Funding Opportunities

Grant Proposal Planning
Proposal Development as a Process
Identifying the Topic
Needs Assessment
Specifying the Organization's Mission
Developing a Program
Targeting a Funding Source
Contacting and Visiting Funding Sources

Writing the Grant Proposal
Appearance and Writing Style
Components of the Proposal
Submitting the Proposal

Writing a Research Report
Consideration of the Audience
Organization of the Report
The Process of Writing

Main Points

Important Terms for Review

Exploring InfoTrac® College Edition and the Internet

For Further Reading

Exercises for Class Discussion

This chapter focuses on two important elements of applied research that are often neglected in introductory research methods texts: the role of grants in research and human service practice and the importance of good writing. The term **grant** refers to the provision of money or other resources to be used for either research or service delivery purposes. Grants are an important funding source for social research and the provision of human services. In fact, the amount of grant monies awarded each year is truly staggering. Among the federal government offices dispensing funds, the National Institute of Justice awarded $97 million in 2002 (NIJ 2003) and the Department of Health and Human Services' research, demonstration, and evaluation budget (RD&E) for 2003 totaled almost $2 billion. (DHHS 2002). Private foundations give out grants worth well over $1 billion each year for projects in the social sciences and human services (U. S. Census Bureau 2002). Given the large role grants play in funding research, demonstration projects, and some activities of nonprofit human service organizations, it is highly likely that most future human service practitioners will be directly involved in grant-funded projects during their careers.

Despite the pervasiveness of grants, preparing a grant proposal without previous experience can feel overwhelming. Grant writing is sometimes perceived as a mystical process with strange jargon and convoluted procedures through which only seasoned professionals with an inside track succeed in receiving funds. However, grants range from complex, multi-million-dollar undertakings to fairly modest projects for small agencies. Some universities offer small research grants specifically for undergraduate student research. So preparing a successful funding proposal is an attainable goal even for the beginning human service professional. A neophyte understandably has many questions: What do I do first? Whom do I contact? What do they want to know? Although the prospect of writing the first grant proposal can be daunting, preparing a fundable proposal involves many of the principles of sound practice and research that are part of professional education. Approached systematically, writing grant proposals can be an interesting challenge rather than something to be feared.

In this space we can neither explore all aspects of grantsmanship nor go into much detail. Instead, we will focus on obtaining grants for agency functions, including both service delivery and research purposes. In fact, grants for service delivery typically include a call for needs assessment data and an evaluation of the service delivery; therefore, many grants combine practice and research activities. Depending on the demands of the funding source, minor differences may arise between preparing a proposal for a research project, service delivery, or a combination of the two. Those serious about seeking grants should consult the listings in For Further Reading at the end of this chapter.

The Grant-Funding Process

Sources of grant money fall into three general categories: government agencies, private foundations, and corporations (Bauer 2004; Smith and McLean 1988). Of these, government agencies are by far the largest source of grant monies. They are also about the only sources of grants of more than a few thousand dollars. Even in the case of smaller grants, it often pays to start first with government sources because many of the private foundations refuse funding automatically unless the researcher can prove that efforts to obtain government funding have failed. Among government agencies, branches of the federal government are the largest source for grant money.

Federal Government Funding Sources

The *Catalog of Federal Domestic Assistance* (which we will discuss in more detail at the end of this section) is a key government publication for communicating information about funding opportunities. The catalog identifies seven types of financial assistance provided by the federal government. One of the most important types of federal support is the project or categorical grant (the terms are synonymous). **Project** or **categorical grants** provide funding, for fixed or known periods, of specific projects including research grants, training grants, experimental and demonstration grants, evaluation grants, and planning grants, among others. Grant seekers design approaches, within specified guidelines provided by the government agency, to meet the need or ameliorate the problem specified by the government agency. The agencies make their requests for programs or research opportunities known through what is called a **Request for Proposals** (RFP), a formal request for people or agencies to submit proposals on how they would conduct some research or establish and run some program. Agencies or researchers then submit proposals in a competition to obtain the grant money. Because these grants are awarded selectively on a competitive basis to those submitting the best proposals within the guidelines established by the granting agency, they are also known as **discretionary grants.**

Another type of grant is generally dispensed to all eligible units. A **formula grant** is an allocation of federal money to states or their subdivisions, in accordance with distribution formulas prescribed by law or administrative regulation, for activities of a continuing nature not confined to a specific project. For example, at times of high unemployment, the federal government commonly sponsors various job-creating activities through formula grants. Because various places in the country experience unemployment in varying levels of severity, the money is allocated by a "formula" (hence the name) that provides most of the funds to those areas hardest hit and pro-rates the remainder of the funds to other areas as needed. Normally, formula grants are channeled through state and local governments until they reach the agency level. This allows each state and locality to tailor its approach to the problems of its particular situation. For example, unemployment in one locale may be concentrated among displaced factory workers and in another among minority teenagers. The most effective approach in the first locale may be re-training programs, but the second locale may benefit more from having its teenagers taught basic job skills, such as showing up regularly and on time for work.

The term *block grant* is sometimes used interchangeably with formula grant but generally refers to a package of funding that is created by consolidating several existing programs into one. **Block grants** are awards allocated to states by formula and funded by annual congressional appropriations. A block grant is often a fixed or capped alternative to more open-ended funding approaches. The state government does the final allocating to state agencies and nonprofit service providers. Block grants are special in that they cover broad areas, such as maternal and child health or elementary and secondary education, and are ongoing year after year. For example, the Community Mental Health Services Block Grant is authorized by the Public Health Service Act for the purpose of improving mental health service systems across the country. A stated goal of the program is to promote cost-effective systems of community-based care for people with serious mental disorders (Substance Abuse and Mental Health Services Administration 2003). Although individual human service agencies do not receive federal block grants directly, this type of grant is still important to human service providers because they may be able to access the funds by submitting proposals to the state or local government office that does receive them.

Though not strictly grants, **federal government contracts** also can be an important source of funds. With contracts, the government decides precisely what it wants and how it wants it done, leaving little flexibility to the researcher or service provider. The government then looks for agencies that can perform the desired tasks at the lowest price. Sources of information about contracts and the rules under which they are awarded are different from grants. Also, the number and variety of contracts is vast, so considerable research may be needed to get involved with the contract side of the federal government. However, despite the obstacles, nonprofit agencies are moving into contracts as a new way to fund research and services.

State Government Grants

Although states have always dispersed some of their own tax revenue through the granting process, the rise of federal block grants and the occasional formula grant have greatly expanded the dispersal of funds at the state level. Because each state disperses these monies differently, we cannot make any blanket statements about how to bid successfully for these funds. Regarding block grants, however, something consistent across all states is a federally mandated series of open meetings to discuss how the grant money should be used. The Community Mental Health Services Block Grant follows this procedure. Although showing up and speaking at these meetings will not ensure that a practitioner or agency will get a grant, it will help to ensure that some money is allocated for the area of its greatest concern. Another way to increase the chances of getting state grant monies is to keep in contact with the state departments and agencies that oversee and fund research and services related to the human services, such as the department of corrections, the department of mental health, and the department of social services. These state agencies may also publish RFPs to solicit grant proposals.

Private Funding Sources

A **foundation** is a nonprofit, legally incorporated entity organized for the purpose of dispersing funds to projects that meet the guidelines of its charter. The number of private foundations is staggering—upwards of 35,000 (Bauer 2004). However, not all foundations are created equal. The largest 20 percent of foundations control 97 percent of all foundation assets, so this narrows the number of likely prospects considerably. Second, most foundations award only small grants. Only about 500 foundations typically give grants in excess of $5,000 each.

Submitting a proposal, no matter how noble the purpose or how well prepared the paperwork, that calls for a grant of $20,000 to a foundation that has never awarded more than $5,000 in any one grant is a waste of time. The person looking for a small grant must begin looking at some of the other characteristics of foundations to sort through the possibilities and find those few most likely to fund the proposal. In general, private funding sources are good places to seek grants for agency activities or applied research because they prefer to fund action programs that produce immediate results rather than research

projects that, at best, have some long-term payoff. Also, the complexity of proposal preparation and submission is much less than that encountered with federal agencies.

There are five distinct types of foundations. *Community foundations* exist to serve their immediate local area. Therefore, if a project is modest in scale and serves some local need, a community foundation may be a good choice. *General-purpose foundations* are often large, such as the Ford Foundation, and operate nationwide. If a project is large in scope, with the potential of having an impact broader than just the local community, these large foundations may be ideal. They particularly like innovative demonstration projects that show the way for other communities to solve various problems. *Special-purpose foundations* carve out a particular area of interest and award grants only to projects that deal directly with that area of specialization. Successful funding from these sources requires some research into which foundations fund what kinds of projects. Fortunately, large foundations usually publish annual reports, much as corporations do, outlining recently funded projects (Krathwohl 1988). From these, we can tell what issues and projects various foundations are interested in and willing to support.

Family foundations are the most difficult to categorize because there are so many—more than 30,000, according to Bauer (2004)—and they are so different. Some are large and have the resources to award fairly substantial grants, whereas others have a cap on grant size of a few thousand dollars. Some are quite general in the projects they fund, whereas others have very narrow interests. For example, some fund only projects that benefit a particular religious or ethnic group, whereas others fund only projects that address a particular problem, such as alcoholism or child abuse.

Corporate foundations are used by some corporations as the conduit for corporate philanthropy. Other corporations engage in philanthropy but do not use the foundation mechanism. In either case, nonprofit agencies are common recipients of corporate giving. To maximize the chances of sharing some of this corporate wealth, grant seekers must understand a few things about corporate giving. As investor owned, profit-making enterprises, corporations are giving away stockholders' money. As such, the directors who make the philanthropic decisions are careful to fund only those activities that they can justify to their stockholders. This tends to mean that the corporation or its employees must stand to benefit in some way from funded projects. For example, a nonprofit child care facility used by many corporate employees might receive a corporate grant or other corporate support. Also, because of this need to benefit, corporate giving is concentrated largely in areas where the corporations have their offices, headquarters, or manufacturing facilities.

Learning about Funding Opportunities

Given all the separate agencies and organizations that disperse grants, how do we find specific funding opportunities? Publications and computer databases can help. The *Catalog of Federal Domestic Assistance* (CFDA), for example, is available on the Web (www.cfda.gov/default.htm), and it describes all federal government programs. Detailed information is provided for a vast array of programs. The CFDA explains the objectives of each program, the eligibility requirements, the steps in the application process, examples of funded projects, and criteria for selecting proposals. The Federal Assistance Award Data System (FAADS) can help search the CFDA by providing information on people and organizations that have successfully applied for grants from programs listed in the CFDA (www.census.gov/govs/www/faads.html).

Grant seekers can search for funding opportunities with the "Grants Database" prepared by the Dialog Corporation and Greenwood Publishing Group on the Web (library.dialog.com) or on a CD-ROM. Oryx Press also has a printed version available, titled *Directory of Research Grants.* This is the most comprehensive source of current information on grants offered by government, corporate, and private funding sources. In addition to its convenience, the database has the advantage of monthly updates and contains an extensive and useful list of Web sites related to obtaining funding for research.

Another useful publication is the *Federal Register.* This daily, magazine-sized volume reports on the ac-

tivities of the federal government and is also available online (www.gpoaccess.gov/fr/index.html). Although it includes a lot of information of little use to grant seekers, new programs are announced first in it, so it is a good resource for the ever-changing opportunities in obtaining federal funding. Guidelines for obtaining funding under the new programs are also first provided in the *Federal Register.* Eventually, this information gets into the CFDA, but because that is only published annually, many months can pass before a new program gets listed in the latest edition.

Many funding agencies publish periodic newsletters or bulletins describing their latest activities and programs. It is easy to get on these mailing lists, which often contain RFPs that may unveil a funding opportunity.

An organization called the Foundation Center (www.fdncenter.org) produces a huge amount of material to help in searching for grants. One of its primary publications is *The Foundation Directory,* which contains information on foundations of all types. Figure 17.1 presents an entry from the directory on one organization that funds research. The entry supplies a considerable amount of information about an organization—information that is useful in the sorting-out process. For example, the financial information gives some idea of the size of grants the foundation typically makes. It also provides information on purpose and activities, types of support, and limitations to further screen potential funders. In these sections, we can learn whether a particular foundation provides grants for research purposes (some do not). Also, procedures for making applications are described and memberships of boards of directors provided. For those in the business of seeking grants, *The Foundation Directory* is an essential tool.

Another publication from the Foundation Center, *Foundation Fundamentals: A Guide for Grant Seekers,* is particularly useful for beginners. It outlines the services of the center, along with information on locating foundations and preparing and submitting proposals to private foundations. A special guide to corporate foundations, *Corporate Foundations Profiles,* is also offered by the Foundation Center. This useful

Figure 17.1 Explanation of Sample Entry from *The Foundation Directory*

Entry number

1228

The Philip L. Graham Fund_

Street address

c/o The Washington Post Co.
1150 Fifteenth St., N.W.
Washington 20071 (202) 334-6640

Person to whom inquiries should be addressed

Contact: Mary M. Bellor, Pres.

Establishment data

Trust established in 1963 in DC.
Donor(s): Katharine Graham, Frederick S. Beebe.‡ The Washington Post Co., Newsweek, Inc. Post-Newsweek Stations.
Foundation type: Independent

Year-end date of accounting period
Assets at market value (M) or ledger value (L)
Total expenditures figure
Amount and number of grants paid
Separate information on amount and number of employee matching gifts, grants to individuals, or loans

Financial data (yr. ended 12/31/94): Assets $5,803,245 (M); expenditures, $2,916,512; qualifying distributions, $2,886,262, including $2,826,485 for 145 grants (high: $300,000; low: $1,000; average: $5,000–$25,000).

Areas of foundation giving

Purpose and activities: Support for raising standards of excellence in journalism. Grants also for arts and culture, education, social welfare with an emphasis on youth agencies, and civic and community affairs.
Fields of interest: Journalism & publishing; arts/cultural programs; early childhood education; human services; youth services; community development.

Types of grants and other types of support

Types of support: Capital campaigns; building/renovation; equipment; endowment funds; program development; seed money; matching funds.

Specific limitations on foundation giving by geographic area, subject focus, or types of support

Limitations: Giving primarily in the metropolitan Washington, DC, area. No support for national or international organizations, or for religious organizations for religious purposes. No grants to individuals, or for medical services, research, annual campaigns operating expenses, conferences, publications, tickets, films, or courtesy advertising; no loans.

Printed material available from the foundation

Publications: application guidelines, program policy statement, grants list.

Application information

Applicant information: Application form not required.
Initial Approach: Letter, telephone, or proposal
Copies of proposal: 1
Deadline(s): Feb. 1, Aug.1, and Nov.1
Board meeting date(s): Spring, summer, fall, and winter
Final notification: 6 months

Officers and trustees or other governing bodies

Officers and Trustees:* Mary M. Bellor, Pres.; Martin Cohen,* Treas.; Donald E. Graham, Katharine Graham, Theodore Lutz, Vincent E. Reed, John W. Sweeterman.

Staff

Number of staff: 1 part-time professional

IRS Identification Number

EIN: 526051781

Selected grants

Selected grants: The following grants were reported in 1993.
$60,000 to Federal City Council, DC, 2 grants: $35,000 (For DC COPE (Committee for Public Education)), $25,000 (To develop staffing and management plan for DC Public Schools).
$25,000 to Youth for Tomorrow, Bristow, VA. For residential school for teenage boys.
$20,000 to Allen Community Outreach Center, DC. For social services to poor.
$20,000 to Archbishop Carroll High School, DC. For computer lab for school programs.
$15,000 to Ellington Fund, DC. For Duke Ellington School for the Arts.
$10,000 to Arizona State University, Walter Cronkite School of Journalism and Telecommunication, Tempe, AZ. For equipment for broadcast department.
$10,000 to Dance Exchange, DC. For community outreach programs.
$10,000 to Family Friends of the National Capital Area, DC. For respite care for medically fragile children.
$10,000 to Youth Leadership Metropolitan Washington, Springfield, VA. For youth leadership training.

Source Reprinted with permission from *The Foundation Directory,* 18th ed., copyright © 1996 by the Foundation Center, 79 Fifth Ave., New York, NY 10003.

volume presents detailed descriptions of the largest 250 corporate foundations and less detailed information on 470 more. This directory shows which corporations have operations in which areas and might therefore be likely prospects for funding. The Foundation Center also publishes *The Foundation Center's Guide to Grant Seeking on the Web* and provides a wide variety of other center materials online.

The Annual Register of Grant Support: A Directory of Funding Sources, like *The Foundation Directory,* is an excellent source of information on grant sources. Of particular interest to human service professionals is that funding sources are organized according to funding purposes. One category is "Special Populations," which includes subcategories for African Americans, Native Americans, Spanish-speaking people, and women. Additional listings for children and youth, community development, crime prevention, and public health and social welfare are covered under "Urban and Regional Affairs." Another good source is *The Grants Register* (Waterlow Specialist 2003).

Grant Proposal Planning

The grant-funding process involves two players: the funding sources, who sift through proposals seeking worthy projects in which to invest, and the agencies with project ideas that deserve funding. Getting the two together is the heart of the granting enterprise. Having described the funding sources, we now turn to the second process, namely, the development of a fundable proposal (Locke, Spirduso, and Silverman 2000; Miner and Miner 2003).

Proposal Development as a Process

Let us explode one myth about obtaining grants: Successful proposals are not started and finished in short order. Rather, they are developed in detail and carefully honed over time. The preparation of grant proposals should be considered an ongoing, continuing function within an agency rather than a sporadic event. All too often, grants are begun in haste and rushed to partial completion to meet some fast-approaching deadline. The result, frequently, is rejection.

When conceptualized as a process instead of a single event, grant development has many principles in common with the research process introduced in Chapter 1. When the grant is for the purpose of conducting a research project, the connection with the research process is obvious, but a sound understanding of research principles is also directly applicable to grants for service delivery. In seeking funds, the prospective grantee must identify a problem, hone it into a well-defined and manageable topic, develop objectives for the project, search the literature to devise a method of intervention, and plan an evaluation strategy. Furthermore, just as one research study leads to new questions for study, lessons learned in one grant-funded project lead to new ideas for further projects.

In this section, we describe a number of key elements of the grant-funding process. These are not a series of sequential steps but a number of separate and interconnected elements that can be accomplished in different orders at different times. Some are ongoing agency activities, while others are specific things that must be done at a particular point. Together, they culminate in and make possible the actual writing of the grant proposal.

To promote the concept of the generation of grant proposals as an ongoing part of agency activities, the use of a *proposal development workbook* (PDW) is recommended (Bauer 2004). This loose-leaf binder becomes the mortar that holds the building blocks of a proposal together. As the proposal develops from a vague idea to a full-blown project— complete with demonstration of need, evidence of community support, funding source possibilities, and much more—the PDW organizes everything that goes into a successful proposal as the various components are obtained or completed. Agency staff should be encouraged to watch for items to contribute. For example, favorable news stories about the proposed project are effective demonstrations of community support that help influence funding decision makers. Some of the materials in the PDW for one project might also be useful for a later project.

Identifying the Topic

Before we can begin filling our PDW, of course, we need an idea that can be developed into a fundable proposal. Problems that need to be solved exist in abundance, and many sources of research problems are discussed in Chapter 4. What tends to be in short supply, however, are innovative ways of attacking them. One approach is to organize brainstorming sessions (Bauer 2004), where members of the staff divide into small groups and develop as many possible solutions or approaches to the selected problem as they can. All proposed solutions are recorded for further consideration. The goal is to generate ideas, not come to a consensus as to which solution is best. In fact, it is desirable to maintain alternative approaches to the problem. One or another may be more palatable politically to a particular funding source, and the chances of obtaining a grant can be significantly enhanced by choosing a solution favored by a funding source.

After brainstorming, the next step is evaluation. Thanks to group dynamics, wildly impractical or just plain stupid ideas usually never make it out of the group. Realistically, however, some ideas will be better than others. We want to sort the best few to save for building into a proposal. One important part of this evaluation is to work out cost-benefit or cost-effectiveness analyses (see Chapter 12). The cost-benefit analyses reveal whether the suggested solutions are economically viable. With any luck, one or more of the considered approaches will show benefits outweighing costs. The cost-benefit analyses of the chosen approach will also be important later as they become one of the arguments for funding the proposal. Cost-effectiveness analyses, of course, allow selecting the approaches that produce the greatest effect for the least cost. Being able to argue that the project for which an applicant is seeking funding is the most cost-effective of the several projects considered can only be looked on favorably by decision makers at the funding source.

Needs Assessment

One of the most important components of a successful grant application is establishing the existence of some problem or need that requires amelioration. All funding sources must operate within their annual budgets, so the competition for available funds is fierce. If an agency can make the case that the problem or need it wishes to address is most pressing, that agency greatly increases its chances of being funded.

There are a variety of ways of making a case for your proposal, and those successful include information from more than one source. The core of the evidence supporting the existence of need will likely come from a *needs assessment survey*. With a properly drawn sample, it is possible to make quite accurate estimates concerning the extent of some need within a given population. Additional supporting evidence can come from *key informants,* or people who are particularly close to and knowledgeable about the problem at issue. *Community forums* can gather testimony about the problem. Examples of individuals suffering from the problem can be used as *case studies,* which illustrate the problem in more human terms than abstract statistics. Finally, data from *public records* may be used as additional evidence of need. Bauer (2004) makes the useful analogy between the grant seeker and a lawyer preparing a case for trial. Each wishes to prepare as persuasive a case as possible to influence a set of decision makers (jury or review panel) to reach the desired conclusion. In the case of obtaining grants, documenting need is a crucial part of the process. Just as it is not enough for a defendant to be innocent of the crime to be found not guilty by a jury, it is not enough for a need to exist in order to convince a funding source to fund a relevant proposal. In both situations, evidence must be gathered and the case presented to the decision makers with great care in order to generate a favorable verdict.

In some cases, it may be possible to obtain a grant to conduct needs assessment research. Recall that needs assessment is one of the focal areas considered in this text. Especially with problems we know little about, funding agencies are sometimes willing to fund a survey to obtain more information. In other cases, a funding agency may require that a needs assessment survey be included as part of a larger funding proposal, which may include a service delivery program that affects the problem. In any event, needs assessment often plays an important part in the grant-funding process.

Specifying the Organization's Mission

Not only must the need for services or research be documented, but the funding source must also be convinced that a particular organization is the proper site for a program to address that problem. This entails demonstrating to the funding source that the problem described in the needs assessment is within the applicant's domain or mission. Many organizations, such as universities, have formal mission statements that appear in official publications. However, such statements are often global in nature and may not be adequate for such a purpose. At a minimum, the mission statement should include how and why the organization was started and its primary goals. Generally, funding sources look more favorably on organizations with a history and a track record of accomplishment related to the project to be funded. A new organization might have to work hard to prove its viability. The mission statement should also address current activities of the agency because organizations change with the changing needs of society—an organization that originated for one purpose may be doing something else today. Finally, the mission statement should include future plans. Funding sources like organizations that appear to be serious and well managed. One way of demonstrating this is by showing careful group plans for the future.

Another way to convince a funding source that an applicant is best suited for a particular project is to focus on the uniqueness of that agency. The goal here is to stand apart from others. There is a tendency to think that one agency is not very different from others that provide similar services. But with some thought (and perhaps another brainstorming session), the staff should be able to come up with some characteristics that make it special. Perhaps it is the geographical location, such as a particularly remote area or proximity to a large minority population. Possibly something is unusual about the clientele or staff. Or maybe the problem-solving approach is different and uniquely successful. With a little careful consideration, the grant seeker should be able to develop unique qualifications to address the documented need.

Developing a Program

The most crucial component of any proposal is the research or service project itself. Having established a need, it is necessary to translate that need into specific outcomes for the project and to develop a plan by which those objectives can be achieved. In the case of a research grant, such as a proposal to evaluate the effectiveness of a client advocacy program in a state department of mental health, the task is fundamentally one of preparing a detailed blueprint of the stages of the research process (presented in Chapter 1). Hypotheses must be developed and a method of testing these hypotheses devised. Issues of subject selection, study design, and data collection and analysis must be taken into account. A service delivery grant requires specification of exactly what will be done to address the need. Direct connections between the goals of the project and the program content must be explicated. Even though service delivery may be the primary emphasis of the proposal, most grants require an evaluation component, so a strategy for monitoring the program and securing data for evaluation purposes must be included.

An important consideration is the time sequencing of the project. Before subjects can be interviewed, interviewers must be trained, and instruments need to be selected or developed. How long will each of these steps take? Must certain staff be hired before the activities can take place? Accounting for all these details requires developing a work plan that shows the flow of procedures from beginning to end of the project and identifies how the various activities coordinate. Although a simple time schedule with beginning and ending dates for various phases may suffice for some projects, the use of graphics, such as a flowchart, is often convincing—and may be preferred. Such charts can clearly portray the relationships among elements of the project, when each element begins and ends, and which elements overlap. Planning the steps of the project and determining the amount of time for each requires a great deal of effort, but it is effort well spent. For one, it forces the agency to analyze how the various parts of the program fit and function together. It also serves to uncover difficulties before the proposal is written and approved, avoiding, for example, the discovery midway through the project that some significant and expensive component was overlooked. Finally, when the time comes to develop the budget and ask for dollars, the plan serves as justification for the resources.

A number of tools have been developed to aid in developing the work plan. Two of the most common are PERT (Program Evaluation Review Technique) and CPM (Critical Path Method). With these techniques, a collection of tasks is specified that results in a final outcome, which in this case is the completed project. Circles, rectangles, and arrows graphically illustrate the progression of events. The technical details of PERT and CPM are beyond the scope of this text, but a variety of computer programs are available that employ these program-planning principles. A major advantage of these programs is that we can readily see the budgetary impact of changing situations by manipulating the variables that affect the budget when we play "what if." For example, we could readily determine how much an extra full- or part-time employee would cost over the life of the program by inputting a single number. Likewise, all other costs can be easily evaluated and a final, accurate budget prepared.

Targeting a Funding Source

By this point, the raw material of a proposal—including a clear idea of the problem, data on the need, the preferred program alternative, and cost estimates for the components of that alternative—have been amassed. Before organizing the final proposal, though, consideration must be given to potential funding sources. As a first step, the most appropriate organizations should be identified from among the myriad government agencies and private foundations. However, sending numerous duplicate proposals to whichever funding sources appear most receptive probably will not work. Each proposal must be tuned specifically for each funding source because each has different rules and needs. This re-

quires research into the various funding sources—their rules of submission, project areas they have funded in the past, and their particular political viewpoints. Having created a list of possible funding agencies, the grant seeker begins to narrow the list. One consideration is whether the organization has any advocates who are associated with the funding agency or can make contact with the agency.

By *advocates,* we refer to individuals who not only will speak on the agency's behalf to funding sources but also offer guidance and advice throughout the funding process. Previously, we described the grant seeker preparing a proposal as analogous to a lawyer preparing a case for trial. That analogy applies once again in the area of advocates to help make the case for the grant. The lawyer uses witnesses to help convince a jury. Advocates are the grant seeker's witnesses, supplying testimony favorable to the proposal to funding sources. Like an attorney, grant seekers need to envision how advocates might be viewed and select those who can make the most favorable impression because advocates can play a key role in the final outcome.

The best advocates are people who are favorably disposed toward the agency and the proposed project and who have some influence on the funding source. In this respect, securing grant funding is a political process, requiring strategies similar to those used by practitioners in community practice. The range of people who could help influence a funding source is vast and difficult to discuss in general terms, but some possibilities include people with membership on both the agency's and the funding source's governing boards, members of the agency's staff (don't forget their spouses) with special contacts at funding sources, politicians at all levels who support the agency's efforts, and agency volunteers who may have useful contacts.

Once the advocates are identified, along with the funding sources they can help with, it is time to put them to use. Advocates can be helpful in a variety of ways. At the initial stage, they can help contact representatives of the funding sources in order to establish a working relationship. They can set up appointments with funding sources; they may even accompany grant seekers when visiting a funding source, and they may know someone at the funding source who can help ensure that the proposal receives a fair and complete review. When the proposal has actually been written, advocates can provide letters of support. All these efforts are intended to increase the likelihood that a proposal will receive attention. Funding agencies have limited resources, and they receive many more proposals than they can possibly fund. No matter how numerous or powerful, no collection of advocates substitutes for a worthy project and a well-prepared proposal, so in all of this we are assuming that those two conditions are met. Advocates are important because a meritorious proposal is in competition with others that are also deserving. It is when decision makers are forced to choose from among numerous worthy proposals that advocates come into play.

Contacting and Visiting Funding Sources

Having identified a few agencies or foundations as likely funding sources, contacting them may be the next step. Doing so can sometimes substantially increase the chances of funding (Miner and Miner 2003; Morth and Johnson 1999). Most agencies and organizations today maintain a Web site, and visiting it is a good start to gathering information—sometimes even including funding guidelines and applications. If the research organization has advocates who are associated with the funding agency or can make contact with the agency, they could make the first contact. Otherwise, contact the funding source by letter. Figure 17.2 contains some of the elements that such a letter might include to inform the source of the agency's intent and obtain some much-needed forms and other information. Assuming that the agency's initial response is not negative, such as "no funds available," it may be worthwhile to arrange for a personal or telephone contact to explore research plans and gather more information about the source. Some funding agencies will also review drafts of a grant proposal and make suggestions for revision and improvement.

In some cases, it may be possible to make an actual visit to the funding agency. This is especially fea-

sible with local agencies, such as a county social service department or school district office, and can accomplish three general purposes. First, it will confirm or reject the selection of this organization as a likely funding source. With large federal agencies that offer funding under numerous special programs, information gained during this visit ensures that the grant seeker is applying to the agency most appropriate for the project. For example, a research proposal would probably be rejected if submitted to a program designed to fund action-oriented projects, even though it might have been funded under some other program controlled by the same agency. Second, the visit supplies additional information on how best to tailor the proposal to the funder's special needs, thus increasing the chances for funding. Third, the visit provides a personal touch for the proposal when it is submitted. Instead of representing a faceless organization, the proposal will be from people who are known personally and who made an impressive presentation of a serious need and their plans to fill it. Whether the grant seeker calls, writes, or visits the organization, he or she should check Table 17.1 for suggestions for what to learn about an agency.

Note that one element in Figure 17.2 requests a list of last year's grant recipients. Before finalizing the grant proposal, the grant seeker should contact one or more of these successful organizations. The range of useful information they can supply is vast. They have experience with the agency, and there is no substitute for that in learning the ins and outs of successful grantsmanship with that particular agency. Each agency develops its own particular style of operating as well as a perspective on problems and ways to solve them. It is important to learn about these bureaucratic idiosyncrasies from past grant recipients in order to tailor the proposal to best fit what the agency is looking for.

Writing the Grant Proposal

Having identified a topic, collected supporting documentation that confirms the need for action or research, formulated a method for addressing the

Figure 17.2 Elements to Be Included in a Letter to a Federal Agency to Obtain Information about Grants

---

Superior Shores Youth Advocacy Center

1415 Voyageur Way
Marquette, Michigan 49855

August 10, 2003

Recipient Name, Title, Address

Dear Sir or Madam:

Our organization is interested in carrying out a project under your program title _____. The project will deal with meeting the needs in the area of _____.

Please add me to your mailing list to receive the necessary application forms, program guidelines and any existing priorities statements or information that you feel would be helpful to me. Please include a list of last year's grant recipients under this program.

If my project is ineligible under your current guidelines or there are not funds available, would you please refer me to a more appropriate agency?

I have enclosed a self-addressed stamped envelope for your convenience in returning the list of successful grantees. Thank you for your cooperation and assistance in this matter.

Sincerely,

Name
Title
Phone number/email

Table 17.1 What to Learn about a Granting Agency

- Does the funding agency have a real commitment to funding in the area of the proposed project, as evidenced by previous grants funded?

- Does the amount of funds requested in the proposed grant fit within the granting agency's typical range of funding?

- What proportion of agency grants go to new projects, as opposed to the continuation of currently running projects? Will this proportion change in the coming year?

- Does a new grant from an agency like ours have a chance for funding, especially when competing against those requesting a continuation of funding?

- To see what has worked in the past, can we review grant proposals that have received funding from this agency in the past?

- What are the most common reasons for rejecting a grant proposal submitted to this agency?

- What is the most common mistake that people make when submitting a grant request to this agency?

- Can we submit a draft of our grant proposal to this agency and receive feedback before submitting the final proposal?

- Are there any packaging guidelines that must be followed or the proposal will not be seriously considered (e.g., length, number of copies, binding, format, etc.)?

- What is the deadline for submitting a grant proposal?

problem, and targeted a funding source, you have completed the groundwork. Actually writing the proposal, with the information gleaned from these earlier steps, should be a relatively straightforward endeavor—but it still requires a great deal of care (Miner and Miner 2003). In a number of places in this book, we emphasize that a very important part of both research and practice is to communicate to others about both plans and accomplishments. Such communication can occur at a number of different points in the research process, of which we will emphasize two in this chapter: preparing a grant proposal and writing a research report. Anyone who cannot prepare a comprehensible and convincing grant proposal will not gain the financial support needed to complete a research project. The research findings of anyone who cannot write a clear and thorough research report—no matter how important—cannot be translated into policies and practices by practitioners. We do not pretend that we can create accomplished writers here, but we hope to offer some useful suggestions and point to useful resources.

Appearance and Writing Style

The old adage that you cannot judge a book by its cover may be true, but people routinely make such superficial judgments anyway. Because of this, both outward appearance and style of presentation in a grant proposal are crucial to success. Because demand for grant monies is great, funding agencies may look for any excuse to reject proposals in order to reduce the number that have to be given full review. Failure to follow any guideline may be seized as a reason not to consider a proposal further. So, to begin with, follow the guidelines to the letter, even if they appear senseless. In particular, be careful about length restrictions. Submitting an overly long proposal, no matter how worthy, may result in rejection.

Reviewers have a limited amount of time to review many proposals, so a proposal should be attractive and capable of being skimmed easily. Uncomplicated sentences and short paragraphs work toward this end. Emphasizing key phrases or the use of bullets (solid dots used to set off a series of points in a text) for highlighting purposes helps, too. Different type styles, boldface headings, and variable margins and spacing further contribute to overall appearance and readability. Include charts and graphs to enhance visual impact and convey information in a small space. For example, a graph depicting the increasing incidence of some problem is far more effective at making the point than a simple reference to that fact in the text. The graph is also less likely to be unintentionally passed over by busy reviewers.

Not long ago, great effort and a professional printing company were required to produce a proposal with these desirable features. The advent of word processing and computerized desktop publishing systems, however, has placed the ability to produce high-quality documents within easy reach of most agencies. Such systems are strongly recommended for producing grant proposals—at least some of the competing grant applicants also will produce a slick and attractive grant request. If an agency does not have this kind of technical support available, it may be worth contracting with another organization that can assist in preparing a polished document. Beyond appearance, the style of the text is important. A dull, lifeless proposal, regardless of merit, has less chance of being funded than one that exudes interest and excitement. Use action words and express emotions wherever appropriate. Interest the reviewers in the problem and in the proposed innovative approach to it by reaching them at an emotional level. Citing dialogue is one effective approach: Presenting possible future clients describing their problems in their *own words* is better received than a third-party description. As a general rule, try to maintain a fairly light, readable style.

As in all writing, a sense of one's audience is crucial to preparing a successful grant proposal. Of particular importance is the fact that review panels for both federal agencies and private foundations may contain at least some nonspecialists (Krathwohl 1988). This means that grant seekers must be careful to communicate their intentions in language that is clear to someone who is not a professional in the field. More specifically, jargon should be avoided or, if unavoidable, explained. Beyond that, no assumptions can be made regarding prior knowledge of the problem, its importance, previous approaches, measurement devices, or analytical techniques. Explain everything in detail and in terms a layperson can understand. Doing so and at the same time not boring the specialists requires a difficult balancing act in writing.

Writing a proposal requires such extreme care because the proposal represents the agency to the funding source and is an indicator of the quality of its personnel and of their work. A great idea presented in a sloppy proposal will not get the funding

it deserves. A worthy idea deserves proper presentation so that funding can be obtained to implement it. The ultimate goal, after all, is not just to get grant money but to finance programs that accomplish some good.

After a draft of the proposal is completed and before it is submitted, it is a good idea to have several members of the agency who were not directly involved in its production proofread it. This step is important because people unfamiliar with the proposal will approach it more as a reviewer will, with no prior knowledge of its content. The proposal will have to stand on its own just as it will during review by the funding source. In addition to looking for the usual typographical and grammatical errors, proofreaders should assess the total package for content and presentation. Is all the needed information included? Is the problem adequately documented by the needs assessment? Does the proposed project logically address the problem identified in the needs assessment? Is the budget adequately detailed to justify the requested funds? These and many other questions regarding the content of the proposal should be addressed at this final proofreading stage.

All these suggestions regarding the appearance, style, and presentation of a proposal should not distract from the central importance of the proposed project itself. No amount of fancy wrappings will make up for an ill-conceived idea. The importance of these matters is to separate one agency's deserving proposal from all the other deserving proposals, to the point that yours gets funding.

Components of the Proposal

A typical proposal to a government agency or major foundation will contain most or all of the components shown in Table 17.2, probably in the order listed. The precise components depend on the requirements of the specific agency or organization and on whether the proposal is to fund research, service delivery, or both. Notice that the order in Table 17.2 is quite different from the grant development sequence because the proposal is organized according to the needs of the reader and not necessarily according to the order in which one prepares the parts.

Table 17.2 Typical Proposal Contents and Sequence

1. Cover letter	6. Methods
2. Title page	7. Evaluation
3. Summary	8. Future funding
4. Problem/Need	9. Dissemination
5. Objectives	10. Budget
	11. Attachments

Table 17.3 Title Page Specifications

1. Title of project
2. Program being applied to
3. Grant program contact person
4. Name, position, and institutional affiliation of principal investigator
5. Name of other sources, if any, to which you have applied for funding for this project
6. Proposed start-up date and anticipated completion date

The Cover Letter. The cover letter is probably the last item to be completed, but because it is the first thing read by those who will evaluate your proposal, it is crucial. One important function of the cover letter is to remind agency personnel of who the grant seeker is and that he or she bothered to visit the funder and take into account their suggestions when designing the proposal. The idea is to show that everything has been done right (according to the funder's views) so that, now, the proposal deserves careful consideration.

Title Page. The title page is often a standard form supplied by the granting organization. Table 17.3 illustrates the common elements of a title page. A good title is one that describes the project and communicates the anticipated results. Thus, the title "Reducing Homicide in Family Disputes" is preferable to "Applying Mental Health Crisis Intervention Techniques to Family Violence" because the first title indicates what the project plans to achieve with the funds, whereas the second merely describes a service. Beyond serving as a label for the proposal, the title page will route the application to the various officials who must process it. The page should clearly identify the applicant's name and address as well as the specific program being applied for and the granting organization contact person.

Summary. Most granting agencies request a brief summary of the proposal so that agency administrators can quickly assess who should receive a copy. This should be no more than a paragraph and should briefly mention all elements of the proposal: research problem or service to be delivered, methods used, and anticipated results.

The Problem or Needs Statement. This is where the applicant really begins to make the case. What should go here has already been discussed in the previous section while analyzing the needs assessment and mission of the organization. What must be done in the proposal is put clearly and coherently into prose, describing what the problem is and why this agency can help solve it.

Objectives. Objectives state very clearly and precisely what the proposal will achieve—exactly what research will be done or what service will be delivered in concrete and achievable terms. No funding agency will be impressed if the objective is to "discover the real truth about spouse abuse." A more concrete objective would be to learn about the role of economic independence in the ability of women to avoid abuse. List all the objectives with no more than a sentence or two devoted to each and present them in the order of their potential importance and contribution, with the most important first. In a research proposal, this section should contain theoretical considerations and the development of hypotheses.

Methods. The proposal should include a complete description of how the applicant plans to conduct research or provide a service. In a research proposal, this section should contain all the mechanics of carrying out the research: sample size, sampling technique, research design, and statistical procedures to be used in analyzing the data.

Evaluation.
Federal funding sources place particular emphasis on evaluation. It is politically (as well as practically) important to gather evidence that shows that the funded activities are achieving the objectives claimed for them. Therefore, virtually all proposals must contain adequate methods for assessing whether and how well the program is achieving its goals. In a service delivery grant, this typically involves conducting research to assess whether the program resulted in the improvements or changes intended. (A review of Chapter 12 along with some of the suggested readings should be helpful in preparing this part of the proposal.)

Future Funding.
A grant, by its very nature, is a one-time dispersal of funds. Human service organizations, on the other hand, typically support ongoing programs that require continuous funding. The disjunction between the one-time grant and the ongoing needs of the program should be addressed in the proposal. What happens when the grant money ends? The agency will want to see that this problem has been thought through and plans made to deal with it. Plans for local funding, other grants, fundraisers, telethons, and so on should be included. Agencies like to see lasting and successful programs develop out of their seed money. Inclusion of money in the budget for future fund-raising efforts is perfectly appropriate.

Dissemination.
Dissemination refers to spreading the word about the research, service delivery program, the grant, the funding source, and, we hope, successes. Inclusion of comments regarding dissemination of results is looked on as an indicator of confidence. Agencies like positive publicity about the good that they do and tend to look favorably on opportunities to obtain it. This is a small item; alone it will not secure funding, but successful grantsmanship is ultimately a result of doing a lot of little things right and better than the competition.

Budget.
A carefully detailed budget is an important part of any grant proposal because granting agencies are punctilious in their accounting demands of grant recipients. Table 4.3 on page 94 provides an example of a research budget for a survey interview, showing the major elements that would be included in a budget. Essentially, every dollar requested must be accounted for. The methods section of the proposal, which spells out precisely what the program will do, provides the guide for developing the budget. All costs that will be incurred must be identified and included. Novice grant seekers often underestimate costs or leave out expenses. Because the developers of the project are usually researchers or practitioners and not financial officers, it is important to seek consultation in determining costs. The grant seeker's agency may have standard formulas for fixing fringe benefit costs, travel, and overhead and may require bidding procedures for purchasing equipment. But the budget must be realistic. Promising the moon on a shoestring budget will not endear the proposal to a funding source. It will merely be seen as the amateurish effort it is. If costs are reasonable and well justified, it may be possible to negotiate reductions if the total amount is too high.

Attachments.
The attachments section provides important supporting evidence for claims made elsewhere in the proposal. Bauer (2004) suggests the following as appropriate for inclusion in the attachments section: needs assessment and supporting research, résumés of key personnel, minutes of advisory committee meetings, names of board members, auditor's financial statement, letters of support from advocates, evidence of tax-exempt status from the Internal Revenue Service, any pictures or diagrams, and copies of any organization publications.

Documentation of community support is also important. Some funding sources demand a demonstration that the community is behind a project, but this should be provided even for those who do not require it. Evidence of community support generally comes from two sources: advisory board minutes and newspaper articles. Many agencies of the type we are discussing here have advisory boards that oversee their operations. These boards—comprised primarily of other professional service providers, former consumers of the agency's services, and people whose expertise lies in the area of fund-raising—hold regular meetings to discuss the activities of the agencies they oversee. Minutes from meetings when the project for which funding is being sought was discussed can be used as evidence of community support. Newspaper articles reflecting positively on the project form the other major source of evidence of community support. Grant seekers can actively seek publicity for the agency and the project they are trying to get funded.

Submitting the Proposal

Public funding sources have quite rigid guidelines, not to mention firm deadlines, that govern the submission process. Applicants, of course, have to obtain these along with all other relevant information from the funding agency. Because deadlines are involved, the proposal should be submitted either in person or by registered mail. In either case, it is a good idea to telephone the funding source to verify receipt.

With many of the private foundations, generalizing about submission procedures is difficult because each foundation has its own peculiar way of doing business. This places an added burden on the grant seeker. In some cases, private foundations do not require the lengthy and detailed proposals we have described. They do not have the resources in the form of reviewers to evaluate such complex documents. Instead, they rely on what is called the *letter proposal* (Miner and Miner 2003). As the name suggests, the letter proposal outlines the need, plans to meet that need, and the grant request, all in a fairly brief letter of no more than a few pages in length. Even something as important as the budget is abbreviated. Usually, the estimated total cost is all that is required. Rather than the voluminous detail characteristic of a federal proposal, each important issue in the letter proposal must fit into a paragraph. Brevity and clarity are the watchwords of a letter proposal.

Because the applicant has done the homework, chances are good that the grant will be approved. But what if it is not? Understandable disappointment aside, rejection is an opportunity to learn. The applicant may contact the funding source and inquire about what was wrong (and right) about the proposal. He or she can learn from them how to do a better job the next time. The only grant seekers never turned down are those who never submit a proposal. It is the nature of the game.

Grantsmanship is an exciting and increasingly essential element of human service research and practice. We hope that this chapter has made the prospect of preparing a grant proposal less daunting. Remember, however, that we have been able to present only a limited amount of material on obtaining grants. We strongly recommend that you read carefully a complete book devoted to grantsmanship.

Writing a Research Report

One of the strengths of the scientific method is the public character of scientific results. Publicizing scientific findings accomplishes several important functions. First, unless research findings are made public, they accomplish little social good. How can others learn from the findings of research if those findings are withheld? Clearly, publication of research findings is necessary in order to apply those findings in developing programs and policies.

Second, publication allows the process of replication to ferret out errors, frauds, and falsehoods that inevitably creep into the products of human endeavor. The self-correcting nature of science that has contributed so much to its success depends on the wide dissemination of research results.

Third, publication of research findings makes attempted suppression of those findings more difficult. Recall that in Chapter 12 we noted that historically this had been a problem for evaluation research reports. A few copies were supplied to a sponsor, who then had complete control over what was or was not done with the results. Broader publicity concerning research findings makes it more likely that such findings will come to the attention of someone who will use them.

Finally, the publication of research findings, like any written publication, is an effort at persuasion, an attempt to influence the readers to accept specific ideas or conclusions. Chapter 3 discusses the idea of advocacy in research and shows that human service researchers are especially likely to advocate some particular use of their research findings. To be effective, advocates must communicate positions to others, and one major mode of communication is through the written word. An interesting, well-written, and smooth presentation is more likely to be persuasive.

Given the central role that communication of research results plays in the entire scientific enterprise, proper preparation of the research report is vital. In this section, we assume that knowledge of appropriate English grammar and usage. The complexity of the English language being what it is, we strongly recommend consulting one or more of the style manuals listed in For Further Reading. No matter how well we think we write, our writing always benefits from regular application of a style manual.

Consideration of the Audience

An important consideration before beginning any writing assignment is the intended audience. For the writing to be most effective, it must be tailored to its specific audience. Although it is possible to identify several distinct audiences for research reports, the most significant distinction is between a *professional audience* and a *lay audience*. Of course, within these two broad categories are several more specific audiences that may require special consideration. Not all professionals are created equal. Even in the social sciences and human services, those pursuing research careers develop a different expertise and professional jargon than those following a more practice-oriented career. Likewise, those concentrating on clinical practice gain different expertise from those in administration or community practice. They may all be professionals within the same discipline, but they do not share the same knowledge. It is important to keep these distinctions in mind when writing reports.

When a report is aimed at an audience of other professionals, we can make certain assumptions such as familiarity with basic concepts of the discipline and knowledge of common statistical terms. Although these assumptions make writing for other professionals easier, such an audience is likely to be more critical of such things as following a proper format, elements of style, and substantive content.

If the intended audience is the lay public or others less familiar with research and the human services, we cannot make those assumptions. Instead, we must minimize the use of professional jargon, which is likely to be meaningless or possibly misleading to such an audience. Occasionally, jargon cannot be avoided. Social science disciplines do not make up jargon for its own sake but to enhance precision or to describe phenomena that everyday language does not have words for. When used, professional jargon should be carefully explained to lay readers. Presentation of data to a lay audience must also be simplified. They probably will not know what a probability coefficient is and may even have difficulty grasping the importance of a percentage table. Instead, the visual impact of graphs and charts helps get the message across. Also, explain fully what each statistic used accomplishes and what the result means. Professionals who do not work routinely with statistics and data analysis may also need some of this sort of assistance. If we believe in the importance of our research and want it to be useful, careful attention to our audience will further that goal immensely.

Because different journals are read by different audiences, requirements of professional periodicals vary from one publication to another. If a research report is being prepared for possible publication, care must be taken to follow the specifications of the particular journal to which the manuscript will be submitted. A helpful resource toward this end is *An Author's Guide to Social Work Journals* (NASW Press Staff 1997). Published by the National Association of Social Workers, the guide includes more than 130 social work, social welfare, and human service journals. Readers will find information on the journal's review process, editorial focus, format, and suggested style guide. In addition, the guide indicates where each journal is abstracted and indexed.

Organization of the Report

Despite the variation depending on the audience, research reports usually include most or all of the following elements.

Title.   The title is an important part of a report and the first element a reader sees. The major function of the title is to give prospective readers an idea of what the study is about so they can decide whether they are interested in reading further. Therefore, a good title informs the reader about the major independent and dependent variables and, possibly, the major findings. A second reason to develop a good title is that online library searches discussed in Appendix A use key words in titles as one means of selecting articles. Therefore, a report with a misleading or poor title may be lost from these searches. The following examples are from a recent issue of a social work journal:

- Socialization and the Belief Systems of Traditional-Age and Nontraditional-Age Social Work Students
- The Korean Protestant Church: The Role in Service Delivery for Korean Immigrants
- The Effect of Short-Term Family Therapy on the Social Functioning of the Chronic Schizophrenic and His Family

Note that each of these titles provides sufficient information for a reader to decide whether to pursue the article further and for a computer retrieval system to identify key words.

Abstract.   Most scientific journals and reports contain an abstract, which is a brief summary of the study that allows the reader to learn enough to decide whether to read the whole report. (Some examples of this type of abstract are presented in Chapter 4.) Abstracts are also often published in reference volumes or online in searchable databases, some of which are discussed in Appendix A. In these collections, the abstracts allow the reader to decide whether to locate the complete articles. Because of their importance and brevity (125–175 words), abstracts must be carefully written. The first sentence

should be a clear statement of the problem investigated by the study. The research methodology and sampling techniques are then indicated. A brief summary of findings and conclusions completes the abstract. Figure 17.3 shows an abstract with its component parts identified.

Introduction and Problem Statement.   The first part of the body of the report states the research problem and its importance, including a literature review of the history of the problem in previous research and theory. This material indicates how the current study flows from that which has gone before. Presentation of the theoretical material sets the stage for presenting the hypotheses that were tested in the study. Of necessity this section must be kept relatively brief. For example, the literature review typically consists of numerous citations of previous work on the topic area, with comments on only the most relevant aspects of each study. This emphasis on brevity should not be overdone, however. Clarity of presentation in this section is a must—without it, the remainder of the report loses its meaning.

Methods.   The methods section describes the sample that was studied and the research techniques employed. It also shows how concepts are operationalized and what measurement devices, such as scales, were used. This section is important because it provides the basis on which the validity and generalizability of conclusions will be judged. It is also the basis for any future replication efforts. As such, this section must be written with sufficient detail so that it can perform both of these functions. Readers must be able to tell precisely what was done in the study and who participated.

Results.   This section is a straightforward presentation of the findings of the study, devoid of any editorializing or comment as to the meaning of the results. That comes later. Typically, the presentation of results involves the use of tables, graphs, and statistics. The one exception to this is the results from a participant observation study, which is likely to have little quantitative data. As noted previously, you

Figure 17.3 Example of an Abstract, with Its Component Parts Identified: 1. Statement of problem, 2. Sample selection, 3. Method of study, 4. Results

507. ARNTZ, A. & VAN DEN HOUT, M.
Psychological treatments of panic disorder without agoraphobia: cognitive therapy versus applied relaxation.
Behavior Research and Therapy, 34(2): 113–21, Feb. 1996.
Dept. of Medical Psychology, Univ. of Limburg, PO Box 616, NL-6200 MD Maastricht, The Netherlands

1 { This study compared two psychological treatments of panic disorder and tested whether cognitive therapy (CT) was superior to applied relaxation (AR); and whether treatment was superior to waiting, Thirty-six outpatients of the community

2 } mental health center with the DSM-III-R diagnosis of panic disorder with no or mild agoraphobia were randomly assigned to CT or AR. Eighteen similar patients who were referred after the treatment conditions were complete constituted a waiting-list group. Treatment consisted if 12 weekly sessions. Patients

3 { self-monitored panic attacks during the whole treatment period, and the following four weeks, and during one week at a half-year follow-up. Questionnaires were filled out before and after treatment, and at four-week and half-year follow-ups. After the first follow-up additional treatment was provided if clinically indicated. One patient dropped out of AR and was replaced.

4 } Treatment was superior to waiting in reducing panic and questionnaire scores. CT was clearly superior to AR in reducing panic frequency, and somewhat less strongly superior to AR in reducing the questionnaire scores. Depending on the assessment point, 77.8–83.3 percent of the CT patients was panic-free after treatment, compared to 50 percent of the AR and 27.7 percent of the waiting-list patients. In conclusion, cognitive therapy for panic is especially effective in reducing the incidence of panic attacks. (Journal abstract, edited.)

should consider your audience and fashion your presentation so the data can be readily understood.

Discussion. In this section, conclusions are drawn regarding the implications of the data presented in the results section. Each tested hypothesis should be related to relevant data and a conclusion stated about the degree of support (or nonsupport) the data provide for it. Beyond that, any broader im-

plications of the findings for research, practice, or social policy should be noted. Any limitations or weaknesses of any of the results should be honestly noted as well. Often, research results raise new questions as they answer others. Therefore, it is common practice to identify opportunities for future research.

References. A list of all works cited in the report is usually presented as the last element of the report.

A variety of formats can be used, but the one known as the *Harvard method* is common in the social sciences. As sources are cited in the body of the text, the author's last name and date of publication are placed in parentheses at the end of the sentence. The references are then listed in alphabetical order by the first author's last name at the end of the report. An alternative format is called the *serial method,* in which the citations are indicated numerically in the body of the text. The references are then presented in the reference section, with each reference identified by the number associated with it in the text.

Preparing a list of references or a bibliography for a grant or research report is generally a difficult and not very pleasant task. All the names of the authors must be spelled correctly, the page numbers and dates must be correct, and the punctuation is not like that used anywhere else. Computer software, however, can take some of the drudgery out of preparing bibliographies. Bibliography-formatting software creates a file of references with all the required information for each reference (still a lot of work). Once the file is complete, the program reformats and prints the information in a variety of popular bibliography styles. In addition, some programs interface with word-processing programs and search documents for citations and make up a correct bibliography from the file of references. It also flags any citations not in the file and any references in the file that are not cited. When revising a long document (such as a book or grant proposal), this feature can save a lot of work and reduce errors. Bibliographic software does not do all of the busywork, but it can reduce the drudgery considerably and greatly enhance the accuracy of the finished product.

The Process of Writing

It is not possible, of course, to cover in a brief chapter all the elements involved in writing. This is done in writing courses and through practice at writing. However, a few points are of special importance.

First, writing is a process rather than a product. We never finish writing, although we may finish a paper or a report because it has to be submitted by a deadline. However, this doesn't mean that we couldn't write and

revise further. Writing aims at the expression and communication of clear thought. It is difficult to write because, in some respects, language is a poor mechanism for communicating the subjective reality of our thoughts. If we hear that someone was almost hit by a car on the way to school this morning, words like "car" and "hit" seem straightforward and comprehensible. But do those words encompass the experienced reality? It was a bright red car, and it was speeding, and the driver seemed not to notice, and . . . How much detail communicates an experience? We say we were frightened by the close call and then realize we cannot make clear the wrenching terror, and so we repeat that we were "really" frightened, using qualifiers, emphasis, and inflection to make our point. The words seem inadequate to communicate the experience, but this is precisely the challenge that any writer confronts: using words to describe a very complex and confusing reality. Researchers face the challenge of using words to describe a very complex theoretical and methodological reality to various audiences.

A second point, which really flows from the first, is that rewriting and revision are an inherent part of the writing process. Few writers are capable of making the first draft the final draft. Most writers, especially professional writers, must rewrite their material several times before they consider it clear, comprehensible, and smooth. (The term "smooth" in this context simply means the writing contains few errors or awkward constructions that distract the reader from the content.) One of the keys to revision is to be able to read the prose through the eyes of the intended audience. Would they understand a particular word, phrase, or sentence? Can they follow the sequential organization in the report? Do they grasp the transitions that move the reader from one sentence to another, from one paragraph to another? What is perfectly clear from the writer's perspective may be muddled and unclear from the reader's. The writer's talent is to perceive his or her writing from that other perspective.

Rewriting is an essential if sometimes tedious task, and it is also creative. As with other creative efforts, the energy and attention needed to create is greater at some times than at others. This means that the best writing is usually not produced in one sitting. Most writers find it useful to approach revisions after they have been away from a paper for some time. This enables them to work on it with fresh insight and attention. For this reason, words written at the last minute, with a deadline rapidly approaching, may not be the best words after all.

Main Points

- Grants have become a very important source of funding for both social research and human services. To gain funding successfully, grant proposals must be written well.
- Sources of grant money fall into three categories: government agencies, private foundations, and corporations, with government the largest source.
- Government funds come in a number of different forms: project (categorical or discretionary) grants, formula grants, block grants, federal contracts, and state government grants.
- Although many foundations fund grants, most fund only small projects and some fund research on only limited subject areas. Corporations tend to fund grants that can be justified to the stockholders, such as for services or improvements from which the corporation or its employees will benefit.
- Many funding sources can be located through online computerized search services.
- The preparation of grant proposals should be considered an ongoing, continuing function of a human service agency. The steps in the grant development process are analogous to the steps in the research process.
- The first step in grant development is to identify a fundable topic; this can be assisted by conducting a needs assessment.
- Once the project has been identified, the next step is to target a funding source that will be interested in the project; this might call for visits to potential funding sources to assess their interest.
- To be successful, grant proposals must be written well, and this requires paying attention to the appearance and to the writing style. Proposals must be neat, interesting to read, and addressed to the audience that will read them.
- A grant proposal should contain all the components necessary to provide a funding source with adequate information to assess it.
- Research reports should also be well written because the communication and publication of scientific results accomplish important functions for science.
- A research report should be written at the level of the audience for whom it is intended. These might be researchers conversant with the jargon of research and statistics, practitioners unfamiliar with such jargon, or the lay public.
- Most research reports include the following elements: title, abstract, introduction and statement of the problem, description of methods and results, discussion of the implications of the findings, and list of references.

Important Terms for Review

block grant
categorical grant
discretionary grants
federal government contracts
formula grants
foundation
grant
project grant
Request for Proposal (RFP)

Exploring InfoTrac® College Edition and the Internet

InfoTrac® College Edition search terms:

block grant
discretionary grant
foundation AND human services
grant proposal
grant writing

InfoTrac® College Edition articles:

Strategies for Grant Writing That Turn Plans into Dollars. Pam Nutt. *Multimedia Schools* Nov–Dec 2001 v8 i6 p28(3) (1,500 words)

Writing a Winning Grant Proposal. Jon M. Shane. *The FBI Law Enforcement Bulletin* May 2003 v72 i5 p12(10) (4,954 words)

Some of the major governmental human service sites have extensive material on grants, including abstracts of funded projects and RFPs that you can examine to better understand the issues of writing successful proposals. For example, the Justice Information Center (www.ncjrs.org) has extensive information available on grants from the National Institute of Justice, the Office of Juvenile Justice and Delinquency Prevention, the Office for Victims of Crime, the Bureau of Justice Assistance, and other grant opportunities from the Department of Justice. Just enter the word "grants" in its search engine.

You can also go to the Web page for the *Catalog of Federal Domestic Assistance* (www.cfda.gov), which, as is pointed out in this chapter, is a government-wide compendium of federal programs, projects, services, and activities that provide assistance or benefits to the public. It contains financial and nonfinancial assistance programs administered by departments and agencies of the federal government. The Internet site has a search engine where you can query the catalog. By entering terms for human service issues, you can quickly locate information about related grant opportunities.

A good way to get a better sense of how to write grant reports is to read some completed studies. One source you might try is the Department of Justice (www.ojp.usdoj.gov/vawo/statistics.htm). You can easily search their databases and review abstracts of completed projects. The references indicate where and how to obtain complete reports. Another excellent location is the National Science Foundation (www.nsf.gov). Click on "Social, Behavioral Sciences" or on "Grants and Awards."

Various granting organizations provide application materials, including instructions for completion, right on the Web. A good example is the Substance Abuse and Mental Health Services Administration (www.samhsa.gov/funding/funding.html). Another site worth exploring for excellent information on grants, including examples of actual grant applications, submission procedures, and budget, is the National Institutes of Health site (grants1.nih.gov/grants/index.cfm). *The Philanthropy News Digest* (fdncenter.org/pnd/) is a high-quality source for keeping grant seekers informed on foundations and funding opportunities.

For Further Reading

Beebe, Linda. *Professional Writing for the Human Services.* Washington, D.C.: NASW Press, 1993. This handbook provides valuable information to help authors improve their writing and publish in professional journals.

Brown, Larissa G., and Martin J. Brown. *Demystifying Grant Seeking: What You Really Need to Do to Get Grants.* San Francisco: Jossey-Bass, 2001. This book takes the reader through the steps of setting up a usable office, making matches between agencies and foundations, writing grant applications, and evaluating the process. The authors use one agency as an example, taking the reader through the entire process.

Chicago Manual of Style, 15th ed. Chicago: University of Chicago Press, 2003. Prepared by the editorial staff of the University of Chicago Press, the Chicago Manual has long been considered the definitive writing reference work. If you take your writing seriously, you should have a copy.

Cuba, Lee. *A Short Guide to Writing about Social Science,* 4th ed. New York: Longman, 2002. This book is a good review of what you need to know about writing research papers and preparing presentations on topics in the social sciences.

Hall, Donald, and Sven Birkerts. *Writing Well,* 9th ed. Reading, Mass.: Addison-Wesley, 1997. Hall, the author of dozens of books, brings his experience and expertise to a book that can help anyone improve his or her writing. Unlike many such books that present the rules in a rather stiff and direct fashion, Hall makes learning to write interesting.

Henson, Kenneth T. *Grant Writing in Higher Education: A Step-by-Step Guide.* Boston: Allyn & Bacon. 2004. This is a practical resource for developing effective grant proposals. Strengths of this resource are sections on preparing budgets and locating funding sources.

McIlnay, Dennis P. *How Foundations Work: What Grant-Seekers Need to Know about the Many Faces of Foundations.* San Francisco: Jossey-Bass, 1998. The author explores the customs and unique cultures of foundations to better understand the qualities that set them apart from other types of organizations. Provides an understanding of foundations with recommendations for grant makers.

Miner, L. E., J. T. Miner, and J. Griffith. *Proposal Planning and Writing,* 2nd ed. Phoenix: Oryx Press, 1998. This is another excellent guide to developing grant proposals for research or other types of grants.

Ogden, Thomas E., and Israel A. Goldberg. *Research Proposals: A Guide to Success,* 3rd ed. San Diego: Academic Press, 2002. This book focuses on research grants and includes topics not found in more general works. It covers the NIH and other sources of research support. The book addresses components of a research proposal such as preliminary studies, research design and methods, and human subjects.

Ries, Joanne B., and Carl G. Leukefeld. *Applying for Research Funding: Getting Started and Getting Funded.* Thousand Oaks, Calif.: Sage, 1995. This book is an excellent overview of the steps in preparing a successful grant application for research in the human services.

Yuen, Francis K. O., and Kenneth L. Terao. *Practical Grant Writing and Program Evaluation.* Belmont, Calif.: Wadsworth, 2003. This brief and practical text covers program planning, grant writing, and program evaluation, with emphasis on the interrelationship between these components. Readers will learn the development and the implementation of grant proposals, program evaluation plans, data collection and analysis, and report writing.

Exercises for Class Discussion

17.1 Portage Bay is a resort-oriented, medium-sized city of about 40,000 persons. Recently, the city council has been receiving numerous complaints from downtown merchants about vagrants and homeless people taking over the parks and public areas along the waterfront mall. A large mental institution is located near the city, and deinstitutionalized patients are accused of driving tourists away and hurting sales. Representatives of several organizations such as the Community Mental Health Center and Community Action Agency counter that the mentally ill are also residents and are being unfairly blamed for the problem. The advocates for the patients contend that the services are inadequate to meet the needs of the homeless in the community. A task force is formed to study the problem and develop a plan to resolve the conflict with the merchants while meeting the community's desire to be compassionate and meet the needs of the homeless. It becomes immediately clear that outside funding will be necessary to do a comprehensive study and to implement a plan of action.

a. Make a list of materials to which the task force might turn to locate funding sources. Do you think government grants or foundation grants would be more appropriate?

b. By using the *Catalog of Federal Domestic Assistance* and the *Monthly Catalog of Government Documents,* identify a list of several potential grant sources related to the problem faced by the city of Portage Bay.

17.2 Request sample grant application forms from organizations in your state that fund human service research projects. Your college or university probably has an office of research and development that can provide the guidelines, or you might contact such agencies as the state departments of mental health, social services, or corrections.

a. Compare the grant applications in terms of the kind and detail of information that each requires.

b. For each application, determine the problems for which the granting organization dispenses funding. What special priorities, if any, does the granting organization specify? Who is eligible to apply for the grant?

17.3 Select a human service–related research article from a recent professional publication and review it from the standpoint of the criteria presented in the discussion of writing a research report.

a. To what audience does the article appear to be addressed (e. g., professional social workers, researchers, or the general public)?

b. Is the title effective?

c. Is there an abstract? If so, does it communicate the necessary information?

d. Examine the organization of the study to determine if it contains the basic components described in the text. How are the problem statement, methods description, results, and discussion handled by the author(s)?

Appendix A

A Guide to Library Use and Information Retrieval

A key part of all scientific research is information retrieval: finding the information to conduct sound research. Information retrieval is central to virtually all the steps in the research process: reviewing existing literature to see what has been done on a particular topic, gaining help in developing a research design, locating existing scales, and so on. Good information retrieval today requires two types of knowledge: how to use the physical library and how to search for information online.

A library is both a repository of information and a gateway for accessing information stored at other sites. Libraries own some of the information products they make available to customers, and libraries assist customers in locating and accessing information resources at other libraries or other locations. However, because of the proliferation of information retrieval technologies these days, finding pertinent information can be a daunting task for those unfamiliar with modern technologies of information retrieval and processing. Effective information retrieval requires a number of things: first, precise definition of what is needed; second, a determination of the best strategy for locating that information; and third, an evaluation of the information found. This appendix focuses primarily on the second step by providing a basic introduction to library usage and online information retrieval technologies. In addition, we point to some specific resources in the library and online that are especially useful to practitioners in the human services.

Organization of the Library

Two key elements in the organization of a library must be understood for effective library use. First, the library contains certain *departments* that perform special functions in the search for information. Second, the library contains a number of important mechanisms for *accessing information*.

Library Departments

One of the most valuable departments in the library for students seeking materials is the *reference depart-*

ment. In most libraries, the reference department contains the basic tools for searching for information: encyclopedias, indexes, abstracts, dictionaries, handbooks, yearbooks, government documents that summarize statistical data, and an array of other such resources. Familiarity with this department is critical. In addition to its materials, the reference department's reference librarians are a valuable asset. Highly trained and knowledgeable about how to locate materials, librarians have as one of their major duties helping library patrons. Working closely with a reference librarian enables students not only to locate a specific item but also to learn the techniques of thorough and efficient searching for materials. Students should probably try to locate materials themselves first but not to hesitate to consult a reference librarian if they have difficulties.

Without access to a very large library, such as at Harvard University or the University of California, Berkeley, we undoubtedly find that some needed books or resource materials are not readily available. This is where the *interlibrary loan department* comes in. Most libraries participate in an interlibrary loan program that permits them to borrow books, copies of journal articles, or other materials from other libraries. Libraries use computers to locate materials in libraries in their region, around the nation, and in some cases around the world. All participating libraries benefit because they can provide a greater range of materials and services to patrons than their own budgets allow. Books are usually sent by mail from one library to another, with the borrower often paying a fee for each item. As a part of their interlibrary loan service, libraries also participate in a periodical reprint service through which library patrons can request a duplicated copy of an article from a periodical.

Libraries also provide *copy machines* for photocopying certain library materials for a nominal fee. Most libraries also have machines that will make copies from microfilm or microfiche because some old journals and newspapers have been put on microforms to save space. Copying materials is important because it gives the researcher a permanent copy of materials that cannot be removed from the library. In using copying equipment, however, researchers should be familiar enough with federal copyright laws to avoid violating them. Normally, reproducing one copy of a journal article or book chapter for private use is permissible.

The *documents division* of the library houses government publications, magazines, pamphlets, and sometimes collections of special books. Many government documents are now issued on microfiche or online. In a small library, the documents division might be integrated with the reference department.

Another library service that gives patrons greater access to materials is the table-of-contents and document-delivery services. *Table-of-contents services* make available the tables of contents of thousands of periodicals, providing author and title as well as other information relevant to accessing the articles. This means that a user can review the contents of many journals rapidly, even journals not owned by the library he or she is using. Two online table-of-contents services are Infotrieve (infotrieve.com) and Ingenta (ingenta.com). *Document-delivery services,* often a part of table-of-contents services, actually deliver copies of articles to patrons. For example, Inside Web (bl.uk/services/current/inside.html) is a product of the British Library and has a searchable database of over 20,000 journals and magazines and 100,000 conference proceedings. It can serve as the library's document delivery service for faculty, staff, and students.

The *stacks* are the part of the library where most books and periodicals are stored. Large universities may have more than one library, so all the books and journals will not necessarily be housed in the same building. Some libraries permit anyone to roam the stacks, whereas others are more restrictive, distributing "stack passes" to a limited number of people, such as university faculty, graduate students, or other serious researchers. Access to the stacks is always desirable because browsing in them is a valuable adjunct to the other ways of finding appropriate resource materials. In the stacks, we can review the table of contents and the index of a book, which provide more information about how useful it will be than does the brief description of the book in the library catalog. In addition, because books on similar topics are normally placed near one another in the stacks, browsing for other, similar books once in the right area of the stacks can be extremely helpful.

Accessing Library Materials and Other Information

Having a library available with ample materials and services is of little use unless we know how to access the materials we want. Those unfamiliar with the library can easily feel overwhelmed because there seem to be so many nooks and crannies, both physical and electronic, in which relevant resources can hide. However, three basic strategies for locating materials can make the search easier:

1. Use the online library catalog (or OPAC: Online Public Access Catalog).
2. Use a variety of *online databases* to search for books, journal articles, government documents, abstracts, indexes, and other materials.
3. Use the Internet and the World Wide Web, which have become increasingly important in the search for information; we have discussed their use in the Exploring the Internet sections in each chapter of this book.

These three strategies provide a good start to discovering the information available in the library and at other locations. A thorough search that locates the most up-to-date sources requires familiarity with all three strategies for accessing information.

Many of these library services are operated by the patrons themselves, although some require assistance from library personnel. Some library services are free or provided at low cost, but other services can be expensive. Some of the document-delivery services, for example, can get rather costly. Check with library personnel to determine precisely which services are available and what costs might be incurred.

Books

The Classification System

Small, local libraries might contain a few thousand books. Small- to medium-sized universities have libraries with hundreds of thousands of volumes.

Large university and public libraries contain millions of books. Despite the tremendous variations in library size, the systems to classify books in them are so flexible that the system used in the smallest library can also be used in the largest, and, despite the tremendous size of some libraries, we can easily retrieve a book if we know how the book is classified.

Most classification systems arrange books according to *subject matter*—first into very general categories (such as humanities, science, or social sciences), then, within each general category, into more precise subcategories. The category of social sciences, for example, is divided into economics, sociology, and so on. In this fashion, the subject matter of a book can be narrowed until it fits into a fairly specific category. Then each book is given a unique *call number*, which contains all the necessary information from the classification system to identify that particular book. Two classification systems are used in the United States: the *Library of Congress System* and the *Dewey Decimal System*. Most college and university libraries use the Library of Congress system (or a variation of it), whereas many smaller public and school libraries use the Dewey system.

The Library of Congress System uses a combination of letters and numbers to classify books (see Table A.1). The first letter in the call number is one of 21 letters of the alphabet used to classify books into the most general categories. The letter *H,* for example, indicates the general category of the social sciences. The second letter (if there is a second letter) further narrows the subject matter within the social sciences. The letter *Q,* for example, indicates that the book falls in the more specific social science subject matter of "Family, Marriage, Women," whereas *V* refers to the subject of "Social Pathology." The letters of the call number are followed by a number that further narrows the subject matter. Within the classification *HV,* for example, numbers 701–1420 refer to works on the topic of "protection, assistance, and relief of children," whereas numbers 5001 to 5840 refer to books on "alcoholism." This number is followed by a letter that is

Table A.1 Library of Congress Classification System

A	General Works
B	Philosophy and Religion
C	History (General—Civilization, Genealogy)
D	History—Old World
E	American History and General U.S. History
F	American History (Local) and Latin America
G	Geography, Anthropology, Folklore, Sports, and Other
H	Social Sciences
	HA Statistics
	HB–HD Economics
	HF Commerce
	HG–HJ Finance
	HM Sociology
	HQ Family, Marriage, Women
	HV Social Pathology
J	Political Science
K	Law
L	Education
M	Music
N	Fine Arts
P	Language and Literature
Q	Science
R	Medicine
S	Agriculture, Forestry, Animal Culture, Fish Culture, Hunting
T	Technology
U	Military Science
V	Naval Science
Z	Bibliography and Library Science

Example: HV
             875
             F6

the first letter of the last name of the author of the book (in cases of multiple authors, it is by the first author's last name). This is followed by a number that further identifies the author. These sets of letters and numbers of the call number provide an identification that is unique to this book: No other book has exactly the same call number. Books are placed on the shelves in the order of their call numbers. All the Hs are placed together, and within the Hs all the HMs go together. Within the HMs, books are arranged according to the other letters and numbers.

Table A.2   Dewey Decimal Classification System

Broad subject areas or classes:

000   Generalities

100   Philosophy and Related Disciplines
200   Religion
300   The Social Sciences
400   Language
500   Pure Sciences
600   Technology (Applied Sciences)
700   The Arts
800   Literature and Rhetoric
900   General Geography and History

Each class can be subdivided into smaller classes or subclasses:

300   The Social Sciences
310   Statistical Method and Statistics
320   Political Science
330   Economics
340   Law
350   Public Administration
360   Welfare and Association
370   Education
380   Commerce
390   Customs and Folklore
Example: 362.7

N34

The Dewey Decimal System arranges books into 10 general categories based on a three-digit number on the top row of the call number (see Table A.2). Numbers in the 300 range make up the social science category. The second and third digits of this top row further narrow the classification within the social sciences. For example, the 360s deal with "welfare and association."

The three-digit number is followed by a decimal point and numbers that indicate narrower classifications. In the second row of the Dewey call number is a letter, which is again the first letter of the author's last name, followed by a number that further identifies the author. This may be followed by a lowercase letter that is the first letter in the first word of the title of the book (excluding "a," "an," and "the"). The Dewey system also provides each book with its own unique call number.

The Library Catalog

With knowledge of the classification system in use at a particular library, anybody can locate any book. To do so, first find the *online library catalog,* which is a listing of all the holdings in the library. In some cases, the library catalog can say not only whether the library owns a particular item but also its status: whether it is checked out, at the bindery, lost, and so on. Some libraries in regional networks list in their online catalogs which libraries in the network own a particular book or other holding. Thus, if a book is not available at one library, the catalog knows where it can be found.

In the library catalog, each library holding has a separate entry or record that can be viewed on computer. To locate a book or other item in the library, find the record of the book, make note of the location (e.g., reference, documents, or stacks) and the call number, and find it on the library shelves. (Remember that books with similar call numbers will be about similar topics, so it is a good practice to browse through books in the immediate vicinity as well.) The record for each book shows the author and title of the book, the subject headings under which it can be found in the library catalog, the library where the book is located, and so on.

To find a record in the catalog, look it up under the author's name, the title of the work, and the subject heading under which it is listed or by key words that appear in the record. Author and title searches are fairly straightforward, but searching by subject can be a little more problematic because it is sometimes difficult to find useful subject headings for the topic. To assist in this task, refer to the *Library of Congress Subject Headings* if the library uses the Library of Congress classification system. If the library uses the Dewey decimal system, then the equivalent is *Sears List of Subject Headings.* Both volumes list headings acceptable for use in a library catalog, cross-referencing a number of different topics. These volumes are located in the library and can also be found online. When using the library catalog to locate books, determine from the title of the book and the brief description of the contents contained in the record whether a book will be useful. It is better to err on the side of jotting down too many call numbers rather than too few.

You are also not limited to searching your own library since Web sites now exist to help review the holdings of libraries across the country and around the world. This is especially useful for those who have access only to small libraries with limited holdings. Exploring other libraries unveils other resources, particularly books and journals, that would simply be otherwise unavailable. The Library of Congress Web site (loc.gov), in addition to locating published materials, provides webcasts, online exhibitions, and other audiovisual resources. Another Web site that provides access to many libraries is LIBDEX (libdex.com), with links to the catalogs of more than 18,000 libraries. The University of Saskatchewan Web site {library.usask.ca/catalogs/world.html) provides links to library catalogs around the world. Finally, OCLC WorldCat (the OCLC Online Union Catalog), which may be accessible through a library's online database system, provides a catalog of books and other materials in libraries worldwide.

Periodicals

One of the most valuable and heavily used resources of the library, in addition to books, is *periodicals.* Periodicals are published periodically, such as weekly or monthly (hence, the name "periodicals"), and usually contain articles by a number of different authors on a variety of topics. Periodicals come in two basic types, although some are a blend of both. *Magazines* are directed at the general public, written in a light and popular style, and are often commercial ventures. *Journals* are professional periodicals that publish articles primarily intended for members of a particular profession. The *American Sociological Review,* the *Journal of Social Service Research,* and the *Journal of the American Medical Association* are examples.

We will focus primarily on journals, but both magazines and journals can be helpful in researching a problem because, first, periodicals tend to be more current than books, especially in reporting research findings, in part because the production process for books is longer than that for periodicals. In addition,

in many scientific fields, including the human services, much research is reported first in journals. In fact, many books contain primarily summaries or assessments of research that has already appeared in journals. Second, the articles in periodicals are brief and specific, offering more information about a particular topic in a shorter form.

The Classification System

Periodicals, like books, can have call numbers, although not all libraries classify their periodicals that way. When periodicals are given a call number, they can be housed in the library in two ways: along with the books in the library by call number or separately from books by call number. When periodicals are classified by call number, you will need to look in the library catalog or other location to find the call number of the periodical you wish. The advantage of classifying periodicals by call number is that periodicals on a similar topic are then near one another. Some libraries, however, do not use periodical call numbers but instead arrange periodicals separately from books in alphabetical order by the title of the journal (excluding the first "the" or "a" in the title). Once we see how the periodicals are stored in a particular library, we can find any periodical because no two have the same title or call number. Each issue of a journal is further identified by a volume number, the year of its publication, and an issue number indicating its place in the sequence of issues making up a particular volume. Some journals also identify their issues with the month or season (for example, Summer) in which it was published. To locate an issue of a journal, then, requires the following information: the call number or name of the journal, year of issue, volume number, and issue number (or month or season of publication).

Periodicals are usually found in one of four locations. First, most libraries store *current periodicals,* the most recent issues, in a separate place where users can browse through them. Typically, the most recent one or two years are kept there. Second, *bound periodicals* contain several issues that have been bound together in one hardcover volume for extended storage. Each bound volume normally contains one year's worth of issues. Third, old volumes are sometimes stored on *microfilm* or *microfiche* or some other space-saving device for long-term storage and are usually kept in large cabinets near the machines that magnify them for viewing. Fourth, a small but growing number of periodicals, especially the more recent issues, can now be found online, sometimes in full-text versions.

A problem can arise when accessing periodicals that, though minor, is irksome to both patrons and librarians: the binding of separate issues that make up a volume of a journal. This means the volume has to be sent to a bindery, which means that the issues in that volume are temporarily unavailable to library patrons. The period is usually brief, but the periodicals are also usually recent ones because the binding is done within the first few years of publication. Students need to be aware that this problem can occur; it is one reason to begin library research on a project early because some recent journals available now may be gone to the bindery a month from now.

Journals Important to the Human Services

Literally hundreds of journals in the library or online contain materials of use to human service researchers and practitioners. Although no one can read all these journals, awareness and occasional perusal of them can uncover much valuable source material. One way to spend free time is to browse through some of these journals, either online or in the current periodicals section of the library. Numerous journals are published primarily for human service professionals. Among the more important are these:

Administration in Social Work
British Journal of Social Work
Child Welfare
Children and Schools: A Journal of Social Work Practice
Clinical Social Work Journal
Exceptional Children
Families in Society
Federal Probation
Health & Social Work

International Journal of Aging and Human Development
International Social Work
Journal of Social Work Education
Journal of Social Service Research
Journal of Sociology and Social Welfare
Policy and Practice of Public Human Services
School Social Work Journal
Smith College Studies in Social Work
Social Security Bulletin
Social Service Review
Social Work
Social Work Abstracts
Social Work in Health Care
Social Work Research
Social Work with Groups
Substance Use and Misuse

Because the human service professions use knowledge developed by many of the behavioral sciences, many journals not published directly for human service providers also can be of great value. Among the more useful are these:

Administration and Policy in Mental Health
American Journal of Orthopsychiatry
American Journal of Public Health
American Journal of Sociology
American Sociological Review
Archives of General Psychiatry
Behavior Therapy
Child Development
Child Psychiatry and Human Development
Clinical Sociology Review
Community Mental Health Journal
Crime and Delinquency
Criminology
Gerontologist
International Journal of Group Psychotherapy
Journal of Abnormal Psychology
Journal of Applied Behavioral Science
Journal of Applied Sociology
Journal of Clinical Psychology
Journal of Consulting and Clinical Psychology
Journal of Counseling Psychology
Journal of Criminal Law and Criminology
Journal of Drug Issues

Journal of General Psychology
Journals of Gerontology (Series A and B)
Journal of Health and Social Behavior
Journal of Marital and Family Therapy
Journal of Marriage and the Family
Journal of Personality and Social Psychology
Journal of Research in Crime and Delinquency
Journal of Studies on Alcohol
Merrill-Palmer Quarterly
Psychological Bulletin
The Public Interest
Social Forces
Social Policy
Social Problems
Social Psychology Quarterly
Sociological Quarterly

Given this diversity in periodicals, how do we find those articles that relate to a particular topic? A variety of online databases are available to assist in this search.

Online Databases

A variety of computerized information-retrieval systems is available to locate professional literature on particular topics. Some services are available to individual users, but the most common approach is to access articles through a library's Web-based service, such as OCLC FirstSearch. Most students are undoubtedly familiar with the basic search process. The user enters one or more search terms that relate to the topic of interest, and the computer displays a list of matching articles or books ranging from literally thousands of citations down to the unwelcome message, "No Matches Found!" By applying some basic search principles, we can avoid these extremes by sifting out the irrelevant material and identifying the best sources.

A first consideration is which specific database to use. Choices vary from one library to another, but library database systems such as FirstSearch even suggest which databases are best for a particular subject area. Table A.3 summarizes some popular databases that human service professionals should consider.

Although there is overlap between them, it is a good idea to try several.

A second consideration is the type of search term to use. The search terms might be key words, subject headings, authors' names, titles of articles, and so on. For a basic search, the user specifies only a few types of search terms such as a key word, author, or title. An advanced search permits the user to refine the search process by entering various combinations of search terms.

Even a basic search needs to be approached carefully. For example, assume a researcher is interested in locating articles on the effectiveness of intervention programs on child abuse. Table A.4 illustrates the consequences of using various strategies. Consider the difference between searching for child abuse as a key word or as a title term. Key words are found in titles, notes, abstracts, summaries, descriptions, and subjects. Key words are also names of people and places that are the subjects of a library resource or a listing in a directory. Consequently, a key word search returns many more citations than a title search. (The number of citations is something to take into consideration if there is a fee for this search service based in part on the number of references provided. Also, the longer list will include many sources not directly relevant and could waste valuable time.) The search engine also distinguishes between entering the words "child" and "abuse" (key word: child and key word: abuse) and entering "child abuse" (key word: child with abuse). The former locates articles about children and various types of abuse such as drug abuse, spouse abuse, and so on as well as child abuse, whereas the latter only returns child abuse articles. Presumably, really important descriptors will appear in the title, but using the title for a search also misses many potentially good articles, so a key word search is generally preferred. However, if the title of the article or at least some terms in it are known, a title search is best for pinpointing a specific study. A final point about searching for key words or subject terms is that some search services provide a dictionary of the terms used in the database. One such database, for example, is ERIC, or Educational Resources Information Center. If a library subscribes to this database, then it also has a volume titled *Thesaurus of ERIC*

Table A.3 Summary of Database Choices

Database	Topics
Cumulative Index to Nursing and Allied Health Literature (CINAHL)	nursing, allied health
ERIC (ERIC) Journal articles and reports in education	adult, career, and vocational education; assessment and evaluation; disabilities and gifted education; educational management; elementary and early childhood education; higher education; information and technology; language and linguistics; reading and communication; teachers and teacher education; urban education
MEDLINE (MEDLINE) All areas of medicine, including dentistry and nursing	clinical medicine, dentistry, education, experimental medicine, health services administration, nursing, nutrition, pathology, psychiatry, toxicology, veterinary medicine
National Criminal Justice Reference Service (NCJRS) Summaries of more than 180,000 criminal justice publications	crime and justice information, research, statistics, funding opportunities
PsycINFO 1887 (PsycINFO_1887) Psychology and related fields since 1887	anthropology, business, education, law, linguistics, medicine, nursing, pharmacology, physiology, psychiatry, sociology
Sociological Abstracts (SocAbs) Abstracts on all aspects of sociology	community development, culture and social structure, demography and human biology, environmental interactions, family and social welfare, health and medicine and law, religion and science, social psychology and group interactions, welfare services, women's studies
Social Sciences Abstracts (SocialSciAbs)	anthropology, economics, geography, law, political science, psychology, sociology
Resource Discovery Network (rdn.ac.uk/)	a collaboration of over seventy educational and research organizations, including the British Library.
WWW Virtual Library (vlib.org/)	widely recognized as among the highest-quality guides to particular sections of the Web
BUBL Link (bubl.ac.uk/link/)	selected Internet resources covering all academic subject areas and catalogued according to DDC (Dewey Decimal Classification)

Descriptors that contains all the subject terms used in the ERIC database. We also noted earlier that other volumes of subject headings can be used when searching the online library catalog.

Another consideration is to move from a basic to an advanced search. An advanced search offers the user control over a wide array of search variables beyond key word, author, and title. One may also broaden or restrict searches by using special features such as "wildcards," which substitute for letters in the search term, and Boolean operators like the words "and," "or," and "not." Before commencing a search, searchers can consult the extensive help service available on the main menu of the online database program as well as with a reference librarian for guidance on conducting an effective search. Finally,

Table A.4   Sample Database Search Results

Database	Type search	Term(s)	Records found:
PsycINFO_1887	Key word	kw: child and kw: abuse.	18,694
PsycINFO_1887	Key word	kw: child w abuse.	14,462
PsycINFO_1887	Title	ti: child w abuse.	1,905
PsycINFO_1887	Key word and title	kw: outcome and (ti: child w abuse).	68
Sociological Abstracts	Key word	kw: child and kw: abuse.	7,884
Sociological Abstracts	Key word	ti: child w abuse.	6,135
Sociological Abstracts	Title	ti: child w abuse.	733
Sociological Abstracts	Key word and title	kw: outcome and (ti: child w abuse).	23

many libraries provide short courses that can improve these skills.

Searching online databases is generally a two-stage process. First, the search program returns a list of identified sources (articles or books) in summary form. Second, by clicking the mouse pointer on a selection, the user is taken to a detailed record that includes a variety of information about the source, including an abstract and descriptors. An *abstract* is a brief description, usually no more than a paragraph, of the contents of a book or an article. A good abstract provides a complete summary of the work, including thesis, description of any data collected, conclusions drawn, and study limitations. Abstracts help locate relevant research and decide whether it is sufficiently useful to warrant reading the entire work. Abstracts also frequently provide the list of key words or descriptors under which each book or article is cataloged, and this is an important assist in searching for other materials on the same topic.

Reference Books for the Human Services

One group of useful books that are, unfortunately, often overlooked is general reference books. Included in this rather broad category are encyclopedias, directories, and bibliographies. Although such works do not substitute for a thorough library search, they can save time and efficiently answer many routine questions. The following is only a partial listing of common reference works:

An Author's Guide to Social Work Journals
Encyclopedia of Adolescence
Encyclopedia of Aging
Encyclopedia of Alcoholism
Encyclopedia of Associations
Encyclopedia of Drug Abuse
Encyclopedia of Psychology
Encyclopedia of Social Work
Encyclopedia of Sociology
National Directory of State Agencies
Public Welfare Directory
The Social Sciences Encyclopedia
Social Service Organizations and Agencies Directory
Social Work Almanac
State Executive Directory Annual

Government Documents

The U.S. government is one of the largest publishers in the world, pouring forth mountains of books, bulletins, circulars, reports, and the like. Practitioners and researchers in the human service field find government documents especially important because the government sponsors much of the research done in this area. The government, for example, commonly funds demonstration projects, program evaluations, and needs assessments and publishes the resulting research reports. Government documents also include information on model programs, funding sources, and bibliographies of topics of interest to human service professionals.

Locating pertinent government documents may at first seem a daunting endeavor. With the aid of a few basic tools, however, the task can be done quickly, thoroughly, and with relatively little pain. The first step is to look in the online library catalog. Most libraries list government documents along with other books in the library catalog, and the documents can be identified through name, title, subject, or key word search in the library catalog. The search for government documents can then go to other online sites. The three best are the U.S. Government's Official Web Portal (firstgov.gov), the U.S. Government Printing Office's GPOAccess (www.gpoaccess.gov), and the Web page of the *Catalog of U.S. Government Publications* (www.gpoaccess. gov/cgp). The Official Web Portal, for example, offers a variety of areas to explore (such as "Government Agencies" or "Data and Statistics") and an advanced search feature where we can enter key words and use various drop-down menus to specify the kind of search we want to do. We can also specify whether we want to search for federal government documents only or for state government documents as well. The Web pages of GPOAccess and the *Catalog of U.S. Government Publications* use similar search procedures.

In addition to these three government Web sites, other government agencies have their own Web sites where documents, reports, and data of various kinds can be found. The following agencies and their Web sites are among the most useful to researchers and practitioners in the social sciences and human services:

Bureau of the Census (www.census.gov)
Department of Health and Human Services (www.hhs.gov)
Department of Justice (www.usdoj.gov)
Bureau of Justice Statistics, Department of Justice (www.ojp.usdoj.gov)

Department of Education (www.ed.gov)
Department of Labor (www.dol.gov)
Women's Bureau, Department of Labor (www.dol.gov/wb)
Commission on Civil Rights (www.usccr.gov)

Government document users find that more and more documents are becoming available directly over the Web without the need of locating a hard copy. Many government documents are available as PDF files, which can be viewed online or downloaded to the user's computer for later viewing or printing. In addition, some documents are available for purchase through government Web sites.

To find government documents in the library, we need to know how and where they are located. Which government documents a particular library possesses depends in part on whether it is a *depository library,* a designation made by the Superintendent of Documents at the U.S. Government Printing Office (GPO). A *regional depository library*, of which there can be up to two in any state, receives everything published by the printing office. *Selective depositories* receive only some government publications (see *List of Classes of U.S. Government Publications Available for Selection by Depository Libraries*). Nondepository libraries have some government documents, depending on what they choose to purchase. A listing of depository libraries and more information about the federal depository library program can be found online at www.gpoaccess.gov/libraries.html.

The *Catalog of U.S. Government Publications* includes a listing of most government publications, along with the information necessary to locate them in the library or to purchase them from the office of the Superintendent of Documents. Every government document submitted to the office of the Superintendent of Documents is given a *Catalog* entry number, and documents are listed in the *Catalog* in order of this number. This number has two components. The first two digits indicate the year the document was published (an entry number of 88-5280 was published in 1988). The second group of digits locates the record in the printed version of the *Catalog*.

This second number is derived from sequencing the publications alphanumerically according to the classification number of the Superintendent of Documents, or SUDOCS number. The SUDOCS number is like the call number in the library catalog for locating books because government documents are filed in the library according to this number. However, while the Dewey Decimal and Library of Congress classification systems classify entries according to subject matter, the SUDOCS system classifies materials according to the agency issuing the materials. In the SUDOCS number "HE 20.7009/a:Ac 7/2/982-87," for example, *HE* means the document was issued by the Department of Health and Human Services. Thus, the *Catalog* entry number helps locate the document in the printed version of the *Catalog,* and the SUDOCS number helps locate where the document is shelved in the library. Many libraries shelve government documents in a separate location from other books and periodicals, but some also mix them together so that the Library of Congress (Dewey Decimal) numbers of books are mixed in with the SUDOCs number of government documents.

Information Literacy and Critical Thinking Skills

A library is a veritable cornucopia of information, and we have tried to provide basic information on how to access that information. However, the best way to learn about any library is to use it. Roam around the stacks, browse through the online library catalog, delve into government documents, and explore the Internet. We have emphasized the ways to systematically access information in the library. However, much useful material can also appear in random and casual rovings through the library. Above all, consult with the reference librarians, who are trained to help students and faculty devise programs and strategies for finding, analyzing, synthesizing, and evaluating information. Such informational literacy is increasingly essential in the modern world, whether it is found in a book, on a CD-ROM, or online. Informational literacy is an important part of critical thinking, which is the

ability to judge the authenticity, accuracy, and worth of information.

This guide to the library has emphasized the library's utility to human service practitioners. However, a library is not meant solely to help write a term paper or complete a research project. A library is a repository of cultural knowledge. It houses research reports on alcoholics along with the epic myths of Homer and the ancient and sacred literature of Hinduism and the Vedas. Literature, philosophy, and theology accompany engineering and celestial mechanics—and the daily newspaper!

Our point is that a library is, in a sense, the storehouse of a culture, and we hope that you use it to its fullest extent throughout your life as a source of enrichment and fulfillment. The search programs and strategies devised for college students with the help of reference librarians are useful long after those years to help find and analyze information about social issues or personal problems and to help people keep current in their chosen fields of endeavor.

For Further Reading

Bolner, Myrtle S., and Gayle A. Poirier. *The Research Process: Books & Beyond,* 2nd ed. Dubuque, Iowa: Kendall/Hunt, 2001. This book provides a comprehensive overview of how to do research in the library and online.

Cuba, Lee. *A Short Guide to Writing about Social Science,* 4th ed. New York: Longman, 2002. This book is mostly about writing term papers and research reports, but it also includes a significant amount of material on using the library and the Internet.

Gates, Jean K. *Guide to the Use of Libraries and Information Sources,* 7th ed. New York: McGraw-Hill, 1993. This book is designed as a text for basic courses in library resources, so it can be an excellent introduction to the library that extends the topics in this chapter considerably.

Hahn, Harley. *Harley Hahn's Internet Yellow Pages.* Emeryville, Calif.: McGraw-Hill Osborne Media, 2003. As the name implies, this book is an excellent resource for finding materials on the Internet.

Reed, Jeffrey G., and Pam M. Baxter. *Library Use: A Handbook for Psychology,* 3rd ed. Washington, D.C.: American Psychological Association, 2003. Focused as it is on psychology, this book is nonetheless a valuable guide to the library for someone preparing to conduct a social research project. Among other things, it covers using abstracting services, doing computer searches, and locating various scales and measurement devices.

Schneider, Gary, and Jessica Evans. *New Perspectives on the Internet, 4th Edition Comprehensive.* Boston: Thomson/Course Technology, 2003. This book is an excellent introduction to the Internet, providing all the information needed to utilize that online source of information.

The Sociology Writing Group. *A Guide to Writing Sociology Papers*, 5th ed. New York: Worth, 2001. This book provides useful guidance in terms of doing library research in the social sciences, organizing time and materials, and preparing and writing analyses based on both quantitative and qualitative data.

Appendix B

Generating Random Numbers

Random numbers have many purposes in social research. For example, they are often used in constructing a probability sample in which elements are selected from a population and placed in the sample on a random basis. In some cases, we do this with a table of random numbers. Such tables of random numbers can be found in many places, such as textbooks on statistics; a few volumes contain nothing but random numbers. Figure B.1 in this appendix contains a spreadsheet-generated table of random numbers.

Spreadsheet software, such as Microsoft Excel, makes generating random numbers easy. Although the specific procedures vary from program to program, the basic approach is the same. Using Excel, the following command is entered into a cell of a spreadsheet, and it generates a random number from 0 to 10,000:

$$=INT(RAND*10001)$$

The formula contains two subcommands. "RAND" returns a decimal value consisting of an evenly distributed random number greater than or equal to 0 and less than 1. The formula multiplies this random decimal by 10,001, resulting in a number that ranges from a low of less than 1.0000 to a high of less than 10,001.0000. The "INT" command drops the decimal portion and displays the integer portion. Hence, the resulting random number ranges from 0 to 10,000. For example, if the random decimal is 0.00002, the result is:

$$= INT(0.00002*10001) = INT(0.20002) = 0$$

If the random decimal is 0.99999, the result is:

$$= INT(.99999*10001) = INT(10000.899) = 10000$$

We can adjust the range of random numbers by simply substituting a different value for 10,001. To generate a list of random numbers, copy the formula into as many cells as needed, using the "Copy" and "Paste" commands. Figure B.1 illustrates 200 random numbers generated by this procedure with Excel. Note that the numbers are displayed in the table with leading zeros, using the "Format Cells" > "Numbers" > "Custom" option found on the Format menu.

An advantage of a spreadsheet is that we can easily order the random numbers from lowest to highest, a feature convenient for such tasks as selecting a random sample from an ordered sampling frame. Note that spreadsheets typically return a new random number every time the worksheet is calculated. So reordering the numbers requires that the cell formulas must first be converted to values. To accomplish this, scroll over the cells containing the random numbers, use "Copy" from the Edit menu, and then paste the selection elsewhere in the worksheet by selecting the "Values" option from "Paste Special" on the Edit menu. Next, select the "Sort" option from the Data menu. The result is a list of random numbers in rank order.

Finally, standard statistical packages, such as Minitab, also generate random numbers. In addition, programs such as SPSS and Minitab have menu commands for selecting a sample of cases from a file. For example, a Census data set may contain several thousand cases, so this feature enables the researcher to conveniently select a smaller, random subset of cases for analysis.

If we are drawing a random sample by hand, using a table of random numbers to do so is straightforward. First, we note the size of the population to determine how many of the random digits we need when selecting each element. For example, if the population does not exceed 9,999 elements, we use four columns of random digits for each of the selections from the sampling frame. If the population exceeds 9,999 elements but not 99,999, we take random digits five columns at a time.

The second step is to select a starting point in the table of random numbers. It is important that we not always start from the same place in the table, such as the upper left corner. If we did, every sample, assuming we used the same number of digits, would select the same elements from the population and, of course, violate the randomness we seek. This problem can be easily avoided by merely starting in the table at some point that is itself randomly determined (close your eyes and point).

Figure B.1 implements this process by showing the selection of a sample of size 6 from a population of size 30. Each case in the population is given a number between 1 and 30. Then we proceed through the table from the randomly selected starting point, taking each set of two digits that is between 1 and 30 until we reach the desired sample size. We just ignore any number between 31 and 99 and any number that is a repeat. We then use this list of random numbers to identify the elements to be included in the sample. When using computers instead of tables to select random samples, each element in a sampling frame is assigned a number, and then the program generates a set of random numbers the size of the sample needed. If there are 2,798 elements in the sampling frame and we need a sample size of 300, the computer generates 300 random numbers between 1 and 2,798. Those 300 cases are our sample. If the whole sampling frame is in a computer file, the computer may be able to both assign the numbers to the sampling frame and select the 300 random cases.

Figure B.1   Random Numbers Generated by Excel

8473	6469	0023	1284	7224
8942	2464	4716	2969	7263
0483	1714	5849	8958	5386
2149	5816	3700	9948	7455
7453	6909	9577	0492	6852
3122	3299	9818	3816	0147
9852	6862	8790	7899	4399
5501	1995	4117	8482	4002
6969	9006	4146	9040	7428
1374	2614	4006	1365	4388
6454	9996	3058	0393	6331
1859	8391	0248	4116	5107
0964	0824	7381	4105	2046
9787	5866	5979	5099	5007
5314	1390	6447	9694	0161
0786	4317	0927	5093	2017
8012	7434	0633	4440	8431
8035	4707	4235	5832	6368
5954	6540	1745	8472	2485
9846	4691	7976	4018	4088
5214	9309	9049	8558	8203
5238	3653	5350	9468	9199
1143	8013	8016	0706	7169
6014	7212	5308	3707	8973
9352	9680	8359	4905	7620
0661	4566	2770	9675	3599
7735	2633	1237	2176	6353
5568	6770	6900	8182	1006
8759	0209	5726	7022	1945
7844	5681	1323	3519	9542
6310	4024	8095	9248	1715
9114	8417	0360	9554	7951
6276	8759	5863	0888	5439
8415	9510	5243	4901	4480
8937	0400	0181	8841	8829
4965	0216	4428	8468	9285
6722	1994	8732	9902	4732
8914	6150	9054	4557	8645
6085	0677	8324	4685	3131
1767	6983	4181	5552	5760

Random
starting point

Sample of 6:
29 04 13 03 07 21

Glossary

Accidental Sampling: samples composed of those elements that are readily available or convenient to the researcher.

Alpha Error: the probability of rejecting a null hypothesis when it is actually true.

Alpha Level: the probability at which the null hypothesis will be rejected; the amount of Type I error (probability of rejecting a true null hypothesis) that is acceptable in a research design, typically $p = .05$ or $p = .01$.

Alphanumeric Variables: variables consisting only of type characters, being without the property of quantitative value, and treated as labels or strings by data analysis programs.

Anonymity: a situation in which no one, including the researcher, can link individuals' identities to their responses or behaviors that serve as research data.

Applied Research: research designed with a practical outcome in mind and with the assumption that some group or society as a whole will gain specific benefits from it.

Area Sampling: a multistage sampling technique that involves moving from larger clusters of units to smaller and smaller ones until the unit of analysis, such as the household or individual, is reached.

Availability Sampling: samples composed of those elements that are readily available or convenient to the researcher.

Available Data: observations collected by someone other than the investigator for purposes that differ from the investigator's but that are available to be analyzed.

Bar Graph: a frequency distribution graph for variables treated as nominal or ordinal, in which each value is plotted on the X axis as a separate bar whose height signifies the frequency of the value.

Baseline: a series of measurements of a client's condition prior to treatment that is used as a basis for comparison with the client's condition after treatment is implemented.

Basic Research: research conducted for the purpose of advancing knowledge about human behavior, with little concern for any immediate or practical benefits that might result.

Beta Error: the probability of failing to reject a null hypothesis that is actually false.

Bivariate Statistics: statistics that describe the relationship between two variables.

Block Grants: awards allocated to states by formula and funded by annual congressional appropriations.

Blocking: a two-stage system of assigning subjects to experimental and control groups whereby subjects are first aggregated into blocks according to one or more key variables and then members of each block are randomly assigned to experimental and control conditions.

Case Study: a detailed, descriptive account of one individual, situation, organization, group, or other entity.

Categorical Grants: grants that provide funding, for fixed or known periods, of specific projects, including research grants, training grants, experimental and demonstration grants, evaluation grants, and planning grants among others.

Categorizing Strategies: attempts in qualitative data analysis to generalize and abstract by generating concepts and even theories from the raw data.

Causality: the situation where an independent variable is the factor—or one of several factors—that produces variation in a dependent variable.

Central Limit Theorem: if random samples are taken from any population with a given mean and standard deviation, the sampling distribution of sample means will be approximately normally distributed and the mean of the sampling distribution will be equal to the population parameter.

Clinical-Research Model: the merger of clinical practice and research through the use of single-subject designs.

Closed-Ended Questions: questions that provide respondents with a fixed set of alternatives from which they are to choose.

Cluster Sampling: a multistage sampling technique that involves moving from larger clusters of units to smaller and smaller ones until the unit of analysis, such as the household or individual, is reached.

Coding: the categorizing of behavior into a limited number of categories.

Coding Scheme: a plan by which the researcher organizes responses to a variable, together with specifications for including the variable in a computer data file.

Common Sense: practical judgments based on the experiences, wisdom, and prejudices of a people.

Computer-Assisted Interviewing (CAI): using computer technology to assist in the completion of questionnaires and interviews.

Computer-Assisted Personal Interviewing (CAPI): face-to-face interviewing in which the interviewer reads questions from the computer monitor and enters responses directly into the computer.

Computer-Assisted Qualitative Data Analysis (CAQDA): using computers to do coding, hypothesis testing, and theory building in qualitative data analysis.

Computer-Assisted Self-Interviewing (CASI): respondents read questions from a survey on a computer screen and enter their responses at the computer keyboard themselves.

Computer-Assisted Telephone Interviewing (CATI): conducting an interview over the telephone, with the interviewer reading questions from the computer monitor and recording answers directly into the computer.

Concepts: mental constructs or images developed to symbolize ideas, persons, things, or events.

Concurrent Validity: a type of criterion validity in which the results of a newly developed measure are correlated with results of an existing measure.

Confidentiality: ensuring that information or responses will not be publicly linked to specific individuals who participate in research.

Construct Validity: a complex approach to establishing the validity of measures involving relating the measure to a complete theoretical framework, including all the concepts and propositions that the theory comprises.

Content Analysis: a method of transforming the contents of documents from a qualitative, unsystematic form to a quantitative, systematic form.

Content Validity: the extent to which a measuring device covers the full range of meanings or forms included in a variable that is being measured.

Context Map: one type of visual display in qualitative data analysis that describes in graphic form the physical or social setting that is the context of the observations.

Contextualizing Strategies: attempts in qualitative data analysis to treat the data as a coherent whole and retain as much of the raw data as possible in order to capture the whole context.

Contingency Control: a multivariate analysis that examines the relationship between an independent variable and a dependent variable in each of the categories of a third, or test, variable.

Contingency Question: a question that is answered only if certain responses were given to a previous question.

Continuous Variables: variables that theoretically have an infinite number of values.

Control Condition: the condition in an experiment that does not receive the experimental stimulus.

Control Group: the subjects in an experiment who are not exposed to the experimental stimulus.

Control Variables: variables whose value is held constant in all conditions of an experiment.

Convenience Sampling: samples composed of those elements that are readily available or convenient to the researcher.

Cost-Benefit Analysis: an approach to program evaluation wherein program costs are related to program benefits expressed in dollars.

Cost-Effective Analysis: an approach to program evaluation wherein program costs are related to program effects, with effects measured in the units in which they naturally occur.

Cover Letter: a letter that accompanies a mailed questionnaire and serves to introduce and explain it to the recipient.

Criterion Validity: a technique for establishing the validity of measures that involves demonstrating a correlation between the measure and some other standard.

Cross-Sectional Research: research based on data collected at one point in time.

Data Analysis: the process of placing observations in numerical form and manipulating them according to their arithmetic properties to derive meaning from them.

Data Archives: a national system of data libraries that lend sets of data, much as ordinary libraries lend books.

Data Display: an organized presentation of data in qualitative data analysis that enables researchers and their audiences to draw some conclusions from the data and move on to the next stage of the research.

Deductive Reasoning: inferring a conclusion from more abstract premises or propositions.

Demand Characteristics: subtle, unprogrammed cues in an experiment that communicate to experimental subjects something about how they should behave.

Dependent Variable: the passive variable in a relationship or the one affected by an independent variable.

Descriptive Research: research that attempts to discover facts or describe reality.

Descriptive Statistics: procedures that assist in organizing, summarizing, and interpreting the sample data on hand.

Dimensional Sampling: a sampling technique designed to enhance the representativeness of small samples by specifying all important variables and choosing a sample that contains at least one case to represent all possible combinations of variables.

Direct Costs: a proposed program budget or actual program expenditures.

Direct Replication: the repeated application of the same treatment by the same clinician to other clients suffering from the same basic problem.

Discrete Variables: variables with a finite number of distinct and separate values.

Discretionary Grants: Grants that provide funding, for fixed or known periods, of specific projects, including research grants, training grants, experimental and demonstration grants, evaluation grants, and planning grants, among others.

Discriminatory Power Score: a value calculated during construction of a Likert scale that indicates the degree to which each item discriminates between high scorers and low scorers on the entire scale.

Double-Blind Experiment: an experiment conducted in such a way that neither the subjects nor the experimenters know which groups are in the experimental condition and which are in the control condition.

Ecological Fallacy: inferring something about individuals from data collected about groups.

Empirical-Practice Model: see Clinical-Research Model.

Ethics: the responsibilities that researchers bear toward those who participate in research, those who sponsor research, and those who are potential beneficiaries of research.

Ethnographic Interview: informal and unstructured interviews that can explore a wide range of topics, last for a long time, and involve a nondirective interviewer.

Evaluability Assessment: a preliminary investigation into a program prior to its evaluation to determine those aspects of the program that are evaluable.

Evaluation Research: the use of scientific research methods to plan intervention programs, to monitor the implementation of new programs and the operation of existing programs, and to determine how effectively programs or clinical practices achieve their goals.

Evidence-Based Practice: the conscientious, explicit, and judicious use of the best evidence in making decisions about human service assessment and intervention.

Experiential Knowledge: knowledge gained through firsthand observation of events and based on the assumption that truth can be achieved through personal experience.

Experiment: a controlled method of observation in which the value of one or more independent variables is changed in order to assess its causal effect on one or more dependent variables.

Experimental Condition: the condition in an experiment that receives the experimental stimulus.

Experimental Group: those subjects who are exposed to the experimental stimulus.

Experimental Stimulus: the independent variable in an experiment that is manipulated by the experimenter to assess its effect on behavior.

Experimental Treatment: the independent variable in an experiment that is manipulated by the experimenter to assess its effect on a dependent variable.

Experimental Variability: variation in a dependent variable produced by an independent variable.

Experimenter's Expectations: expectations of experimenters about how they wish an experiment to come out that may be inadvertently communicated to experimental subjects.

Explanatory Research: research with the goal to determine why or how something occurs.

External Validity: the extent to which causal inferences made in an experiment can be generalized to other times, settings, or people.

Extraneous Variability: variation in a dependent variable from any source other than an experimental stimulus.

Face Validity: the degree to which there is a logical relationship between the variable and the proposed measure.

Federal Government Contracts: an important source of research and practice funds other than through grants; with contracts, it is the government that decides precisely what it wants and how it wants it done.

Field Experiments: experiments conducted in naturally occurring settings as people go about their everyday lives.

Field Notes: detailed, descriptive accounts of observations made in a given setting.

Field Research: a type of qualitative research that involves observations of people in their natural settings as they go about their everyday lives.

Filter Question: a question whose answer determines which question a survey respondent answers next.

Focus Group: an interview with a whole group of people at the same time, especially for the purpose of seeking people's subjective reactions and levels of meaning that are important to people's behavior.

Formative Evaluation Research: evaluation research that focuses on the planning, development, and implementation of a program.

Formula Grant: an allocation of federal money to states or their subdivisions in accordance with distribution formulas prescribed by law or administrative regulation, for activities of a continuing nature not confined to a specific project.

Foundation: a nonprofit, legally incorporated entity organized for the purpose of dispersing funds to projects that meet the guidelines of its charter.

Fraud (Scientific): the deliberate falsification, misrepresentation, or plagiarizing of data, findings, or the ideas of others.

Frequency Polygon: a frequency distribution graph of an interval- or ratio-level variable in which interval midpoints are plotted on the X axis, the corresponding frequencies are plotted on the Y axis, and the resulting points are connected by a line.

Grant: the provision of money or other resources for either research or service delivery purposes.

Grounded Theory: a research methodology for developing theory by letting the theory emerge from the data, or be "grounded" in the data.

Group Depth Interview: an interview with a whole group of people at the same time, especially for the purpose of seeking people's subjective reactions and levels of meaning that are important to people's behavior.

Guttman Scale: a measurement scale in which the items have a fixed progressive order and that has the characteristic of reproducibility.

Histogram: a graph for depicting the frequency distribution of an interval or ratio level variable in which intervals of the variable are plotted on the X axis and frequencies are depicted as bars on the Y axis.

Human Services: professions with the primary goal of enhancing the relationship between people and societal institutions so that people may maximize their potential.

Hypotheses: testable statements of presumed relationships between two or more concepts.

Idiographic Explanations: explanations that focus on a single person, event, or situation and attempt to specify all of the conditions that helped produce it.

Independent Variable: the presumed active or causal variable in a relationship.

In-Depth Interview: informal and unstructured interviews that can explore a wide range of topics, last for a long time, and involve a nondirective interviewer.

Index: a measurement technique that combines a number of items into a composite score.

Indicator: an observation assumed to be evidence of the attributes or properties of some phenomenon.

Inductive Reasoning: inferring something about a whole group or class of objects from knowledge of one or a few members of that group or class.

Inferential Statistics: procedures that allow us to make generalizations from sample data to the populations from which the samples were drawn.

Informed Consent: telling potential research participants about all aspects of the research that might reasonably influence their decision to participate.

Internal Validity: an issue in experimentation concerning whether the independent variable actually produces the effect it appears to have on the dependent variable.

Interpretive Approaches: the perspective that social reality has a subjective component to it, that social reality arises out of social interaction and the exchange of social meanings, and that science must gain knowledge of that subjective dimension.

Interval Measures: measures that classify observations into mutually exclusive categories with an inherent order and equal spacing between the categories.

Interview: a technique in which an interviewer reads questions to respondents and records their verbal responses.

Interviewer Falsification: the intentional departure from the designed interviewer instructions, unreported by the interviewer, that can result in the contamination of data.

Interview Schedule: a document used in interviewing, similar to a questionnaire, that contains instructions for the interviewer, specific questions in a fixed order, and transition phrases for the interviewer.

Item: a single indicator of a variable, such as an answer to a question or an observation of some behavior or characteristic.

Judgmental Sampling: a nonprobability sampling technique in which investigators use their judgment and prior knowledge to choose people for the sample who best serve the purposes of the study.

Jury Opinion: an extension of face or content validity that uses the opinions of other investigators, especially those knowledgeable about the variables involved, to assess whether particular operational definitions are logical measures of a variable.

Laboratory Experiments: experiments conducted in artificial settings and constructed in such a way that selected elements of the natural environment are simulated and features of the investigation are controlled.

Latent Coding: coding of more abstract or implicit meanings in a document or medium in which the coder must infer whether a representation in a document is an instance of some broader phenomenon.

Level of Measurement: rules that define permissible mathematical operations on a given set of numbers produced by a measure.

Likert Scale: a measurement scale consisting of a series of statements followed by four response alternatives, typically these: strongly agree, agree, disagree, or strongly disagree.

Longitudinal Research: research based on data gathered over an extended time period.

Manifest Coding: coding the more objective or surface content of a document or medium.

Matching: a process of assigning subjects to experimental and control groups in which each subject is paired with a similar subject in the other group.

Matrix Display: A visual display in qualitative data analysis that looks very much like a contingency table with its rows and columns but contains text rather than numerical quantities in the cells of the table.

Matrix Question: a question designed so that response alternatives are listed only once and each question or statement is followed by a box to check or a number or letter to circle.

Measurement: the process of describing abstract concepts in terms of specific indicators by the assignment of numbers or other symbols to these indicants, in accordance with rules.

Measures of Association: statistics that describe the strength of relationships between variables.

Measures of Central Tendency: statistics, also known as averages, which summarize distributions of data by locating the "typical" or "average" value.

Measures of Dispersion: statistics that indicate how dispersed or spread out the values of a distribution are.

Memos: attempts at theorizing in qualitative data analysis in which the researcher writes down ideas about the meanings of the codes that are emerging from the data and the relationships between the various codes.

Misconduct (Scientific): scientific fraud, plus such activities as carelessness or bias in recording or reporting data, mishandling data, and incomplete reporting of results.

Missing Data: incomplete data found in available data sets.

Multidimensional Scale: a scale designed to measure complex variables composed of more than one dimension.

Multistage Sampling: a multiple-tiered sampling technique that involves moving from larger clusters of units to smaller and smaller ones until the unit of analysis, such as the household or individual, is reached.

Multitrait–Multimethod Approach: a particularly complex form of construct validity involving the simultaneous assessment of numerous measures and concepts through the computation of intercorrelations.

Multivariate Statistics: statistics that describe the relationships among three or more variables.

Narrative Analysis: similar to profiles but with interviews, autobiographies, life histories, letters, and other personal materials used to form a descriptive narrative of a person's life or circumstances.

Needs Assessment: the collection of data to determine how many people need particular services and to assess the level of services or personnel that already exist to fill that need.

Network Analysis: a context map that shows connections and relationships between individuals, groups, statuses, or organizations by the use of lines and arrows.

Nominal Definitions: verbal definitions in which one set of words or symbols is used to stand for another set of words or symbols.

Nominal Measures: measures that classify observations into mutually exclusive categories but with no ordering to the categories.

Nomothetic Explanations: explanations that focus on a class of events and attempt to specify the conditions that seem common to all those events.

Nonprobability Samples: samples in which the probability of each population element's being included in the sample is unknown.

Nonreactive Observation: observation in which those under study are not aware they are being studied and the investigator does not change their behavior by his or her presence.

Normal Distribution: a symmetrical, unimodal distribution in which the mode, median, and mean are identical and have the same proportion of cases between the same two ordinates.

Null Hypothesis: a statement in statistical hypothesis testing that states that no relationship exists between two variables in the population or that there is no difference between a sample statistic and a population parameter.

Numeric Variable: a variable that has the property of quantitative value or a variable in a computer data file that can be used in computations.

Observational Techniques: the collection of data through direct visual or auditory experience of behavior.

Open-Ended Questions: questions without a fixed set of alternatives, leaving respondents completely free to formulate their own responses.

Operational Definitions: definitions that indicate the precise procedures or operations to be followed in measuring a concept.

Opportunity Costs: the value of forgone opportunities incurred by funding one program as opposed to some other program.

Ordinal Measures: measures that classify observations into mutually exclusive categories that have an inherent order to them.

Panel Study: research in which data are gathered from the same people at different times.

Paradigms: general ways of thinking about how the world works and how we gain knowledge about the world.

Participant Observation: a method in which the researcher is a part of, and participates in, the activities of the people, group, or situation being studied.

Pie Chart: a circular graph depicting the frequency distribution of a variable, with the number of degrees of the circle for each section or slice representing the proportionate number of cases for each value of the variable.

Pilot Study: a trial run on a small scale of all procedures planned for a research project.

Population: all possible cases of what one is interested in studying.

Positivism: the perspective that the world exists independently of people's perceptions of it and that science uses objective techniques to discover what exists in the world.

Predictive Research: research that attempts to make projections about what will occur in the future or in other settings.

Predictive Validity: a type of criterion validity wherein scores on a measure are used to predict some future state of affairs.

Preexperimental Designs: crude experimental designs that lack the necessary controls of the threats to internal validity.

Pretest: a preliminary application of the data-gathering technique to assess the adequacy of the technique.

Privacy: the ability to control when and under what conditions others will have access to your beliefs, values, or behavior.

Probability Samples: samples in which each element in the population has a known chance of being selected into the sample.

Probes: follow-up questions used during an interview to elicit clearer and more complete responses.

Profiles: vignettes of a person's experience, usually taken from in-depth interviews, that are stated largely in the person's own words with relatively little interpretation or analysis by the researcher.

Project Grants: grants that provide funding, for fixed or known periods, of specific projects, including research grants, training grants, experimental and demonstration grants, evaluation grants, and planning grants, among others.

Proportional Reduction in Error (PRE): a property of a measure of association that permits estimation of how much the independent variable contributes to reducing error in predicting values of the dependent variable.

Propositions: statements about the relationship between elements in a theory.

Pure Research: research conducted for the purpose of advancing our knowledge about human behavior with little concern for any immediate or practical benefits that might result.

Purposive Sampling: a nonprobability sampling technique wherein investigators use their judgment and prior knowledge to choose people for the sample who best serve the purposes of the study.

Qualitative Research: research that focuses on data in the form of words, pictures, descriptions, or narratives.

Quantitative Research: research that uses numbers, counts, and measures of things.

Quasi-Experimental Designs: designs that approximate experimental control in nonexperimental settings.

Questionnaire: a set of written questions that people respond to directly on the form itself without the aid of an interviewer.

Quota Sampling: a type of nonprobability sampling that involves dividing the population into various categories and determining the number of elements to be selected from each category.

Random Assignment: a process for assigning subjects to experimental and control groups that relies on probability theory to equalize the groups.

Random Errors: measurement errors that are neither consistent nor patterned.

Ratio Measures: measures that classify observations into mutually exclusive categories with an inherent order, equal spacing between the categories, and an absolute zero point.

Reactivity: the degree to which the presence of a researcher influences the behavior being observed.

Reductionist Fallacy: inferring something about groups, or other macro levels of analysis, based on data collected from individuals.

Reflective Remarks: reflections, interpretations, connections, or other thoughts that occur to the researcher and that are added to field notes while transcribing field notes or coding the data.

Reliability: the ability of a measure to yield consistent results each time it is applied.

Representative Sample: a sample that accurately reflects the distribution of relevant variables in the target population.

Request for Proposals (RFP): A formal request for people or agencies to submit proposals on how they would conduct some research or establish and run some program.

Research Design: a detailed plan outlining how a research project will be conducted.

Research Hypothesis: the alternative statement to the null hypothesis, stating that a relationship is present between variables at the population level or that there is a difference between a sample statistic and a population parameter.

Respondent-Driven Sampling: a variation of snowball sampling.

Response Bias: responses to questions that are shaped by factors other than the person's true feelings, intentions, and beliefs.

Response Pattern Anxiety: the tendency for people to become anxious if they have to repeat the same response all the time and to change their responses to avoid doing so.

Response Rate: the percentage of a sample that completes and returns a questionnaire or agrees to be interviewed.

Response Set: the tendency for people to agree or disagree with statements regardless of the content of the statements.

Sample: one or more elements selected from a population.

Sampling Distribution: a theoretical distribution of all possible values of a sample statistic, which is distinguished by being a normal distribution whose mean is the population parameter.

Sampling Error: the extent to which the values of a sample differ from those of the population from which it was drawn.

Sampling Frame: a listing of all the elements in a population.

Sampling Validity: an approach to establishing validity of measures through determining whether a measuring device covers the full range of meanings that should be included in the variable being measured.

Scale: a measurement technique, similar to an index, that combines a number of items into a composite score.

Science: a method of obtaining objective knowledge about the world through systematic observation.

Secondary Analysis: the reanalysis of data previously collected for some other research project.

Semantic Differential: a scaling technique that involves respondents rating a concept on a scale between a series of polar-opposite adjectives.

Simple Random Sampling: a sampling technique wherein the target population is treated as a unitary whole and each element has an equal probability of being selected for the sample.

Single-System Designs: quasi-experimental designs featuring continuous or nearly continuous measurement of the dependent variable on a single research subject over a time interval that is divided into a baseline phase and one or more additional phases during which the independent variable is manipulated; experimental effects are inferred by comparing the subject's responses across baseline and intervention phases.

Snowball Sampling: a type of nonprobability sampling characterized by a few cases of the type we wish to study leading to more cases, which, in turn, lead to still more cases until a sufficient sample is achieved.

Social Desirability Effect: people's tendency to give socially desirable, popular answers to questions in order to present themselves in a good light.

Social Research: a systematic examination (or re-examination) of empirical data collected by someone firsthand, concerning the social or psychological forces operating in a situation.

Sociogram: a context map that shows connections and relationships between individuals, groups, statuses, or organizations by the use of lines and arrows.

Stakeholders: all the people who have an interest in whether a social program operates or how well it does so.

Statistics: procedures for assembling, classifying, and tabulating numerical data so that some meaning or information is derived.

Stratified Sampling: a sampling technique wherein the population is subdivided into strata with separate sub-samples drawn from each strata.

Summated Rating Scales: scales in which a respondent's score is determined by summing the numbers of questions answered.

Summative Evaluation Research: evaluation research that assesses the effectiveness and efficiency of programs and the extent to which program effects are generalizable to other settings and populations.

Survey: a term used both to designate a specific way of collecting data and to identify a broad research strategy; survey data collection involves gathering information from individuals, called respondents, by having them respond to questions.

Survey Research: a broad research strategy that involves asking questions of a sample of people, in a fairly short period of time, and testing hypotheses or describing a situation based on their answers.

Systematic Errors: measurement errors that are consistent and patterned.

Systematic Replication: an attempt to extend a treatment to different settings, practitioners, client disorders, or any combination of these conditions.

Systematic Sampling: a type of simple random sampling wherein every *n*th element of the sampling frame is selected for the sample.

Table Elaboration: a multivariate analysis that examines the relationship between an independent variable and a dependent variable in each of the categories of a third, or test, variable.

Targeted Sampling: a variation on quota and purposive sampling in which procedures are used to ensure that people or groups with specified characteristics will appear in the sample.

Theoretical Sensitivity: having data collection and analysis closely guided by emerging theoretical issues.

Theory: a set of interrelated propositions or statements, organized into a deductive system, that offers an explanation of some phenomenon.

Thurstone Scale: a measurement scale consisting of a series of items with a predetermined scale value to which respondents indicate their agreement or disagreement.

Time Sampling: a sampling technique used in observational research in which observations are made only during specified preselected times.

Traditional Knowledge: knowledge based on custom, habit, and repetition.

Trend Study: research in which data are gathered from different people at different times.

True Experimental Designs: experimental designs that utilize randomization, control groups, and other techniques to control threats to internal validity.

Type I Error: the probability of rejecting a null hypothesis when it is actually true.

Type II Error: the probability of failing to reject a null hypothesis that is actually false.

Unidimensional Scale: a multiple-item scale that measures one, and only one, variable.

Units of Analysis: the specific objects or elements whose characteristics we wish to describe or explain and about which data are collected.

Univariate Statistics: statistics that describe the distribution of a single variable.

Unobtrusive Observation: observation in which those under study are not aware they are being studied and the investigator does not change their behavior by his or her presence.

Validity: the degree to which a measure accurately reflects the theoretical meaning of a variable.

Variables: operationally defined concepts that can take on more than one value.

Verification: the process of subjecting hypotheses to empirical tests to determine whether a theory is supported or refuted.

Verstehen: the effort to view and understand a situation from the perspective of the people actually in that situation.

References

Achen, C. H. *The Statistical Analysis of Quasi-Experiments.* Berkeley: University of California Press, 1986.

Adams, S., and M. Orgel. *Through the Mental Health Maze: A Consumer's Guide to Finding a Psychotherapist.* Washington, D.C.: Health Research Group, Public Citizen, 1975.

Alexander, C. J. Gay and Lesbian Parenting: A Unique Opportunity for Sexual Minority Research. *Journal of Gay and Lesbian Social Services* 7 (1997): 87–91.

Alfonso, S. D., and S. F. Dziegielewski. Self-Directed Treatment of Panic Disorder: A Holistic Approach. *Journal of Social Work Research and Evaluation* 2 (2001): 5–18.

Alford, R. R. *The Craft of Inquiry: Theories, Methods, Evidence.* New York: Oxford University Press, 1998.

Allen-Meares, P. Content Analysis: It Does Have a Place in Social Work Research. *Journal of Social Service Research* 7 (Summer 1984): 51–68.

Altman, L. Falsified Data Found in Gene Studies. *The New York Times on the Web* (October 30, 1996), Retrieved January 11, 2001 from the World Wide Web: www.nytimes.com.

Amato, P. R. Family Processes in One-Parent, Step-Parent, and Intact Families: The Child's Point of View. *Journal of Marriage and the Family* 49 (May 1987): 327–337.

Amato, P. R., and A. Booth. *A Generation at Risk: Growing Up in an Era of Family Upheaval.* Cambridge, Mass.: Harvard University Press, 1997.

American Association for Public Opinion Research Standards Committee. *Interviewer Falsification in Survey Research: Current Best Methods for Prevention, Detection, and Repair of Its Effects* (3d draft). American Association for Public Opinion Research. http://www.aapor.org/interviewfalse.pdf (April 21, 2003).

American Sociological Association *Code of Ethics* (Approved by ASA Membership in spring of 1997). [Accessed: June 21, 2003] <http://www.asanet.org/members/ecoderev.html>.

Anderson, A. Scientific Misconduct Still an Unknown. *Nature* 340 (1989): 3.

Anderson, B., B. Silver, and P. Abramson. The Effects of the Race of the Interviewer on Race-Related Attitudes of Black Respondents in SRC/CPS National Election Studies. *Public Opinion Quarterly* 52 (1988): 289–324.

Anderson, J. E., and R. Stall. Increased Reporting of Male-to-Male Sexual Activity in a National Survey. *Sexually Transmitted Diseases* 29 (November 2002): 643–646.

Annis, R. C., and B. Corenblum. Effect of Test Language and Experimenter Race on Canadian Indian Children's Racial and Self-Identity. *Journal of Social Psychology* 126 (December 1986): 761–773.

Archer, D., B. Iritiani, D. D. Kimes, and M. Barrios. Faceism: Five Studies of Sex Differences in Facial Prominence. *Journal of Personality and Social Psychology* 45 (1983): 725–735.

Arches, J. Social Structure, Burnout, and Job Satisfaction. *Social Work* 36 (May 1991): 202–206.

Armstrong, G. . . . Like That Desmond Morris? In *Interpreting the Field,* ed. D. Hobbs and T. May. Oxford, U.K.: Oxford University Press, 1993.

Armstrong, J. S., and E. J. Luck. Return Postage in Mail Surveys: A Meta-Analysis. *Public Opinion Quarterly* 51 (Summer 1987): 233–248.

Arnold, D. O. Dimensional Sampling: An Approach for Studying a Small Number of Cases. *American Sociologist* 5 (1970): 147–150.

Aronson, E., M. B. Brewer, and J. Carlsmith. Experimentation in Social Psychology. In *The Handbook of Social Psychology,* 3d ed., G. Lindzey and E. Aronson. New York: Random House, 1985.

Ashcraft, N., and A. E. Scheflen. *People Space: The Making and Breaking of Human Boundaries.* New York: Doubleday, 1976.

Bachman, J. G., and P. M. O'Malley. Yea-Saying, Nay-Saying, and Going to Extremes: Black–White Differences in Response Styles. *Public Opinion Quarterly* 48 (1984): 491–501.

Backstrom, C. H., and G. D. Hursh-Cesar. *Survey Research,* 2d ed. New York: Macmillan, 1981.

Bahl, A. B., S. A. Spaulding, and C. B. McNeil. Treatment of Noncompliance Using Parent–Child Interaction Therapy: A Data-Driven Approach. *Education and Treatment of Children Special Issue: Level 1 Research: Improving Our Education and Treatment through Simple Accountability Procedures* 22 (May 1999): 146–156.

Bailey, K. *Methods of Social Research,* 3d ed. New York: Free Press, 1987.

Bailey, R. C., Y. Hser, S. Hsieh, and M. D. Anglin. Influences Affecting Maintenance and Cessation of Narcotics Addiction. *Journal of Drug Issues* 24 (1994): 249–272.

Balassone, M. L. A Research Methodology for the Development of Risk Assessment Tools in Social Work Practice. *Social Work Research and Abstracts* 27 (1991): 16–23.

Bales, R. F. *Interaction Process Analysis.* Cambridge, Mass.: Addison-Wesley, 1950.

_____. Some Uniformities of Behavior in Small Social Systems. In *Readings in Social Psychology,* rev. ed., ed. G. E. Swanson, T. M. Newcomb, and E. L. Hartley. New York: Henry Holt and Company, 1952.

Barlow, D., and M. Hersen. Single-Case Experimental Designs: Uses in Applied Clinical Research. *Archives of General Psychiatry* 29 (1973): 319–325.

_____. *Single-Case Experimental Designs: Strategies for Studying Behavior Change,* 2d ed. New York: Pergamon Press, 1984.

Barlow, D. H., M. G. Craske, J. A. Cerny, and J. S. Klosko. Behavioral Treatment of Panic Disorder. *Behavior Therapy* 20 (1989): 261–282.

Barlow, D. H., S. C. Hayes, and R. O. Nelson. *The Scientist Researcher: Research and Accountability in Clinical and Educational Settings.* Boston: Allyn & Bacon, 1992.

Barlow, H. *Introduction to Criminology,* 7th ed. New York: HarperCollins, 1996.

Barnes, H. E., ed. *An Introduction to the History of Sociology.* Chicago: University of Chicago Press, 1948.

Bauer, D. G. *The "How To" Grants Manual: Successful Grantseeking Techniques for Obtaining Public and Private Grants.* Westport, Conn.: Praeger, 2004.

Baum, M. I. Gays and Lesbians Choosing to Be Parents. In *Gay and Lesbian Mental Health: A Sourcebook for Practitioners,* ed. C. J. Alexander et al. New York: Harrington Park Press/Haworth Press, 1996.

Baumrind, D. Research Using Intentional Deception. *American Psychologist* 40, no. 2 (February 1985): 165–174.

Beauchamp, T. L., R. R. Faden, R. J. Wallace Jr., and L. Walters, eds. *Ethical Issues in Social Science Research.* Baltimore, Md.: Johns Hopkins University Press, 1982.

Becerra, R. M., and R. E. Zambrana. Whose Side Are We On? *Social Problems* 14 (1967): 239–247.

_____. Methodological Approaches to Research on Hispanics. *Social Work Research and Abstracts* 21 (Summer 1985): 42–49.

Bedell, J. R., J. C. Ward Jr., R. P. Archer, and M. K. Stokes. An Empirical Evaluation of a Model of Knowledge Utilization. *Evaluation Review* (9 April 1985): 109–126.

Bell, A. P., and M. S. Weinberg. *Homosexualities: A Study of Diversity among Men and Women.* New York: Simon & Schuster, 1978.

Bell, W. *Contemporary Social Welfare,* 2d ed. New York: Macmillan, 1987.

Benton, T. *Philosophical Foundations of the Three Sociologies.* Boston: Routledge & Kegan Paul, 1977.

Berg, B. *Qualitative Research Methods for the Social Sciences,* 5th ed. Boston: Allyn & Bacon, 2004.

Berger, R. L. Ethics in Scientific Communication: Study of a Problem Case. *Journal of Medical Ethics* 20 (1994): 207–211.

Berk, R., and P. Rossi. *Thinking about Program Evaluation.* Newbury Park, Calif.: Sage, 1990.

Berk, R. A., et al. Social Policy Experimentation: A Position Paper. *Evaluation Review* 9 (August 1985): 387–430.

Bernard, H. R. *Research Methods in Anthropology: Qualitative and Quantitative Approaches,* 3d ed. Walnut Creek, Calif.: AltaMira Press, 2001.

Berry, S. H., and D. E. Kanouse. Physician Response to a Mailed Survey: An Experiment in Timing of Payment. *Public Opinion Quarterly,* 51 (Spring 1987): 102–114.

Berry, M. An Evaluation of Family Preservation Services: Fitting Agency Services to Family Needs. *Social Work* 37 (1992): 314–321.

Billups, J. O., and M. C. Julia. Changing Profile of Social Work Practice. *Social Work Research and Abstracts* 23 (Winter 1987): 17–22.

Binder, A., G. Geis, and D. Bruce. *Juvenile Delinquency: Historical, Cultural, and Legal Perspectives.* New York: Macmillan, 1988.

Black, M. M., and A. Ponirakis. Computer-Administered Interviews with Children about Maltreatment: Methodological, Developmental, and Ethical Issues. *Journal of Interpersonal Violence* 15 (July 2000): 682–695.

Blaikie, N. *Approaches to Social Enquiry.* Cambridge, Mass.: Polity, 1993.

Bloom, M., and J. Orme. Ethics and the Single-System Design. *Journal of Social Service Research* 18 (1993): 161–180.

Bloom, M., J. Fischer, and J. G. Orme. *Evaluating Practice: Guidelines for the Accountable Professional,* 3d ed. Boston: Allyn & Bacon, 1999.

Bogdan, R. C., and S. K. Biklen. *Qualitative Research for Education: An Introduction to Theory and Methods,* 2d ed. Boston: Allyn & Bacon, 1992.

Bogdan, R., and S. J. Taylor. *Introduction to Qualitative Research Methods.* New York: Wiley, 1975.

Bohrnstedt, G. W. Measurement. In *Handbook of Survey Research,* ed. P. H. Rossi, J. D. Wright, and A. B. Anderson. New York: Academic Press, 1983.

Bonnie, R. J. and R. B. Wallace, eds. *Elder Mistreatment: Abuse, Neglect, and Exploitation in an Aging America.* Washington D.C.: National Academy Press, 2003.

Borgatta, E., and G. Bohrnstedt. Levels of Measurement: Once Over Again. In *Social Measurement: Current Issues,* ed. G. Bohrnstedt and E. Borgatta. Beverly Hills, Calif.: Sage, 1981.

Bourgois, P. *In Search of Respect: Selling Crack in El Barrio.* Cambridge: Cambridge University Press, 1995.

Bourgois, P., M. Lettiere, and J. Quesada. Social Misery and the Sanction of Substance Abuse: Confronting HIV Risk among Homeless Heroin Addicts in San Francisco. *Social Problems* 44 (May 1997): 155–173.

Boynton, P. M. "I'm Just a Girl Who Can't Say No"? Women, Consent, and Sex Research. *Journal of Sex and Marital Therapy,* 29 (Suppl. 1, 2003): 23–32.

Bradburn, N. M. Response Effects. In *Handbook of Survey Research,* ed. P. H. Rossi, J. D. Wright, and A. B. Anderson. New York: Academic Press, 1983.

Bradburn, N. M., and S. Sudman. *Improving Interview Method and Questionnaire Design.* San Francisco: Jossey-Bass, 1979.

Brajuha, M., and L. Hallowell. Legal Intrusion and the Politics of Fieldwork. *Urban Life* 14 (1986): 454–479.

Brent, E. E., and A. Thompson. *Methodologist's Toolchest Version 3.0.* Columbia, Mo.: Idea Works, 2000.

Bridge, R. G. *Nonresponse Bias in Mail Surveys.* Defense Advanced Research Projects Agency R-1501. Santa Monica, Calif.: Rand, 1974.

Bronowski, J. *The Origins of Knowledge and Imagination.* New Haven, Conn.: Yale University Press, 1978.

Brown, S. V. The Commitment and Concerns of Black Adolescent Parents. *Social Work Research and Abstracts* 19 (1983): 27–34.

Brunner, G. A., and S. J. Carroll. Effect of Prior Telephone Appointments on Completion Rates and Response Content. *Public Opinion Quarterly* 31 (1967): 652–654.

Brunswick-Heineman, M. The Obsolete Scientific Imperative in Social Work Research. *Social Service Review* 55 (1981): 371–397.

Bryson, M. The *Literary Digest* Poll: Making of a Statistical Myth. *The American Statistician* 30 (November 1976): 184–185.

Buetow, S. A., R. M. Douglas, P. Harris, and C. McCulloch. Computer-Assisted Personal Interviews: Development and Experience of an Approach in Australian General Practice. *Social Science Computer Review* 14 (1996): 205–212.

Burch, G., and V. Mohr. Evaluating a Child Abuse Intervention Program. *Social Casework* 61 (1980): 90–99.

Burgess, R., and L. Youngblade. Social Incompetence and the Intergenerational Transmission of Abusive Parental Practices. In *Family Abuse and Its Consequences: New Directions in Research,* ed. G. Hotaling, D. Finkelhor, J. Kirkpatrick, and M. Strauss. Newbury Park, Calif.: Sage, 1988.

Bushery, J. M., J. W. Reichert, K. A. Albright, and J. C. Rossiter. Using Date and Time Stamps to Detect Interviewer Falsification. [Accessed: June 21, 2003] http://www.amstat.org/sections/srms/proceedings/papers/1999_053.pdf. Washington D.C.: U.S. Census Bureau, 1999.

Cahalan, D. The *Digest* Poll Rides Again! *Public Opinion Quarterly* 53 (1989): 129–133.

Campbell, D. T., and D. W. Fiske. Convergent and Discriminant Validity by the Multitrait-Multimethod Matrix. *Psychological Bulletin* 56 (1959): 81–105.

Campbell, D. T., and J. C. Stanley. *Experimental and Quasi-Experimental Designs for Research.* Chicago: Rand McNally, 1963.

Cannell, C. F., and R. L. Kahn. Interviewing. In *The Handbook of Social Psychology,* 2d ed, vol. 2., ed. G. Lindzey and E. Aronson. Reading, Mass.: Addison-Wesley, 1968.

Carise, D., W. Cornely, and O. Gurel. A Successful Researcher–Practitioner Collaboration in Substance Abuse Treatment. *Journal of Substance Abuse Treatment* 23 (2002): 157–162.

Carlock, C. J., and P. Y. Martin. Sex Composition and the Intensive Group Experience. *Social Work* 22 (1977): 27–32.

Carroll, L. *Through the Looking Glass.* New York: Random House, 1946.

Cartwright, A., and W. Tucker. An Attempt to Reduce the Number of Calls on an Interview Inquiry. *Public Opinion Quarterly* 31 (1967): 299–302.

Catlin, G., and S. Ingram. The Effects of CATI on Costs and Data Quality: A Comparison of CATI and Paper Methods. In *Telephone Survey Methodology,* ed. R. G. Groves et al. New York: Wiley, 1988.

Cavan, S. *Liquor License.* Chicago: Aldine, 1966.

Ceci, S. J., D. Peters, and J. Plotkin. Human Subjects Review, Personal Values, and the Regulation of Social

Science Research. *American Psychologist* 40 (September 1985): 994–1002.

Centers for Disease Control and Prevention. Update: AIDS—United States, 2000. *Morbidity and Mortality Weekly Report* 51 (July 12, 2002): 592–595.

Chaiken, M. R., and J. M. Chaiken. Offender Types and Public Policy. *Crime and Delinquency* 30 (April 1984): 195–226.

Champion, D. J. *Basic Statistics for Social Research,* 2d ed. Scranton, Pa.: Chandler, 1981.

Charmaz, K. The Grounded Theory Method: An Explication and Interpretation. In *Contemporary Field Research,* ed. R. M. Emerson. Prospect Heights, Ill.: Waveland Press, 1983.

Chen, H., and P. H. Rossi. The Multi-Goal, Theory-Driven Approach to Evaluation: A Model Linking Basic and Applied Social Science. *Social Forces* 59 (1980): 106–122.

Children's Research Center. *The Improvement of Child Protective Services with Structured Decision Making: The CRC Model.* San Francisco: National Council on Crime and Delinquency, 1999.

Christie, R., and F. L. Geis. *Studies in Machiavellianism.* New York: Academic Press, 1970.

Clark, H. W. Bridging the Gap between Substance Abuse Practice and Research: The National Treatment Plan Initiative. *Journal of Drug Issues* 32 (Summer 2002): 757–768.

Clandinin, D. J., and F. M. Connelly. *Narrative Inquiry: Experience and Story in Qualitative Research.* San Francisco: Jossey-Bass, 2000.

Clum, G. A. *Coping with Panic: A Drug-Free Approach to Dealing with Anxiety Attacks.* Belmont, Calif.: Brooks/Cole, 1990.

Coe, J. A. R., and G. M. Menon, eds. *Computers and Information Technology in Social Work.* Binghamton, N.Y.: Haworth Press, 2000.

Coe, R. D., and D. H. Hill. Food Stamp Participation and Reasons for Nonparticipation: 1986. *Journal of Family and Economic Issues* 19 (Summer 1998): 107–130.

Coehlo, R. J. *An Experimental Investigation of Two Multi-Component Approaches on Smoking Cessation* (Ph.D. diss., Michigan State University, 1983).

Cohen, J. *Statistical Power Analysis for Behavioral Sciences,* 2d ed. Hillsdale, N.J.: Lawrence Erlbaum Associates, 1988.

Cohen, M. R., and E. Nagel. *An Introduction to Logic and Scientific Method.* New York: Harcourt, 1934.

Colley, G., B., C. H. Johnson, B. Morrow, I. B. Ahluwalia, M. E. Gaffield, L. Fischer, M. Rogers, and N. Whitehead. *PRAMS 1997 Surveillance Report.* Atlanta: Ga.: Division of Reproductive Health, National Center for Chronic Disease Prevention and Health Promotion, Centers for Disease Control and Prevention, 1999.

Committee on the Status of Women in Sociology. *The Treatment of Gender in Research.* Washington, D.C.: American Sociological Association, 1986.

Cook, T. D. Postpositivist Critical Multiplism. In *Social Science and Social Policy,* ed. L. Shotland and M. M. Mark. Beverly Hills, Calif.: Sage, 1985.

Cook, T. D., F. L. Cook, and M. M. Mark. Randomized and Quasi-Experimental Designs in Evaluation Research: An Introduction. In *Evaluation Research Methods,* ed. L. Rutman. Beverly Hills, Calif.: Sage, 1977.

Cochrane Collaboration. *The Cochrane Library* [Accessed: October 13, 2003] <http://www.update-software.com/Cochrane/> (2003).

Corcoran, K., and J. Fischer. *Measures for Clinical Practice: A Sourcebook.* New York: Free Press, 1987.

Corcoran, K. and J. Fischer, eds. *Measures for Clinical Practice: A Sourcebook,* 3d ed. New York: Free Press, 2000.

Corry, J. Children's TV Found Dominated by White Men. *New York Times,* July 15, 1982, 14.

Cote-Arsenault, D., and R. Marshall. One Foot In—One Foot Out: Weathering the Storm of Pregnancy after Perinatal Loss. *Research in Nursing and Health* 23 (2000): 473–485.

Coulton, C. J. Developing an Instrument to Measure Person–Environment Fit. *Journal of Social Service Research* 3 (1979): 159–174.

Council on Social Work Education. *Handbook of Accreditation Standards and Procedures,* 4th ed. Washington, D.C.: Council on Social Work Education, 1994.

Couper, M. P. Web Surveys: A Review of Issues and Approaches. *Public Opinion Quarterly* 64 (Winter 2000): 464–494.

Couper, M. P., and B. Rowe. Evaluation of a Computer-Assisted Self-Interview Component in a Computer-Assisted Personal Interview Survey. *Public Opinion Quarterly* 60 (1996): 89–105.

Cournoyer, B. R., and G. L. Powers. Evidence-Based Social Work: The Quiet Revolution Continues. In *Social Workers' Desk Reference,* ed. A. R. Roberts and G. J. Greene. Oxford: Oxford University Press, 2002, 798–807.

Couvalis, G. *The Philosophy of Science: Science and Objectivity.* London: Sage, 1997.

Cox, D. E., and C. N. Sipprelle. Coercion in Participation as a Research Subject. *American Psychologist* 26 (1971): 726–728.

Crabb, P. B., and D. Bielawski. The Social Representation of Material Culture and Gender in Children's Books. *Sex Roles* 30 (1994): 69–79.

Crockenberg, S., and B. Soby. Self-Esteem and Teenage Pregnancy. In *The Social Importance of Self-Esteem,* ed. A. Mecca, N. Smelser, and J. Vasconcellos. Berkeley: University of California Press, 1989.

Cronbach, L. J. Coefficient Alpha and the Internal Structure of Tests. *Psychometrica* 16 (1951): 197–334.

Cronbach, L. J., and P. Meehl. Construct Validity in Psychological Tests. *Psychological Bulletin* 52 (1955): 281–302.

Dailey, R. M., and R. E. Claus. The Relationship between Interviewer Characteristics and Physical and Sexual Abuse Disclosures among Substance Users: A Multilevel Analysis. *Journal of Drug Issues* 31 (Fall 2001): 867–888.

Davis, D. W. Nonrandom Measurement Error and Race of Interviewer Effects among African Americans. *Public Opinion Quarterly* 61 (1997): 183–207.

Davis, L. V. Beliefs of Social Service Providers about Abused Women and Abusing Men. *Social Work* 29 (May/June 1984): 243–250.

Dawson, J. A., and J. J. D'Amico. Involving Program Staff in Evaluation Studies: A Strategy for Increasing Information Use and Enriching the Data Base. *Evaluation Review* 9 (April 1985): 173–188.

Decker, S. H., and B. Van Winkle. *Life in the Gang: Family, Friends, and Violence.* Cambridge: Cambridge University Press, 1996.

DeKeseredy, W. S. Current Controversies on Defining Nonlethal Violence against Women in Intimate Heterosexual Relationships. *Violence Against Women* 6 (July 2000): 728–746.

DeKeseredy, W. S., and L. MacLeod. *Woman Abuse: A Sociological Story.* Toronto: Harcourt Brace, 1997.

deLeeuw, E., and W. Nicholls II. Technological Innovations in Data Collection: Acceptance, Data Quality, and Costs. *Sociological Research Online* 1, no. 4 (1996), Accessed at http://www.socresonline.org.uk/socresonline/1/4/leeuw.html.

DeMaio, T. J. Social Desirability and Survey Measurement: A Review. In *Surveying Subjective Phenomena,* 2d, ed. C. F. Turner and E. Martin. New York: Russell Sage Foundation, 1984.

DeMartini, J. Basic and Applied Sociological Work: Divergence, Convergence, or Peaceful Coexistence? *Journal of Applied Behavioral Science* 18 (1982): 203–215.

Denzin, N. *The Research Act: A Theoretical Introduction to Sociological Methods,* 3d ed. Englewood Cliffs, N.J.: Prentice Hall, 1989.

Department of Health and Human Services. *Research, Demonstration, and Evaluation Activities FY 2003 Plan and Budget* [Accessed: October 13, 2003] <http://aspe.hhs.gov/progsys/rde/general.htm> (February 2002).

Deutch, S. J., and F. B. Alt. The Effect of Massachusetts's Gun Control Law on Gun-Related Crimes in the City of Boston. *Evaluation Quarterly* 1 (1977): 543–567.

DeVault, M. L. *Liberating Method: Feminism and Social Research.* Philadelphia: Temple University Press, 1999.

DeVellis, R. F. *Scale Development: Theory and Applications,* 2d ed. Thousand Oaks, Calif.: Sage, 2003.

DeWalt, K. M., and B. R. DeWalt. *Participant Observation: A Guide for Fieldworkers.* Walnut Creek, Calif.: AltaMira Press, 2001.

Dignan, M., R. Michielutte, P. Sharp, J. Bahnson, L. Young, and P. Beal. The Role of Focus Groups in Health Education for Cervical Cancer among Minority Women. *Journal of Community Health* 15 (1990): 369–375.

Dobratz, B. A., and S. L. Shanks-Meile. *"White Power, White Pride!" The White Separatist Movement in the United States.* New York: Twayne Publishers, 1997.

Dohan, D., and M. Sánchez-Jankowski. Using Computers to Analyze Ethnographic Field Data: Theoretical and Practical Considerations. *Annual Review of Sociology* 24 (1998): 477–516.

Dotson, L. E., and G. F. Summers. Elaboration of Guttman Scaling Techniques. In *Attitude Measurement,* ed. G. F. Summers. Chicago: Rand McNally, 1970.

Dowd, N. E. *In Defense of Single-Parent Families.* New York: New York University Press, 1997.

Dunford, F., D. Huizinga, and D. Elliott. *The Omaha Domestic Violence Police Experiment.* Washington, D.C.: National Institute of Justice, 1989.

Durkheim, E. *Rules of the Sociological Method.* Trans. S. Solovay and J. Mueller. Chicago: University of Chicago Press, 1938.

Earnest, C. Single Case Study of EEG Asymmetry Biofeedback for Depression: An Independent Replication in an Adolescent. *Journal of Neurotherapy* 3 (Spring 1999): 28–35.

Eckenwiler, L. A. Pursuing Reform in Clinical Research: Lessons from Women's Experience. *Journal of Law, Medicine & Ethics* 27 (1999): 158–70.

Edlesen, J. L. Rapid Assessment Instruments for Evaluating Practice with Children and Youth. *Journal of Social Service Research* 8 (1985): 17–31.

Edwards, A. L. *Techniques of Attitude Scale Construction.* New York: Appleton-Century-Crofts, 1957.

Edwards, A. L., and F. P. Kilpatrick. A Technique for the Construction of Attitude Scales. *Journal of Applied Psychology* 32 (1948): 374–384.

Eichler, M. *Nonsexist Research Methods: A Practical Guide.* Boston: Allen & Unwin, 1988.

Ellickson, P., and R. Bell. Challenges to Social Experiments: A Drug Prevention Example. *Journal of Research in Crime and Delinquency* 29 (1992): 79–101.

Elliott, D. S., and D. Huizinga. Social Class and Delinquent Behavior in a National Youth Panel: 1976–1980. *Criminology* 21 (1983): 149–177.

Elms, A. C. Keeping Deception Honest: Justifying Conditions for Social Scientific Research Strategies. In *Ethical Issues in Social Science Research,* ed. T. L. Beauchamp, R. R. Faden, R. J. Wallace Jr., and L. Walters. Baltimore: Johns Hopkins University Press, 1982.

Engler, R. L., J. W. Covell, P. J. Friedman, P. S. Kitcher, and R. M. Peters. Misrepresentation and Responsibility in Medical Research. *New England Journal of Medicine* 17 (November 26, 1987): 1383–1389.

Epstein, I., and T. Tripodi. *Research Techniques for Program Planning, Monitoring, and Evaluation.* New York: Columbia University Press, 1977.

Erikson, K. T. A Comment on Disguised Observation in Sociology. *Social Problems* 14 (1967): 366–373.

Estroff, S. E. *Making It Crazy: An Ethnography of Psychiatric Clients in an American Community.* Berkeley: University of California Press, 1981.

Eysenbach, G., and J. E. Till. Ethical Issues in Qualitative Research on Internet Communities. *Information in Practice BMJ* (November 2001): 1103–1105.

Fahrenberg, J. Ambulatory Assessment: Issues and Perspectives. In *Ambulatory Assessment: Computer-Assisted Psychological and Psychophysiological Methods in Monitoring and Field Studies,* ed. J. Fahrenberg and M. Myrtek. Seattle, Wash.: Hogrefe & Huber, 1996.

Farley, R. *Blacks and Whites: Narrowing the Gap.* Cambridge, Mass.: Harvard University Press, 1984.

Federal Bureau of Investigation. *Uniform Crime Reports: Crime in the United States, 1991.* Washington, D.C.: U.S. Government Printing Office, 1992.

Federal Register 64 (June 17, 1999): 116.

Feldman, M. S., J. Bell, and M. T. Berger. *Gaining Access: A Practical Guide for Qualitative Researchers.* Walnut Creek, Calif.: AltaMira Press, 2003.

Feldman, R. A., and T. E. Caplinger. Social Work Experience and Client Behavioral Change: A Multivariate Analysis of Process and Outcome. *Journal of Social Service Research* 1 (1977): 5–33.

Fernandez, M., and H. S. Ruch-Ross. Ecological Analysis of Program Impact: A Site Analysis of Programs for Pregnant and Parenting Adolescents in Illinois. *Journal of Applied Sociology* 15 (1998): 104–133.

Ferree, M., and E. Hall. Visual Images of American Society: Gender and Race in Introductory Sociology Textbooks. *Gender and Society* 4 (1990): 500–533.

Festinger, L., H. Riecken, and S. Schachter. *When Prophecy Fails.* New York: Harper & Row, 1956.

Fielding, N. G. Automating the Ineffable: Qualitative Software and the Meaning of Qualitative Research. In *Qualitative Research in Action,* ed. T. May. Thousand Oaks, Calif.: Sage, 2002.

Fienberg, S., M. Martin, and M. Straf, eds. *Sharing Research Data.* Washington, D.C.: National Academy Press, 1985.

Fletcher, L. A., D. J. Erickson, T. L. Toomey, and A. C. Wagenaar. Handheld Computers: A Feasible Alternative to Paper Forms for Field Data Collection. *Evaluation Review* 27 (April 2003): 165–178.

Flick, U. *An Introduction to Qualitative Research*, 2d ed. Thousand Oaks, Calif.: Sage, 2002.

Fontana, A., and J. H. Frey. Interviewing: The Art of Science. In *Handbook of Qualitative Research,* ed. N. K. Denzin and Y. S. Lincoln. Thousand Oaks, Calif.: Sage, 1994.

Fortune, A. E. Communication in Task-Centered Treatment. *Social Work* 24 (1979): 390–397.

Fowler, F., Jr., and T. Mangione. *Standardized Survey Interviewing.* Newbury Park, Calif.: Sage, 1990.

Fox, R. J., M. R. Crask, and J. Kim. Mail Survey Response Rate: A Meta-Analysis of Selected Techniques for Inducing Response. *Public Opinion Quarterly* 52 (1988): 467–491.

Fox, S., and D. Schwartz. Social Desirability and Controllability in Computerized and Paper-and-Pencil Personality Questionnaires. *Computers in Human Behavior* 18 (July 2002): 389–410.

Frankfort-Nachmias, C., and D. Nachmias. *Research Methods in the Social Sciences*, 6th ed. New York: Worth Publishers, 2000.

Fredman, N., and R. Sherman. *Handbook of Measurements for Marriage and Family Therapy.* New York: Brunner/Mazel, 1987.

Frey, J. H. An Experiment with a Confidentiality Reminder in a Telephone Survey. *Public Opinion Quarterly* 50 (Summer 1986): 267–269.

Fricker, R. D., and M. Schonlau. Advantages and Disadvantages of Internet Research Surveys: Evidence from the Literature. *Field Methods* 14 (November 2002): 347–367.

Frisch, M. B., and R. L. Higgins. Instructional Demand Effects and the Correspondence among Role-Play, Self-Report, and Naturalistic Measures of Social Skill. *Behavioral Assessment* 8 (Summer 1986): 221–236.

Fulford, K. W. M., and K. Howse. Ethics of Research with Psychiatric Patients: Principles, Problems, and the Primary Responsibilities of Researchers. *Journal of Medical Ethics* 19 (1993): 85–91.

Galison, P., and D. Stump, eds. *The Disunity of Science: Boundaries, Contexts, and Power.* Stanford, Calif.: Stanford University Press, 1996.

Galtung, J. *Theory and Methods of Social Research.* New York: Columbia University Press, 1967.

Garfield, E., and A. Welljams-Dorof. The Impact of Fraudulent Research on the Scientific Literature. *Journal of the American Medical Association* 263 (1990): 1424–1426.

Gelles, R. J. Methods for Studying Sensitive Family Topics. *American Journal of Orthopsychiatry* 48 (1978): 408–424.

_____.What to Learn from Cross-Cultural and Historical Research on Child Abuse and Neglect: An Overview. In *Child Abuse and Neglect: Biosocial Dimensions,* ed. R. J. Gelles and J. B. Lancaster. New York: Aldine de Gruyter, 1987.

Gibbs, L. Evaluation Researcher: Scientist or Advocate? *Journal of Social Service Research* 7 (Fall 1983): 81–92.

_____. *Scientific Reasoning for Social Workers: Bridging the Gap between Research and Practice.* New York: Macmillan, 1991.

_____. *Evidence-Based Practice for the Helping Professions: A Practical Guide with Integrated Multimedia.* Pacific Grove, Calif.: Brooks/Cole-Thomson Learning, 2003.

Gibelman, M., and S. R. Gelman. Learning from the Mistakes of Others: A Look at Scientific Misconduct in Research. *Journal of Social Work Education* 37 (2001): 241–254.

Gilligan, C. *In a Different Voice: Psychological Theory and Women's Development.* Cambridge, Mass.: Harvard University Press, 1982.

Gilmore, S., and A. Crissman. Video Games: Analyzing Gender Identity and Violence in This New Virtual Reality. *Studies in Symbolic Interaction* 21 (1997): 181–199.

Gingerich, W. Rethinking Single-Case Evaluation. In *Advances in Clinical Social Work Research,* ed. L. Videka-Sherman and W. Reid. Silver Spring, Md.: NASW Press, 1990.

Ginsburg, H., and S. Opper. *Piaget's Theory of Intellectual Development,* 3d ed. Englewood Cliffs, N.J.: Prentice Hall, 1988.

Glaser, B. *Theoretical Sensitivity.* Mill Valley, Calif.: Sociology Press, 1978.

Glaser, B., and A. Strauss. *Awareness of Dying.* Chicago: Aldine, 1965.

Glaser, J., J. Dixit, and D. P. Green. Studying Hate Crime with the Internet: What Makes Racists Advocate Racial Violence? *Journal of Social Issues* 58 (2002): 177–193.

Gold, R. L. Roles in Sociological Field Observations. *Social Forces* 36 (1958): 217–223.

Goldberg, G. S., R. Kantrow, E. Kremen, and L. Lauter. Spouseless, Childless Elderly Women and Their Social Supports. *Social Work* 31 (March/April 1986): 104–112.

Goldfried, M. R., and B. E. Wolfe. Psychotherapy Practice and Research: Repairing a Strained Alliance. *American Psychologist* 51 (October 1996): 1007–1016.

Goldsmith, D. J., V. M. McDermott, and S. C. Alexander. Helpful, Supportive, and Sensitive: Measuring the Evaluation of Enacted Social Support in Personal Relationships. *Journal of Social and Personal Relationships* 17 (2000): 369–391.

Goode, W. J., and P. K. Hatt. *Methods in Social Research.* New York: McGraw-Hill, 1952.

Gorden, R. L. *Interviewing: Strategies, Techniques, and Tactics,* 4th ed. Chicago: Dorsey Press, 1987.

Gordon, M. M. *The Scope of Sociology.* New York: Oxford University Press, 1988.

Gottman, J. M. *Time-Series Analysis: A Comprehensive Introduction for Social Scientists.* New York: Cambridge University Press, 1981.

_____. Observational Measures of Behavior Therapy Outcome: A Reply to Jacobson. *Behavioral Assessment* 7 (Fall 1985): 317–321.

Gottman, J. S. Children of Gay and Lesbian Parents. In *Homosexuality and Family Relationships,* ed. F. W. Bozett and M. B. Sussman. New York: Harrington Park Press, 1990.

Gouldner, A. The Dark Side of the Dialectic: Toward a New Objectivity. *Sociological Inquiry* 46 (1976): 3–16.

Goyder, J. Face-to-Face Interviews and Mailed Questionnaires: The Net Difference in Response Rate. *Public Opinion Quarterly* 49 (Summer 1985): 234–252.

Graham, K., L. LaRocque, R. Yetman, T. J. Ross, and E. Guistra. Aggression and Barroom Environments. *Journal of Studies on Alcohol* 41 (1980): 277–292.

Graham, K. R. *Psychological Research: Controlled Interpersonal Research.* Monterey, Calif.: Brooks/Cole, 1977.

Gray, B. H. The Regulatory Context of Social and Behavioral Research. In *Ethical Issues in Social Science Research,* ed. T. L. Beauchamp, R. R. Faden, R. J. Wallace Jr., and L. Walters. Baltimore: Johns Hopkins University Press, 1982.

Greene, J. C. Qualitative Program Evaluation. In *Handbook of Qualitative Research,* ed. N. K. Denzin and Y. S. Lincoln. Thousand Oaks, Calif.: Sage, 1994.

Greene, P. D. Handheld Computers as Tools for Writing and Managing Field Data. *Field Methods* 13 (May 2001): 181–197.

Greenfield, T. K., and C. C. Attkisson. The UCSF Client Satisfaction Scales II: The Service Satisfaction Scale-30. In *The Use of Psychological Testing for Treatment Planning Outcomes Assessment,* 2d ed., ed. M. E. Maruish. Mahwah, N.J.: Lawrence Erlbaum Associates, 1999.

Greenley, J. R., and R. A. Schoenherr. Organization Effects on Client Satisfaction with Humaneness of Service. *Journal of Health and Social Behavior* 22 (1981): 2–18.

Gribble, J. N., H. G. Miller, and S. M. Rogers. Interview Mode and Measurement of Sexual Behaviors: Methodological Issues. *Journal of Sex Research* 36 (February 1999): 16–24.

Grichting, W. L. Do Laws Make a Difference? *Journal of Social Service Research* 2 (1979): 245–265.

Grigsby, R. K., and H. L. Roof. Federal Policy for the Protection of Human Subjects: Applications to Research on Social Work Practice. *Research on Social Work Practice* 3 (October 1993): 448–461.

Groth-Marnat, G. *Handbook of Psychological Assessment.* New York: Van Nostrand, 1984.

Groves, R. M. *Survey Errors and Survey Costs.* New York: Wiley, 1989.

Groves, R. M., P. B. Blemer, L. E. Lyberg, J. T. Massey, W. L. Nicholls, and J. Waksberg, eds. *Telephone Survey Methodology.* Somerset, N.J.: Wiley, 1988.

Groze, V. Adoption and Single Parents: A Review. *Child Welfare* 70 (1991): 321–332.

Groze, V. K., and J. A. Rosenthal. Single Parents and Their Adopted Children: A Psychosocial Analysis. *Journal of Contemporary Human Services* (1991): 130–139.

Guba, E. G., and Y. S. Lincoln. Competing Paradigms in Qualitative Research. In *Handbook of Qualitative Research,* ed. N. K. Denzin and Y. S. Lincoln. Thousand Oaks, Calif.: Sage, 1994.

Gubrium, J. F., and J. A. Holstein. *The New Language of Qualitative Methods.* New York: Oxford University Press, 1997.

Guttman, L. A Basis for Scaling Qualitative Data. *American Sociological Review* 9 (1944): 139–150.

———. The Basis for Scalogram Analysis. In *Measurement and Prediction,* ed. S. A. Stouffer et al. Princeton, N.J.: Princeton University Press, 1950.

Halfpenny, P. *Positivism and Sociology: Explaining Social Life.* London: Allen & Unwin, 1982.

Harlow, E., and S. A. Webb, eds. *Information and Communication Technology in the Welfare Services.* London: Taylor and Francis, 2003.

Harris, A. R., S. H. Thomas, G. A. Fisher, and D. J. Hirsch. Murder and Medicine: The Lethality of Criminal Assault 1960–1999. *Homicide Studies Journal* 6 (May 2002): 128–166.

Harris, F. N., and W. R. Jenson. Comparisons of Multiple-Baseline across Persons Designs and AB Designs with Replication: Issues and Confusions. *Behavioral Assessment* 7 (Spring 1985): 121–127.

Harrison, W. D. Role Strain and Burnout in Child-Protective Service Workers. *Social Service Review* 54 (1980): 31–44.

Hayes, S. C., D. H. Barlow, and R. O. Nelson-Gray. *The Scientist Practitioner: Research and Accountability in the Age of Managed Care.* Boston: Allyn & Bacon, 1999.

Heckathorn, D. D. Respondent-Driven Sampling: A New Approach to the Study of Hidden Populations. *Social Problems* 44 (May 1997): 174–199.

Heise, D. R. The Semantic Differential and Attitude Research. In *Attitude Measurement,* ed. G. F. Summers. Chicago: Rand McNally, 1970.

Henry, G. *Practical Sampling.* Newbury Park, Calif.: Sage, 1990.

Hepworth, D. H., and J. Larsen. *Direct Social Work Practice.* Belmont, Calif.: Wadsworth, 1990.

Higgins, P. C., and J. M. Johnson. *Personal Sociology.* New York: Praeger, 1988.

Hirschel, J., I. Hutchison III, and C. Dean. The Failure of Arrest to Deter Spouse Abuse. *Journal of Research in Crime and Delinquency* 29 (1992): 7–33.

Holstein, J. A., and J. F. Gubrium. Phenomenology, Ethnomethodology, and Interpretive Practice. In *Handbook of Qualitative Research,* ed. N. Denzin and Y. Lincoln. Thousand Oaks, Calif.: Sage, 1994.

———. *The Active Interview.* Thousand Oaks, Calif.: Sage, 1995.

Holstein, J. A., and J. F. Gubrium, eds. *Inside Interviewing: Conceptual Issues and Methodological Considerations.* Thousand Oaks, Calif.: Sage, 2003.

Holsti, O. R. *Content Analysis for the Social Sciences and Humanities.* Reading, Mass.: Addison-Wesley, 1969.

Holtgrave, D. R., ed. *Handbook of Economic Evaluation of HIV Prevention Programs.* New York: Plenum Press, 1998.

Honey, M. *Creating Rosie the Riveter: Class, Gender, and Propaganda.* Amherst: University of Massachusetts Press, 1984.

Hooker, E. The Adjustment of the Male Overt Homosexual. *Journal of Projective Techniques* 21 (1957): 18–31.

Horowitz, R. Community Tolerance of Gang Violence. *Social Problems* 34 (December 1987): 437–450.

Huber, B. New Human Subjects Policies Announced; Exemptions Outlined. *ASA Footnotes* 9 (1981): 1.

Hudson, W. W., and S. L. McMurtry. Comprehensive Assessment in Social Work Practice: The Multi-Problem Screening Inventory. *Research on Social Work Practice* 7 (January 1997): 79–98.

Hughson, J. Among the Thugs: The "New Ethnographies" of Football Supporting Cultures. *International Review for the Sociology of Sport* 33 (1998): 43–57.

Hummel-Rossi, B., and J. Ashdown. The State of Cost-Benefit and Cost-Effectiveness Analyses in Education. *Review of Educational Research* 72 (Spring 2002): 1–30.

Humphreys, L. *Tearoom Trade: Impersonal Sex in Public Places.* Chicago: Aldine-Atherton, 1970.

Hyman, H. *Interviewing in Social Research.* Chicago: University of Chicago Press, 1954.

Irwin, D. M., and M. M. Bushnell. *Observational Strategies for Child Study.* New York: Holt, Rinehart & Winston, 1980.

Israel, T. Studying Sexuality: Strategies for Surviving Stigma. *Feminism & Psychology* 12 (2002): 256–260.

Jackson, B. O., and L. B. Mohr. Rent Subsidies: An Impact Evaluation and an Application of the Random-Comparison-Group Design. *Evaluation Review* 10 (August 1986): 483–517.

James, J., and R. Bolstein. The Effect of Monetary Incentives and Follow-Up Mailings on the Response Rate and Response Quality in Mail Surveys. *Public Opinion Quarterly* 54 (1990): 346–361.

Janssen, P. P., W. B. Schaufeli, and I. Houkes. Work-Related and Individual Determinants of the Three Burnout Dimensions. *Work and Stress* 13 (1999): 74–86.

Jayaratne, S, and R. Levy. *Empirical Clinical Practice.* New York: Columbia University Press, 1979.

Jeger, A. M., and R. S. Slotnick. Community Mental Health: Toward a Behavioral-Ecological Perspective. In *Community Mental Health and Behavioral Ecology,* ed. A. M. Jeger and R. S. Slotnick. New York: Plenum, 1982.

Jekielek, S. M. Parental Conflict, Marital Disruption, and Children's Emotional Well-Being. *Social Forces* 76 (1998): 905–935.

Jenkins-Hall, K., and C. A. Osborn. The Conduct of Socially Sensitive Research: Sex Offenders as Participants. *Criminal Justice and Behavior* 21 (1994): 325–340.

Joe, G. W., K. M. Broome, G. A. Rowan-Szal, and D. D. Simpson. Measuring Patient Attributes and Engagement in Treatment. *Journal of Substance Abuse Treatment* 22 (June 2002): 183–196.

Johnson, F. C. Practice versus Research: Issues in Teaching of Single-Subject Research Skills. *Journal of Education for Social Work* 17 (1981): 62–68.

Johnson, S. M., and G. White. Self-Observation as an Agent of Behavioral Change. *Behavioral Therapy* 2 (1971): 488–497.

Joint Initiative of Mental Health Professional Organizations. *Mental Health Bill of Rights Project: Principles for the Provision of Mental Health and Substance Abuse Treatment Services.* 1997. American Psychological Association. [Accessed: June 21, 2003] <http://helping.apa.org/spreadtheword/rights.html>.

Jones, J. H. *Bad Blood: The Tuskegee Syphilis Experiment,* exp. ed. New York: Free Press, 1992.

Jones, M. A. *A Second Chance for Families: Five Years Later, Follow-Up of a Program to Prevent Foster Care.* New York: Child Welfare League of America, 1985.

Jorgensen, D. *Participant Observation: A Methodology for Human Studies.* Newbury Park, Calif.: Sage, 1989.

Kadushin, A., and G. Kadushin. *The Social Work Interview: A Guide for Human Service Professionals,* 4th ed. New York: Columbia University Press, 1997.

Khang, S. W., and B. A. Iwata. Computer Systems for Collecting Real-Time Observation Data. In *Behavioral Observation: Technology and Applications in Developmental Disabilities,* ed. T. Thompson, D. Felce, and F. J. Symons. Baltimore: Brooks Publishing, 1999.

Kalra, V. S., E. A. Fieldhouse, and S. Alam. Avoiding the New Deal: A Case Study of Nonparticipation by Minority Ethnic Young People. *Youth & Policy* 72 (Summer 2001): 63–79.

Kamerman, J. B. *Death in the Midst of Life: Social and Cultural Influences on Death, Grief, and Mourning.* Englewood Cliffs, N.J.: Prentice Hall, 1988.

Kang, M-E. The Portrayal of Women's Images in Magazine Advertisements: Goffman's Gender Analysis Revisited. *Sex Roles* 37 (1997): 979–996.

Karoly, L. A., et al. Investing in Our Children: What We Know and Don't Know about the Costs and Benefits of Early Childhood Interventions. Santa Monica, Calif.: Rand, 1998.

Kassebaum, G., D. Ward, and D. Wilner. *Prison Treatment and Parole Survival.* New York: Wiley, 1971.

Katz, J. *Experimentation with Human Beings.* New York: Russell Sage Foundation, 1972.

Kaye, B. K., and T. J. Johnson. Research Methodology: Taming the Cyber Frontier: Techniques for Improving Online Surveys. *Social Science Computer Review* 17 (1999): 323–337.

Kazdin, A. E. *Single-Case Research Designs.* New York: Oxford University Press, 1982.

Kelle, U. Computer-Assisted Analysis of Qualitative Data. In *A Companion to Qualitative Research,* ed. U. Flick, E. von Kardoff, and I. Steinke. Thousand Oaks, Calif.: Sage, 2004.

Kelly, J. R., and J. E. McGrath. *On Time and Method.* Beverly Hills, Calif.: Sage, 1988.

Kemeny, J. G. *A Philosopher Looks at Science.* Princeton, N.J.: Van Nostrand, 1959.

Kennet, J., L. Burgio, and R. Schulz. Interventions for In-Home Caregivers: A Review of Research 1990 to Present. *Handbook of Dementia Caregiving,* ed. R. Schulz. New York: Springer, 2000.

Kenny, G. K. The Metric Properties of Rating Scales Employed in Evaluation of Research: An Empirical Examination. *Evaluation Review* 10 (June 1986): 397–408.

Kimmel, A. *Ethics and Values in Applied Social Research.* Newbury Park, Calif.: Sage, 1988.

King, N. M. P., G. E. Henderson, and J. Stein, eds. *Beyond Regulations: Ethics in Human Subjects Research.* Chapel Hill: University of North Carolina Press, 1999.

King, S. Researching Internet Communities: Proposed Ethical Guidelines for the Reporting of Results. *The Information Society* 12 (1996): 119–127.

Kirk, J., and M. L. Miller. *Reliability and Validity in Qualitative Research.* Beverly Hills, Calif.: Sage, 1986.

Kirk, S., and H. Kutchins. *The Selling of DSM: The Rhetoric of Science in Psychiatry.* New York: Aldine de Gruyter, 1992.

Kirsch, I. S., et al. *Adult Literacy in America: A First Look at the Results of the National Adult Literacy Survey.* Washington, D.C.: U.S. Department of Education, NCES, 1993.

Kish, L. *Survey Sampling.* New York: Wiley, 1965.

Kline, D. The Power of the Placebo. *Hippocrates: The Magazine of Health and Medicine* 2 (May/June 1988): 24–26.

Klockars, C. B. Dirty Hands and Deviant Subjects. In *Deviance and Decency: The Ethics of Research with Human Subjects,* ed. C. B. Klockars and F. W. O'Connor. Beverly Hills, Calif.: Sage, 1979.

Knorr, K. *The Manufacture of Knowledge: An Essay on the Constructivist and Contextual Nature of Science.* Oxford, U.K.: Pergamon Press, 1981.

Kogan, L. S. Principles of Measurement. In *Social Work Research,* ed. N. A. Polansky. Chicago: University of Chicago Press, 1975.

Kohfeld, C., and L. Leip. Bans on Concurrent Sale of Beer and Gas: A California Case Study. *Sociological Practice Review* 2 (April 1991): 104–115.

Korbin, J. E. Child Maltreatment in Cross-Cultural Perspective: Vulnerable Children and Circumstances. In *Child Abuse and Neglect: Biosocial Dimensions,* ed. R. J. Gelles and J. B. Lancaster. New York: Aldine de Gruyter, 1987.

Korn, J. H. *Illusions of Reality: A History of Deception in Social Psychology.* Albany: State University of New York Press, 1997.

Krasucki, C., P. Ryan, T. Ertan, R. Howard, J. Lindesay, and A. Mann. The FEAR: A Rapid Screening Instrument for Generalized Anxiety in Elderly Primary Care Attenders. *International Journal of Geriatric Psychiatry* 14 (1999): 60–68.

Krathwohl, D. R. *How to Prepare a Research Proposal: Guidelines for Funding and Dissertations in the Social and Behavioral Sciences,* 3d ed. New York: Distributed by Syracuse University Press, 1988.

Krippendorff, K. *Content Analysis: An Introduction to Its Methodology,* 2d ed. Thousand Oaks, Calif.: Sage, 2003.

Krueger, R. A. and M.A. Casey. *Focus Groups: A Practical Guide for Applied Research,* 3d ed. Thousand Oaks, Calif.: Sage, 2000.

Kuhn, T. *The Structure of Scientific Revolutions,* 2d ed. Chicago: University of Chicago Press, 1970.

Kuo, W. H., and Y. Tsai. Social Networking, Hardiness, and Immigrants' Mental Health. *Journal of Health and Social Behavior* 27 (June 1986): 133–149.

Lally, J. J. Social Determinants of Differential Allocation of Resources to Disease Research: A Comparative Analysis of Crib Death and Cancer Research. *Journal of Health and Social Behavior* 18 (1977): 125–138.

Lamb, S., M. R. Greenlick, and D. McCarty, eds. *Bridging the Gap between Practice and Research: Forging Partnerships with Community-Based Drug and Alcohol Treatment* Washington, D.C.: National Academy Press, 1998.

Landrine, H. Race and Class Stereotypes of Women. *Sex Roles* 13 (July 1985): 65–75.

Lansford, J. E., R. Ceballo, A. Abbey, and A. J. Stewart. Does Family Structure Matter? A Comparison of Adoptive, Two-Parent Biological, Single-Mother, Stepfather, and Stepmother Households. *Journal of Marriage and Family* 63 (2001): 840–851.

Lantz, H. R., R. Schmitt, M. Britton, and E. C. Snyder. Pre-Industrial Patterns in the Colonial Family in America: A Content Analysis of Colonial Magazines. *American Sociological Review* 33 (1968): 413–426.

Lavrakas, P. J. *Telephone Survey Methods: Sampling, Selection, and Supervision.* Beverly Hills, Calif.: Sage, 1987.

Lawless, E. J. Methodology and Research Notes: Women's Life Stories and Reciprocal Ethnography as Feminist and Emergent. *Journal of Folklore Research* 28 (1991): 35–60.

Lee, R. M. *Unobtrusive Methods in Social Research.* Philadelphia: Open University Press, 2000.

Lenihan, K. *Unlocking the Second Gate.* Department of Labor R&D Monograph 45. Washington, D.C.: U.S. Government Printing Office, 1977.

Leo, R. A. Trial and Tribulations: Courts, Ethnography, and the Need for an Evidentiary Privilege for Academic Researchers. *American Sociologist* 26 (Spring 1995): 113–134.

————. The Ethics of Deceptive Research Roles Reconsidered: A Response to Kai Erikson. *American Sociologist* 27 (Spring 1996): 122–128.

Lessler, J. T., R. A. Caspar, M. A. Penne, and P. R. Barker. Developing Computer Assisted Interviewing (CAI) for the National Household Survey on Drug Abuse. *Journal of Drug Issues* 30 (Winter 2000): 9–33.

Levin, J., and J. L. Spates. Hippie Values: An Analysis of the Underground Press. *Youth and Society* 2 (1970): 59–73.

Levin, J. R. Single-Case Research Design and Analysis: Comments and Concerns. In *Single-Case Research Design and Analysis: New Directions for Psychology and Education*, ed. T. R. Kratochwill and J. R. Levin. Hillsdale, N.J.: Lawrence Erlbaum, 1992.

Lewis, K. G. Children of Lesbians: Their Point of View. *Social Work* 25 (1980): 198–203.

Likert, R. A. Technique for the Measurement of Attitudes. *Archives of Psychology* 21 (1932): 140.

Lipsey, M. W. Design Sensitivity: Statistical Power for Applied Experimental Research. In *Handbook of Applied Social Research Methods,* ed. L. Bickman and D. Rog. Thousand Oaks, Calif.: Sage, 1997.

Locke, L. F., S. J. Silverman, and W. W. Spirduso. *Reading and Understanding Research.* Thousand Oaks, Calif.: Sage, 1998.

Locke, L. F., W. W. Spirduso, and S. J. Silverman. *Proposals That Work: A Guide for Planning Dissertations and Grant Proposals,* 4th ed. Thousand Oaks, Calif.: Sage, 2000.

Lockhart, L. L. Spousal Violence: A Cross-Racial Perspective. In *Black Family Violence: Current Research and Theory,* ed. R. L. Hampton. Lexington, Mass.: Lexington Books, 1991.

Lofland, J., and L. H. Lofland. *Analyzing Social Settings,* 3d ed. Belmont, Calif.: Wadsworth, 1995.

Loisel, P., M. Durand, B. Diallo, B. Vachon, N. Charpentier, and J. Labelle. From Evidence to Community Practice in Work Rehabilitation: The Quebec Experience. *Clinical Journal of Pain* 19 (2003): 105–113.

Luebke, B. Out of Focus: Images of Women and Men in Newspaper Photographs. *Sex Roles* 20 (1989): 121–133.

Lyddon, W. J., and J. V. Jones Jr., eds. *Empirically Supported Cognitive Therapies: Current and Future Applications.* New York: Springer Publishing, 2001.

Lynch, K. B., et al. Successful Program Development Using Implementation Evaluation. *Journal of Prevention and Intervention in the Community* 17 (1998): 51–64.

Lynch, M., and D. Bogen. Sociology's Asociological "Core": An Examination of Textbook Sociology in Light of the Sociology of Scientific Knowledge. *American Sociological Review* 62 (1997): 481–493.

Mactavish, J. B., M. J. Mahon, and Z. M. Lutfiyya. "I Can Speak for Myself ": Involving Individuals with Intellectual Disabilities as Research Participants. *Mental Retardation* 38 (June 2000): 216–227.

Magura, S., and B. S. Moses. *Outcome Measures for Child Welfare Services: Theory and Applications.* Washington, D.C.: Child Welfare League of America, 1986.

Mandell, N. The Least-Adult Role in Studying Children. *Journal of Contemporary Ethnography* 16 (1988): 433–467.

Manson, S. M. Recent Advances in American Indian Mental Health Research: Implications for Clinical Research and Training. In *Mental Health Research and Practice in Minority Communities: Development of Culturally Sensitive Training Programs,* ed. M. R. Miranda and H. H. L. Kitano. Rockville, Md.: U.S. Department of Health and Human Services, DHHS Publication No. (ADM) 86–1466, 1986.

Marascuilo, L., and P. L. Busk. Combining Statistics for Multiple-Baseline AB and Replicated ABAB Designs across Subjects. *Behavioral Assessment* 10 (1988): 1–28.

Marin, G., and B. VanOss Marin. *Research with Hispanic Populations.* Newbury Park, Calif.: Sage, 1991.

Marquart, J. W. Doing Research in Prison: The Strengths and Weaknesses of Full Participation as a Guard. In *Extreme Methods: Innovative Approaches to Social Science Research,* ed. J. M. Miller and R. Tewksbury. Boston: Allyn & Bacon, 2001.

Marshall, E. How Prevalent Is Fraud? That Million-Dollar Question. *Science* 290 (December 2000): 1662.

Martinez, T. A. Popular Culture as Oppositional Culture: Rap as Resistance. *Sociological Perspectives* 40 (1997): 265–286.

Martini, R., and H. J. Polatajko. Verbal Self-Guidance as a Treatment Approach for Children with Developmental Coordination Disorder: A Systematic Replication Study. *Occupational Therapy Journal of Research* 19 (Fall 1998): 157–181.

Marx, K. *Selected Writings in Sociology and Philosophy,* ed. T. B. Bottomore and M. Rubel. Baltimore: Penguin, 1964 (originally published 1848).

Maslach, C. Burned-Out. In *A Sociological Framework for Patient Care,* 2d ed., ed. J. R. Folta and E. S. Deck. New York: Wiley, 1979.

Mathios, A., R. Avery, C. Bisogni, and J. Shanahan. Alcohol Portrayal on Prime-Time Television: Manifest and Latent Messages. *Journal of Studies on Alcohol* 59 (1998): 305–310.

Maton, K. I., F. A. Hrabowski, and G. L. Greif. Preparing the Way: A Qualitative Study of High-Achieving African American Males and the Role of the Family. *American Journal of Community Psychology* 26 (1998): 639–668.

Mavis, B. E., and J. J. Brocato. Postal Surveys versus Electronic Mail Surveys: The Tortoise and the Hare Revisited. *Evaluation and the Health Professions* 21 (1998): 395–408.

Maxwell, C. D., J. H. Garner, and J. A. Fagan. The Effects of Arrest on Intimate Partner Violence: New Evidence from the Spousal Assault Replication Program. *Research in Brief.* Washington, D.C.: National Institute of Justice, U. S. Department of Justice, July 2001.

Maxwell, J. A. *Qualitative Research Design: An Interactive Approach.* Thousand Oaks, Calif.: Sage, 1996.

Mayo, J. K., R. C. Hornick, and E. G. McAnany. *Educational Reform with Television: The El Salvador Experience.* Palo Alto, Calif.: Stanford University Press, 1976.

McCandlish, B. Against All Odds: Lesbian Mother Family Dynamics. In *Gay and Lesbian Parents,* ed. F. Bozett. New York: Praeger, 1987.

McCord, J. A. Thirty-Year Follow-Up of Treatment Effects. *American Psychologist* 33 (1978): 284–289.

McDowell, I., and C. Newell. *Measuring Health: A Guide to Rating Scales and Questionnaires,* 2d ed. New York: Oxford University Press, 1996.

McFall, R. M. Effects of Self-Monitoring on Normal Smoking Behavior. *Journal of Consulting and Clinical Psychology* 35 (1970): 135–142.

McGranahan, D. V., and I. Wayne. German and American Traits Reflected in Popular Drama. *Human Relations* 1 (1948): 429–455.

McKillip, J. *Need Analysis: Tools for Human Services and Education.* Beverly Hills, Calif.: Sage, 1987.

McLanahan, S., and G. Sandefur. *Growing Up with a Single Parent: What Hurts, What Helps.* Cambridge, Mass.: Harvard University Press, 1994.

McLellan, et al. The Fifth Edition of the Addiction Severity Index. *Journal of Substance Abuse Treatment* 9 (1992): 199–213.

McMurtry, S. L., and W. W. Hudson. The Client Satisfaction Inventory: Results of an Initial Validation Study. *Research on Social Work Practice* 10 (2000): 644–663.

Melton, G. B., and J. N. Gray. Ethical Dilemmas in AIDS Research: Individual Privacy and Public Health. *American Psychologist* 43 (1988): 60–64.

Mendes, H. A. Single Fatherhood. *Social Work* 21 (1976): 308–312.

Merriam, S. B. *Qualitative Research and Case Study Applications in Education.* San Francisco: Jossey-Bass, 1998.

Miles, M. B., and A. M. Huberman. *Qualitative Data Analysis: An Expanded Sourcebook,* 2d ed. Thousand Oaks, Calif.: Sage, 1994.

Miller, D. C., and N. J. Salkind. *Handbook of Research Design and Social Measurement,* 6th ed. Thousand Oaks, Calif.: Sage, 2002.

Miller, J. M., and R. Tewksbury. *Extreme Methods: Innovative Approaches to Social Science Research.* Boston: Allyn & Bacon, 2001.

Miller, L. P. The Application of Research to Practice: A Critique. *American Behavioral Scientist* 30 (September/October 1987): 70–80.

Miner, J. T., and L. E. Miner. A Guide to Proposal Planning and Writing. In *Directory of Research Grants,* 28th ed. Westport, Conn.: Oryx Press, 2003.

Mitchell, J. V. *The Ninth Mental Measurements Yearbook.* Lincoln: University of Nebraska Press, 1985.

Mitsos, S. B. Personal Constructs and the Semantic Differential. *Journal of Abnormal and Social Psychology* 62 (1961): 433–434.

Moe, K. Should the Nazi Research Data Be Cited? *Hastings Center Report* 14 (December 1984): 5–7.

Molina, E. Informal Non-Kin Networks among Homeless Latino and African American Men: Form and Functions. *American Behavioral Scientist* 43 (January 2000): 663–685.

Moos, M., N. Bartholomew, and K. Lohr. Counseling in the Clinical Setting to Prevent Unintended Pregnancy: An Evidence-Based Research Agenda. *Contraception* 67 (2003): 115–132.

Morash, M., and J. R. Greene. Evaluating Women on Patrol: A Critique of Contemporary Wisdom. *Evaluation Review* 10 (April 1986): 230–255.

Morgan, D. L. *Focus Groups as Qualitative Research,* 2d ed. Thousand Oaks, Calif.: Sage, 1994.

Morse, J. M. and P. A. Field. *Qualitative Research Methods for Health Professionals,* 2d ed. Thousand Oaks Calif.: Sage, 1995.

Morth, M., and P. J. Johnson. *Foundation Fundamentals: A Guide for Grantseekers,* 6th ed. New York: The Foundation Center, 1999.

Moser, C. A., and G. Kalton. *Survey Methods in Social Investigation,* 2d ed. New York: Basic Books, 1972.

Murray, L., R. Donovan, B. L. Kail, and L. J. Medvene. Protecting Human Subjects during Social Work Research: Researchers' Opinions. *Social Work Research and Abstracts* 16 (1980): 25–30.

Nabors, L. A., M. D. Weist, E. W. Holden, and N. A. Tashman. Quality Service Provision in Children's Mental Health Care. *Children's Services: Social Policy, Research, and Practice* 2 (1999): 57–79.

Nagel, E. *The Structure of Science.* New York: Harcourt, Brace & World, 1961.

NASW Press Staff. *An Author's Guide to Social Work Journals,* 4th ed. Washington, D.C.: National Association of Social Workers, 1997.

National Association of Social Workers. *Code of Ethics.* 1999. National Association of Social Workers. [Accessed: June 21, 2003] <http://www.socialworkers.org/pubs/code/code.asp>.

National Commission for the Protection of Human Subjects of Biomedical and Behavioral Research. *The Belmont Report: Ethical Principles and Guidelines for the Protection of Human Subjects of Research.* Washington, D.C.: Department of Health, Education, and Welfare, 1978.

National Institute of Justice. Funding Opportunities: *National Institute of Justice Awards in Fiscal Year 2002.* [Accessed: July 30, 2003] <http://www.ojp.usdoj.gov/nij/pdf/2002.pdf> (July 2003).

Neelon, V. J., M. T. Champagne, J. R. Carlso, and S. G. Funk. The NEECHAN Confusion Scale: Construction, Validation, and Clinical Testing. *Nursing Research* 45 (November–December 1996): 324–330.

Nelsen, J. Ethics, Gender, and Ethnicity in Single-Case Research and Evaluation. *Journal of Social Service Research* 18 (1994): 139–152.

Nelsen, J. C. Issues in Single-Subject Research for Nonbehaviorists. *Social Work Research and Abstracts* 17 (1981): 31–37.

Nelson, K. Populations and Outcomes in Five Family Preservation Programs. In *Family Preservation Services: Research and Evaluation,* ed. K. Wells and D. Biegel. Newbury Park, Calif.: Sage, 1991.

Nelson-Gardell, D. Child Report of Treatment Issue Resolution: Pilot of a Rapid Assessment Instrument. *Child Abuse and Neglect* 21 (1997): 309–318.

Nesbary, D. *Survey Research and the World Wide Web.* Boston: Allyn & Bacon, 2000.

Neuendorf, K. A. *The Content Analysis Guidebook.* Thousand Oaks, Calif.: Sage, 2002.

Newman, J. C., D. C. DesJerlais, C. F. Turner, and J. Gribble. The Differential Effects of Face-to-Face and Computer Interview Modes. *American Journal of Public Health* 92 (February 2002): p. 294ff.

Newman, K. S., and M. M. Chin. High Stakes: Time Poverty, Testing, and the Children of the Working Poor. *Qualitative Sociology* 26 (Spring 2003): 3–34.

Nielson, J. M., ed. *Feminist Research Methods.* Boulder, Colo.: Westview Press, 1989.

Nigro, G. N., et al. Changes in the Facial Prominence of Women and Men over the Last Decade. *Psychology of Women Quarterly* 12 (June 1988): 225–235.

Nugent, W. R., J. D. Sieppert, and W. Hudson. *Practice Evaluation for the 21st Century.* Belmont, Calif.: Wadsworth, 2001.

Nyden, P., A. Figert, M. Shibley, and D. Burrows. *Building Community: Social Science in Action.* Thousand Oaks, Calif.: Pine Forge Press, 1997.

O'Connell, A. A. Sampling for Evaluation: Issues and Strategies for Community-Based HIV Prevention Programs. *Evaluation and the Health Professions* 23 (June 2000): 212–234.

O'Farrell, T. J., and W. Fals-Stewart. Alcohol Abuse. *Journal of Marital and Family Therapy* 29 (January 2003): 121–146.

Office of Research Integrity. *Report on 2001 Annual Report on Possible Research Misconduct.* Washington, D.C.: Department of Health and Human Services, <ori.hhs.gov> (August 2002).

Ogilvie, D. M., P. J. Stone, and E. S. Shneidman. Some Characteristics of Genuine versus Simulated Suicide

Notes. In *The General Inquirer: A Computer Approach to Content Analysis in the Behavioral Sciences,* ed. P. J. Stone, D. C. Dunphy, M. S. Smith, and D. M. Ogilvie. Cambridge, Mass.: MIT Press, 1966.

Ogles, B. M., M. J. Lambert, and K. S. Masters. *Assessing Outcome in Clinical Practice.* Boston: Allyn & Bacon, 1996.

O'Hare, T. Integrating Research and Practice: A Framework for Implementation. *Social Work* 36 (May 1991): 220–223.

Oksenberg, L., L. Coleman, and C. F. Cannell. Interviewers' Voices and Refusal Rates in Telephone Surveys. *Public Opinion Quarterly* 50 (Spring 1986): 97–111.

Ollendick, T. H. Cognitive Behavioral Treatment of Panic Disorder with Agoraphobia in Adolescents: A Multiple Baseline Design Analysis. *Behavior Therapy* 26 (1995): 517–553.

Olsen, V. Feminism and Models of Qualitative Research. In *Handbook of Qualitative Research,* ed. N. Denzin and Y. Lincoln. Thousand Oaks, Calif.: Sage, 1994.

Orme, J. G., and T. D. Combs-Orme. Statistical Power and Type II Errors in Social Work Research. *Social Work Research and Abstracts* 22 (1986): 3–10.

Orme, J. G., and R. M. Tolman. The Statistical Power of a Decade of Social Work Education Research. *Social Service Review* 60 (1986): 619–632.

Orne, M. T. On the Social Psychology of the Psychological Experiment: With Particular Reference to Demand Characteristics and Their Implications. *American Psychologist* 17 (1962): 776–783.

Orr, L. L. *Social Experimentation: Evaluating Public Programs with Experimental Methods.* Thousand Oaks, Calif.: Sage, 1998.

Ortner, S. B. The Founding of the First Sherpa Nunnery and the Problem of 'Women' as an Analytic Category. In *Feminist Re-visions,* ed. V. Patraka and L. Tilly. Ann Arbor: University of Michigan Women's Studies Program, 1984.

Osgood, C. E., G. J. Suci, and P. H. Tannenbaum. *The Measurement of Meaning.* Urbana: University of Illinois Press, 1957.

Patterson, C. Families of the Lesbian Baby Boom: Parent's Division of Labor and Children's Adjustment. *Developmental Psychology* 31(1995): 115–123.

Patton, M. Q. *Creative Evaluation.* Beverly Hills, Calif.: Sage, 1981.

_____. Evaluation's Political Inherency: Practical Implications for Design and Use. In *The Politics of Program Evaluation,* ed. D. J. Palumbo. Newbury Park, Calif.: Sage, 1987.

_____. *Qualitative Research and Evaluation Methods,* 3d ed. Thousand Oaks, Calif.: Sage, 2002.

Pepler, D. J., and W. M. Craig. A Peek behind the Fence: Naturalistic Observations of Aggressive Children with Remote Audiovisual Recording. *Developmental Psychology* 31 (1995): 548–553.

Perkins, C., and P. Klaus. National Crime Victimization Survey. *Bureau of Justice Statistics Bulletin* (April 1996): 1–8.

Pescosolido, B. A., E. Grauerholz, and M. A. Milkie. Culture and Conflict: The Portrayal of Blacks in U.S. Children's Picture Books through the Mid- and Late-Twentieth Century. *American Sociological Review* 62 (1997): 443–464.

Peterson, R. R. A Re-Evaluation of the Economic Consequences of Divorce. *American Sociological Review* 61 (1996): 528–536.

Peterson, S., and T. Kroner. Gender Biases in Textbooks for Introductory Psychology and Human Development. *Psychology of Women Quarterly* 16 (1992): 17–36.

Peterson, S., and M. Lach. Gender Stereotypes in Children's Books: Their Prevalence and Influence on Cognitive and Affective Development. *Gender and Education* 2 (1990): 185–197.

Peyrot, M. Coerced Voluntarism: The Micropolitics of Drug Treatment. *Urban Life* 13 (January 1985): 343–365.

Phillips, D. P. The Impact of Mass Media Violence on U.S. Homicides. *American Sociological Review* 48 (August 1983): 560–568.

Piliavin, I., S. Masters, and T. Corbett. Factors Influencing Errors in AFDC Payments. *Social Work Research and Abstracts* 15 (1977): 3–17.

Piquemal, N. Free and Informed Consent in Research Involving Native American Communities. *American Indian Culture and Research Journal* 25 (2001): 65–79.

Plake, B. S., J. C. Impara, and Robert A. Spies, eds. *The Fifteenth Mental Measurements Yearbook.* Lincoln: University of Nebraska Press, 2003.

Polsky, N. *Hustlers, Beats, and Others.* Chicago: Aldine, 1967.

Pound, E. T. Nurse's Clues Shut Down Research. *USA Today,* July 13, 2000, 3A.

Powdermaker, H. *Stranger and Friend: The Way of an Anthropologist.* New York: Norton, 1966.

Prentice, D. A., and D. T. Miller. When Small Effects Are Impressive. In *Methodological Issues and Strategies in Clin-*

ical Research, 2d ed., ed. A.E. Kazdin. Washington, D.C.: American Psychological Association, 1998.

Prothro, J. W. Verbal Shifts in the American Presidency: A Content Analysis. *American Political Science Review* 50 (1956): 726–739.

Purcell, P., and L. Stewart. Dick and Jane in 1989. *Sex Roles* 22, nos. 3–4 (1990): 177–185.

Rabinow, P., and W. M. Sullivan, eds. *Interpretive Social Science: A Second Look.* Berkeley: University of California Press, 1987.

Rapee, R. M., M. G. Craske, and D. H. Barlow. Subject-Described Features of Panic Attacks Using Self-Monitoring. *Journal of Anxiety Disorders* 4 (1990): 171–181.

Rapp, L. A., C. N. Dulmus, J. S. Wodarski, and M. D. Feit. Screening of Substance Abuse in Public Welfare and Child Protective Service Clients: A Comparative Study of Rapid Assessment Instruments vs. the SASSI. *Journal of Addictive Diseases* 18 (1999): 83–88.

Ratzan, R. M. The Experiment That Wasn't: A Case Report in Clinical Geriatric Research. *Gerontologist* 21 (1981): 297–302.

Rawson, R. A., and C. Branch. Connecting Substance Abuse Treatment and Research: "Let's Make a Deal." *Journal of Drug Issues* 32 (Summer 2002): 769–782

Rea, L., and R. Parker. *Designing and Conducting Survey Research.* San Francisco: Jossey-Bass, 1992.

Reamer, F. G. *Social Work Values and Ethics.* New York: Columbia University Press, 1995.

Reece, R., and H. Siegal. *Studying People: A Primer in the Ethics of Social Research.* Macon, Ga.: Mercer University Press, 1986.

Reese, H. W., and W. J. Fremouw. Normal and Normative Ethics in Behavioral Science. *American Psychologist* 39 (1984): 863–876.

Reid, P. N., and J. H. Gundlach. A Scale for the Measurement of Consumer Satisfaction with Social Services. *Journal of Social Service Research* 7 (1983): 37–54.

Reid, W. The Social Agency as a Research Machine. *Journal of Social Service Research* 2 (1978): 11–23.

Reinharz, S. *Feminist Methods in Social Research.* New York: Oxford University Press, 1992.

Reiss, A. K., and L. Rhodes. An Empirical Test of Differential Association Theory. *Journal of Research in Crime and Delinquency* 4 (1967): 28–42.

Rennison, C. M., and M. R. Rand. *Criminal Victimization 2002. National Crime Victimization Survey.* Washington, D.C.: Bureau of Justice Statistics, U.S. Department of Justice, <http://www.ojp.usdof.gov/bjs/abstract/cv02.htm> (2003).

Reverby, S. M., ed. *Tuskegee's Truths: Rethinking the Tuskegee Syphilis Study.* Chapel Hill and London: University of North Carolina Press, 2000.

Reynolds, P. D. *Ethical Dilemmas and Social Science Research.* San Francisco: Jossey-Bass, 1979.

Ridley, S. M., R. A. McWilliam, and C. S. Oates. Observed Engagement as an Indicator of Child Care Program Quality. *Early Education and Development* 11 (March 2000): 133–146.

Riedel, M. *Research Strategies for Secondary Data: A Perspective for Criminology and Criminal Justice.* Thousand Oaks, Calif.: Sage, 2000.

Robinson, J., P. Shaver, and L. Wrightsman, eds. *Measures of Personality and Social Psychological Attitudes.* San Diego: Academic Press, 1991.

Roscoe, P. B. The Perils of "Positivism" in Cultural Anthropology. *American Anthropologist* 97 (1995): 492–504.

Rosen, A. The Scientific Practitioner Revisited: Some Obstacles and Prerequisites for Fuller Implementation in Practice. *Social Work Research* 20 (June 1996): 105–111.

Rosenhan, D. L. On Being Sane in Insane Places. *Science* 179 (1973): 250–258.

Rosenthal, R. Covert Communication in the Psychological Experiment. *Psychological Bulletin* 67 (1967): 356–367.

———. "Replication in Behavioral Research." In *Replication Research in the Social Sciences,* ed. J. Neuliep. Newbury Park, Calif.: Sage, 1991.

Rosnow, R. L. The Volunteer Problem Revisited. In *Interpersonal Expectations: Theory, Research, and Applications,* ed. P. D. Blanck. New York: Cambridge University Press, 1993.

Rossi, P. H., R. A. Berk, and K. J. Lenihan. *Money, Work, and Crime: Experimental Evidence.* New York: Academic Press, 1980.

Rossi, P. H., H. E. Freeman, and M. W. Lipsey. *Evaluation: A Systematic Approach,* 6th ed. Thousand Oaks, Calif.: Sage, 1999.

Rudd, M. D., M. H. Rajab, and D. T. Orman. Effectiveness of an Outpatient Intervention Targeting Suicidal Young Adults: Preliminary Results. *Journal of Consulting and Clinical Psychology* 64 (1996): 179–190.

Ruggles, P. *Drawing the Line: Alternative Poverty Measures and Their Implications for Public Policy.* Washington, D.C.: Urban Institute Press, 1990.

Rule, J. B. *Insight and Social Betterment: A Preface to Applied Social Science.* New York: Oxford University Press, 1978.

Runcie, J. F. *Experiencing Social Research,* rev. ed. Homewood, Ill.: Dorsey Press, 1980.

Russell, B. On the Notion of Cause, with Applications to the Free-Will Problem. In *Readings in the Philosophy of Science,* ed. H. Feigel and M. Brodbeck. New York: Appleton-Century-Crofts, 1953.

Russell, M. *Clinical Social Work: Research and Practice.* Newbury Park, Calif.: Sage, 1990.

Rutman, L. Introduction. In *Evaluation Research Methods,* 2d ed., ed. L. Rutman. Beverly Hills, Calif.: Sage, 1984.

Ryden, M. B., et al. Development of a Measure of Resident Satisfaction with the Nursing Home. *Research in Nursing and Health* 23 (2000): 237–245.

Sackett, D. L., W. S. Richardson, W. Rosenberg, and R. B. Haynes. *Evidence-Based Medicine: How to Practice and Teach EBP.* New York: Churchill Livingstone, 1997.

Sackett, D. L., S. E. Straus, W. S. Richardson, W. Rosenberg, and R. B. Haynes. *Evidence-Based Medicine: How to Practice and Teach EBM,* 2d ed. Edinburgh: Churchill Livingstone, 2000.

Saltzman, L. E., J. L. Fanslow, P. M. McMahon, and G. E. Shelley. *Intimate Partner Violence Surveillance: Uniform Definitions and Recommended Data Elements Version I.0.* Atlanta, Ga.: Centers for Disease Control and Prevention, National Center for Injury Prevention and Control, 1999.

Scarce, R. (No) Trial (But) Tribulations: When Courts and Ethnography Conflict. *Journal of Contemporary Ethnography* 23 (1994): 123–149.

Schafer, A. On Using Nazi Data: The Case Against. *Dialogue* 25 (Autumn 1986): 413–419.

Scheaffer, R. L., W. Mendenhall, and L. Ott. *Elementary Survey Sampling,* 5th ed. Belmont, Calif.: Wadsworth, 1996.

Scheper-Hughes, N. *Death without Weeping: The Violence of Everyday Life in Brazil.* Berkeley: University of California Press, 1992.

Schiebinger, L. L. *Has Feminism Changed Science?* Boston: Harvard University Press, 1999.

Schiffman, S., M. Reynolds, and F. Young. *Introduction to Multidimensional Scaling.* New York: Academic Press, 1981.

Schmidt, F. L. Statistical Significance Testing and Cumulative Knowledge in Psychology: Implications for Training Researchers. In *Methodological Issues and Strategies in Clinical Research,* 2d ed., ed. A. E. Kazdin. Washington, D.C.: American Psychological Association, 1998.

Schuckit, M. *Drug and Alcohol Abuse,* 3d ed. New York and London: Plenum, 1989.

Schuman, H., and S. Presser. The Open and Closed Question. *American Sociological Review* 44 (1979): 692–712.

Schutte, N. S., and J. M. Malouff. *Sourcebook of Adult Assessment Strategies.* New York: Plenum, 1995.

Scott, J. *A Matter of Record: Documentary Sources in Social Research.* Oxford: Polity Press, 1990.

Scott, R. A. The Selection of Clients by Social Welfare Agencies: The Case of the Blind. In *Human Service Organizations,* ed. Y. Hasenfeld and R. A. English. Ann Arbor: University of Michigan Press, 1975.

Seale, C. Using Computers to Analyse Qualitative Data. In *Doing Qualitative Research: A Practical Handbook,* ed. D. Silverman. Thousand Oaks, Calif.: Sage, 2000.

Segal, S. P. Research on the Outcome of Social Work Therapeutic Intervention: A Review of the Literature. *Journal of Health and Social Behavior* 13 (1972): 3–17.

Seidman, I. E. *Interviewing as Qualitative Research,* 2d ed. New York: Teachers College Press, 1998.

Seiler, L. H., and R. L. Hough. Empirical Comparisons of the Thurstone and Likert Techniques. In *Attitude Measurement,* ed. G. F. Summers. Chicago: Rand McNally, 1970.

Shadish, W. R., T. D. Cook, and D. T. Campbell. *Experimental and Quasi-Experimental Designs for Generalized Causal Inference.* Boston: Houghton Mifflin, 2002.

Shapin, S. Here and Everywhere: Sociology of Scientific Knowledge. *Annual Review of Sociology* 21 (1995): 289–321.

Sheafor, B. W., and C. R. Horejsi. *Techniques and Guidelines for Social Work Practice,* 6th ed. Boston: Allyn & Bacon, 2003.

Shearing, C. D. How to Make Theories Untestable: A Guide to Theorists. *American Sociologist* 8 (1973): 33–37.

Sheley, J. F. A Study in Self-Defeat: The Public Health Venereal Disease Clinic. *Journal of Sociology and Social Welfare* 4 (1976): 114–124.

Sherman, L. *Policing Domestic Violence: Experiments and Dilemmas.* New York: Free Press, 1992.

Sherman, L., and R. A. Berk. The Specific Deterrent Effects of Arrest for Domestic Assault. *American Sociological Review* 49 (1984): 261–271.

Shiffman, S., M. Hickox, J. A. Paty, M. Gnys, J. A. Kassel, and T. J. Richards. Progression from Smoking Lapse and Relapse: Prediction from Abstinence Violation Effects, Nicotine Dependence, and Lapse Characteristics. *Journal of Consulting and Clinical Psychology* 64 (1996): 933–1002.

Shiffman, S., et al. Remember That? A Comparison of Real-Time versus Retrospective Recall of "Smoking Lapses." *Journal of Consulting and Clinical Psychology* 65 (1997): 292–300.

Shilts, R. *And the Band Played On: Politics, People, and the AIDS Epidemic.* New York: St. Martin's Press, 1987.

Shireman, J. F., and P. R. Johnson. A Longitudinal Study of Black Adoptions: Single Parent, Transracial, and Traditional. *Social Work* 31 (May/June 1986): 172–176.

Shulman, L. A Study of Practice Skills. *Social Work* 23 (1978): 274–280.

Shupe, A. D., Jr., and D. G. Bromley. Walking a Tightrope: Dilemmas of Participant Observation of Groups in Conflict. *Qualitative Sociology* 2 (1980): 3–21.

Sieber, J., ed. *Sharing Social Science Data: Advantages and Challenges.* Newbury Park, Calif.: Sage, 1991.

Siegel, D. Defining Empirically Based Practice. *Social Work* 29 (1984): 325–329.

Singer, E., D. R. VonThurn, and E. R. Miller. Confidentiality and Response: A Quantitative Review of the Experimental Literature. *Public Opinion Quarterly* 59 (1995): 446–459.

Siweki, J., M. L. Gourlay, D. C. Slawson, and A. F. Shaughnessy. How to Write an Evidence-Based Clinical Review Article. *American Family Physician* 65 (January 2002): 251–258.

Skidmore, W. *Theoretical Thinking in Sociology.* Cambridge: Cambridge University Press, 1979.

Skinner, H. A. Benefits of Sequential Assessment. *Social Work Research and Abstracts* 17 (1981): 21–28.

Smart, B. *Sociology, Phenomenology, and Marxian Analysis: A Critical Discussion of the Theory and Practice of a Science of Society.* Boston: Routledge & Kegan Paul, 1976.

Smith, A. W. Problems and Progress in the Measurement of Black Public Opinion. *American Behavioral Scientist* 30 (March/April 1987): 441–455.

Smith, C. P. Content Analysis and Narrative Analysis. In *Handbook of Research Methods in Social and Personality Psychology,* ed. H. T. Reis and C. M. Judd. Cambridge: Cambridge University Press, 2000.

Smith, H. W. *Strategies of Social Research,* 2d ed. Englewood Cliffs, N.J.: Prentice Hall, 1981.

Smith, M. F. *Evaluability Assessment: A Practical Approach.* Boston: Kluwer Academic Publishers, 1989.

Smith, P. R. How Do We Understand Practice? A Qualitative Approach. *Families in Society: The Journal of Contemporary Human Services* 79 (September 1998): 543–550.

Smith, S. H., and D. D. McLean. *ABCs of Grantsmanship.* Reston, Va.: American Alliance for Health, Physical Education, Recreation, and Dance, 1988.

Smith, T. W. That Which We Call Welfare by Any Other Name Would Smell Sweeter: An Analysis of the Impact of Question Wording on Response Patterns. *Public Opinion Quarterly* 51 (Spring 1987): 75–83.

———. The Polls—A Review: The Holocaust Denial Controversy. *Public Opinion Quarterly* 59 (1995): 269–295.

Squire, P. Why the 1936 *Literary Digest* Poll Failed. *Public Opinion Quarterly* 52 (1988): 125–133.

Stacey, J., and T. J. Biblarz. (How) Does the Sexual Orientation of Parents Matter? *American Sociological Review* (April 2001): 159–183.

Stein, J. *Fiddler on the Roof.* New York: Crown, 1964.

Stevens, S. S., ed. *Handbook of Experimental Psychology.* New York: Wiley, 1951.

Stott, C., and S. Reicher. How Conflict Escalates: The Inter-Group Dynamics of Collective Football Crowd "Violence." *Sociology* 32 (1998): 353–377.

Straus, M., and R. J. Gelles. How Violent are American Families? Estimates from the National Family Violence Resurvey and Other Studies. In *Family Abuse and Its Consequences: New Directions in Research,* ed. G. Hotaling, D. Finkelhor, J. Kirkpatrick, and M. Straus. Newbury Park, Calif.: Sage, 1988.

Straus, M. A., S. L. Hamby, S. Boney-McCoy, and D. B. Sugarman. The Revised Conflict Tactics Scales (CTS2): Development and Preliminary Data. *Journal of Family Issues* 17 (May 1996): 283–316.

Strauss, A. L. *Qualitative Analysis for Social Scientists.* Cambridge and New York: Cambridge University Press, 1987.

Strauss, A., and J. Corbin. Grounded Theory Methodology: An Overview. In *Handbook of Qualitative Research,* ed. N. K. Denzin and Y. S. Lincoln. Thousand Oaks, Calif.: Sage, 1994.

Street, D., R. D. Vinter, and C. Perrow. *Organizations for Treatment: A Comparative Study of Institutions for Delinquents.* New York: Free Press of Glencoe, 1966.

Stum, K., and M. M. Chu. Gang Prevention and Intervention in a Rural Town in California: At-Risk Youth and the Community Policing School Partnership Program. *Journal of Gang Research* 7 (Fall 1999): 1–12.

Substance Abuse and Mental Health Services Administration. *Community Mental Health Services Block Grant Program.* [Accessed: July 30, 2003] <http://www.mentalhealth.org/publications/allpubs/KEN95-0022/default.asp> (April 2003).

Sudman, S. Time Allocation on Survey Interviews and Other Field Occupations. *Public Opinion Quarterly* 29 (1965): 638–648.

———. *Applied Sampling.* New York: Academic Press, 1976.

———. Mail Surveys of Reluctant Professionals. *Evaluation Research* 9 (June 1985): 349–360.

Sudman, S., and N. M. Bradburn. *Asking Questions.* San Francisco: Jossey-Bass, 1982.

Suen, H. K., and D. Ary. Poisson Cumulative Probabilities of Systematic Errors in Single-Subject and Multiple-Subject Time Sampling. *Behavioral Assessment* 8 (Spring 1986): 155–169.

Sullivan, C. The Provision of Advocacy Services to Women Leaving Abusive Partners. *Journal of Interpersonal Violence* 6 (1991): 41–54.

Sullivan, T. J. *Introduction to Social Problems*, 6th ed. Boston: Allyn & Bacon, 2003.

Sulzer-Azaroff, B., and G. Mayer. *Behavior Analysis for Lasting Change.* Fort Worth, Tex.: Holt, Rinehart and Winston, 1991.

Sutherland, E. *Criminology.* Philadelphia: Lippincott, 1939.

Taber, M., and I. Shapiro. Social Work and Its Knowledge Base: A Content Analysis of the Periodical Literature. *Social Work* 10 (October 1965): 100–107.

Teitelbaum, L., and B. Mullen. The Validity of the Mast in Psychiatric Settings: A Meta-Analytic Integration. *Journal of Studies on Alcohol* 61 (March 2000): 254–261.

Thorne, B. *Gender Play: Girls and Boys in School.* New Brunswick, N.J.: Rutgers University Press, 1993.

Thrasher, E., and C. Mowbray. A Strengths Perspective: An Ethnographic Study of Homeless Women with Children. *Health and Social Work* 20 (1995): 93–101.

Thurstone, L. L., and E. J. Chave. *The Measurement of Attitudes.* Chicago: University of Chicago Press, 1929.

Timberlake, E. M. Children with No Place to Call Home: Survival in Cars and on the Streets. *Child and Adolescent Social Work Journal* 5, no. 4 (1994): 268.

Timms, N., and J. Mayer. *The Client Speaks.* London: Routledge & Kegan Paul, 1971.

Tjaden, P., and N. Thoennes. Prevalence, Incidence, and Consequences of Violence against Women: Findings from the National Violence against Women Survey. *Research in Brief.* Atlanta, Ga.: National Institute of Justice, Centers for Disease Control and Prevention, 1998.

Tolman, R. The Development and Validation of a Nonphysical Abuse Scale. *Violence and Victims* 4 (1989): 159–177.

Toseland, R. W., and W. J. Reid. Using Rapid Assessment Instruments in a Family Service Agency. *Social Casework* 66 (1985): 547–555.

Touliatos, J., B. F. Perlmutter, M. A. Strauss, and G. W. Holden, eds. *Handbook of Family Measurement Techniques.* Thousand Oaks, CA: Sage, 2000.

Tourangeau, R., and T. W. Smith. Asking Sensitive Questions: The Impact of Data Collection Mode, Question Format, and Question Context. *Public Opinion Quarterly* 60 (1996): 275–304.

Tran, T. V., and L. F. Williams. Effect of Language of Interview on the Validity and Reliability of Psychological Well-Being Scales. *Social Work Research* 18 (March 1994): 17–25.

Treas, J., and A. VanHilst. Marriage and Remarriage Rates among Older Americans. *Gerontologist* 16 (1976): 132–140.

Tuffrey-Wijne, I. The Palliative Care Needs of People with Intellectual Disabilities: A Literature Review. *Palliative Medicine* 17 (2003): 55–62.

Turnbull, J. E., and B. Dietz-Uhler. The Boulder Model: Lessons From Clinical Psychology for Social Work Training. *Research on Social Work Practice* 5 (October 1995): 411–429.

Turner, C. F., L. Ku, S. M. Rogers, L. D. Lindberg, J. H. Pleck, and F. L. Sonenstein. Adolescent Sexual Behavior, Drug Use, and Violence: Increased Reporting with Computer Survey Technology. *Science* 280 (May 8, 1998): 867–873.

Tye, M. C. Lesbian, Gay, Bisexual, and Transgender Parents: Special Considerations for the Custody and Adoption Evaluator. *Family Court Review* (January 2003): 92–103.

Tyson, K. An Empowering Approach to Crisis Intervention and Brief Treatment for Preschool Children. *Families in Society* 80 (January/February 1999): 64–77.

Varmus, H. Evaluating the Burden of Disease and Spending the Research Dollars of the National Institutes of Health. *New England Journal of Medicine* 340 (June 17, 1999): 1914–1915.

Vinokur, A., L. Oksenberg, and C. Cannell. Effects of Feedback and Reinforcement on the Report of Health Information. In *Experiments in Interviewing Techniques,* ed. C. Cannell, L. Oksenberg, and C. Converse. Ann Arbor: University of Michigan Institute for Social Research, 1979.

Wagenaar, A. C., and M. B. T. Wiviott. Effects of Mandating Seatbelt Use: A Series of Surveys on Compliance in Michigan. *Public Health Reports* 101 (September/October 1986): 505–512.

Ward, D. A., and G. G. Kassebaum. On Biting the Hand That Feeds: Some Implications of Sociological Evaluations of Correctional Effectiveness. In *Evaluating Social Programs: Readings in Social Action and Education,* ed. C. H. Weiss. Boston: Allyn & Bacon, 1972.

Warriner, K., J. Goyder, H. Gjertsen, P. Hohner, and K. McSpurren. Charities, No; Lotteries, No; Cash, Yes:

Main Effects and Interactions in a Canadian Incentives Experiment. *Public Opinion Quarterly* 60 (1996): 542–562.

Warwick, D. P., and C. Lininger. *The Sample Survey: Theory and Practice.* New York: McGraw-Hill, 1975.

Waterlow Specialist Information Publishing. *The Grants Register 2004: The Complete Guide to Postgraduate Funding Worldwide,* 22d ed. New York: Palgrave Macmillan, 2003.

Watters, J. K., and P. Biernacki. Targeted Sampling: Options for the Study of Hidden Populations. *Social Problems* 36 (1989): 416–430.

Webb, E. J., D. T. Campbell, R. D. Schwartz, L. Sechrest, and J. B. Grove. *Nonreactive Measures in the Social Sciences.* Boston: Houghton Mifflin, 1981.

Weber, M. Science as a Vocation. In *Max Weber, Essays in Sociology,* ed. H. H. Garth and C. W. Mills. New York: Free Press, 1946 (originally published 1922).

_____. *The Theory of Social and Economic Organization.* Trans. A. M. Henderson and T. Parsons. New York: Free Press, 1957 (originally published 1925).

Weber, R. P. *Basic Content Analysis,* 2d ed. Beverly Hills, Calif.: Sage, 1990.

Weeks, M. F. Computer-Assisted Survey Information Collection: A Review of Basic Methods and Their Implication for Survey Operations. *Journal of Official Statistics* 4 (1992): 445–466.

Weinberg, M. Sexual Modesty, Social Meanings, and the Nudist Camp. In *Sociology and Everyday Life,* ed. M. Truss. Englewood Cliffs, N.J.: Prentice Hall, 1968.

Weinstein, R. M. "The Mental Hospital from the Patient's Point of View: The Pitfalls of Participant-Observation Research." In *Deviance and Mental Illness,* ed. W. R. Gove. Newbury Park, Calif.: Sage, 1982.

Weiss, C. *Evaluation Research: Methods for Assessing Program Effectiveness.* Englewood Cliffs, N.J.: Prentice Hall, 1972.

Weiss, C. H. *Evaluation: Method for Studying Programs and Policies,* 2d ed. Upper Saddle River, N.J.: Prentice Hall, 1998.

Weiss, R. L., and P. E. Frohman. Behavioral Observation as Outcome Measures: Not through a Glass Darkly. *Behavioral Assessment* 7 (Fall 1985): 309–315.

Weitzman, E. B., and M. B. Miles. *Computer Programs for Qualitative Data Analysis.* Thousand Oaks, Calif.: Sage, 1995.

Weitzman, L. J. *The Divorce Revolution: The Unexpected Social and Economic Consequences for Women and Children in America.* New York: Free Press, 1985.

_____. The Economic Consequences of Divorce Are Still Unequal: Comment on Peterson. *American Sociological Review* 61 (1996): 537–538.

Wells, G. L., and E. A. Olson. Eyewitness Identification. In *Annual Review of Psychology,* vol. 54, ed. S. T. Fiske. Palo Alto, Calif.: Annual Reviews Inc., 2003.

Wells, K., and D. Biegel. *Family Preservation Services: Research and Evaluation.* Newbury Park, Calif.: Sage, 1991.

Wells, W. D., and G. Smith. Four Semantic Rating Scales Compared. *Journal of Applied Psychology* 44 (1960): 393–397.

West, S. G., J. C. Biesanz, and S. C. Pitts. Causal Inference and Generalization in Field Settings: Experimental and Quasi-Experimental Designs. In *Handbook of Research Methods in Social and Personality Psychology,* ed. H. T. Reis and C. M. Judd. Cambridge: Cambridge University Press, 2000.

Whalen, J., and D. H. Zimmerman. Observations on the Display and Management of Emotion in Naturally Occurring Activities: The Case of "Hysteria" in Calls to 9–1–1. *Social Psychology Quarterly* 61 (1998): 141–159.

Whyte, *Street Corner Society,* 2d ed., Chicago: University of Chicago Press, 1955.

_____. W. F. Freedom and Responsibility in Research: The Springdale Case. *Human Organization* 17 (1958): 1–2.

Wilson, S. R., N. Brown, C. Mejia, and P. W. Lavori. Effects of Interviews Characteristics on Reported Sexual Behavior of California Latino Couples. *Hispanic Journal of Behavioral Sciences* 24 (February 2002): 38–62.

Wilson, T. Normative and Interpretive Paradigms in Sociology. In *Understanding Everyday Life: Toward the Reconstruction of Sociological Knowledge,* ed. J. Douglas. New York: Aldine, 1970.

Wingard, D. Trends and Characteristics of California Adoptions: 1964–1982. *Child Welfare* 66 (July/August 1987): 303–314.

Witkin, B. R. *Assessing Needs in Educational and Social Programs.* San Francisco: Jossey-Bass, 1984.

Wolfe, V. V., et al. Negative Affectivity in Children: A Multitrait-Multimethod Investigation. *Journal of Consulting and Clinical Psychology* 55 (April 1987): 245–250.

Wolfgang, M. E. Confidentiality in Criminological Research and Other Ethical Issues. *Journal of Criminal Law and Criminology* 72 (1981): 345–361.

Wood, J. M., S. O. Lilienfeld, and H. N. Garb. The Rorschach Test in Clinical Diagnosis: A Critical Review, with a Backward Look at Garfield (1947). *Journal of Clinical Psychology* 56 (March 2000): 395–420.

Woodruff, S. I., T. L. Conway, and C. C. Edwards. Increasing Response Rates to a Smoking Survey for U.S. Navy Enlisted Women. *Evaluation and the Health Professions* 23 (June 2000): 172–181.

Wysocki, D. K. Feminist Methods: The Use of the Internet to Find Difficult-to-Reach Populations. Paper presented at the annual meetings of the Midwest Sociological Society, Minneapolis, April 1999.

Yammarino, F. J., S. J. Skinner, and T. L Childers. Understanding Mail Survey Response Behavior: A Meta-Analysis. *Public Opinion Quarterly* 55 (Winter 1991): 613–639.

Yin, R. K. *Case Study Research: Design and Methods*, 3d ed. Thousand Oaks, Calif.: Sage, 2002.

Zalaquett, C. P., and R. J. Wood, eds. *Evaluating Stress: A Book of Resources.* Lanham, Md.: Rowman & Littlefield, 1997.

Zelenski, J. M., C. L. Rusting, and R. J. Larsen. Consistency in the Time of Experiment Participation and Personality Correlates: A Methodological Note. *Personality and Individual Differences* 34 (2003): 547–558.

Name Index

Subject Index